LIFE AND DEATH MATTERS

LIFE AND DEATH MATTERS

Human Rights, Environment, and Social Justice

Second Edition

Barbara Rose Johnston, editor

Walnut Creek, CA

green press
INITIATIVE

Left Coast Press is committed to preserving ancient forests
and natural resources. We elected to print this title on 30% post
consumer recycled paper, processed chlorine free. As a result,
for this printing, we have saved:

6 Trees (40' tall and 6-8" diameter)
2 Million BTUs of Total Energy
550 Pounds of Greenhouse Gases
2,650 Gallons of Wastewater
161 Pounds of Solid Waste

Left Coast Press made this paper choice because our printer,
Thomson-Shore, Inc., is a member of Green Press Initiative,
a nonprofit program dedicated to supporting authors, publishers, and suppliers in their efforts to reduce their use of fiber
obtained from endangered forests.

For more information, visit www.greenpressinitiative.org

Environmental impact estimates were made using the Environmental Defense
Paper Calculator. For more information visit: www.papercalculator.org.

Left Coast Press, Inc.
1630 North Main Street, #400
Walnut Creek, CA 94596
www.LCoastPress.com

Copyright © 2011 by Barbara Rose Johnston.

ISBN 978-1-59874-338-8 hardcover
ISBN 978-1-59874-339-5 paperback

Library of Congress Cataloging-in-Publication Data

Johnston, Barbara Rose.
Life and death matters: human rights, environment, and social justice / Barbara Rose Johnston, editor. — 2nd ed.
    p. cm.
Includes index.
ISBN 978-1-59874-338-8 (hardcover : alk. paper)—ISBN 978-1-59874-339-5 (pbk. : alk. paper)
  1. Economic development—Environmental aspects—Developing countries. 2. Environmental policy—Developing countries. 3. Human rights—Developing countries. I. Johnston, Barbara Rose. II. Title.
    HC59.72.E5L54 2010
    333.7—dc22

2010036303

Printed in the United States of America

∞™ The paper used in this publication meets the minimum requirements of American National Standard for Information Sciences—Permanence of Paper for Printed Library Materials, ANSI/NISO Z39.48–1992.

Cover design by Andrew Brozyna. Photos used to illustrate the title for this second edition include an image of Maya A'chi protestors at the Chixoy Dam on September 8, 2004 (photo credit Bert Jannssens). This protest involved an occupation by some 800 members of the dam-affected communities and resulted in the agreement of the Guatemalan government to initiate a reparations negotiation process. The middle image is a radiation hazard warning sign on the chain-link fence surrounding Trinity site ground-zero in White Sands, New Mexico, where the world's first atomic bomb was detonated (photo credit Barbara Rose Johnston). The final image is meant to illustrate the end goal of most human rights and environment struggles to achieve social justice, which, for many people, involves the struggle to retain, regain, and restore the means to support a culturally-meaningful and locally sustainable way of life. This image is from Nepal, where a woman is working her terraced farm on the slopes above the Modi khola river, one of the major tributaries of the Kaligandaki River of the Gandaki basin. The image was taken on the trail to Chhomrong and to the Annapurna base camp (photo credit Ted Edwards).

Contents

Part V Development, Degradation, and Conflict

Part VI Postwar Matters

Part VII Problems That Push the Parameters of Time and Space

ACKNOWLEDGMENTS

The idea of producing a book that offers a "then and now" perspective was both exciting and daunting, especially given the immense changes to cases, places, and, indeed, the world during the decade that passed between the first and second editions. Making this idea a reality was immensely difficult, in part because so much had changed, in part because of the considerable time needed to write when events rapidly eclipse conclusions. The authors were amazing in their willingness to write, rewrite, update, and update again. They also gracefully suppressed their frustration over the need to abstract original essays to create space for new updates and over the time that this process took. Thank you, all of you.

Thanks are also due the panelists and audience attending the November 2008 session "Pulse of the Planet: Human Rights, Environmental Quality, and Social Justice" at the AAA meetings; my co-organizer for that session, Gregory Button; and our discussant, Alison Dundes Rentlen. This dynamic session was both a capstone to the previous six months practicum in op-ed writing and, with its success, the launch of another two years of similar work turning scholarly analysis into advocacy-oriented commentary on public policy. With the encouragement of Jeffrey St. Clair, many of these presentations have been published as commentaries in the online political magazine, CounterPunch, and some are reprinted in this volume.

I gratefully acknowledge the support of The Christensen Fund, whose human rights and environment grant to the Center for Political Ecology helped sustain both the revision of this book and my related efforts to assert the notion that biocultural health is the primary indicator of sustainability. The Fund's support allowed me to write "Pulse of the Planet" commentary essays, elements of which were worked into this book, and to help to draft policy and publications as an advisor to UNESCO on water and cultural diversity.

Many of the contributing authors received institutional support for their research and writing as well as assistance from colleagues. These individual acknowledgments are listed in chapter endnotes.

Although a decade of feedback from faculty and students has encouraged and shaped this revision, I especially profited from the critical review comments of Alexander Ervin at the University of Saskatchewan (Saskatoon, Canada) and his former students Travis Morpak and Nick Hazen; teleconference "lectures" with Leslie Sponsel and his students at the University of Hawai'i (Manoa); visiting lectures and discussion with Anne Ferguson, Tracy Dobson, Bill Derman, Bob Hitchcock, and other colleagues and students at Michigan State University; feedback from Carole Nagengast and her students at the University of New Mexico; and the enthusiastic support for this topic and its continued relevance offered by Laura Nader and her students at the University of California, Berkeley.

To my long-suffering, incredibly patient editor at Left Coast Press, Jennifer Collier, and publisher, Mitch Allen, thanks is too small a word. The first edition of this book was published by these two people under the AltaMira imprint, and, I am happy to say, this revised version is now in their hands.

And to my family and friends who endured my "sorry, I can't, maybe when the book is done" excuses for far too many years, as you know, the work is never done. But, on this front, please know, the next round is on me!

Barbara Rose Johnston, December 2010

CHAPTER 1

Human Rights, Environmental Quality, and Social Justice[1]

Barbara Rose Johnston

The right to health, a decent existence, work, and occupational safety and health; the right to an adequate standard of living, freedom from hunger, an adequate and wholesome diet, and decent housing; the right to education, culture, equality and non-discrimination, dignity, and harmonious development of the personality; the right to security of person and of the family; the right to development; the right to meaningful remedy . . . all are rights established by existing United Nations covenants. These rights represent the ideal that governments should strive for in providing for their citizens' basic life requirements, to which all humans are entitled. Guaranteeing these rights requires strategies and structures that insure equitable access to and sustainable use of critical resources—sociopolitical systems that insure environmental quality and social equity.[2]

This ideal of fundamental human rights remains elusive. In fact, it is difficult to think of a single society existing in today's world that retains a self-sufficient, locally controlled, equitable, and environmentally sustainable way of life. This has not always been the case.

For much of human history social groups developed rules and tools for insuring access to critical resources in ways that allowed survival of the group. Some 2.5 million years ago the ancestral *Homo habilis* emerged in Africa. Some 200,000 years ago, *Homo sapien sapiens* gathered plants, hunted animals, and lived in small mobile communities in the forests and savannas of Africa. By 40,000 years ago our human ancestors had developed ways to live in the heat of the world's deserts, the extreme cold of arctic and mountain terrains, in shady forests, lush and fertile river valleys, and along the coastal shores. And 10,000 years ago humans had fashioned ways to survive and thrive in every major ecosystem on this planet. They developed ways to cultivate and store food to allow for the lean times. They settled in larger numbers in villages, towns, and cities, where their ideas, values, ways of living, and language

9

grew increasingly complicated and diverse. Unlike other creatures whose response to harsh or varied conditions prompted biological change, humans generally relied on their ingenuity to survive. They created innovative ways to live and communicate and thus passed knowledge down to their children.

This cultural diversity—the multitude of ways of living and communicating knowledge—gave humans an adaptive edge. Other creatures adjusted to change in their environment through biological adaptation, a process that requires thousands of life spans to generate and reproduce adaptive mutation to the level of the population. Humans developed analytical tools to identify and assess change in their environment, to search out or devise new strategies, and to communicate and incorporate new strategies throughout their group. And humans developed strategies for resource use and regulation that served as core elements of a broader social, cultural, political, and economic system that defined and protected basic rights.

For the human species, culture is our primary adaptive mechanism. No individual social group can survive without the means to communicate, the ability to learn, and a set of values and rules governing interaction, relationships, and rights among its members. As society changes, new rules and rights are defined, and the ideas that frame human-rights propositions vary according to society's need. However, despite immense cultural variation, all human groups share the need for rights that insure the basic parameters necessary for human survival: maintaining bodily health, material security, and social relations and having the opportunity for the development of a cultural and moral life—those aspects of life that allow one to be human.[3]

In the past, when human groups faced deteriorating conditions adaptive success was dependent on time to develop biological responses or, more typically, behavioral responses that recognize changing environmental conditions, identify causality, search out or devise new strategies, and incorporate new strategies in ways that allow the society to survive and thrive. Often the strategy of choice was simply to go somewhere else.

The environmental constraints faced by our ancestors were in large part defined by the biophysical parameters of nature, such as water availability, soil fertility, altitude, and temperature. Today human survival is increasingly constrained by the biodegenerative products of humanity: growing deserts; decreasing forests; declining fisheries; poisoned food, water, and air; and climatic extremes and weather events such as floods, hurricanes, and droughts. Although environmental degradation is by no means new, this new array of biodegenerative conditions presents a number of seemingly insurmountable challenges.

Biodegenerative problems are complex, creating multiple assaults on systemic viability. For example, adaptive responses may be inhibited by the cumulative and synergistic nature of toxic pollution—substances work their way up the food chain at increasing levels and cause mutation at the cellular level—producing not only biophysical change but also intergenerational degenerative change.[4]

Biodegenerative problems are increasingly global, as a matter of scale or as part of a broader global trend. Changes in upper atmospheric composition, for example, have global impact, and these changes present a host of problems tied to fluctuating weather patterns and increased ultraviolet radiation. Other environmental crises may be localized, yet their origins and consequences are tied to global forces and conditions. Water quality problems might involve place-specific issues, such as contamination from human waste, agricultural chemicals, industrial solvents, or mining by-products, all of which generate localized crises. Yet these local crises contribute to

a global trend of water scarcity. Today, in 2010, nearly one billion people lack access to improved sources of water, and 2.6 billion lack even a "simple" improved latrine.[5]
The long-lived nature of many degenerative threats poses crises that defy our conception of time. The nuclear hot spots of the world—places where nuclear weapons were developed, tested, and their waste stored—will continue to contaminate life processes for tens of thousands of years. Our ability to contain, reduce, or even remove their threat is not only limited by our knowledge, technology, and money, but it is also seriously inhibited by the changing nature of sociopolitical systems. Who is responsible for managing the radioactive legacy of defunct regimes?

Human survival skills are challenged in seemingly insurmountable ways by these new biodegenerative conditions. Human adaptation to changing environmental circumstances requires time, space, and the means to implement change. Yet time is an increasingly scarce commodity, especially given the rapid pace of degenerative change. Space is similarly problematic, especially when the threat is global in nature. And the means to implement change may elusive or impossible—especially when customary knowledge and traditions fail to protect, and technoinnovation falls short in achieving true sustainable remedy. The synergistic and cumulative effects of some forms of biodegenerative change produce conditions that may not be reversible no matter how much we believe in human ingenuity. Even when remedies are identified (such as strategies to reduce carbon emissions), implementation on a global scale requires commitment and cooperation that are difficult to achieve. Traditionally, when all else failed, people abandoned their homes, villages, and cities. Yet today migration is less and less a viable option; there are few frontiers, few unmapped spaces to disappear into.

Biodegenerative conditions further complicate the human-environmental relationship. Humans not only need to contend with access and use rights of critical resources such as water, food, and shelter, but they also must contend with the environmental quality issues and their adverse consequences. Such challenges are further exacerbated when sociocultural dynamics and histories are factored in, producing systemic vulnerability.

Human Environmental Rights Abuse

Human environmental rights are those rights that insure basic human survival. They include those universal rights pertaining to minimum biological requirements necessities such as access to food, water, and shelter, as well as those rights that support and sustain life over months, years, and generations—those relative rights that allow the production and reproduction of sociocultural, political, and economic systems that define critical resources and manage access and use in ways that insure social and ecosystemic viability. They include both the rights of the individual and the rights of groups to survive and thrive.

In past eras, when economies and societies were place-based, these rights were mutually interdependent. In today's world, where communities are often multicultural, where cultural identity is fluid and involves membership in multiple communities, where economic ways of life are shaped and constrained by global as well as local forces and conditions, and where the loci of control over local resources are rarely in local user hands—individual and group efforts to secure basic human environmental rights conflict with broader systemic efforts to manage and use environmental resources. These conflicts produce human environmental rights abuses: powerless groups (race, ethnicity, class, gender) and their rights to land, resources, health, and environmental protection are socially and legally sanctioned casualties of broader state and multinational agendas to protect national security and develop national resources (agricultural land, minerals, timber, water, energy).

At one level, human environmental rights abuse occurs because people happen to be living in the wrong place. Beneath their homes lie economic or strategic mineral resources. Their lives are spent in the "empty, open spaces" far from densely populated regions and thus become the logical place for military exercises, weapons testing, the storage or disposal of hazardous wastes. They live on the frontier, in the peripheral regions, and on the borders between "political nations" and find themselves caught in the middle during times of war or civil unrest. Their isolation attracts those who are seeking economic, political, and environmental alternatives. For these and many more reasons, resident peoples become displaced, alienated from their traditional holdings, and experience increasing difficulty in maintaining individual, household, and community health.[6]

At another level, human environmental rights abuse occurs because people are in the way of progress, and "national" needs supersede individual and community concerns. Thus people find themselves forcibly relocated while governments and industry build dams, expand export-oriented intensive agriculture, develop international tourist facilities, and set aside "wilderness" to save the biocommons and attract foreign ecotourism dollars.[7]

Still, at another level, human environmental rights abuse occurs because it is socially, culturally, and legally acceptable to protect the health of some people, while knowingly placing other humans at risk. Thus, women and children, and racial, ethnic, and other powerless groups, experience a contradictory application of occupational health and safety regulations, and of environmental protection measures. The State may disregard its own laws in the name of national security or economic interests. Environmental and occupational health and safety policies may vary greatly between "home" and foreign manufacturing locales. Information about hazardous materials may be available in one setting to some people but purposefully withheld from other people.

Such abuse is justified and legitimized by ethnocentric notions: the belief that the values, traditions, and behavior of your own cultural group are superior, and other groups are biologically, culturally, and socially inferior. Ethnocentric notions are produced and reproduced in a discourse of debasement that serves to dehumanize (they are subhuman: savage, primitive, backward, ignorant, lazy people, illegal aliens) and, thus, to legitimize immoral behavior.[8]

If cultural diversity is a primary adaptive mechanism in human survival, ethnocentricism plays a key role in the demise of peoples and their unique ways of life. While the ideal of human rights is to insure that all humans—irrespective of nationality, religion, sex, social status, occupation, wealth, property, or any other differentiating ethnic, cultural, or social characteristic—are guaranteed the conditions necessary for a life of dignity in the contemporary world, at the experiential level, ethnocentric prejudices, conflicting interests, greed, and simple brutality intercede between law and practice.

In short, human environmental rights are abused when political and economic institutions and processes wrest control over traditionally held resources without negotiation or compensation. Human environmental rights are abused when political and economic institutions and processes degrade environmental settings, place individuals and populations at risk, withhold information about that risk, and rationalize selective exposure on the basis of national security, national energy, and national debt. And, even in the context of strong legal protection for human rights and environmental quality, human environmental rights are abused when cultural forces and economic greed co-opt and corrupt the implementation of legal structures. This *culpability gap*—the distance between governing ideals that protect the basic rights to life and the actual reality of vulnerable and disenfranchised peoples—is an increasingly significant factor in social conflict.[9]

Human Environmental Rights Abuse and the Struggle for Environmental Justice

If a generalized norm can be derived from the study of human environmental rights abuse, it is this: Life-threatening situations prompt people to act, organize, and seek to transform the conditions of their life. Through formal and informal political means, people seek remedy and change in local, national, and international governance. Collectively this social justice environmentalism has two parallel goals: (1) empowerment, through transformation in decision-making systems to allow people living with the problem to gain greater control in defining the nature of the crisis, devise equitable responses, and prohibit its reoccurrence—and (2) accountability, whereby institutions and organizations that played a significant role in creating the problem acknowledge their culpability and (through their efforts to respond) carry a greater share of the burden for repairing the conditions and consequences resulting from environmental crisis.

Information flows and communications technology play a key role in these human environmental rights struggles, especially in the shaping of informal political arenas where individuals, groups, and communities can voice their complaints, exchange information, generate support, encourage political action, and apply political pressure. Cell phone, digitalized video, and internet access allow has helped shape a rights-protective place in cyberspace.[10] These techno-innovations and the communication flows they engender are mechanisms that insure that the experience of human environmental crises is rarely experienced in singular silent fashion. Abuses can be instantaneously reported and protests voiced from around the world.

Previously isolated communities and organizations have formed networks and issue-based coalitions that cross class, race, culture, and national lines, creating a broader base of power to renegotiate relationships with government and industry.[11] This informal political sector seeks equal protection of civil and human rights; access to information; rights of the worker and the community to know the risks and dangers involved in industrial activity; the right to request and receive environmental and community health safeguards and monitor conditions; the right to question the reasons for and benefits from development; and, the right to say no. Their struggles often involve documenting the human context of environmental crisis, using this information in ways to establish culpability and force changes in the status quo to prevent future abuses. They seek strong systems of law and regulation and user representation in policy formation, and a restructuring of the cultural values and assumptions on which decision-making systems are built.[12]

As a result of advocacy efforts, human environmental rights issues are increasingly emerging as pivotal issues in formal political arenas. International human rights treaties, covenants, and law; regional human rights instruments; trade agreements and related forums; national constitutions and laws have all been used by advocacy groups to force acknowledgment of culpability, halt impending human environmental rights abuses, and renegotiate the human and environmental conditions.[13]

The social conflicts emerging from human environmental rights abuse contexts involve such questions as: Who has the authority to define resource use—the "State" in its actions or granting of permits to outside economic interests, or the affected communities? Who are affected peoples? Who participates in shaping development and other decision-making agendas? Who has the authority to evaluate, modify, assess, or reassess the implications of state-sponsored or sanctioned change? Who holds social and environmental culpability when sanctioned change brings adverse affects? Who is responsible for remediation? How do we respond to human environmental crises that are the legacy of past governments? What is the basis for determining socially just measures of compensation?

These questions testify to the dysfunctional nature of state and international governance, whereby decisions are often made to further the interests and agendas of entities (governments, corporations) and forces (economic development, national security) in ways that adversely affect the rights and futures of local communities. Huge social, political, economic, and geographic distance typically exists between those who decide and those who pay the price of decisive actions. Confronting this distance—organizing, communicating, and actively confronting and engaging culpable agencies and parties—represents an effort to bridge the culpability gap. However, the asking of these questions also threatens the stability of existing power structures and thus can prompt severe responses. Backlash is inevitable.

Eric Wolf has argued that "the arrangements of a society become most visible when they are challenged by crisis."[14] Those who suffer the most are typically those with the least power in society—either the power to insulate themselves from the threat or, later, the power to rebuild their lives. Not only does the experience of crisis expose the power relations of society, but it also tests the viability of political systems. The common experience and urgent need to respond blurs previous lines of cleavage—the cultural notions and historical relationships that divide groups in society are temporarily pushed aside as people struggle to survive a common threat. They act, organize, and transform the conditions of their life, and thus new leaders emerge, new networks and coalitions are formed, and community identity is reshaped.

In other words, in responding to human environmental crisis new opportunities emerge to rearrange the hierarchies of power in society.

This observation is borne out in communities across the world, where people are linked in environmental justice struggles to secure access to information, the right of the worker and the community to know the risks and dangers involved in industrial activity, the right to request and receive environmental and community health safeguards, the right to monitor and repair degenerative conditions, the right to question the reasons for and benefits from development, and, increasingly, the right to say "no." Such struggles often involve documenting the human context of environmental crisis, using this information in ways to establish culpability, and forcing changes in the status quo to prevent future abuses. They seek strong systems of law and regulation as well as user representation in policy formation. In short, these environmental quality and social justice movements seek a restructuring of the cultural values and assumptions on which decision-making systems are built.

Such efforts typically involve conflict between individuals, communities, peoples, and/or the State over rights to define, use, and control resources. For the State, the "nation" is the salient population for whom decisions are made. For resident communities living in the path of change, the community is the salient group. In the resolution of these power struggles, compensatory or remedial action taken by government and industry may serve, intentionally or unintentionally, to co-opt the goals of the movement and deflate the power of movement leadership. Disinformation campaigns, corporate greenwashing, publicly acknowledging culpability but responding to problems and victims in relatively minor ways, and creating regulatory and decision-making frameworks that give the image of addressing the concern but are implemented in limited and restrictive fashion are all actions that neutralize a potential threat to the status quo.[15]

Resolving human environmental crises requires fundamental transformations in local, national, and international decision-making systems that, first, allow people living with the problem to gain greater control in defining the nature of the crisis, devising equitable responses, and prohibiting recurrence; and, second, allow institutions and organizations that played a significant role in creating the problem to acknowledge their culpability and (through their efforts to respond) to carry a greater share of the burden for resolving the consequence. The struggle to achieve these transformations in decision-making systems requires confronting, challenging, and changing the status quo. Backlash is inevitable. Thus, we come to what may be the crucial question of our time: Can we build environmentally sound and socially just solutions to our problems in ways that minimize or prevent the incidence of violent conflict?

Human Rights and the Environment: Building an International Framework?

The planetary right to a healthy environment was a key concept emerging from the 1990 global Earth Day activism and the subsequent 1992 United Nations Earth Summit in Rio de Janeiro. Attended by representatives of 172 governments and 2,400 nongovernmental organizations, Earth Summit explored the relationship between economic development and environmental degradation, adopting three major agreements (Agenda 21, the Rio Declaration on Environment and Development, the Statement of Forest Principles) and two legally binding conventions (the United Nations Framework Convention on Climate Change and the United Nations Convention on Biological Diversity). Earth Summit accords also called on the UN to negotiate an international legal agreement on desertification, hold talks on preventing the depletion of certain fish stocks, devise a program of action for the sustainable development of small-island developing states, and establish other mechanisms for ensuring the implementation of the Rio accords.

While the Rio Declaration and Agenda 21 did not contain many explicit references to human rights, a petition presented by the Sierra Club Legal Defense Fund (now Earth Justice Fund) on the relationship between human rights and the environment was accepted by the UN General Assembly in the lead up to the Rio meetings.[16] In 1990 Mme. Fatma Zohra Ksentini was designated a Special Rapporteur by the UN Commission for Human Rights Sub-Commission on Prevention of Discrimination and Protection of Minorities and charged with the study of the problem of the environment and its relation to human rights. Her resulting work produced a statement of *Draft Principles on Human Rights and the Environment*.[17] To consider the fundamental issues and address the question of whether a new treaty was needed, the Special Rapporteur invited the international community, including governments, indigenous peoples, nongovernmental organizations, and other members of civil society to submit case materials illustrating the intersect between human rights abuse and the environment.[18]

Mme. Ksentini's final report, submitted to the UN Economic and Social Council in July 1994, identified the legal foundations for the right to a satisfactory environment as present in existing human rights covenants, especially the right to life, sustainable and environmentally sound development, and participatory democracy. Her review and findings on the varied dimensions of the human rights/environment intersect included:

1. There is a special relationship between fragile habitats and indigenous peoples that is increasingly problematic, threatened by an escalation of human rights violations including right to life, to health, to traditional lands, and to the promotion and protection of culture especially as a result of development projects and their associated displacement of indigenous peoples.

2. The many instruments created by UN treaties and dimensions of international law that prohibit attacks against the environment in periods of armed conflict, especially the use of environment as an instrument of war, are increasingly ignored demonstrating the failure of such instruments in protecting the environment.

3. There is a core relationship between the environment and international peace and security that is seriously threatened by the fact that "nuclear weapons and biological and chemical substances can eliminate much if not all of life. There are now many methods of altering the climate and destroying essential foodstuffs, and the deprivation that would certainly follow would create social unrest and instability. Population pressures, with or without intentional environmental degradation, will inevitably lead to States vying with each other for resources essential for survival."

4. Pollution of the air, water and land from various sources, especially industrial disasters (oil spills, Bhopal, Chernobyl), transboundary transfer of hazardous waste (including the dumping of nuclear and other radioactive waste), deforestation, climate change, loss of biodiversity, has generated a disproportionate impact on the health and well-being of vulnerable peoples. Indigenous peoples, individuals and groups who are marginalized by poverty, women, children, disabled persons, and environmental refugees are especially vulnerable to the crises generated by such environmental abuse.[19]

Presented to UN Commission on Human Rights in 1995, the declaration of *Draft Principles on Human Rights and the Environment* proposed a substantive right to "a secure, healthy, and ecologically sound environment" and included the concept of intergenerational equity. The Commission, with the expressed concern of its members from the United States and European countries, rejected this articulation of a new substantive right. Instead, the report and its guiding principles were distributed across the UN system with the recommendation that all agencies of the UN and its' member states address its' concerns.[20]

The Ecopolitical Climate That Influenced This Book

The UN human rights and environment initiative was part of a new era of environmental justice advocacy that sought the protection of biocultural diversity through rights-based governance. In the decade that followed Earth Summit, the right to a healthy environment was not only explored in international initiatives as described above but also formally recognized in the enactment of more than 90 national constitutions as either a justiciable right or a noted element of the constitutional rights to life, health, and family life.[21]

Consider, for example, President William Jefferson Clinton's September 24, 1996, address to the 51st UN General Assembly speech to the United Nations General Assembly, in which he outlined his plan to achieve security for America. Security meant the ability to enjoy fundamental rights and was achieved by increased involvement in international treaties. Clinton's goals declared in this speech included pursuing unconditional extension of the Nuclear Non-Proliferation Treaty; ratification of START II and Chemical Weapons Convention to ban poison gas worldwide; adoption of a Comprehensive Test Ban Treaty and a global ban on the production of fissile material for weapons; ratification of the Convention on Certain Conventional Weapons; outlawing indiscriminate use of antipersonnel landmines; and, strengthen the Biological and Toxin Weapons Convention.[22] On a national level, security meant embracing transparency, accountability, and diplomacy, and a priority of addressing historical injustice. Thus, the President, following an order to declassify and review previous administration's records, apologized to Guatemala for the U.S. role in facilitating the 1954 coup and apologized to native Hawaiian's for the overthrow of the Kingdom of Hawaii on January 17, 1893 and the deprivation of the rights of Native Hawaiians to self-determination. He issued letters of apology, expanded compensation, authorized commemorative work to memorialize the abuses suffered in Japanese internment camps, and restructured federal relationships with American Indian tribes to recognize their sovereign rights to self-determination. He declassified documents, established commissions to study, and authorized measures to provide redress, including letters of apology to African American men abused in Tuskegee syphilis experiments and to native Alaskans, Marshall Islanders, and other groups who had been abused as human subjects in radiation experiments. And, through environmental justice policy, science, and programs, the Clinton administration established and provided remedial attention to the many human and environmental issues of the day.[23]

This is the ecopolitical world in which the first edition of *Life and Death Matters: Human Rights and the Environment at the End of the Millennium* was written. It was a time of increasing awareness that local environmental crises are influenced and shaped by broader global forces, that resources are finite, and that human action has stimulated profound, degenerative, planetary change. In facing such dire threats, it was also a time of hopeful optimism, when the United States and other governments took leadership roles in promoting the notion that true security can be achieved through international cooperation and transparent governance that prioritizes environmental health and human rights. In such a climate we saw the possibilities for real progress in recognizing and providing redress for historical wrongs. In such a climate we believed in the possibility that these corrective actions at home and abroad might serve a cautionary role and encourage action that insures a more sustainable future.

This promise and the potential role of the scholar advocate were a core focus of the November 1994 American Anthropological Association annual meeting in Atlanta, Georgia. The conference theme explored anthropology and human rights, and contributors to this book participated in a "human rights and environment" session that considered the sociocultural and political factors that often generate environmental crisis; the historical conditions and relationships that make some people more vulnerable than others; and, the varied forms of response to the life-threatening situations that result.

Our presentations and the discussion that followed were very much influenced by a recent publication by Robert Kaplan, an *Atlantic Monthly* article entitled "The Coming Anarchy: How Scarcity, Crime, Tribalism, and Disease Are Rapidly Destroying the Social Fabric of Our Planet." Using examples from West Africa, Asia, and the Middle East, Kaplan argued that population growth, environmental degradation, and subsequent competition for increasingly scarce resources are interrelated factors that contribute to increased aggression and violent conflict in many places around the globe. With photographs, interviews, and descriptions, Kaplan painted a picture of life in some of the more desperate regions of the world: environmental hot spots, where people act solely through self-interest; where power lies in cultural, ethnic, and religious group membership; and where the state and other governmental institutions are weak (or nonexistent), while cultural-based institutions are strengthening (or dominate). Regions, he argued, are no longer sharply defined by political borders, but rather reflect ethnic affiliation and the fluid movement of populations. Given current population rates and continually escalating levels of resource extraction and consumption, Kaplan suggested that the criminal anarchy characterizing life in these crisis areas may represent the shape of things to come in a "few decades hence" for the entire planet. "The coming upheaval," Kaplan predicted, "in which foreign embassies are shut down, states collapse, and contact with the outside world takes place through dangerous, disease-ridden coastal trading posts, will loom large in the century we are entering."[24]

Kaplan's article was one of the most reproduced essays of the year, and his vision and conclusions were matter for much heated debate. Will the events of the next 50 years be characterized by environmental scarcity leading to cultural and racial clashes, to a remaking of the geopolitical map reflecting "geographic destiny and the transformation of war"? Are cultural allegiances simply a matter of immediate family and "guerrilla comrades"? Is humanity doomed to employ cultural strategies for self-serving ends?

In response and in reaction to Kaplan's provocative framing, we took a critical look at how people in communities, organizations, and governmental institutions respond to the human environmental crises that structure their lives. *Life and Death Matters* documented a broad range of responses (including individual, community, state, and international responses) that include denial, migration, and the formation of social and political movements, as well as efforts to renegotiate power and consequence from within existing systems, efforts to transform systems, and efforts to build new hierarchies of power. In some cases, we found Robert Kaplan's vision validated: people *do* use cultural notions and mechanisms in an attempt to respond to human environmental crises, and at times these responses are reactionary, repressive, abusive, and violent. One can draw identifiable connections between ineffective response and the rise of violent conflict. However, other cases suggest that although chaos and anarchy may be inevitable byproducts of human environmental crisis, neither is necessarily the endpoint. There is much more to the story.

Life-threatening situations tear at the fabric of culture and society. Some people are caught in an escalating cycle of degradation and human rights abuse: they die, they flee, they passively accept their lot. Others fight to survive in more violent ways, embracing and engaging in confrontational politics and actions. Sometimes the common experience and urgent need to respond blurs previous lines of cleavage: new leaders emerge, innovative networks and coalitions are formed, community identity is reshaped. Organization, activism, and the changes that these sociopolitical movements promote all threaten the status quo. Conflict, and the chaos and anarchy that conflict engenders, is inevitable—hence Kaplan's vision. However, the process of shaping solutions requires confronting and engaging problems—for substantive change emerges from what appears, at a temporal glance, to be anarchy.

The human environmental crises plaguing our planet are difficult to define, to understand, and to resolve—because they are, by their very nature, the manifestation of historical processes and events with consequences that, as observed earlier, are both synergistic and cumulative. If we are to recognize and support the new strands of order emerging from the chaos and anarchy of our times, we must refocus our questions. Kaplan asked an important question: Is the violent anarchy that plagues Africa today the shape of things to come for the entire planet tomorrow? In the first edition of this book we rephrased the question to ask: How are people responding to these crises? What works in what settings? What doesn't work? What are the social and environmental consequences of inadequate response to human environmental crisis? What structural mechanisms are employed, or needed, to resolve crises successfully?

We found that, although response to human environmental rights abuse is varied, generalized strategies in the response continuum can be recognized and include *passive victimization* where abuse is endured with no significant struggle to fight back; *passive resistance* with nonconfrontational efforts to renegotiate conditions in subtle ways; *nonviolent protest, political advocacy, and action* to adjust conditions and affect change within existing systems through confrontation, negotiation, and the development of further rights-protective problem-solving mechanisms; *confrontational protest, advocacy, and actions* aimed at transforming conditions *and* structures of power; and *reparation* with efforts to repair, restore, and rebuild in the aftermath of structural transformations of conditions and power. Depending on the conditions and options available and the consequences of previous efforts, societal action to human environmental crisis may include any or all categories in the response continuum.

We also found that a continued history of institutional denial or inadequate response to human environmental rights abuse may force people toward action on the violent end of the response continuum. Thus, we argued in the first edition of this book: if we, as a species, are to survive and even thrive, we must approach human environmental crisis by listening and learning how to see reality from the multiplicity of vantage points that structure each and every crisis and by devising strategies and creating opportunities that let us bridge the distance between those who struggle to survive in the midst of environmental crisis and those who helped create the chaos that has fundamentally transformed life.

This Second Edition and the Ecopolitical Climate That Shaped It

The title and the topics addressed in the first edition of this book reflected an understanding that the life-and-death struggles of people in the distant corners of this planet are struggles that matter: to those involved, to those intimately and distantly responsible, and to the many who will, unless lasting solutions are found, experience similar difficulties sooner or later. This advocacy-oriented work was strongly influenced by the promise of 1990s-era rights-based governance. It was our hope that in documenting, assessing, and interpreting human environmental crisis and response to those crises we might generate understandings that encourage meaningful remedy and forestall or prevent future crises. In our social documentation we sought environmental justice.

In 2007, when I asked my authors to consider revising this collection, our views of the world were also influenced by the culture of power in national and international governance—though this era of governance operated under a very different notion security and approach to its achievement.

Consider, for example, the meaning and implications of the term *security* articulated in September 2000 in the Project for a New American Century's "Rebuilding America's Defenses"—a political strategy document that served as the key architecture for Paul Wolfowitz, Donald Rumsfeld, and Dick Cheney in their respective roles in the new George W. Bush administration.[25] This plan for American security would be achieved through geostrategic expansion, including the direct imposition of U.S. "forward bases" throughout Central Asia and the Middle East to ensure strategic resource access and economic domination, while strangling any potential rival or any viable alternative to America's vision of a free-market economy. It also called for global military policing using various instruments of military intervention including punitive and preemptive bombings. And new weapons systems are called for, including the Star Wars missile shield, laser-guided and hypersonic weapons with global reach, weather/climatic warfare weapons (High Altitude Auroral Research Program), weaponization of space, high-energy weapons, and the development of a new generation of nuclear weapons.

This notion of achieving security through militarism was a pre-9/11 feature of the George W. Bush presidency, as evidenced by his administration's stance on international governance, especially treaties that attempted to restrict militarism. In February 2001 the Bush administration refused to join 123 nations in their pledge to ban the use and production of antipersonnel bombs and mines. In March 2001 the Bush administration announced its intent to withdraw from the Kyoto process on climate change. In April 2001 the United States—opposing resolutions supporting lower-cost access to HIV/AIDS drugs, acknowledging a basic human right to adequate food, and calling for a moratorium on the death penalty—failed in its bid for reelection to the UN Human Rights Commission. In July 2001 the United States opposed the UN Agreement to Curb the International Flow of Illicit Small Arms. That same month the United States walked out of a London conference to discuss a 1994 protocol designed to strengthen the 1972 Biological and Toxin Weapons Convention (in November 2001 UN Ambassador John Bolton announced that the protocol was dead). Also that month, the New York Times reported: "In its first six months, the Bush administration has been examining ways to escape permanently from an unratified international agreement banning nuclear tests, just as it has moved to scrap the Antiballistic Missile Treaty and has rebelled against a global warming pact that it believes would cripple American industry."[26] In August 2001 the Bush administration formally refused signing the Land Mine Treaty. In September 2001 the United States withdrew from the International Conference on Racism. In October 2001, when Great Britain became the 42nd nation to ratify the International Criminal Court, the United States continued its opposition, adopting legislation that prohibited U.S. military personnel from obeying the jurisdiction of the proposed ICC. In December 2001 the United States officially withdrew from the 1972 Antiballistic Missile Treaty.[27] By February 2002, with congressional approval, George W. Bush had formally adopted contingency plans that included a first strike "pre-emptive" nuclear weapons policy against the so-called axis of evil (Iraq, Iran, Libya, Syria, and North Korea), as well as Russia and China.

When President Bush gave his October 21, 2004, address to the UN General Assembly, he offered the world his vision for security:

> In this young century, our world needs a new definition of security. Our security is not merely found in spheres of influence, or some balance of power. The security of our world is found in the advancing rights of mankind. . . . These rights are advancing across the world—and across the world, the enemies of human rights are responding with violence. Terrorists and their allies believe the Universal Declaration of Human Rights and the American Bill of Rights, and every charter of liberty ever written, are lies, to be burned and destroyed and forgotten. They believe that dictators should control every mind and tongue in the Middle East and beyond. They believe that suicide and torture and murder are fully justified to serve any goal they declare. And they act on their beliefs.[28]

With this assertion that terrorists and their allies reject the fundamental rules of any and all forms of society, the United States attempted to legitimize its own rejection of the laws that protect fundamental human rights.

As the United States and the nations of world attempted governance through security state militarism, unbridled plunder took hold.[29] Massive expansion of extractive industry (oil, mining, deforestation) occurred while the world's attention was largely focused on terrorist acts and nation-state reprisals. And when natural or humanitarian disasters occurred (hurricanes, drought, famine) attention and resources were often too little, too late.

Our Approach to Revision and Additional Thoughts on the Meaning of Security

It was in this rights-repressive climate that contributors to this book worked on a second edition. Given the massive changes that have occurred in this past decade, the deeper dimensions of ulcerating crisis, and the many new human rights and environment issues that are now apparent, both revision and expansion were needed. For these and other reasons it has taken another four years to revise, update, and revise again the case studies in this book.

This second edition, as did the original edition, incorporates a seven-part conceptual structure that addresses Economic Development; Biodiversity: Preserving What, for Whom?; Mineral Wealth vs. Biotic Health; Agriculture and Agri-Conflict;

Development, Degradation, and Conflict; Postwar Matters; and Problems That Push the Parameters of Time and Space. Case-specific essays are summarized, revised, and further expanded; 1990s-era text, appearing in sections titled "End of the Millennium," communicates a sense of the problems in a world where human rights and the environment were emerging concerns or central goals of governance. This world stands in sharp and, at times, painful contrast to our current vantage point, explored in new sections titled "View from the 21st Century." Because new issues have emerged in the past decade, several new chapters and brief vignettes ("Snapshots") have also been added. These new essays and vignettes were crafted between 2008 and 2010, when writers were very much aware that a new political administration in the United States was on the horizon, or in its early days, and that a return to rights-based governance was again a possibility. With new political leadership, new agendas, policies and possibilities emerge.

Collectively the chapters in this second edition offer a sense of place, problems, dynamics of engagement, and envisioned future from the perspectives of the mid-1990s and 2010. We identify some of the driving forces behind change, the controlling processes that influence change, and the profound consequences that occur when such change abuses the fundamental rights of people and their environment. We consider some of the human environmental consequences of moving from a rights-based notion of governance to a "war on terror" security framework. And, we ask, given this history and its consequences: What trends are on the horizon?

As this book goes to press, a new National Security Strategy has been articulated by a new U.S. President, Barack Obama. In this 2010 vision of security the consequential damages of a decade of militarism and the associated rejection of internationalism and rights-based governance are acknowledged, with the administration reserving "the right to act unilaterally if necessary to defend our nation and our interests."[30] The overriding policy focus, however, is one that seeks "security through peace," with armed conflict considered a last resort, to be used only when diplomacy is exhausted. Thus the Obama vision of security, as articulated in this National Security Strategy, is a state of peace achieved through international cooperation and governance with prioritized actions that secure the basic means to support life: health, education, food, the environment—coupled with a renewed attention to the home front, recognizing that peace begins at home. To achieve such goals, the administration has emphasized science-based policy, as opposed to the previous administration's reliance on policy-driven science, and has aggressively promoted people-centered economics—government policy that addresses the economic well-being of its citizens, in addition to industry and market-driven priorities.

Whether these approaches are effective in addressing the complex and profound human environmental crises of our times—manifested through violence, war, plunder, pollution, environmental disasters, resource scarcity, poverty, and degenerative health—remains to be seen.[31] Consider, for example the BP oil spill in the Gulf of Mexico and its threat to aquatic and coastal life throughout the region. Given ocean currents and the marine food chain, this disaster will most assuredly generate profound change on a planetary scale. And consider the controlling processes that set the stage for this disaster. The regulatory approaches that prioritize profit over environmental safeguards and the government oversight mechanisms that depend on oil industry reporting and assurances (they are the experts, their technology is safe) are the same controlling processes that structure the government/industry relationship in the coal and nuclear industries.

Do we have what it takes to build a world system, a national government, a local community reality that not only responds in reaction to emergent crises and ulcerating conditions but also anticipates the potentially destructive consequences of today's decisions—the driving forces behind tomorrow's human environmental crises? We argue that such visionary thinking can be shaped only with thoughtful attention to the historical relationships, actions, and biocultural consequences that got us to this pivotal place in human history.

Notes

1. This essay is a revision of material published in the first edition of *Life and Death Matters* (Johnston 1997); the chapter "Human Environmental Rights" in *Human Rights: New Perspectives, New Realities*, 2nd ed., Adamantia Pollis and Peter Schwab, Eds. (New York, NY: Praeger Publishers, 2000, 95–103); and the preface to the *Endangered Peoples of the World* series of books (cf. *Endangered Peoples of Southeast and East Asia*, Leslie Sponsel, Ed. [Westport CT: Greenwood Press, 2000]). Since the initial version of this introductory paragraph was drafted significant expansion in human rights law has occurred, especially with regard to the recognition of the rights of cultural groups, indigenous peoples, and ethnic minorities; the right to remedy and reparation for historical cases of injustice experience by such groups; and the recognition that human rights are abused not only by individuals but also by processes such as development and militarism. See, for example, "Basic Principles and Guidelines on the Right to a Remedy and Reparation for Victims of Gross Violations of International Human Rights Law and Serious Violations of International Humanitarian Law" adopted and proclaimed by the United Nations General Assembly (2005 A/RES/60/147); and the United Nations Declaration on the Rights of Indigenous Peoples (2007 A/RES/61/295). As discussed later in this chapter, increasingly regional human rights courts are accepting and ruling on historical injustices resulting from state-sponsored processes (development, militarism).

2. As noted in Mme. Fatima Zaire Ksentini's preliminary report on Human Rights and the Environment prepared for the Sub-Commission on the Prevention of Discrimination and Protection of Minorities (UN Doc.E/CN.4Sub2/1991/8). Many of conceptual ideas in this essay were originally developed as a contribution to Ksentini's study and later refined in *Who Pays the Price? The Sociocultural Context of Environmental Crisis*, Barbara Rose Johnston, Ed. (Washington, D.C.: Island Press, 1994); and, note 1, Johnston 1997, 2000.

3. After Jennifer Shirmer, "The Dilemma of Cultural Diversity and Equivalency in Universal Human Rights Standards," in *Human Rights and Anthropology*, Theodore Downing and Gilbert Kushner, Eds., Cultural Survival Report 24 (Cambridge, MA: Cultural Survival, 1988, 91–106).

4. The first major work to draw attention to these issues was Theo Colburn, Dianne Dumanoski, and John Peterson Meyers, *Our Stolen Future* (New York: Plume Books, 1997), findings that were most recently confirmed by the President's Cancer Panel 2008/2009 Annual Report *Reducing Environmental Cancer Risk, What Can We Do Now*, National Cancer Institute; accessed 5/14/2010, http://deainfo.nci.nih.gov/advisory/pcp/pcp08-09rpt/PCP_Report_08-09_508.pdf.

5. As reported by World Health Organization, "Water, Sanitation and Health"; accessed 5/2/2010, www.who.int/water_sanitation_health/en/. For cross-cultural comparative studies examining local conditions as part of a global crisis in water access and use, see *Water, Culture, & Power: Local Struggles in a Global Context*, John Donahue and Barbara Rose Johnston, Eds. (Covello, CA: Island Press, 1998).

6. See, for example, the various issues of *Cultural Survival Quarterly* and Cultural Survival's *State of the Peoples: A Global Human Rights Report on Societies in Danger* (Boston: Beacon Press, 1993).

7. For a review of the socioenvironmental impacts of large-scale hydroelectric dam projects, see Patrick McCully's *Silenced Rivers: The Ecology and Politics of Large Dams* (London: Zed Press, 1996); Thayer Scudder, *The Future of Large Dams: Dealing with Social, Environmental, Institutional and Political Costs* (London: Earthscan, 2005); and *Dams and Development: A New Framework for Decision Making*, Final Report of the World Commission on Dams, November 16, 2000; accessed 5/10/2010, www.dams.org/report/. For political ecological analysis of agribusiness and other export-oriented development strategies, see Susan Stonich, *"I Am Destroying the Land!" People, Poverty, and Environment in Honduras* (Boulder, CO: Westview, 1994); and Daniel Faber, *Environment under Fire: Imperialism and the Ecological Crisis in Central America* (New York: Monthly Review Press, 1993).

8. George Appell has conducted a cross-cultural comparative analysis of human rights abuses, finding that dehumanizing discourse is characteristically used as a means of legitimizing unequal social relations. See his article "Dehumanization in Fact and Theory Processes of Modernization and the Social Science," in *Social Science Models and Their Impact on Third World Societies*, John A. Lent, Ed., Studies in Third World Societies Publication No.45 (Williamsburg, VA: College of William and Mary, 1991). This discussion is heavily influenced by John Bodley's seminal work *Victims of Progress* (Mountain View, CA: Mayfield Publishing, 1982, 1999)—especially his ideas on the role of ethnocentrism in justifying oppressive state policies. For historical examples of the use of ethnocentric philosophy to justify government action, see Bodley's *Tribal Peoples and Development Issues* (Mountain View, CA: Mayfield Publishing, 1988).

9. The linkages between environmental scarcity and violent conflict have shaped the "environmental security" field. See, for example, Norman Meyers, *Ultimate Security: The Environmental Basis of Political Stability* (Covello, CA: Island Press, 1996) and the work of Thomas Homer-Dixon, especially *Environmental Scarcity and Global Security* (New York: Foreign Policy Association, 1993); and *Environment, Scarcity, and Violence* (Princeton, NJ: Princeton University Press, 1999).

10. Information technology and communications technology play a significant role in disrupting and transforming traditional power structures—as tools that transform information flows (especially access to and control over critical information) and as structural forums that shape cyberspace as political space. Nevertheless, free uncensored access to the tools and space is still, for the most part, restricted to first-world actors. In 1995 some 40 million people in 100 countries had access to the internet. Yet, of the 500,000 "host" internet computers, 70% were based in the United States, and more than 50% of the world's internet-connected computers were in the United States (reported by Mike Holderness, "The Internet and the South," in *Earth Island Journal*, Winter 1996–97:40–42). By 2010 these ratios had changed, with Asia and Europe reporting greater numbers of people using the internet, and Africa, the Middle East, and Oceania/Australia still lagging far behind. Africa currently hosts only 4.8% of the world's internet users, the Middle East 3.2%, and Oceania 1.2%. In many of these places access is further constrained by the lack of digital cable line, unstable phone lines, and slow transmission rates. In China, which has the largest number of the world's internet users, access is predominantly urban and restricted through the use of server filter and monitoring systems. In the United States, although 74% of the people have internet access, less than 10% of Native Americans are estimated to have access to broadband technology allowing internet access (see Internet World Stats; accessed 5/14/2010, www.internetworldstats.com/stats.htm; and New Media, Technology, and Internet Use in Indian Country: Quantitative and Qualitative Analyses, Native Public

Media and the New America Foundation report; 5/14/2010, www.nativepublicmedia.org/Broadband-Advocacy/).

11. Examples are numerous. For instance, increased awareness of development impacts and the rights of dam-affected peoples has led to a rise in protests, calls for remediation, and a strengthening of local and regional movements. See the Movement of Dam-Affected Peoples in Brazil (MAB), African Rivers Network, Latin American Network Against Dams and for Rivers, Communities and Water (REDLAR), and the Himalayan and Peninsular Hydro-Ecological Network (HYPHEN). These movements have been supported through the efforts of international advocacy groups (such as International Rivers), events (such as the four regional consultations of the World Commission on Dams and the 1997, 2003, and 2010 "Rivers for Life" international meetings of dam-affected peoples), and strengthened by the free and prior informed cosnet requirements in UN treaties (see Indigenous Peoples Declaration adopted by the UN General Assembly in 2007, note 1).

12. For an excellent tactical essay on building international environmental justice links, see Chris Kiefer and Medea Benjamin's essay "Solidarity with the Third World: Building an International Environmental Justice Movement," in R. Hofrichter, Ed., *Toxic Struggles: The Theory and Practice of Environmental Justice* (New York: New Society Publishing, 1993, 226–36). For an analysis of social movements in the southern hemisphere, see Ponna Wignaraja, Ed., *New Social Movements in the South: Empowering the People* (London: Zed Books, 1992). For a rare, successful case of community activism against a government-endorsed chemical multinational development scheme, see Claude Alvares's edited volume *Unwanted Guest: Goans vs. Du Pont* (New Delhi: The Other India Press, 1991). For an examination of the role of NGOs in stimulating World Bank reform, see Jonathan Fox and L. David Brown, Eds., *The Struggle for Accountability: The World Bank, NGOs, and Grassroots Movements* (Boston, MA: MIT Press, 1998).

13. Neil Popovic, "In Pursuit of Environmental Human Rights: Commentary on the Draft Declaration of Principles on Human Rights and the Environment," *Columbia Human Rights Law Review* (27:3, Spring 1996).

14. Eric Wolf, 1990:590. "Distinguished Lecture: Facing Power—Old Insights, New Questions," *American Anthropologist* (92:586–96, 1990).

15. For example, government recognition of indigenous land rights in Brazil has been inconsistently enforced with greater protection provided during times of global interest on the issue (during and after the 1992 UNCED Conference in Rio de Janeiro, for example). In January 1996 the government revised rules for indigenous land demarcation, giving greater voice to those who illegally occupy indigenous lands. Violent conflicts have increased, as have the number of people killed in land conflicts. With millions of landless poor in Brazil, the politics surrounding indigenous reserves intensify. Families move on their own into the reserves, prompting violent conflicts with indigenous peoples. Landed interests push for reducing reserve size, especially when faced with the possibility of seeing current holdings acquired by the government to use for agrarian reform. For a mid-1990s perspective, see Stephan Schwartzman, Ana Valeria Araujo, and Paulo Pamkarau, "Brazil: The Battle over Indigenous Land Rights," *NACLA Report on the Americas* (March/April 1996). For a current view, search Google news for "Avatar" and "Xingu." Human environmental rights conflicts are intensifying as the region embarks on a new generation of hydrodevelopment projects and expansion of plantation agriculture for biofuel.

16. See United Nations General Assembly resolution 42/186, dated December 11, 1987, and Sub-Commission on Prevention of Discrimination and Protection of Minorities, 1989/108, dated August 31, 1989.

17. E/CN.4/Sub.2/1994/9, Annex I, accessed on line, May 5, 2010, http://daccess-ods.un.org/access.nsf/Get?Open&DS=E/CN.4/2005/96&Lang=E. This Declaration of Draft Prin-

ciples was also published in the first edition of *Life and Death Matters*. The Declaration is still in draft form; it has never been formally adopted by the General Assembly. In November 2000 the right to a healthy environment was recognized as an aspect of the right to health (United Nations Committee on Economic, Social, and Cultural Rights, General Comment 14, "The Right to the Highest Attainable Standard of Health," 11/8/2000, UN Doc E/C.12/2000/4, para 9). The Draft Principles were taken up jointly by UNEP and OHCHR in 2002, in an expert forum on Ecosystem Services and Human Well-Being in 2008 and a High-level Expert Meeting on the "The New Future of Human Rights and Environment: Moving the Global Agenda Forward" in 2009. Meeting documents and reports accessed 5/5/2010; www.unep.org/environmentalgovernance/Events/HumanRightsandEnvironment/tabid/2046/language/en-US/Default.aspx. Water, with its key role in sustaining the dignity and the equal rights of human beings and life itself, was recognized as an essential human need under the 1981 *Convention on the Elimination of All Forms of Discrimination Against Women* and the 1989 *Convention on the Rights of the Child* [CEDAW Article 14(2)(h) and CROC Article 24(2)(c)]. In 2003 the right to drinkable water and adequate sanitation were recognized as an essential part of the right to health and the right to an adequate standard of living in the *International Covenant on Economic, Social, and Cultural Rights* (United Nations Committee on Economic, Social and Cultural Rights, General Comment 15, "The Right to Water", 20/1/2003, UN Doc E/C.12/2002/11 and General Comment 14, as footnote 3). In this covenant, the United Nations expressly stated that the human right to water entitles everyone to sufficient, safe, acceptable, accessible, and affordable water for personal and domestic uses (General Comment 15, as footnote 5). On July 28, 2010, the UN General Assembly, with a vote of 122 votes in favor and zero votes against (41 nations abstaining), adopted a resolution declaring safe and clean drinking water and sanitation as human rights essential to the full enjoyment of life and all other rights.

18. For an example of contributions to the UN study, see Johnston 1994, note 2.

19. E/CN.4/Sub.2/1994/9, quote from Chapter III, section C, paragraph 12.

20. UN Commission on Human Rights, Resolution on Human Rights and the Environment C.H.R. res. 1995/14, ESCOR Supp. (No. 4) at 66, U.N. Doc. E/CN.4/1995/14 (1995), accessed 5/5/2010; www.unhchr.ch/Huridocda/Huridoca.nsf/TestFrame/fc9e5e01445 c4ce2802566db004032bc?Opendocument. Presumably, implementation of this proposed substantive right would require a major restructuring of priorities and the related goals and agenda of governance from its current primary mission of developing and protecting economic security, and such changes might pose a conflict of interest and threat to the national security and sovereign rights of member states. See Mattei and Nader, note 29.

21. For a review of how human rights and environment concerns have been addressed in case law, see "Human Rights and the Environment: What Specific Environmental Rights Have Been Recognized?" Dinah Shelton, *Denver Journal of International Law and Policy*, 35:1: 129–70, 2006.

22. Signing the Comprehensive Nuclear Test Ban Treaty on September 24, 1996, President Clinton submitted it to the Senate in 1997. In October 1999 the Senate rejected it, 48 for, 51 against, 1 present. It remains on the Senate Foreign Relations Committee's calendar and would require a two-thirds Senate vote to send the treaty back to the President for disposal or to give advice and consent for ratification. The Bush administration opposed ratification and actively sought funding to develop and test a new generation of nuclear weapons, including low-yield weapons, earth-penetrating weapons, enhanced radiation weapons, and agent defeat weapons. In an April 2009 speech in Prague, President Barack Obama announced his intent to aggressively pursue ratification.

23. For an example of significant directives, see: "Executive Order 12898 of February 11, 1994. Federal actions to address environmental justice in minority populations and low-income populations" by President William Jefferson Clinton; accessed 3/13/2010, www.epa.gov/fedreg/eo/eo12898.htm. For one example of how implementation of this policy shaped new funding and prompted a subsequent refocus of environmental social science work, consider the emergence of environmental anthropology, an effort largely driven by the Society for Applied Anthropology Environmental Anthropology project, which I helped organize and directed (1996–2000). To view to the SfAA-EPA Cooperative Agreement, project brochures, reports, conference papers, and other publications, see www.sfaa.net/eap/abouteap.html. For an evaluation of the project and its outcomes, see "Backyard Anthropology and Community Struggles to Reclaim the Commons? Lessons from the SfAA Environmental Anthropology Project," Barbara Rose Johnston, *Practicing Anthropology* (Volume 23:3, 2002).

24. Robert D. Kaplan, "The Coming Anarchy: How Scarcity, Crime Overpopulation, Tribalism, and Disease Are Rapidly Destroying the Social Fabric of Our Planet," *The Atlantic Monthly*, February 1994, accessed 9/6/10, www.theatlantic.com/magazine/archive/1994/02/the-coming-anarchy/4670/.

25. "Rebuilding America's Defenses: Strategy, Forces, and Resources for a New Century" is a report resulting from a series of papers and discussions authored by a conservative group men who were concerned with decline in the strength of America's defenses and the potential ramifications that this post–Cold War "peace dividend" might bring. The principal author is Thomas Donnelly. Paul Wolfowitz is listed as a contributor to the report. The project's stated goal was to build on the vision pursued by Secretary of Defense Dick Cheney, whose 1992 Defense Policy Guidance included strategies to insure the international dominance of the United States, to anticipate and preclude threats to that dominance from other rival powers, and to build an international security order that reflected American principles and sustained American interests; accessed 5/5/2010, www.newamericancentury.org/RebuildingAmericasDefenses.pdf.

26. "White House Wants to Bury Pact Banning Tests of Nuclear Arms," Thom Shanker and David E. Sanger, *The New York Times*, July 7, 2001; accessed 5/5/2010, CommonDreamns.org, www.commondreams.org/headlines01/0707-01.htm.

27. See "The US: Rogue Nation," Richard Du Boff, Centre for Research on Globalisation, December 22, 2001; accessed 5/5/2010, www.globalresearch.ca/articles/DUB112B.html.

28. President George W. Bush, Address to the United Nations General Assembly, October 21, 2004.

29. To consider the driving forces behind this new era of natural resource extraction and consumption, see Mattei and Nader's analysis of the mechanisms used by powerful elites to survive the vagrancies of political change while maintaining their ability to plunder through their control of the "rule of law": Ugo Mattei and Laura Nader, *Plunder: When the Rule of Law Is Illegal* (Hoboken, NJ: Wiley-Blackwell, 2008).

30. National Security Strategy, May 2010. Document posted on the White House Blog, "A Blueprint for Pursuing the World that We Seek"; accessed 5/31/2010, www.whitehouse.gov/blog/2010/05/27/a-blueprint-pursuing-world-we-seek.

31. See *Amnesty International Report 2010: The State of the World's Human Rights*; accessed 5/28/2010, http://thereport.amnesty.org/.

CHAPTER 2

Distant Processes: The Global Economy and Outer Island Development in Indonesia[1]

Lorraine V. Aragon

SECTION I: End of the Millennium

The View of a Highland Sulawesi Farmer

During my 1986–89 fieldwork in highland Central Sulawesi, I was relaxing with my friend Tina Mase' on the veranda of her family's field house, a one-room bamboo and bark structure on wooden stilts, gazing out over the swidden rice fields and vast mountain silhouettes that stretched before and below us in a late afternoon at the start of the harvest season. Chewing on her betel nut and tobacco leaf quid, Tina Mase' broke our calm silence by asking: "Ronald Reagan, he is president of the United States, right?" It struck me that few of my college students in the United States would be able to provide the name of Indonesia's president. Tina Mase' is an elementary school educated grandmother in her 40s with seven of her 10 children still living. In addition to household work and childcare, Tina Mase' farms rain-fed crops of rice, corn, and vegetables on steep mountain slopes. Her husband, Tama Mase', also farms, builds houses, and hunts game animals. They both tend coffee trees and harvest the beans, which he carries to the coast to trade for cash or supplies. Tina Mase' continued: her political questioning. "And Father Suharto, he is president of . . . out there?" She paused midsentence, looked me straight in the eyes, and then nodded slowly in the direction of one of those faraway mountain ranges in the distance. This interchange startled me not because I was surprised by a rural Indonesian's knowledge about the United States. Millions of Indonesians after all, watch Bill Cosby on television in urban areas, listen to cassette tapes of American pop musicians, and regularly view Hollywood action films. But Tina Mase's words reveal just how distant western Central Sulawesi highlanders feel from the government capital in Jakarta, from the province of

Central Sulawesi, and from the political nation as a whole. Indonesia is one of the most rapidly developing nations in the world, but the path of development has been created without the participation, or sometimes even the knowledge, of the hundreds of ethnic minority groups in the hinterlands. The established ways of life of millions of people in the so-called outer islands hinge on their elusion of, or at least partial control over, expanding development projects linked to global market forces.

The Periphery Meets the Center

Millions of North Americans begin their mornings with a "cup of java" and regularly purchase clothes, running shoes, tropical wood furniture, or toys manufactured in Java or Bali, the most populous islands of Indonesia. Few of them know that Indonesia is the fourth most populous nation in the world with a per capita economic growth rate some three times the world average. International economists cite Indonesia as "among the world's outstanding examples of poverty reduction."[2] What remains relatively unexamined is the political and economic relationship between the state and its multiethnic hinterlands, peoples and lands that are radically affected by economic projects controlled from the center. The Indonesian national development program is founded on, and literally fueled by, regional inequities that often entail the rapid debasement of lands occupied by ethnic minorities on the less populated "outer islands" of the archipelago.

For many decades, the peoples of western Central Sulawesi, one of those outer island ethnic minority regions, have participated indirectly in the global economy by growing and selling coffee for export. Now they are confronting new development programs, including transmigration, timber harvesting, and tourism, which more severely threaten their ecological and cultural environments. Many indigenous Central Sulawesi people are startled by these transformations and are cautious about the initiatives of a powerful military-based government. Ultimately, environmental and human rights violations in Indonesia are affected by choices made by foreign consumers and legislators. Multilateral approaches to human rights and development policies could help attenuate disruptive regional violence and facilitate the cause of Indonesian national stability as well as international investment.

International Business and Human Rights Problems in Indonesia

President Clinton's 1994 visit to Jakarta for the Atlantic-Pacific Economic Cooperation (APEC) meetings highlighted Indonesia's increasing importance to American foreign trade. It also drew national attention to Indonesia's most troubling human rights problems. As during his earlier 1994 diplomatic encounter with China, President Clinton was concerned about human rights violations in Asia—but he did not wish to jeopardize the United States' potential trade opportunities in this rapidly expanding region. Indonesia's gross national product grew at an average of 6% annually from 1970 to 1992, and the United States and Japan were Indonesia's two biggest trading partners.[3] The Clinton administration took the stance that commercial engagement would lead to more progress on human rights than would disengagement.[4]

Indonesia is no exception to the general rule that a state's economic development most adversely affects the environment and human rights of its marginal populations, particularly its ethnic minority groups. The historical basis for Indonesia's asymmetrical development, however, is geographic as well as demographic. Untapped natural resources are most abundant in the "outer islands" of the archipelago outside of the most densely populated islands of Java, Bali, and Madura. Given that about 60% of the nation's population is clustered on those three "inner islands," which constitute only 7% of the country's land mass, the remaining 6,000 inhabited islands appear in the eyes of the government to be relatively unoccupied and unproductive. It views the outer islands—home to most of Indonesia's over 300 ethnic minority groups—as primary locales for "human development" (*pembangunan masyarakat*) as well as resource development for the purposes of mining, forestry, tourism, oil extraction, and plantation agriculture.[5]

The Indonesian program for economic development (*pembangunan*) is implemented by civil service and military personnel in their dual role as security and development forces and has two matching facets: first, the creation of large Indonesian businesses that pull foreign cash into the national economy and, second, the management or guidance (*pembinaan*) of more "modern" citizens who will cooperatively participate in the growing economy. These twin goals create the potential for large-scale environmental and cultural debasement in Indonesia. Economic development projects, often funded by foreign aid monies or multinational companies, have made territorial consolidation in the outer islands a priority for President Suharto. Possibilities for profitable development, especially mineral and offshore oil extraction, have led to the relatively recent incorporation of regions such as Irian Jaya (the western half of New Guinea subsumed in 1969) and East Timor (seized by military occupation in 1975), despite the resistance of indigenous inhabitants. Organizations such as Human Rights Watch and Amnesty International have publicized these most dramatic environmental and human rights crises, yet events in other outer island areas have received less international attention, largely because few outsiders have observed them.[6]

Indonesia's political boundaries are a legacy of centuries of Dutch colonialism. Some of the ethnic groups held under Indonesian military rule have ancient historical and cultural ties to one another, but many do not. This situation creates a potential tension between the interests of minorities in the hinterlands and those of the central government on Java, which sets national development policies. Local responses to incipient human environmental rights problems in western Central Sulawesi illustrate the varied perceptions of development programs held by local villagers, entrepreneurs, Indonesian government officials, and social scientists. This case can be matched with parallel examples from other Indonesian regions where ethnic minorities have sought to negotiate for their community rights or to evade development initiatives designed without their input. Ultimately, western consumers, businesses, and governments play a large role in providing incentives for ecological and cultural degradation in Indonesia, yet the contexts for western policy formulation leave the foreigners involved largely unaware of their effects on Indonesian minorities. It is important, therefore, when governments formulate foreign policy, technology transfer agreements, and human rights positions, that they include state–minority ethnic relations in the equation. As several Asian governments have correctly pointed out, western governments have no right to exercise neocolonial demands in the human rights arena. Such issues benefit more from multilateral discussion and the participation of nongovernmental organizations (NGOs). Western citizens and their governments, however, do have the right to raise human rights issues and withhold their business from companies profiting from unethical development ventures.

Tourism, Transmigration, and Roads Forward in Central Sulawesi

The one western visitor I met in Central Sulawesi during fieldwork in the late 1980s commented that Palu, the provincial capital, was one of the least attractive cities he had ever visited during his 30 years of travel in Indonesia. Tourist development, we thought, was not likely to arise in a province with few impressive "traditional" buildings and even fewer paved roads, flush toilets, or other amenities. But we had grossly underestimated the vision of Indonesian and western entrepreneurs.

In 1992 a European man married to an Indonesian woman purchased land from a coastal fishing village and built a scuba-diving resort beside a coral reef. That reef formerly was considered a village right of way, but locals accepted the passage of resident foreigners who occasionally stopped by for a few hours to swim, snorkel, and watch colorful tropical fish. The new resort, by contrast, privatized the previously open beach. Bungalow accommodations, priced comparably to Palu's urban hotel rooms, catered to European backpacking tourists. Once the facility was listed in a major guidebook along with provincial bus routes, a stream of tourists arrived. I asked the European businessman how the coastal inhabitants, members of the Bugis and Kaili ethnic groups, felt about moving their houses to accommodate the resort. He smiled proudly and answered: "No problem, they all work for me." The new owners first asked the locals to evacuate a portion of their village to create space for the bungalows. Then they hired cooperative villagers as cooks, maids, and custodians. The resort began sponsoring guided trekking tours, including one to a distant highland area where the indigenous peoples' previous experience of westerners had been confined to an occasional Protestant missionary. A nurse told me that the influx of tourist dollars into the highland economy was severely inflating prices for transportation services and local commodities, including clinic medicines.

Meanwhile, the European entrepreneur and his wife were receiving unprecedented support from provincial military officials. Although the resort's charges for scuba diving were a bargain for European tourists, the daily fees far exceeded the average monthly income of a local Indonesian family. In the long run the owners and government officials issuing permits stood to profit from these tourism activities, while the villagers, even if some had new access to cash, stood to lose their land rights, privacy, and coastal subsistence patterns.

Another relic of Dutch colonialism is the policy of "transmigration," designed to control overpopulation by moving peasants from the densely populated inner islands to sparsely populated outer islands. This policy has been pursued with vigor by postwar independent Indonesian governments. Now new transmigration sites were targeted for the forested interior. The low-population areas of western Central Sulawesi selected by the government for new transmigration sites are locales known to the indigenous people for their potential health risks. In one of these targeted areas, Banggaiba, residents suffered from an unusually high incidence of malaria, insufficient access to clean water, and no health care clinics. Another area was known for schistosomiasis, a liver disorder transmitted by water-borne parasites. Local people in these regions said they hoped that better health care and water purification facilities would arrive with the transmigration programs. Research indicates, however, that interisland transmigration often results in poorer health and higher mortality for the migrants, as well as altered ecological habitats conducive to disease transmission.[7]

Between 1989 and 1993 electric lines had progressed 80 km up into the Kulawi district highlands, and the road extended 20 km deeper into the forest. I was told that some government officials had made a deal with the villagers of the area: if the locals voted 100% for the government party (GOLKAR) in the 1993 election, the government would arrange for a vehicle road to enter their region, probably with the ulterior motive of accessing timber or minerals. The new roadbed, however, was not paved, and following heavy rains the deforested trail became a morass of sticky mud useless even for foot travel. Soon locals began cutting new walking trails through the forest, coping with the development-induced landslides much as they would any other "natural" disaster.

The Charms of Development

This situation illustrates some processes that "selectively victimize" Indonesian ethnic minorities and degrade their environment.[8] Many rural residents initially are attracted to development proposals. The government promises advancement and new opportunities to obtain cash and imported goods. Central Sulawesi highlanders, who have long lived without electricity or vehicle roads and exchanged subsistence crop surpluses primarily with relatives, now find themselves labeled as impoverished and "backward" (*terbelakang*) by development project leaders who tour the region. Under pressure to "make progress" from international economists and foreign investors, the New Order Indonesian government promotes economic development as an abstract value to the citizenry. Pervasive Indonesian media campaigns and community education programs equate economic development with moral righteousness. These so-called guidance (*pembinaan*) programs seek to draw Indonesia's ethnic minorities into a national culture. Members of smaller ethnic minorities see that citizens of the nation's "more advanced" (*lebih maju*) ethnic groups own a range of possessions that they themselves cannot afford. Thus Central Sulawesi villagers often are anxious to participate in development programs and cannot foresee the environmental and human rights problems that may accompany the projects. I heard people say that they would love to attract wealthy foreign tourists and have a vehicle road and forestry or building projects, as well as the infrastructure improvements promised by government transmigration programs. Although these pleas for "progress" are troubling,[9] foreign observers are in no position to dismiss Indonesian villagers' desires to improve their families' and communities' fragile socioeconomic status. Nor should we dismiss the government's desire to improve Indonesia's economic status in the world. Rather, members of Indonesia's smaller ethnic groups need more information, participation, and options with regard to development schemes that are transforming their regions.

Local responses in Central Sulawesi confirm that Indonesian villagers are open to both internally and externally generated change.[10] What villagers are *not* open to is unwarranted risk to their subsistence or severe social disruption. Resistance to development programs often rises dramatically as actual costs and benefits become increasingly understood by the individuals affected. Because the Indonesian government circulates only positive or neutral data, locals gain knowledge about their future far too slowly.[11]

Blaming Tourists, Migrants, and Swidden Farmers

Indonesian villagers have limited information to guide them in assigning responsibility for damages once they become apparent. In the case of tourism, Central Sulawesi residents assume that tourists who flaunt local cultural rules are powerful independent agents—wealthy people who hold the political power to obtain passports and visas that are unattainable for the average Indonesian citizen. Highland villagers generally know little about tourists' and tribal art collectors' motivations. They also are unaware of their own government's promotion of Indonesian tourism with advertisements that promise views of exotic tribes and "lost worlds."[12] Villagers envision what they have to gain from development but rarely what they have to lose—ancestral land rights, fish and game habitats, cultural autonomy, subsistence.

Central Sulawesi highlanders generally blame problems associated with transmigration on the other ethnic groups who have been relocated to their region rather than on government policies. The expansion of inter-island transmigration sites is carving away the ancestral domains of indigenous inhabitants with efforts to establish wet-rice agriculture in steep and infertile areas that often are better suited to their prior swidden farming uses. Additionally, "local transmigration" (*resetelmen penduduk*) programs are moving "isolated ethnic minorities" (*suku terasing*) into model villages near the coast, where the government can supervise them more closely. Many of these new houses and villages are neglected or abandoned, because, as Michael Dove puts it, the people are asked "to change too much, too fast, in exchange for too little."[13]

Indonesia's policy on "isolated ethnic minorities" condemns as antithetical to development goals and national security three cultural features that characterize several indigenous Central Sulawesi groups. First, they supposedly lack "religion" (*agama*), meaning that they have not yet converted to Islam, Protestantism, Catholicism, Hinduism, or Buddhism. World religion is considered a necessary step in the modernization of "backward" groups and a protection from communism. Moreover, the government closely regulates all official religious organizations, which can be useful to spread government messages to local congregations. The other two cultural characteristics are the subsistence strategy of shifting cultivation—the regular movement of rice and other rain-fed crop fields throughout an otherwise intact forested environment—and the movement of farmhouses with shifting fields. The Indonesian government perceives shifting cultivation as a potential threat to national security, unproductive in terms of crop harvests, and problematic in terms of government taxation, supervision, and military mobilization. Swidden or dry-rice fields allow for the regrowth of forests and the periodic use of land where irrigated agriculture is not feasible. The government claims that swidden farming is detrimental to the environment and, ironically, often replaces swiddened forests with transmigration projects or timber concessions that do far more ecological damage. The government also overlooks the significant contributions of forest peoples to the national economy, including their harvest of wild forest products such as rattan and resins.[14]

In essence, just as most Americans are unaware of the human rights violations leading to the inexpensive Indonesian products they consume, most Indonesians do not comprehend the global market forces and central government strategies behind development projects. Despite promises of local progress, these programs really are aimed at solving national problems, including uneven population distribution, military security, and economic advancement. Until the larger forces propelling change in the outer islands are better known to local villagers, they will not be able to negotiate effectively for greater local participation.

National versus Local Rights

According to the 1945 Indonesian constitution the government has rights to all "natural forest" and assigns concessions averaging 100,000 hectares for approximately 20 years to timber companies.[15] In one western Central Sulawesi highland region where logging concessions have been operating for years, the forest has been widely clear-cut despite official Indonesian regulations that require "selective felling."[16] November 1994 international news briefs indicated that forest fires raging in Kalimantan and Sumatra were set by ethnic minority peoples protesting the logging of their lands. This drastic means by which swidden farmers try to reestablish claims to land cleared by timber companies has been reported for over a decade.[17] Interior villagers learn too late that loggers will remove not only "valuable trees" but also locally useful species that timber companies define as "troublesome plants" growing in "unoccupied" territories. One of the greatest problems faced by swidden farmers whose ancestral territories are desired by developers is that their long fallow cycles ensure that they will be absent from most of their customary homelands at any given time. This situation provides developers with many opportunities to seize legally unoccupied land.

In western Central Sulawesi there is often a resigned acceptance of new development projects and local peoples' inability to reject government proposals. Aggressive actions by foreign human rights activists or mobilized resistance by local ethnic minorities are potentially dangerous; government response can be severe, and so Central Sulawesi highlanders have a long, and in certain respects successful, history of choosing detached or passive resistance strategies. Historical evidence indicates that many ethnic minorities in Indonesia adopted their interior locales and difficult subsistence strategies precisely to avoid overbearing state control, including from Dutch colonialists and previous coastal rulers. But primary forest land is increasingly scarce. When government-approved enterprises build roads to their villages and request "hospitality" for army troops and nonlocal workers, minority communities have few realistic options.

Although unrestrained tourism in new locations such as Sulawesi may evoke cultural conflicts and resentment among local populations, cautious tourism development that allows residents a significant part in planning and economic gains may provide indigenous communities with increased employment options and national visibility. Such cooperative tourism in the outer islands may also allow regional minorities to maintain greater control over cherished lands that otherwise would be targeted for more ecologically destructive logging, mining, or transmigration projects. The aim is not to stall national development in Indonesia, but rather to couple international economic initiatives with efforts to augment local participation while safeguarding environmental and human rights.

Government Officials, Foreign Investors, and the Future

The Indonesian government is faced with a difficult balancing act to meet the often-conflicting demands of foreign investors and its own socially heterogeneous, multiethnic populations. But given Indonesia's unprecedented economic growth and rising middle class, it is unlikely that objections to development from either outside or inside the nation will turn this tide of change. Nevertheless, resistance and insurgency in the islands—expressed most violently in East Timor and Irian Jaya but also among indigenous farmers, urban workers, and students in Kalimantan, Sulawesi, Sumatra, Bali, and even Java—indicates that the Indonesian government stands to improve its negotiations with minorities who seek greater local autonomy and their share of development decisions and profits.

Although the Indonesian military, through the application of force, has been capable of suppressing past outbreaks of resistance, a greater openness to local input could help Indonesia elude future political turmoil and resulting resource depletion. Riots, such as those occurring near a Freeport-McMoran Copper and Gold mine in Irian Jaya in March 1996 or those resulting in the death of students protesting an increase of public transportation fares in South Sulawesi in April 1996, create international opprobrium as well as national embarrassment. Even the Javanese, who make up the majority of Indonesians, view governmental exercises of force as a sign of weakness rather than political strength.

Beyond investor demands and government development programs lies the purchasing pressure of foreign consumers and businesses who seek inexpensive labor and raw materials. The unprincipled pursuit of precious metals, low-cost toys, running shoes, clothes, and teak furniture has helped to create many of the environmental and human rights crises now facing Indonesia. Commercial engagement without adequate research and ethical considerations also undermines any leverage on human rights that foreign nations might gain through diplomacy. At the 1994 APEC meetings the Clinton administration witnessed or signed 15 agreements for projects worth over $40 billion to U.S. companies involved in telecommunications, energy, transportation, and the environment. One of these projects was a $104 million agreement between Motorola and Indonesia's Ministry of Forestry. Motorola agreed to provide a "state-of-the-art, integrated, radio communication system" designed to "improve forestry management" by minimizing "rain forest destruction and illegal exploitation." At first glance this project appears to be a laudable program designed to protect Indonesia's vast tropical rain forest, the second largest in the world. This technology, however, could readily be used to track and eliminate members of ethnic minorities who attempt to cultivate their ancestral lands in the face of development programs aimed to usurp their occupation.

At the end of October 1994 the Indonesian government signed an agreement with the United Nations High Commission for Human Rights to develop a national action plan to improve human rights. This positive step came in the wake of a series of news magazine shutdowns, persecutions of East Timor dissidents, and other indications of regression in the human rights arena. Public commitments to human rights must be matched with a form of international commercial engagement that no longer ignores the distant processes through which wealthy foreigners obtain inexpensive clothes, handmade furniture, exotic vacations, and gourmet coffee.

In 1996 *The New York Times* exposed human rights violations at an Indonesian Nike sport shoe factory, catalyzing a "Justice: Do It Nike!" call-in campaign.[18] When U.S. citizens learn about human rights and environmental safety violations tacitly supported by U.S.-based companies manufacturing overseas, businesses can be lobbied and laws proposed to prohibit the import of products created under ignoble conditions. Even a few such actions could resonate overseas to affect the

Indonesian government's development policies. Economic development that respects the environmental and human rights concerns of local populations drawn into the global economy will help to undercut violence between the Indonesian state and its minority communities, thereby enhancing the political equilibrium of the nation as well as future international investments.

SECTION II: View from the 21st Century

The Troubling Questions of a Muslim Cleric

During a 2003 visit to the civil war–damaged district of Poso in Central Sulawesi, I was asked to explain U.S. war policies to a classroom of Muslim students. The Poso District had experienced episodes of grisly violence that became polarized along Christian and Muslim lines.[19] After mid-2000 the district capital of Poso City remained a woeful site of burned and looted buildings, with the main roads under Indonesian military supervision. An estimated 1,000 people were killed, and roughly 150,000 more were displaced by physical violence and arson. Periodic bombings, militia attacks, and so-called mystery killings dominated local news stories and people's hushed conversations. The Poso District and Central Sulawesi province in general were avoided by most foreigners, which restricted outsiders' knowledge of heinous local conditions, and the province remained a low national priority.

I traveled through the Poso District in May 2003 with a team of young Indonesian NGO activists whose charge was to implement postconflict humanitarian programs with Poso counterparts. We met first with the staff of a local Muslim micro-credit association, then saw a newly constructed elementary school in a mixed Muslim and Christian village. The NGO team was to announce a bank-funded college scholarship program for socially active students at several Poso community colleges. These educational institutions had become largely segregated by religious affiliation. After the team leader described the scholarship competition to a packed classroom at a private Muslim university in Poso City, he invited the audience to question their visitor from the United States—me. I was asked questions such as "How do U.S. people view Poso?" and "What do Americans think about Indonesia? What is their opinion of Islam?" More pointed questions were posed by the instructor, a middle-aged Muslim cleric with a Qur'an resting on his desk: "Isn't it true that Osama bin Laden had nothing to do with the events of the World Trade Center? And that the World Trade Center events have no proven connection to Afghanistan or Iraq? Aren't 9/11 events just an excuse for the U.S. to make war against Muslim people?"

In the 1980s I had been impressed by the political and cultural knowledge that ordinary Indonesians had about the United States. Here I was blindsided on two accounts: first by the elements of disinformation that this cleric and some Muslim political leaders I met in 2003 and 2004 swallowed in full confidence; and second by the way in which improbable ideas about 9/11 and U.S. motivations were marshaled along with more feasible ones to ask critical questions that few Americans posed about the Afghanistan and Iraq wars.

World opinions on relations between Muslim and Christian peoples changed significantly during the first years of the new millennium. Certainly, my ability to travel freely and sustain a fieldwork program in Indonesia was hindered. Yet, in terms of economic interconnections, my new-millennium story about the global economy's links with human rights and the environment in Indonesia is continuous with observations from the end of the last millennium. Although violent conflict in Indonesia in the late 1990s and early 2000s often are examined primarily in instrumentalist political terms, evidence suggests that land ownership transformations and deforestation driven by global economy collaborations are critical factors. Thus the path of economic development framed my response to the Muslim cleric and his students.

Indonesia's Decade of Living Dangerously

Dramatic economic, political, and environmental transformations affected Indonesia after 1997. These included the debilitating monetary crisis of 1998, violent street demonstrations leading to the resignation of President Suharto, and prodemocracy, anticorruption, and political decentralization movements. Dyspeptic anti-Chinese riots in the 1990s were overtaken by secessionist movements in Aceh, Timor, and Papua (formerly Irian Jaya). Then post-Suharto communal violence, of which the Poso conflict was just one case, peaked in several regions between 1999 and 2002. Then came the October 2002 nightclub bombings in Bali and a series of other high-profile bombings by jihadist groups. Most prominent in the international media was the December 2004 tsunami and related floods that killed more than 127,000 people.[20] Indonesia was a mess.

By the end of the millennium Indonesia's failed governance policies and human rights violations in the seized province of East Timor came home to roost. An internationally monitored referendum vote allowed the brutalized residents of this former Portuguese colony to secede and become Timor Leste, the world's first newly independent nation of the 21st century. By contrast, repercussions of the tsunami included humanitarian interventions and unprecedented political gains aimed at solving long-running civil wars in oil-rich Aceh.[21]

In the wake of these complexly layered and tumultuous events, Indonesia's dire need for foreign currency encountered developed nations' continued hunger for tropical resources, especially luxury items, timber, and fuel. In the 21st century Indonesia's land and sea resources are being tapped at an ever-faster pace. While enriching to some businessmen, government officials, and labor migrants, the land transformations are detrimental to many local farmers and foragers, especially ethnic minorities in the outer islands. Deforestation, transmigration, and the alienation of customary family and village lands preceded several communal conflicts. In such regions as Central Sulawesi and Maluku, where the interests of Muslims and Christians rubbed against each other, conflict became interpreted through the lens of religious distrust, fear, and militarization and linked by some to the U.S.-declared "war on terror."[22]

By 2003 Indonesian tourism was deeply compromised by bombing fears and official "travel warnings." The owners of the western Central Sulawesi scuba diving resort described above struggled; they avoided mentioning the Poso violence to their European customers, who innocently booked their diving vacations over the Internet. The owners decided to sell the resort, but one set of potential buyers pulled out, apparently concerned about regional security. A great irony was that Western reactions to the bombings harmed exactly those Indonesians who had been most engaged with foreigners' cultural and political interests. For example, before the 2002 nightclub bombing, tourism accounted for roughly half of Bali's economy.[23] After the bombing, many were rapidly impoverished. The late 1990s' monetary crisis and political unrest combined with the Bali bombings to make tourism in the Toraja region of South Sulawesi drop from over 230,000 annual domestic and foreign tourists in the mid-1990s to less than 30,000 in 2004, with less than 6,000 of those being foreigners bringing foreign currency into the economy.[24] The fragile and fickle nature of tourism dependency was exposed.

After the bombings, economically struggling Hindus and Christians wondered why *they* were being so severely punished when it was just a few radical Muslims from other islands who had committed the isolated crimes. Observers noted that the United States did not slap long-term travel warnings on London or Madrid, European sites of comparable jihadist group bombings in public venues. The United States claims that Indonesia was a much-appreciated, moderate Muslim ally in the "war on terror" rang hollow in Southeast Asia on multiple levels. In reality, much of the population was unwilling to endorse either the U.S.-led wars on Muslim-majority countries, or the Indonesian militants who condoned violent jihad and suicide bombings on the soil of their own Muslim-majority nation.[25] In the harrowing years after President Suharto's resignation in May 1998, three weak civilian presidents ruled in quick succession, only to see a military general, Susilo Bambang Yudhoyono, win the elections of 2005 and 2009. The new democratic system of competitive elections thus returned Indonesia to its familiar pattern of military leadership.

Cash Cropping Shifts, Oil Palm in Kalimantan, and Unnatural Disasters

Millions of North Americans still begin their mornings with a "cup of java." Several fine specialty coffees sold in the U.S. (including Sumatra Mandailing, Sulawesi Kalosi, and Java Mocha) are grown in Indonesia. But compared to the early 1990s, coffee comes from other tropical locations, such as Vietnam, Ethiopia, and Latin America, where it is produced even more cheaply or transported more directly. As competition forced down prices, rural Indonesian farmers sought to plant, often on the advice of government officials allied with big businesses, whatever new cash crop appeared to promise quick income. This continued the government's goal, discussed in my 1997 chapter, to convert shifting, subsistence farming to permanent fields serving export markets.

Cash-cropping practices worldwide adjust surprisingly quickly to market price and currency shifts. Easily tended tree crops that mature and produce rapidly in tropical conditions are considered golden. By the late 1990s small cash-cropping farmers in Central Sulawesi responded to changing world prices by reducing coffee production in favor of a relatively new (for them) tree crop—cocoa or cacao. During the same period, lowland peat-soil forests in Kalimantan were increasingly cleared of mature hardwoods, burned, and seeded with oil palm trees (*Elaeis guineensis*), in high demand because of a burgeoning European market for biofuel. Palm oil prices rose almost 70% during 2007, and yet world demand still outstrips the supply of cooking and fuel oils for global markets.[26] The result is an unprecedented rate of deforestation in the service of cash crops.

Accomplished by both large timber concessions and smallholder farmers, rampant clear-cutting of forests in Kalimantan is linked with over a decade of widely reported "wildfires."[27] The smoke has been so dense and vast as to cause respiratory problems and airplane flight cancellations, not only in Indonesia but in angered neighboring nations such as Malaysia and Singapore. Analysts have argued cogently that the fires and Indonesian monetary crises are closely related, because the seemingly natural disasters in fact "are generated by the particular political economy of natural resource-based development in Indonesia" begun in the late 1960s.[28] Suharto's government granted large land concessions to forestry and other development businesses. In exchange, Suharto family members and associates received subsidiary interests. Oil palm and other tree crop plantations were established with full support from the World Bank, which by the 1990s discovered that the impoverished families it helped the Indonesian government "transmigrate" into the outer islands for subsistence rice faming had neither escaped poverty nor managed local forests in a sustainable manner.[29]

Clear-cutting and burning of forests has been the preferred local Southeast Asian strategy for initiating mono-crop plantations of both cacao and oil palm trees. Similar clearing methods have been used for centuries by local subsistence farmers, but with only hand tools used on scattered small plots and long fallow periods to encourage diverse forest re-growth. The recent, industrial-scale draining, felling, and burning of peat-swamp forests in Indonesia causes high carbon dioxide emissions, roughly two billion tons per year. A dysfunctional marriage between timber concessions in mature-tree forests and the newly favored, unshaded tree crop business has emerged in Indonesia.

In 1950–2000 Indonesia's forest cover was reduced nearly by half, from 162 to 98 million hectares. In three of the largest islands, Sulawesi, Sumatra, and Kalimantan, most of the biologically diverse lowland forests were cleared by loggers. Coincidentally, illegal logging has been rampant, accounting for approximately two-thirds of Indonesia's 60 million cubic meters per year domestic wood demand in 2000. That year, the United States imported more than $450 million of Indonesian timber, including perhaps $330 million from illegal sources.[30] Indonesia's rate of rainforest destruction, which Greenpeace sets at 2% annually, now rivals that of Brazil.[31]

By 2007 landslides and floods, undeniably linked to local deforestation, gained the attention of Indonesian leaders.[32] New government pledges and regulations supporting forest preservation and community management faced resistance from entrenched logging ventures. These enterprises enmesh businessmen, government officials, military, migrants, local labor, gangsters, and a host of disreputable side businesses such as prostitution all within a vertically integrated "twilight zone between legality and illegality."[33] There is a great deal of money at stake in the timber and tree-crop industries and an uneasily controlled mercenary muscle behind it. Similar patterns of illegal logging—often marshaled simply to supply cheap wood hand tools for Walmart and J.C. Penney—exist in Russia, China, Africa, and Latin America.[34]

As during the 1990s promises of "economic development" in the early 21st century remain seductively attractive to many Indonesian citizens. But when expectations are unfulfilled, blame for poorly understood economic losses often is directed at new migrants or nearby residents of different ethnicity and religion. In more religiously and ethnically homogenous regions such as South Sumatra, Suharto development policies resulted in numerous conflicts between villagers and development companies.[35] In one Sumatran case farmers did not understand how oil palm company loans from the World Bank caused banks to hold land titles even though oil palm companies were supposed to return land plots to the farmers who worked them.[36]

Despite significant post-Suharto gains in press and political speech freedoms, many Indonesian citizens continue to fear government authorities and military troops who are stationed to protect government-supported businesses. Indonesian NGO leaders describe how "vertical conflicts" between government-connected businesses and locals often turn into "horizontal conflicts" between resident groups compelled to compete over reduced resources or incentives (such as security jobs) provided by the concessions.

Chocolate, Migration, and Land Alienation—The Sulawesi Case

Recent books and marketing campaigns extol the historic charms and antioxidant health benefits of chocolate, processed from seeds of the tropical American tree *Theobroma cacao*.[37] But there is bad news about chocolate, and it does not concern obesity, cholesterol, or constipation. Increasingly prolific histories of the tree tend to ignore how cacao plantations cause the elimination of diverse tropical forests and frequently friction among nearby social groups. Even buying from politically correct "fair trade" companies generally does not mitigate the intrinsically damaging ecological process known as "the cocoa cycle."[38] Like oil palms, cacao trees grow and fruit rapidly and prolifically when planted on newly clear-cut tropical forest land. Short-term, bottom-line thinking leads cacao plantations to "eat" old growth tropical forests.

In Indonesia longtime residents and indigenous peoples residing near such land are unlikely to have the chainsaws, political authority, or community desire to fell large swaths of locally shared heritage forests. By contrast, newly arriving migrant laborers, who have no historical or cultural attachment to the topography at hand, are more easily persuaded to clear-cut, plant cacao, and reap the economic rewards of escalating commodity prices. Governments of developing nation-states both actively and passively support the predations of migrant cash-croppers on tropical forests with the understanding that it boosts regional and national economies. This volatile combination of agronomic and social degradation in the global south feeds insouciant culinary appetites in the global north.

In the late 1990s the World Bank plan for Indonesia was to establish "nuclei" of government estates within a "plasma" of local smallholder farmers who would be trained to plant and sell the same crop to the government-run plantation.[39] This plan presumes local farmers will make the "rational choice" to plant the most profitable crop that requires the least amount of labor. Cacao tree cultivation is far easier than farming rice, much less highly perishable vegetables, and cacao bean demand and prices became extremely high in the late 1990s. By the early 2000s prices paid to Central Sulawesi farmers for dried cacao beans were about double what they received for coffee beans and many times what they received for rice paddy. In 2003 one farmer I knew sold a single cacao harvest for the equivalent of about U.S. $3,500, a terrific sum of wealth representing many times the average annual income in the region.

The residents of Central Sulawesi, Indonesia, with whom I lived in the mid-1980s, began to plant a few cacao trees in their gardens by the early 1990s. Until then, each family farmed from one to four acres of rice on a mountain slope and planted other crops in adjacent fallow gardens or forests. Living in homemade houses without electricity, three days' walk from the nearest town with stores, their needs for cash were few. Since Dutch merchants introduced it in the 1950s shade-grown coffee had been their primary cash crop, overshadowing trade in tree resins. Once a year, villagers harvested coffee trees planted under forest canopies outside their settlements.

They thereby generated enough cash to buy salt, soap, and clothes, as well as to pay their taxes and children's school fees. Sales of coffee also financed foods and gifts for rituals such as weddings and funerals.[40]

When I returned to the Central Sulawesi highlands in 1993, the price of cacao was as high as coffee. Several women showed me how the cacao trees planted in their yards fruited more quickly than the coffee trees they maintained farther away in the mountain forests. Cheerfully we broke open the peachy-gold pods so that the edible fruit around the beans would rot away. My friends might have heard that allowing the fruit to ferment slowly around the bean improves the quality of the chocolate produced. By the 1990s tens of thousands of voluntary migrants, mostly from more heavily populated South Sulawesi, had entered Central Sulawesi mountain areas, seeking plots of forest land to clear and plant cacao. The Indonesian government already had appropriated large areas land for transmigration projects: during the Suharto presidency (1966–98), roughly 85,000 families (about 340,000 individuals) were moved from other islands into Central Sulawesi province.[41] During the same period about 4.6 million of the province's 6.8 million hectares were assigned, often with overlapping extraction rights, to over 130 private or government-connected businesses in the fields of forestry, plantations, or mining.[42]

New roads were built to get the transmigrants into the undeveloped areas and to get the valuable timber or crops they produced out of the mountains. Voluntary migrants, sensing future "good fortune," followed roughly the same paths as the official transmigrants. Government agricultural agents promoted seedlings of cash crops such as cacao and new hybrid seeds of staples such as wet rice. District officials made bargains with village headmen, who conceded land in their jurisdiction to transmigrants in exchange for a cut of the agriculture or timber businesses planned for the site. Cacao bean production in Central Sulawesi grew by more than 100-fold from 1988 to 2002, by which time it amounted to nearly 90% of the province's valued foreign exchange income.[43] Much shared customary village land shifted to private ownership, as various pathways to land alienation through sale, seizure, or de facto permanent "borrowing" led to disharmony between locals and migrants.

Once baby cacao trees were planted on newly cleared forest land, about 1,500 per two and a half acres, migrants knew that within three years they could harvest and sell enough cacao beans to buy themselves more land, maybe also a new car or nice cement house. Acquiring new forest is essential to long-term cacao farming success, because cacao trees soon decline in production through lost fertility and tree mortality caused by pests and diseases, including the pod borer (*Acrocercops cramerella*) and Vascular-Streak Dieback (VSD). Although properly shaded and tended cacao trees can live for 40 years, most cacao trees planted under commercial conditions become diseased within 15 or 20 years.[44] By 2003 I saw many cacao trees in Central Sulawesi with shriveled brown leaves and pods, the work of the pod borer. My local friends recognized that they faced a challenging pest, but they understood neither its physiology nor the implications of its appearance. Several told me with confidence that government agricultural agents promised to sell them pesticides that would take care of the problem—when they could save up enough money to buy it. A foreign forestry specialist I met just shook his head sadly, saying there was no quick fix for the pod-borer problem. The only economical, and therefore inevitable, solution for Indonesians would be to shift to yet more newly cleared forest land. For the highlanders I knew, that movement would be within their, or their spouses', ancestral lands, which would be planted with cacao in lieu of rice. That would reduce their food security. For incoming migrants, by contrast, that newly planted land could be anywhere; that is, in other people's ancestral forests. Both the foreign forestry expert and an Indonesian who worked for the Nature Conservancy independently told me they shed tears when they saw one of the few remaining "world class" forests in a national park decimated with chainsaws to plant cacao.

How had this happened in a protected conservation area? A locally transmigrated group experienced conflict and social problems at their new residential site so the government welfare office transferred them to live in the forest conservation area under the promise that they would not clear-cut the old growth trees. Initially, they didn't. Then a migrant group owning chainsaws came in, paid or pushed off the resettled "native" group, and cleared it for cacao plantations.

Increasingly, scholars have recognized the contentious political nature as well as the time and space relativity of identity categories such as "native" (imagined as natural conservationists) and "newcomer" (imagined as inherently destructive). These terms feed sometimes problematically into rapidly changing and contested sets of policy decisions by government officials, forestry experts, human rights NGOs, and self-proclaimed indigenous people.[45] Yet there is little doubt that the economic conditions and "social facts" generating these binary categories provide people who are competing for limited resources rationales to suspect and violently "defend themselves against" members of other groups.

The rapid cacao explosion, social displacement, and consequent deforestation in Sulawesi are neither local nor strictly Indonesian phenomena. Rather they are a tiny epicycle in the historically global process of cacao boom and bust. This process began in Central and South America in the 1700s but has shifted from Brazil and western Africa to eastern Indonesia. The economics and disease profiles of cacao tree production invariably entail boom and bust cycles, irrespective of the kind of market pressures for luxury chocolate that bear down on Indonesian forests suitable for growing cacao trees.[46]

Deforestation, Conflict, and Displacement: Another Side of the Sulawesi Case

The social policy tool that makes this resource exploitation process happen both quickly and dangerously is migrant labor. Migrants are the catalysts of forest removal. Deforestation in Indonesia thus bears more generally on the nation's past domestic migration policies and on public debates about how migration (and now corrections to involuntary migration propelled by violence) should be handled by government and multinational organizations.

On the basis of her research in Africa, Malkki argues that nationalist discourses on the nation-state presume the cultural sedentarism, or rootedness, of citizens. Those groups involved in migration or territorial displacement become marked as pathological, even of suspect moral character.[47] Yet, in Indonesia an active maritime crossroads hosting many diasporas long preceded contemporary nation-states, with their controlled territorial boundaries and "uplifting" citizenship programs. On this historically fluid situation, the postcolonial Indonesian government imposed interisland migration, or transmigration, as a national development tool. Transmigration in Central Sulawesi, irrespective of the intent of particular migrants, rapidly accelerated deforestation, road building, voluntary migration, and land alienation—four developmental processes that contributed to increased communal tensions. Those processes also are part of a trend that marginalizes rural and upland regions while it aids plantations and other development agendas.[48]

To complicate matters, members of some Indonesian groups, notably the Bugis of South Sulawesi, routinely describe migration as part of their ethnic heritage and portray themselves as avatars of the nation's development goals and its majority religion, Islam. The post-1998 episodes of violence that occurred in Indonesia among some members of notably migratory groups, such as the Bugis, Butonese, Mandar, and Madurese, in opposition to some members of more sedentary non-Muslim groups who conceive themselves as "indigenous" (including Pamona, Mori, and Lore in Central Sulawesi) provides an opportunity to rethink postconflict "displacement" in relation to nation-state policies on ethnic minorities, domestic migration regimes, ethnic nationalism, and transnational religious networks.[49] Such rethinking makes gradual penetration by the standardized infrastructure of the modern Indonesian state and global capital a more visible part of the rapidly changing social and ecological matrix within which post-Suharto social frictions and violence emerged.

Between 2000 and 2004 I interviewed a wide variety of people who encountered, or were displaced by, the Poso District conflict. Those involved in transmigration programs revealed how primary forests initially were viewed as mere obstacles to migrants' rice agriculture plans. Subsequent voluntary migrants were more oriented toward cash crops. They began to see remaining forests as the most fertile land for mono-crop production. My interviews showed a diverse array of experiences by Poso farmers and merchants, whose seemingly straightforward efforts to "make a living" ensnared them in native-migrant rivalries over land and incomprehensible violence.

In December 2004 I met a man from a Hindu Balinese transmigrant family who had moved to the Poso District in 1979 when he was just a 10-year-old boy. The family was resettled along the coastal road with other Balinese near another transmigration village that was assigned to Muslim Javanese. At the time his family arrived, the Balinese man observed that there were few villages nearby and that at first there was "too much forest," including abundant ebony, mahogany, and other hardwoods. The transmigrants did not know the wood was valuable and felled trees to clear the ground for wet-rice fields, then burned the timber for cooking fires. Starting in 1985 and 1986 cacao plants were introduced by the Indonesian government to the Balinese and nearby Javanese transmigrants. Cacao prices were low, so people didn't bother with it much. Only when cacao prices rose 10-fold, from Rp.1,100 per kilo to a peak of Rp.13,000 per kilo in 1999, did they pick the trees, and plant more like crazy. Still the Balinese transmigrant said that the indigenous people of Poso did not plant much cacao because they were unfamiliar with it. Then, during the 1998 financial crisis, "those with cacao trees had their opportunity. In six months, you could buy a car." In 2003 it was easier to plant only cacao and stop growing rice for food. Rice for food was imported from other regions. The Balinese man said that his transmigrant village remained uninvolved with the Muslim-Christian fighting in Poso, but the neighboring Muslim Javanese village did not.

By contrast, most Muslim refugees I encountered at either refugee camps in the district or private homes outside the district had come to Poso as voluntary economic migrants during the 1990s. Almost invariably they would tell me about several locations on Sulawesi Island where they tried to make a living before they moved to Poso. These stories suggest that the island and district had become routine destinations for a class of highly mobile but relatively poor, landless, and uneducated laborers by the end of the Suharto regime. The narratives described Indonesian human rights problems that began with widespread rural poverty, changed provincial locations with government-backed land development schemes, and then led to "unexpected" religious violence impacting both the migrants and other poor locals.

Some of the migrants began as timber workers for Poso forestry concessions. In one case a voluntary Javanese migrant who arrived without capital was able to obtain more than one hectare of land and over a thousand fruiting cacao trees in just a few years. This and other comparable stories suggested that Poso government authorities were supporting the migrants through the allocation of local fallow and forest lands that could be used for cacao tree seedlings.[50] By contrast, aside from civil servants who fled Poso City, most displaced Protestants had been subsistence food farmers with only a small area of their inherited fields reserved for cash crops. They noted that Muslim migrants increasingly had arrived to buy land and cash-crop plots up to 20 times larger than the one to two hectares traditionally farmed for food by locals. My ethnographic interviews with Muslim migrants and Protestant "natives" revealed how the outcomes of broader demographic and agricultural changes were diversely perceived.[51] Muslim migrants said they were "just trying to make a living," that in the Poso District there were large parcels of "empty" forest land, which they had been able to make more productive and profitable. In their view, local Protestants had welcomed them into the region because they were hard workers, skilled at cash cropping, and able to introduce better prices for useful trade goods through their interregional migrant networks. Migrants claimed they had no idea their neighbors resented them until the very day they were threatened with violence and forced to flee.

In September 2003 at a Muslim refugee barracks, I listened to the story of a young ethnic Mandar man born in South Sulawesi 20 years earlier. He had recently migrated voluntarily to a Protestant majority town. He said he was just a farmer, didn't know how to fish or trade, and had been given a plot of teak by the regional government. But, he added, because the land was part of a forest conservation area, he owned no official title and the land was not legally his to return to. In 2000 his Protestant neighbors told him he had better flee. His uncle who stayed was killed. His house was destroyed as soon as he left it. This narrative is indicative of how government agents oversaw the illegal logging of official conservation forests, using landless migrant farmers to accomplish the deed "off the record."

One of the key policy issues involved here is that local heritage or "customary village lands" in much of Indonesia are legally untitled and shared in rotation by members of kinship groups whose ancestors first used the land for subsistence farming, foraging, or hunting.[52] If an individual stops using the land, its new allocation is decided by elders. Customarily, no land could be alienated by sale. Now land can be legally privatized by government officials for "national development," although this often creates considerable resentment among local people who then blame migrants drawn into the government's economic plans. One "indigenous" Poso woman told me her people originally just "gave" away their fallow land to the new migrants, thinking it would create gratitude and future good relations. Their thanks, she said bitterly, was that the migrants later chased them off their own ancestral land. Clearly, her Protestant group's understandings about "indigenous" landuse rights, "ownership," and ongoing reciprocity did not match the cultural understandings of migrants who sought outright possession and saw themselves entitled to "formerly empty land" once they had worked to plant it with permanent cash crops.

By contrast, I met a group of young Muslims in Poso City who denied that there were any "indigenous people" in the region who deserved special recognition or rights. One said: "There are no original Poso people, other than people like us. There is no Poso language. We all speak Indonesian; that's it. Some of us were born here, some of us weren't, but we—or our parents—are all from someplace else." They claimed that Poso City had never been anything but a place occupied by recent migrants, mainly Muslims like them. This vision of Poso as a migrant frontier territory, where Indonesians from elsewhere claim to be equal stakeholders, corresponds practically, if on a smaller political scale, with the government position that all Indonesian citizens are officially considered indigenous people. In the young men's view, the rural highlanders who came downhill to Poso City were just migrants like everybody else, not indigenous peoples or, as they said disparagingly, "lords of the land."

The refugee narratives suggest the extent to which the Poso conflict became a battle that must be assessed, at least partially, in terms of competing territorial claims and civil rights among those who are recent migrants and those who claim to be natives. These zero-sum claims emerged in the late Suharto era as outer island forests became more potentially profitable for timber and export cash crops. At the same time, migrants supported by pro-Muslim development activities penetrated both the rural agricultural sector and urban business-state collaborations. Both migrant and host communities became enmeshed in collaborative relations with powerful forest-clearing businesses and government agents.[53] My argument is that these unsustainable economic collaborations provided a necessary support for the militant ideologies and political mismanagement that many see as the sufficient conditions of Indonesia's post-Suharto regional and transnational "religious" wars. I return, then, to my inquisition at the Muslim campus.

My Answers to the Muslim Cleric, Students, and Policy Analysts

I began my answer to Muslim college students in Poso City by confessing, with some embarrassment, that most U.S. citizens do not have a thorough knowledge of world geography and districts in Indonesia such as Poso. I added that U.S. media do not present much news about events abroad, including Indonesia, in part because overseas reporters are costly and in part because Americans are most eager to consume local news stories. I explained that our schools have been weak in teaching world geography and history. I wanted Poso students to know that there is freedom of religion in the United States and that the nation has a significant Muslim minority, although American Muslims live in specific, usually urban, regions. I explained that most immigrants who became U.S. citizens were European Christians, so most of their descendants do not know much about Islam. I added that most educated U.S. citizens recognize that Indonesia is a Muslim majority country where the prevalent forms of Islam are moderate and peaceful. I said that the attacks of 9/11 unfortunately drew many Americans into negative feelings about all Muslims. I added that Americans need to recognize that there are many varieties of Islam and Muslims, just as Indonesians need to recognize that there are many varieties of Christianity and Christians.

I tried to explain that after the attacks of September 2001, which resulted in over 3,000 deaths, Americans felt very threatened and turned to their recently elected leaders to protect the nation from further attacks. When those leaders told them that wars in Afghanistan and later Iraq were necessary to prevent more attacks on the United States, many citizens and legislators accepted that assessment, at least initially. Those who did not agree with the decisions to go to war were overruled.

There was no opportunity to raise conflict-related resource and global economy issues at the Muslim campus forum, but I did try to enlist Indonesian and multinational NGO staff in such discussions. Generally, those not already focused on environmental, fossil fuel, or migrant issues were unwilling to entertain the plausibility of their relevance. For many, the corruption of greedy political leaders or the machinations of religious militants were the only factors that clearly mattered. When I described some of the horrific burned forests and migrant squatting I observed in Kalimantan with a policy expert in Jakarta, I was told: "This is happening all over Indonesia. So is corruption. The only thing that makes places like Poso different is the penetration of jihadist militias."

In this way, I suggest, violent conflict is too quickly and exclusively explained by essentialist ideas of religious ideology or universal human greed. Neither factor is irrelevant. The religious ideologies that legitimize violent struggles over resources are instrumental, as are the political and institutional weaknesses (such as biased police, army, and judges) that allow initial acts of violence to escalate unchecked. Yet, such conventional political analyses foreclose opportunities to examine the processes that link resource struggles, environmental transformations, and violent politics. Thus, it is easy to overlook the linkages between resource consumption and political privileges at one end of the globe and far-away conditions of human rights abuse perpetrated by national state agents and local collaborators whose intergroup relations may be contentious.

Those regions in Indonesia where communal conflict emerged in the late 1990s, and where exclusivist religious or ethnic ideologies became suddenly more widespread, were largely areas experiencing high rates of deforestation and domestic migration, in conjunction with population demographics that made political fights over available resources competitive. Also telling are reports that the most successful efforts to reduce militant radicalism in Poso have focused on education, vocational training in auto mechanics or fishing, and in-kind assistance rather than large cash grants, which are liable to corrupt mismanagement that further undermines public trust in government.[54] These programs coincidentally move young men away from sectarian competition over land.

Environmental and Analytic Trends on the Horizon, Indonesia and Beyond

At the start of the new millennium, around the world nations are juggling perceived economic development needs with new understandings of what environmental stability and planetary survival require. Given Indonesia's large remaining forest acreage and exponential deforestation rate, it was apt that the December 3–15, 2007, UN-sponsored Climate Conference on carbon emissions targets was held in Bali, Indonesia.[55] As fossil fuel supplies decline and worldwide demand grows (especially in China and South Asia), food and biofuel industries based on plant oils such as palm and soybean will be in direct price and supply competition. In 2007, as U.S. farmers grew more corn for ethanol and Asian farmers rerouted palm oil for biodiesel, vegetable oil and related food prices skyrocketed, especially for Asian consumers. Supplies of corn and soy-based foods declined precipitously that year, leading to food riots and protests in countries as widely dispersed as Indonesia, Pakistan, Guinea, Mauritania, Mexico, Morocco, Senegal, Uzbekistan, and Yemen.[56]

The most immediate responses to this crisis came from the European Union. The EU environment commissioner admitted that an earlier EU plan to obtain 10% of its road fuels from plant oils, largely palm oil from Indonesia and Malaysia, could lead to unacceptable rainforest destruction, food price increases, and land alienation with little or no reduction in carbon dioxide emissions.[57] The EU then proposed a certification program for biofuels to insure that new supplies are not generated by counter-productive and unethical methods of palm oil production. Australia, which has given tax rebates to biofuel manufacturers and importers, also reconsidered its policies on supporting palm oil fuels from Indonesia and Papua New Guinea.[58]

Southeast Asian responses to the promised European policy shift range from fear that their oil palm biodiesel factories will tank to the dismissal of EU pronouncements as just "tough talk" that will not lead to action.[59] Indonesia's Vice President, Jusuf Kalla, laid the blame squarely on market demands by developed nations. Although Kalla was perhaps not wrong, he was politically prudent in downplaying Indonesian state collaboration. According to Kalla, son of an automobile magnate and an avid road-builder, developed countries "contribute greatly" to Indonesian forest destruction and so they should take more responsibility rather than simply blaming Indonesia for poor forest management policies.[60] Surely, ending the intensive and unsustainable methods of clear-cutting and burning is crucial to curtailing dire social and ecological consequences described in this chapter.

On the subject of human-nature interactions, recent studies have examined the ecological politics of conservation parks and border zones in Asia and the Pacific.[61] Severe tensions often exist between those who plan and promote plant and animal conservation policies and those who advocate for the survival of local peoples. Recent investigations have required a stark reconsideration of familiar ideas about "traditional societies" and "indigenous peoples." Both their romantic status in international human rights political projects and their political connection with environmental movements, often as not, are promoted and funded by more affluent peoples and distant nations who do not directly pay the full price of local conservation schemes.[62] "Conservation," and "sustainability," like "development" and "globalization," must be understood as universalizing projects, which support some interests more than others and may encounter diverse local responses or resistance.[63]

The issues of political scale—local, national, transnational—and their interactions are critical. Efforts have been made to follow NGOs participating in transformational social movements, and to track commodities through the entire pathway from growers to consumers. These studies highlight the structural violence committed in the production of luxury goods such as diamonds, gold, exotic animal products, and even increasingly ubiquitous digital tools such as computers, cell phones, and ipods.[64] At their best these investigations "study up" institutions of the global economy without sacrificing fieldwork-based local knowledge about "gift exchange" (or partially commoditized) societies, whose members bear the brunt of human rights violations and ongoing land rights alienation.[65]

Two significant legal debates that remain largely beyond public consciousness concern intellectual property and land titling initiatives that are now expanding worldwide. New intellectual and cultural property laws being written for developing nations such as Indonesia will affect human rights and the environment through policy initiatives related to bioengineered agriculture, pharmaceuticals, and local arts production. Although some state agents and individual or business producers will benefit, the new laws, as currently proposed, will favor those farthest along in the commodification process and will potentially exclude marginal groups or draw them into fractious legal wrangling over cultural boundaries and proprietary ownership of what often were nonrivalrous resources in the public domain.[66]

A related legal issue for Indonesia, which also results from international trade pressures that affect most "developing" nations, is the largely unpublicized effort to expand private land titling, or cadastral registration. Although some progressive lawyers in Indonesia believe that rural residents could be better protected if they owned legal titles to their family land, that shift would effectively terminate the environmental and economic flexibility that now exists among families and groups where access to land resources is shared in rotation over generations. Those customary systems generally restrain new and intensive land uses that result in deforestation, while providing food security to rural groups. Moreover, there are genuine debates in Indonesia about whether it is easier for land to be confiscated by powerful outsiders when local individuals do, or do not, own transferable land certificates.

Increasingly, it is critical for us to connect the dots between innocent, sometimes painful local experiences and these distant transnational systems of value and actions. As with the Muslim cleric or Jakarta policy expert who knows little about, or places scant emphasis on, the social disruptions impelled by Indonesia's deforestation processes, American consumers of Indonesian chocolate, palm oil, or wood products generally see no links between their consumer behaviors and global south circumstances or anger. Primordial religious or ethnic differences become enlarged, even fetishized, as the most conscious and visible sources of conflict, conclusions that have their own real-world effects on violence and diplomacy. Our present hope must be that accessibly portraying those connections, their dysfunctional potential, and other options will prompt new discussions and a reassessment of choices on individual, network, and national scales.

After the "great recession" of 2008, with U.S. and world economic crises compounding widespread food shortages and crop diversions for the biofuel industry recognized as price-increase and shortage factors, there is renewed public attention to the goal of food security instead of mere agronomic efficiency.[67] Proposed policy changes often are described as measures to support better-balanced national economies, but we should also note the larger values and social ideals at stake. Prioritizing "emergent technologies" will not be an automatic solution to food and energy crises, which are long-term problems of scale and distribution rather than simple abundance or bottom-line economics. Well-fed people, satisfying labor conditions, biodiversity, and fair access to local resources could stand as preeminent social goals above and beyond familiar calls for cheap products, technological "progress," and high investment returns. Then, our descendants may be around next millennium when they can reevaluate ever-changing visions of how life and death matters.

Notes

1. I am grateful to the following organizations for fieldwork support: Fulbright-Hays program and the National Science Foundation, 1986 and 1989; the Association for Asian Studies and the Wenner-Gren Foundation for Anthropological Research, 1993; and the Wenner-Gren Foundation for Anthropological Research, the John D. and

Catherine T. MacArthur Foundation Research and Writing Program, and the Koninklijk Instituut voor Taal-, Land- en Volkenkunde in Leiden, Netherlands, 2002–2004. I also thank the Indonesian Institute for Sciences (LIPI) and Tadulako University in Palu for research permits and finally, acknowledge Stuart Kirsch for excellent comments on an earlier version of this chapter.

2. See Edwin S. Mills, *Growth and Equity in the Indonesian Economy,* Background Paper No. 1 (Washington, D.C.: United States-Indonesia Society, 1990: xi).

3. Ibid., 1–11.

4. This position matches the widespread claim among Asian governments that economic development will "naturally" lead to greater democracy and political freedoms. Counter-examples exist in many countries ("Human Rights and the Underside of 'Progress' in the Urban Peripheries of Asia," panel presented at the Association for Asian Studies annual meeting, March 26, 1994, Boston). See also Michael Hirsh with Ron Moreau, "Making It in Mandalay, Burma: Where Trade Meets Human Rights—Again," *Newsweek,* June 19, 1995, 46. See Jusuf Wanandi, "Confrontation on Human Rights," *Indonesian Quarterly* 21:3 (1993, 245–49) for a position against economic sanctions.

5. See William H. Frederick and Robert L. Worden, Eds., *Indonesia: A Country Study* (Washington, D.C.: Federal Research Division, Library of Congress, 1993), and Lorraine V. Aragon, "Multiculturalism: Some Lessons from Indonesia," *Cultural Survival Quarterly* 18:2/3 (1994, 72–76). A summary critique of Indonesian development programs can be found in Marcus Colchester, "Unity and Diversity: Indonesia's Policy toward Tribal Peoples," *The Ecologist* 16:2/3 (1986, 89–98).

6. See, for example, Amnesty International, *Power and Impunity: Human Rights under the New Order* (New York: Amnesty International USA, 1994). By contrast, see J. Kadjat Hartojo, "Indonesia's Political Modernization and Economic Development," *Indonesian Quarterly* 18:3 (1990, 253–61) for a compelling explanation of why the Indonesian army became so involved with economic development and why the political process must admit greater public participation.

7. See Bakir Bakir Abisudjak and Rusydi Kotanegara, "Transmigration and Vector-Borne Diseases in Indonesia," in *Demography and Vector-Borne Diseases,* Michael W. Service, Ed. (Boca Raton, FL: CRC Press, 1989, 207–23); P. M. Laksono, "Perception of Volcanic Hazards: Villagers versus Government Officials in Central Java," in *The Real and Imagined Role of Culture in Development: Case Studies from Indonesia,* Michael R. Dove, Ed. (Honolulu: University of Hawaii Press, 1988, 191–98); Mariel Otten, "'Transmigrasi': From Poverty to Bare Subsistence," *The Ecologist* 16:2/3 (1986, 71–76); M. Sudomo, "Ecology of Schistosomiasis in Indonesia with Certain Aspects of Control," *Southeast Asian Journal of Tropical Medicine and Public Health* 15:4 (1984, 471–74); Kartini Binol, "Transmigration and Health in Connection with Tropical Diseases in Indonesia," *Southeast Asian Journal of Tropical Medicine and Public Health* 14:1 (1983, 58–63).

8. See Barbara R. Johnston, "Human Rights and the Environment," *Practicing Anthropology* 16:1 (1994, 9), and Barbara R. Johnston, Ed., *Who Pays the Price? The Sociocultural Context of Environmental Crisis* (Washington, D.C.: Island Press, 1994).

9. Appell notes that "every act of development or modernization necessarily involves an act of destruction." See George N. Appell, "Costing Social Change," in *The Real and Imagined Role of Culture in Development: Case Studies from Indonesia,* Michael R. Dove, Ed. (Honolulu: University of Hawaii Press, 1988, 272). See also Marcus Colchester, "The Struggle for Land: Tribal Peoples in the Face of the Transmigration Programme," *The Ecologist* 16:2/3 (1986, 99–110), and related articles in the same issue.

10. See Michael R. Dove, "Introduction: Traditional Culture and Development in Contemporary Indonesia," ibid., 23–24, 31.

11. Ibid., 27–28.

12. See the Garuda National Airlines advertisements discussed in Paul Taylor and Lorraine Aragon, *Beyond the Java Sea: Art of Indonesia's Outer Islands* (Washington, D.C.: National Museum of Natural History and Abrams Press, 1991, 52) and also in Shelley Errington, "Unraveling Narratives," in *Fragile Traditions: Indonesian Art in Jeopardy,* Paul M. Taylor, Ed. (Honolulu: University of Hawaii Press, 1994, 139–64).

13. Dove, note 10, p. 19.

14. See Carl L. Hoffman, "The 'Wild Punan' of Borneo: A Matter of Economics," ibid., 89–118. A good overview of the "isolated ethnic minorities" issue that considers Indonesian government policies from an Indonesian anthropological perspective can be found in Koentjaraningrat, "Pendahuluan" ("Introduction"), *Masyarakat Terasing di Indonesia (Isolated People in Indonesia)*, Koentjaraningrat, 3d ed. (Jakarta: PT Gramedia Pustaka Utama, 1993, 1–18).

15. See Malcolm Gillis, "Indonesia: Public Policies, Resource Management, and the Tropical Forest," in *Public Policies and the Misuse of Forest Resources*, Robert Repetto and Malcolm Gillis, eds. (Cambridge: Cambridge University Press, 1988, 43–113), and Kathryn G. Marshall, "The Economy," in *Indonesia: A Country Study*, William H. Frederick and Robert L. Worden, Eds. (Washington, D.C.: Federal Research Division, Library of Congress, 137–205).

16. Anna Lowenhaupt Tsing describes an instance of this in *In the Realm of the Diamond Queen: Marginality in an Out-of-the-Way Place* (Princeton, NJ: Princeton University Press, 1993, 167).

17. Dove, note 10, p. 15.

18. Edward A. Gargan, "An Indonesian Asset Is Also a Liability," *The New York Times,* March 16, 1996; two columns by Bob Herbert, "Nike's Pyramid Scheme," *The New York Times,* June 14, 1996, p. A17, and "Nike's Bad Neighborhood," *The New York Times,* June 14, 1996, p. A15, were followed by a response from Nike CEO Philip H. Knight, "Nike Pays Good Wages to Foreign Workers," *The New York Times,* June 21, 1996, p. A18.

19. See Lorraine V. Aragon, "Communal Violence in Poso, Central Sulawesi: Where People Eat Fish and Fish Eat People," *Indonesia* 72 (October 2001, 45–79); International Crisis Group, "Jihad in Central Sulawesi," Indonesia Backgrounder Report, 2/4/2004; www.crisisgroup.org; Lorraine V. Aragon, "Elite Competition in Central Sulawesi," in *Renegotiating Boundaries: Local Politics in Post-Soeharto Indonesia*, Henk Schulte Nordholt and Gerry Van Klinken, Eds. (Leiden: KITLV Press, 2007, 39–66); Dave McRae, "Criminal Justice and Communal Conflict: A Case Study of the Trial of Fabianus Tibo, Dominggus da Silva, and Marinus Riwu," *Indonesia* 83 (April 2007, 79–117); and Lorraine V. Aragon, "Reconsidering Displacement and Internally Displaced Persons from Poso," in *Conflicts, Violence, and Displacement in Indonesia*, Eva-Lotta Hedman, Ed. (Ithaca: SEAP Press, 2008, 173–205).

20. See also Arief Budiman, Ed., *State and Civil Society in Indonesia* (Monash: Center of Southeast Asian Studies, 1990); Ingrid Wessel and Georgia Wimhöfer, Eds., *Violence in Indonesia* (Hamburg: Abera, 2001); Edward Aspinall and Greg Fealy, Eds., *Local Power and Politics in Indonesia: Decentralization and Democratization* (Singapore: ISEAS, 2003); Maribeth Erb, Priyambudi Sulistiyanto, and Carole Faucher, Eds., *Regionalism in Post-Suharto Indonesia* (London: Routledge, 2005); and *Renegotiating Boundaries: Local Politics in Post-Soeharto Indonesia*, Henk Schulte Nordholt and Gerry Van Klinken, Eds. (Leiden: KITLV Press, 2007).

21. See Barry Bearak, "The Day the Sea Came," *The New York Times Magazine* (November 27, 2005, 46–101); Anthony Reid, Ed., *Verandah of Violence: The Background to the Aceh Problem* (Singapore: Singapore University Press, 2006); and Eva-Lotta E. Hedman, "Back to the Barracks: *Relokasi Pengungsi* in Post-Tsunami Aceh," *Indonesia* 80 (October 2005, 1–19).

22. Lorraine V. Aragon, "Mass Media Fragmentation and Narratives of Violent Action in Sulawesi's Poso Conflict," *Indonesia* 79 (April 2005, 1–55).

23. Leo M. Howe, *The Changing World of Bali: Religion, Society and Tourism* (London: Routledge, 2005, 3).

24. Kathleen M. Adams, *Art as Politics: Re-Crafting Identities, Tourism, and Power in Tana Toraja, Indonesia* (Honolulu: University of Hawaii Press, 2006, 15–17).

25. See reports at the International Crisis Group's website: www.crisisgroup.org. Also, John Sidel's *Riots, Pogroms, Jihad: Religious Violence in Indonesia* (Ithaca, NY: Cornell University Press, 2006).

26. Keith Bradsher, "A New, Global Oil Quandary: Costly Fuel Means Costly Calories," *The New York Times*, January 19, 2008: A1.

27. Paul K. Gellert, "A Brief History and Analysis of Indonesia's Forest Fire Crisis," *Indonesia* 65 (April 1998, 63–85).

28. Ibid., p. 64; Christopher Barr, "Bob Hasan, the Rise of Apkindo, and the Shifting Dynamics of Control in Indonesia's Timber Sector," *Indonesia* 65 (April 1998, 1–36).

29. Ibid., pp. 77–80, and World Bank reports in Gellert, note 27; see also *Borneo in Transition: People, Forests, Conservation, and Development*, Christian Padoch and Nancy Lee Peluso, Eds. (New York: Oxford University Press, 1996). Generally, the migrants used intensive farming methods developed for their natal home's rich volcanic soils at their new locations, generally areas with nonvolcanic, thin tropical forest soils.

30. Forest Watch Indonesia and Global Forest Watch, *The State of the Forest:* Indonesia (Bogor: Forest Watch Indonesia, and Washington D.C.: Global Forest Watch, 2002); and Dave Currey et al., *Timber Trafficking: Illegal Logging in Indonesia, Southeast Asia and International Consumption of Illegally Sourced Timber* (London: Emerson Press, Environmental Press and Telapak Indonesia, 2001).

31. "Indonesia Deforestation Fastest in the World: Greenpeace," *Reuters*, May 3, 2007.

32. "Vice President Wants Change in Forest Management Strategy," *Jakarta Post*, December 17, 2007.

33. John F. McCarthy, "Sold Down the River: Renegotiating Public Power over Nature in Central Kalimantan," in *Renegotiating Boundaries: Local Politics in Post-Soeharto Indonesia*, Henk Schulte Nordholt and Gerry Van Klinken, Eds. (Leiden: KITLV Press, 2007, 151–76). Also, Human Rights Watch, "Without Remedy: Human Rights Abuse and Indonesia's Pulp and Paper Industry" (New York: Human Rights Watch, 2003).

34. Raffi Khatchadourian, "The Stolen Forests: Inside the Covert War on Illegal Logging," *The New Yorker* (October 6, 2008, 64–73).

35. Elizabeth Fuller Collins, *Indonesia Betrayed: How Development Fails* (Honolulu: University of Hawaii Press, 2007).

36. Ibid., pp. 56–58.

37. See, for example, Theresa Greaden, *Chocolate without Guilt* (Chapel Hill: Graeden Enterprises, 2002) and Mort Rosenblum, *Chocolate: A Bittersweet Saga of Dark and Light* (New York: North Point Press, 2005).

38. Fair Trade organizations' objections to big candy business-linked chocolate plantations usually concern abusive child labor practices, including slavery, such as those identified in Ivory Coast in 2005 by the U.S. State Department and the ILO. Higher prices paid to cacao farmers and improved work standards are positive measures, but cacao's usual environmental impacts often are left unconsidered in these equations.

39. Gellert, note 27, p. 79.

40. Lorraine V. Aragon, *Fields of the Lord: Animism, Christian Minorities, and State Development in Indonesia* (Honolulu: University of Hawaii Press, 2000).

41. Arianto Sangaji, "The Masyarakat Adat Movement in Indonesia," in *The Revival of Tradition in Indonesian Politics: The Deployment of Adat from Colonialism to Indigenism,* Jamie S. Davidson and David Henley, Eds. (London: Routledge, 2007, 319–36); sourced from *Sulawesi Tengah dalam Angka 1998* (Palu: BPS and Bappeda Propinsi Sulawesi Tengah, 1999, 88).

42. Sangaji, note 41, p. 326. Sangaji's data are from a database compiled in 2004 by the Yayasan Tanah Merdeka NGO, Palu, from official Indonesian government documents.

43. Sangaji, ibid., p. 326.

44. François Ruf and P. S. Siswoputranto, Eds., *Cocoa Cycles: The Economics of Cocoa Supply* (Cambridge: Woodhead Publishing, 1995).

45. See also Tania M. Li, "Adat in Central Sulawesi: Contemporary Deployments," in *The Revival of Tradition in Indonesian Politics: The Deployment of Adat from Colonialism to Indigenism,* Jamie S. Davidson and David Henley, Eds. (London: Routledge, 2007, 337–70); Mahmood Mamdani, "Beyond Settler and Native as Political Identities; Overcoming the Political Legacy of Colonialism," *Comparative Studies in Society and History* 43: 651–64.

46. Ruf and Siswoputranto, *Cocoa Cycles,* note 45; and *Agriculture in Crisis: People, Commodities and Natural Resources in Indonesia,* Françoise Gérard and François Ruf, Eds. (Montpellier: Cirad, 2001).

47. Liisa H. Malkki, "National Geographic: The Rooting of Peoples and the Territorialization of National Identity among Scholars and Refugees," in *Culture, Power, Place: Explorations in Critical Anthropology,* A. Gupta and J. Ferguson, Eds. (Durham, NC: Duke University Press, 1997, 52–74).

48. Tania Murray Li, Ed., *Transforming the Indonesian Uplands: Marginality, Power and Production* (Amsterdam: Harwood Academic Publishers, 1999).

49. Aragon, note 19, "Reconsidering Displacement and Internally Displaced Persons from Poso," and "Communal Violence in Poso, Central Sulawesi."

50. Aragon, note 19, "Communal Violence in Poso," Lorraine V. Aragon, "Migrasi, Komoditi Expor, dan Sejarah Perubahan Hak Pemakaian Tanah di Sulawesi Tengah," in *Berebut Tanah: Beberapa Kajian Berspektif Kampus dan Kampung,* Anu Lounela, and R. Yando Zakaria, Eds. (Yogyakarta: INSISTPress, 2002, 271–82) and Tania Murray Li, *The Will to Improve: Governmentality, Development, and the Practice of Politics* (Durham, NC: Duke University Press, 2007).

51. Here I follow local use of terms indicating that someone is "native," "indigenous," or "original" rather than a "newcomer," recognizing that those categories are constructed, flexible, and political. The first three terms connote a range of ideas, from "first settlers" to the colonial and more chauvinistic term "sons of the soil," to simply labeling current residents who are descended from people with no known foreign origins.

52. On local categories of land and use rights, see Lorraine V. Aragon, *Fields of the Lord: Animism, Christian Minorities, and State Development in Indonesia* (Honolulu: University of Hawaii Press, 2000).

53. See Anna Lowenhaupt Tsing, *Friction: An Ethnography of Global Connection* (Princeton, NJ: Princeton University Press, 2005).

54. International Crisis Group, "Indonesia: Tacking Radicalism in Poso," Asia Briefing No.75, www.crisisgroup.org, 1/22/2008.

55. "Set of Simple Numbers Will Help Shape Two Years of Post-Bali Climate Talks," *Jakarta Post,* December 17, 2007.

56. Bradsher, note 26.

57. Roger Harrabin, "EU Rethinks Biofuels Guidelines," *BBC News,* January 14, 2008.

58. "Australia Should Follow EU Biofuel Lead," *Northern Queensland Register (Australia)*, January 17, 2008.

59. Naveen Thukral, "EU's Stand on Palm-biofuel to Hit Asian Plants," *Reuters*, January 15, 2008.

60. "Vice President," note 32.

61. Pam McElwee, "Lost Worlds and Local People: Protected Areas Development in Viet Nam," *Conservation and Mobile Indigenous People: Displacement, Forced Settlement, and Sustainable Development*, D. Chatty and M. Colchester, Eds. (Oxford: Berghahn Press, 2002, 296–312); Paige West, *Conservation Is Our Government Now: The Politics of Ecology in Papua New Guinea* (Durham, NC: Duke University Press, 2006); Janet Sturgeon, *Border Landscapes: The Politics of Akha Land Use in China and Thailand* (Washington, D.C.: Island Press, 2006); also Tania Li, note 45.

62. Peter J. Brosius, "Analyses and Interventions: Anthropological Engagements with Environmentalism," *Current Anthropology* 1999, 40(3): 277–309. See also Tsing, note 53.

63. Donna Haraway, *Simians, Cyborgs, and Women: The Reinvention of Nature* (New York: Routledge, 1991); Arturo Escobar, "Constructing Nature: Elements for a Poststructural Political Ecology," in *Liberation Ecologies: Environment, Development, Social Movements*, R. Peet and M. Watts, Eds. (London: Routledge, 1996, 46–68); and Arturo Escobar, "After Nature: Steps to an Antiessentialist Political Ecology," *Current Anthropology* 1999, 40: 1–30; Paul Greenough and Anna Tsing, Eds., *Nature in the Global South: Environmental Politics in South and Southeast Asia* (Durham, NC: Duke, 2003).

64. Tsing, note 53; Elizabeth Grossman, *High Tech Trash: Digital Devices, Hidden Toxics, and Human Health* (Washington, D.C.: Island Press, 2006).

65. See Marcel Mauss's classic work, *The Gift* (New York: W.W. Norton, 1990).

66. Lorraine V. Aragon and James Leach, "Arts and Owners: Intellectual Property Law and the Politics of Scale in Indonesian Arts," *American Ethnologist* 2008, 35(4): 607–31.

67. James Surowiecki, "The Perils of Efficiency," *The New Yorker* (November 24, 2008, 46).

CHAPTER 3

Uncommon Property Rights in Southwest China

Section I: Lindsey Swope, Margaret Byrne Swain,
Fuquan Yang, and Jack D. Ives[1]
Section II: Bryan Tilt

SECTION I: The End of the Millennium

In northwestern Yunnan Province, Lijiang County sits on the edge of the Tibetan Plateau. Until the modern airport was opened in August 1995, it took two long days by road from Kunming, the provincial capital, to reach Lijiang City. The western and northern boundary of the county is the Jinsha Jiang (Yangtse River). The crowning feature of the Lijiang landscape is its sacred mountain, Yulong Xue Shan (Jade Dragon Snow Mountains, 5,595 m), in conjunction with the Tiger-Leap Gorge, which has cut a chasm almost 4,000 m deep between the Yulong summits and the neighboring Haba Xue Shan (5,400 m). This enormous landscape has produced a great range of vegetation, from rich agricultural terraces with oranges and bananas through a series of altitudinal forest belts, to bare rock and talus slopes and the southernmost glaciers and permanent snowfields in Eurasia. Wildlife includes snow leopard, red panda, bears, wolves, and endemic pheasants, although several of these species are seriously endangered.[2]

People of seven nationalities inhabit the area, with Naxi (numbering 300,000) as a clear majority.[3] Until recently extreme poverty was widespread, with most people involved in subsistence farming and earning an estimated per capita annual income as low as U.S. $40 per year. The physical environment brings many obstacles to economic development. Agriculture is limited by the mountainous terrain characterized by poor quality and a short growing season at higher elevations. Many villages are not linked by roads, making access to markets difficult. There are, however, abundant natural resources, including timber, medicinal herbs, and considerable hydroelectric power potential. Recent policies established by central and provincial governments have encouraged the development of tourism as the primary economic activity in the region, as a means both to improve standards of living and to protect a fragile environment.

Policies to encourage a tourist economy were designed while severe environmental disturbances were occurring between 1985 and 1989, when the entire region of northwestern Yunnan was progressively "opened" to the world market. At the same time that economic regulations were eased, forest policy was confused and unpoliced. The Yi, and neighboring Tibetan and Naxi villagers, began a process of excessive logging. During this short boom period, individual per capita income from illegal logging in the Yi village of Hei Shui exceeded 1,700 yuan (U.S. $1.00 = about 8 yuan). Additional Tibetan and Yi people moved into the area; many were able to acquire large trucks for transporting illegally cut logs. The improved (though still unsurfaced) road south to Lijiang City was choked with lumber trucks day and night. Logging occurred in forests throughout the region, including within the Yulong Xue Shan Nature Preserve, established in 1979 as a means to protect the Yunnan monkey, the high mountain duck, and other wildlife habitat. Deforestation was claimed to have contributed to soil erosion, increased runoff of water and sediments, and flooding in the lower reaches of the drainage. Because Lijiang County borders on the upper reaches of the Yangtse River, the health and extent of the forest cover not only affects villages in the immediate area but also may have serious implications for the heavily populated Sichuan basin located downstream.

By 1990 the central government began to react strongly to the devastation caused by both illegal and legal logging. It began strengthening the forest laws and, in places, vigorously enforcing them. Degradation slowed, though the extreme poverty of the rural population results in continued use of forested areas to practice traditional agriculture, collect fuel wood and other forest products, and—through timber harvest—acquire scarce capital. Increasingly, for villagers and the national government, tourism came to be seen as a viable economic development alternative.[4]

Forest Ownership and Management Policy

We need village laws like in old times, and different levels of government should work together to forcefully control illegal logging. The Forestry Bureau has tried but is unsuccessful. Besides, they do not know what the local situation is, and would give the same punishment if someone is rich and cutting trees to make money or poor and cutting because they need to build a house.[5]

According to official policy, the forests of Lijiang are managed by the village communities. Villagers want to conserve their forests but told us that they cannot control the deforestation, because they do not feel empowered to do so, even though the forests belong to them in the form of village collectives. They are affected by the reduction in quantity and quality of the forests because of reduced availability of firewood, building materials, compost, and, in some cases, access to legitimate income.

Continued pressure for development stems from both national and local sources. Lijiang County is relatively remote from the main production centers of China, is populated by ethnic minority groups, and is viewed by the national government as lagging behind the rest of the nation. Official Chinese policy urges minorities to "catch up" to the majority Han population and improve their economic standing.[6] Most of China's remaining natural resources are located in the rural, marginal regions of the country, and areas such as Lijiang are the focus of the national government's resource-use plans. Development enterprises that exploit natural resources are encouraged both for national interests and as a means of helping minority populations. Of course, the resulting environmental degradation usually far outweighs economic improvements for locals. Recent economic restructuring, such as the Household Responsibility System[7] and the introduction of a market economy, also encourages locals to increase their income, and the forests are a means to this end.

Currently, the village forests in Lijiang County are held as common property in the form of village collectives. Forests are not a completely public, "open-access" resource; the idea of "property" implies the exclusion of nonowners.[8] Rather the resource is shared among a group of users who have equal rights of access to the goods and services it provides.[9] To accommodate access by multiple users, a viable common-property management system requires a set of institutional arrangements. This governing instrument should incorporate both administrative and managerial duties by recognizing the rights of users to determine the rules governing the resource as well as to make decisions regarding the resource and its management. In Lijiang the Forest Bureau determines how much of the forest may be logged and is responsible for protecting the forest and prosecuting offenders. However, the forest area is large and the Forest Bureau staff is small. Thus villagers, whose rights to use forest resources are determined by outsiders, find themselves in the unique situation of being alienated from the decision-making system while at the same time being responsible for enforcing that system. The introduction of a market economy has increased the demand beyond sustainable limits, and the result in this open-access situation is extreme overexploitation of the resource. Villagers feel they do not have the power to improve the situation, despite being official owners of the resource, because the Forest Bureau has usurped their management rights and responsibilities.

In fall 1993 a team of researchers from the University of California, Davis and the Yunnan Academy of Social Sciences surveyed villagers' attitudes and perceptions of their forest resources. In Yu Hu and Jiazi (Naxi villages) deforestation is acknowledged and the harm to the environment is recognized, but there is no effort to mitigate it. People expressed feeling powerless to effect positive change. In the village of Hei Shui (a Yi village) the introduction of tourism has led to stricter government oversight by the Tourism Bureau and the Forestry Bureau. The forest is patrolled more regularly for illegal loggers, and those caught are thrown into jail (in other villages, guilty parties are only reprimanded). In Wen Hai (Naxi), village leaders responded to the impending crisis by rallying the villagers to conserve their resource.

Love-Suicide Meadow: Is Tourism the Answer?

Between 1985 and 1989 it was still possible to walk through Lijiang's Yulong Xue Shan Nature Preserve and enjoy peace and serenity in solitude. By 1993 word had spread along tourism channels of prospects for a beautiful and tragically romantic trip—and the trek to Love-Suicide Meadow, a subalpine meadow at about 3,500 m elevation on the east slope of the Yulong Xue Shan, became increasingly popular. Lijiang is the site of the mythical Kingdom of the Naxi. This "kingdom" bears several names, including "the forgotten kingdom," "the love-suicide center of the world," and "the kingdom of powerful and brave women." According to folklore the Naxi forebears (an ancient culture called the *Dongba*, also the name for Naxi high priests, or male shamans) developed a literary script in pictograph form (the *lubberluraqt*), which preceded creation of the Chinese script. Thanks to the efforts of the Dongba priests, who protected the literature as well as traditional forms of painting, music, dance, and religion, many hundreds of the early Naxi pictographs have survived and have become the object of serious and extensive research. Today there are five Dongbas working at the Dongba Research Institute translating the pictographs, including one that gives the legend of Love-Suicide Meadow.[10] The Queen of the Kingdom of Love-Suicide called on the girl Kaimeijjiumiji (believed to have been the first suicide), to join her in paradise.

Kaimeijjiumiji!

There is so much suffering in this human world, you see it all around you. Farmers begin to worry about what they shall eat for supper when they have barely finished their breakfast. They work hard in the fields all day only to return home in the evening tired and hungry. Herdsmen do not have meat to eat, even though they herd many yaks and sheep. Girls have no beautiful clothes for themselves, even though they weave from morn till dark for harsh task masters. And lovers cannot share that splendid ecstasy of life even though they know their heart's desire.

Kaimeijjiumiji!

By seeing the world your eyes are suffused with so much suffering. You must come to my kingdom to see the lovely flowers in the meadows. Your feet are injured from walking in the human world. You must come to me where you can walk barefoot in the cool grass. Come to live in this world of gentle breeze and refreshing clouds. Come here and fill your hair with garlands of flowers. Where the birds will sing with you in chorus. Here you will be able to weave beautiful clothes from the clouds of the morning. Here you can eat the white pine sugar of the meadow. Here you can drink the rich milk that flows from the mountain spring. Come to us and live in harmony with nature, with birds and animals and enjoy a life of youth everlasting, of rapture that never falters.

Under the Ming and Yuan dynasties (before 1723) the ethnic minorities of present-day southwest China were ruled according to a code named *suisushizheng* ("rule minority people according to a policy of no interference with their traditional customs"). After 1723 the Qing Emperor Yongzheng introduced a new policy for ethnic minorities called *giatuguiliu* ("conversion to the official system of the central government"). This new policy caused serious cultural conflict between Confucianized political institutions and the diverse traditions of many ethnic minorities in the southwest. The traditional Naxi marriage and family system was based on matrilineal and patrilineal modes, with marriage being a free choice of love partners; teenage love relations were open and predominant. As part of the imposition of Han-style customs, all indigenous traditions and institutions came to be looked down on as primitive and barbarian. The Han-style marriage contract arranged during infancy was enforced; cremation of the dead was forbidden; there was even an attempt to eliminate the wearing of the Naxi woman's costume. In particular, under Han Confucian morality, childbirth before marriage was considered shameful and virginity was emphasized.

Despite heavy political suppression and Confucian ideological influence, remnants of the Naxi way of life survived. Free love before marriage continued to exist, together with the Han-enforced marriage arrangements by parents. In this way, a highly romanticized sexual relationship developed informally. Nevertheless, the two, frequently mutually exclusive approaches to marriage often came into conflict. The love-suicide pact became the dramatic response of young lovers unwilling to face forced separation for a loveless marriage with prearranged and unknown partners.

In some instances these events were group contracts with participation of several couples. In anticipation of this ultimate act, the lovers would spend several days visiting beautiful natural locations; high mountain meadows with a backdrop of spectacular snow peaks became favored places. By the 18th century the Love-Suicide Meadow above the White River section of the Yulong Xue Shan became the most revered place. From this meadow, Yunshanping (Meadow in the Spruce Forest), can be seen one of the most magnificent landscapes in southwest China, including the highest summit (Sanzi-dou, Fan Peak) of the Naxi sacred mountain. Although Yunshanping is the most famous meadow for ritual suicide, many other sites were also used: the *hualeibu* cliff, for instance, above the village of Yu Hu, from which place views of the Tiger-Leap Gorge can be obtained. And near Yunshanping, the valleys of the White and Black Rivers are frequently mentioned in the Dongba religious scripts.

The suicides, dressed in their finest clothes, as if for a wedding, sang sad and beautiful love songs (*Yeqbee*) accompanied on traditional instruments. They built simple rustic shelters decorated with garlands of flowers, feasted, and indulged in physical love. When the food was eaten they would hang themselves on rope suspended from tree limbs or jump over the cliffs to their deaths. The lovers believed that after death they would be transported over the mountaintop to a paradise (a kind of *Shambala*, or Shangri-la) where they would live forever in perpetual youth and in good health. They would dwell deep in the mountains in harmony with nature. Stags would assist in plowing the fields; they would be awoken in the mornings by colorful pheasants; during the days they would ride on red tigers or sing together with wild animals. At night bright stars and the moon would cast sufficient light so that lamps would not be necessary. Clothes and pine sugar would be available in abundance. Above all they would be totally removed from the bitterness and sorrows of the world. In turn they would call on young lovers in the common world to escape from their suffering and so join them.

In the 1930s groups of up to 10 couples committed this tragic ritual. Love suicides occurred until as recently as the 1950s. In that decade artifacts of the rituals were still being discovered in the meadow, including instruments that were used by the suicides. The local Naxi revere the meadow even today; no one should whistle in the meadow for fear that the spirits of the young lovers will seduce him or her, and so that person will commit suicide in a form of ecstasy; it would be impossible to escape.

Love-Suicide Meadow Today

The Love-Suicide Meadow remained a much-revered site of myth and mystery—quiet, sad, and dramatically romantic. Save for the suicides, the only occasional visitors were herders who brought their animals, or farmers from distant villages who came to collect herbs. The first certain human impacts occurred about 60–70 years ago, when the Yi people from Ninglang County to the east immigrated to the vicinity. They established small subsistence villages in the forests below the meadow and began to practice their traditional slash-and-burn agriculture (swidden). The first disturbance of the forest was not particularly significant and did not reach the actual meadow.[11] Whereas the "opening" of northwestern Yunnan between 1985 and 1989 meant settlers pouring into the area and excessive logging in the nature preserve, the meadow remained scarcely touched.

With the 1990 tightening of forest laws, access to the forests of the Yulong Xue Shan Nature Preserve became controlled, and income from logging and timber sales dried up. By 1994 tourism development had become the dominant economic activity in the region. The headquarters to the Nature Preserve is situated immediately below the Love-Suicide Meadow on the main road from Lijiang City north to Daju, the northern "gateway" to the Tiger-Leap Gorge. A modern hotel and restaurant opened in October 1993. Tourists, mainly domestic, but with an increasing trickle of foreigners, began to visit the hotel, driving the unsurfaced road from Lijiang City by taxi or minibus. Some of them would walk to the meadow and picnic. The nearest of the three Hei Shui natural villages is only a 20-minute walk from the hotel and base of the trail to the meadow. Yi entrepreneurs, with government assistance, began to offer horses for hire. Typically, Yi women, appareled in their spectacular traditional regalia, lead the tourists seated on gaily decorated horses. Business began to flourish. Soon, however, Yi women were in fierce competition for clients.

The Yulong Xue Shan Nature Preserve staff estimate that 4,000 people visited the meadow in 1990; 5,200 in 1991; 7,500 in 1992; and more than 10,000 in 1993. By 1994 the Yi villagers had acquired 56 horses and were building temporary shacks along the road adjacent to the hotel. A modern chairlift began operation, complete with parking lot, restaurants, and a program to widen and surface the road from Lijiang City. This novel mechanization severely undercut the Yi entrepreneurs. A series of compromises between the Yi villagers and the Tourist Bureau of Lijiang Prefecture were attempted, and the Yi villagers replaced individual family competition with a strict schedule of equal allocation of clients and fixed prices. This approach reduced the importance of female costumes in the competition, and most of the horse attendants became indifferently dressed males. The compromises, however, caused serious damage to the meadow, and the short trail from the chairlift to the meadow became a quagmire. This type of environmental damage added to the existing damage of tourist litter. Tourists liberally cast litter across the forest floor, especially plastic bags and bottles, which domestic animals can ingest and choke to death on. Eventually, the Tourist Bureau and the Nature Preserve staff instigated more secure restrictions on the use of horses.

By October 1995 the Yi villagers had 104 horses, most idle, and no subsistence food crops. The short-lived tourist boom had led many of them to neglect their traditional subsistence farming. During the boom period Yi horse owners had been able to earn up to 1,600 yuan per month for each horse; a good day could bring 100 yuan. But the idle horses had become a burden on their owners, who could hardly afford to feed them. Horses are not traditional to Yi subsistence agriculture, and consequently their acquisition has become a serious liability.

Tourist visits to the meadow continue to increase. Only one year after opening, the lift, financed jointly by a Hong Kong business company and the Prefecture Tourist Bureau, had been amortized. During the 1995 Spring Festival several thousand tourists visited the meadow each day. The economic participation of Yi villagers is now concentrated on the meadow itself, where booths have been set up, operated by Yi women who hire out Yi and Naxi costumes to tourists for photographs and sell trinkets. At the base of the chairlift small tourist lodges for overnight stays are being constructed.

Two Yi dance teams, composed primarily of girls, perform for tourists daily in the meadow, but the prospects of this element of the tourist trade to degenerate into prostitution is greatly feared. Other jobs available for Yi men involve litter collection and the management of tourists to minimize environmental damage.

Naxi villagers, whose ancestors created the legends and traditions of Love-Suicide Meadow, participate in the tourist development in quite a different manner. Farmers from Jiazi village, 15 km east of the meadow, bring their surplus products (fruit, chickens, and pigs, for example) to sell to the hotel, tourists, and associated traders. Some Naxi women from the Lijiang Old Town come by bus to sell traditional *liangfen* (black bean curd).

Conclusion

In Lijiang, the Forest Bureau is not effective in enforcing the laws and protecting the forest, with the exception of Hei Shui, where tourism related to the Nature Preserve and Love-Suicide Meadow provides an incentive to do so. Villagers are excluded from decision-making systems that would invest them with resource management responsibility. No one is in control, and illegal logging proliferates. Those management decisions that are enforced are typically those that serve the "public interest"— interests defined by officials far removed from the actual minority nationality village (whose cultural needs may be overlooked or deemed insignificant).[12] This situation supports the contention that development in areas occupied by minority nationality groups often comes at the expense of the environment,[13] despite the local government's stated aspirations.

Local villagers have responded in a range of ways to the problems of deforestation, and tourism plays a central role. Capitalizing on the unique aspects of Naxi tradition, history, and legend in a spectacular natural setting, tourism has had a marked effect on the region. Its economic potential is exemplified by the rapid amortization of the costs of installing the chairlift and by the large and increasing number of visitors. Tourist visits in 1995 to Lijiang City and County exceeded over 700,000 overnight stays (more than 20,000 of those foreign tourists), and five new hotels were under construction. Major infrastructure improvements were attempted, including a high-quality road network. Lijiang Old Town was nominated as a World Cultural Heritage Site, and there are prospects for a World Heritage nomination for the Yulong Xue Shan-Tiger-Leap Gorge–Haba Xue Shan region.

Placed in broader regional perspective, sustainable development and maintenance of the entire Yulong Xue Shan Nature Preserve, and the enhancement of living standards and cultural security in a large number of mountain villages, including Naxi, Yi, and Tibetan peoples, are at risk. Increasing environmental degradation attributable to tourism development makes problematic any assertion that tourism is truly the answer to economic issues in Lijiang. A significant underlying issue is who controls the access to environmental, scenic, and cultural resources, and who pays the price for their degradation.

SECTION II: View from the 21st Century

Civil Society and Environment in China (by Bryan Tilt)

Public campaign slogans are a common feature of contemporary Chinese life. One widespread billboard features the smiling face of Deng Xiaoping, architect of China's liberal economic reforms, above a bold caption: "Development is the ultimate truth" (*Fazhan cai shi ying daoli*). As Mao Zedong's successor, Deng Xiaoping and his allies represented a radical break with China's socialist past. Beginning in 1978 Deng and other top political leaders announced a wave of liberal economic policies known as Reform and Opening (*gaige kaifang*), which have brought sweeping changes to the nation over the past three decades, including the return of private smallholder farming under the Household Responsibility System, the privatization and expansion of industrial production, an exponential increase in foreign trade and investment, and the rise of an urban consumer class. China's gross domestic product has grown nearly 10% annually over that period, and its economy is expected to be largest in the world, surpassing the United States, within two decades.

Along with obvious social changes, such rapid economic growth has also caused major changes in China's biophysical environment. Water quality in most major Chinese rivers is so terrible that half of the river sections that undergo routine monitoring earn the lowest rating in the nation's environmental quality standards for surface water. The World Bank reported in 2001 that 16 of the world's 20 most polluted cities were in China. Sulfur dioxide emissions, mostly from coal-fired industrial plants, cause acid rain across much of the country.[14] Meanwhile, the nation continues to expand its hydroelectric capacity by building large dams, resulting in ecosystem fragmentation and the displacement of rural populations. The environment may well be the first and most meddlesome check on China's meteoric economic growth.

Such widespread environmental degradation has not gone unnoticed by Chinese leaders or by the citizenry. One recent journalistic report on the rise of citizen protests over environmental issues ran under the title "Tempers Flare in China."[15] In my own research on environmental issues in rural Sichuan and Yunnan Provinces, I have talked with many villagers who are angered by the effects of pollution on their lives and livelihoods and by the requisitioning of their land for development projects. Civil action over environmental issues—including litigation, petitioning, public protest, and media coverage—is on the rise.

Here, I explore some of the ways in which Chinese civil society engages with environmental problems. With the term *civil society* I refer to an intermediate realm between the family and the state characterized by collective action around shared values, interests, and goals.[16] As the Chinese Communist Party has liberalized the nation's economy over the past three decades, it has also gradually reduced the scope of its administrative power, increasing the space within which civil society organizations may operate.[17] Yet the Chinese case presents special challenges in thinking about civil society in regard to the environment, since there is little precedent for the protection of individual rights and the single-party nature of the political system severely constrains collective action. In short, a set of empirical questions arises: Where do civil-society strategies come from? What cultural values, historical precedents, and legal statutes underpin them? In what social and political contexts are they deployed? How do various facets of civil society in China engage with the nation's seemingly intractable environmental problems?[18]

I consider these questions by examining two case studies involving key pieces of China's environmental crisis: the development of large hydropower dam facilities and the growing problem of industrial air and water pollution. I suggest that the civil society movements that are currently working to achieve more equitable environmental outcomes comprise both "pillars" and "processes." Pillars are sturdy, well-established social norms grounded in historical precedent that undergird civil society. Processes are the array of strategies that individuals and institutions use on the ground to accomplish their desired ends. Examining the role of civil society in addressing China's environmental crisis is interesting from a theoretical perspective, given the nation's unique social and political context. It is also important from a pragmatic perspective, as China's 1.4 billion citizens, approximately one-fifth of humanity, undergo some of the most radical and far-reaching environmental changes in history.

Dams and Development on Yunnan's Angry River

China's legacy of dam building stretches back deep into its dynastic past. The Dujiangyan, for example, was constructed on the Chengdu Plain of southwest China 2,200 years ago; heralded as an engineering marvel, it is still used effectively today for flood control and irrigation. In modern times the construction of dams of all sizes is an integral part of the story of China's rise to industrial might. In 1949, on the eve of the socialist revolution that brought the Chinese Communist Party to power, China had only a handful of hydrostations and reservoirs. By 1985 the country had built more than 80,000 dams for hydroelectricity, irrigation, flood control, and navigation. Although much of China's growing energy demand is met by coal-fired power plants, the hydropower industry currently provides about 10% of the nation's electricity output.

The exploitation of hydropower presents some unique political and geographical challenges in China today, particularly in regard to the distribution of hydropower potential and electricity demand. Beginning in the late 1970s, as China's economy reconnected with the world after decades of self-reliance, Deng Xiaoping proposed a coastal development strategy that would use central policy to create Special Economic Zones (SEZs) along China's east coast to serve as hubs of export-driven manufacturing. The strategy succeeded in attracting vast amounts of foreign capital and transforming many coastal cities into manufacturing centers to serve the global economy.[19]

But the hydropower resources needed to fuel this industrial boom are not located in the floodplains and river deltas of the east. Most of the nation's great rivers have their headwaters in the vast, arid interior regions of western China, which largely have been left behind in China's rush to develop its east coast. Chinese scholar Hu Angang has characterized this pattern of uneven development as "one country with four worlds": the high-income areas of the eastern coastal region, including Beijing, Shanghai, and the Pearl River Delta; the middle-income areas consisting of second-tier cities on the east coast; the low-income and primarily agricultural areas of central China; and the western regions with low-income and substandard living conditions.[20]

The western regions are home to China's vast hydropower potential. The massive Three Gorges Dam project, located on the middle reach of the Yangtze, has garnered scholarly and popular attention from around the world. Meanwhile, however, a 13-dam cascade has been planned the Nu River, in a remote corner of Yunnan Province, with comparatively little attention.[21] The development is to be spearheaded by a public-private consortium including China Huadian Corporation (one of five corporations formed when the nation's power industry was liberalized and the State Power Corporation of China was disbanded) and the provincial government of Yunnan.[22] The Nu (literally "angry river") originates at more than 5,500 m high on the Qinghai-Tibet Plateau, then flows through the province of Yunnan and Myanmar (Burma), where it is known as the Salween. The Nu winds through the Gaoligong mountain range, where the Nature Conservancy operates a nature reserve with the cooperation of the provincial government. Several areas in northwest Yunnan were also named UNESCO World Heritage Sites in 2003; home to 7,000 plant species and 80 species of rare or endangered animals, the region is one of the most biodiverse temperate ecosystems in the world. To the Chinese this place is the mythical Shangri-la; to the Tibetans it is home to many sites of spiritual significance; and to Western science it is a biodiversity hotspot famous for the richness of its flora and fauna.[23]

In addition to its biodiversity, northwest Yunnan is an area of tremendous ethnic and cultural variation. China considers itself a "unified, multiethnic state" (*tongyi duo minzu guojia*). In addition to the dominant Han majority, which makes up about 93% of the nation's population, there are 55 so-called minority nationalities (*shaoshu minzu*) that received formal recognition by the central government following an ethnic identification project conducted during the 1950s.[24] The southwest region—and Yunnan Province in particular—is China's poorest region, long considered the ethnic, cultural, and economic frontier of the nation.

Various places with high concentrations of ethnic minorities have received the designation of "autonomous region" (*zizhi qu*), "autonomous prefecture" (*zizhi zhou*), or "autonomous county" (*zizhi xian*), but the ability of officials within these entities to practice self-governance or to influence central policy remains extremely limited. Tibet, for example, is recognized as a provincial-level autonomous region (*zizhi qu*), but the potential for a secessionist movement causes the central government to keep a tight rein on the region. Moreover, China has been reluctant to accord its minority nationalities "indigenous" status under such frameworks as the UN Convention on Biodiversity, which recognizes the rights of indigenous people for autonomy and self-determination. Although national discourse depicts the Han and minority nationalities living in harmony with one another, antipathy often lurks just below the surface. The Tibetan riots of 2008 and the 2009 riots among the Muslim Uighur minority in the western province of Xinjiang are recent examples.

Government census statistics show a marked overlap between minority populations and poverty.[25] In the Nu River gorge infrastructure is poorly developed; villagers most often cross the river by zip-line. Reaching the remotest villages requires more than a day's hike from any road. Not surprisingly, many of the official government documents on the Nu River projects describe the dams as part of a poverty alleviation strategy in a region that is otherwise culturally and economically backward. Even the local government in Nujiang Prefecture, which is accustomed to relying on central government subsidies as a main revenue source, is strongly in favor of the projects. But careful inspections of the planning documents reveal an interesting fact: the vast majority of electrical power will be sent eastward to coastal cities such as Shanghai and Guangzhou, where industrial, commercial and residential demands remain high. This plan, officially termed "Send Western Electricity East" (*xi dian dong song*) will be facilitated by high-voltage direct-current (DC) transmission lines, cutting-edge technology which Chinese engineers have helped to develop. Thus, existing economic disparities between regions are likely to be exacerbated by the Nu River projects.[26]

Meanwhile, China's National Development and Reform Commission (NDRC), the comprehensive planning agency that operates under the supervision of the State Council, maintains that many of the planning documents for the Nu River cascade are to be considered state secrets, since the Nu is a transboundary river. This move, coupled with the complex public-private structure of the hydropower industry and the lucrative stakes involved, has veiled the decision-making process from public view. More than a dozen minority nationalities live in the Nu River watershed, including the Nu, Lisu, Naxi, Yi, Dai, Bai, and Zang (Tibetans). Approximately 50,000 live within the areas that would potentially be inundated, should all 13 dams be built, a small number compared to the estimated 1.5 million displaced by the Three Gorges Project, but a significant number in the context of global dam development. Recent studies on the social effects of dam construction around the world suggest that displacement and resettlement, particularly by force or coercion, result in a cascade of subsequent negative effects on employment and income, social networks, and health and well-being.[27]

Many scholars and activists look to the nearby Upper Mekong watershed (known as the *Lancang* in Chinese) as a model for understanding the potential ecological, economic, and social effects of hydropower development on the Nu. The two rivers, along with the upper Yangtze (known as the *Jinsha*), flow parallel to each other in northwest Yunnan, only dozens of kilometers apart in places. Two dams currently exist on the Upper Mekong: the Manwan, which was completed in 1995, and the Dachaoshan, which was completed in 2003. Two other dams, the Jinghong and the Xiaowan, are under construction, and several more are in various stages of planning. The Manwan hydropower station was initially a joint project of the Yunnan provincial government and the Ministry of Water Resources and Electric Power but is now operated by a private entity called Hydrolancang, a subsidiary of China Huaneng Group, which holds a state-granted monopoly on hydropower development in the region. Daming He, a hydrologist and geographer at Yunnan University and one of the founders of the Asian International Rivers Center, conducted an environmental impact study of the Manwan Dam shortly after its completion, in cooperation with Xiaogang Yu, an anthropologist at Yunnan Academy of Social Sciences, who conducted a study on the social impacts of Manwan.[28]

Their findings were striking. Four counties, encompassing 8 townships and 114 villages, were significantly affected by the Manwan Dam, and more than 7,000 people had to be resettled. In total more than 6,000 *mu* of farmland were inundated by the reservoir.[29] Some of the most productive paddy fields with intensive irrigation systems were inundated, resulting in decreased yields of rice and other staple grains and a shift to the production of maize, sugar cane, and other dryland crops. The per-capita incomes of Manwan resettlers have fallen to less than half of the provincial average. Many residents now seek wage-earning jobs outside their home communities in construction, tourism, and related industries, sending remittances back to their households. Most ironically, villages adjacent to the Manwan Dam have experienced chronic shortages of electricity. Although every resettled village has been connected to the power grid, most of the electrical power is sent eastward to Guangdong Province, and the electricity available locally must be purchased for several times its previous cost.[30] China's decision to regulate the Upper Mekong has also agitated its neighbors downstream in mainland Southeast Asia. Cambodian officials in particular are concerned about the decreased flow of water into Tonle Sap Lake, a crucial wetland area, fishery, and migratory bird habitat that relies on the seasonal flux in the hydrograph of the Mekong.

Concerned by the largely unacknowledged social costs of dam construction in Yunnan, Xiaogang Yu founded Green Watershed in 2002, an NGO backed in part by foreign funding agencies. The mission of Green Watershed is to represent the rural people whose lives and livelihoods depend on southwest China's rivers. In a bold move Yu reached out to villagers whose lands were in the potentially inundated areas of the Nu River projects. Green Watershed even went so far as to organize trips for these villagers to visit the Manwan facility on the Upper Mekong in order to view the social impacts for themselves and to travel to Beijing to a United Nations conference on hydropower.[31] Such actions raised the ire of both private hydropower development interests and officials within the National Development Reform Commission, and ultimately it resulted in Yu's temporarily losing his passport. Green Watershed also came under close scrutiny by central and provincial government authorities. As often happens in cases of dissent in China, Yu's work received a warmer reception abroad than at home: in 2006 he was awarded the Goldman Environmental Prize, a prestigious international award given to grassroots environmental activists.

Yu has been joined in the struggle by a wide array of journalists, conservationists, and activists from China and abroad. Serendipitously, Yu's work as a scholar and activist has also coincided with an important legislative milestone in Chinese environmental law, which may change the course of hydropower development on the Nu River. In 2003 the State Council passed a new Environmental Impact Assessment Law, which requires all significant development projects to undergo more rigorous regulatory oversight from SEPA as well as public hearings involving potentially affected stakeholders. Invoking the new law Premier Wen Jiabao called a temporary halt to the Nu River hydropower projects in early 2004 in order to allow for more complete environmental reviews. For now, the future of hydropower development on the Nu River is uncertain as scientists, journalists, and activists seek greater transparency in the decision-making process and a seat at the table for potentially affected individuals and communities.

Industrial Pollution in Rural Sichuan

I have focused a great deal of my research for the past decade on understanding another interesting phenomenon with far-reaching consequences for China's environment: rural industry. Although the situation seems like a contradiction in terms, rural industrialization was in fact part of the carefully planned Reform and Opening policies initiated by the central government. After agricultural reforms were completed in the early 1980s, and farming once again became the task of households rather than communes, the countryside saw a marked rise in surplus labor. To absorb this rural labor force, and to generate revenues for local township and village governments, central policymakers encouraged peasants to "leave the land, but not the countryside" (li tu bu li xiang) by working in rural factories. These so-called township and village enterprises became a primary engine of economic growth in the countryside.

Although it has undoubtedly lifted millions of peasants out of poverty, the rural industrialization process has also proven ecologically disastrous. Air quality and water quality in many villages rival that of urban areas, and the health, welfare, and livelihoods of the nation's 800 million rural residents are in jeopardy. The State Environmental Protection Administration (SEPA), China's ministry-level environmental science and regulatory agency, has focused a great deal of its pollution enforcement efforts on the rural industrial sector since the late 1990s.[32] While conducting fieldwork in rural Sichuan Province I have had the opportunity to observe the pollution-enforcement process unfold in one community called Futian Township, located at the western edge of Panzhihua Municipality.

Futian is home to approximately 4,100 people. A mixed ethnic community of Han Chinese and Yi minorities, it lags behind the national and provincial averages on most development indicators, including income, educational attainment, and poverty rates. Three township enterprises have been key to Futian's development path in recent years: a zinc smelter, which produces refined zinc that is alloyed with other metals to produce consumer goods and construction materials; a coking plant, which produces coke, a hard, porous carbon material used for industrial operations such as steel smelting; and a coal-washing plant, which rinses coal to reduce its sulfur content before it is used in industrial boilers. Residents of Futian must cope daily with noxious plumes of black, sulfurous smoke and river water that is contaminated by untreated effluents from the factories. Although these factories were initially established as communal assets managed by the township government, they have been sold to private investors in recent years, a common process under the Reform and Opening policies.

The story of pollution enforcement in Futian is related in part to the deepening of China's commitment to environmental protection at the central government level. Although many in the West criticize China for its obvious and egregious environmental problems, the nation is currently stepping up its investment in environmental protection. For example, during the Ninth National People's Congress in 1998, amid massive cuts in the national bureaucracy, SEPA not only survived but was promoted to ministerial status.[33] Chinese pollution standards are similar to, if slightly more lax than, developed countries such as the United States. Total nationwide expenditures on environmental protection have risen steadily over the past 30 years, from a fraction of GDP in the 1980s to 1.4% of GDP in 2005.[34] Several recent laws and policies are geared toward combating industrial pollution from rural factories, including Decisions Concerning Certain Environmental Protection Issues (1996) and Regulations Concerning Environmental Protection at Township and Village Enterprises (1997). Day-to-day enforcement of pollution laws is carried out by Environmental Protection Bureaus (EPBs), which are located within municipal and county-level governmental units. Numbering about 2,500 nationwide, the EPBs represent the frontline defense against pollution and the extension of SEPA's authority to the most peripheral areas of the country.

As I followed the Futian case I soon learned that many of the key drivers in the pollution-enforcement process were exogenous to the state and had more to do with civil society. In early 2000 a coalition of local farmers, led by a charismatic Han man in his 30s, began lodging complaints with the township government and with the district EPB over water emissions from the local coal-washing plant. Agricultural lands in Futian's central village are irrigated by a small tributary to the Jinsha River, the headwaters of the Yangtze. Farmers in the village had observed for years that untreated effluents released during periods of heavy operation at the coal-washing plant would literally turn the stream black. Health concerns were only secondary, since most agricultural households rely on well water for drinking. The farmers' primary complaint was that the pollution threatened their livelihoods, since contaminated water could not be used for irrigation or for watering stock animals, including water buffalo, goats, and donkeys.[35]

After several months of letters, telephone calls, and visits from angry villagers, the EPB fined the owner of the coal-washing plant. EPB officials used part of the fee to provide compensation for the approximately 100 agricultural households affected by the emissions. However, the average household received only 50 yuan, hardly enough to offset the financial losses caused by the effluents.[36] As one farmer remarked, "Fifty yuan! What are you going to do with fifty yuan? They ruin your crop and then they give you fifty yuan!"

Soon the media entered the melee. In late 2002 a news crew from Sichuan Television Station, which is operated by the provincial government, was alerted by the coalition of local farmers and arrived in Futian to film an exposé program on pollution enforcement for a soft-news television segment called *Ten Minutes Tonight* (*Jinwan Shifen*). A reporter wielding a hidden camera interviewed the owner of the zinc smelter, a man in his 50s who had moved to the township from the neighboring province of Guizhou in order to invest in local industry. Oblivious to the fact that he was being filmed, the owner of the smelter explained that his factory was immune to regulation, because it constituted a vital source of tax revenue for the local government. He wasn't worried about environmental regulators, he maintained, because his smelter was so lucrative, both to him personally and to the township government.

The investigative reporter also interviewed several workers from the smelter. When the broadcast aired on television, it showed some very damning evidence of environmental infractions, including wide-angle shots of the factory belching thick, black smoke into the sky. The township mayor and the Communist Party Secretary also appeared on the program, discussing the status of the township's industrial development and its impact on the local environment and the health of the township's citizens. No one could have predicted it at the time, but this media scrutiny would have immediate and lasting consequences. Officials from the EPB conducted an unannounced inspection in early 2003 and ordered the closure of all factories in the township for noncompliance with emissions standards pending further notice. Over the course of several months it became clear that the factories would not reopen. The factory owners sold off some of the most valuable pieces of equipment, and villagers scavenged what remained: zinc ore slag, bits of coal for heating and cooking, metal scraps and bricks for construction, and cylindrical crucibles from the zinc smelter to be used as irrigation spouts in the terraced rice paddies. The loss of township factories has been a major point of controversy in Futian; environmental quality has improved, but residents' incomes have fallen and township finances have been dramatically reduced.[37]

I found it noteworthy that EPB officials, while guided by policies and directives from SEPA, were also profoundly influenced by various aspects of Chinese civil society. Factories in Futian were known to be in violation of national emissions standards; these environmental infractions went on for years with minimal sanction, mostly in the form of pollution discharge fees. But the tipping point in this case happened when the informal citizens' group, concerned about the effects of pollution on their livelihoods, took action by complaining to the appropriate officials and alerting the media. Television coverage of the Futian case constituted a major loss of "face" (*mianzi*) for local EPB officials, who appeared incompetent at best and blatantly corrupt at worst. In Chinese society "face" is possessed by people in positions of power; it is a form of moral authority that aids officials in accomplishing their tasks and exacting the compliance of people under their charge.[38] In my interviews with several regulatory officials at the EPB, they conceded that the agency had been deeply shamed by the public airing of their failings on television, and they resolved to step up their enforcement efforts. The scientist in charge of environmental monitoring at the EPB remarked, "This is a war, and I'm on the front line."

Pillars and Processes of Environmental Civil Society

The two cases I have briefly reviewed indicate a growing role for civil society in identifying and addressing environmental problems in China. Yet the nature of civil society illustrated here bears little resemblance to what students of Western political history might expect to see. Indeed, there is little of the formal civic institutions, voluntary associations, and open social dialogue that are considered part and parcel of the civil society of the West.[39] This situation is perhaps not very surprising, given the nature of politics in China: from the 1989 crackdown on the student-led democracy movement in Tiananmen Square, to the more recent suppression and persecution of members of the Falungong religious sect, China's top political leaders have shown time and again that, despite new openness in the economic arena, social order is more important than individual liberty when it comes to politics. The two cases reviewed here, hardly unequivocal environmental victories, reveal a certain caution and circumspection on the part of civil society actors. Environmental civil society in China is undoubtedly still in its infancy. How, then, are we to analyze its role in contemporary China and to judge its successes or failures?

Although the concept may take a unique form in China's peculiar political, cultural, and economic context, *civil society*, I have suggested, comprises two key elements, pillars and processes, which I examine in some detail below. Pillars are sturdy, well-established social norms grounded in historical precedent that undergird civil society; processes are the array of strategies and tactics that individuals and institutions use to accomplish their desired ends.

Pillars   At least two pillars serve to support China's burgeoning environmental civil society. The first, ironically, is a deep historical legacy of public mobilization and protest that is grounded in millennia-old social norms. As early as the 12th century B.C.E. rulers of the Zhou Dynasty governed the nation based on the "mandate of heaven" (tianming), an idea that served to legitimize their rule so long as they governed virtuously. As a corollary, however, imperial subjects had the right to rebel if their leaders made unjust demands or ruled ineffectively; hence the dynastic cycle waxed and waned over the centuries as a given ruling family obtained, then lost, the mandate of heaven.[40] Even during the Cultural Revolution (1966–1976), the height of the socialist experiment and the point at which the power of the Chinese state was nearly absolute, this tradition of public engagement in civic affairs remained viable. Citizens were encouraged to purge intellectuals and other "bad elements" from their midst and also to "struggle" against corrupt leaders who abused their power. For all its brutality, the Cultural Revolution kept alive this tradition of justified public protest. Civil society mobilizations today—whether they seek to address political, religious, economic, or environmental issues—bear the stamp of this legacy.[41]

The second pillar of environmental civil society is more formal and institutional in nature. China's recent economic reforms have been remarkable in their speed and scope; political reforms, meanwhile, have been incremental but significant, resulting in a growing framework of codified individual rights and a growing consciousness of these rights on the part of the populace. Two key laws in this regard are the Administrative Litigation Law (1989), which allows individuals to bring lawsuits against governmental units and officials, and the Organic Law of Villagers' Committees (1998), which established a system of self-government by which villagers elect rural cadres. The effectiveness of such laws in fostering meaningful public participation in the governing process is widely questioned, but official statistics show a 10-fold increase in litigation of all types over the past two decades, indicating increased public participation in the legal system.[42]

As public consciousness grows regarding the rule of law and the contractual obligations that bind citizens to the state, a greater discursive space is beginning to open within which the processes of civil society may operate. The political scientists Kevin O'Brien and Lianjiang Li describe this growing phenomenon as "rightful resistance":

> A form of popular contention that operates near the boundary of authorized channels employs the rhetoric and commitments of the powerful to curb the exercise of power, hinges on locating and exploiting divisions within the state, and relies on mobilizing support from the wider public. In particular, rightful resistance entails the innovative use of laws, policies, and other officially promoted values to defy disloyal political and economic elites.[43]

Rightful resistance differs from open rebellion against existing power structures, which in contemporary China can prove politically ineffectual and downright dangerous. Rightful resistance must remain within the bounds of legality set by the government and, if it is to be successful, must invoke some of the ideas and discourses of the government itself. In this sense rightful resistance straddles "the border between what is usually considered popular resistance and institutional participation."[44] In both case studies presented in this chapter individuals and organizations used central policy as the foundation on which to accomplish their environmental goals. In the case of dam construction in Yunnan scholars and activists invoked the newly promulgated Environmental Impact Assessment Law to force a more thorough review of the Nu River projects. In Sichuan villagers concerned about their livelihoods petitioned the Environmental Protection Bureau on the basis of several antipollution laws.

Processes   These pillars support a variety of processes, or strategies, for mobilizing civil society organizations around environmental interests. The people and organizations involved in the cases described in this chapter employed a variety of strategies, including the formation of nongovernmental organizations (NGOs), the mobilization of popular protest, and use of the media.

The first process, the formation of environmental NGOs, is a relatively new phenomenon in China. Green Watershed, the NGO described briefly in the Nu River case study, was established to help mitigate some of the social costs of hydropower development in Yunnan. The organization followed in the path of Friends of Nature, a group founded in 1994 and widely cited as the country's first environmental NGO. These groups occupy shaky political ground. The central government is still extremely hesitant to grant complete autonomy to non-State actors, a discomfort that is embodied nicely by the fact that the Chinese term "nongovernmental organization" (*fei zhengfu zuzhi*) sounds suspiciously like "antigovernmental organization" (*fan zhengfu zuzhi*). While environmental NGOs in China currently number in the hundreds, these groups are subject to a dizzying set of controls and regulations from the State Council and Central Committee. These controls include allowing no more than one organization of a type to be registered with the Ministry of Civil Affairs, and requiring each social organization to be affiliated with an approved governmental unit.[45]

As a result often only a very fine line exists between formal organizing under the banner of an environmental NGO and the next process that I would like to discuss: less formal, ad hoc mobilization on the part of concerned citizens. In the case of industrial pollution in Sichuan, concerned villagers focused their efforts on influencing regulatory officials in the Environmental Protection Bureau by lodging complaints and by alerting the provincial media to the environmental infractions of local factories.[46] Cultural norms, including the EPB officials' aversion to losing "face," played a key role in this process. Notably, the political economy of China's rural industrial sector was also a crucial element in the enforcement process. Factories were formerly held by the township government as collective assets, which meant that any criticism of the factory was ultimately criticism of the state. When the factories were privatized as part of Reform and Opening, however, industry and state were effectively decoupled, which allowed citizens to complain about industrial pollution without posing any direct affront to state power. Similarly in the Yunnan case, the disbanding of the State Power Corporation of China, and the formation of several corporate power distribution entities, provided some maneuvering space for scholars and activists who questioned the logic of damming the Nu River. Liberal economic reforms are undoubtedly nudging China's political and legal systems toward greater openness.

Finally, the media constitutes a vital avenue for fostering the development of environmental civil society. Environmental issues are increasingly considered nonsensitive by government officials, which means that covering industrial accidents or infractions has become relatively routine.[47] The vast majority of this media coverage is conducted through legal channels, since all major television stations and print media are managed by the government. The Sichuan case reviewed here is just one of many examples. Another is a chemical plant explosion that released more than 100 tons of benzene into the Songhua river upstream from the major northeastern city of Harbin in 2005; local officials attempted to cover up the incident. But a deluge of media reports via newspapers and popular television programs brought the issue to the public's attention and ultimately resulted in the firing of Xie Zhenhua, the minister of SEPA, the highest-ranking official ever to lose his job over an environmental accident.[48] More dynamic information technologies, such as the Internet, will undoubtedly facilitate the public's ability to gain information about environmental issues, although currently only about 5% of the Chinese populace—mostly well-off, educated, urban people—have regular access to the Internet.[49] All these processes point to a growing desire for transparency and public participation in environmental decision making.

Concluding Thoughts

By examining two case studies—hydropower development on Yunnan's Nu River and industrial pollution in Sichuan—I described some of the environmental challenges facing China today and some of the ways in which civil society helps to address them. I have suggested that we can use "pillars" and "processes" as heuristic devices to understand how environmental civil society in China both draws on historical and cultural precedent and adapts to present circumstances through the use of creative strategies. Understanding the role of environmental civil society in China today is crucial as the nation grows to superpower status. From the transboundary effects of regulating great rivers, to the protection of biological and cultural diversity, to the greenhouse gases emitted by an overheated economy, China's environmental crisis affects us all.

A common saying in Chinese politics holds that there are "policies from above, and countermeasures from below" (*shang you zhengce, xia you duice*). In other words, no matter how solid a grip the central government appears to have on its citizens and on local officials, its control is never absolute; individuals and organizations at the margins always have strategies for getting what they need from the political system. Nevertheless, I wish to end on a slightly cautionary note. Civil society actors—whether in religious, social, or environmental arenas—occupy a very tenuous space in Chinese politics. If the two case studies in this chapter tell us anything, it is that greater openness in environmental decision making will come slowly and incrementally by working within, rather than overturning, existing power structures. Indeed, "the roots of Chinese rightful resistance lie in the rich soil of central policy."[50] The consolidated nature of political power in China may even prove over the long term to be an asset for environmental protection, once the central government and the populace decide to change course.

Notes

1. This chapter, "circa 1997," is an abstracted version of a longer essay originally titled "Uncommon Property Rights in Southwest China: Trees and Tourism" by Lindsey Swope, Margaret Byrne Swain, Fuquan Yang, and Jack D. Ives, *Life and Death Matters: Human Rights and the Environment at the End of the Millennium* (Alta Mira, 1997, 26–42).

2. Jack D. Ives and He Yaohua, "Environmental and Cultural Change in the Yulong Xue Shan, Lijiang District, NW Yunnan, China," in *Montane Mainland Southeast Asia in Transition,* proceedings of a symposium, Chiang Mai University, Thailand, Nov. 12–16, 1995, B. Rerkasem, Ed. (Chiang Mai University, 1996, 1–18).

3. Han, Yi, and Tibetan are the other nationality populations in the study area.

4. The first edition version of this chapter included a section on the problems of deforestation and villager response to national efforts to regulate and control local timber harvest, with data derived from a joint University of California–Davis and Yunnan Academy of Social Science research project examining the relationships between poverty, development, and environment in poor mountain ethnic communities. Funding for this study was provided by the Ford Foundation and the United Nations University as part of a larger study on poverty and gender relations in Lijiang County. Dr. Jack Ives (Dept. of Environmental Studies, University of California, Davis) and He Yaohua (Yunnan Academy of Social Sciences) were the principal investigators on the project.

5. These comments were made by various informants during village surveys in Lijiang County.

6. Colin Mackerras, *China's Minorities: Integration and Modernization in the Twentieth Century* (New York: Oxford University Press, 1994).

7. The Household Responsibility System returned agricultural production responsibility from village collective organizations to individual households. For a detailed discussion, see Elizabeth Croll, "Some Implications of the Rural Economic Reforms for the Chinese Peasant Household," in *The Re-Emergence of the Chinese Peasantry*, Ashwani Saith, Ed. (London: Croom Helm, 1987).

8. A. P. Grima and Fikret Birkes, "Natural Resources: Access, Rights-to-Use, and Management," in *Common Property Resources: Ecology and Community-Based Sustainable Development,* Fikret Birkes, Ed. (London: Bellhaven Press, 1989, 36).

9. See C. Ford Runge, "Common Property and Collective Action in Economic Development," in *Making the Common Work*, D. W. Bromley, Ed. (San Francisco: ICS Press, 1992, 17–39) and Elinor Ostrom, *Governing the Common: The Evolution of Institutions for Collective Action* (Cambridge: Cambridge University Press, 1990).

10. Fuquan Yang, *Mysterious Suicide for Love among Naxi People (Shenquidexunqing)* (Hong Kong: Joint Publishing Company, 1993) (Taipei: Hanyang Publishing House, republished 1995).

11. In 1985 tree-ring counts indicated trees exceeding 900 years of age; comparison with 1930s photographs taken by Dr. Joseph Rock showed little noticeable change in the meadow.

12. Nicholas Menzies and Nancy Peluso, "Rights of Access to Upland Forest Resources in Southwest China," *Journal of World Forest Resource Management* 6 (1991, 18).

13. Mackerras, note 6.

14. For a thorough overview of China's current environmental crisis, see Elizabeth Economy, *The River Runs Black: The Environmental Challenge to China's Future* (Ithaca, NY: Cornell University Press, 2004). See also Jianguo Liu and Jared Diamond, "China's Environment in a Globalizing World: How China and the Rest of the World Affect Each Other," *Nature* 435 (2005, 1179–86).

15. Jean-Francois Tremblay, "Tempers Flare in China," *Chemical and Engineering News* 83: 39 (September 26, 2005, 21–28). For an interesting case of citizen protest over environmental pollution, see also Jun Jing, "Environmental Protests in China," in *Chinese Society: Change, Conflict and Resistance*, 2nd ed., Elizabeth Perry and Mark Selden, Eds. (New York: Routledge, 2003).

16. Adam B. Seligman, *The Idea of Civil Society* (New York: Free Press, 1992).

17. Robert P. Weller, "Introduction: Civil Institutions and the State," in *Civil Life, Globalization, and Political Change in Asia: Organizing between Family and State*, Robert P. Weller, Ed. (New York: Routledge, 2005). See also Kin-Man Chan, "The Development of NGOs under a Post-Totalitarian Regime: The Case of China," in *Civil Life, Globalization, and Political Change in Asia: Organizing between Family and State*, Robert P. Weller, Ed. (New York: Routledge, 2005).

18. I have avoided using the term *environmental justice* in this chapter, because many of the connotations of this term do not fit well with the Chinese case. First, as Robert Bullard reminds us in his recent edited volume, one of the key axioms in environmental justice struggles is "race matters." (See Robert D. Bullard, *The Quest for Environmental Justice: Human Rights and the Politics of Pollution* [San Francisco: Sierra Club Books, 2005, 2].) Much of the work on environmental justice in the United States has focused on how racial minorities and people of low socioeconomic status bear a disproportionate share of the health risks associated with environmentally polluting industries and activities. But although China exhibits great ethnic and cultural diversity, race is a trope that does not work so well in the Chinese context. Second, much of the recent work on environmental justice in the United States is conducted under a growing legal framework supported by Executive Order 12898, which makes clear legal mandates on federal agencies. No similar statutes exist in China.

19. The most dramatic example of the effects of global capital on eastern China is the city of Shenzhen. In 1978, before its designation as an SEZ, Shenzhen was a medium-sized city with a population of about 300,000. Today, its population, drawn from all corners of China and the world, numbers nearly 5 million, and its bustling economy is driven by manufacturing, banking, and trade.

20. Angang Hu, "Yige Zhongguo, Sige Shijie: Zhongguo Diqu Fazhan Chayu de Bupingdengxing" ["One China, Four Worlds: The Inequality of Uneven Political Development in

China"], in *Dierci Zhuanxing: Guojian Zhidu Jianshe*, A. Hu, S. Wang, and J. Zhou, Eds. (Beijing: Qinghua University Press, 2003).

21. Jim Yardley, "Seeking a Public Voice on China's Angry River," *The New York Times* (New York: December 26, 2005).

22. For an excellent overview of the political decision-making process behind hydropower development in southwest China, see Darrin Magee, "Powershed Politics: Hydropower and Interprovincial Relations under Great Western Development," *The China Quarterly* 185 (2006, 23–41).

23. Ralph Litzinger, "The Mobilization of 'Nature': Perspectives from North-west Yunnan," *The China Quarterly* 178 (2004, 488–504).

24. The anthropologist Fei Xiaotong, who studied in Britain under Branislaw Malinowski, played a key role in the ethnic identification project. The goal was to classify each minzu according to Marx's schema as primitive, slave, feudal, bourgeois-capitalist, socialist, or communist. (See Stevan Harrell, "Introduction: Civilizing Projects and the Reaction to Them," in *Cultural Encounters on China's Ethnic Frontiers*, Stevan Harrell, Ed. [Seattle: University of Washington Press, 1995].) Various places with high concentrations of *minzu* have received the designation of "autonomous region" (*zizhi qu*), "autonomous prefecture" (*zizhi zhou*), or "autonomous county" (*zizhi xian*), but the ability of officials within these entities to practice self-governance, or to influence central policy, remains extremely limited. Tibet, for example, is recognized as a provincial-level autonomous region (*zizhi qu*), but the potential for a secessionist movement causes the central government to keep a tight rein on the region. China has been reluctant to accord its minority nationalities "indigenous" status under such frameworks as the UN Convention on Biodiversity, which recognizes the rights of indigenous people for autonomy and self-determination.

25. See Shaoguang Wang and Angang Hu, *The Political Economy of Uneven Development: The Case of China* (Armonk, NY: M.E. Sharpe, 1999).

26. Darrin Magee, "Powershed Politics: Hydropower and Interprovincial Relations under Great Western Development," *The China Quarterly* 185 (2006, 23–41). Interestingly, two key rationale for building large dams—hydropower generation and flood control—are at odds with each other in Yunnan. Southwest China's monsoonal climate means that summer, with its heavy rains, would be peak time for electricity generation. But engineers and public officials also recognize that water would need to be stored behind the dams during this time to prevent flooding downstream.

27. Growing global concern about the social costs of large dam projects, and about how to solicit meaningful participation from those most affected, resulted in the formation of the World Commission on Dams in 1998, which produced the first systematic assessment of large dams around the world. (See World Commission on Dams, *Dams and Development: A New Framework for Decision Making* [London: Earthscan, 2000]; see also Thayer Scudder, *The Future of Large Dams: Dealing with Social, Environmental, Institutional, and Political Costs* [London: Earthscan, 2005].)

28. The environmental and social impact studies were sponsored by Oxfam Hong Kong during the summer of 2000 and were jointly completed by Professors Daming He, Xiaogang Yu, Lihui Chen, Jiaji Guo, Shu Gan, and Qin Li. Findings were incorporated into a document entitled "Reasonable and Equitable Utilization of Water Resources and Water Environment Conservation in International Rivers in Southwest China," a key component of China's 9th National Five Year Plan for Science and Technology.

29. The *mu* is the standard unit in China for measuring land area. One mu is equal to 0.066 hectare or 0.165 acre.

30. See Daming He and Lihui Chen, "The Impact of Hydropower Cascade Development in the Lancang-Mekong Basin, Yunnan," *Mekong Update and Dialogue* 5:3 (2002, 2–4).

31. Darrin Magee, *New Energy Geographies: Powershed Politics and Hydropower Decision Making in Yunnan, China* (Seattle: Dissertation Completed at the University of Washington, 2006).

32. Bryan Tilt and Pichu Xiao, "Industry, Pollution and Environmental Enforcement in Rural China: Implications for Sustainable Development," *Urban Anthropology and Studies of Cultural Systems and World Economic Development* 36:1–2 (2007, 115–43). For an overview of policy and regulations governing pollution in the rural industrial sector, see Xiaoying Ma and Leonard Ortolano, *Environmental Regulation in China: Institutions, Enforcement, and Compliance* (Lanham, MD: Rowan and Littlefield, 2000).

33. Before 1998 the agency was known as the National Environmental Protection Administration (NEPA). For an excellent overview of the evolution and the current structure of the Chinese environmental protection bureaucracy, see Abigail R. Jahiel, "The Organization of Environmental Protection in China," *The China Quarterly* 156 (1998, 757–87). In addition, the geographer Joshua Muldavin has traced the effects of the Reform and Opening policies on China's environmental bureaucracy. (See Joshua Muldavin, "The Paradoxes of Environmental Policy and Resource Management in Reform-Era China," *Economic Geography* 76:3 [2000, 244–71].)

34. Z. Zhang, "Shiyi Wu Guihua Xiade Huanjing Touzi" ["Environmental Investment in the 11th Five-year Plan"], *Huanjing [Environment]* 310 (2005, 38–40).

35. See Bryan Tilt, "Perceptions of Risk from Industrial Pollution in Rural China: A Comparison of Occupational Groups," *Human Organization* 65:2 (2006, 115–27).

36. The exchange rate was approximately USD 1 = RMB 8.2. China's pollution levy system is the primary instrument through which EPB officials exact environmental compliance from factories. Article 18 of the Environmental Protection Law states that "in cases where the discharge of pollutants exceeds the limit set by the state, a compensation fee shall be charged according to the quantities and concentration of the pollution released." (See Hua Wang and Dasgupta Wheeler, "Financial Incentives and Endogenous Enforcement in China's Pollution Levy System," *Journal of Environmental Economics and Management* 49:1 [2005, 174].)

37. For a more thorough examination of the politics of pollution control in this case, see Bryan Tilt, "The Political Ecology of Pollution Enforcement in China: A Case from Sichuan's Rural Industrial Sector," *The China Quarterly* 192 (2007, 915–32).

38. Yunxiang Yan, *The Flow of Gifts: Reciprocity and Social Networks in a Chinese Village* (Stanford, CA: Stanford University Press, 1996, 133–38).

39. Robert Hefner, "On the History and Cross-Cultural Possibility of a Democratic Ideal," in *Democratic Civility: The History and Cross-Cultural Possibility of a Democratic Ideal*, Robert Hefner, Ed. (London: Transaction Press, 1998, 3–52). See also Adam B. Seligman, *The Idea of Civil Society* (New York: Free Press, 1992).

40. John Bryan Starr, *Understanding China: A Guide to China's Political Economy, History, and Political Structure* (New York: Hill and Wang, 1997, 52–54).

41. See Elizabeth J. Perry, "'To Rebel Is Justified': Cultural Revolution Influences on Contemporary Chinese Protest," in *The Chinese Cultural Revolution Reconsidered: Beyond Purge and Holocaust*, Kam-yee Law, Ed. (New York: Palgrave MacMillan, 2003, 274). Of course, any form of dissent in Chinese society is also shaped by the Confucian ethos, with its emphasis on social harmony and its privileging of the good of society over the rights of the individual.

42. Minxin Pei, "Rights and Resistance: The Changing Contexts of the Dissident Movement," in *Chinese Society: Change, Conflict and Resistance*, 2nd ed., Elizabeth J. Perry and Mark Selden, Eds. (New York: Routledge, 2003, 23–46). See also Kevin J. O'Brien and Lianjiang Li, "Suing the Local State: Administrative Litigation in Rural China," *The China Journal* 51 (2004, 75–96).

43. Kevin J. O'Brian and Lianjiang Li, *Rightful Resistance in Rural China* (Cambridge: Cambridge University Press, 2006, 2).

44. Ibid.

45. Kin-man Chan, "Development of NGOs under a Post-Totalitarian Regime: The Case of China," in *Civil Life, Globalization, and Political Change in Asia: Organizing between Family and State*, Robert P. Weller, Ed. (London: Routledge, 2005). The current status of environmental NGOs in China is described in detail in Guobin Yang, "Environmental NGOs and Institutional Dynamics in China," *The China Quarterly* 181 (2005, 46–66).

46. Similar citizen protests happen every day in rural China. Although it is extremely difficult to estimate the frequency with which environmental protests occur, in part because of the ambiguous definition of what constitutes "protest," data published by the central government show a marked increase in citizen complaints to environmental protection bureaus beginning in the late 1990s and culminating with more than 600,000 per year presently (2010) (Mol and Carter 2006, 161). (See Arthur P. J. Mol and Neil T. Carter, "China's Environmental Governance in Transition," *Environmental Politics* 15:2 [2006, 161].)

47. Ibid.

48. "China Fires Water Monitor," *The New York Times* (December 3, 2005).

49. See Guobin Yang, "Environmental NGOs and Institutional Dynamics in China," *The China Quarterly* 181 (2005, 58–59). Moreover, thousands of "Internet police" with a mandate from the Party to control and censor material on the Internet (felicitously dubbed the "Great Firewall of China") makes it difficult to get opposing viewpoints. For example, one rarely hears the Tibet issue talked about in terms other than those espoused by the central government: "the peaceful liberation of Tibet" (*Xizang heping jiefang*).

50. Kevin J. O'Brian and Lianjiang Li, *Rightful Resistance in Rural China* (Cambridge: Cambridge University Press, 2006, 5).

SNAPSHOT: China Ecocities.doc—Huangbaiyu: Eco-Cities in the Chinese Countryside[1]

Shannon May

Many people in rural Chinese households are still responsible for their own basic needs. During harsh weather and environmental conditions, their days are consumed with the struggle to survive. During the two coldest months in the eastern mountain villages of Liaoning Province, households must allocate five labor hours per day to the single task of building and managing the fires necessary to warm a room from the frigid −30°C temperatures outside, and another six labor hours to prepare, chop, and haul wood fuel in preparation for next year's winter.

Recently rural residents have witnessed the income of their urban comrades outpace their own by three to one. When urban in-kind subsidies are included, the gap jumps to six to one, the largest income disparity in the world. Yet even this calculation does not fully account for the economic opportunity cost of being born in rural China. Those 11 household labor hours a day in the dead of winter necessary to avoid freezing to death are hours that cannot be spent earning income to pay for education and healthcare. Can rural urbanization be done in a way that both increases quality of life and economic opportunity for rural Chinese and positively affects the globe's carbon calculus?

The integrated waste and energy systems of eco-cities hold this promise. In an eco-city, human habitat is designed with the recognition that the city, as the earth, is a closed system. Taking metric tons of carbon dioxide equivalents as the unit of measurement through which to approximate ecological hazard, eco-cities strive for a carbon-neutral footprint. Rather than burning carbon-based fuels for energy procured by each household, biogas systems can take human, animal, or agricultural wastes from the household and return converted gas for heating and cooking. Eco-cities in the countryside may prove to be the bridges that cross the socioeconomic chasm between rural and urban populations without the hazard of ecological collapse. In the mountains of eastern Liaoning, this solution is being tested with the China-United States sustainable-development demonstration village of Huangbaiyu. It is held up as a model for China's 600,000 villages, because it meets national goals of land consolidation and global goals of limiting carbon emissions.

The plan for Huangbaiyu village includes grey water infrastructure, solar-powered electricity, and a biogas plant fueled by agricultural waste to fuel stoves for heating and cooking. The houses would be built only with materials that could be safely returned to earth or recycled and would have running water for the first time. Households spread across four valleys and seven ravines would be consolidated into a single village, with centralization allowing economic efficiency in building, operating, and providing water and energy. Such changes would halt the use of forested lands for fuel, reduce the carbon footprint of the community, and free up former residential lands for more productive endeavors. Has the promise been delivered? Ethnographic evidence raises troubling questions.

One problem came in the shift from wood to agricultural waste as a fuel source: although the design was ecologically sound, implementation ended up devastating the local economy. Government leaders and project planners assumed they knew what "waste" was in an agricultural economy that they were not a part of and did not fully understand. The corn stalks and cobs that were (mis)taken for waste by the development team are in fact the critical winter food supply for one of the leading cash crops in the area: cashmere goats. Already being recycled, so to speak, by the 30% of the local population whose household income depends on selling cashmere fiber each spring, the corn stalk "waste" already equals food, and without it herds have no fuel and families no income.

Another problem was that the soil near streams within the watershed that was deemed inefficient for cash crops was incorporated into the housing plan, and in the middle of the new eco-city development a lake was created as a community gathering point and scenic spot. While these lands are poor agriculturally, they are rich for aquaculture, for which they were used. Yet these pools had no place in the master plan, because fish were not considered a cash crop. Thus the 10% of households who depended on this income fell victim to another measure intended to improve their quality of life.

At the heart of the promise of eco-cities in the countryside is that public infrastructure will liberate families from the burden of survival and free their time for more productive pursuits. This infrastructure also carries the cost of regular cash payments. In the case of the Huangbaiyu biogas plant, which ended up depriving many families of income from cashmere goats, these utility payments totaled 15–20% of the median household's annual income. This cost clearly competes with other expenses, including health care, education, and an adult son's wedding. Moreover, while a biogas plant may free up hundreds of labor hours per year per household, there is no employment to be had in the dead of winter. Chopping down wood and burning fuel is in fact the most economical use of one's time, saving the family from paying for services with cash that is dear. Family mountain forest lands are sustainably managed over 8–10 year cycles for household use in Huangbaiyu. A biogas plant would thus impoverish the local community while meeting its second goal of global sustainability—lowered carbon emissions.

So here is the rub of sustainable development: whom does it sustain?

Current best practices in the field of sustainable design emphasize designing from the perspective of a bird, the soil, the water. But they erase the *people* of Huangbaiyu from the ecosystem, leaving only nature—and gaze of the designers. Thus, the eco-city development model of ecosystem dynamics did not recognize the necessities of local human survival. In failing to see that "waste" was, in fact, a critical resource already employed in ways that sustained lives and livelihoods, development meant to improve lives left the people of Huangbaiyu further impoverished.

As fears of a planet in peril lead environmentalists and politicians to understand carbon as a commodity that must be regulated and that has a value rising in direct proportion to our anxieties about a risky and unknown future climate, subsistence economies will most certainly be thrown into turmoil. We must recognize that there is no environmental policy that is not at the same time an economic policy. Any environmental policy that does not admit this imperils populations even as it seeks to safeguard the Earth. If subsistence use of natural resources is to be altered, then other means for families not only to subsist but also to thrive must be designed at the same time. Otherwise, programs to save the planet from industrialization will do so on the broken backs of the world's rural poor.

Note

1. Earlier versions of this essay were published as "A Sino-U.S. Sustainability Sham" in the April 2007 issue of *Far Eastern Economic Review* and as "Ecological Crisis and Eco-Villages in China" *CounterPunch*, www.counterpunch.org/may11212008.html, 11/21-23/08. For more information see Shannon May, *Practices of Ecological Citizenship: Global Dreams for a Chinese Village* (Ph.D. Dissertation, University of California, Berkeley, 2010), which further investigates the logical design.

CHAPTER 4

African Wildlife: Conservation and Conflict

Robert K. Hitchcock

Over the past several decades a dramatic upsurge has taken place in activities designed to conserve biodiversity, especially wildlife, in Africa.[1] The problem has been that conservation efforts have sometimes had negative effects on local people, including violations of basic human rights[2] (see Table 4.1). As a result, many Africans called for a new approach to wildlife preservation, management, and development, one that does not cause them harm but that instead leads to improvements in their standards of living.[3]

Biodiversity is on the decline in some parts of Africa as some species have been driven to extinction or reduced in number and as habitats have been altered by a combination of human and environmental factors.[4] A major worry of biologists in Africa is that the ability of ecosystems to carry out vital functions such as maintenance of soil fertility, water retention, and the cycling of nutrients will be reduced by the loss of biodiversity. In response, African governments, along with nongovernment organizations (NGOs) and international aid agencies, have devised various policies and programs to counteract the problems. Biodiversity preservation strategies employed in Africa range from endangered species protection legislation, control of trade in wildlife products, and enforcement of conservation laws (species conservation) to the declaration and gazettement of national parks, game reserves, and other kinds of conservation areas (spatial conservation).

Attempts have also been made to implement projects aimed at balancing conservation and development. The basic assumption behind these kinds of projects, which are known as integrated conservation and development projects (ICDPs) or community-based natural resource management (CBNRM) projects, is that people will be more likely to conserve resources if they are able to gain direct benefits from them.[5] This chapter examines the social and environmental impacts of wildlife

Table 4.1 Conservation Efforts in Africa That Have Had Negative Effects on the Well-Being of Local Populations

Project	Country	General Comments
Central Kalahari	Botswana	Over 1,700 people were resettled out of the Central Kalahari Game Reserve in 1997 and 2002; in spite of a High Court decision against the government in 2006, people continue to be arrested for hunting and entering the reserve; restrictions on access to water continue.
Korup National Park	Cameroon	Resettlement of villagers was done but was underfunded; assistance and infrastructure promised was not forthcoming; the majority of the benefits from the project went to people living away from the park rather than to residents.
Tsavo National Park	Kenya	None of the benefits from use of the park by tourists went to the people removed from there; beatings, shootings of hunters and gatherers occurred.
West Caprivi	Namibia	Local Khwe in conflict with Mbukushu and Kavango peoples in the vicinity of what was a game reserve (now Bwabwata National Park) with government ministry backing.
Virunga Volcanoes National Park	Rwanda	Gorilla protection in the park led to kidnapping of local children, intimidation of nearby residents, and restrictions on access to area; gorillas have been under pressure from human populations, which have led to a reduction in the numbers of mountain gorillas and hardships for local people.
Kruger National Park	South Africa	Local people were moved out of the park and mines were planted to prevent ingress; antipoaching efforts were used to intimidate people under the apartheid regime of South Africa.
Ngorongoro Conservation Area	Tanzania	Use of the region's grazing resources by Maasai was restricted; cultivation of crops was banned; benefits from tourism went to district councils but were not decentralized to communities.
Kibale Forest Reserve	Uganda	30,000 residents were evicted in a six-day operation and had to leave possessions for which they were not compensated; intimidation of people has occurred.

preservation and management activities in Africa, with special emphasis on human rights and environmental justice.

Problems with Biodiversity Conservation Efforts

In the past a major problem with biodiversity conservation programs in Africa, from the perspective of local people, was that they tended to result in dispossession or to prevent people from engaging in resource procurement activities. As one Ju/'hoan woman in the Nyae Nyae region of northeastern Namibia, put it: "Government first took away our right to hunt and then tried to remove us from our traditional territories." Efforts to control hunting and collection of wild plants and the setting aside of parks and reserves generally exacerbated poverty and resource stress among local communities in Africa.[6]

Some people in Africa feel threatened by what they perceive to be coercive conservation. Beginning with the creation of colonial institutions, local people were subjected to the imposition of restrictive wildlife laws and periodic search-and-seizure operations. This was particularly true of foragers and small-scale farmers who hunted and gathered wild plants and animals to supplement their subsistence and incomes.[7] In the 1970s and 1980s, as the concern over the loss of elephants, rhinoceros, and other large mammal species increased, African governments increased their efforts to put pressure on people whom they defined as poachers. Local people were arrested and jailed by police, wildlife department officials, and military personnel. In some cases suspected poachers were badly mistreated during questioning or while they were in custody.[8] In some cases local people were shot and killed as antipoaching operations were conducted. Field data suggest that at least some of those shot were simply gathering wild plants, obtaining water, or visiting friends.[9] Some officials have suggested off the record that there may have been as many as 96 people shot and killed in a single year in one country in southern Africa. The shoot-to-kill policy angered local people and has resulted, in some cases, in attacks on game scouts and tourists. It has also led to what some people believe are politically motivated spearings of rhinoceros and other large mammals.[10]

The antipoaching operations arguably have served to slow down the rate of destruction of such endangered or threatened species as rhinoceros and elephant.[11] But is the mistreatment and killing of people the most effective way to promote conservation? Some local people in Africa have suggested that the actions of government and military agencies are genocidal in intent. Others have said that preservationist actions have been undertaken in order to get them off the land so that it can be used for other purposes, including ranching and recreation. Still others have argued that the arrests and killings have actually had the effect of exacerbating poaching problems.[12] One Tyua Bushman man from the Nata River region of northeastern Botswana had this to say about wildlife laws:

> Our lives depend mostly on meat, and the laws have kept us from eating. I believe that when God created man, he provided all animals to be the food of the Masarwa. The Bamangwato depend on their cattle to provide their food. The Kalanga depend on their crops. White people live on money, bread, and sugar. These are the traditional foods of these groups of people, so it can be seen that the law is against us, the Masarwa, because it has prevented us from eating. The people who made the law knew that they

were depriving us of our food. Even if we raise cattle, we cannot do it as well as the Bamangwato. We cannot raise crops like the Kalanga, and we cannot make money like the white people do. These are the ways of other people.

African communities argue that it is possible to promote development and enhance the conservation status of wildlife without engaging in actions that result in the mistreatment and deaths of local people. As a Tyua woman from northeastern Botswana put it: "Just because these people say that they are helping preserve the environment does not mean that they should be able to violate our human rights." It is possible, they argue, to promote development and enhance the conservation status of wildlife without engaging in actions that result in the mistreatment and deaths of local people.

Causes and Consequences of Wildlife Decline in Africa

Africans, especially poor ones residing in remote areas, have taken the brunt of preservationist efforts to protect wildlife. As Eric Edroma, the Director of Uganda National Parks, said at a conference on natural resource management in Libreville, Gabon, in 1993, "African voices are heard rarely in the halls of the offices of environmental organizations." Other African speakers argued that the role of the average African peasant in the decline of Africa's game populations has been grossly overstated and that the people who are interested in the well-being of Africa's wildlife should look much more carefully at the root causes.[13]

A significant cause of wildlife decline in various parts of Africa over the past several decades has been military activity. In Angola and northern Namibia in the 1970s and 1980s game populations were decimated by military personnel in what some consider one of the worst atrocities against wildlife in the 20th century.[14] South Africa, long considered to be a leader in environmental protection, was at the center of what some local people in Angola and Namibia have described as a "wildlife holocaust." Testimony at a series of hearings in South Africa in September–October 1995 suggested that military operatives killed large numbers of rhinoceros for their horns and elephants for their tusks, which were then smuggled out of the region and sold on the black market. The funds that they obtained in exchange were used to carry out covert operations and to enrich individuals, some of them high military officers. An internal inquiry conducted in 1988 cleared South African Defense Force (SADF) officers of any wrongdoing, but subsequent investigations indicated that there had been a whitewash and that SADF officers were directly involved in the poaching and smuggling operations.

Members of Angola's National Union for the Total Independence of Namibia (UNITA), funded by South Africa for over 20 years and by the United States until 1975, was responsible for the slaughter of thousands of elephants in Angola and the near total decimation of rhinoceros. Wildlife continued to be killed in southern Angola by former UNITA fighters and government soldiers in spite of the fact that peace accords were signed in 2002.[15] One way to deal with the problem, according to members of local indigenous peoples' advocacy organizations, is to do a better job of controlling the spread of weapons and promoting strategies that reduce conflict.[16] The South African Police have an Endangered Species Protection Unit that has investigated cases of alleged poaching and smuggling by refugees from Mozambique. This unit has called for tighter customs controls and for closer investigations of individuals and businesses moving goods from one country to another.

Heightened refugee flows arising from civil conflicts in Africa have contributed significantly to the destruction of wildlife in areas where people have taken refuge; for example, in southern Somalia and northern Kenya in the late 1980s and early 1990s and in the Democratic Republic of Congo, Tanzania, and Burundi as a result of refugees fleeing the genocide in Rwanda in 1994. Wildlife losses at the hands of well-armed militias also occurred in 2007–2008 in the eastern Democratic Republic of Congo. One way to get around this problem, according to NGOs working with refugees, is to disarm people and promote greater cooperation between the various refugee agencies and wildlife departments; another is to punish those who take part in massive human rights violations, for example, by using the World Court or international tribunals.

Community-Based Natural Resource Management Projects

Members of local communities, staffs of nongovernment organizations, and African researchers and development personnel have advocated alternative strategies that will help rather than hurt Africa's people. Some NGOs, with the support of government environmental agencies, are engaged in promoting projects that aim to increase local incomes and raise standards of living while at the same time bringing about biodiversity conservation.

The World Wildlife Fund (WWF–US), The Worldwide Fund for Nature (WWF–International), Conservation International (CI), the African Wildlife Foundation (AWF), Endangered Wildlife Trust (EWT), and other environmental NGOs are involved in projects that combine conservation and development and that operate at the local level. These community-based resource management (CBNRM) projects are found in a wide variety of habitats in Africa, from tropical forests to savannas and from Afromontane habitats to coastal marine regions. Some are located on the peripheries of protected areas in what are sometimes referred to as buffer zones, and others are in rural areas under customary systems of land tenure, such as those in the communal areas of Botswana, Malawi, Namibia, Zambia, and Zimbabwe. CBNRM projects are also being implemented in specially designated reserve areas that allow for multiple use (for example, hunting, collecting of medicinal plants and firewood, small-scale cultivation of domestic crops, and tourism).[17]

Despite their intentions, some of these projects have had unforeseen negative effects on the well-being of local people. One example is a forestry conservation project established in the late 1980s in the Kibale Forest Reserve and the Kibale Game Corridor in western Uganda.[18] Financed in part by the European Community (EC), now the European Union (EU), this project led to the eviction of some 30,000 people at the hands of armed parks officers, police, and paramilitary personnel. The residents were forced out so quickly that many of them had to abandon their household possessions. No arrangements were made before their eviction to ascertain their assets or to adjudicate their claims; as a consequence, the few compensation payments that eventually were made were minimal.

A major problem with integrated conservation and development projects has been that they have generally underestimated the costs of compensating people for their losses and have not been able to come up with strategies that restore lost livelihoods and income. In the WWF-UK program in Korup National Park in

Cameroon, for example, some villagers were moved outside the park. Although there were plans to resettle six villages, only two were established, and much of the assistance and infrastructure that had been promised was not forthcoming. The majority of the benefits from the project have not gone to people residing inside or on the peripheries of the park but instead to people living some distance away.[19]

Overall, CBNRM projects in Africa have had mixed results. Although they have sometimes led to an expansion of incomes and employment for local people, they have also had costs ranging from reduced land and resource availability to impoverishment and expanded rates of wildlife depletion.[20] In the case of the Dzanga-Sangha Dense Forest Special Reserve and the Dzangha-Ndoki National Park in the Central African Republic (CAR), Baka Pygmy communities were included in a project sponsored in part by the WWF–US and the U.S. Agency for International Development (USAID). Some of the Baka in the forest reserve work as tourist guides; others sell goods that they obtain from the forest on the commercial market. A local NGO was established, and it receives some of the park gate receipts and plays a role in park management. Unfortunately, logging companies are still allowed to extract timber in the area, and high rates of illegal wildlife offtake continue.[21]

Resettlement in the name of wildlife conservation and tourism promotion has been advocated by a number of African governments and environmental NGOs. An example is the Central Kalahari Game Reserve, the second largest game reserve in Africa.[22] In February 1996 Botswana government ministers announced at a community meeting in the central Kalahari that the residents of the reserve would be required to leave the area. Local people argued that they should be allowed to stay where they were, that the Central Kalahari Game Reserve was established originally as a means of protecting the land-and-resource use rights of local people. They also suggested that resettlement could have a whole series of negative effects on both the people who were moved and those residing in the areas where resettlement occurs.[23]

In the late 1980s and early 1990s the Botswana government had pursued a policy of "freezing" development in the Central Kalahari Game Reserve. When the borehole at !Xade, the largest community in the reserve, broke down, it took months before it was fixed. Buildings and roads were not maintained in the reserve except for those going to Department of Wildlife and National Parks camps. Even drought relief feeding programs were slower in the central Kalahari than elsewhere in Botswana, a situation that threatened the well-being of people in several parts of the reserve.

Pressures were also brought to bear on people in the central Kalahari through selective enforcement of wildlife laws and what some people perceived to be intimidation. Data collected on households in the central Kalahari and adjacent areas reveal that up to two-thirds of the resident adult males of some communities have been arrested at one time or another by game scouts from the Department of Wildlife and National Parks, police officers, or Botswana Defense Force (BDF) personnel. One result of high rates of arrest was a considerable withdrawal of sources of much-needed labor from households and communities. This was especially problematic if the person arrested and jailed was a breadwinner or a hunter. Families who had a member arrested often faced both economic and nutritional difficulties. In some cases, people who formerly had been self-sufficient economically had to seek government assistance as destitutes. Local people claimed that people in remote areas such as the central Kalahari tended to be arrested more frequently and receive higher fines and jail sentences than did people who reside in towns and villages, some of whom actually engage in greater amounts of hunting than do remote area residents.[24]

Even more disturbing were incidents in which people claimed that they were tortured or received inhumane or degrading punishment when suspected of poaching or when being questioned about others who might be engaged in illegal hunting. According to one report, the most common form of torture included a "rubber ring" placed tightly around the testicles and a plastic bag placed over the face of a person.[25] There were cases where people died of injuries inflicted on them by game scouts, as occurred at !Xade in August 1993 when a 40-year-old man died after being questioned. Community leaders in the central Kalahari have argued that authorities have stepped over the line from antipoaching to persecution.

The central Kalahari case provides an excellent example of some of the responses that Africans are employing to deal with the negative effects of wildlife preservation and management efforts. The Bushmen (Basarwa, Khwe) have begun to organize at the grassroots level, to protest the ways that they are being treated, forming indigenous advocacy organizations such as the San nongovernment organization First People of the Kalahari (FPK), established in 1992. The FPK spoke out at international meetings on issues ranging from poverty to cultural preservation and stressed that they wished to be treated with greater respect by officials of the Department of Wildlife, National Parks, and other Botswana government agencies.

San spokespersons also attended international meetings, including those of the Working Group on Indigenous Peoples (WGIP) of the United Nations in Geneva and the Permanent Forum on Indigenous Issues (PFII) in New York, where they argued forcefully that they should have land and resource rights, the right to practice their own culture and learn their own languages, and the right to have a say in decision making about development planning. They pointed out that the kinds of treatment that some San had received were potentially in violation of international human rights law, especially the severe forms of torture and what they felt were tantamount to extrajudicial executions. Human rights organizations such as Amnesty International, Survival International, and the International Work Group for Indigenous Affairs took note of these allegations, as did the U.S. Department of State.[26] The defense that some people offered when charged with crimes such as violations of the fauna conservation laws was that they committed these acts "because they were hungry." Poverty and hunger, however, are *not* considered to be extenuating circumstances under Botswana law. As a result, people are jailed or fined for what in essence is an "economic crime."[27]

San, Nama, and other indigenous groups in Africa have sought to use the media and have requested the help of intergovernmental organizations such as the United Nations as well as NGOs, including environmental ones. They have stressed how much damage forced relocation does to local communities. Indeed, extensive research by social and natural scientists and development workers shows that involuntary community relocation of people with strong ties to the land has nearly always resulted in a reduction in the standards of living of those who were moved.[28] While some of the people moved may temporarily be better off, over the longer term conditions can be expected to worsen, in part because of increased competition for natural resources and employment opportunities.

One of the effects of the resettlement out of conservation areas has been an increase in interethnic tensions and community conflict. This can be seen around some of the national parks in Africa. There are also cases where ethnic tensions surfaced including conflict resulting from efforts to improve the livelihoods of resettled communities through community-based natural resource management projects. For example, Bakonjo people closest to the boundaries of the Rwenzori Mountains National Park—the legendary "Mountains of the Moon"—in western Uganda were underrepresented in the park management institutions established by the Rwenzori Mountains Conservation and Development Project (RMCDP), a situation that generated tension. In efforts to involve resident peoples in the management of park resources, Bakonjo project stakeholders expressed a sense of marginalization and lack of power in decision making, especially in relation to the Batoro, another of the ethnic groups in the region.[29] Clearly, it is important to pay careful attention to ensuring that the various ethnic groups in an area are able to participate effectively in conservation and natural resource management activities.

One of the sources of conflict in ICDPs in Africa has been what local people sometimes perceive to be inequities in the distribution of benefits, particularly employment opportunities. In some ecotourism projects in Africa, for example, management-level positions are occupied by expatriates, while lower-paying and less important jobs go to local people. In Botswana tourism companies generally hire Bushmen only for such menial positions as camp cleaners or occasionally as trackers for safari hunters.[30] The notion that tourism will provide a windfall of benefits to local people in the central Kalahari, a claim made by both the government and environmental NGOs,[31] is highly unlikely.

One of the strategies employed by Africans in their efforts to deal with environmental and development agencies is to request that they observe international standards such as those pertaining to the resettlement of populations.[32] As John Hardbattle of First People of the Kalahari and other community leaders in Africa have argued, African governments should be open to negotiation with local people and practice planning that is grassroots oriented rather than top-down. They have also advocated the establishment of more community-based organizations (CBOs), which should be given greater say in policy formulation. Some indigenous NGOs, such as First People of the Kalahari, the Working Group of Indigenous Minorities in Southern Africa (WIMSA), and the /Khomani San of South Africa, pressed for legal cases against the governments of their countries, with some degree of success. The /Khomani were able to get rights to land and benefits from the Kgalagadi Transfrontier Park in an out-of-court settlement in South Africa in 1980, and the San and Bakgalagadi won a landmark legal case against the government of Botswana in the High Court in December, 2006.

The country where the CBNRM approach had been developed to the greatest extent is the Republic of Zimbabwe. Under the Parks and Wildlife Act of 1975, the Zimbabwe government began to devolve authority over benefits from wildlife to district councils and local communities under the Communal Areas Management Program for Indigenous Resources (CAMPFIRE). CAMPFIRE has been implemented in over half of the districts of the country, and it has been cited as a model of community empowerment and wildlife management.[33] One of the problems with CAMPFIRE is that many of the decisions about resource management come from outside the local communities that are supposed to benefit most from the program. In the Tsholotsho District, when communities were forced out of a newly designated wildlife management area, some Tyua Bushmen attempted to move across the border but were arrested, and others, including women collecting bush foods and water, were shot.[34]

The imposition of the ivory ban by the Convention on Trade in Endangered Species of Flora and Fauna (CITES) in 1989 had adverse effects on the economies of Tyua and Ndebele households engaged in commercial hunting and ivory carving.[35] Ironically, the elephant populations in western Zimbabwe and northern Botswana were on the rise at the time of the ban, so much so that crop damage by elephants became a major problem in the early 1990s. Tyua and other rural Zimbabweans are not allowed to hunt or to shoot animals that raid their fields; they must depend instead on Department of National Parks and Wildlife Management (DNPWLM) game scouts to deal with problem animals. As one Tyua woman put it, referring to a situation in which women had been arrested for collecting resources in an area allocated to a private company by the local district council, an allocation that occurred without the knowledge or consent of local people: "We are not allowed to protect our crops and our children from wild animals, and we are even arrested and shot at for collecting thatching grass and firewood." The gender effects of wildlife management projects must be considered much more carefully in the future, since women in general tend to bear greater costs and receive fewer benefits than men.[36]

CBNRM projects were based on a number of key assumptions. First, southern African governments would be willing to devolve authority over wildlife resources to the local level and would enact legislation to make this possible. Second, local people would be willing to participate in community based conservation and development. Third, government authorities and nongovernment organizations would be willing to consult local people and involve them in planning and decision making. Fourth, if local people had the rights over wildlife resources and got the benefits from them, they would work to conserve them. Fifth, since CBNRM combines wildlife conservation and rural development, both human and wildlife populations would benefit.

A characteristic feature of some of these projects was that local people were able to get some cash income, employment, and, in a number of cases, meat from animals that were obtained in their areas. In some places local communities could contract out the rights to wildlife to private companies who then paid them for the right to bring in hunters or tourists. These companies would sometimes employ local people as guides or safari camp assistants. The clients of the companies would also purchase products from local people, including handicrafts, thus enabling local people to generate some income. CBNRM projects have also had their downsides. Sometimes safari operators took advantage of local people and did not provide the benefits that they promised. Governments also may go back on agreements with local communities, as did the Zimbabwe government when the Mugabe regime tightened its control over the populace.

Some ecologists and social scientists working on CBNRM projects realized that the promotion of biodiversity conservation could affect human populations. An increase in the number of large mammals such as elephants or lions was not viewed all that positively by local people, including the Tyua in western Zimbabwe and the Ju/'hoansi in northeastern Namibia. There were incidents in Tsholotsho, Zimbabwe, and Nyae Nyae, Namibia, in which lions preyed on people's livestock and elephants destroyed water points and gardens. Local people argued that if the governments of Zimbabwe and Namibia were promoting CBNRM, then people should be compensated for wildlife-related damages.

Compensation programs for involuntary resettlement, damage to the land and assets of individuals and communities, and the re-establishment or improvement of the lives of people affected by development projects have varied tremendously over the past 50 years. The systems for handling losses suffered by people have ranged from no compensation whatsoever to relatively substantial packages aimed at improving the standards of living of project-affected people. On balance, these programs have failed to restore the livelihoods of people affected by projects, and in a number of cases they have made people worse off.

Resettlement is a complicated process, one that is often extremely hard on the people who are relocated. A major problem with compensation and resettlement projects is that planners generally have tended to focus attention on loss of residences (that is, homes) rather than on loss of access to the means of production (especially land, grazing resources, and wild resources on which people depend for subsistence and income). A second major problem is that in nearly all cases, the effect on populations has been seriously underestimated. The World Bank arguably has had the most comprehensive guidelines on resettlement and social impact assessment. The problem with these guidelines is that they call for the *restoration* of livelihoods of people affected by projects, but they do not argue for *improvement* of the standards of living of people who have been affected by projects. The World Commission on Large Dams has argued for the need to improve the livelihoods of project-affected people (PAP), as has the World Bank.

Frequently cash is used as the primary means of compensation for lost assets. But cash payments generally do not restore the incomes of resettled people. Problems include the fact that recipients sometimes expend their money very quickly; the frequent lack of local opportunities for investment of the cash resources; and the control of the cash, which sometimes is appropriated by adult males in the household for their own use, disadvantaging women and children.

Human Rights in Africa

It is useful to differentiate the types of rights of concern of African peoples. They include: civil and political rights; social, economic, and cultural rights; rights to development; planetary (environmental) rights; and the right to peace. There is a major debate in the literature about cultural relativity and the issue of individual rights versus group (collective) rights. There is also a concern with sustainability.

Security rights include the rights to be free from torture, execution, and imprisonment, or rights relating to the integrity of the person. This set of rights is especially important in light of the frequency of allegations of alleged torture and mistreatment of suspected poachers by game scouts and other government officials in southern African countries such as Angola, Botswana, Namibia, South Africa, Zambia, and Zimbabwe.

Subsistence rights are those rights related to the fulfillment of basic human needs (for example, water, food, shelter, and access to health assistance and medicines). The denial of the right to hunt, gather, and fish, according to some African peoples, is an example of restrictions on subsistence rights. An important right cited by indigenous people, including the G/wi and G//ana and the Bakgalagadi of the Central Kalahari Game Reserve region in Botswana, is the right to water. In January, 2002, the Government of Botswana stopped delivery of water to the people in the Central Kalahari, and water points (boreholes) were made inaccessible as part of an effort to get people to move to settlements on the periphery where the Government was providing services, including water. The denial of water rights was part of the legal case brought against the Botswana Government, and these rights continue to be an issue in the Central Kalahari even after the High Court of Botswana ruled in favor of the right of return to the Central Kalahari in December, 2006.

Cultural rights include the rights of people to practice their own cultural activities, ceremonies, and customs, and to speak and teach their own languages. An issue of significance to local people in Africa is the right to the benefits from the crafts that they produce. The egg of the ostrich (*Struthio camelus*), the largest bird in southern Africa, is an important wild resource that the San and other groups exploit extensively in the Kalahari Desert region of Namibia and Botswana. These eggs are a prized commodity because of their nutritional value—just one holds the equivalent of about two dozen chicken eggs. But the shells are also used to created a massive number of critical material and cultural goods, including canteens and valuable beads and ornaments. They are sometimes used in gift exchanges, which according to the Ju/'hoan San are known as *hxaro*, that reinforce social alliances and represent trade partnerships. The manufacture and sale of ostrich eggshell items is also an important source of income for a sizable number of San and Bakgalagadi households in the Kalahari. A problem facing women and other people who manufacture and utilize ostrich eggshell products extensively is that the government of Botswana established an Ostrich Policy in 1994 requiring people to buy licenses from the Department of Wildlife and National Parks to procure and sell ostrich-related products. It also restricted collection of ostrich eggshells to the period April–August. Women in rural Botswana are worried that they will be arrested, and they have been. Some women, such as those in West Hanahai in Ghanzi District, have attempted to establish ostrich user groups, but it has taken them years to get the license necessary to exploit and sell ostrich products. Only a few people, some of them high government officials and elites, have been able to obtain the required permits for ostrich eggshell product exploitation and sale.

The Ostrich Management Plan has the potential to harm rural women and their families. It is an example of how crucial it is to incorporate women more directly into the planning and implementation of wild resource development projects to ensure that these initiatives do not favor males over females and that equity and broad-based community participation are achieved.

Intellectual property rights (IPR) are those rights of groups to their unique knowledge and cultural information, such as knowledge of the properties of plants, animals, and other items that are part of peoples' belief systems, ideologies, and oral history. Much of this information is informal and is transmitted orally from one generation to the next. Indigenous peoples in southern Africa have sought to get governments, international organizations, and multinational corporations to recognize their intellectual property rights and compensate them for the exploitation of culturally significant. In this era of globalization, there have been numerous controversies over the acquisition of intellectual property and biological property by private entities (for example, transnational pharmaceutical companies). Limited progress is being made as indigenous peoples have sought legal assistance to contest being denied compensation or royalties for the utilization of drugs developed from plants that they identified as having important medicinal or physiological properties. Some have reached agreements with governments and private companies that will allow them the right to a percentage of the benefits from the procurement, production, and marketing of these valuable plant products. Note that the issue of intellectual property rights extends far beyond wild plant and animal products; it is associated with the marketing of valuable culturally significant products that have tremendous potential in terms of providing substantial returns while at the same time putting at risk resources, both human and natural, that could go a long way toward enhancing the well-being of humanity and contributing to the continuity of global biodiversity.

Conclusions

The degree to which conservation and development projects are beneficial to local people is dependent in part on the extent to which they can take part in project activities. Many of the NGO-sponsored projects initiated in Africa have not been as proactive as they should have been in terms of incorporating local people, including women, children, the elderly, and indigenous minorities, into decision making. For this reason, some African communities have sought to plan and implement their own projects and have come up with their own sets of rules by which conservation and development will be conducted.

Fledgling grassroots social and environmental movements are springing up in many parts of Africa that seek a better balance between conservation and development as well as greater flows of benefits to local people (as opposed to elites and outsiders). Some of these movements have achieved some success, for example, in the efforts to prevent the government of Botswana from implementing a water development project in the Okavango Delta, the "jewel of the Kalahari," and the actions of women's associations in Kenya, Tanzania, Swaziland, Lesotho, and South Africa to promote organic agriculture, soil conservation schemes, and small-scale business activities.[37]

Effective conservation and development activities in Africa can come about only when coercion gives way to cooperation—and when local people are given support, information, and technical assistance. Africans are more than willing to cooperate with those organizations that place human rights on an equal footing with species preservation. What they are seeking, they say, is a more participatory process, one in which direct links are made among human rights, the environment, and democratic governance. Successful conservation can come about, they maintain, only if local people are involved in formulating and implementing policies and programs that incorporate safeguards against abuses and that place strong emphasis on equity and social justice.

Notes

1. Wildlife conservation efforts in Africa have been discussed in the following publications: Stuart A. Marks, *The Imperial Lion: Human Dimensions of Wildlife Management in Africa* (Boulder, CO: Westview Press, 1984); David Anderson and Richard Grove, Eds., *Conservation in Africa: People, Policies and Practice* (Cambridge: Cambridge University Press, 1987); Agnes Kiss, Ed., *Living with Wildlife: Wildlife Resource Management with Local Participation in Africa* (Washington, D.C.: World Bank, 1990); Jonathan S. Adams and Thomas O. McShane, *The Myth of Wild Africa: Conservation without Illusion* (New York: Norton, 1992); Raymond Bonner, *At the Hand of Man: Peril and Hope for Africa's Wildlife* (New York: Alfred A. Knopf, 1993); Christopher B. Barrett and Peter Arcese, "Are Integrated Conservation-Development Projects (ICDPs) Sustainable? On the Conservation of Large Mammals in Africa," *World Development* 23:7 (1995, 1073–84); Clark C. Gibson and Stuart A. Marks, "Transforming Rural Hunters into Conservationists: An Assessment of Community-Based Wildlife Projects in Africa," *World*

Development 23:6 (1995, 941–57); Robert K. Hitchcock, John E. Yellen, Diane J. Gelburd, Alan J. Osborn, and Aron L. Crowell, "Subsistence Hunting and Resource Management among the Ju/'hoansi of Northwestern Botswana," *African Study Monographs* 17:4 (1996, 153–208); Roderick P. Neumann, *Imposing Wilderness: Struggles over Livelihood and Nature Preservation in Africa* (Berkeley and Los Angeles: University of California Press, 1998); Clark G. Gibson, *Politicians and Poachers: The Political Ecology of Wildlife Policy in Africa* (Cambridge: Cambridge University Press, 1999); C. J. M. Musters, H. J. de Graaf, and W. J. ter Keurs, "Can Protected Areas Be Expanded in Africa?" *Science* 287 (2000, 1759–60); David Hulme and Marshall Murphree, Eds., *African Wildlife and Livelihoods: The Promise and Performance of Community Conservation* (London: James Currey, 2001); William Beinart and JoAnn McGregor, Eds., *Social History and African Environments* (Oxford: James Currey, 2003); Christo Fabicius and Eddie Koch, Eds., with Hector Magome and Stephen Turner, *Rights, Resources and Rural Development: Community-Based Natural Resource Management in Southern Africa* (London: Earthscan, 2004); Brian Child, *Parks in Transition: Biodiversity, Rural Development, and the Bottom Line* (Sterling, VA: Stylus Publishing, 2004); Jim Igoe, *Conservation and Globalization: A Study of National Parks and Indigenous Communities from East Africa to South Dakota* (Belmont, CA: Thomson/Wadsworth, 2004); Monique Borgerhoff Mulder and Peter Coppolillo, *Conservation: Linking Ecology, Economics, and Culture* (Princeton, NJ: Princeton University Press, 2005).

2. Human rights violations in the context of conservation programs have been dealt with in the following publications: Nancy L. Peluso, "Coercing Conservation? The Politics of State Resource Control," in Ronnie D. Lipschutz and Ken Conca, Eds., *The State and Social Power in Global Environmental Politics* (New York: Columbia University Press, 1993, 46–70); Marcus Colchester, *Salvaging Nature: Indigenous Peoples, Protected Areas, and Biodiversity Conservation,* United Nations Research Institute for Social Development, Discussion Paper 55 (Geneva: UN Research Institute for Social Development, World Rainforest Movement, and Worldwide Fund for Nature, 1994); Robert K. Hitchcock, "Centralization, Resource Depletion, and Coercive Conservation among the Tyua of the Northeastern Kalahari," *Human Ecology* 23:2 (1995, 169–98). General discussions of human rights and environmental justice can be found in Human Rights Watch, *Indivisible Human Rights: The Relationship of Political and Civil Rights to Survival, Subsistence, and Poverty* (New York: Human Rights Watch, 1992); Human Rights Watch and Natural Resources Defense Council, *Defending the Earth: Abuses of Human Rights and the Environment* (Washington, D.C.: Human Rights Watch and Natural Resources Defense Council, 1992); Aaron Sachs, *Eco-Justice: Linking Human Rights and the Environment,* WorldWatch Paper 127 (Washington, D.C.: WorldWatch Institute, 1995); Aaron Sachs, "Upholding Human Rights and Environmental Justice," in Lester Brown et al., Eds., *State of the World 1996* (Washington, D.C.: WorldWatch Institute, 1996, 133–51); Nancy Lee and Michael Watts, Eds., *Violent Environments* (Ithaca, NY: Cornell University Press, 2001); Mac Chapin, "A Challenge to Conservationists." *World Watch Magazine* 11–12 (2004, 17–31); Mark Dowie, "Conservation Refugees: When Protecting Nature Means Kicking People Out," *Orion* 24:6 (2005, 16–27); Michael Cernea and Kai Schmidt-Soltau, "Poverty Risks and National Parks: Policy Issues on Conservation and Resettlement," *World Development* 34:10 (2006, 1808–1930).

3. See Hanne Veber, Jens Dahl, Fiona Wilson, and Espen Waehle, Eds., ". . . *Never Drink from the Same Cup*," *Proceedings of the Conference on Indigenous Peoples in Africa, Tune, Denmark, 1993,* IWGIA Document No. 74 (Copenhagen: International Working Group for Indigenous Affairs and the Center for Development Research, 1993); Alan Barnard and Justin Kenrick, Eds., *Africa's Indigenous Peoples: 'First Peoples' or Marginalized Minorities?* (Edinburgh: Center for African Studies, University of Edinburgh, 2001); Robert K. Hitchcock and Diana Vinding, Eds., *Indigenous Peoples' Rights in Southern Africa* (Copenhagen: International Work Group for Indigenous Affairs, 2004).

4. The environmental crisis in Africa has been discussed in the following publications: Rodger Yeager and Norman N. Miller, *Wildlife, Wild Death: Land Use and Survival in Eastern Africa* (Albany: State University of New York Press, 1986); Mort Rosenblum and Doug Williamson, *Squandering Eden: Africa at the Edge* (New York: Harcourt, Brace, Jovanovich, 1987); Lloyd Timberlake, *Africa in Crisis: The Causes, the Cures of Environmental Bankruptcy* (London: Earthscan Publications, 1988); Daniel Stiles, Ed., *Social Aspects of Dryland Management* (Nairobi: UN Environment Program and New York: John Wiley and Sons, 1995); David S. G. Thomas, Deborah Sporton, and Jeremy Perkins, "The Environmental Impact of Ranches in the Kalahari, Botswana: Natural Resource Use, Ecological Change, and Human Response in a Dynamic Dryland System," *Land Degradation and Development* 11:4 (2000, 327–41); David S. G. Thomas and Chasca Twyman, "Equity and Justice in Climatic Change: Adaptations amongst Natural Resource Dependent Societies," *Global Environmental Change* 15 (2005, 115–24); Deborah Sporton and David S. G. Thomas, Eds., *Sustainable Livelihoods in Kalahari Environments: Contributions to Global Debates* (Oxford: Oxford University Press, 2002); Andrew Simms and Hannah Reid, *Africa—Up in Smoke? The Second Report from the Working Group on Climate Change and Development* (London: New Economics Foundation and International Institute for Environment and Development, 2005).

5. For a discussion of some of these efforts, see Associates in Rural Development, *Decentralization and Local Autonomy: Conditions for Achieving Sustainable Resource Management* (Burlington, VT: Associates in Rural Development and Washington, D.C.: U.S. Agency for International Development, 1992); Michael Brown and Barbara Wyckoff-Baird, *Designing Integrated Conservation and Development Projects* (Washington, D.C.: Biodiversity Support Program and World Wildlife Fund, 1992); Michael Wells and Katrina Brandon, with Lee Hannah, *Parks and People: Linking Protected Area Management with Local Communities* (Washington, D.C.: World Bank, World Wildlife Fund, and U.S. Agency for International Development, 1992); World Conservation Monitoring Center (WCMC), *Global Biodiversity: Status of the Earth's Living Resources* (Cambridge: WCMC, 1992); Biodiversity Support Program, *African Biodiversity: Foundation for the Future, A Framework for Integrating Biodiversity Conservation and Sustainable Development* (Washington, D.C.: World Wildlife Fund, the Nature Conservancy, World Resources Institute, and U.S. Agency for International Development, 1993); World Wildlife Fund, *Community-Based Conservation in Southern Africa: Training Cases* (Washington, D.C.: World Wildlife Fund, 1993); International Institute for Environment and Development, *Whose Eden? An Overview of Community Approaches to Wildlife Management* (London: International Institute for Environment and Development and Overseas Development, 1994); Ruth Norris and Robert K. Hitchcock, *Final Evaluation: Social Science and Economics Program (Formerly Wildlands and Human Needs Program)* (Alexandria, VA: Automation Research Systems, 1994); Evelyn S. Wilcox, *Lessons from the Field: Marine Integrated Conservation and Development* (Washington, D.C.: World Wildlife Fund, 1994); S. D. Turner, *Common Property Resources and the Rural Poor in Sub-Saharan Africa* (Rome: International Fund for Agricultural Development, Special Programme for Sub-Saharan African Countries Affected by Drought and Desertification, 1995); For comparative information, see Nancy Peluso, *Rich Forests, Poor People: Resource Control and Resistance in Java* (Berkeley and Los Angeles, University of California Press, 1992); Clare D. Fitgibbon, Hezron Mogaka, and John H. Fanshawe, "Subsistence Hunting in Arabulo-Sokole Forest, Kenya and Its Effects on Mammal Populations," *Conservation Biology* 9:5 (1995, 1116–26); Stuart Coupe, Viv Lewis, Zadoc Ogutu, and Cathy Watson, Eds., *Living with Wildlife: Sustainable Livelihoods for Park-Adjacent Communities in Kenya* (Herndon, VA: Stylus Publishing, 2002); Barrett and Arcese, note 1.

6. Perhaps the best example of the social and economic stress brought about by the creation of a national park is that of Colin Turnbull in his book *The Mountain People* (New York:

Simon and Schuster, 1972), which chronicles the cultural dissolution of the Ik, who were removed from Kidepo National Park in northern Uganda.

7. Hunter-gatherers in particular had to give up foraging activities or face arrest and lengthy jail terms; see, for example, Daniel Stiles, "Sustainable Development in Tropical Forests by Indigenous Peoples," *Swara* 16:5 (1993, 24–27), as well as the section on Sub-Saharan Africa (pp. 161–78) in Marc S. Miller, Ed., *State of the Peoples: A Global Human Rights Report on Societies in Danger* (Boston: Beacon Press, 1993); Susan Kent, Ed., *Cultural Diversity among Twentieth-Century African Foragers: An African Perspective* (Cambridge: Cambridge University Press, 1996); Robert Gordon and Stuart Sholto Douglas, *The Bushman Myth: The Making of a Namibian Underclass* (Boulder, CO: Westview Press, 2000); Robert K. Hitchcock, "'We Are the First People': Land, Natural Resources, and Identity in the Central Kalahari, Botswana," *Journal of Southern African Studies* 28:4 (2002, 797–824).

8. See, for example, Alice Mogwe, *Who Was (T)here First? An Assessment of the Human Rights Situation of Basarwa in Selected Communities in the Gantsi District*, Occasional Paper No. 10 (Gaborone, Botswana: Botswana Christian Council, 1992); Casey Kelso, "Hungry Hunter-Gatherers Tortured," and Casey Kelso, "The Inconvenient Nomads Deep Inside the Deep," *Weekly Mail*, July 24–30, 1992, 12; Anonymous, "Wildlife Atrocities Exposed: Basarwa Speak Out," *Mokaedi*, Sept. 1992; Anonymous, "Human Rights Abuses against Basarwa," *Mmegi: The Reporter*, May 29–June 4, 1992; Kenneth Good, "The State and Extreme Poverty in Botswana: The San and Destitutes," *Journal of Modern African Studies* 37:2 (1999, 185–205); Kenneth Good, *Bushmen and Diamonds: (Un)Civil Society in Botswana* (Uppsala: Nordiska Afrikainstitutet, 2003); Peluso, note 2; Hitchcock (1995), note 2.

9. See Douglas B. Lee, p. 49, "Okavango Delta: Africa's Last Refuge," *National Geographic* 178:6 (Dec. 1990, 38–69). Data on impacts of antipoaching operations include interview data obtained in 1989, 1990, 1991, 1995, 1997, and 2005 in northern, eastern, central, and southwestern Botswana; see, for example, Robert K. Hitchcock and Rosinah Rose B. Masilo, *Subsistence Hunting and Resource Rights in Botswana: An Assessment of Special Game Licenses and Their Impacts on Remote Area Dwellers and Wildlife Populations* (Gaborone, Botswana: Natural Resource Management Project and Dept. of Wildlife and National Parks, 1995); for western Zimbabwe, see Robert K. Hitchcock and Fanuel M. Nangati, *Zimbabwe Natural Resources Management Project Community-Based Resource Utilization Component: Interim Assessment* (Harare, Zimbabwe: U.S. Agency for International Development and Dept. of National Parks and Wildlife Management, 1992); Heena Patel, *Sustainable Utilization and African Wildlife Policy: The Case of Zimbabwe's Communal Areas Management Program for Indigenous Resources (CAMPFIRE)* (Boston, Massachusetts: Indigenous Environmental Policy Center, 1998); Mogwe, note 8; Hitchcock, note 2.

10. Henry Fosbrooke, Daniel Stiles, personal communications. See also Richard Bell, "Monitoring of Illegal Activity and Law Enforcement in African Conservation Areas," in R. H. V. Bell and E. McShane-Caluzi, Eds., *Conservation and Wildlife Resources in Africa* (Washington, D.C.: U.S. Peace Corps, 1986, 297–315); L. Talbot and P. Olindo, "Amboseli and Maasai Mara, Kenya," in Kiss, note 1, p. 70; K. M. Homewood and W. A. Rodgers, *Maasailand Ecology: Pastoral Development and Wildlife Conservation in Ngorongoro, Tanzania* (Cambridge: Cambridge University Press, 1991); P. Arcese, J. Hando, and K. Campbell, "Historical and Present-Day Anti-Poaching Efforts in Serengeti," in A. R. E. Sinclair and P. Arcese, Eds., *Serengeti II: Research, Conservation, and Management of an Ecosystem* (Chicago: University of Chicago Press, 1995, 506–33). The work in Ngorongoro shows that although the environment has generally been protected, the socioeconomic status of the Maasai is in a serious state of decline; see J. Terrence McCabe, Scott Perkin, and Claire Schofield, "Can Conservation and

Development Be Coupled Among Pastoral People? An Examination of the Maasai of the Ngorongoro Conservation Area," *Human Organization* 51:4 (1992, 353–66).

11. For a classic discussion of the utility of antipoaching efforts, see Dennis Holman, *Massacre of the Elephants* (New York: Holt, Rinehart, and Winston, 1967). Antipoaching in Kenya in the period between following World War II was discussed by Edward Steinhart, "National Parks and Anti-Poaching in Kenya, 1947–1957," *The International Journal of African Historical Studies* 27:1 (1994, 59–76); Mark and Delia Owens in their book *The Eye of the Elephant: Life and Death in an African Wilderness* (New York: Houghton Mifflin, 1992) discuss various antipoaching actions in the North Luangwa National Park of Zambia along with efforts to promote alternative economic opportunities for local populations. See also N. Leader-Williams and S. D. Albon, "Allocation of Resources for Conservation," *Nature* 336 (1988, 533–5); N. Leader-Williams, S. D. Albon, and P. S. M. Berry, "Illegal Exploitation of Black Rhinoceros and Elephant Populations: Patterns of Decline, Law Enforcement, and Patrol Effort in Luangwa Valley, Zambia," *Journal of Applied Ecology* 27:3 (1990, 1055–87); Dale Lewis, Gilson B. Kaweche, and Ackim Mwenya, "Wildlife Conservation Outside Protected Areas—Lessons from an Experiment in Zambia," *Conservation Biology* 4 (1990, 171–80); E. Millner-Gulland and N. Leader-Williams, "A Model of Incentives for the Illegal Exploitation of Black Rhinos and Elephants: Poaching Pays in Luangwa Valley, Zambia," *Journal of Applied Ecology* 29:2 (1992, 388–401); Gibson and Marks, note 1.

12. This was argued, for example, by San speakers at a conference on indigenous peoples in Africa (see Veber et al., note 3) and at two National Institute for Research seminars on Basarwa (San, Bushmen) held at the University of Botswana in Gaborone, Botswana, in August and October, 1995, as well as a conference on Khoe and San peoples held at the University of Botswana in September, 2003.

13. See the African Training for Leadership and Advanced Skills (ATLAS) Project, *Natural Resource Management in Africa: Issues in Conservation and Socioeconomic Development* (New York: The African-American Institute, 1993).

14. See S. R. Galster, "Big Game Smugglers: The Trail Leads to South Africa," *The Nation* 256:6 (1993, 195–8); Judith Matloff, "South Africa Decimated Rhinos, Elephants in 1970s for Wars," *Christian Science Monitor,* Jan. 19, 1996, p.1.

15. See Kyle Owen-Smith, "Caprivi Faces Wildlife Ruin," and "Frontier Dealing Could Wreck Caprivian Hopes," *The Namibian,* March 29, 1996, pp. 1–2, 7–8.

16. For a discussion of the situation in West Caprivi, see Robert K. Hitchcock and Marshall W. Murphree, *Report of the Field Assessment Team, Phase III of the Mid-Term Assessment of the LIFE Project, USAID/Namibia Component* (690–0251.73) (Windhoek, Namibia: U.S. Agency for International Development, 1995); Julie J. Taylor, "The Politics of Identity, Authority, and the Environment: San, NGOs, and the State in Namibia's West Caprivi," Ph.D. dissertation, Oxford University, 2007; Julie J. Taylor, "Rendering the Land Visible," *Cultural Survival Quarterly* 31:4 (2007, 10–15).

17. Assessments of some of these projects can be found in Wells and Brandon, note 5; Brown and Wyckoff-Baird, note 5; World Wildlife Fund, note 5; International Institute for Environment and Development (1994), note 5; Norris and Hitchcock, note 5; and David Western and R. Michael Wright, Eds., *Natural Connections: Perspectives in Community Based Conservation* (Washington, D.C.: Island Press, 1994); David G. Anderson and Eeva Berglund, Eds., *Ethnographies of Conservation: Environmentalism and the Distribution of Privilege* (New York: Berghahn Books, 2003); Brian Child and Martha West Lyman, Eds., *Natural Resources as Community Assets: Lessons from Two Continents* (Madison, WI: Sand County Foundation and Washington, D.C.: The Aspen Institute, 2005); Hulme and Murphree, note 1; Borgerhoff Mulder and Peter Coppolillo, note 1.

18. See Patricia Feeney, *The Impact of a European Community Project on Peasant Families in Uganda*, Briefing Paper No. 6 (London: OXFAM UK/Ireland, 1993).

19. See S. Gartlan, *The Korup Regional Management Plan: Conservation and Development in the Ndian Division of Cameroon* (London: World Wildlife Fund United Kingdom, 1985); R. Moorehead and T. Hammond, "An Assessment of the Rural Development Program of the Korup National Park Project," Report to CARE–United Kingdom (London, 1992); Patrick Sweeting et al., *Evaluation Report: Korup National Park Project, Cameroon* (Geneva: Worldwide Fund for Nature International, 1992).

20. See John A. Hoyt, *Animals in Peril: How "Sustainable Use" Is Wiping Out the World's Wildlife* (Garden City, NY: Avery Publishing Group, 1994); Colchester, note 2; Norris and Hitchcock, note 5; Barrett and Arcese, note 1; Gibson and Marks, note 1. Note that Wildlife Conservation Society and a number of other conservation organizations take strong exception to some of the generalizations made about the human rights impacts of conservation and especially relocation and resettlement activities; see, for example, Kent Redford and E. Fearn, Eds., *Protected Areas and Human Displacement: A Conservation Perspective*, Working Paper No. 29 (New York: Wildlife Conservation Society, 2007).

21. See Richard W. Carroll, "The Development, Protection, and Management of the Dzangha-Sangha Dense Forest Special Reserve and the Dzangha-Ndoko National Park in Southwestern Central African Republic," Report to the World Wildlife Fund–U.S. (Washington, D.C., 1992); Anna Kretsinger, "Recommendations for Further Integration of BaAka Interests in Project Policy, Dzanga-Sangha Dense Forest Reserve," Report to the World Wildlife Fund–U.S. (Washington, D.C., 1993); G. Doungoube, "The Dzanga-Sangha Dense Forest Reserve," in *Rural Development and Conservation in Africa: A Series of Briefing Papers for Development Organizations* (Geneva and Washington, D.C.: Africa Resources Trust, World Conservation Union, Worldwide Fund for Nature, and World Wildlife Fund–U.S.); Colchester, note 2, pp. 32–33.

22. See Suzanne Daley, "Botswana Is Pressing Bushmen to Leave Reserve," *The New York Times,* July 14, 1996; Robert K. Hitchcock, "Traditional African Wildlife Utilization: Subsistence Hunting, Poaching, and Sustainable Use," In *Wildlife Conservation by Sustainable Use*, Herbert H. T. Prins, Jan Geu Grootenhuis, and Thomas T. Dolan, Eds. (Boston: Kluwer Academic Publishers, 2000, 389–415); Robert K. Hitchcock, "'Hunting Is Our Heritage': The Struggle for Hunting and Gathering Rights among the San of Southern Africa," in *Parks, Property, and Power: Managing Hunting Practice and Identity within State Policy Regimes*; David G. Anderson and Kazunobu Ikeya, Eds., *Senri Ethnological Studies 59* (Osaka: National Museum of Ethnology, 2001, 139–56); Sidsel Saugestad, *The Inconvenient Indigenous: Remote Area Development in Botswana, Donor Assistance, and the First People of the Kalahari* (Uppsala: Nordic Africa Institute, 2001); Sidsel Saugestad, "Improving their Lives': State Policies and San Resistance in Botswana." *Before Farming* 2005/4:1–11; Kgosi Motshabi and Sidsel Saugestad, Eds., *Research for Khoe and San Development: International Conference, University of Botswana, September 10–12, 2003* (Gaborone, Botswana: University of Botswana and University of Tromso, 2004).

23. See the minutes of the *kgotla* (public council) meeting at !Xade, Central Kalahari Game Reserve, Feb. 17, 1996, on file at the Ghanzi District Council, Ghanzi, Botswana, and the Ministry of Local Government, Lands, and Housing, Gaborone, Botswana; and the report by Ditshwanelo, *When Will This Moving Stop? Report on a Fact-finding Mission of the Central Kgalagadi Game Reserve, April 10–14, 1996* (Gaborone, Botswana: Ditshwanelo, Botswana Center for Human Rights, 1996). The Government of Botswana (www.gov.bw) has extensive discussions of the Central Kalahari Game issue on its official website, as does Survival International (www.survival.org).

24. Interviews of residents of the Central Kalahari Game Reserve and surrounding areas and of officials in the Ghanzi District Council and the Government of Botswana were conducted in 1988–1991 and 1995. See Robert K. Hitchcock, "The Central Kalahari Game Reserve:

A Case Study in Remote Area Research and Development," in *Monitoring, Research, and Development in the Remote Areas of Botswana* (Gaborone, Botswana: Ministry of Local Government and Lands, 1988); American Anthropological Association Committee for Human Rights, *Population Relocation and Survival: The Botswana Government's Decision to Relocate the People of the Central Kalahari Game Reserve* (Washington, D.C.: American Anthropological Association, 1996). Subsequent interviews were done in 2000, 2004, and 2005. See Robert K. Hitchcock and Wayne Babchuk, "Kalahari San Foraging, Territoriality, and Land Use: Implications for the Future," *Before Farming: The Archaeology and Anthropology of Hunter-Gatherers,* 2007/3, 169–81.

25. Mogwe, note 8, p. 12.

26. Survival International, "Botswana: Kalahari Peoples Threatened with Expulsion from Game Reserve," *Urgent Action Bulletin,* UAB/BOT/1/APR/1989 (1989); Survival International, Letter to the President of Botswana, April 1996; U.S. Dept. of State, *Country Report on Human Rights Practices for 1993* (Washington, D.C.: Government Printing Office, 1993, 13–14); Survival International, *Bushmen, Botswana: Bushman Land Carved Up for Diamond Exploration* (London: Survival International, 2003a); Survival International, *Bushmen, Botswana: Diamonds Bring Despair for the Bushmen* (London: Survival International, 2003b); Stephen Corry, "Bushmen: The Final Solution and Blaming the Messenger," *Before Farming* 2003/2 (14): 1–4; James Suzman, "Kalahari Conundrums: Relocation, Resistance, and International Support in the Central Kalahari, Botswana," *Before Farming* (2003–2004, 12–20); Julie J. Taylor, "Celebrating Victory Too Soon? Reflections on the Outcome of the Central Kalahari Game Reserve Case," *Anthropology Today* 23:5 (2007, 3–5); Survival International and Ditshwanelo, the Botswana Center for Human Rights, estimate that some 90 people have been arrested for hunting illegally in the Central Kalahari Game Reserve in the past five years (up to 2008), and some of these individuals have been mistreated while in custody; at least four of them have died in detention. Some of the websites that have information on the San include the Kalahari Peoples Fund (www.kalaharipeoples.org); the International Work Group for Indigenous Affairs (www.iwgia.org); Survival International (www.survivalinternational.org); Indigenous Peoples of Africa Coordinating Committee (IPACC) (www.ipacc@iafrica.com).

27. Mogwe, note 8, p. 13.

28. See, for example, Art Hansen and Anthony Oliver-Smith, Eds., *Involuntary Migration and Resettlement: The Problems and Responses of Dislocated People* (Boulder, CO: Westview Press, 1982); Forest Peoples Project, *Indigenous Peoples and Protected Areas in Africa: From Principles to Practice* (Moreton-in-March: Forest Peoples Project, 2002); Michael Cernea and Hari Mohan Mathur, Eds., *Can Compensation Prevent Impoverishment? Reforming Resettlement through Investments and Benefit-Sharing* (New York: Oxford University Press, 2008).

29. See Norris and Hitchcock, note 5, pp. 35–43. Background information on the Rwenzoris, the groups residing there, can be found in Kenneth Ingham, *The Kingdom of Tora in Uganda* (London: Methuen, 1975); B. K. Taylor, *The Western Lacustrine Bantu: The Konjo* (London: International African Institute, 1962); Guy Yeoman, *Africa's Mountains of the Moon: Journeys to the Snowy Sources of the Nile* (New York: Universe Books, 1989); Guy Yeoman, "Uganda's New Rwenzori National Park," *Swara* 15:2 (1992, 16–22).

30. See Robert K. Hitchcock, "Cultural, Economic, and Environmental Impacts of Tourism among Kalahari Bushmen," in Erve Chambers, Ed., *Native Tours: Comparative Perspectives on Tourism and Community* (Albany: State University of New York Press, 1997, 93–128); Megan Biesele and Robert K. Hitchcock, *The Ju/'hoan San of Nyae Nyae Since Independence: Development, Democracy, and Indigenous Voices in Namibia* (New York: Berghahn Books, 2010).

31. See, for example, Kalahari Conservation Society, *Management Plan for Central Kalahari and Khutse Game Reserves* (Gaborone, Botswana: Kalahari Conservation Society, 1988) and the speech by President Ketumile Masire on environmental issues in Botswana (Carnegie Endowment for International Peace, Washington, D.C., June 13, 1996).

32. World Bank, "Operational Directive 4.30: Involuntary Resettlement," in *The World Bank Operational Manual* (Washington, D.C.: World Bank, 1990); World Bank, *Involuntary Resettlement Sourcebook: Planning and Implementation in Development Projects* (Washington, D.C.: World Bank, 2004).

33. See, for example, Adams and McShane, note 1, pp. 178–83, 242–43; Hitchcock and Nangati, note 9; Bonner, note 1, pp. 253–78; Gordon Edwin Matzke and Nontokozo Nabane, "Outcomes of a Community Controlled Wildlife Utilization Program in a Zambezi Valley Community," *Human Ecology* 24:1 (1996, 65–85); Ignatius Mberengwa, Ignatius, "The Communal Areas Management Program for Indigenous Resources (CAMPFIRE) and Rural Development in Zimbabwe's Marginal Areas: A Study in Sustainability," Ph.D. Dissertation, University of Nebraska, Lincoln, Nebraska, 1999; Rosaleen Duffy, *Killing for Conservation: Wildlife Policy in Zimbabwe* (Oxford: James Currey and Bloomington: Indiana University Press, 2000).

34. This information was obtained during interviews in Tsholotsho and Bulalima-Mangwe Districts in western Zimbabwe in July, 1992.

35. Hitchcock, note 2, p. 193.

36. See Malcolm L. Hunter, Robert K. Hitchcock, and Barbara Wyckoff-Baird, "Women and Wildlife in Southern Africa," *Conservation Biology* 4:4 (1990, 448–51); and Norris and Hitchcock, note 5. On the rights to wildlife products such as ostrich eggshell beads, see the discussion in Robert Hitchcock and Rosinah Rose Masilo (1995), note 9. On intellectual property rights, especially regarding the succulent Hoodia, see Anonymous, "It's Prickly and Sour, But This Plant Could Cure Obesity," *Mail and Guardian*, Sunday, January 5, 2003, p. 1; Ginger Thompson, "Bushmen Squeeze Money from a Humble Cactus," *The New York Times*, April 1, 2003; WIMSA, *The San of Southern Africa: Heritage and Intellectual Property* (Windhoek: Working Group of Indigenous Minorities in Southern Africa, 2003); Roger Chennels, "San Hoodia Case: A Report for GenBenefit," www.uclan. ac.uk/genbenefit; Fanie R. van Heerden, R. Martinhus Horak, Vinesh J. Maharaj, Robert Vieggaar, Jeremiah V. Senabe, and Philip J. Gunning, "An Appetite Suppressant from Hoodia Species," *Phytochemistry* 68 (2007, 2545–53).

37. See Robert K. Hitchcock, "Zenzele: Swazi Women Say, 'Do It Yourself,'" *Ndiza Natsi* 3:11 (1985, 22–25); Alan Durning, *Action at the Grassroots: Fighting Poverty and Environmental Decline* (Washington, D.C.: Worldwatch Institute, 1989); Caroline M. Ross, *Can the Poor Influence Policy? Participatory Poverty Assessments in the Developing World* (Washington, D.C.: The World Bank, 1999); Thayer Scudder, *The Future of Large Dams: Dealing with Social, Environmental, Institutional, and Political Costs* (London: James and James Science Publishers, 2005); Jeffrey Sachs, *The End of Poverty: How We Can Make it Happen in Our Lifetime* (London: Penguin Books, 2005).

CHAPTER 5

Nature, Development, and Culture in the Zambezi Valley[1]

Bill Derman, with the assistance of Mike Makina (Mushumbi Pools) and Lazarus Zhuwao (Basiyao, Zimbabwe)

SECTION I: The End of the Millennium

Royal ancestral spirits, known in the Zambezi Valley as *mhondoros*, have guided the conduct and conscience of Zambezi Valley communities. These representatives of the past speak through their contemporary mediums. They serve a critical role in both past and present events by facilitating discussion on controversial issues. In addition, they examine whether current practice is or is not consistent with past understandings and current community practice. The *mhondoros* are arguably no longer as respected as in the past, although when difficulties arise—drought, murder, famine—they are consulted. Their comments represent many older residents' sentiments about current environment and development projects in the Zambezi Valley. Yet the perspectives of *mhondoros* were not sought in either the planning or implementation stage of the Mid-Zambezi Rural Development Project. This case demonstrates why local participation and democratic processes have an environmental significance that has, all too often, been ignored.

The *mhondoro* Karembera had this to say about the Mid-Zambezi Project:

> I wasn't told about it. What happened was the District Councilor[2] came with his friend to peg [demarcate with stakes] an area which included my tsopero [a sacred place]. I waited to see if they would inform me but they did not. On the fourth day I travelled around my territory. When I reached the place where I conduct tsopero, I found a peg. I asked a local leader what is this and he said it's a peg for a residential plot. I asked him, who did this? He said it was the Councilor. I told him to call the Councilor but the Councilor said he would not come that way. The Councilor said he would come at his own time when he heard that I am angry.[3]

We then asked if the *mhondoro* was told that your people (meaning those living within the boundaries of the *mhondoro*) could no longer cultivate on the river banks and what were his thoughts about that decision:

That is not a good idea because here in Mbire [the valley] the sun is very hot. When the river is in flood it spills into the valleys. When the water dries it is when my people will grow their crops and the crops we sell there. Do you know snuffing tobacco? Here we don't grow it on this land [upland] but along the river banks and now this crop is beginning to disappear [snuff tobacco is an essential part of the sacred paraphernalia as well as being a cash crop]. If you want to know how bad are their plans, they will tell you that we will put you in prison if you cultivate there.[4]

The issues are clear: a large development project in the name of protecting a fragile ecology has sought to bar valley residents from cultivating along the rivers, the source of both water and good land. In addition, a project meant to benefit citizens did not inform their leaders nor consult with them about how to proceed. How did this happen, and what are the implications? How does a government come to override the views and aspirations of its own citizens in the name of both environment and development? This is not an unusual story, yet it demonstrates the multiple and often unforeseen consequences of disempowering local communities. Ignoring local knowledge and institutions can intensify environmental degradation and social conflict.

The Zambezi Valley and Zimbabwe

The Zambezi Valley, which traverses the northern border of Zimbabwe, serves as one of the most important wildlife reservoirs in Central and Southern Africa. It provides extraordinary tourism opportunities, including Victoria Falls, Lake Kariba, and several national parks and safari areas. The valley also has been the site for some of Africa's bitterest conflicts between poachers and national park rangers in the difficult and ultimately unsuccessful campaign to protect the last remaining black rhinos. At the same time, the valley is characterized by the poverty of many of its human residents.

   Contrary to popular images, the valley is not exemplary of wilderness in Zimbabwe; instead, it represents a very large ecosystem experiment. In 1959 a large dam and lake were created, known as Kariba. The human-created lake flooded the prime agricultural lands of a people known as the Tonga, altering irrevocably the valley's ecology. Downstream of Kariba to the east, many communities were removed to create a habitat for animals, while, further east, major projects to create environments more favorable for human settlement are under way. These changes do not take place without debate. One major unresolved issue centers on the best economic use of the semiarid lands of the Zambezi Valley. On one side are those who argue that wildlife programs are both more economical and sustainable in the longer term. On the other side are those who contend that with appropriate land-use planning and water management, intensive agricultural systems are viable. Both are human-designed programs to utilize the environment in quite distinct ways. Another long-term ecological and human experiment has been the effort to control and eradicate the tsetse fly, the vector for both human and bovine trypanosomiasis (sleeping sickness). The measures used to eradicate the fly have included the mass destruction of wild animals, the movement of human populations, aerial spraying, ground spraying, and the like. This long-term effort remains a site of contestation between development planners and valley residents, since the presence of tsetse reduces to some measure the possibilities of keeping livestock. In short, the Zambezi Valley continues to be a site of multiple social, cultural, and ecological experiments whose outcomes remain unknown.[5]

   It is clear that for wildlife and environmental programs to succeed, they will have to incorporate the multiple developmental needs of valley residents. Two different strategies have emerged. The first, which has attracted much international attention, is the Communal Areas Management Program for Indigenous Resources (popularly known as CAMPFIRE). Less attention has been given to the second, the Mid-Zambezi Valley Rural Development Project (MZVRDP), which began in 1987 and which technically ends in December 1996. This second project, while lacking the intense international scrutiny and criticism that CAMPFIRE received, is apparently the model of choice for future land-use planning and programs in the valley. The principles underlying both programs reflect how divergent approaches can be utilized in the same ecological and geographic area. In the case of the Mid-Zambezi Project, they demonstrate why investment in top-down, blueprint types of projects can lead to both disillusionment with a government and greater ecological degradation than if the project had been planned and implemented in a more democratic fashion. It has led to the vast deforestation of what had been a dryland forest area with gallery forest along seasonal rivers. The government has attempted to bar people from the centuries-old practices of cultivating along the riverine areas, practices that have made living possible in this drought-prone environment. Democracy and participation must be more than slogans in examining development projects in fragile environments when the longer-term sustainability of an environment is envisioned.

Zimbabwe's independence, gained through a guerrilla war and sustained until recently by a socialist ideology, has led many scholars to conduct research in this strikingly beautiful but glaringly inequitable nation.[6] The inequities derive primarily from colonialist alienation of one-half of the best land from African residents and the differential infrastructure put into place in the former European areas (now called Large Scale Commercial Farmers) and the Tribal Trust Lands (now called Communal Areas). This structural inequality persists. Increasingly small numbers of black Zimbabweans are becoming large-scale commercial farmers.[7] Land, and the nature of the war for independence, remains a critical focal point for contemporary research, along with the contemporary situation in the communal areas. Unfortunately, the commercial areas have not been adequately researched.[8] The current land categories in Zimbabwe are classified as: large-scale commercial farm land (40% of the total area); small-scale commercial farm land (4%); communal lands (42%); and national parks and safari areas (14%).

The commercial farms are located in the regions of highest rainfall and good soils. The European colonialists seized the best lands for themselves, a historical legacy that has been difficult to overcome. Moreover, there remains a dual property regime in which the commercial areas are privately owned and are fully commoditized, whereas the communal areas are owned by the national government and managed by a combination of newly created local structures emphasizing the elected Rural District Councils. The "traditional authorities" of chiefs and headmen, while legally barred from allocating land, are, in practice, quite influential.

The communal lands were created along racial lines to hold the indigenous African populations. Issues of sustainability, adequacy, viability, or economies of scale were not considered.[9] The large-scale farm areas were created to be vast in order to deny Africans the best lands. The small-scale commercial areas served the rising elite of black Zimbabwean farmers. These, on the whole, have been nonviable as farming enterprises. The national parks and safari areas are important in understanding the role of tourism and wildlife utilization.

Indeed, there has been a long perceived historical conflict between livestock and wildlife. The Zambezi River valley supports a large population of tsetse flies, which carry both human and bovine trypanosomiasis (sleeping sickness). Since the discovery that sleeping sickness was carried by the tsetse fly there have been continuous efforts to eliminate or at least diminish the presence of the fly. Since the discovery of the vector, efforts have been directed to eliminate wild animals that might carry the disease and to destroy tsetse habitats. These indiscriminate killings came to an end in the 1950s; however, it was not until the 1980s that a linkage was made between tsetse control and land-use planning. In practice, this meant opening up new sections of the valley for increased human and livestock habitation.[10]

The European Economic Community (EEC) funded a Regional Tsetse and Trypanosomiasis Control Programme (RTTCP) to investigate the best methods to control and eliminate the fly belt in Zimbabwe, Zambia, Malawi, and Mozambique. The government's aim was to expand the frontiers of prosperous communal farming. Tsetse control was to support these rural development programs, which relieve the population pressure in other parts of the country. Perhaps most importantly, alternative land-use options were not seriously entertained by the GOZ and the EEC in these critical years. The EEC aerially sprayed the length of the Zambezi Valley, stopping only in 1988 because of the development of alternative cost-competitive techniques.[11] In light of the range of potential long- and short-term consequences of tsetse eradication or reduction, new studies were commissioned to examine land-use in the valley. The basis of such policies—which remained unstated—was that the division of land between communal and large-scale commercial lands would remain unchanged. In addition, land for land-poor communal farmers had to be found in "marginal" areas such as the Zambezi Valley. The European Economic Community consultancy proposed a series of projects that, at least in hindsight, had contradictory objectives of both large-scale projects and emphasis on environmental conservation. Among the projects they proposed was the Mid-Zambezi Valley Rural Development Project.

The Mid-Zambezi Valley Rural Development Project

The MZVRDP was the first major postindependence development project in the Zambezi Valley. It was initiated in 1987 with funding from the African Development Bank, and it was staffed entirely by Zimbabweans. The project was supposed to run for five years but, because it was not completed in that time frame, it was granted first a three-year, then another one-year, extension. It is expected to terminate in December 1996.

The MZVRDP resettled populations from other, more crowded rural areas to either commercial farm land or to frontier areas. The political rationale for the project was to be able to claim that 7,600 households were being resettled, thus demonstrating the government's ongoing commitment to resolving historic land grievances.[12] It was designed to fit within the larger land-use planning strategy recommended by the EEC to the government of Zimbabwe and the government's developmental objectives. The MZVRDP was to provide boreholes, schools, clinics, roads, and improved agriculture for all residents—both new and old. Planning documents stated that the valley was so underdeveloped and so many critical aspects of infrastructure were missing that *any* intervention would be better than none.[13] The project was originally recommended by an FAO (Food and Agriculture Organization) team conducting a land-use study of the entire valley in response to the question What would the valley look like if the tsetse fly were indeed eliminated?[14]

Resettlement projects within the government of Zimbabwe ordinarily fall within the purview of the Department of Rural and Urban Development (Derude), which is located in the Ministry of Local Government and Rural and Urban Development (MLGRUD).[15] This department was given primary responsibility for the MZVRDP's implementation. Most members of Derude were trained by the Department of Rural and Urban Planning at the University of Zimbabwe, and there were strong continuities with colonial planning. The Department of Agricultural Extension and Technical Services (Agritex) drew up the project plans in collaboration with Derude following the guidelines for an Accelerated Model A Resettlement Scheme.[16] This entailed an allocation of 5-hectare arable plots to eligible household heads, setting aside lands for grazing, and consolidating villages. The project has involved resettling and reorganizing the local population into consolidated villages grouped around boreholes. Arable plots were found for 7,600 households through aerial photograph identification. Planners thought that there were only 3,600 resident families living in the project area, but this turned out to be a gross underestimate. As a result of this miscalculation, the government's objective of providing land for new settlers could not be achieved.

The project's planning process exemplifies how government and the project related to the proposed beneficiaries. Government planners believed that they had a successful model for rural development programs and thus felt that it was unnecessary to consult with valley residents.[17] This model and its accompanying procedures were strikingly similar to that used by the Rhodesian colonial state and were so viewed by many valley residents. The model was virtually identical to that proposed in the Native Land Husbandry Act of 1951, which was detested by black Rhodesians. The act attempted to compartmentalize the land into areas for concentrated villages, fields, and grazing areas. It was ultimately withdrawn because of widespread opposition and the incapacity of the Rhodesian government to implement it.

Employing colonial terminology, the MZVRDP named the new villages, calling peoples' homesteads "residentials" and fields "arables." In addition, grazing areas were delimited. The identification of arable, residential, and grazing areas was carried out by Agricultural Research and Technical Services (Agritex) in the Ministry of Agriculture. The principles were simple: vegetative complexes were used to identify arable areas, grazing areas were set aside along the rivers, and residentials were located where boreholes were sunk. Although the practice of riverine cultivation was central to human adaptation and agriculture in the valley, the project set out to rupture this agro-ecological adaptation by prohibiting riverine or stream-bank cultivation, moving the designated arables away from rivers, and allocating riverine land for grazing areas.

This contemporary planning pattern has its roots in the colonial period. During the 1930s colonial officials believed that there was an immediate soil conservation crisis, which they regarded as a result of destructive African agricultural practices.[18] They blamed overpopulation and poor farming methods in the reserves for creating degraded soils, deforestation, and low agricultural productivity. Overstocking of cattle was added to the causes of rapid soil deterioration, and thus compulsory destocking became part of agricultural policy toward African producers. Scientists and Rhodesian agricultural specialists thought that there was a growing ecological crisis of erosion because of African cultivation practices. Their views became part of the scientific and knowledge system of those attempting to understand and alter African agricultural systems. There has been little analysis and study, for example, of the ecological outcomes of a tobacco-led agricultural export economy.[19]

As the practice of stream-bank cultivation was regarded as one of the major factors promoting erosion, laws were enacted during the colonial period to prohibit it. The all-white Parliament of Rhodesia passed the Water Act of 1927 (amended in 1976) to control use of Zimbabwe's wetlands. This concern with water use and erosion was reinforced by the Stream Bank Protection Regulation, which formed part of the 1942 Natural Resources Act (amended in 1975). This law prohibits cultivation within 100 feet (now 30 meters, but often interpreted as 100 meters) of the normal flow of a stream or wetland.

The policies on stream banks and wetlands grew out of studies conducted in the high plateau. Nevertheless they were applied nationwide regardless of ecological variation and river slope. While the regulation has been enforced in other portions of Zimbabwe's communal lands, it was not enforced, until recently, in the Zambezi Valley. To make matters more difficult in the valley, normal flow was defined by Agritex planners as the flood stage of the rivers, which meant that large areas of alluvial soils were, in principle, to remain unutilized for cultivation.

Colonial policies reflected the view that African knowledge and practices were inimical to progress. The MZVRDP planners, in essence, accepted these views, especially as they pertained to riverine cultivation. As a consequence, local voices and knowledge were not incorporated into the design or implementation of the project, although they have had a decided impact on its operation. Indeed, from the valley residents' perspective the most objectionable part of the project has been the effort to ban riverine cultivation.

Riverine Cultivation in the Zambezi Valley

Stream-bank cultivation in the Zambezi is not a single practice. It encompasses both rainy and dry season cultivation and involves the cultivation of current river beds and former river beds, as well as the use of stream banks. Rainy season areas of cultivation are referred to as *fields*, and the dry season areas are termed either *fields* or *gardens*. They are gardens when they are small in size or contain vegetables rather than maize or snuff tobacco. Rainy-season crops include maize, with smaller areas of sorghum, squash/pumpkins, and, increasingly, cotton. In the dry season farmers cultivate maize, sweet potatoes, and a range of vegetables for sale and household use. Depending on the depth of ground water, most gardens are now hand irrigated during the long dry season from hand-dug wells. It has become increasingly difficult for women to sustain these gardens as they have been moved away from the rivers and as the increasing numbers of livestock drink from the shallow wells, thereby filling them in. Because of the large number of migrants into the valley, riverine land for rainy season cultivation is hard to obtain. Riverine cultivation allows people to have harvests if the rains are poor, as often occurs in the valley. When the rains are heavy and damage or destroy a crop, then the moist soil of these gardens permits a reliable dry-season harvest.

When the MZVRDP was initiated, residents were told that their lands would be demarcated and they would get schools, boreholes, clinics, tractors, and even electricity. They were *not* told that the project would decide where they were to live and farm. Indeed, the project got under way when peggers entered two areas in the valley and began demarcating arables. When residents inquired what they were doing, they were told not to ask questions or else they would be arrested. That night all the pegs were pulled out of the ground by local residents (who remained anonymous) and placed at District Council offices. The District Councils and Administrators along with project staff then had to explain the project to valley residents.[20]

The most contested part of the MZVRDP was the moving of residents away from the rivers and converting these most highly valued riverine lands to grazing areas. Valley residents describe this process as "throwing away land." In general, it is the long-term residents, often from the most influential families, who own or have user rights to large tracts of riverine land. More recent migrants have obtained access only to riverine gardens, and thus have had much less of a stake in this issue. The major cash crop in the valley is cotton, which for the most part is cultivated in the uplands, away from the alluvial riverine soils. Although many migrants were able to keep their existing lands, which were located away from the rivers, those with lands along the rivers were relocated. In addition, wealthier migrants who owned cattle are not as opposed to the project's setting aside of grazing areas. Even though residents do not speak with one voice, project and Agritex personnel, who overwhelmingly come from outside the valley, tend to listen to the wealthier, cotton-growing, cattle-owning families.

In 1990 a new Ward Councilor was elected for one of the project wards, or political districts. As part of his platform he argued that the MZVRDP needed to be changed. At an early meeting following his election, he made known his views on what he thought the relationship should be between the government and its citizens, and between the project staff and valley residents:

> The Mid-Zambezi Project has distorted our lives and brought problems in the valley because of not listening to the dwellers of this area who know best about what they want. Some of you have been threatened by the VIDCO Chairmen [heads of Village Development Committees] and Councilors that failure to cooperate with the project will result in your losing your land. Most of you have become afraid to say anything at meetings. . . . The project did not spend time listening to anybody. People were frightened and got nervous until the whole project was viewed as a bad idea. Resettlement has allocated sacred land, taken good soil for cattle grazing which people don't have.[21]

He spoke clearly and forthrightly about the importance of local knowledge and participation to the success of development efforts, including the project. His activities and speeches did not go unnoticed. In a letter to the District Administrator reporting on the activities of this Council, the Resettlement Officer observed that this Councilor:

> involves Spirit Mediums and Kraal Heads [*sabhukus*] in development issues. I feel he does this to get their support. These people tend to give him the wrong advice which he fails to object to. As far as I have observed traditional leaders oppose changes and this could be the reason why the Councillor goes to meetings with negative attitudes. These leaders have their role in society and if properly used can help in mobilization other than as advisors. The Councillor made this mistake from the very start and I cannot find a way out.

I feel that the Councillor needs to be told as to who to consult on developmental issues.[22]

The Resettlement Officer expressed the prevailing view that local authorities and local practices were not relevant to development. But the Ward Councillor attempted to incorporate spirit mediums and *sabhukus* into the discussion of local development. It is not without irony that *sabhukus* and chiefs have been given increased authority over all issues. Indeed, it is strongly rumored that the Village Development Committees will be ended. Thus, a Ward Councilor who actually tried to represent his constituents and engage in an appropriate process of consultation found his hand slapped. In the final irony, the agency responsible for resettlement, Derude, has been ended. The first and only project manager for the project has taken early retirement.

While valley residents do not speak with one voice on most issues, there is strong consensus that riverine cultivation is essential to the valley economy and to household well-being. Almost all those who can obtain access to riverine gardens and fields do so, be they project employees, Ward Councilors, Village Development Committee chairmen, or virtually everyone else.[23] Notably, those charged with moving people away from rivers, Ward Councilors, VIDCO Chairs, and the like, all have riverine fields and gardens.

On several occasions, farmers and researchers have debated the rationale that stream-bank cultivation causes erosion. In general, officials, planners, and technicians uniformly asserted that riverine cultivation causes erosion. When questioned as to how the erosion process worked in the relatively flat valley, the answers they gave were appropriate to steeply sloped river beds and not to those that characterized most of the valley. Valley residents were far more nuanced in their explanations of why riverine cultivation did not usually cause erosion. They pointed to how their crops and cultivation practices held the soil in place. They described their practices of shifting their fields and the rationale that underlay these moves. They identified and recognized erosion as a natural process that could be affected by human action. A former Ward Councilor, whom I first interviewed in 1990, asked me if I believed that stream-bank cultivation was causing erosion and causing the rivers to stop flowing. I reversed the question and asked him if he and his family found themselves unable to cultivate their riverine fields and gardens because of soil erosion. He laughed and said no. Since he was an elder, I asked him what change had there been in the land that he has continuously cultivated for 16 years. He replied, "None," continuing: "They are just as fertile now as when I first returned to the village after the war." Although the processes of erosion are at least partially understood, they are not necessarily acted on by younger farmers, many of whom were expanding cotton cultivation in riverine fields despite the cautions on pesticide bottles not to use these chemicals near water or fish.

The MZVRDP's commitment to a blueprint planning approach has made real dialogue very difficult between residents, technicians, planners, and other development personnel. The structure of the resettlement program and its shortage of resources (including trained people) have made it difficult for project personnel to learn and incorporate the results of relevant. The outcome to date in the Zambezi Valley has been a pattern of serious resistance by valley residents to different aspects of the MZVRDP but especially to the notion of ceasing riverine cultivation. An attempt was made to bar residents from having livestock. The maximum number was to be two oxen per household has been totally ignored, and the project has given up any effort to limit livestock in the project area.

Ongoing Contestation

A fascinating dimension of this process of project implementation has been the outspoken opposition to the project by some residents, combined with much foot-dragging and resistance. This is a major reason why the project fell so far behind schedule. A workshop organized by the District Councilor to resolve problems in two wards along the Manyame River was attended by local leaders and Government Department Heads, including the Mid-Zambezi Project, Tsetse Control and Eradication, and the Department of Co-operatives as well as many residents (older men). The representative of the Mid-Zambezi Project spoke. He stated:

> Most people think that the MZVRDP is for we the employees, but the project is yours. You got arables, boreholes, roads, clinics and schools. All these facilities are for the community, not for us the employees. When we ask people to come and help us on the construction of the school, few people come to do the work. This has become a major problem for school construction especially in this ward. . . . These works should be done by you, the parents. The school is yours! . . . This project has its time period. When the period is over we are going to leave some of these schools incomplete and you will be to blame.

Following a brief discussion the representative from Tsetse Eradication and Control complained, in a similarly accusatory tone, that community members steal tsetse fly traps. These speeches make clear that local populations are resisting central components of the government's strategy for this area. Local populations have not taken ownership of a project, which, they are told, was meant to benefit them. It is more than likely that the speakers are not familiar with the project's history and really do believe what they say. In the first instance, people are resisting building schools. Education is highly valued, and school attendance is relatively high; however, many residents don't know which school to work on since they are or were in the process of moving. In the second instance of stolen tsetse fly-cloth traps, there has been increasing conflict between cattle owners and cultivators. In addition, there is much cross-border movement between Mozambique and Zimbabwe, and it is possible that Mozambicans are more responsible for the thefts.

Many residents have supported elements of the project. More recent migrants to the valley who did not have clear rights to land or who had relatively small areas were delighted to receive more secure tenure and larger areas. Most residents supported the construction of roads and boreholes. They have also supported increased numbers of stores and markets. The project has created centers of temporary employment for the construction of roads, boreholes, schools, and the clearing of one acre for new fields. This has intensified economic activity in the valley. Moreover, there has been a dramatic increase in the numbers of cement or brick dwellings and livestock. This reflects the residents' use of savings for their homes and agricultural production. This intensified economic activity has also meant that the valley continues to draw migrants into the valley. These migrants and kin of residents settle on unpegged or nonallocated land, thus undermining all efforts at land-use planning. To add to the confusion, one ward in the project area remained undemarcated and unpegged until 1995. In this ward, the local *mhondoro* opposed pegging, as did many of the family heads.

The *mhondoro* named Chidyamauyu has been responsible for the territory of a major spirit (known as Nehanda) whose medium died during the war for an independent Zimbabwe. In 1993 and 1994 the project made a concerted attempt to have Chidyamauyu accept the project in Nehanda's territory (his was outside the project). This was his account of the project's efforts:

> I am the only one who looks after Ambuya Nehanda [the other royal ancestral spirit]. If you want me to tell you the wrong things which are done by Government to the *mhondoros* Chiefs I can tell you. But if you are after the pegging and you are just hiding, that is what I don't want. Chief Matsiwo came here hiding by saying that he had been sent by

his children. And yet it was him and Maziofa [the Project Manager for the Mid-Zambezi Project]. You should not take me that way. I fought for this country for eight years. When I went to Mozambique I had been with this Medium Nehanda. I represented all the *mhondoros* of Dande [the Shona term for this part of the valley]. If you come with an idea of destroying this area by pegging, that is what I don't want to hear. Even if it is [president] Mugabe telling me [to accept the pegging] then I will tell him to stop it. If we are talking of pegging it is a very disturbing issue. The Government has just used its powers without asking. . . . When they started their war [against the Rhodesians] they asked us, the *mhondoros* and the *mambos* [the chiefs]. The chiefs gave them their children to go to war until today some of their children didn't return home. . . . The Government has forgotten us, the *mhondoros* and the chiefs, the owners of the land.[24]

In the end, the project proceeded. Its supporters were able to carry it forward only after the election of a new, younger Ward Councilor who was told in no uncertain terms that the area would not get a new clinic or schools without the project. Nonetheless, he did genuinely support the project. He said in his campaign that it would bring development to his ward. After eight years the value and worth of the project should have been demonstrated, but it had not been. The pegging is in process as of July 1996. It should be completed by October. People have yet to begin to move to take up their new arables and residentials, although in this ward they have been given greater input into land-use planning. Let us briefly examine the broader ecological changes in the valley and how new plans continue to rely on blueprint models.

Since the mid-1980s the eastern Zambezi Valley has been transformed from a verdant zone to a deforested, dust-filled region, with thousands of new farms. The contemporary patterns of migration into the valley (not only the east) are historically rooted in an effort by the Rhodesian government to reorganize what were then called the Reserves and to find new areas for displaced farmers. In addition, the use of frontiers for human settlement results from the growing scarcity of good farm land and pasture in the communal lands of Zimbabwe. It is indicative of the land-scarcity in other portions of Zimbabwe that so many migrants choose the drought-prone Zambezi Valley in which to settle. The current government, with the assistance of the European Economic Community, Food and Agriculture Organization, Overseas Development Administration, and the African Development Bank, has continued to press for the intensification of population and production in the Eastern Valley. This is being done through a new generation of projects only slightly different from the Mid-Zambezi Valley Rural Development Project.

Consider, for example, the Dande Irrigation Project, a plan to irrigate much of the marginal land where people have just been resettled. The project requires construction of a dam, tunnel, diversions, roads, and other infrastructure, and this infrastructure will cause the displacement of some 600 households. Billed as poverty alleviation, the development plan assumes that beneficiaries, in exchange for marginal land and irrigation, will give up their upland and riverine fields. If they don't do this, then they will be removed from the project. This is clearly a top-down, blueprint approach to development.

All development interventions and projects in the valley claim that the standards of living will be raised and that the environment will be protected. This has been the case since colonial times. At the same time, farmers' knowledge is discounted, community social structures are regarded as irrelevant, and planners ignore them. Meanwhile the division of lands into arables, residentials, and grazing areas takes no account of microecological variations. Past and present projects, with the exception of CAMPFIRE, do not begin with the assumption that valley residents are knowledgeable agents who are making a living in a tough environment. I even have heard social scientists, planners, and project implementers argue that valley residents are used to moving because of the needs of their system of shifting cultivation. While considerable movement took place in both precolonial times and even during colonial years, this kind of voluntary movement involved searching for new fields and villages, as well as fissioning of kin groups. It had a decidedly different character than that which took place following establishment of the Native Land Husbandry Act of 1951, which proposed to determine the size of people's fields, how many animals they could own, and where they could be employed. During the war, the Rhodesians forced valley residents into keeps (which were equivalent to strategic hamlets created by the United States in Vietnam). Past mobility was similarly different from the coercive resettlement continued within the MZVRDP and now, in our estimation, the new irrigation proposals. On the more pragmatic side, a large-scale irrigation project involves heavy management costs and operations, which may be beyond the capacity of the different project management entities that are to be established. Most importantly, these projects will prevent communities from creating the organization and structures necessary to manage their natural resources on a sustainable basis.

However, there is no turning back to earlier land-use systems. Because of the heavy in-migration to the valley, there is a dramatic shift from a more diverse natural resource management system to primary reliance on cotton and maize. These population and agricultural changes are profoundly altering both the valley's ecology and relationships between people and nature. To date, centralized planning has not worked. Efforts to control in-migration have been ineffective, and alternative solutions need to be generated. New efforts are required to see if local populations regard current patterns of in-migration into the valley as a major problem and what solutions can be found to reduce it in those areas where local communities find it objectionable or unmanageable. It is ironic that government officials who had attempted to solve these kinds of problems find themselves virtually powerless to stop these processes. Thus, although in the past they disempowered local communities, now they need to re-empower them to find solutions.

Conclusions

The Mid-Zambezi Valley Rural Development Project illustrates how a complex mix of developmental, environmental, and political objectives have override local knowledge and local practices. Unfortunately, this experience is not unique in the annals of large-scale development projects that plan lives for people deemed "underdeveloped" or "undeveloped" in ways that would not be done for wealthier or more powerful individuals. Although it is perhaps too early in the process to draw final conclusions, it is already clear that the project has missed accomplishing its central goals. Partly, this was due to the ambitious, if not unrealistic, nature of those goals and the contradictory means employed to achieve them. The nature of the planning process and the incorporation (or rather the lack thereof) of environmental concerns demonstrates once again the importance of finding and following appropriate democratic means and structures in the design and implementation of large-scale development projects.[25] This process is now far more complicated than before, owing to the dual pressures of development projects and continued in-migration. Let us examine these in turn: government-sponsored (if externally funded) development projects send a message that local peoples cannot generate the resources and expertise necessary to improve their own livelihoods and standards of living. In short, external intervention combined with government takes responsibility for valley residents' development. The assumption is that different agencies of government and development assistance agencies can "know" how to develop a region. This message is precisely wrong. The true message is not that external assistance and governments aren't necessary, but that the responsibility lies ultimately with local populations, village communities, and their organizations to generate, within their capacities, the means to determine their futures. Governments and development assistance organizations can facilitate a process, though to date they have intervened far too deeply so that communities, villages, and local organizations have acquiesced and shifted the ultimate responsibility for change to others.[26]

Second, the Zambezi Valley, particularly the eastern valley, is now threatened by blueprint and inappropriate approaches to its environment. The central government's and donors' continued emphasis on large projects, combined with land scarcity and sustained drought in southern Zimbabwe, mean that migrants are drawn to the valley to find adequate land, pasture, and employment in the valley. These processes are leading to increased populations of humans, cattle, goats, and other animals. The major cash crop remains cotton, which requires extensive land areas and essentially mines the soil while utilizing large quantities of pesticides. Deforestation has proceeded at a frightening pace. This all can work while cultivable land remains available and when rainfall is adequate. The system, however, remains highly vulnerable. Potential solutions are complex, involving greater community controls to now regulate, if possible, overgrazing conflicts between livestock and agriculture, deforestation, and experimentation to use more drought-resistant crops. Failure to address these issues will lead to the continued encroachment on the National Parks and Wild Life estate, which in turn is viewed globally and nationally as one of Zimbabwe's treasures. It will also lead to a deteriorating living standard for valley residents and increased dependence by these residents on government during drought years.

SECTION II: View from the 21st Century

Since this book was originally published Zimbabwe has experienced economic decline, multiple health crises, and violent elections. What happened?

In 1997 Zimbabwe was, at least in broad public consciousness, a relatively progressive African developmental state. Numerous critiques, such as mine, were circulated by social, environmental, and agricultural scientists in the hope that they could be used to improve policy. The period from 1997 to 2000 showed a marked bifurcation. On the one hand, civil society expanded, the union movement grew bolder, new publications emerged, and an opposition party was formed. This broad coalition, called the Movement for Democratic Change, included the union confederation (Zimbabwe Congress of Trade Unions), academics, members of numerous civil society organizations, some farm workers, and farm owners. Almost from its inception it was able to contest elections on a national basis. On the other hand, the ruling party, Zimbabwe African National Union–Patriotic Front (ZANU–PF), hardened its stance in response to a controversial and unconstitutional intervention in Congo's civil war, to economic decline, and to internal dissent seeking a change of leadership. In this period of ferment, and as part of civil society, a new group led by law professors at the University of Zimbabwe began lobbying for a new constitution, one that would be far more democratic than the one in existence. The government responded by forming its own national constitutional commission to write a new constitution. This constitution formed the basis of Zimbabwe's first nationwide referendum. However, the constitution was defeated—but, according to most observers, not because of the constitution's content, which was a dramatic improvement, but because it became in the public's mind a referendum on President Mugabe's rule.

The referendum was defeated in February 2000, with parliamentary elections slated for April. Land occupations began in March 2000, and the government claimed that they were spontaneous. The opposition newspapers—*The Daily News, The Financial Gazette, The Zimbabwe Independent,* and *The Zimbabwe Standard*—all reported invasions led by the ruling party and war veterans (closely linked to the president, and the army). During this period I was doing research on water reform and water law, and I visited many farms, including farms owned by white commercial farmers—thus I can verify the land occupations. The war veterans and the newly formed ZANU–PF youth militias made many rural areas "no go," especially in the Mashonaland provinces, areas for opposition party members. In particular they targeted teachers who were supporting the Movement for Democratic Change (MDC). There was in 2000 a climate of extreme violence, including murder, beatings, torture, kidnappings, and all-night indoctrination sessions, combined with control of voters' rolls and other forms of election manipulation. Not unexpectedly, ZANU–PF won control of the parliament, not least because the president appointed 20 additional members to parliament who voted with the ruling party. MDC brought multiple election fraud and violence cases to the courts, but most of them had yet to be heard in 2009.

Subsequent presidential and parliamentary elections (2005) were marked by violence, abductions, torture, beatings, and election manipulation. However, the severe economic crises of 2008 led to the electoral defeat of ZANU–PF by a divided MDC opposition in March. This occurred in the context of continued violence and changing of voting-district boundaries to favor the rural over the urban. The presidential ballots disappeared while the leaders of ZANU–PF decided what to do. They announced that neither candidate, Mugabe (ZANU–PF) or Tsvangirai (MDC), had a majority of the vote (a third candidate, Simba Makoni, drew votes from both candidates), and a run-off election was scheduled for June 27, 2008. Violence spread through most of the country between March 29 and June 27. In January–December 2008 the Human Rights Forum recorded 6 politically motivated rape cases, 107 murders, 137 kidnappings (abductions), 1,913 cases of assault, 19 cases of disappearance, 629 people forced from their homes, and thousands of violations of freedoms of association and expression. According to the Forum there "was an organized and well-orchestrated plan of action and collusion between private individuals and state security institutions to annihilate the MDC party structures countrywide so as to instill fear in the electorate. . . ."[27] Rather than risk more violence against the MDC, Tsvangirai withdrew from the presidential race; however, his action, not surprisingly, was not accepted, and he remained on the ballot. Although some nations in southern Africa accepted his victory, there was increasing pressure internationally to reject the election. In a compromise negotiated by former President of South Africa, Thabo Mbeki, a government of national unity was formed, with Robert Mugabe continuing as President and Morgan Tsvangirai in a new post of Prime Minister. This was an unstable situation, with continuing violence and economic decline in the midst of a cholera epidemic.[28]

In June 2000 I returned again to Marirahoko, a small-resettled village in the MZVRDP where Mike Makina (my coresearcher since 1990), his wife Netsai, and their family lived, which I used as a base for many of my research visits. On the way there, near Mvurwi, an old commercial farming center, I discovered that there had been a battle between the police and members of the ruling party, ZANU–PF, who had been attempting to free several of their comrades from jail. The police had attempted to remain professional but were forced by the president not to intervene on the land issue. Nonetheless, the ZANU–PF members had been jailed for attacking farmer owners and farm workers as part of the farm occupations. Later, near Mushumbi Pools, in the valley, we encountered a large gathering of residents; however, given the potential for violence, we did not stop. Heather[29] and I finally arrived and set up camp in Mike and Netsai's homestead and made coffee. Mike arrived at dusk with the story of the meeting. In the chilly winter's evening we sat around the *mopane* wood fire while Mike described how the local war-veteran leaders had called the meeting, a rally of sorts meant to energize the local community in support of the ruling party and to denounce members of the opposition party. Following the chanting of slogans two local men, brothers, one of whom had been given a small tractor by a white commercial farmer, were identified as local supporters of the Movement for Democratic Change (MDC), the new national opposition party that was now making dramatic inroads into rural Zimbabwe. Speeches were made, and the two men were verbally abused; then the abuse turned to beating and threats to kill them. At this point a local spirit medium startled the assemblage by asserting that no blood should be spilled; as a spirit medium and a war veteran, he demanded that no one be killed in his area. Everyone was Zimbabwean and valley citizens, and so no one should spill blood. Then the meeting ended, and everyone returned home.

This was just one of many such events, and later ones did not end peacefully. In general, the tolerance for any perspective other than that of the ruling party was stamped out in the rural areas, although forums for debate did continue in Zimbabwe's two largest cities, Harare and Bulawayo.

On this trip I did not visit Chikafa or Basiyao, where Lazarus Zhuwao, my other co-researcher, lived. He had been ill with AIDS, off and on, for several years and died in 1997. He died from AIDS. The dramatic rise in AIDS characterized my years of valley research. When I first began working in the valley AIDS cases were very rare, but in Chikafa, for example, the head teacher and all the teachers had died or were very ill. At that time antiretrovirals were not available, and AIDS was an illness that could not be named. Lazarus' father did not name the disease either at his funeral.

When I visited the valley again in 2004 members of the Movement for Democratic Change were now regarded by local political leaders as traitors and collaborators with the external enemies of Zimbabwe—primarily meaning the United Kingdom, led by Tony Blair, with the United States government not far behind. Alternative sources of information to the government-owned and -run radio and television networks in the rural areas had disappeared. *The Daily News*, an alternative daily newspaper, had enjoyed widespread popularity before its printing presses were bombed; it then was denied a license to publish under new media laws. The other weekly newspapers did not circulate widely outside urban areas. There was unceasing government racial propaganda, which blamed whites for Zimbabwe's growing ills and the United States and the United Kingdom for economic problems through sanctions. Thus, the ruling party became moderately successful in displacing the national political issues of governmental dictatorship, corruption, and impoverishment with national sovereignty, anticolonization, and explicit racism against Zimbabwean white citizens. Nonetheless, the urban areas all voted for the opposition party, and rural areas, under severe coercion, voted for the ruling party.

In the world of neoliberalism Zimbabwe stands out for its effort to remain apart from globalization while pursuing regressive, race-based, and dictatorial policies hiding under the cloak of anticolonialism.[30] The initial policies of racial reconciliation disintegrated in the most recent series of elections.[31] In a return to the use of state violence the ruling party, ZANU–PF, claimed that it was simply continuing the liberation war (*chimurenga*) because of continued colonial efforts to resubjugate Zimbabwe. In a sharp reversal of international engagements, the ruling party returned to the tropes of colonialism and race combined with a "selective rendition of the liberation history deployed as an ideological policing agent in the public debate."[32] After 2000 ZANU–PF's focus had become fast-track land reform.

Although issues of land distribution and ownership had existed, and there had been sporadic efforts to address the continued colonial legacy of white-owned private commercial farmland and black-owned communal "tribal" lands, the government decided to break with this past by forcing virtually all white farm owners from their lands. I have concluded that the overwhelming purpose of the farm occupations was political in the sense that it was intended to prevent farm workers from exercising their right to vote, to block farm owners from supporting the Movement for Democratic Change, and to provide land to the party faithful (and whole farms to the most powerful).

This new land reform program has been called *fast-track*, because rather than Zimbabweans being provided planning and services before resettlement, they were urged to take the land with the promise of services to follow. Multiple processes determined who obtained the farm land: provincial differences, political differences, and rapid shifts in national directions. Much of these processes was hidden, and the outcomes reflected intense competition for the best and richest farms, especially those closest to major cities. And many of the best and largest farms were appropriated by senior government and military officials.

In more recent fieldwork on processes of water reform I met many black farmers who were successful on their own farms and did not want the burdens of large-scale farms. Other young male Zimbabweans joined the farm occupations just to see if there was something in it for them, but almost all left, either because they were chased by the "chefs" (the powerful) or no resources were provided for farming.

Before the farm occupations there had been approximately 450,000 farm workers on the large-scale commercial farms, plus approximately 334,000 children and other family members. Farm workers are always among the poorest paid and most exploited categories of any population. However, dispossessing them of work, schools, and homes in the name of the Third Chimurenga seems especially horrendous. Indeed, more people lost their homes and work through fast-track then gained them through resettlement on what had been commercial farms. This action can be partly explained by the notions that most farm workers supported the opposition party and/or weren't really Zimbabwean (meaning Shona, Zimbabwe's largest Indigenous group). This combination of stereotypes made farm workers especially vulnerable to violence and dispossession.

While destroying the agricultural sectors (which did need to be changed) President Mugabe and the ruling party claimed to be the unsuccessful victims of destructive policies of the United Kingdom, Tony Blair, globalization, and the United States. Zimbabwe's rulers take pride, if not delight, in resisting the trends of good governance, human rights, and a free media in order to promote their version of a revolution. The central argument used to defend the "revolution" has been the resistance to Western efforts to protect former white landowners and reestablish Zimbabwe as a colony of the United Kingdom. The result has been a set of devastating economic policies that have turned Zimbabwe from a relatively successful nation to one of overwhelming poverty (except for a few people). Indeed, the steep decline of all economic indicators has caught the world's attention. Examples are the reduction in life expectancy from 56 to 33 and one of the world's highest rates of inflation. (In October 2008 it was 231,000,000%; a newly printed 8-billion-dollar note was worth only $.10 shortly after having been issued.) The World Food Programme said that more than 5 million people needed food aid, and half the population was chronically malnourished. Hundreds of thousands Zimbabweans continue to seek work and refuge in neighboring states. In general, the economy is shrinking rapidly; this includes food production, export crop production, and industrial production—and scarcities of fundamental commodities are increasing, including food, fuel, and transport. In addition, mass emigration of citizens is occurring. Internationally, Zimbabwe's lines of credit have dried up; it must pay cash for most imports and indeed, owing to its credit unworthiness, pays a higher price for imports. Given the rate of inflation and decline in exports, the International Monetary Fund (IMF), in a gross understatement, has judged Zimbabwe's economic policies to be "unsound." Although the government has paid off some of its debts to the World Bank, it has been suspended from obtaining additional loans, which has only intensified the economic crisis. Although many social scientists viewed Zimbabwe's government with increasing criticism in the 1990s, they were hardly prepared for the turn in 2000.

The Mid-Zambezi Valley Rural Development Project (MZVRDP) and Its Successor, The Dande Irrigation Project (DIP), 2007

Owing to the growing political repression and the inability of the Zimbabwe government to repay its loans, large-scale "development" projects such as the Mid-Zambezi have ceased. Virtually all Western bilateral and multilateral donors have withdrawn from Zimbabwe except for humanitarian engagements. However, Chinese interest in Africa in general and in Zimbabwe in particular has been growing, but recent economic crises have limited Chinese involvement.

The Mid-Zambezi Project was stopped in 1995 with much of the work undone. Land delineation was never completed, and kin of resettled residents moved in behind the resettlers. Such resettlement, often sanctioned by local headmen, effectively defeated all efforts to achieve land-use planning and to end riverine cultivation. The areas not resettled were fundamentally left unaltered, thereby implicitly recognizing the failure of earlier efforts. As in other areas in the broader Zambezi Valley and Gokwe, large numbers of immigrants flocked into the area for pasture, cotton cultivation, and expanded economic opportunities.[33] The central government has been unable to control such flows, and systemic conflicts have arisen between longer-term residents and newer migrants. Perhaps, if sizeable areas of the large-scale commercial farms had been opened earlier for immigrants, it might have decreased pressure on fragile lands and soils, increased sustainable agriculture, addressed profound imbalances between white and black land ownership, and decreased conflicts in Zimbabwe's frontier areas. This action, however, was not taken, and so the legitimacy of fast-track land reform was accepted.

In a puzzling choice, the national government proposed, developed, and began implementing another large-scale development project, called the Dande Irrigation Project (DIP), on top of the MZVRDP. Planning for this new project began before the other was completed. The DIP is based on a high dam located on the escarpment above the valley; canals are to bring the water to the valley and to new double-cropped, irrigated perimeters, where people are currently living and farming. The DIP calls for a cropping shift away from maize, cotton, and vegetables to primarily tomatoes.

Even though I had discontinued my research on the MZVRDP to focus on the implementation of water law and water reforms, one of the watersheds that I focused on was the Manyame Catchment, which includes the Dande River and therefore the proposed project. In addition, a graduate student, Pinnie Sithole, at the University of Zimbabwe had focused, under my direction, his Master's thesis on local understandings of the project in the area of Chitsungo, which would be most affected.[34] Funding for the DIP was to be provided by the African Development Bank, the same funder as for the MZVRDP, with the contract for the dam and irrigation works awarded to a Chinese company. In the midst of much controversy construction started on the dam and its reservoir. As always, claims of sacred sites, disruption of graves, and lack of consultation with the ancestors dogged construction. Pinnie Sithole's interviews with local officials and project implementers reflected their supreme indifference to the consequences of the project for those already resettled and to any engagement with the local populations. Indeed, he found that local government personnel refused to discuss the project with local people for fear of creating opposition. And, typically, they blamed the local population for resisting new seed varieties and for consulting the custodians of the land, the *mhondoros*. However, the inability of the Zimbabwe government to meet its share of the costs has brought the DIP to a halt and effected the return of Chinese construction workers and engineers to China. The dam and the lake are unfinished, and the construction of irrigated perimeters was not begun.

The Dande Irrigation Project continued the same patterns of state-peasantry relations as previous projects. The government chose to control land issues in Zimbabwe's communal areas, paying, once again, no attention to local land tenure and local aspirations. Zimbabwe's communal areas have been all but ignored in comparison to fast-track land reform. It is fast-track that is currently reshaping Zimbabwe's landscape and agrarian relations.

After Fast-Track?

All land reform discussions and implementation in southern Africa take place in the shadow of Zimbabwe, including the highly contentious debates in Namibia and South Africa. The regional and international focus on Zimbabwe's land reform has produced fervent ideological debates but little empirical study even now. In any event, it will be quite difficult to separate the consequences of land reform from the more general decline of all dimensions of Zimbabwe's economy. And, as critics have noted, the decline in the economy is inextricably bound to the haphazard, violent, and chaotic means by which land reform was implemented. But there remain a small if shrinking number of defenders of President Mugabe's approach to Zimbabwe. In the words of two defenders of Zimbabwe's path, Sam Moyo and Paris Yeros, struggling to find a revolutionary path in this violence:

> If independence bequeathed a neo-colonial state in Zimbabwe, the late nineties saw a rebellion against neo-colonialism. There was an incipient radicalization of the state from 1997 onwards marked by its interventionist role in the economy, the suspension of structural adjustment, and the listing of 1,471 farms for expropriation. The basis of this radicalization is to be found in the economic, social, and, ultimately, political crisis of the late 1990s, a robust crisis which was organically driven by social forces within and without the ruling party. The extent and direction of this radicalisation was unpredictable at the time and remained subject to both internal and external contradictions in the form of a hostile and subversive reaction by imperialist forces, namely Western states, the International Financial Institutions (IFIs), and their domestic allies.[35]

They use the language of the old left while not considering the realities of who holds power and why in the Zimbabwean state. They argue for a unification of the proletariat, semiproletariat, and peasantry across the rural-urban divide in a context in which no political organizations are permitted to function outside the existing political party without repression and surveillance. They view what they term the *radicalised* state as the vehicle to accomplish this goal of unification while most scholars, including a host of socialist and leftist ones, have long ago dismissed any progressive and leftist realities or possibilities in the current president and his closest advisors. The idea that there is anything leftist in the current crises of Zimbabwe discredits the left.

Concluding Reflections

In the Zimbabwe of the new millennium there has been a return to the use of state violence in the name of national sovereignty and anticolonialism. The ruling party, ZANU–PF, claims that it is simply continuing the liberation war because of continued colonial efforts to resubjugate Zimbabwe (for which there is little or no evidence). In a sharp reversal of international engagements, the ruling party has returned to the tropes of colonialism and race. In place of more complex and historically rooted understandings, there has emerged a new, according to Terry Ranger, patriotic historiography.[36] Ruling party intellectuals are in control of virtually all media, including television, radio, and newspapers. With control over the major news sources they produce new historical interpretations privileging some voices while silencing others. Indeed, long-standing liberation figures are denied burial in the national cemetery if they did not completely side with fast-track land reform and other current elements of party policy and practice. The government-controlled media consistently put forward the ruling party perspective and attempt to create a reality that is at odds with the daily life of hardship and misery. The terms *terrorist* and *terrorism* are occasionally used against the opposition party. The term, however, that should be employed against the government is *state violence,* or *state-directed terror,* launched in the name of progressive causes and masking the appropriation of all resources and the enrichment of a few. Vast numbers of reports, publications, and testimonials describe the systematic use of torture and violence against real and potential political opponents, who are, for the most part, political activists seeking to advance democracy and human rights against a government based on the strategic use of violence. How the government used its power to coerce the implementation of the Mid-Zambezi project now pales in front of its current project, to keep the ruling party in power forever.

Notes

1. The research on the Mid-Zambezi Rural Development Project could not have been possible without the support of a Senior Research Fulbright Fellowship, a Wenner-Gren Foundation grant, a Social Sciences Research Council grant from their African Agriculture Project, Michigan State University, and the Centre for Applied Social Sciences of the University of Zimbabwe.

2. Zimbabwe is divided into provinces, districts, and wards. The Councilor is an elected official from the ward.

3. The interview was conducted on April 23, 1991, by Lazarus Zhuwao.

4. According to the project all land is divided between arables (fields), residentials (homesteads), and grazing areas. The project pegged these areas without discussion or approval by local populations and threatened to arrest those who cultivated outside the arable areas.

5. For a consideration of these issues see John Barrett, "Economic Issues in Trypanosomiasis Control: Case Studies from Southern Africa by John Barrett," Ph.D. dissertation, University of Reading, 1994, p. 31; Bill Derman, "The Unsettling of the Zambezi Valley: An Examination of the Mid-Zambezi Rural Development Project," Centre for Applied Social Sciences Working Paper, Sept. 1990; S. Metcalfe, "The Zimbabwe Communal Areas Management Programme for Indigenous Resources (CAMPFIRE)," *Natural Connections: Perspectives in Community Based Conservation*, David Western and R. Michael Wright, Eds. (Washington, D.C.: Island Press, 1994); "Livestock, Wildlife and the Forage Commons: Prospects for Rangelands Reform in a Semi-Arid Communal Area of Zimbabwe" (CASS Occasional Paper–NRM: University of Zimbabwe, 1995); Marshall Murphree, "Communities as Resource Management Institutions," International Institute for Environment and Development Gatekeeper Series, No. 36 (London: IIED, 1993); "Traditional and State Authority/Power in Zimbabwe" (CASS Occasional Paper Series–NRM: University of Zimbabwe, 1995); "Optimal Principles and Pragmatic Strategies: Creating an Enabling Politico-Legal Environment for Community Based National Resource Management (CBNRM)" (Harare: Centre for Applied Social Sciences, 1995); Marshall Murphree and David H. M. Cumming, "Savanna Land Use: Policy and Practice in Zimbabwe," in *The World's Savannas: Economic Driving Forces, Ecological Constraints and Policy Options for Sustainable Land Use* (London: Parthenon Press, 1993, 39–177); John Peterson "Campfire: A Zimbabwean Approach to Sustainable Development and Community Empowerment through Wildlife Utilization" (Zimbabwe: Centre for Applied Social Sciences, University of Zimbabwe, 1991).

6. The best-known work is that of David Lan, who explored the interaction of the ideology of the peasants of Dande (the local term for the eastern portion of the Zambezi Valley) with that of the guerrillas who lived among them during the war of liberation; see *Guns and Rain: Guerrillas and Spirit Mediums in Zimbabwe* (Berkeley and Los Angeles: University of California Press, 1985). Before the war one can cite the following anthropological studies of the Shona and Tonga: Elizabeth Colson, *Social Organization of the Gwembe Tonga* (Manchester: Manchester University Press, 1960); A. K. H. Weinrich, *The Tonga People on the Southern Shore of Kariba* (Gweru, Zimbabwe: Mambo Press, 1977); Marshall Murphree, *Christianity and the Shona* (London: Athlone Press, 1969);

and Thayer Scudder, *The Ecology of the Gwembe Tonga* (Manchester: Manchester University Press, 1962). More recent are the works of Michael Bourdillon: *The Shona Peoples: An Ethnography of the Contemporary Shona, with Special Reference to Their Religion* (revised ed.) (Gweru, Zimbabwe: Mambo Press, 1982) and "Guns and Rain: Taking Structural Analysis Too Far?" *Africa* 57:2 (1987, 263–74); Angela Cheater, *Idioms of Accumulation: Rural Development and Class Formation among Freeholders in Zimbabwe* (Gweru, Zimbabwe: Mambo Press, 1984); and Pamela Reynolds, *Dance Civet Cat: Child Labour in the Zambezi Valley* (London: Zed Books, 1991). The best-known anthropological studies are those of Thayer Scudder and Elizabeth Colson, *The Social Consequences of Resettlement* (Manchester: Manchester University Press, 1971), focusing on the Tonga displaced by Kariba Dam conducted on the Zambian side. Their research is summarized in Elizabeth Colson, *The Social Consequences of Resettlement* (Manchester: Manchester University Press, 1971); and Thayer Scudder and Elizabeth Colson, "Long-Term Research in Gwembe Valley, Zambia," in Robert V. Kemper and Anna Royce, Eds., *Chronicling Cultures: Long Term Field Research in Anthropology* (Walnut Creek, CA: AltaMira Press, 2002, 197–238).

7. There have been numerous efforts to address this question, including an ambitious resettlement program, the 1992 Land Acquisitions Act, which permits the national government to confiscate up to one-half of commercial farm land and give it to others without specifying how it should be done, and most recently a National Commission on Land Tenure, which is to address the questions of multiple tenurial systems within the nation. See Mandivamba Rukuni and Carl Eicher, Eds., *Zimbabwe's Agricultural Revolution* (Harare: University of Zimbabwe Press, 1994).

8. Blair Rutherford from McGill University is the only anthropologist that I know examining a large-scale commercial farm. See Blair Rutherford, "Traditions of Domesticity in 'Modern' Zimbabwean Politics: Race, Gender, and Class in the Government of Commercial Farm Workers in Hurungwe District," Ph.D. dissertation, McGill University, 1996. There is also the earlier valuable study by Rene Loewenson, *Modern Plantation Agriculture: Corporate Wealth and Labour Squalor* (London: Zed Books, 1992).

9. Government of Zimbabwe, *Report of the Commission of Inquiry into Appropriate Agricultural Land Tenure Systems*, under the Chairmanship of Prof. Mandivamba Rukuni, Vol. 2: Technical Reports (Harare, Zimbabwe: The Government Printer, 1994, 107).

10. Barrett, 1994, note 5, p. 31.

11. Ibid.

12. There is a large and important literature that reviews the land question in Zimbabwe. There are relatively good statistics to demonstrate that, overall, the government did not meet its own specified commitments to acquire land from commercial farmers to give to communal area farmers. The government has said that this is due to the lack of funds for the purchase of such land. This question has become moot since 1992, when Parliament passed the Land Acquisition Bill, whose intent is to acquire 6.9 million hectares from the large-scale commercial sector to add to the resettlement and state farm sectors. The government's initial efforts to acquire land have been met with a great deal of opposition and skepticism because of the lack of clear guidelines and data base for the GOZ to systematically acquire and productively redistribute land. For a much more detailed treatment of these issues see Sam Moyo, *The Land Question in Zimbabwe* (Zimbabwe: SAPES Books, 1995); Michael Bratton, "Land Redistribution," in Rukuni and Eicher, 1994, note 7; and Michael Roth, "Critique of Zimbabwe's 1992 Land Act," in Rukuni and Eicher, note 7.

13. The two primary project documents are the Food and Agriculture Organization of the United Nations, *Zimbabwe: Mid-Zambezi Valley Rural Development Project Preparation Report* (Main Text and Annexes), No. 119/85 AF-ZIM 10, Oct. 1985, and the African Development Fund, *Appraisal Report: Mid-Zambezi Valley Rural Development Project, Zimbabwe*, Agriculture and Rural Development Dept., July 1986. It has often been argued

by personnel of the Dept. of Rural and Urban Development that much of the fault lies in the documents that had not been properly prepared. The implication is that they were rushed through without a real project preparation document, which left DERUDE the unenviable task of implementing a project without sufficient design.

14. The FAO study sought to develop an overall plan for the valley, anticipating the successful eradication of the tsetse fly by the EEC aerial and ground spraying program. It was anticipated that much of the valley would be opened for livestock, and thus there would be a great need for such planning. The consultants did not appreciate the historical legacy of land-use planning in Zimbabwe that would lead to projects such as the MZVRDP.

15. There are a few examples of the management placed in the hands of the parastatal Agriculture and Rural Development Authority (ARDA). Indeed, DERUDE has been phased out, replaced by the District Development Fund at District Level and by ARDA at the national level.

16. There are four different types of resettlement schemes. In general they are voluntary, and Zimbabwean citizens apply to become eligible. Accelerated Type A means that the government provided no support (either logistical or monetary) for citizens having to move their residences or fields.

17. Jocelyn Alexander, "State, Peasantry, and Resettlement in Zimbabwe," *Review of African Political Economy* 21:61 (1994, 325–44); Bill Derman, "Changing Land Use in the Eastern Zimbabwe Valley: Socio-Economic Considerations," Report Prepared for WWF-Zimbabwe and the Centre for Applied Social Sciences, University of Zimbabwe, 1995; Michael Drinkwater, *The State and Agrarian Change in Zimbabwe's Communal Areas* (London: Macmillan, 1991); and A. H. J. Helmsing, N. D. Mutizwa-Mangiza, D. R. Gaspar, C. M. Brand, and K. H. Wekwete, *Limits to Decentralization in Zimbabwe: Essays on the Decentralization of Government and Planning in the 1980s* (Harare: Dept. of Urban and Rural Planning, University of Zimbabwe, 1991).

18. The origin and practice of conservation and centralization have been the subject of an important historical debate between Ian Phimister and William Beinart, "Soil Erosion, Conservationism, and Ideas about Development in Southern Africa," *Journal of Southern African Studies* 11:2 (1984, 52–83). Phimister leans toward viewing the emphasis on conservation as one more way by which the colonialists attempted to control and dispossess Africans. Beinart suggested that conservation was indeed important in its own right and couldn't just be reduced to economic interest, although economic interests were important.

19. Government planners relied on the results of the controversial scientific findings of agricultural research during the 1930s and 1940s, which blamed only African cultivators for land degradation without examining the consequences of land alienation and the policies of permanent cultivation using hybrid maize promoted by the Dept. of Agriculture.

20. The history of this process forms part of the larger study of the MZVRDP. For partial accounts see Derman 1990, note 5; and Bill Derman, "Recreating Common Property Management: Government Projects and Land Use Policy in the Mid-Zambezi Valley, Zimbabwe," CASS Occasional Paper, NRM 1993 (University of Zimbabwe).

21. This Ward Councilor was sent a severe reprimand by Derude and the District Administrator for his district (letter of the RO to the District Administrator of Guruve District, April 19, 1990.)

22. See note 21.

23. There are areas in the project where riverine cultivation is not possible, because there are not sufficient water resources during the dry season or the soils are too sandy. These areas tend to be away from the base of the escarpment and the major rivers. A relatively low percentage of the population is located in these areas.

24. These quotes are from an interview conducted by Lazarus Zhuwao and Marja Spierenburg. Zhuwao has worked with me since 1990. Marja Spierenburg is a Dutch anthropologist who has written an excellent paper on the role of Chidyamauyu: Marja Spierenburg, "The Role of the Mhondoro Cult in the Struggle for Control Over Land in Dande (Northern Zimbabwe): Social Commentaries and the Influence of Adherents," Centre for Applied Social Sciences Occasional Paper–NRM Series (Harare 1995).

25. This issue is explored in greater detail in Bill Derman and James Murombedzi, "Democracy, Development, and Human Rights in Zimbabwe: A Contradictory Terrain," *African Rural and Urban Studies* 1:2 (1994, 119–44).

26. A second major emphasis of contemporary development practice and research has been the Communal Areas Management Program for Indigenous Resources, better known by its acronym CAMPFIRE. This program has become justly renowned for its efforts to redress and redirect the flow of wildlife resources from national government and tourist interests to local communities that live with wildlife. For an account of the contrasts between CAMPFIRE and other valley projects, see Derman 1995, note 17.

27. The Zimbabwe Human Rights NGO Forum (also known as the Human Rights Forum) has been in existence since January 1998. Nongovernmental organizations working in the field of human rights came together to provide legal and psychosocial assistance to the victims of the Food Riots of January 1998 and since then documents and supports victims of violence. Their web page, www.hrforumzim.com/, contains an enormous amount of information on violence and torture in Zimbabwe. There are currently 16 organizations that are members of this coalition.

28. There has been a large and expanding literature on the ongoing crises in Zimbabwe. I and a colleague have written two pieces dealing with the violence and the land question: Bill Derman and Anne Hellum, "Land, Identity and Violence in Zimbabwe," in *Citizenship, Identity, and Conflicts over Land and Water in Contemporary Africa,* Rie Odgaard and Espen Sjaastad, Eds. (London, Durban, and East Lansing: James Currey, University of Kwazulu Press and Michigan State University Press, 2007, 161–86); Bill Derman and Anne Hellum, "Land Reform and Human Rights in Contemporary Zimbabwe: Balancing Individual and Social Justice through an Integrated Human Rights Framework," in *World Development* 32:10 (2004, 1785–1805). For a defense of the land reform see Sam Moyo, who tries to make the case that something revolutionary will come from this process: S. Moyo and P. Yeros, "Land Occupations and Land Reform in Zimbabwe: Toward the National Democratic Revolution," in S. Moyo and P. Yeros, Eds., *Reclaiming the Land: The Resurgence of Rural Movements in Africa, Asia, and Latin America* (London: Zed Press, 2005). For a balanced, accurate assessment of the crisis see Brian Raftopoulos, "The Crisis in Zimbabwe, 1998–2008," in Brian Raftopolous and Alois Mlambo, Eds., *Becoming Zimbabwe: A History from the Pre-Colonial Period to 2008* (Capetown: Jacana and Weaver, 2009, 201–32). There have been a number of first-hand accounts of the farm invasions on white-owned farms. The best is Catherine Buckle, *Beyond Tears: Zimbabwe's Tragedy* (Johannesburg: Jonathan Ball, 2003). A number of websites have tracked the vast human rights violations for the past decade. The best one is Zimbabwe Human Rights NGO Forum, www.hrforumzim.com/, accessed 5/20/2010, which has a complete archive and up-to-date information.

29. Heather Holtzclaw was a graduate student at Michigan State University whose original research on farm workers had been rendered impossible by the farm occupations, so she turned her attention to the invasions. Her Ph.D. thesis is entitled "The Third Chimurenga? Political Violence and Survival in Zimbabwe's Commercial Farming Communities,"(East Lansing, Michigan State University, 2004).

30. Methuseli Moyo, "Ahead of the Game," in *Focus on Africa,* January–March 2008, 10–12; George Shire, "An Unending Explosion," *Focus on Africa,* January–March 2008, 12–13.

Baffour Ankomah, editor of *The New African Magazine*, has been a very vocal proponent of Zimbabwe's president. See his interview in May 2007 and the brief selection below.

31. Eric Worby, "Maps, Names, and Ethnic Games: The Epistemology and Iconography of Colonial Power in Northwestern Zimbabwe," *Journal of Southern African Studies* 20:3 (1994, 371–92), and "What Does Agrarian Wage-Labour Signify? Cotton, Commoditisation, and Social Form in Gokwe, Zimbabwe," *Journal of Peasant Studies* 23:1 (1995, 1–29).

32. Eric Worby, note 30; Vupenyu Dzingirai, "'CAMPFIRE Is Not for Ndebele Migrants': The Impact of Excluding Outsiders from CAMPFIRE in the Zambezi Valley, Zimbabwe," *Journal of Southern African Studies* 29:2 (2003, 445–59); Pius S. Nyambara, "Immigrants, 'Traditional' Leaders, and the Rhodesian State: The Power of 'Communal' Land Tenure and the Politics of Land Acquisition in Gokwe, Zimbabwe, 1963–1979," in *Journal of Southern African Studies* 27:4 (2001, 771–91).

33. Brian Raftopolous, "Nation, Race, and History," in *Zimbabwean Politics in Zimbabwe: Injustice and Political Reconciliation*, Brian Raftopoulos and Tyrone Savage, Eds. (Harare: Weaver Press, 2005, 160).

34. Pinimidzai Sithole, "Planning and Practice at the Crossroads: A Case of the Dande Irrigation Project in the Zambezi Valley, Zimbabwe," dissertation submitted in partial fulfillment of the requirements of the Master of Sociology and Social Anthropology Degree to the Department of Sociology, University of Zimbabwe, 2004.

35. S. Moyo and P. Yeros, "Land Occupations and Land Reform in Zimbabwe: Towards the National Democratic Revolution," in S. Moyo and P. Yeros, Eds., *Reclaiming the Land: The Resurgence of Rural Movements in Africa, Asia, and Latin America* (London: Zed Press, 2007, 104).

36. Terence Ranger, "Nationalist Historiography, Patriotic History, and the History of the Nation: The Struggle over the Past in Zimbabwe," *Journal of Southern African Studies*, 30:2 (2004, 215–34).

CHAPTER 6

The Master Thief: Gold Mining and Mercury Contamination in the Amazon

Leslie E. Sponsel[1]

SECTION I: The End of the Millennium

In 1987 in the town of Boa Vista in northern Brazil, José Altino Machado, a founder and leader of a union of gold miners in the Amazon, swallowed some mercury in front of television cameras to demonstrate its harmlessness. He stated:

> the mercury we employ is inert: it is the same as that in teeth, the same that old people used to cure constipation; it goes in and goes out of the organism. There is no relation with the mercury in Japan (Minamata). . . . It does not contaminate. Even "garimpeiros" [goldminers] who inhale mercury vapours, they are not poisoned. . . . We will measure mercury levels in the waterways. I challenge someone to show me a person, just one person, contaminated by mercury in the Amazon. . . . The point is, as they (ecologists and government) cannot do anything against a citizen pursuing a better way of living, they make up this story of river pollution and shut down all "garimpos." These ecologist "boys" do not realize they are being used as political instruments.[2]

In 1991 an internationally recognized leader for the human rights of the Yanomami and winner of the Global 500 Prize of the United Nations Environmental Program, Davi Kopenawa Yanomami, spoke to the UN:

> My Yanomami people now, they see what is happening to our community, and they see what is happening to our relatives in other communities. They are terrified by the miners, and by the [polluted] rivers. The miners invaded our reserve and came to our communities feigning friendship; they lied to us, they tricked us Indians, and we were taken in. Then their numbers grew; many more arrived, and they began bringing in machinery that polluted the river. The pollution killed the fish and the shrimp, everything that lived in our rivers.[3]

These are just two of the many voices in a complex and ugly arena of desperate conflict. Other miners and indigenes as well as anthropologists, politicians, officials, missionaries, environmentalists, and advocates of human rights also offer critical perspectives.[4]

This chapter focuses on one aspect of this conflict—the human and environmental impact of the use of mercury for mining gold by the informal mining sector. The ancient Roman god Mercury was considered to be a master thief, among other things, and so is the metal named after him. In the Amazon today, mercury not only helps steal gold, but it also steals the health of human populations and ecosystems and will continue to do so far into the future.

Gold Rush

For over 6,000 years gold has been one source of wealth, prestige, and power. Greed for gold was a pivotal concern in the discovery, exploration, and colonization of the New World by European kingdoms. In the process, entire peoples, societies, and environments were degraded and destroyed. This holocaust continues today, and the Amazon is one of its last frontiers.[5]

Brazil has experienced gold rushes since the 17th century, and in the mid-18th century it was the world's biggest producer of gold. However, since 1980 the Amazon has been the stage for the largest gold rush ever. During the 1980s gold production in the Brazilian Amazon exceeded U.S. $2 billion per year. Serra Pelada (Stripped Mountain), a huge, deep, open-pit mine worked by up to 100,000 miners, is likely the richest single gold discovery of this century. Since 1980 this mine has produced over half a billion dollars, with an average of a ton of gold per month. This mine is a symbol of hope for poor miners throughout the Amazon Basin who would like to become instant millionaires, and it has even stimulated some confidence in Brazil's ability to repay its enormous international debt.[6] Amazonian gold is not, however, confined by Brazilian borders. By the late 1980s some 30,000 people were prospecting and mining in southern Venezuela. An estimated 4.5 million people are involved directly or indirectly in gold mining in the Amazonian region, working some 2,000 mining sites scattered over 250,000 sq km. Major mining centers include the Gurupí (Maranahao), Serra Pelada (Pará), Cumaru (Pará), Mato Grosso, Tapajós (Pará/Amazonas), River Madeira (Rondonia), and Roraima.[7] Much of this mining activity occurs illegally in the traditional homelands and protected territories of indigenous peoples.

The timing of this modern gold rush reflects not so much new discoveries as a sharp increase in the price of gold. During the 1970s the price of an ounce of gold rose steadily from U.S. $35 to around U.S. $300. During the 1980s the price ranged from U.S. $300 to U.S. $500, although it briefly soared to U.S. $850 in January 1980. In the 1990s the price remained substantially higher than in the 1970s.[8] An increase in production followed: between 1980 and 1992 world gold production rose by 78%. In Brazil analysts estimate that about 100 tons per year of gold were produced during the 1980s; however, this is only a rough estimate, because the activity is illegal, and most of the gold is sold in the black market to avoid taxes.[9] Other factors influenced the timing of the gold rush. For example, a severe drought struck northeastern Brazil beginning in 1979, spurring a massive migration to the Amazon Basin in search of new lands and gold.[10]

Many miners are poor, landless, and suffering from rampant inflation. Many pursue mining as a seasonal alternative when their farming or ranching activities allow. Informal mining has probably had a greater impact on the economy than formal mining. Some three to four million people are indirectly involved in mining as family members, storekeepers, boat operators, airplane pilots, mechanics, carpenters, traders, cooks, prostitutes, drug dealers, and so on.[11]

The invasion of the Amazon during the 1970s and 1980s by more than a million gold miners was orchestrated, not spontaneous. Gold mining is part of a largely hidden agenda of nation-states and the militaries, a combined geopolitical and economic development strategy to conquer, control, integrate, and exploit the Amazon.[12] This agenda is a continuation of European colonization and industrialization, but with some new components. One common denominator is the exploitation of minerals—the "geological imperative"—which Davis and Mathews define as a "search for mineral and petroleum resources . . . a unique historical phenomenon related to the specific distribution of wealth and power which presently exists in the world. The chief elements in these phenomena are large multinational mineral and energy corporations, and the powerful governments and international lending and development institutions on which they depend. Their *raison d'être* is profit-maximization and private economic gain."[13] By the 1970s the geological imperative led the military government of Brazil, in collaboration with the U.S. Geological Survey and supported by USAID, to initiate a series of development projects, including a huge aerial survey to detect and map major mineral deposits in the Amazon (Project Radam). Project Radam revealed that the Amazon had one of the most diverse and richest mineral profiles on the planet.[14]

Northern Trench Project (Calha Norte), a secret military master plan begun around 1986, developed infrastructure to facilitate mining, including roads, airstrips, military bases, hydroelectric dams, and agricultural colonization schemes. A main goal was to "Brazilianize" this zone of the Amazon to help the military control the border security, including combating drug traffic and guerrilla incursions from neighboring countries. According to anthropologist Linda Rabben "the Calha Norte program seems ineffective at achieving its stated objectives but all too efficient at facilitating devastation of the environment and destruction of the Indians."[15] A parallel but short-lived project was pursued in Venezuela.

These infrastructural developments provided the springboard for the seemingly spontaneous invasion of "illegal" small-scale miners throughout the Brazilian Amazon and into Yanomami territory. Meanwhile, FUNAI (the Brazilian National Indian Foundation, the agency in charge of protecting and assisting the indigenous population of Brazil), was administering mineral leases on indigenous lands. In some cases official announcements by the government publicized the existence of gold in the Amazon.[16] The government's agenda was candidly exposed in March 1975 by General Fernando Ramos Pereira, then governor of the northern province of Roraima: "I am of the opinion that an area as rich as this—with gold, diamonds, and uranium—cannot afford the luxury of conserving a half a dozen Indian tribes who are holding back the development of Brazil."[17] This statement proved prophetic for many indigenous societies.[18]

Mining and Mercury Contamination

The Amazon region contains some of the most ancient geological formations on the planet, its bedrock dating back some 2.8 billion years. Gold occurs in two basic types of deposits. Lode deposits are concentrations of gold in solid rock, usually as veins. Placer deposits occur in sand, gravel, and other sediments associated with streams and rivers. They contain particles of gold eroded from a lode.

Lode deposits are mined by tunneling or sinking a shaft, often a major operation requiring the organization and resources of a mining company. In contrast, placer deposits can be worked by screening or panning sediments with water along a stream or river. This method accounts for only about 17% of the gold production.[19] About 83% is produced through using heavy equipment for hydraulic techniques. High-pressure hoses wash away the sediment, which is channeled into troughs or sluices. These are riffled to catch the heavy particles of gold. River beds may also be dredged or vacuumed with huge pumps from floating rafts. Prospectors often follow placer deposits upstream to the lode.[20]

Gold mining causes localized deforestation, biodiversity reduction, game depletion and displacement, mercury and other pollution, river and stream bank destruction, siltation, and the degradation of fisheries. Enormous amounts of waste result because, on average, about 9 *tons* of waste are left for every *ounce* of gold extracted. Placer mining has a disproportionately large impact on aquatic ecosystems. About 2 cubic meters of sediments enter water courses per gram of gold extracted by miners. Mining wastes can silt water courses, reduce sunlight penetration and thereby diminish photosynthesis and productivity of aquatic plants, clog the gills of fish, and produce other negative consequences. Water may become undrinkable for tens of kilometers downstream. Other metals associated with gold, plus chemicals used in the processing, may pollute soils and water bodies for decades or even centuries.[21] Human waste in water courses is yet another pollution problem.

Although cattle ranching, pioneering agriculture, logging, roads, and hydroelectric dams are the main causes of deforestation in the Amazon, mining also contributes in at least two ways. Localized deforestation degrades the soil and drainage, inhibiting forest regeneration, and mining profits may be invested in economic schemes such as cattle ranching, which involve deforestation far from mining sites.[22]

One of the most pernicious and longest lasting consequences of gold mining is contamination with mercury, a highly toxic metal, yet until the recently relatively little scientific research had been conducted into its consequences on human health and ecosystems. Although little is known about the dynamics of mercury contamination in tropical compared to temperate ecosystems, the movement of mercury through the environment most certainly reflects the basic laws of ecology—namely, that everything is interconnected, is interdependent, and must go somewhere.[23]

Today, worldwide, about 400–500 tons of mercury are released into the environment every year by small-scale gold miners. These miners introduce about 90–120 tons per year of mercury into the Brazilian Amazon alone.[24] This is a substantial portion of the global anthropogenic load (releases of mercury from all sources, not just gold mining)—estimated to range around 1,000–6,000 tons per year of mercury.[25]

Liquid, elemental, or metallic mercury (Hg) is used to amalgamate (alloy or agglutinate) with smaller gold particles (Au_2Hg, Au_3Hg, and Au_4Hg) so that they will be heavier and more likely to be trapped in the riffles of sluices. The liquid mercury is poured over crushed rock or sediments. Then the amalgam of mercury and gold is separated from remaining waste by hand. Cloth at the bottom, often a shirt, is also used to collect the amalgam. Some of this mercury is washed away with the water into streams and rivers, where it may settle in the sediments. Next, the amalgam is heated with a blowtorch to vaporize the mercury as a white gas, leaving the gold. The mercury vapors go into the local atmosphere and with rainfall return to the surrounding vegetation, soils, and waters, the amount depending on the level of dust particles and humidity. About 1.32 kg of metallic mercury is used to produce 1 kg of gold, with 0.72 kg lost to the atmosphere as vapor and 0.60 kg (almost half) lost directly to the stream or river as metallic mercury.[26] Later, in shops where it is sold, the gold is again subjected to heating to remove the remaining mercury. Inside shops and within 100 m around them, high levels of mercury contamination occur—shop owners may show higher levels of metallic mercury in their hair than even the miners.[27]

The metallic or inorganic mercury from gold mining is eventually deposited in the soil and sediments of water courses. Indeed, puddles of mercury are common on soils and rock surfaces at the shores of mining areas.[28] Metallic mercury (Hg) becomes organic, or methylated (CH_3Hg+), by microorganisms, in fish guts, and through other biological routes. Demethylation (when methylmercury is transformed into metallic mercury and methane by microorganisms) also occurs, but apparently at a slower rate than methylation.[29]

The waters of the Amazon differ in their chemistry; however, they are rich in such metals as iron and manganese, which stimulate methylation of inorganic mercury, as do the high humic acids and overall acidity of black waters in particular. This type of water may be especially liable to high levels of mercury contamination. Curiously, the Tapajós River changed from clear to white water because of extensive siltation from mining upstream. This change in water types would in turn profoundly alter the biological and cultural ecology of the area.

Mercury enters the food chain in various ways: from water through respiration, by absorption of water from the body surface, and by ingestion of food such as through bottom-feeding fish. The mercury is increasingly concentrated at higher levels of the food chain (biomagnification). In the Amazon River piscivorous (fish-eating) animals include such birds as heron and kingfishers as well as caiman (alligator), river turtles, freshwater dolphins, river otters, and even some species of wild cats. Several species are already endangered. Mercury may also cause reproductive failure in animals. Huge fish kills have already been reported in the waters of Pará and Mato Grosso in 1985–86, probably as a result of mercury poisoning. Thus, mercury contamination must be added to the growing number of threats to the rich biodiversity in the Amazon. This region has the highest diversity of freshwater fish in the world, with an estimated 2,500–3,000 species.[30]

Inorganic mercury can attach to particles of sediments in water courses and be transported by currents over vast distances. Likewise, fish migrations can extend over hundreds or even thousands of kilometers. In such ways, mercury contamination can be spread surprisingly far beyond the original point of pollution.[31]

The Tapajós River basin is the oldest and most productive gold mining region in the Brazilian Amazon, and it is highly contaminated. Studies have shown fish to contain up to 3.82 ppm of mercury, and most exceed the allowable limit of 0.5 ppm for Brazil.[32] A longitudinal study of hair samples from local fishing villages revealed miners with mercury levels up to 31.8 ppm. Higher levels of metallic mercury contamination have been found in gold shop workers, and higher levels of methylmercury contamination in riverine fishers than in miners.[33]

The Tucuruí reservoir in Pará, Brazil, is 250 km downstream along the Tocantins River from Serra Pelada and other mining sites. Mercury emissions from Serra Pelada have been estimated at 590 tons between 1980 and 1986. Studies have shown the Tucuruí reservoir, fish, and hair samples from local residents to be highly contaminated. Fish from the reservoir are sold in towns, including in the delta of the Amazon, 300 km away.[34] In the contaminated Madeira River area, fish 180 km downstream from the mining show mercury levels above the safety limit.[35]

Fish is the cheapest form of high-quality protein and also the only regular source of it for millions of poor people in villages, towns, and cities along the rivers of the Amazon. Fish are also an extremely important part of the cultural ecology of many indigenous and peasant societies. Contamination of fisheries jeopardizes their income, nutrition, and health. For instance, the harvest value of the piramutaba catfish (*Brachyplatysoma vaillantii*), once the most important species of fish exported from the Amazon, declined from U.S. $13 million to U.S. $3 million annually because of depletion.[36]

Metallic mercury contamination in the human body can occur in many ways: inhalation of vapors; absorption through the skin while handling slurries of mercury and gold; ingestion with subsequent absorption in the intestinal tract when dust that is carrying mercury lands on the hands, food, or eating utensils; and so on. The principal indirect path is the regular consumption of contaminated foods, most commonly fish containing methylmercury from polluted waters. Obviously gold miners and buyers are likely to suffer direct contamination with metallic mercury, while the people in river villages and towns who depend on fish suffer indirect contamination with the much more dangerous form methylmercury.

Mercury poisoning produces a different combination of symptoms depending on whether metallic (inorganic, elemental) mercury or methylmercury is the cause and whether the poisoning is acute or chronic. There are also differences depending on age class—fetus, children, or adults—which in turn reflect differences in body size, nutritional needs, absorption rates, and physiological vulnerability. Symptoms develop gradually, and early on they may be hard to distinguish from other causes, such as malaria. By the time the poisoning is noticeable, irreversible damage has already occurred. Among the many symptoms of chronic poisoning by methylmercury are skin irritations, low fever, headaches, nausea, diarrhea, fatigue, insomnia and irritability, marked decline in sensory acuity (vision, hearing, smell, touch), and eventually blindness, loss of ability to speak properly, memory loss, premature senility, manic depression, kidney problems, crippling and severe tremors, brain damage, and death.

Pregnant women may be spared from poisoning, because the methylmercury rapidly crosses the placenta to accumulate in the fetus. Thus mercury concentrations can be higher in the fetus than in the mother, who may even appear normal. Still births, spontaneous abortions, gross birth defects, paralysis, physical impairment, and mental retardation are among the abnormalities that result from mercury poisoning of the fetus.[37] A child weighing 20 kg need eat regularly only 10 to 20 g of a contaminated carnivorous fish to develop mercury poisoning.[38]

The first longitudinal clinical study of the health hazards of mercury in the Amazon was based on monitoring, for five years (1986–91), 55 patients with symptoms of mercury poisoning from the Tapajós, Pará/Amazonas, region of Brazil. Of these 33 had direct occupational exposure to mercury at mines and in gold shops, with a mean of 13.1 years (range 2–44). For gold shop workers and miners, respectively, mean blood and urine levels of mercury were 5.1 and 61.0 ppm, and 2.2 and 35.4 ppm. The higher level for shop workers may reflect the fact that they do more burning of mercury than miners do, and in an enclosed area with variable ventilation. Furthermore, even urbanites with no direct exposure to the gold industry also showed elevated levels of mercury: a resident living above a gold shop had a blood level of 5.6 ppm. Normal levels of mercury should not exceed 1.5 ppm in the blood and 15.0 ppm in the urine for unexposed patients. Thus, based on the means the subjects in this study showed abnormal mercury levels elevated by a factor of 1.5–3.4 or more in the blood and 2.7–4.0 in the urine. But some individuals had much higher levels. Symptoms included dizziness, headache, palpitations, tremor, numbness, insomnia, dyspnea (difficult breathing), nervousness, poor vision, diminished appetite, forgetfulness, weakness, hair loss, cramps, chest pain, abdominal pain, fatigue, pruritus (itching), impotence, weight loss, and edema.[39]

Such elevated levels and symptoms, present even in persons not directly involved in the gold industry, are serious enough. However, extensive medical studies have not been made on people involved in or impacted by gold mining in the Amazon, and the symptoms of mercury poisoning are readily confused with other diseases. As a result, ailments and death caused by mercury contamination may be underestimated.[40]

Responses: Indigenes

The varied responses of indigenous societies to gold mining fall into two broad categories depending on whether the society has had sustained experience with the national society. Societies such as the Yanomami, who have had very little previous contact, are extremely vulnerable and may be devastated. Those such as the Mundurucú, who have had substantial previous contact, are more adaptable and may themselves engage in mining to some degree. However, in either case, mining has had many serious negative consequences.[41]

Yanomami   The Yanomami have been an independent population for around 2,000 years, according to evidence from genetics and linguistics. Until recently they were one of the more isolated and traditional indigenous societies remaining in the Amazon and had an adaptive and sustainable society. Then in the early 1970s a portion of the Northern Perimeter Highway (Perimetral Norte) penetrated nearly 225 k into the southern portion of their ancestral territory. As predicted, road construction precipitated the spread of epidemic diseases and a population crash in contacted villages. But even worse was the illegal invasion of 40,000–100,000 gold miners in the 1980s, which peaked in 1987. The situation in Yanomami territory in Venezuela has been deteriorating rapidly as well.[42]

The Yanomami did not have sustained contact experience and had not developed immunological resistance against many western diseases, which quickly become devastating epidemics. Miners have inadvertently introduced new diseases such as tuberculosis and significantly increased preexisting diseases such as malaria and onchocerciasis (African river blindness). Through prostitution the miners have introduced sexually transmitted diseases and, possibly, purposefully introduced AIDS to the Yanomami. Studies of hair samples for mercury contamination have revealed increased levels among Yanomami in gold mining areas, from 0.3–1.4 ppm before the mining invasion[43] to 1.4–8.14 ppm in 1990.[44]

In Brazil from 1988–95 some 2,280 Yanomami died, about a quarter of the population, as a direct result of the invasion of miners, leaving somewhere between 9,000 and 10,000.[45] In Venezuela, government census data indicate 2,955 Yanomami (including Sanema) deaths, a decline from 12,082 in 1982 to 9,127 in 1992 (24.5%).[46] Illness and death on such a massive scale severely disrupts economy, society, psychology, and religion. The Yanomami are increasingly an endangered people threatened with biological and cultural extinction.[47]

Beyond the indirect violence of disease, the miners have given or traded guns to Yanomami in order to aggravate conflicts between villagers and villages. Miners have also attacked the Yanomami. The most notorious incident is the 1994 Hashimu massacre, in which at least 12 Yanomami were brutally killed and mutilated. Although the murderers have been identified, they have never been brought to justice.[48] Surprisingly, the Yanomami have been relatively restrained in their violence against the miners.

For the first time Yanomami are experiencing poverty, inequality, theft, alcoholism, and prostitution. They sorely need outside help at the national and international levels. A few human rights advocacy organizations, such as CCPY (Commission for the Creation of the Yanomami Park, now Pro-Yanomami Commission), have been providing some of the needed help, but they are severely constrained by limited personnel and resources as well as government obstacles.

In short, multiple factors that interact in synergy are attacking Yanomami life, rendering them an endangered people. In 1992 the Brazilian government demarcated the Yanomami territory; however, this legal and physical process has not been effectively enforced.[49] The Brazilian and Venezuelan governments not only have failed to protect the human rights of the Yanomami, including the provision of adequate health care, but also have violated their basic human rights. They have allowed, and in some ways even facilitated, the entrance of miners into the territory of the Yanomami nation. This is a clear case of ethnocide, genocide, and ecocide.[50]

There is nothing inevitable about the degradation and destruction of indigenes and ecosystems through contact with "civilization" and "economic development." It is a moral choice made by policy makers in government, bank, and corporate offices in Brazil, the United States, and other countries, as well as a result of public apathy.[51]

Mundurucú In sharp contrast to the Yanomami, the Mundurucú, peoples of the savanna and forest of the upper Tapajós River in Brazil, have long been involved in small-scale extraction of resources for trade, initially tapping natural rubber trees for the latex, and in recent decades gold mining. Tapping and later mining allowed the Mundurucú to obtain some of the western things they value, including tools and medicines. Until recently they retained their traditional, reciprocal exchange system. With the development of rubber tapping in the 19th century the Mundurucú simply added a barter-credit system to their new patron-client relationship with traders and missionaries. However, gold mining and money have been not simply additive, but transformative too. The very nature of social relations as well as their economy has changed profoundly. Even food and time have become monetized.

The mining started around 1959, when gold was discovered in and near the Mundurucú reservation. Many Mundurucú moved to the upper Tapajós River and the Cururú River to small, temporary camps for mining for several weeks or months each year. Thus, mining did not completely replace traditional subsistence and economic activities like hunting and swidden farming. The miners usually pan alone or in pairs scattered along widely separated streams, and although they may dig up stream beds, they do not use hydraulic hoses and other machinery. They do use mercury to amalgamate the gold particles, but they do not have the typical miners' attitude of quickly getting in, striking it rich, and getting out. Moreover, other sources of cash are also exploited, including rubber tapping and wage labor.[52] It seems likely that these factors combine to reduce the environmental impact of Mundurucú mining.

Amarakaeri   Gold mining first came to the Madre de Dios area of southeastern Peru in the 1930s and again since the 1970s. The Amarakaeri have integrated gold mining into their economy while maintaining their sustainable subsistence and other aspects of their cultural identity. Their small-scale mining of placer deposits focuses on sandy beaches exposed in the dry season; the people move inland during the wet season. They use a large metal sieve mounted on a sloping wooden board. Water is supplied by hand-carried buckets and in some cases by pumps. They also use mercury. Unlike other miners in the area, the Amarakaeri have a sustainable subsistence economy, maintain legal right to their ancestral land, use gold mining as a complementary component of their economy, and do not attempt to maximize their profits.[53]

Kayapo   The Kayapo of Brazil, with their Cumaru mine, is one of the few examples of an indigenous society that has maintained control of the mineral wealth in its territory and benefits from it, although not without serious costs. In 1980 some 10,000 gold miners invaded the Gorotire Kayapo reserve. The Kayapo asked for government intervention and negotiated a 10% royalty on mine production. Initially, they invested their earnings in demarcating their lands. They also developed a video project to archive their ceremonies and other aspects of their culture. However, this success story is tempered by some tragic consequences. For instance, a survey of Kayapo children in 1988 revealed a mean level of mercury in their blood of 4.74 ppm, whereas 2 ppm is an acceptable upper limit. Miners working upstream at Cumaru have 4.97 ppm in their blood.[54]

Ye'kuana   In the Upper Orinoco River region of the Amazon of southern Venezuela, the Ye'kuana have exercised the fundamental human right to self-determination by demarcating their ancestral territorial boundaries and then mapping these with a Global Positioning System receiver in a small airplane. They are also documenting their history of settlement, land, and resource use to gain legal title from the government and secure their territory before the gold miners invading Yanomami lands move further north into Ye'kuana territory. This is an extremely promising model in applied cultural ecology that could be developed and implemented by other indigenous groups.[55]

Response: Miners

The response of the miners to controversy over their illegal invasion of indigenous territory, mercury contamination, and other problems has been mixed. They have organized into unions and become a significant force in provincial elections and politics. Miners are sometimes represented as frontier heroes, as in the giant concrete statue of a gold miner erected in Boa Vista. For the most part, however, the miners have tended to ignore, deny, or minimize the human and environmental problems they create, a stance reinforced by government action or lack of action. Miners have rarely been held accountable for criminal actions, and there has been little effort to educate them about the human and environmental dimensions of their gold mining in the Amazon.[56]

   If the miners were willing to accept lower profits, they could mine without mercury; most recognize this possibility but reject it.[57] Alternatively, relatively simple and inexpensive measures can minimize mercury exposure and environmental pollution.[58] Naturally, it is easier to clean up mining sites where mercury contamination is concentrated than to clean up sediments and water where it is widely dispersed. Several remedial measures have been proposed, including natural and absorbent coverings.[59] But the logistics, the labor, the amounts of material required, the expense, miner apathy, ecological impact, and the possibility of introducing additional hazards render these measures problematic.[60]

There are no federal laws to regulate the importation, sale, and use of mercury in Brazil, and miners can readily purchase it.[61] Most of the mercury now comes from the Netherlands, Germany, and England.[62] In any case, a ban on mercury could be difficult to enforce and could simply make its use clandestine and spur smuggling and black market sales.[63] Ironically, the well-being of the gold miners themselves has been neglected in this crisis, even though their often-illegal activity precipitated it. They face an alien environment, disease, natural hazards, and violence from other miners and also possibly from indigenes. Miners have inadequate or no health care,[64] and sanitation is poor. They are a hundred times more likely to get malaria than other workers in the Amazon because mining creates ponds that provide breeding grounds for mosquitoes.[65] Federal and provincial authorities do not enforce the laws in this frontier region. Also, most of the miners are not getting rich; they are often exploited by those who finance, equip, and supply them. Conditions of semislavery, including child labor, exist in some mining camps.[66]

Increased attention to the needs, problems, interests, and rights of the miners could improve the situation for all parties. For example, if both the health and the health care of the miners were better, this would reduce the health problems for peoples with whom the miners interact, like the Yanomami.[67]

Response: Government

On at least one occasion the federal government of Brazil publicly acknowledged the potential health and environmental hazards of mining with mercury.[68] However, federal and provincial governments have tended to ignore, deny, or minimize the problems. When the government has taken action, usually as a result of international pressure, it has been completely inadequate. For example, in 1990, President Fernando Collar de Mello of Brazil bombed 13 landing strips used to transport miners, equipment, supplies. But at least 156 landing strips were untouched.[69] Several attempts were made to expel miners from Yanomami territory, but many miners simply returned.[70]

The recent gold rush in the Amazon, like its predecessors in earlier centuries, has been difficult for the government to control and regulate. The informal mining sector is diffuse, transitory, and clandestine, and miners work deposits in remote, rugged terrain, usually well beyond police and military control.[71] The number of miners is twice that of soldiers in the Brazilian army.[72] Thus a lack of will is compounded by difficult logistics.

Another important factor is that Amazonian countries continue to experience severe economic and political problems that render concerns for indigenous and environmental welfare secondary at best. Had Brazil developed effective agrarian reform and economic development programs, it would have greatly reduced the poverty and landlessness that drove many into mining.[73] About half of Brazil's arable land belongs to just 1% of the landowners, whereas around 3% is divided among 3.1 million small farmers.[74] These underlying causes of the mining crisis must be addressed.

The failure of Brazil and Venezuela to regulate mining and to maintain national security has brought criticism from human rights and environmental organizations. Moreover, neither government gains much from unregulated mining, since the miners sell most of their gold on the black market to avoid taxes.[75] The decline of fisheries that sustain so many villages and towns, threats to the health of the workforce, and the ecological degradation that could have severe negative effects on Amazon's important tourist industry, all should be further incentives for mining regulation.

Response: Populace

Political, economic, and personal preoccupations, compounded by ignorance, ethnocentrism, and racism toward indigenous peoples, render most of the public apathetic to both the mining crisis and its human and environmental impacts. The populace needs to be better informed of the full human and environmental costs of gold mining and to understand that these costs are greatly increased by inadequate government responses. Consumers throughout the world should be better informed and reduce the demand for gold, or even boycott it.[76] Meanwhile, residents of the Amazon themselves are the least powerful and least able to make such choices as substituting meat for fish.[77] But they can avoid eating the most contaminated predatory fish, and particularly pregnant women and children should take precautions.

Response: International

The international community clearly is part of the problem in the Amazon. Conveniently, the international and national business interests involved in the mining—for example, those supplying mercury—are almost invisible, although they include companies from Canada, the United States, and Europe.[78] Thus the international community also must be part of the solution: only concerted, systematic, and sustained international action will give Amazon's indigenous peoples any chance to survive. Consumer boycotts of their products and stocks, for example, could force them to take remedial action. Humanitarian assistance is also critical; CCPY, together with such agencies as Doctors without Borders (Medicins du Monde), has provided medical assistance to the Yanomami in Brazil, though much more is needed.[79]

Missionaries, who have a long-term presence in the region, have also provided emergency medical, education, and other humanitarian assistance. They are linked to large national and international organizations that could have substantial power to affect change. Problems with missionary work include constraints of limited personnel and resources. Additionally, education is problematic if it is not bilingual and bicultural to perpetuate the indigenous heritage. Missionaries like anthropologists are a heterogeneous group, and some individuals in either group may behave unethically and jeopardize or even violate human rights.[80]

Response: Anthropology

Many government officials and missionaries, as well as some anthropologists, assume that the cultural extinction of indigenous peoples is inevitable in the face of "civilization" and "progress." From their perspective the Yanomami and other indigenes must change or perish. Others, however, realize that there is nothing inevitable about cultural extinction; rather it is a moral choice of policy makers. From this point of view, self-determination is the pivotal group-right for indigenous societies.[81] In the late 1960s this position, together with moral outrage at atrocities committed against indigenous peoples, motivated the development of anthropological advocacy organizations such as the Anthropology Resource Center, Cultural Survival, International Work Group for Indigenous Affairs, and Survival International.[82]

In the case of the Yanomami, the American Anthropological Association (AAA) took various actions, including resolutions at the annual convention and the establishment of the special Yanomami Commission, which had significant success.[83] The AAA also developed an explicit and systematic approach to human rights research, education, and advocacy in its Commission for Human Rights (1992–95), which has become a permanent Committee for Human Rights. Individual anthropologists have followed their personal and professional conscience in taking action on behalf of groups in the Amazon and elsewhere. Others take action by educating their students and initiating letter writing or other campaigns.[84]

Human Rights

The entire episode of gold mining in the Amazon can be seen as a complex chain reaction of human rights violations extending back to the problems of impoverished peoples seeking economic security. Human rights are universal, indivisible, and interconnected.[85] Three international conventions being drafted explicitly treat the linkage between human rights and environment: the UN Declaration of Principles on Human Rights and the Environment (see the appendix to this volume), the UN Declaration on the Rights of Indigenous Peoples, and the Inter-American Declaration on the Rights of Indigenous Peoples of the Organization of American States.

The 1994 draft of the UN Declaration of Principles on Human Rights and the Environment includes the following articles relevant to the gold mining situation in Brazil:

2. All persons have the right to a secure, healthy and ecologically sound environment;

5. All persons have the right to freedom from pollution, environmental degradation and activities that adversely affect the environment, threaten life, health, livelihood, well-being or sustainable development within, across or outside national boundaries;

14. Indigenous peoples have the right to control their lands, territories and natural resources and to maintain their traditional way of life;

20. All persons have the right to effective remedies and redress in administrative or judicial proceedings for environmental harm or the threat of such harm.

Recently the United Nations agreed in principle to recognize that "all individuals are entitled to live in an environment adequate for their health and well-being." Furthermore, Brazil was one of the nations incorporating this principle into its national constitution.[86] The 1988 Constitution of Brazil also has excellent and extensive environmental clauses, according to Nickel and Viola.[87]

Written or oral statements are one thing; actions are too often quite another. At all levels, government actions contradict their statements.[88] Thus, for example, in 1985 the Inter-American Commission for Human Rights of the Organization of American States charged that in the case of the Yanomami the Brazilian government had violated numerous articles it agreed to in the "American Declaration of the

Rights and Duties of Man." In particular this commission charged that the Brazilian government was liable for failing to take timely and effective measures to protect the human rights of the Yanomami during the construction of the Northern Perimeter Highway and in allowing the invasion of gold miners into Yanomami territory.[89] The Brazilian government finally allowed this commission to send representatives to assess the Yanomami situation in late 1995—some 15 years after the original request.[90]

The Brazilian government has violated numerous other international agreements ranging from the UN Convention on Genocide, the UN World Charter for Nature, the International Labour Organization's Convention 107 on Tribal and Indigenous Populations, the ILO Convention on Tribal and Indigenous Peoples No. 169, the 1992 Rio Charter and Agenda 21, and others.[91]

Gold mining and mercury contamination clearly link human rights and the environment. Miners' illegal invasion of indigenous territory, together with the resulting degradation and destruction of their interrelated population, society, culture, and environment, involves a multitude of serious human rights abuses. Mercury contamination violates the most fundamental of all rights—the right to life. Obviously this right necessarily depends on a safe and healthy environment, and that is absolutely endangered by mercury contamination.

One of the causes of the disparity between what national governments say and what they do is simple hypocrisy: states sign human rights conventions as part of their public relations management while promoting a hidden agenda that often not only fails to protect human rights but actually violates them. In other words, a major Achilles heel of international conventions on human rights is that the very political body that has the authority and power to protect and advance rights is often the agent of the violation of rights. National sovereignty prevents intervention by other nations or international organizations. Moreover, the human rights framework does not address the relatively recent development of multinational corporations that may abuse the rights of local communities, albeit with the complicity of the government.[92] Advocacy organizations also tend to be reactive rather than proactive. Another obstacle is inadequate flow of information from frontier zones such as the Amazon Basin. Despite these weaknesses, rights conventions remain an important weapon against inhumanities.

Conclusions

Given the hazardous human health, economic, and environmental consequences of mercury use in gold mining, its use should be immediately and strictly prohibited. Since this is unlikely to happen for political, economic, and logistical reasons, feasible measures are adoption of simple, inexpensive technology by workers on placer mines and in gold shops to reduce mercury emissions; deployment of technological remedies to clean up mining sites; avoidance of the consumption of contaminated carnivorous fish (especially by mothers and children); and continual environmental and health monitoring and treatment.[93]

Ann Misch in *World Watch* labels mercury contamination in the Amazon "a public health disaster of frightening proportions."[94] Any economic and social benefits of mining may eventually be outweighed by its human and environmental costs for many generations.[95] Even if gold prices fall, mining will be an attractive economic alternative so long as poverty persists and mercury is available, affordable, and unregulated. Each year miners invade new river areas of the Amazon, and nearly every mining company in the world is exploring for gold somewhere, some constructing facilities for cyanide-heap leaching of gold-bearing sediments.[96]

A high priority should be given to long-term research on the detection, monitoring, assessment, and treatment of the human and environmental impacts of mercury contamination. Because of the human and environmental variability in mining areas and their hinterlands, results from one place cannot be readily extrapolated to others.[97] Research has barely begun on the biogeochemical cycling of mercury in forest and aquatic ecosystems of the tropics.[98] The behavior and ecology of fish is also critical in understanding routes of mercury biomagnification.[99] Field studies on indigenous and peasant subsistence fishing that anthropologists, geographers, and biologists have pioneered in the Amazon illuminate the pathways of methylmercury contamination in humans through fishing and fish consumption.[100] Anthropological, economic, political, legal, and psychological research is sorely needed on all the interest groups involved in gold mining in search of ways to try to reduce or resolve aspects of the crisis.[101]

SECTION II: View from the 21st Century

What has transpired with the human and environmental impacts of gold mining activity and associated mercury contamination in the Amazon during the decade since the original publication of this essay? The short answer to this question is more of the same. If anything, the situation has gotten worse, because the demand for and price of gold have soared, as has poverty.[102] In general, supply has responded accordingly. The need and greed that drives gold mining continues,[103] and so does the accompanying mercury contamination and other negative effects.[104] Increased research is documenting the multifarious and nefarious impacts of gold mining.

Although gold prices oscillate, the general trend is toward a substantial increase. For instance, prices per ounce of gold at the London market were $34.94 in 1970, $675.30 in 1980, $410.11 in 1990, and $284.45 in 2000.[105] At the same time, annual gold production increased, fluctuating from 1,480 metric tons in 1970, 1,220 in 1980, 2,180 in 1990, and 2,590 in 2000.[106] The demand for gold continues for industry, electronics, dentistry, and most of all for jewelry, as well as for secure investments. Prices often increase during wars and energy and economic crises. Thus by 2010 the price of gold has soared to record highs of $1,200 per ounce.

In recent years the major gold fields in the Amazon have included the Alto Rio Negro, Western Roraima, Trombetas, Amapa, Tapajos, Gurupi, Sierra Pelada, Cumaru, Alto Floresta, and the Rio Madeira (all in Brazil), as well as the Beni in Peru and the Madre de Dios in Bolivia. During the 1980s and 1990s the density of dredges along the Madeira in Rondonia, Brazil, was so great that it disrupted the normal flow of boat traffic. Schools of migratory fish were frightened by the dredges and swam back downstream. But the Tapajos Valley was the most affected area in the entire Amazon, with thousands of its streams excavated.[107] Biomedical investigations in three Tapajos villages revealed that more than 80% of the children had levels of mercury concentration in their hair sufficient to adversely affect brain development.[108] Research in the Upper Beni River region of the Bolivian Amazon found that gold mining has affected areas 150 km downstream from the mining.[109]

In the last 10 years there has also been a shift in the main regions of gold mining in the Amazon: Peru has surpassed Brazil, although approximately 500 mining sites remain active in Brazil. Now Peru ranks sixth in gold production after China,

South Africa, United States, and Indonesia. Peru is followed by Russia, Canada, Papua New Guinea, and Ghana.[110] Brazil's gold rush has declined since the early 1990s, but new deposits are still being discovered that trigger a local gold rush, with thousands of miners invading areas such as in Apui in Brazil in early 2007.[111] Moreover, mining has spread in the upper Madre de Dios region of Peru, which is now the most heavily mined region in the Amazon. During the dry season several thousand miners blast away hundreds of kilometers of river levees, banks, beds, floodplains, and lakes, resulting in widespread mercury contamination. The increased sedimentation and turbidity of the waterways has turned them from mostly clear waters to turbid slurries, probably killing many fish adapted to clear water, although research has not yet been done to document this matter. Floodplains have been turned over for alluvial gold with mechanized operations that include tractors and large sluices along the Inambari, Colorado, and other tributaries of the Madre de Dios. The landscape has been reduced to a giant gravel pit that can be detected from satellite images. It is unknown just how far downstream the contamination and sedimentation reaches, but because mercury combines with sediments it can be carried long distances, even to the Atlantic Ocean. There may also be significant amounts of mercury buried in sediments along riverbanks and floodplains disturbed by mining, and these may be mobilized later as sediments shift with flooding and erosion.[112]

In Brazil the Yanomami situation remains grave and urgent, and government agencies remain negligent. Although today there are hundreds of illegal miners rather than several tens of thousands here, the impact on the Yanomami people, sociocultural system, and ecosystems remains severe. During the short period of 2000–2004, when the URIHI—Yanomami Project was able to provide medical care, the incidence of diseases was dramatically reduced. But the Yanomami have little access to health care, and failure of Brazilian government agencies to provide adequate care may be considered genocide by default. In 2004 the Yanomami established, with support from the Rainforest Foundation, the Hutukara Yanomami Association, led by Davi Kopenawa Yanomami, to defend their human rights.[113]

Meanwhile in Venezuela hundreds of miners entered the Caura River area, threatening the indigenous Ye'kuana, Sanema (a Yanomami subgroup), and Hoti. Eventually, the military expelled most of the miners. Under the presidency of Hugo Chavez, Venezuela's Amazon region has been militarized, discouraging illegal wildcat mining in some areas. Elsewhere, it causes widespread damage and presents a huge challenge for the state. Illegal small-scale miners, settlements, and clandestine landing strips are even being built in the national parks.[114] Furthermore, the disease introduced by miners in Venezuela spreads across the border into Brazil through the Yanomami social network.[115]

Anthropologists and others are increasingly studying mining as the energy and environmental crises increased awareness of the limits of natural resources and of industrial growth.[116] Writing from a cultural materialist point of view, Ricardo Godoy portrayed mining as an economic base that powerfully influences the structure and the superstructure. The latter includes the beliefs and rituals as well as ideology associated with mining; the former encompasses the deployment of technology and capital in the exploration, development, and production phases of the mining process. The structural level deals with demography, labor recruitment and migration, mining communities, and their political organization. Godoy also noted the economic and ecological impact of mining. He stressed that anthropologists are strategically positioned by method and inclination to contribute to the research on the small-scale sector of mining in the so-called Third World.[117]

Subsequent researchers have pursued aspects of Godoy's framework in various ways. For example, Marieke Heemskerk has written on the impact of gold mining on the Maroon people of Suriname. She notes that, although this activity jeopardizes economic, ecological, and physical security in the long run, the Maroon pursue mining because of the immediate economic opportunities it offers.[118] Heemskerk problematizes antipoverty policies that promote women's self-employment in artisanal gold mining, arguing that short-term economic considerations fail to anticipate the greater costs for their health, culture, and society in the long term. Although women's participation in the informal labor market associated with gold mining can be profitable and socially empowering, it is also risky, because it is not regulated by public standards for wages, social organization, health, and safety. She calls for government policy interventions to improve public health care, especially prevention campaigns for malaria and AIDS.[119]

Heemskerk concludes that stricter law enforcement and environmental awareness campaigns are unlikely to promote more sustainable use of resources in Suriname and elsewhere in the Amazon. Instead, she advocates policies that stabilize national economies and promote people-centered development in rural regions.[120]

Alisson F. Barbieri and colleagues disclose the serious situation in the Northern Mato Grosso, an area that has had one of the highest incidence of malaria in the Americas since the early 1990s. There, agricultural colonization, cattle ranching, urbanization, and small-scale gold mining all contribute to the spread of the disease. Miners are especially prone to malaria, because they use water to process the gold and live in crowded conditions, and their high level of mobility spreads the disease into new areas. The disruption of the ecology of the insect vectors transmitting malaria in mining areas generates high malaria endemism. As mining declines, so, too, does malaria, but new road construction will increase access by miners as well as others to new areas, which is likely to increase the frequency of malaria unless effective public health and other policy measures are implemented.[121]

Garry D. Peterson and Heemskerk have investigated the long-term impacts on forest cover after gold miners abandon an area. They note that gold miners clear 48–96 km^2 of old-growth forest every year in Suriname and that by 2010 the accumulated deforestation is predicted to total 750–2,280 km^2. Large portions of previously mined areas persist as bare ground, grasses, and standing water, providing a reservoir for the breeding of insect vectors of diseases such as malaria. Although the areas mined are relatively small, they are concentrated in selected regions and the recovery of the forest is very slow and qualitatively inferior, implying a significant reduction of both biodiversity and ecosystem services in the affected areas.[122]

Since the 1990s gold mining activity has increased markedly throughout the forests of the Guianas. Estimates range between 3,000–4,000 mining sites, with over 100,000 people involved directly and indirectly. The mining undermines other forest business, such as trade in non-timber forest products and ecotourism, and malaria and other diseases have worsened greatly in the area.[123]

All the news isn't bad, though. A promising development initiated in 2002 is the Global Mercury Project (GMP) of the Global Environment Facility (GEF) of the United Nations Industrial Development Organization (UNIDO). Among its aims is to reduce mercury emissions by creating alternatives to mercury amalgamation.[124] Medical research on and care for miners and their associates are supposed to be another component of this initiative. Participating countries include Brazil, Sudan, Tanzania, Zimbabwe, Laos, and Indonesia. Yet, mining management, regulations, and controls comparable to those in countries such as the United States and Canada are unlikely to be implemented in the Amazon any time soon.[125] Nor are the rules in those wealthy countries unproblematic. Community capacity-building strategies need to complement and reinforce regulatory efforts. Otherwise, the reduction of mercury emissions may result in further impoverishing the poor people who rely on gold mining for survival.[126]

Other international initiatives include the Guianas Program of the World Wildlife Fund to reduce mercury emissions; the development of a comprehensive ban on mercury export from the countries of the European Union; a resolution by the Association for Tropical Biology and Conservation requesting that the government of Venezuela halt the rampant invasion of the Caura River area by illegal gold miners; and the continuing action of human rights advocacy organizations such as Survival International on behalf of the Yanomami in Brazil. Various organizations, such as Amazon Watch, Communities and Small-Scale Mining (CASM), Instituto Socioambiental, Mercury Watch, Mining Watch, Survival International, and World Rainforest Movement, have been monitoring the gold mining situation in the Amazon and disseminating information to the public.[127]

Anthropologists and other professionals have debated the character and scope of appropriate forms of engagement. Some researchers try to be neutral, while others become involved as consultants or advocates for local communities, corporations, or states.[128] All aspects of gold mining need more systematic and penetrating study, ranging from the frontier culture of mining regions and its social and environmental impacts to the corporate culture and behavior of the organizations behind the mining; the role of the state, regulations, and enforcement; and direct and indirect violence associated with mining.[129] Human rights are implicated in some ways and degrees in most of these aspects.[130] The most elemental right is the community's right to self-determination, whether it opposes mining, is interested in some measure of partnership with miners, or decides to seek redress for damages.[131]

Even as researchers and nongovernmental organizations pay more attention to the costs of mining, governments sometimes deny them access to areas of the Amazon. For instance, the government of Brazil, apparently concerned about national sovereignty and biopiracy, is considering requiring foreigners to apply for a special permit to enter the Amazon. Furthermore, in 2007 Marc Van Roosmalen, a prominent Brazilian biological scientist and conservationist, was actually jailed for his advocacy, although he was later released in response to national and international outrage. Amazon researchers may be pressured to compromise their professional, ethical, and moral integrity by censoring their findings if governments claim that gold and the other natural wealth of the region are matters of national security. It is even conceivable that critics or opponents of mining and other extractive industries may be stigmatized as threats to national security or even as terrorists.[132]

The myths as well as the realities of the Amazon as El Dorado and as savior of national economies will continue to drive the gold rush and other extraction industries there.[133] Yet, the time bombs of mercury contamination must be recognized as a global human and environmental tragedy for decades or centuries.

Worldwide, about 13 million people in over 30 "developing" countries work in small-scale mining while an additional 80–100 million people depend on this sector for their livelihood.[134] Future research on small-scale gold mining and mercury contamination among the regions of the world should yield useful comparative information and insights for understanding and attending to this widespread phenomenon.[135] Tragically, the "Master Thief" continues not only uninhibited but also encouraged and facilitated by the geopolitical circumstances and pretenses of the post-9/11 era.

Notes

1. Some of the background and information for this essay were kindly provided by Bruce Albert, Nelly Arvelo-Jimenez, Jean Chiappino, Marcus Colchester, Gustavo A. Eskildsen, Rebecca Holmes, Gail Gomez, Marco Antonio Lazarin, Jacques Lizot, Paula Loya, Sergio Milano, Peggy Overbey, Abel Perozo, Linda Rabben, Haydee Seijas, Patrick Tierney, and Terrence Turner. The following organizations were also helpful: Amanaka'a, American Anthropological Association, Brazilian Embassy, Commission for the Creation of the Yanomami Park and its successor The Pro-Yanomami Commission, Cultural Survival, Indian Law Resource Center, Instituto Venezolano de Investigaciones Cientificas, Survival International, and World Rainforest Movement. To these and others I am most grateful; however, only I am responsible for any deficiencies or other problems in this essay.

2. Quoted Marcello M. Veiga, John A. Meech, and Raphael Hypolito, "Educational Measures to Address Mercury Pollution from Gold-Mining Activities in the Amazon," *Ambio* 24:4 (1995, 216–17).

3. Quoted from Terence Turner and Davi Kopenawa Yanomami, "I Fight Because I Am Alive: An Interview with Davi Kopenawa Yanomami," *Cultural Survival Quarterly* 15:2 (summer 1991, 1). See also Davi Kopenawa Yanomami, "Letter to All the Peoples of the Earth," *Cultural Survival Quarterly* 13:4 (1989, 68–69).

4. Dennison Berwick, *Savages: The Life and Killing of the Yanomami* (London: Hodder and Stoughton, 1992); J. Butler, "Land, Gold, and Farmers: Agricultural Colonization and Frontier Expansion in the Brazilian Amazon," Ph.D. dissertation, University of Florida, Gainesville, 1985; David Cleary, *Anatomy of the Amazon Gold Rush* (Iowa City: University of Iowa Press, 1990a); Susanna Hecht and Alexander Cockburn, *The Fate of the Forest: Developers, Destroyers and Defenders of the Amazon* (New York: Verso, 1989); A. Feijao and J. A. Pinto, *Garimpeiros in South America: The Amazon Gold Rush* (Pará, Brazil: Union of Amazon Garimpeiros and Merchants Bank of the Future, 1990); Gordon MacMillan, *At the End of the Rainbow? Gold, Land, and People in the Brazilian Amazon* (New York: Columbia University Press, 1995); Alcida Rita Ramos, *Sanuma Memories: Yanomami Ethnography in Times of Crisis* (Madison: University of Wisconsin Press, 1995).

5. MacMillan, note 4, p. 178; Carlos Prieto, *Mining in the New World* (New York: McGraw-Hill, 1973); Amnesty International, *The Americas: Human Rights Violations against Indigenous Peoples* (London: Amnesty International, 1992); John H. Bodley, *Victims of Progress* (Mountain View, CA: Mayfield Publishing Co., 1990); Hecht and Cockburn, note 4.

6. David Cleary, "Gold Mining and Mercury Use in the Amazon Basin," *Appropriate Technology* 17:2 (1990b, 17–19); Marshall C. Eakin, "The Role of British Capital in the Development of Brazilian Gold Mining," in Thomas Greaves and William Culver, Eds., *Miners and Mining in the Americas* (Dover, NH: Manchester University Press, 1985, 1–28); John Hemming, *Red Gold: The Conquest of the Brazilian Indians* (Cambridge: Harvard University Press, 1978, 377–408). Serra Pelada closed in the late 1980s because it became structurally unsound.

7. Marcus Colchester, *Venezuela: Violations of Human Rights, Report to the International Labour Office on the Observation of ILO Convention 107* (Chadlington: Forest Peoples Programme, World Rainforest Movement, 1995, 19–27); Veiga, Meech, and Hypolito, note 2, pp. 216–17; Cleary, note 4.

8. Jed Greer, "The Price of Gold: Environmental Costs of the New Gold Rush," *The Ecologist* 23:3 (1993, 91–96).

9. John E. Young, "For the Love of Gold," *World Watch* 6:3 (1993, 19–26). See also John E. Young, *Mining the Earth*, Worldwatch Paper 109 (Washington, D.C.: Worldwatch, 1992).

10. Michael Goulding, Nigel J. H. Smith, and Dennis J. Mahar, *Floods of Fortune: Ecology and Economy along the Amazon* (New York: Columbia University Press, 1996, 50). See also MacMillan, note 4, pp. 30, 34–37.

11. MacMillan, note 4, pp. 59–60, 76, 162; Berwick, note 4; Cleary, note 4; Hecht and Cockburn, note 4.

12. Shelton Davis, *Victims of the Miracle: Development and the Indians of Brazil* (New York: Cambridge University Press, 1977).

13. Shelton H. Davis and R. O. Mathews, *The Geological Imperative: Anthropology and Development in the Amazon Basin of South America* (Irvine, CA: Program in Comparative Culture Occasional Papers No. 5, 1976) 3.

14. Davis, note 12, pp. 89–90.

15. Linda Rabben, "Brazil's Military Stakes Its Claim," *The Nation* 250:10 (March 12, 1990, 341).

16. Neil Hollander and Robert MacLean, "Mud-Caked Amazonian Miners Wallow in Newfound Wealth and Power," *Smithsonian* 15:1 (1984, 89–96). Also see Cleary, note 4; Davis, note 12, pp. 105–10; J. Mallas and N. Benedicto, "Mercury and Goldmining in the Brazilian Amazon," *Ambio* 15 (1986, 247). For numerous other examples of contradictions and complicity in government practices see Ramos, note 4, pp. 271–312.

17. Davis, note 12, p. 103.

18. For further discussion of the geopolitics of the Brazilian region, see Bruce Albert, "Indian Lands, Environmental Policy and Military Geopolitics in the Development of the Brazilian Amazon: The Case of the Yanomami," *Development and Change* 23 (1992, 35–70); Elizabeth Allen, "Calha Norte: Military Development in Brazilian Amazonia," *Development and Change* 23 (1992, 71–99); MacMillan, note 4; Lucio Flavio Pinto, "Calha Norte: The Special Project for the Occupation of the Frontiers," *Cultural Survival Quarterly* 13:1 (1989, 40–41); Rabben, note 15; Marcio Santilli, "The Calha Norte Project: Military Guardianship and Frontier Policy," *Cultural Survival Quarterly* 13:1 (1989, 42–43); Dave Treece, "The Militarization and Industrialization of Amazonia: The Calha Norte and Grande Carajas Programmes," *The Ecologist* 19:6 (1989, 225–28). For a discussion of geopolitics in Venezuela, see Nelly Arvelo-Jimenez, "The Political Struggle of the Guayana Region's Indigenous Peoples," *Journal of International Affairs* 36:1 (1982, 43–54).

19. Veiga, Meech, and Hypolito, note 2, p. 218.

20. *Appropriate Technology*, Special Issue on "Small-Scale Mining," 17:2 (Sept. 1990, 1–35).

21. MacMillan, note 4, pp. 156–57; Young, note 9, pp. 20, 24.

22. Leslie E. Sponsel, Thomas N. Headland, and Robert C. Bailey, Eds., *Tropical Deforestation: The Human Dimension* (New York: Columbia University Press, 1996); MacMillan, note 4, pp. 92–97, 157.

23. Olaf Malm et al., "An Assessment of Hg Pollution in Different Goldmining Areas, Amazon Brazil," *The Science of the Total Environment* 175 (1995, 127–40). Useful sources on mercury include Leonard J. Goldwater, *Mercury: A History of Quicksilver* (Baltimore: York

Press, 1972); Patricia A. D'Itri and Frank M. D'Itri, *Mercury Contamination: A Human Tragedy* (New York: John Wiley & Sons, 1977); Martin Lodenius, Ed., Special Issue "Mercury Pollution and Gold Mining in Brazil," *The Science of the Total Environment* 175:2 (Dec. 11, 1995, 85–162); Jerome O. Nriagu, Ed., *The Biogeochemistry of Mercury in the Environment* (New York: Elsevier, 1979); Carl J. Watras and John W. Huckabee, Eds., *Mercury Pollution: Integration and Synthesis* (Boca Raton, FL: Lewis Publishers, 1994). Also see *Water, Air, and Soil Pollution,* Special Issue on Mercury 56:1 (April 1991, 843).

24. Greer, note 8, p. 92.

25. Rodolf Reuther, "Mercury Accumulation in Sediment and Fish from Rivers Affected by Alluvial Gold Mining in the Brazilian Madeira River Basin, Amazon," *Environmental Monitoring and Assessment* 32 (1994, 239–58); and A. W. Andren and J. O. Nriagu, "The Global Cycle of Mercury," in Jerome O. Nriagu, Ed., *The Biogeochemistry of Mercury in the Environment* (New York: Elsevier, 1979, 1–22).

26. Wolfgang Christian Pfeiffer and Luiz Drude de Lacerda, "Mercury Inputs to the Amazonian Basin," *Environmental Technology Letter* 9 (1988, 325–30).

27. Roald Hoffman, "Winning Gold," *American Scientist* 82:1 (Jan.–Feb. 1994, 15–17).

28. Malm et al., note 23, p.128; Jerome Nriagu et al., "Mercury Pollution in Brazil," *Nature* 356 (April 2, 1992, 389).

29. E. Salati, "The Climatology and Hydrology of Amazonia," in Ghillean T. Prance and Thomas E. Lovejoy, Eds., *Amazonia* (New York: Pergamon, 1985, 18–48); Emilio F. Moran, *Through Amazonian Eyes: The Human Ecology of Amazonian Populations* (Iowa City: University of Iowa Press, 1993); Olaf Malm, Fernandeo J. P. Branches, et al., "Mercury and Methylmercury in Fish and Human Hair from the Tapajós River Basin, Brazil," *The Science of the Total Environment* 175 (1995, 143); F. M. D'Itri, "What We Have Learned Since Minamata," *Environmental Monitoring and Assessment* 19 (1991, 173–76).

30. Greer, note 8, p. 92; Hecht and Cockburn, note 4, p. 145; Goulding et al., note 10, p. 73.

31. Goulding et al., note 10, p. 94; Greer, note 8, p. 92.

32. Hirokatsu Akagi et al., "Methylmercury Pollution in the Amazon, Brazil," *The Science of the Total Environment* 175 (1995, 85–95).

33. Malm et al., note 23, p. 148; Olaf Malm, Wolfgang C. Pfeiffer, et al., "Mercury Pollution Due to Gold Mining in the Madeira River Basin, Brazil," *Ambio* 19:1 (1990, 14).

34. Tuika Leino and Martin Lodenius, "Human Hair Mercury Levels in Tucuruí Area, State of Pará, Brazil," *The Science of the Total Environment* 175 (1995, 199); Ilkka Aula et al., "The Watershed Flux of Mercury Examined with Indicators in the TuCururúi Reservoir in Pará, Brazil," *The Science of the Total Environment* 175 (1995, 97–107).

35. Reuther, note 25, p. 239; Malm et al., note 23, p. 13; and Luis A. Martinelli et al., "Mercury Contamination in the Amazon: A Gold Rush Consequence," *Ambio* 17:4 (1988, 252–54).

36. Goulding et al., note 10, pp. 87, 93. For example, see Janet Chernela, *The Wano Indians of the Brazilian Amazon: A Sense of Space* (Austin: University of Texas Press, 1993) and Leslie E. Sponsel and Paula Loya, "Rivers of Hunger? Indigenous Resource Management in the Oligotrophic Ecosystems of the Rio Negro, Venezuela," in C. M. Hladik et al., *Tropical Forests, People and Food: Biocultural Interactions and Applications to Development* (London: Parthenon, 1993, 435–46).

37. L. Chang, "Pathological Effects of Mercury Poisoning," in J. O. Nriagu, Ed., *The Biochemistry of Mercury* (New York: Elsevier, 1979, 519–68); and K. Khera et al., "Teratogenic and Genetic Effects of Mercury Toxicity," in J. O. Nriagu, Ed., *The Biochemistry of Mercury* (New York: Elsevier, 1979, 503–12).

38. Nriagu et al., note 28.

39. Fernando J. P. Branches et al., "The Price of Gold: Mercury Exposure in the Amazonian Rain Forest," *Clinical Toxicology* 31:2 (1993, 295–306).

40. Branches et al., note 39. Also see Malm et al., note 23, p. 144.

41. Marcus Colchester, Ed., *The Health and Survival of the Venezuelan Yanoama* (Copenhagen: International Work Group for Indigenous Affairs Document No. 53, 1985, 59–72).

42. Spielman et al., "Regional Linguistic and Genetic Differences among the Yanomama Indians," *Science* 184 (1974, 637–44); R. Brian Ferguson, *Yanomami Warfare: A Political History* (Santa Fe, NM: School for American Research Press, 1995); R. J. A. Goodland and H. S. Irwin, *Amazon Jungle: Green Hell to Red Desert? An Ecological Discussion of the Environmental Impact of the Highway Construction Program in the Amazon Basin* (New York: Elsevier, 1975); Alcida R. Ramos and Kenneth I. Taylor, *The Yanomama in Brazil 1979* (Copenhagen: International Work Group for Indigenous Affairs Document No. 37, 1979); Colchester, note 7.

43. Lawrence H. Hecker et al., "Heavy Metal Levels in Acculturated and Unacculturated Populations," *Archives of Environmental Health* 29 (1974, 181–85).

44. M. B. Castro, B. Albert, and W. C. Pfeiffer, "Mercury Levels in Yanomami Indians' Hair from Roraima, Brazil," in Cep Consultants, Eds., *Proceedings of the 8th International Conference on Heavy Metals in the Environment* (Edinburgh: 1991, 367–70).

45. CCPY, Update 83, Dec. 15, 1995.

46. "Censo Indigena de Venezuela de 1982," *Boletin Indigenista Venezolano* XXI, pp. 227–39; 1992 personal communication from Rebecca Holmes.

47. See also Colchester note 7, pp. 35–38.

48. Bruce Albert, "Gold Miners and Yanomami Indians in the Brazilian Amazon: The Hashimu Massacre," in Barbara Rose Johnston, Ed., *Who Pays the Price? The Sociocultural Context of Environmental Crisis* (Washington, D.C.: Island Press, 1994, 47–55); Zeze Weiss and Martin D. Weiss, *The Yanomami Massacres and the Role of a Powerful Anti-Native Alliance* (New York: Amanaka'a Amazon Network, 1993).

49. Linda Rabben, "Demarcation—And Then What?" *Cultural Survival Quarterly* 17:2 (1993, 12–14); Nelly Arvelo-Jimenez and Andrew L. Cousins, "False Promises," *Cultural Survival Quarterly* 16:1 (1992, 10–13).

50. Leslie E. Sponsel, "The Yanomami Holocaust Continues," in Barbara Rose Johnston, Ed., *Who Pays the Price? The Sociocultural Context of Environmental Crisis* (Washington, D.C.: Island Press, 1994, 37–46).

51. Bodley, note 5, Chapter 10; Davis, note 12, pp. 167–68. An excellent firsthand account of the history of the Yanomami crisis is Ramos, note 4, pp. 271–312. Berwick, note 4; MacMillan, note 4; Ramos and Taylor, note 42; Survival International, *Yanomami: Survival Campaign* (London: Survival International, 1991); and Tierney, note 4, are also important contributions on the Yanomami crisis. For ethnographies of the Yanomami, see Jacques Lizot, *Tales of the Yanomami: Daily Life in the Venezuelan Forest* (New York: Cambridge University Press, 1985); and Ramos, note 4.

52. Brian Burkhalter, *Amazon Gold Rush: Markets and the Mundurucú Indians* (Ann Arbor, MI: University Microfilms International, 1983); S. Brian Burkhalter and Robert F. Murphy, "Tappers and Sappers: Rubber, Gold, and Money Among the Mundurucú," *American Ethnologist* 16:1 (1989, 100–16); Robert F. Murphy, *Headhunter's Heritage: Social and Economic Change among the Mundurucú Indians* (Berkeley and Los Angeles: University of California Press, 1960).

53. Andrew Gray, *And after the Gold Rush? Human Rights and Self-Development of the Amarakaeri of Southeastern Peru* (Copenhagen: International Work Group for Indigenous Affairs Document No. 55, 1986, 33–35, 57, 62, 104).

54. Hecht and Cockburn, note 4, pp. 143, 158. Also see Terrence Turner, "The Kayapo Revolt against Extractivism: An Indigenous Amazon People's Struggle for Socially Equitable or Ecologically Sustainable Production," *Journal of Latin American Anthropology* 1:1 (1995, 98–121). For other cases of indigenes and gold mining see Kaj Århem, "Dance of the Water People," *Natural History,* Jan. 1992, pp. 46–53; Bruce Albert, Ed., "Bresil: Indiens et Developpments en Amazonie," *Ethnies* 5:11–12 (Paris: Revue de Survival International, 1990, 1–46); Gray, *op. cit.,* note 53; and MacMillan, note 4, pp. 29–30.

55. Nelly Arvelo-Jimenez and Keith Conn, "The Ye'kuana Self-Demarcation Process," *Cultural Survival Quarterly* 18:4 (1995, 40–42).

56. Veiga et al., note 2, pp. 216–20; Albert, note 48.

57. Evelyn J. Caballero, "Gold from the Gods: Traditional Small-Scale Mining from Benguet Province, Philippines," Ph.D. dissertation, University of Hawaii, 1992; Cleary, note 4, pp. 225–28; Cleary, note 6, p. 19.

58. Veiga et al., note 2, pp. 216, 219. Raphael Hypolito, "The Hypolito Retort—Making Mercury Recovery Safe," *Appropriate Technology* 17:2 (1990, 20).

59. Marcello M. Veiga and John A. Meech, "Gold Mining Activities in the Amazon: Clean-Up Techniques and Remedial Procedures for Mercury Pollution," *Ambio* 24:6 (1995, 371–75).

60. Malm et al., note 23, p. 138.

61. Mallas and Benedicto, note 16, p. 249.

62. Veiga et al., note 2, p. 216.

63. Cleary, note 6, p. 19. Branches et al., note 39, p. 304. Also see *Appropriate Technology.*

64. MacMillan, note 4, pp. 71–72, 79–80.

65. Branches et al., note 39, p. 302.

66. Gray, note 53, p. 57. See also A. Sutton, *Amazonian Slavery: A Link in the Chain of Brazilian Development* (London: Anti-Slavery International, 1994).

67. MacMillan, note 4, pp. 71–72, 80. These considerations should not in any way be taken as condoning the illegal presence of miners and the human and environmental horrors they cause.

68. Hecht and Cockburn, note 4, pp. 119–21.

69. Berwick, note 4, p. 234.

70. CCPY, Update 86, "New Law Brings Avalanche of Claims to Indian Lands," May 1996, pp. 1–4.

71. Eakin, note 6, p. 12.

72. Veiga et al., note 2, p. 218.

73. Hecht and Cockburn, note 4, pp. 121, 147. See also Macmillan, note 4.

74. Monica Bergamo and Gerson Camarotti, "Brazil's Landless Millions," *World Press* 43:7 (1996, 46–47).

75. Eakin, note 6, p. 24.

76. Young, note 9, 1993.

77. Leino and Lodenius, note 34, p. 124.

78. Colchester, note 7, p. 21; Weiss and Weiss, note 48.

79. Survival International, "Yanomami Health Aid," *Survival International News* 10 (1985, 3).

80. Thomas N. Headland and Darrell L. Whiteman, Eds., Special Issue "Missionaries, Anthropologists, and Human Rights," *Missiology* XXIV:2 (April 1996, 161–299). Patrick

Tierney, *Darkness in El Dorado: How Anthropologists and Journalists Devastated the Amazon* (New York: W.W. Norton, 2000).

81. Christian Bay, "Human Rights on the Periphery: No Room in the Ark for the Yanomami?" *Development Dialogue* 1–2 (1984, 23–41); Bodley, note 5, Chapter 10.

82. Bodley, note 5; Ellen Messer, "Anthropology and Human Rights," *Annual Review of Anthropology* 22 (1993, 221–49); Marc S. Miller, Ed., *State of the Peoples: A Global Human Rights Report on Societies in Danger* (Boston: Beacon Press, 1993); Leslie E. Sponsel, "Relationships among the World System, Indigenous Peoples, and Ecological Anthropology in the Endangered Amazon," in L. E. Sponsel, Ed., *Indigenous Peoples and the Future of Amazonia: An Ecological Anthropology of an Endangered World* (Tucson: University of Arizona Press, 1995, 263–93); Robin Wright, "Anthropological Presuppositions of Indigenous Advocacy," *Annual Review of Anthropology* 17 (1988, 365–90).

83. American Anthropological Association, *Report of the Special Commission to Investigate the Situation of the Brazilian Yanomami* (Washington, D.C.: American Anthropological Association, 1991).

84. Cara Elmore and Leslie Gross, "A Massacre and a Lesson about Life," *NEA Today* (National Education Association) 13:5 (1994, 29); George P. Nicholas, "The Yanomami in the Classroom," *Cultural Survival Quarterly* 16:2 (1992, 28–30).

85. Jack Donnelly, *Universal Human Rights in Theory and Practice* (Ithaca, NY: Cornell University Press, 1989). Andrew Gray, "International Protection of Indigenous Rights: The Subsurface—Forgotten or Ignored?" *International Work Group for Indigenous Affairs Newsletter* 3 (July–Aug.–Sept. 1993, 2–3); W. Paul Gormley, *Human Rights and Environment: The Need for International Cooperation* (Leyden: A. W. Sijthoff, 1976); W. Paul Gormley, "The Legal Obligation of the International Community to Guarantee a Pure and Decent Environment: The Expansion of Human Rights Norms," *Georgetown International Environmental Law Review* 3 (1990, 85–116); Human Rights Watch and Natural Resources Defense Council, *Defending the Earth: Abuses of Human Rights and the Environment* (New York: Human Rights Watch, June 1992); James W. Nickel, "The Human Rights of a Safe Environment," *Yale Journal of International Law* 18 (1993, 281–95); James W. Nickel, and Eduardo Viola, "Integrating Environmentalism and Human Rights," *Environmental Ethics* 16 (1994, 265); Henn-Juri Uibopuu, "The International Guaranteed Right of an Individual to a Clean Environment," *Comparative Law Yearbook* 1 (1977, 101–20); Arthur H. Westing, "Human Rights and the Environment," *Environmental Conservation* 20:2 (1993, 99–100).

86. Westing, note 85, p. 99.

87. Nickel and Viola, note 85, p. 266.

88. For example, see Brazilian Embassy, *Brazilian Policy on Indigenous Populations* (Washington, D.C.: Brazilian Embassy, 1993).

89. Inter-American Commission on Human Rights, *Annual Report of the Inter-American Commission on Human Rights 1984–1985* (Washington, D.C.: Organization of American States, 1985).

90. CCPY, Update 83, Dec. 15, 1995.

91. Also see Nelly Arvelo-Jimenez et al., "Indian Policy," in John D. Martz and David J. Myers, Eds., *Venezuela: The Democratic Experience* (New York: Praeger Publications, 1977, 323–34); and Colchester, note 7 on repeated violations of the ILO Convention 107 in Venezuela.

92. Donnelly, note 85. See also Ellen Messer, "Anthropology and Human Rights in Latin America," *Journal of Latin American Anthropology* 1:1 (1995, 48–97).

93. Malm et al., note 23, p. 149.

94. Ann Misch, "The Amazon: River at Risk," *World Watch* 5:1 (1992, 37).

95. Cleary, note 4, p. 17; Ronald Fuge et al., "Mercury and Gold Pollution," *Nature* 357 (June 4, 1992, 369). Also see Duane A. Smith, *Mining America: The Industry and the Envionment, 1800–1980* (Lawrence: University of Kansas Press, 1987). For benefits see Cleary, note 4, pp. 211–22.

96. Greer, note 8, pp. 91–94.

97. MacMillan, note 4, p. 160.

98. Malm et al., note 23, p. 149.

99. Michael Goulding, *The Fishes of the Forest: Explorations in Amazonian Natural History* (Berkeley and Los Angeles: University of California Press, 1980); Goulding et al., note 10; Nigel Smith, *Man, Fishes, and the Amazon* (New York: Columbia University Press, 1981).

100. For example, see Smith, note 99; and Sponsel and Loya, note 36.

101. See Al Gedicks, *The New Resource Wars: Native and Environmental Struggles against Multinational Corporations* (Boston: South End Press, 1993).

102. Gavin M. Mudd, "Global Trends in Gold Mining: Toward Quantifying Environmental and Resource Sustainability," *Resources Policy* 32:1–2 (2007, 42–56); Samuel J. Spiegel, Annalee Yassi, Jery M. Spiegel, and Marcello M. Veiga, "Reducing Mercury and Responding to the Global Gold Rush," *The Lancet* 366:9503 (2008, 2070–72); D. Cleary and I. Thornton, "The Environmental Impact of Gold Mining in the Brazilian Amazon," in *Issues in Environmental Science and Technology 1: Mining and its Environmental Impact*, R. E. Hester and R. M. Harrison, Eds. (London: Royal Society of Chemistry, 1994, pp. 17–29); Ronald Eisler, "Mercury Hazards from Gold Mining to Humans, Plants, and Animals," in *Reviews of Environmental Contamination and Toxicology*, George W. Ware, Ed. (New York: Springer-Verlag, 2004, 139–98); and Gavin M. Mudd, "Gold Mining and Sustainability: A Critical Reflection," in *Encyclopedia of Earth*, Cutler J. Cleveland, Ed. (Washington, D.C.: Environmental Information Coalition, National Council for Science and the Environment 2008, www.eoearth.org/article/Gold_mining_and_sustainability:_A_critical_reflection).

103. Samuel J. Spiegel, Annalee Yassi, Jery M. Spiegel, and Marcello M. Veiga, "Reducing Mercury and Responding to the Global Gold Rush," *The Lancet* 366:9503 (2008, 2070–72).

104. D. Cleary and I. Thornton, "The Environmental Impact of Gold Mining in the Brazilian Amazon," in *Issues in Environmental Science and Technology 1: Mining and its Environmental Impact*, R. E. Hester and R. M. Harrison, Eds. (London: Royal Society of Chemistry, 1994, 17–29); Ronald Eisler, "Mercury Hazards from Gold Mining to Humans, Plants, and Animals," in *Reviews of Environmental Contamination and Toxicology*, George W. Ware, Ed. (New York: Springer-Verlag, 2004,139–98); Gavin M. Mudd, "Gold Mining and Sustainability: A Critical Reflection," in *Encyclopedia of Earth*, Cutler J. Cleveland, Ed. (Washington, D.C.: Environmental Information Coalition, National Council for Science and the Environment, 2008), www.eoearth.org/article/Gold_mining_and_sustainability: _A_critical_reflection.

105. The Financial Forecast Center, www.neatideas.com/data/index.htm, and the World Gold Council, www.gold.org.

106. United States Geological Survey, http://minerals.usgs.gov/ds/s005/140/gold.pdf.

107. Michael Goulding, Ronaldo Bartem, and Efrem Ferreira, *The Smithsonian Atlas of the Amazon* (Washington, D.C.: Smithsonian Books 2003, 60, 140, 152).

108. Phillipe Grandjean, Roberta R. White, Ann Nielsen, David Cleary, and Elizabeth C. de Oliveira Santos, "Methylmercury Neurotoxicity in Amazonian Children Downstream

from Gold Mining," *Environmental Health Perspectives* 107 (1999, 587–91). Also see Yumiko Uryu, Olaf Malm, Iain Thornton, Ian Payne, and David Cleary, "Mercury Contamination of Fish and Its Implications for Other Wildlife of the Tapajos Basin, Brazilian Amazon," *Conservation Biology* 15:2 (2001, 438–46).

109. Laurence Maurice-Bourgoin, Irma Quiroga, Jean Loup Guyot, and Olaf Malm, "Mercury Pollution in the Upper Beni River, Amazonian Basin, Bolivia," *Ambio* 28 (1999, 302–06).

110. Gold Sheet Links, www.goldsheetlinks.com.

111. World Gold Council, www.gold.org/discover/news/article/5744/.

112. Goulding, note 7, pp. 61–62, 64, 141, 159.

113. Rainforest Foundation, www.rainforestfoundation.org. For more information on the Yanomami situation in Brazil see Bruce Albert and Gale Goodwin Gomez, *Saude Yanomami: Um Manual Ethnolinguistico* (Belem: Museu Parense Emilio Goeldi, 1997); John D. Early and John F. Peters, *The Xilixana Yanomami of the Amazon: History, Social Structure, and Population Dynamics* (Gainesville: University of Florida Press, 2000); Gale Goodwin Gomez, "Forest Disturbance and Health Risks to the Yanomami," in *Human Health and Forests: A Global Overview of Issues, Practice and Policy,* Carol J. Pierce Colfer, Ed. (London: Earthscan Publications, 2008, 239–58). John F. Peters, *Life among the Yanomami: The Story of Change among the Xilixana on the Mucajai River of Brazil* (Peterborough, Ontario: Broadview Press, 1998); Pro-Yanomami Commission (CCPY), www.projanomami.org.br; Linda Rabben, *Brazil's Indians and the Onslaught of Civilization: The Yanomami and Kayapo* (Seattle: University of Washington Press, 2004); and Survival International London, www.Survival-International.org. Unfortunately, comparable initiatives and information apparently have not been generated in Venezuela.

114. Rhett A. Butler, 2007, "Proposed Gold Mine Proves Controversial in French Guiana Rainforest," www.mongabay.com/2007/1107-french_guiana.html.

115. Goodwin Gomez, note 14.

116. Ricardo Godoy, "Mining: Anthropological Perspectives," *Annual Review of Anthropology* 14 (1985, 199–217).

117. See, for example, Communities and Small-Scale Mining (CASM), www.casmsite.org.

118. Marieke Heemskerk, "Maroon Gold Miners and Mining Risks in the Suriname Amazon," *Cultural Survival Quarterly* 25:1 (2001, 25–29).

119. Marieke Heemskerk, "Self-Employment and Poverty Alleviation: Women's Work in Artisanal Gold Mines," *Human Organization* 62:1 (2003, 62–73); Marieke Heemskerk, "Risk Attitudes and Mitigation among Gold Miners and Others in the Suriname Rainforest," *Natural Resources Forum* 27:4 (2003, 267–78).

120. Marieke Heemskerk, "Livelihood Decision Making and Environmental Degradation: Small-Scale Gold Mining in the Suriname Amazon," *Society and Natural Resources* 15 (2002, 327–44).

121. Alisson Barbieri, Diana Oya Swayer, and Britaldo Silveira Soares-Filho, "Population and Land Use Effects on Malaria Prevalence in the Southern Brazilian Amazon," *Human Ecology* 33:6 (2005, 847–74).

122. Garry D. Peterson and Marieke Heemskerk, "Deforestation and Forest Regeneration Following Small-Scale Gold Mining in the Amazon: The Case of Suriname," *Environmental Conservation* 28 (2001, 117–26). Also see David S. Hammond, *Tropical Forests of the Guiana Shield: Ancient Forests in a Modern World* (Cambridge: CABI Publishers, 2005).

123. Butler, note 15.

124. Spiegel, note 2.

125. Ali, Saleem H., *Mining, the Environment, and Indigenous Development Conflicts* (Tucson: University of Arizona Press, 2003).

126. Spiegel, note 2.

127. Amazon Watch, www.amazonwatch.org; Association for Tropical Biology and Conservation, www.atbio.org; Communities and Small-scale Mining (CASM), www.casmsite.org; Instituto Socioambiental in Brazil, www.socioambiental.org/e/; Mercury Watch, http://web.uvic.ca/~hgwatch/Hg_watch_main.htm; Mines and Communities (MAC), www.minesandcommunities.org; Mining Watch Canada, www.miningwatch.ca; Survival International London, www.Survival-International.org; and World Rainforest Movement, www.wrm.org; World Wildlife Fund (WWF) Guianas Program, www.wwf-guianas.org.

128. Leslie E. Sponsel, "Advocacy in Anthropology," *International Encyclopedia of the Social and Behavioral Sciences*, N. J. Smelser and Paul B. Baltes, Eds. (Oxford: Pergamon Press, 2001, 204–06).

129. A. Gedicks, "Resource Wars against Native Peoples in Colombia," *Capitalism, Nature, and Socialism* 14:2 (2003, 85–119).

130. Chris Ballard and Glenn Banks, "Resource Wars: The Anthropology of Mining," *Annual Review of Anthropology* 32 (2003, 287–313).

131. Saleem Ali and Larissa Behrendt, Eds., "Mining Indigenous Lands: Can Impacts and Benefits Be Reconciled?" *Cultural Survival Quarterly* 25:1 (2001, 8).

132. Stephen G. Baines, "Dispatch II: Anthropology and Commerce in Brazilian Amazonia: Research with the Waimiri-Atroari Banned," *Critique of Anthropology* 11:4 (1991, 395–400).

133. David Cleary, "Toward an Environmental History of the Amazon: From Prehistory to the Nineteenth Century," *Latin American Research Review* 36:2 (2001, 64–96); Candace Slater, "All That Glitters: Contemporary Amazonian Gold Miners' Tales," *Society for the Comparative Study of Society and History* (1994, 720–42); Candace Slater, *Entangled Edens: Visions of the Amazon* (Berkeley and Los Angeles: University of California Press, 2002); John Hemming, *Tree of Rivers: The Story of the Amazon* (New York: Thames and Hudson, 2008); Ballard and Banks, note 29; Michael Klare, *Resource Wars: The New Landscape of Global Conflict* (New York: Harry Holt, 2002).

134. CASM, note 117. Also see Roger Moody, *Rocks and Hard Places: The Globalization of Mining* (New York: Zed Books, 2007).

135. Earthworks Action, www.earthworksaction.org; International Institute for Environment and Development (IIED) "Mining, Minerals and Sustainable Development," www.iied.org; Debora Cynamon Kligerman, Emilio Lebre La Rovere, and Maria Albertina Costa, "Management Challenges on Small-Scale Gold Mining Activities in Brazil," *Environmental Research* Section A, 87 (2001, 181–98); M. Sengupta, *Environmental Impacts of Mining: Monitoring, Restoration, and Control* (Boca Raton, FL: Lewis Publishers, 1993); Zero Mercury Global Campaign, www.zeromercury.org.

CHAPTER 7

War on Subsistence: Mining Rights at Crandon/Mole Lake, Wisconsin

Al Gedicks

SECTION I: The End of the Millennium

On March 29, 1995, the United States Army Corps of Engineers held a public hearing on the Mole Lake Sokaogon Chippewa Reservation, in Wisconsin, to take comments on Exxon/Rio Algom's proposed underground zinc-copper mine next to the reservation. Tribal members testified about the historical origins of their present reservation and the significance of the wild rice that they harvest from Rice Lake on the reservation. Fred Ackley, a tribal judge, recalled the history of the creation of the reservation at the hearing:

> The government asked our chief why he wanted this reservation in this spot. Our chief walked over and gave him a handful of wild rice and he said: "This is the food of Indian people. This is why I want my reservation here on this lake. There are six or seven other lakes in this area where my people have been harvesting food for a long time." So he wanted his reservation right here on this lake for the wild rice.
> Through the hard times that we've had to live as Indian people here in Mole Lake, we realized that money and everything else that the white people had, didn't count. Because what the Great Spirit gave us was the food for our people—subsistence to go on another year, to have another offspring, to bury another elder. Also, he taught us how to pray for that every year. We've been doing that every year here in Mole Lake. We still pray for everything we get. We do it our way.

Charles Ackley, the son of Chief Willard Ackley, still harvests and sells wild rice. He testified about the threat to wild rice from the proposed mine: "East of us here, where this mine is supposed to take place, is all spring fed. And if they start fooling around underground, they're going to be a lot of lakes going dry east of us here. And suppose that Exxon taps into our underground water spring? What is going to happen to our water situation in our community? And do we all want to risk that . . .?" Rose Van Zile is a grandmother and a veteran wild rice harvester:

Right now I'm saying I don't want this mine here. I don't want it to be part of my every-day life. When I grow old, I'd like to have my grandchildren here to comfort them, the way my grandparents comforted me and gave me the enjoyment of going to school, coming home, having my dinner and relaxing and knowing that I have a safe place to come home to every night. And when I rest I don't have to worry about the water or the wild rice.

I went out there for 23 years of my life and I picked rice. I still do today. And yes, I'm mad. I'm damned mad at this mining. To me, no mining in Mole Lake. That's what I say. That's what my grandson is going to say. That's what my children are going to say. No mining in Mole Lake. Thank you very much.

Indian tribes in the northern portions of Wisconsin, Minnesota, and Michigan are seriously threatened by sulfide mining operations in ways that are difficult for non-Indians to perceive. For Indian people, natural resource harvest is more than a means to provide food. It is a cultural activity that renews both the Indian person and the resource that is harvested.[1]

Recent court rulings have upheld the reserved rights of the Lake Superior Chippewa Nation to hunt, fish, and gather on public lands ceded to the U.S. govern-ment in 19th-century treaties.[2] For the past decade Chippewa (Ojibwa) spearfishers have had to defend those treaty rights against those northern Wisconsin residents who accused the Chippewa of depleting the fish populations. After disproving the racially motivated charges and peacefully resisting mob violence, the Chippewa now face the prospect of toxic contamination of their fish, deer, and wild rice resources as a result of large-scale mining projects in the Chippewa's ceded treaty lands. In 1975 Texas-based Exxon Minerals Co. discovered one of the 10 largest zinc-copper sulfide deposits in North America, adjacent to the Mole Lake Sokaogon Chippewa Reservation near Crandon, Wisconsin. Situated at the headwaters of the Wolf River in Forest County, Exxon proposed the largest of a series of metallic sulfide mines planned for northern Wisconsin. The Crandon/Mole Lake mine would extract ap-proximately 55 million tons of sulfide ore over 30 years.

In 1993, after prolonged opposition by environmental and Native American groups, Kennecott Copper (a subsidiary of London-based Rio Tinto Zinc) began an open-pit copper sulfide mine on the Flambeau River outside Ladysmith, Wisconsin. The Flambeau mine is tiny in comparison to the Exxon project. But it represents the "foot in the door" the mining industry has been after since 1968 when Kennecott first discovered the orebody at Ladysmith. In 1982 Exxon Minerals suggested that the state could host up to 10 major metal mines by the year 2000.[3]

Exxon's proposed underground shaft mine would disrupt far beyond its surface area of 550 square acres. Over its lifetime, the mine would generate an estimated 44 million tons of wastes—the equivalent of eight Great Pyramids of Egypt.[4] When metallic sulfide wastes have contact with water and air, the potential result is sulfuric acids plus high levels of poisonous heavy metals such as mercury, lead, zinc, arsenic, copper, and cadmium. After a decade of strong local opposition, Exxon withdrew from the project in 1986, citing depressed metal prices.[5] Exxon then returned in September 1993 to announce its intention to mine with a new partner—Canada-based Rio Algom—in their new Crandon Mining Co. Canada's mining industry newspaper, noted: "The only objections raised at the Crandon press conference . . . came from native Americans who expressed concern over archaeological aspects of the site. No objections were heard from environmental groups."[6] The paper's char-acterization of the objections from Native Americans as insignificant, compared to the possible objections from nonnative environmental groups, is all too typical of the way native cultures have been ignored by the dominant society.

Mining vs. Native Subsistence

The threat of annihilation has been hanging over this community since 1975. The mental stress and mental anguish are unbearable at times.[7] —Wayne LaBine, Sokaogon Chippewa tribal planner

The planned mine lies on territory sold by the Chippewa Nation to the United States in 1842, and directly on a 12-square mile tract of land promised to the Mole Lake Sokaogon Chippewa in 1855.[8] Treaties guaranteed Chippewa access to wild rice, fish, and some wild game on ceded lands. The Mole Lake Reservation (formed in 1939) is a prime harvester of wild rice in Wisconsin. The rice, called *manomim* ("gift from the creator"), is an essential part of the Chippewa diet, an important cash crop, and a sacred part of the band's religious rituals.[9] "Rice Lake and the bounty of the lakes harvest lie at the heart of their identity as a people. . . . The rice and the lake are the major links between themselves, Mother Earth, their ancestors, and future generations."[10]

Any contamination or drawdown of water would threaten the survival of both fish and wild rice. The Chippewa were not reassured when Exxon's biologist mistook their wild rice for a "bunch of lake weeds." Later, Exxon maintained that any pollutants from the mine would travel along the rim of Rice Lake and cause no harm to the delicate ecology of wild rice. The tribe asked the U.S. Geological Survey to perform a dye test to determine the path of potential pollutants. The results showed the dye dispersing over the entire lake. Exxon's own environmental impact report blandly mentioned that "the means of subsistence on the reservation" may be "rendered less than effective."[11]

Sokaogon chairman Arlyn Ackley recalled Exxon's previous attempt to develop the ore body:

Exxon claimed it would be an "environmentally safe" mine in the 1970s. They claimed it wouldn't harm our sacred wild rice beds or water resources. We had to spend our own money on tests to prove their project would in fact contaminate our subsistence harvest areas and lower the water level of Rice Lake. Exxon's claims of environmentally safe mining were unfounded.

I think these companies are willing to lie. Their history is one of pollution, destruction, and death. Just last month, more than 70 Yanomami Indians were massacred by miners in the Amazon forest. As far as we are concerned, Exxon and Rio Algom are of the same mind set. Let it be known here and now that these companies are prepared to plunder and destroy our people and lands for their insatiable greed. They may be more polite in North America, but they are no less deadly to Native people.[12]

Half the projected mine waste is rocky "coarse tailings," which would be dumped to fill up the mine shafts. The other half is powdery "fine tailings," which would be dumped into a waste pond covering 350 acres (about 350 football fields), at least 90 feet tall. The water table beneath these ponds is as close as 15 feet down. As proposed, it would be the largest toxic waste dump in Wisconsin history.[13] To control leakage into wells and streams, Exxon plans to place a liner under the waste pond. The U.S. Environmental Protection Agency (EPA) admits that tailings ponds are "regulated . . . loosely" and that leaks from even the best of dumps "will inevitably occur."[14] The U.S. Forest Service says that "there are currently no widely applicable technologies" to prevent acid mine drainage.[15] The mining industry cannot point to a single example of a metallic sulfide mine that has been successfully reclaimed (returned to a natural state).[16] The half-mile-deep mine shafts would also drain groundwater supplies, in much the same way that a syringe draws blood from a patient. The wastewater would be constantly pumped out of the shafts, "drawing down" water levels in a four-square-mile area. This "dewatering" could lower lakes by several feet, and dry up wells and springs.[17]

The potential threat to the economy and culture of the Sokaogon Chippewa from Exxon's proposed mine must also be evaluated in the context of the cumulative environmental threats facing both Indian and non-Indian communities in the north woods. These Indian nations already suffer a disproportionate environmental risk of illness and other health problems from eating wildlife contaminated with such industrial pollutants as airborne polychlorinated biphenyls (PCBs), mercury, and other toxins deposited on land and water. "Fish and game have accumulated these toxic chemicals," according to a 1992 EPA study, "to levels posing substantial health, ecological, and cultural risks to a Native American population that relies heavily on local fish and game for subsistence. As the extent of fish and game contamination is more fully investigated by state and federal authorities, advisories suggesting limited or no consumption of fish and game are being established for a large portion of the Chippewa's traditional hunting and fishing areas."[18]

The Watershed Alliance to End Environmental Racism

They put us here years and years ago on federal land and now that we're here—they discover something—and they either want to take it from us or move us away from it. We don't want to do this. This is where I belong. This is my home. —Myra Tuckwab, Sokaogon Chippewa tribal member[19]

If Exxon had limited the conflict over the mine to a contest between itself and the Sokaogon, the construction of the mine would be a foregone conclusion. Multinational mining companies have a long record of overwhelming native peoples whose resources they have sought to control.[20] In each case, the corporation has sought to reduce its political and financial risks by limiting the arena of conflict so that the victims are completely exposed to the reach of the corporation—while only one tentacle of the corporation's worldwide organization is exposed to the opposition.[21]

The nature of this proposed mine, however, posed a number of environmental and social threats that were of major concern to native residents, environmental groups, sportfishing groups, and other Indian tribes. The nearby Menominee, Potawatomi, and Stockbridge-Munsee nations would be severely affected by the mine pollution and the social upheaval brought by new outsiders. With Mole Lake, they formed the Nii Win Intertribal Council. Unlike in the last Exxon battle, the tribes have considerably more revenues available from casino proceeds that can be used to fight Exxon's current proposal. Nii Win immediately began hiring lawyers and technical experts to challenge Exxon/Rio Algom's mine permit application. They also purchased a Nii Win house on a seven-acre parcel, across the road from the Exxon mine site, to monitor all activities at the site. The Oneida Nation, which is downstream from the mine near Green Bay, also joined the opposition. In the distant and recent past, these tribes have survived relocation, termination, and assimilation, against overwhelming odds. They now see the mine as one more threat to their cultures and their future generations. All five tribes are working in alliance with environmental and sport-fishing groups within a campaign called Watershed Alliance to end Environmental Racism (WATER). Conflict over treaty spearfishing pitted Chippewa against some white fishers from 1984 to 1992[22] but now the mining conflict finds them on the same side, opposing an outside threat.

Opening Up the Mine Permit Process

Our reservation is directly adjacent to this mine project. The mine water will flow through it. How can the DNR possibly discuss socioeconomic impacts without even notifying our tribe of this meeting? Our people stand to lose our very existence. Our wild rice beds will be devastated. Our cultural and spiritual traditions will be seriously damaged—or destroyed. . . . Yet the DNR has the arrogance to assume we don't need to be invited to the table. —Arlyn Ackley, Sokaogon Chippewa Tribal Chairman[23]

One of the symptoms of environmental racism, along with the disproportionate impact that racial minorities experience from environmental hazards, is the exclusion of minorities from participation in the decision-making process. One of the objectives of the WATER campaign is to provide statewide press advisories of any activity by the Wisconsin Department of Natural Resources (DNR) or the Crandon Mining Co. (CMC) relating to the mine permitting process.

In January 1994 the DNR had planned a series of meetings with officials and consultants of the CMC to determine the scope of the social and environmental studies that would be part of the company's mine permit application. Although the DNR did not notify any of the affected Indian and non-Indian communities, word leaked out and WATER issued a statewide press advisory that was picked up over the wire services. On the morning of the first meeting, the headline in the state's largest morning newspaper was: "Indian leaders blast DNR over meetings on mining project." The DNR's mine project coordinator, Bill Tans, said Chippewa leaders were not invited because the meetings were not set up for public comment.[24] Tans explained that the tribes would have an opportunity to comment at the time of CMC's publication of a Notice of Intent and a scope of study for its mine permit application in April 1994. However, this effectively excluded tribes from determining the agenda for the proposed studies. It also contributes to a "psychology of inevitability" about the mine because all the planning is done behind closed doors and presented to the public as an accomplished fact. As a result of the negative publicity, the DNR agreed to notify the tribes in advance of any planned meetings with CMC.

Even before Exxon/Rio Algom filed its notice of intent to seek mining permits, the WATER campaign had announced a statewide emergency rally to stop the proposed mine at the state capitol in Madison. In March 1994, over 400 people rallied and listened as Frances Van Zile, an *Anishinabekwe* (Chippewa woman), spoke about the role of women as the "Keepers of the Water" in her culture:

This isn't an Indian issue, nor is it a white issue. It's everybody's issue. Everybody has to take care of that water. The women are the ones who are the keepers of that water. I ask all women to stand up and support that and realize that if it wasn't for the water none of us would be here today because when we first started out in life, we were born in that water in our mother's womb. And I'll bet you everybody here turned on that water today to do something with it. And that's what they're going to pollute. That's what they're going to destroy. I'm not going to have any more wild rice if that water drops down three feet from the mine dewatering. That is important to my way of life—to all Anishinabes' way of life.

And they're taking that away—they're going to destroy our way of life.

Next, demonstrators marched to the headquarters of the Wisconsin DNR and to the Wisconsin Manufacturers and Commerce Association—one of the chief lobbying organizations for mining companies and mining equipment manufacturers in Milwaukee. The WATER campaign intended to put corporate and governmental decision makers on notice that the resistance to this mine project could reach the centers of corporate and governmental power. Sokaogon Chippewa tribal members Fred Ackley and Frances Van Zile dramatically illustrated this strategy when they attended Exxon's annual shareholder meeting in Dallas, Texas, the following month.

The Exxon Shareholder Campaign

We see our shareholder actions as a vehicle to give access to corporate board rooms for communities like Mole Lake.[25] —Toni Harris, Sinsinawa Dominican Sisters of Wisconsin

In addition to environmental and fishing groups, the WATER campaign included various church groups that held stock in several mining companies and were willing to raise issues of social and corporate responsibility through shareholder resolutions. Shortly after Exxon announced its intention to seek mining permits at Crandon/Mole Lake, the Sinsinawa Dominican Sisters of Wisconsin, along with six other religious congregations, filed a resolution on behalf of the Sokaogon Chippewa and the other affected Native communities. The resolution specifically asked Exxon to provide a report to shareholders on the impact of the proposed mine on indigenous peoples and on any sacred sites within indigenous communities. It also called on Exxon to disclose "the nature of and reason(s) for any public opposition to our Company's mining operations wherever they may occur."[26]

Exxon immediately informed the U.S. Securities and Exchange Commission, which has regulatory authority over shareholder resolutions, that it intended to omit the Sinsinawa resolution from its 1994 proxy statement. The company argued that the resolution is moot because Exxon and Wisconsin DNR had prepared impact studies for the previously proposed mine in 1986.[27] Sister Toni Harris responded that the studies Exxon referred to did not address the specific questions raised in their resolution. "Most significantly," said Harris, the 1986 impact statement "was criticized as inadequate by the U.S. Department of the Interior and the Environmental Protection Agency."[28] The SEC ruled that the Sinsinawa resolution was not "moot" and that Exxon could not exclude the resolution from stockholder consideration.

With the SEC victory in hand, the Chippewa were able to challenge Exxon on its home turf. Fred Ackley and Frances Van Zile explained to shareholders that the very existence of their culture was at stake in this proposed mining investment. The resolution received an impressive 6% of the vote, or 49 million shares (most shareholder resolutions of this type receive less than 3%). While the resolution was defeated, the Chippewa won enough votes to reintroduce the resolution at the 1995 shareholders meeting.[29]

The Wolf River: Ecology and Economics

> Crandon Mining Company's proposed construction and operation of a hardrock metallic sulfide mine at the headwaters of the Wolf River seriously threatens this magnificent river. Water quality and tremendous ecological diversity is imperiled, including bald eagle, wild rice, lake sturgeon, and trout habitat. The Wolf River is the lifeline of the Menominee people and central to our existence. We will let no harm come to the river.[30] —John Teller, Menominee Tribal Chairman

"The environment comes first," says Jerry D. Goodrich, president of the Crandon Mining Company. "If we can't protect the Wolf, there'll be no Crandon mine."[31] The Wolf River is at the center of the northeastern Wisconsin tourist economy and the meeting ground between Indians and sportfishers who have a history of bitter disagreement over Chippewa spearfishing.[32] It is the state's largest whitewater trout stream, supporting brown, brook, and rainbow trout fisheries. Over 50,000 tourists are attracted to the area every year to enjoy trout fishing, whitewater rafting, and canoeing.[33] The lower half of the river is designated a National Wild and Scenic River.

During Exxon's first attempt to develop the Crandon/Mole Lake deposit, the Wolf River became a rallying point for both environmental and tribal opposition. The Menominee Indian Nation strongly opposed the mine, partly because the Wolf River runs through their reservation. Exxon's proposal called for dumping over 2,000 gallons of wastewater per minute into the trout-rich streams that drain into the Wolf River. A biological consultant to environmental groups concluded: "The discharge of waste water from the Crandon Project to Swamp Creek could result in the bioaccumulation of heavy metals in aquatic organisms and changes in the natural species composition of the area."[34] By the time that the DNR held public hearings on the draft environmental impact statement in June 1986, more than 10,000 signatures had been collected on petitions asking the governor, the legislature, and the DNR to oppose any dumping into the Wolf River. The Langlade County board passed a similar resolution. This mobilization of public sentiment became a major turning point in the first Exxon battle because the widely perceived economic threat to the Wolf River tourism industry outweighed potential economic benefits from the mine.

Shortly after Exxon announced that it would once again seek permits for the mine, the Wolf River Territory Association, a group of business people promoting the area for tourism, passed a resolution against it. Herb Buettner, owner of the Wild Wolf Inn and president of the Wolf River chapter of Trout Unlimited, warned that the mine "would wipe out the Wolf River trout stream and create a pile of tailings that in 50 years would be a Superfund site."[35]

CMC's statements about environmental preservation did not reassure those familiar with Exxon's strong opposition to DNR's proposed classification of the upper Wolf River as an Outstanding Resource Water (ORW) under the provisions of the federal Clean Water Act. If this status were granted, any water discharged into the Wolf would have to be as clean as the water in the river, or cleaner. The first indication that Exxon might revive its Crandon project came in May 1988 when James D. Patton, Exxon Minerals' manager of regulatory affairs, wrote to Wisconsin DNR Secretary Carroll Besadny warning that DNR's proposed classification of the Wolf River "could create a significant potential roadblock to any future resumption of the Crandon project."[36] Exxon's intense lobbying against the designation was counteracted by the combined forces of the Menominee Tribe and the Wolf River Watershed Alliance. The Wolf River received ORW status in November 1988.

The 1989 Exxon Valdez oil spill raised additional doubts about Exxon's ability to manage a high-risk mining venture in this ecologically sensitive watershed. Adding to doubts about Exxon's environmental record is the fact that Crandon Mining Co.'s first public relations officer, J. Wiley Bragg, handled public relations for Exxon in Alaska after the Exxon-Valdez spill.[37] Before the first public hearing on Exxon's mine permit application, the WATER campaign ran a series of local newspaper ads that asked: "Will the Wolf River Be Exxon's Valdez? What If It Happened Here?" The ads urged citizens to attend the DNR public hearing and voice concerns about the proposed mine. More than 300 people, including Native Americans, local property owners, fishers, small business owners, and environmentalists, packed into the Nashville Town Hall in April 1994. The DNR stayed past midnight and still was not able to accommodate all those who wanted to speak. Of the 300 people who attended the hearing, only a handful spoke in favor of the project; two-thirds of the people who testified mentioned their concern about the Wolf River, local lakes and streams, or groundwater.

Some mine opponents accused the DNR of manipulating the order in which testimony was heard and preventing several knowledgeable anti-mining citizens from speaking until the media and the majority of the audience had left. Among those who had registered early in the evening but was not called until last was Wisconsin Public Intervenor Laura Sutherland. The Public Intervenor is an office in the Wisconsin Department of Justice empowered to protect public rights in the natural resources of the state. Despite Exxon's objections, the Citizens Advisory Committee, which oversees the Public Intervenor, unanimously directed the Public Intervenor to review Exxon's mine proposal. One of Sutherland's principal concerns was the fact that "the DNR has never before permitted *any* discharge into ORW waters and this mine proposal, therefore, presents the possibility of a dangerous precedent."[38] Although Sutherland's testimony was not covered in the press immediately, the *Milwaukee Journal* featured her testimony in a front-page story the following week, followed by a strong editorial that warned: "The loss of recreation and tourism from a degraded environment could end up outweighing any economic gains from the mine."[39]

Before the DNR meeting, Crandon Mining Company president Jerry Goodrich sent out a letter to local residents warning: "Certain groups opposed to mining and other industry development are planning to bus people in from Green Bay, Madison, Milwaukee and other distant locations to pack the hearing with opponents of the Crandon Project (or, at least, people who will say they are opponents of the project)."[40] It was the classic "outside agitator" ploy. It backfired when the WATER campaign took out ads in local newspapers that asked: "Can We Trust Exxon to Tell the Truth?" The ad pointed out: "There were NO busloads of opponents, there were never any planned. In fact, 68% of those who gave oral statements were from Forest County and the area immediately downriver of the project. The only people that came from 'distant locations' were the employees of Exxon temporarily living near Crandon. Mr. Goodrich, where do you get your misinformation?"[41]

In April 1995 the national conservation group American Rivers placed the Wolf River on its list of the nation's 20 most threatened rivers because of the possibility of pollution from Exxon/Rio Algom's proposed mine. The Menominee, along with the River Alliance of Wisconsin and the Mining Impact Coalition of Wisconsin, provided the documentation on the threat from mine pollution. The very next day Exxon announced it was abandoning plans to dump treated wastewater into the

Wolf River and instead would build a 40-mile pipeline and divert the wastewater into the Wisconsin River. Mine opponents were quick to point out that the new plan threatens pollution of both the Wolf *and* Wisconsin rivers, because tailings from the mine would still be stored at the headwaters of the Wolf. Because the Wisconsin River is not as clean as the Wolf, the company would not have to spend as much treating the discharge. In addition, the plan could actually increase groundwater depletion in the area of the mine because of the amount of water necessary to pump the wastes to Rhinelander.[42] Whatever the motivation for the change of plans, Exxon had retreated from claims that it could meet the stringent requirements for a water body with Outstanding Resource Water designation.

In all these activities, the WATER campaign is developing a multifaceted counterstrategy to Exxon's ecologically and culturally destructive mine plans. Through intertribal organization, alliance building with environmental and sportfishing groups, mass demonstrations, shareholder resolutions, and mass media publicity, the Sokaogon Chippewa hope to increase the political and financial risks of the project for Exxon and Rio Algom. This was why the Sokaogon and the Nii Win Intertribal Council invited the Indigenous Environmental Network (IEN) to hold their fifth annual "Protecting Mother Earth Conference" on the Mole Lake Reservation in June 1994, in conjunction with a regional gathering coordinated by the Midwest Treaty Network. IEN conferences brought together community-based indigenous activists from throughout the Americas and the Pacific Islands to work together to protect indigenous lands from contamination and exploitation. Previous efforts have helped defeat a proposed landfill on the Rosebud Lakota Reservation in South Dakota and incinerator and asbestos landfill on Dine (Navajo) land in Arizona.[43]

International Networking

There'll be decades of fallout regardless of who wins this battle. This is one of the great events. We want to put Mole Lake and Exxon on the map.[44] —Walter Bresette, Red Cliff band of Lake Superior Chippewa

Approximately 1,000 people gathered on the Mole Lake Reservation during the five-day conference. On the last day over 300 native and nonnative people participated in a "spirit walk" to the proposed mine site where they conducted a spiritual ceremony while trespassing on Exxon's property. Exxon called the Crandon police but no arrests were made. The police were reluctant to interrupt the ceremony.

The Mole Lake gathering also featured a Wisconsin Review Commission to review the track records of Exxon and Rio Algom around the world. The commission included groups representing farmers, churches, workers, civil rights activists, women, small businesses, tribal governments, and recreational groups. A similar commission was assembled in the 1970s by the Black Hills Alliance to investigate uranium mining companies that wanted to mine in the sacred Black Hills of the Lakota (Sioux).

The panel, chaired by Wisconsin Secretary of State Douglas LaFollette, heard testimony from Native people who came from Alaska, New Mexico, Colombia, and Ontario. Testimony focused on people who have been directly affected by Exxon's mining and oil drilling activities and its chemical and oil leaks.

Nearly all the testimony was delivered by Native peoples from North and South America, which reflects the fact that a disproportionate amount of resource extraction occurs on Native lands. Native Eyak fisher Dune Lankard explained how the Exxon Valdez spill damaged the resource-based cultures of local Native peoples on Prince William Sound:

> I grew up fishing since I was five years old on the ocean. I thought I had the most incredible way of life in the world and I never believed once that anyone could ever kill the ocean. So when it happened, I was in shock. They leave you with the social impacts—the suicide, the alcohol, the drug abuse, the loss of jobs, the loss of a way of life, the loss of language, the loss of subsistence. How do you add all that up? How do you compensate somebody for taking everything away from you?[45]

After the oil spill Eyak government leaders complained that Exxon simply refused to recognize their Native group. The company took the position that the Eyak were not adversely affected by the oil spill, and it consequently refused to provide food and services that were provided for Natives elsewhere.[46] Exxon was fined $5 billion in punitive damages for economic losses from the spill in 1995. The company is appealing the fine.

Some of the most damning testimony came from Armando Valbuena Gouriyù, a Wayuu Indian from the Guajira peninsula, on the northern tip of Colombia, where Exxon operates the El Cerrejòn open-pit coal mine in a joint venture with the Colombian government. It is the largest coal mine in the western hemisphere. Valbuena worked there from 1983 until Exxon fired him for his union organizing activities in 1988. The construction of the mine had a devastating effect on the lives of approximately 90 Wayuu *apushis* (matrilineal kinship groupings), who saw their houses, corrals, cleared ground, and cemeteries flattened for the construction of a road from El Cerrejòn to the new port of Puerto Bolivar, with no respect for indigenous rights.[47] The excavation of the open pit has also caused the adjoining rivers and streams to dry up, along with people's drinking wells. The total area affected is roughly 94,000 acres.[48] Colombian army troops and armored tanks were called in three times to break miners' strikes.[49] In 1992 the London-based Survival International, an international Native rights organization, named Exxon to its list of the top 10 companies who were doing serious damage to tribal peoples' land in the Americas.[50] Current Crandon Mining Company president Jerry Goodrich was vice president at El Cerrejòn when more than 30 workers died during work there.[51]

The Wisconsin Review Commission released its report on the track records of Exxon and Rio Algom on March 24, 1995—the sixth anniversary of the Exxon Valdez oil spill. In releasing the report Wisconsin Secretary of State Douglas La Follette urged the state legislature to approve the mining "bad actor" legislation that would require the state to consider a company's past performance before approving state mine permits. "Past violations," La Follette said, "are taken into account for everything from driver's licenses to gaming licenses, but not permits for potentially harmful mining developments."[52] The commission presented its citizens' hearing panel as a model for public participation in the absence of governmental action, as well as for multinational citizens' tracking of multinational corporations.

Exxon was offered the opportunity to respond to the charges in the report before its publication but chose not to do so. Instead, Exxon criticized the report for being "obviously biased. . . . The mine will be developed with today's technology and shouldn't be judged by things that were done under old technology."[53]

The Movement to Ban Sulfide Metal Mining

Exxon could not have imagined the opposition this project would generate. It has united people from all over the state in defense of our resources. . . . Thanks to this legislation they are being mobilized.[54] —Bob Hudek, Executive Director, Wisconsin Citizen Action

The typical industry response to any criticism about mine waste problems was that "new technologies" would solve any potential problems. The WATER campaign decided to create a petition drive that would force the industry and the Wisconsin DNR to disclose how these "new technologies" would solve the fundamental problems of acid mine drainage from metallic sulfide mines. The petitions, with over 10,000 signatures, asked the Natural Resources Board, the citizen board that oversees the DNR, to use its rule-making authority to ban the mining of sulfide mineral deposits because of the well-known releases of acid drainage from sulfide metallic wastes and the responsibility of the DNR to prevent pollution resulting from the leaching of waste materials.

Although DNR Secretary George Meyer told the board that it did not have the authority to ban metallic sulfide mining, he admitted that his staff could find no examples of successfully reclaimed metallic sulfide mines.[55] The board denied the petition, but mine opponents won a stunning victory when a Rusk County judge overturned it and asked the DNR to come up with rules to ban metallic sulfide mining.[56] The DNR appealed the decision. The Wisconsin Appeals Court ruled in favor of the DNR, saying that the legislature did not authorize the DNR to ban metallic sulfide mining.

Meanwhile, mine opponents worked with state Rep. Spencer Black (D-Madison) to introduce a mining moratorium bill that would prohibit the opening of a new mine in a sulfide ore body until a similar mine has been operated elsewhere and closed for at least 10 years without pollution from acid mine drainage. Despite a well-organized grassroots lobbying campaign and an overwhelming Assembly vote (95–4) to bring the bill out of committee for consideration, the powerful mining lobby convinced the Republican-controlled Senate to adjourn a week early to avoid sending the bill back to the Assembly for a final vote.[57] Mine opponents responded to the legislative setback by launching a statewide Mining Moratorium Pledge Campaign asking every candidate for state legislative office to pledge to support the moratorium bill in the next legislative session.

The Federal Environmental Review Process

Even if the mining company makes substantial financial commitments for restoration of the site, there will more than likely be damages not provided for with financial assurances. The neighbors, particularly the tribes, will receive a relatively meager proportion of the short term economic benefit, but by virtue of the location of their lands, will inherit the brunt of the environmental problems and economic bust cycle. It seems unfair that a large and powerful, but temporarily involved, interested party can reap the benefits, but leave the majority of the costs to less powerful interests who cannot reasonably move from the area to escape long term costs.[58] —Janet Smith, U.S. Department of the Interior, Fish and Wildlife Service, Green Bay, Wisconsin

The construction of the proposed Crandon mine would involve the filling of approximately 30 acres of wetlands. Under the provisions of the Clean Water Act, the U.S. Army Corps of Engineers (COE) must review such projects. In November 1994, the Fish and Wildlife Service of the U.S. Department of the Interior (DOI) expressed serious reservations about the project because "it could potentially result in a diminishment of Indian interests in exchange for benefits for the general public. The courts have held that federal agencies cannot subordinate Indian interests to other public purposes except when specifically authorized by Congress to do so."[59]

The DOI recommended that the affected tribes play a greater role in identifying environmental impacts and "impacts to Indian trust resources" as defined in the treaties with the federal government. Furthermore, the DOI recommended that the COE be the sole lead agency for the federal environmental impact statement (EIS) "so that the impacts to Indian trust resources can be appropriately assessed in a purely federal forum. The state does not have the authority to assess impacts to Indian trust lands and thus should have no role in doing so."[60] The COE's decision to conduct its own EIS has provided mine opponents with two separate opportunities to argue their case.

The public hearings held by the COE on the Crandon project brought out overwhelming public opposition in the capital city of Madison, in Crandon itself, and on the Sokaogon Chippewa reservation. At the hearing on the reservation tribal members expressed their determination to stop Exxon's proposed mine. Bill Koenen, a tribal member and environmental specialist, testified as his three sons stood beside him: "Our children will be right behind us to help us defend our sacred land and wild rice beds." And Robert Van Zile, a traditional pipe carrier, reflected the views of many who spoke when he said, "If I have to defend this land with my life, I will."[61]

While Exxon has claimed that its Crandon mine studies are "one of the most thorough environmental studies in state history,"[62] the COE determined that the groundwater models used by Exxon to predict water drawdown around the mine are scientifically inadequate and proposed additional studies by an independent consultant.[63]

Tribal Sovereignty and Regulatory Authority

This move by the Thompson/Klauser administration to fight clean water comes as no surprise. Klauser was Exxon's chief lobbyist when the mining industry helped rewrite Wisconsin's water quality laws that govern mining. They eliminated the Public Intervenor's Office, made the administration of the DNR a political appointment, and are even appealing the state judicial decision that gives the DNR authority to determine what kinds of mining are to be allowed. Thompson will not let anything interfere with Exxon's proposed mine—not State or Federal law, not the will of the citizens, and not the concern for clean water.[64] —Sandy Lyon, WATER Campaign

In 1984 the EP announced that it would pursue government-to-government relations with tribes.[65] In 1994–95 three Wisconsin Indian tribes asked the EPA for greater regulatory authority over reservation air and water quality. The Forest County Potawatomi asked for tougher air pollution standards on its reservation under the federal Clean Air Act[66] and the Sokaogon Chippewa and Oneida were granted independent authority to regulate water quality on their reservations. The EPA can designate tribes as independent regulators of surface water quality as it can to states. Tribal regulatory authority would affect all upstream industrial and municipal facilities, including Exxon's proposed mine in the Swamp Creek watershed. Because Swamp Creek flows into the tribe's Rice Lake, the Sokaogon have to give approval for any physical, chemical, or biological upstream activity that might degrade their wild rice beds.[67]

At public hearings on the tribal requests, local citizens, lake associations, and the Wolf River Watershed Alliance testified in support of tribal regulatory authority. Many of the local lake property owners associations expressed extreme dissatisfaction with the way in which Republican Governor Tommy Thompson and his chief aide, James Klauser, a former Exxon lobbyist, paved the way for mining by making the DNR Secretary a political appointment and eliminating the Public Intervenor's Office. The experts hired by the Public Intervenor had raised serious questions about the scientific adequacy of Exxon's groundwater studies and their waste disposal plans. Many citizens applauded the tribe for trying to preserve clean water for everybody.[68]

Some local business people testified in opposition, charging that the regulations would "shut down northern Wisconsin." This was the same kind of misinformation used by those who opposed Chippewa off-reservation spearfishing during the turmoil lasting from 1984 to 1992. The Wisconsin Mining Association, representing some of the largest mining equipment companies in Milwaukee, warned that tribal water quality authority "could be the most controversial and contentious environmental development affecting the state in decades."[69]

Within a week of EPA approval of Sokaogon Chippewa and Oneida water quality authority, Wisconsin Attorney General James Doyle sued the EPA in federal court, demanding that the federal government reverse its decision to let Indian tribes make their own water pollution laws. Several Republican state legislators have called on Congress to change the Clean Air Act to disallow tribal authority over clean-air standards.[70] Once again, mainstream politicians are using scare tactics to suggest that Indian sovereignty over reservation resources is an economic threat to small business owners while they ignore the serious potential for long-term damage to the resources and economic base of northern Wisconsin. In response, the Wolf River Watershed Alliance filed an *amicus* brief supporting EPA's approval of requests by the Sokaogon Chippewa and Oneida tribes. "If the state is stupid enough to appeal this thing, we'll certainly write a brief detailing all the instances where the state has been derelict in its authority or abdicated its responsibility," said Robert Schmitz, president of the alliance.[71] Meanwhile, a federal court ruling in Montana has upheld the right of Indian tribes to set water-quality standards on their reservations.[72]

Save Our Clean Waters Speaking Tour

Exxon executives seriously underestimated the depth and extent of public opposition.[73] The Wolf River Watershed Education Project was an effort to bring the issue to the public that would be directly affected by the mine—whether environmentally, economically, or culturally. The project built on previous joint efforts of grassroots environmental groups, sportfishing groups, and Native American nations. When Exxon announced its plan to divert mine wastewater into the Wisconsin River, the project expanded to include that watershed.

Beginning on Earth Day, two speaking tours simultaneously went up the Wolf and Wisconsin rivers, stopping in communities along the way. Major goals of the tour included building momentum for a rally at the Hat Rapids dam on the Wisconsin River, the site where Exxon/Rio Algom proposes to discharge treated wastewater, and mobilizing public support for legislative passage of a moratorium on sulfide mining. The 12-day tours drew over 1,000 people in 22 cities and towns, and a parade past Exxon/Rio Algom corporate headquarters in Rhinelander, Wisconsin, drew some 1,000 people. Exxon responded with radio and full-page newspaper advertisements in cities and towns along the Save Our Clean Waters speaking tour.[74] Company spokespeople accused mine opponents of spreading misinformation and half-truths about the project, without themselves specifically identifying a single example. The WATER Campaign responded with its own radio ads. The text of one ad read as follows: "The DNR couldn't find a single metallic sulfide mine anywhere that had been closed without polluting the water. In light of this fact, it makes you wonder. Why should Wisconsin's water be the proving ground for Exxon's experiment?"

At the same time, two independent experts retained by the Wisconsin DNR raised serious concerns about virtually every aspect of the Exxon's waste disposal plan. The DNR has asked the company to do further testing to determine the potential for acid generation and toxic metal releases from mine wastes.[75] This research will involve additional costs and will upset the company's permit timetable by at least two years, providing ample opportunities to mobilize even greater public opposition to the project.

Whatever the final outcome, the coming together of the five tribes with their nonnative neighbors, environmental, and sportfishing groups to oppose Exxon/Rio Algom has transformed this local battle into what *The New York Times* has described as "one of the country's fiercest grass-roots environmental face-offs."[76]

Conclusion

> Resource extraction plans . . . proposed for Indigenous lands do not consider the significance of these economic systems, nor their value for the future. A direct consequence is that environmentally destructive programs ensue, many times foreclosing the opportunity to continue the lower scale, intergenerational economic practices which had been underway in the Native community.[77] —Winona La Duke, Anishinabe (Chippewa) activist

Mining, by its very nature, constitutes an assault on the physical, social, and cultural environment. When this assault occurs in ecologically sensitive areas inhabited by native peoples who rely on traditional subsistence economies, the results can be disastrous. In the past, this corporate assault on Native cultures has frequently gone unnoticed and unreported. Chippewa resistance to Exxon's proposed mine emerged at a time when Native peoples all around the world were actively opposing large-scale destructive development projects on or adjacent to their lands. Their initial efforts to oppose Exxon were favorably viewed by some of their non-Indian neighbors and an effective Native–environmental alliance was born. With the emergence of the Watershed Alliance to end Environmental Racism, a new level of political organization and resistance has emerged to challenge the unquestioned assumptions of global industrialization—and the inevitable disappearance of Native subsistence cultures.

SECTION II: View from the 21st Century[78]

Mining Rights at Crandon/Mole Lake, Wisconsin"[79]

In the aftermath of the successful 1996 "Save Our Clean Waters Speaking Tour," the Mole Lake Chippewa joined with their non-Indian neighbors in Nashville (which covers half the mine site and includes the reservation), not only to fight the mine proposal but also to chart economic alternatives to mining development. In December

1996 the Nashville town board signed a local mining agreement with Exxon/Rio Algom, after a number of illegally closed meetings and despite the objections of a majority of township residents. The former town board was replaced in the April 1997 election by an anti-mining board, which included a Mole Lake tribal member. In September 1998 the new town board rescinded the local agreement. Without this agreement from the town, the state cannot grant a mining permit. The mining company sued the town for violation of contract. The township countersued the company, charging that the local agreement "resulted from a conspiracy by the mining company and the town's former attorneys to defraud the town of its zoning authority over the proposed mining operation."[80] To raise funds to defend itself the town set up its own website to explain how people can donate money for a legal defense fund in what the town called a 'David and Goliath" showdown. In January 2002 a state appeals court upheld the 1996 local agreement.

Cooperative relations between the town and the Mole Lake tribe were further strengthened when they received a U.S. $2.5 million grant from the federal government to promote long-term sustainable jobs in this impoverished community. Together with surrounding townships, the Menominee Nation, the Lac du Flambeau Tribe, and Mole Lake formed the Northwoods NiiJii Enterprise Community (*NiiJii* being the Chippewa word for "friends"). Now Indians and non-Indians are working together to provide a clear alternative to the unstable "boom and bust" cycle that mining would bring to their communities. If successful, the unique project could bring in an additional U.S. $7 to $10 million to these communities over the next decade. This effort, combined with casinos that have made the tribes the largest employers in Forest County, has dampened the appeal of mining jobs for many local residents. Indian gaming, although not providing an economic panacea for many tribes, has enabled some tribes to finance legal and public relations fights against the mining companies. One of these fights used federally recognized tribal sovereignty to enhance environmental protection of reservation lands.

Tribal Water and Air Regulatory Authority

Tribal lands were ignored in the original versions of many federal environmental laws of the 1970s, including the Clean Air Act and the Clean Water Act. To remedy this exclusion, amendments to these laws have been enacted to give tribes the same standing as states to enforce environmental standards. In 1995 the Mole Lake Chippewa became the first Wisconsin tribe granted independent authority by the U.S. Environmental Protection Agency (EPA) to regulate water quality on their reservation. The tribe's wild rice beds are just a mile downstream from the proposed Crandon mine. Tribal regulatory authority would affect all upstream industrial and municipal facilities, including the proposed mine. Because Swamp Creek flows into the tribe's rice lake, the tribe has to give approval for any upstream discharges that might degrade their wild rice beds.

Wisconsin Attorney General James Doyle immediately sued the EPA and the tribe in federal court, demanding that the federal government reverse its decision to let Indian tribes make their own water pollution laws. A petition urging Doyle to drop the lawsuit was signed by 26 environmental groups, 2 neighboring townships, and 454 people in 121 communities around the state. In April 1999 the U.S. District Court in Milwaukee dismissed the Wisconsin lawsuit and upheld the tribe's right to establish water-quality standards to protect its wild rice beds. The state appealed this decision. Four townships downstream from the proposed mine signed on as "friends of the court" on the side of the EPA and the tribe. In June 2002 the U.S. Supreme Court let stand the lower court decision.

Meanwhile, after five years of opposition from the state of Wisconsin and the state's largest business lobby, the Forest County Potawatomi won approval of their Class I air quality designation from the EPA. This allows the tribe to designate their 11,000 acres as Class I, the highest air designation possible. No new facilities that release more than 250 tons of particulate per year are permitted. The mine is expected to emit about 247 tons of particulates into the air each year. If either tribal air or water quality standards should be violated by the proposed mine, the tribes can deny air or water quality permits necessary for mine approval.

The Mining Moratorium Campaign

Besides building local alliances among the tribes, environmental groups, and sport-fishing groups, the Wolf Watershed Educational Project's speaking tours in 1996–97 built public support for legislative passage of a sulfide mining moratorium bill that would prohibit the opening of a new mine in a sulfide ore body until a similar mine had been opened for 10 years elsewhere and closed for 10 years without pollution from acid mine drainage. The movement for a sulfide mine ban originally developed out of the Rusk County Citizens Action Group in Ladysmith (site of Rio Tinto's Flambeau mine) and was developed into a piece of legislation at the initiative of the Menominee Nation's Mining Impacts and Treaty Rights office with the assistance of State Representative Spencer Black (D-Madison). The legislation became a rallying point for the Native American, environmental group, and sport-fishing group coalition as well as for the powerful pro-mine lobby in the state.

The mining companies and pro-mining Wisconsin Association of Manufacturers & Commerce (WMC) responded to the speaking tours and the moratorium campaign with newspaper ads, radio ads, a U.S. $1 million blitz of television ads, and a U.S. $ 1 million lobbying effort. Nevertheless, in March 1998, the legislature passed the moratorium bill after initially successful attempts to weaken it, and pro-mining Republican Governor Tommy Thompson was forced to sign the bill to ensure his re-election. The Crandon project appeared doomed to many when the mining moratorium law was signed; yet the new law did not stop the mine permit process but rather provided another hurdle at the projected end of the permit process in about 2004.

The upsurge in environmental activism around the state, however, convinced Exxon to turn the Crandon project over to its partner Rio Algom. The Canadian company put the wastewater pipeline to the Wisconsin River on the back burner, instead proposing on-site waste treatment in perpetuity. It submitted three "example mines" to meet the criteria of the moratorium law (even though two of the mines had not been both open and closed for periods of 10 years). In May 2002 the Wisconsin Department of Natural Resources (WDNR) rejected the only example mine that had been both open and closed for periods of 10 years, because it failed to demonstrate that it had operated without harm to the environment. Finally, in August 2002 the WDNR concluded that potentially polluted groundwater from the mine may travel 22 times faster and reach pollution levels five times higher than the company's predictions, thus threatening local drinking water.[81]

A Broader Anticorporate Movement

The movement against the Crandon mine has linked up with other environmental issues in northern Wisconsin, partly because of other vulnerabilities of the project. The Crandon mine would need enormous amounts of electrical power to process the ores, but it does not have adequate access to electricity. Proposed transmission lines from Duluth, Minnesota, would take power from hydroelectric dams that flood Manitoba Cree lands, transmit it on high-voltage lines that threaten northwestern Wisconsin farmers and the Lac Courte Oreilles Chippewa Reservation, and use it to power the Crandon mine at Mole Lake.[82] The transmission lines came under heavy criticism from a new rural alliance called Save Our Unique Lands (SOUL), in the process casting a shadow over the Crandon mine's future electrical needs. In public hearings on the transmission lines project conducted by Wisconsin's Public Service Commission (PSC) in 2000, virtually all the testimony was critical of the project, prompting one official to comment that in his 16 years at the PSC, "no other project has met such strong and organized opposition from protestors."[83]

The alliance against the transmission lines closely resembles the grassroots Native/non-Native alliance against the Crandon mine, and successful concurrent opposition by central Wisconsin farmers and the Ho-Chunk (formerly Winnebago) Nation to a groundwater pumping plant proposed by the Perrier Corporation. The three rural anticorporate alliances cooperated closely, holding a large rally in April 2000 at the state capitol, and organizing high school and college students to join the growing statewide movement, in the spirit of anticorporate protests that emerged in Seattle and globally in 1999–2000.

In 2000 Rio Algom was purchased by the London-based South African company Billiton, which merged the following year with Australian mining giant BHP to form the largest mining company, BHP Billiton. Company spokesman Marc Gonsalves soon reported that the company had received an "endless stream of emails" from Crandon mine opponents around the world.[84] Mine opponents proposed a ban on cyanide use in Wisconsin mines to prevent the kind of mine-spill disaster that struck in Romania in 2000. They also proposed a bill to end "special treatment" for the mining industry in state environmental laws.

Beginning in December 2000 the Wolf Watershed Educational Project had demanded that BHP Billiton withdraw applications for mining permits and open a dialogue to negotiate the sale of the site. An alliance of environmental groups, conservation groups, and local and tribal governments released a detailed proposal calling for the purchase of the Crandon mine site (more than 5,000 acres of land and mineral rights) as a conservation area devoted to sustainable land-management practices, tribal cultural values, and tourism suitable to this environmentally sensitive area. The main goal of the purchase would be to end permanently the controversy over permitting the Crandon mine by taking the land out of the hands of mining companies.

"Our proposal will support low-impact sustainable development instead of destructive mining at the headwaters of the Wolf River," said Chuck Sleeter, board chairman of the town of Nashville. "We want to protect natural and cultural resources and grow our economy wisely, instead of endangering it with risky, short-term mining."[85] Less than a year after the mine opponents' proposal BHP Billiton sold the Nicolet Mineral Company to the former site owners, a local logging company. The company unsuccessfully attempted to search worldwide for a multinational firm that would serve as a partner.

On October 28, 2003, Mole Lake and Potawatomi leaders announced that the two neighboring tribes had jointly purchased and divided the 5,000 acre Crandon mine property for U.S. $16.5 million. Mole Lake acquired the Nicolet Minerals Company, and quickly dropped mine permit applications. The bombshell announcement not only brought the 28-year battle to a dramatic end; it demonstrated that tribal gaming revenue could be used for the benefit of northern Wisconsin's environment and economy. It also showed the power of the tribes' cultural renaissance and their work in alliance with non-Indian neighbors. The alliance had driven down the site price by tens of millions of dollars, by driving away potential mining company partners.

As he tacked up a giant "SOLD" sign on the company, Potawatomi mine opponent Dennis Shepherd exclaimed: "We rocked the boat. Now we own the boat." The tribes held a large celebration powwow, where they honored Natives and non-Natives who had opposed the mine. The less wealthy of the two tribes, Mole Lake, inherited a mortgage from the company and set up a Wolf River Protection Fund to help pay for its half of the purchase.

Negotiating Debt Repayment with BHP Billiton

Permanent control over the mine site was contingent on Mole Lake's payment of its outstanding U.S. $8 million debt owed to BHP Billiton, due in April 2006. By the fall of 2005 it was clear that Mole Lake was not going to raise the U.S. $8 million through its fundraising efforts. At that point the Wolf Watershed Educational Project (WWEP) offered to contact BHP Billiton and propose that the company cancel Mole Lake's outstanding debt, so that the tribe's resources could be directed toward cleaning up the Crandon mine site (capping the exposed drill holes, and so on) and restoring the land for tribal cultural preservation and conservation.

The tribal council gave the go ahead, and WWEP sent a letter to the CEO and the entire board of directors of BHP Billiton, proposing debt cancellation for Mole Lake as a way to offset the company's horrendous track record with mining operations on indigenous lands, such as its disastrous Ok Tedi mine in Papua New Guinea. The letter made it clear that if the company rejected the debt cancellation proposal, the WWEP was prepared "to continue its longstanding campaign to highlight your corporate record in indigenous communities, as we did with the previous owners Exxon and Rio Algom."[86] WWEP had already contacted Oxfam America and enlisted their support for such a campaign if BHP Billiton rejected the proposal.

Shortly after receiving the WWEP letter, the company contacted the tribe's attorney and asked for a meeting with the tribe to discuss some financial settlement. On May 31, 2006, the Mole Lake Sokaogon Chippewa Tribal Council and BHP Billiton spokesperson Gibson Pierce announced the establishment of the BHP Billiton Fund for the Sokaogon People.[87] It was not a debt cancellation. Instead, the tribe borrowed the money to pay off the mortgage payment to the mining company. BHP Billiton then donated the money back to the tribe through a trust fund that can be used for tribal education or environmental projects. It was a negotiated solution that kept the ownership of the mine property in the hands of the Mole Lake Chippewa and Forest County Potawatomi tribes.

The fierce rural grassroots alliance that emerged in Wisconsin has left a strong impression on the international mining industry. The *Mining Environmental Management Journal* portrays the Wolf Watershed Educational Project as "an example of what is becoming a very real threat to the global mining industry."[88] And the industry-sponsored Fraser Institute in Vancouver, British Columbia, has rated Wisconsin at or near the bottom of its annual "mining investment attractiveness score" for the period of 1998 to 2003 because of the state's "well publicized aversion to mining."[89]

A New Era of Resource Colonialism and Resistance

A number of significant changes have affected the ability of indigenous and rural communities to defend their lands and cultures from unwanted mining projects promoted by multinational mining corporations and development-oriented host governments. During the 1990s, under pressure from the World Bank and the International Monetary Fund, more than 90 countries changed their mining laws in an effort to attract foreign mining investment. These changes included the removal of restrictions on foreign ownership, reduced taxes, easier and faster acquisition of exploration and mining rights, and the privatization of state-owned mining companies. They are part of a broader package of neocolonial measures, more often called "neoliberal reforms," designed "to open up new opportunities for the international mining industry in areas that were formerly either closed de jure because of political restrictions, or closed de facto since political-economic risk was sufficiently high to deter prudent investment."[90] This has resulted in a major geographical shift in mining investment from the traditional targets , such as North America and Australia, to South America, South East Asia, and Africa.

It is estimated that in the next 20 years about half of all gold and copper mined will come from territories used or claimed by indigenous people.[91] These regions include Amazonia, the high Andes, and parts of northern Canada, Indonesia, Papua New Guinea, the Solomons, the Philippines, southwest Africa, and Nevada. These new resource frontiers are frequently regions of high biodiversity that perform critical ecological functions, including climate regulation, soil protection, flood control, and water purification.[92] A recent study by the World Wide Fund for Nature reported a strong correlation between areas of high biodiversity and areas of high cultural diversity.[93] The Declaration of Belem, issued in 1988 by the International Society of Ethnobiology, explicitly affirms the existence of an "inextricable link" between cultural and biological diversity, "a link residing in indigenous peoples' knowledge of, and stewardship over, a large part of the world's most diverse ecosystems."[94] The late geographer Bernard Nietschmann proposed a Rule of Indigenous Environments: "Where there are indigenous peoples *with a homeland* there are still biologically rich environments."[95]

Dramatic increases in the price of gold and copper also provided major incentives for new mining investments. In 1980 gold had hit an all-time high of $850 an ounce. Over $90 billion was invested in the mining sector from 1990–2001, mostly in gold and copper. Gold accounted for 66% of all mining exploration expenditures in 1997.[96] Gold prices have now risen to over $1,000 an ounce. In 2009 new gold mining projects accounted for more than 28% of the value of all new mining projects.[97] The dramatic expansion of mining worldwide was also made possible by improved exploration techniques, such as airborne geophysical prospecting and deeper drilling techniques, which facilitated the discovery of hidden orebodies.[98]

New processing technologies have cut costs and allowed companies to economically extract very low-grade ores that are dispersed in the ground and cover huge areas. These technologies require open pit mining where large quantities of rock are blasted, bulldozed, and pulverized so that the gold and copper can be extracted using cyanide (sulfuric acid in the case of copper) and other toxic chemicals to separate the minerals. As the higher-grade ore reserves are exhausted, the direct energy and water requirements of mining and processing rise rapidly as more ore must be mined and processed for each ton of metal recovered. The extraction, processing, and refining of minerals from the earth consume close to 10% of world energy.[99] A significant share of this energy comes from the burning of fossil fuels such as coal and oil whose carbon dioxide (CO_2) emissions are major causes of global climate change. The effects of climate change are already wreaking havoc on indigenous and poor communities because of their disproportionate dependence on healthy ecosystems for both subsistence and culture.

Large amounts of water are also used throughout the mining process. In many cases mining companies must "dewater" the mine sites by pumping out underground water at staggering rates to keep the mine accessible as it drops below the water table. In Nevada, for example, Barrick Gold of Toronto operates the vast Goldstrike mine, located 1,600 feet below the aquifer. Barrick must pump nearly 10 million gallons a day to continue mining. Some of the water is used to dilute the cyanide that is used to extract the microscopic bits of gold in the heap leach ore piles. Most of the water pumped from the pits will go into the Humboldt River system, either directly into the river, or into settling ponds where it is expected to sink back into the aquifer. When mining is done, there will be a net loss to northern Nevada's aquifer. According to *The New York Times*, "Government scientists estimate that it could take 200 years or more to replenish the groundwater that it [Barrick Gold] and neighboring mine companies have removed."[100]

Nevada is the driest state in the nation and has one of the fastest-growing populations, in Las Vegas. The most directly affected community is the Western Shoshone people, whose subsistence economy and culture are threatened by mines in their traditional territories.[101] In 2008 Barrick Gold received approval from the Bureau of Land Management (BLM) for expansion of the Cortez Hills gold mine on Mount Tenabo, a sacred site for the Western Shoshone people. In December 2009 the federal Ninth Circuit Court of Appeals issued an injunction against the construction and operation of the Cortez gold mine, noting that conservationists and Western Shoshone tribal members were likely to succeed in showing that the BLM violated federal environmental law in failing to properly analyze environmental impacts from the mine on groundwater, air quality, and other resources.[102]

Large volumes of water are also lost in the disposal of mine waste in large storage ponds that scar the landscape, take up far larger expanses of land than the mines, and must be perpetually monitored for releases of toxic metals. Nevada's gold mines are responsible for more toxic mercury releases than any other industry. This amounted to 9,000 pounds of mercury released directly into the air by Nevada mines, representing 25% of all mercury air pollution in the United States west of Texas.[103] Mercury is a highly toxic metal that can damage the human nervous system and harm developing fetuses, infants, and children. Since 2002 the Idaho Department of Health and Welfare has warned people to limit the number of fish they eat from a southern Idaho reservoir where environmental officials have detected mercury levels in the reservoir that are 150 times the highest levels ever found in lakes in the northeastern United States, which have been affected by mercury from coal-fired power plants.[104] Some scientists suspect that gold mines across the border in Nevada are responsible.

The Rights to Self-Determination and Prior, Informed Consent

As the international mining industry has expanded into new resource frontiers, indigenous groups and other local communities have increasingly asserted their right to control their own development and their right to the protection and control of their lands, territories, and natural resources. This right has been recognized in numerous international treaties and international human rights law. To effectively exercise sovereignty over their lands, territories, and natural resources, indigenous peoples have asserted a right to prior informed consent in their dealings with governments and mining companies. This fundamentally challenges the power imbalance between mining companies and affected communities in decision making about potential mining operations:

> "Unlike the traditional mining model, in which mining companies typically negotiated agreements with governments that focused on the needs of the company, the principle of prior informed consent focuses on the needs of the community. It promotes partnership and dialogue, and allows communities to shape, or in some cases to reject, the development of the mining activity." Thus, "prior informed consent is intended to promote a more sustainable form of development, in which the short-term mining interests do not compromise the community's long-term needs for survival."[105]

The legal foundations of the right to prior informed consent are based on international treaties as well as explicit recognition in a country's constitution.[106] For example, the International Labour Organization Convention 169 requires governments to consult with indigenous and tribal peoples within their countries regarding development projects affecting indigenous lands. Article 13.2 defines territory as including "the total environment of the areas which the people concerned occupy or otherwise use."[107] This convention has been ratified by 13 Latin American States. Article 30 of the United Nations Declaration on the Rights of Indigenous Peoples, adopted by the UN General Assembly in 2007, goes beyond "consultation" and explicitly recognizes the right of indigenous peoples to "require that States obtain their free and informed consent prior to the approval of any project affecting their lands, territories and other resources."[108] While the right to prior informed consent may be more developed in the context of indigenous rights, it is just as likely to be invoked by non-indigenous as indigenous communities.

Indigenous Rights and the War on Terrorism

Indigenous assertions of their rights to their lands and resources are increasingly being defined as serious national security concerns by governments around the world. This did not just begin in the period after 9/11. Third World governments have not hesitated to suppress indigenous resistance movements with draconian national security laws accompanied by massive human rights violations. The Mayan Zapatista Army of National Liberation (EZLN) has repeatedly been labeled a terrorist organization by both Mexican and U.S. authorities since the January 1994 uprising to protest the beginning of the North American Free Trade Agreement. What has changed, according to one Asian indigenous leader, is that September 11 has "provided an excuse for governments to reinforce such draconian laws and to justify many of their unlawful actions, which were hitherto condemned as illegal and violations of human rights."[109] States all around the world are increasingly defining protest actions such as barricades, dismantling camps of mining prospectors, and dam builders as acts of terrorism. This criminalization of protest is designed to limit the options of those opposed to the new resource colonialism. Rodolfo Stavenhagen, the former UN special rapporteur for the human rights of indigenous peoples, has reported that indigenous resistance to large scale mines in the Philippines has resulted in the militarization of indigenous communities and grave human rights abuses as members of indigenous communities are accused of rebellion or engaging in "terrorist" activity.[110]

"In the United States," says Jose Aylwin, a lawyer and co-director of an indigenous rights organization in Chile, "there is a perception of indigenous activists as destabilizing elements and terrorists," and their demands and activism have begun to be cast in a criminal light.[111] The growing activism in the Andean countries, in Central America and parts of Mexico (Chiapas) is depicted as a threat to the security and hegemony of the United States in a 2004 report of the U.S. National Intelligence Council (NIC):

> Increasing portions of the population are identifying themselves as indigenous peoples and will demand not only a voice but, potentially, a new social contract. Many reject globalization as it has played out in the region, viewing it as a homogenizing force that undermines their unique cultures and as a U.S.-imposed neoliberal economic model whose inequitably distributed fruits are rooted in the exploitation of labor and the environment.[112]

The NIC works with 13 government agencies, including the CIA. The report describes a number of potential counterinsurgency scenarios, which Pedro Cayuqueo, director of a Mapuche Indian newspaper in Chile, compares to the so-called low-intensity warfare doctrine that was the basis of U.S. intervention in the Central American wars of the 1980s.[113] According to Col. John Waghelstein, commander of the Army's Seventh Special Forces, the term "low intensity" is misleading because it involved "political, economic, and psychological warfare, with the military being a distant fourth in many cases." Low-intensity conflict, he says, "is total war at the grassroots level."[114]

An antiterrorist law that dates from the U.S.-supported dictatorship of the late General Augusto Pinochet (1973–90) has already been used against Mapuche Indians who have protested against the construction of a series of hydroelectric dams and the invasion of timber companies developing tree farms on Mapuche land. Mapuche leaders have been charged under a statute that prohibits "generating fear among sectors of the population." These charges were filed after groups of Mapuches burned forests or farmhouses or destroyed forestry equipment and trucks. "Clearly this is a conflict in which serious crimes have been committed," said Sebastian Brett, a representative of Human Rights Watch in Chile. "But that does not mean you can call the people involved terrorists. These are crimes . . . against property, and they stem from a wide sense of grievance among Mapuches that they have illegally been deprived of their lands."[115] The government has convicted many Mapuche leaders and sentenced them to prison terms of up to 10 years.[116]

Indigenous demands for a new "social contract" in Latin America are not new. As a historically oppressed and excluded population, indigenous groups have demanded recognition of their land claims by states for decades. In addition to land claims, indigenous movements have demanded "recognition as distinct peoples in state constitutions; recognition of their languages . . . their right to control their own development; and their right to the protection and control of their lands, territories, and natural resources."[117] Many Latin American states have responded to these claims by recognizing indigenous rights in their recently revised political constitutions. In several cases, notably Brazil, Bolivia, Colombia, Ecuador, Nicaragua, and Panama, states have recognized the right of indigenous communities to be consulted before the development of extractive resource projects in their territories. However, state recognition of this right does not always guarantee that states will act in accordance with this right.

Nevertheless, in the minds of some key supporters of the war on terrorism this democratic opening to indigenous rights in Latin America and elsewhere is reminiscent of America's war against Indians on the frontier. In the 19th century many Americans believed that it was America's Manifest Destiny to spread democracy by territorial expansion and the subjugation of indigenous peoples. Today the 9/11-inspired war on terrorism has become an all-purpose justification for American global interventionism.[118] In a provocative essay right-wing intellectual Robert Kaplan argues that an "overlooked truth about the war on terrorism" is that "the American military is back to the days of fighting the Indians."[119] Kaplan uses the term *Indian Country* to refer to the battlefields of America's global war to tame the unruly (read democratic) frontier:

> Indian country has been expanding in recent years because of the security vacuum created by the collapse of traditional dictatorships and the emergence of new democracies—whose short-term institutional weaknesses provide whole new oxygen systems for terrorists. Iraq is but a microcosm of the earth in this regard. To wit, the upsurge in terrorism in the vast archipelago of Indonesia, the southern Philippines and parts of Malaysia is a direct result of the anarchy unleashed by the passing of military regimes.[120]

Indigenous struggles for land, resources, and the right to exercise control over their own territories hardly constitutes "anarchy" or terrorism. If anything, countries that recognize and respect indigenous rights are more, not less, stable than those that suppress indigenous peoples. The development of indigenous organizations in Ecuador provides compelling evidence, as documented by Selverston-Scher, "that ethnic political movements may contribute to the development of the participatory citizenship that is essential to democracy" and to democratic stability.[121] Brysk cites the experience of Peru with the Sendero Luminoso (Shining Path) guerrilla movement to argue that "higher levels of violence result from grievances that are not channeled through ethnic movements."[122] In a similar vein Van Cott poses the critical question about indigenous rights and democratic stability: "Which is more destabilizing to democratizing societies: the efforts of an ethnic group to emphasize its distinctiveness, or the strategy of a state to forcibly create a unitary, homogenous 'nation' from a diverse, multiethnic, multilingual population?"[123] The possibility that the actions of a state to exclude indigenous rights from the national agenda may itself be a major source of political instability never occurs to Kaplan.

From Kaplan's perspective the events of September 11, 2001, started America's "Second Expeditionary Era" (the first had begun during the imperialist conquests of Cuba, Puerto Rico, Panama, the Philippines, Hawai'i, Wake Island, and Guam in 1898), in which the U.S. Army Special Operations Command was deployed in 65 countries "to manage an unruly world."[124] Kaplan singles out Colombia as "the possessor of untapped oil reserves" that is "crucially important to American interests" to illustrate "the imperial reality of America's global situation."[125] What

Kaplan fails to mention is that a significant part of Colombia's oil reserves are on indigenous lands where U.S. oil companies such as Occidental Petroleum have failed to obtain the consent of those indigenous communities before oil exploration and production.[126]

Since President Clinton's approval of a $1.6 billion "Plan Colombia" aid package in 2000, the United States has been providing military training and assistance to the Colombian armed forces, which are aligned with both drug traffickers and right-wing death squads.[127] Over the last decade about 300,000 people have died a violent death in Colombia.[128] Another 4.3 million Colombians have been displaced as a result of the violence over the past two decades, the second largest internally displaced population in the world after Sudan.[129] The principal victims in Colombia's ongoing civil war have been peasant, indigenous, and Afro-Colombian communities caught in the crossfire between armed groups on the left and the right. Nonetheless, as Kaplan notes, the situation in Colombia is "still so remote from public consciousness."[130]

And that's precisely how Kaplan would like to keep it. "In Indian Country," writes Kaplan, "it is not only the outbreak of a full-scale insurgency that must be avoided, but [also] the arrival in significant numbers of the global media." As one general officer told Kaplan, "you want to whack bad guys quietly and cover your tracks with humanitarian-aid projects."[131] Indeed, "the best information strategy is to avoid attention-getting confrontations in the first place and to keep the public's attention as divided as possible."[132]

However, keeping a low profile may be more difficult as the United States expands its military presence in South America. In October 2009 the United States and Colombia announced an agreement permitting the United States to establish seven new military bases in Colombia. In response to criticism from Venezuela, Ecuador, and Nicaragua about the increasing U.S. military presence in the region, the United States says this is simply an extension of the already existing relation between the United States and Colombia under Plan Colombia and does not constitute a new "offensive" capability.[133] However, the U.S. Air Force states that the Palanquero air base would allow the military to "conduct full spectrum operations throughout South America" and expand its "expeditionary warfare capability."[134] As the Pentagon confronts indigenous and rural movements opposing the expansion of extractive resource activities in the Amazon and the Andes, it will be more difficult to keep American taxpayers and consumers ignorant about the real costs of extracting oil, gold, copper, timber, and other resources from indigenous lands.

Notes

1. Great Lakes Indian Fish and Wildlife Commission, *Sulfide Mining: The Process and the Price: A Tribal and Ecological Perspective* (Odanah, WI: 1996, 17).

2. Great Lakes Indian Fish and Wildlife Commission, *A Guide to Understanding Chippewa Treaty Rights* (Odanah, WI: Sept. 1991, 1–2).

3. Ron Seely, "Mining Has Strong Potential in Wisconsin," *Wisconsin State Journal*, Jan. 31, 1982.

4. Wisconsin Department of Natural Resources, *Final Environmental Impact Statement, Exxon Coal and Minerals Co. Zinc-Copper Mine, Crandon, Wisconsin* (Madison, WI: Nov. 1986, ii). The weight of the Great Pyramids was calculated from figures provided in the *World Book* (1987, vol. 15, 810a).

5. Al Gedicks, "The Sokaogon Chippewa Take on Exxon," Chapter 3 in *The New Resource Wars: Native and Environmental Struggles against Multinational Corporations* (Boston: South End Press, 1993).

6. "Rio, Exxon Team Up in Wisconsin," *The Northern Miner* 79:29 (Sept. 20, 1993).

7. Testimony before the U.S. Army Corps of Engineers, Public Hearing, Mole Lake Sokaogon Chippewa Reservation, March 29, 1995.

8. Edmund Jefferson Danziger, *The Chippewas of Lake Superior* (Norman: University of Oklahoma Press, 1978, 153).

9. Thomas Vennum, Jr., *Wild Rice and the Ojibway People* (St. Paul: Minnesota Historical Society Press, 1988); Robert P. W. Gough, "A Cultural-Historical Assessment of the Wild Rice Resources of the Sokaogon Chippewa," in COACT Research, Inc., *An Analysis of the Socio-Economic and Environmental Impacts of Mining and Mineral Resource Development on the Sokaogon Chippewa Community* (Madison, WI: 1980).

10. Wisconsin DNR, *Final Environmental Impact Statement, Exxon Coal and Minerals Co., Zinc-Copper Mine, Crandon, Wisconsin* (Madison, WI: Nov. 1986, 108). The importance of subsistence activity can be seen in the fact that 86% of the Chippewa families rely to a great extent on hunting and fishing for food, while over 90% rely on gardening, ricing, and picking wild plants. Ibid.

11. Exxon, *Forecast of Future Conditions: Socioeconomic Assessment, Crandon Project.* Prepared for Exxon Minerals by Research and Planning Consultants, Inc. (Oct. 1983, 316).

12. Masinaigan (Talking Paper), "Chippewa Leaders Voice Concerns about Proposed Wisconsin Mine" (Odanah, WI: Great Lakes Indian Fish and Wildlife Commission, Fall 1993).

13. Laura Sutherland, "Comments on Exxon/Rio Algom's Notice of Intent," *Wisconsin Public Intervenor* (Feb. 1994, 2).

14. Jack Schmidt, "Problems with Tailings Ponds: Incomplete Regulation, Inconsistent Review, Threats to Water," *Down to Earth* (newspaper) (Helena, MT: July/Aug. 1982).

15. U.S. Forest Service, *Acid Drainage from Mines on the National Forests: A Management Challenge* (Washington, D.C.: Dept. of Agriculture, 1993, 3).

16. This was confirmed by a Wisconsin Department of Natural Resources Report: "An Overview of Mining Waste Management Issues in Wisconsin," Bureau of Solid and Hazardous Waste Management, July 1995.

17. Wisconsin Department of Natural Resources, *Final Environmental Impact Statement, Exxon Coal and Minerals Co., Zinc-Copper Mine, Crandon, Wisconsin* (Madison, WI, Nov. 1986, 131).

18. U.S. Environmental Protection Agency, *Tribes at Risk: The Wisconsin Tribes Comparative Risk Project* (Washington, D.C.: Oct. 1992, ix).

19. Cited in Al Gedicks, *The New Resource Wars: Native and Environmental Struggles Against Multinational Corporations* (Boston: South End, 1993, 63).

20. Anthropology Resource Center (ARC), "Transnational Corporations and Indigenous Peoples," *ARC Newsletter* 5:3 (Sept. 1981); Julian Burger, *Report from the Frontier: The State of the World's Indigenous Peoples* (London and Cambridge, MA: Zed Books and Cultural Survival, 1987); Michael C. Howard, *The Impact of the International Mining Industry on Native Peoples* (University of Sydney: Transnational Corporations Research Project, Feb. 1988).

21. Ralph Nader, "Approaching Strategy for Confronting the Corporate Threat," *Akwesasne Notes* (Rooseveltown, NY: Mohawk Nation) 14:6 (Winter 1982, 9).

22. Rick Whaley and Walter Bresette, *Walleye Warriors: An Effective Strategy against Racism and for the Earth* (Philadelphia: New Society, 1993).

23. James E. Causey, "Indian Leaders Blast DNR over Meetings on Mining Project," *Milwaukee Sentinel*, Jan. 10, 1994.

24. Ibid.

25. WATER Press Release, "Religious Investors Group Wins SEC Action against Exxon Crandon Project," Feb. 7, 1994.

26. Exxon, Proxy Statement (1994, 16).

27. Ibid.

28. Sister Toni Harris, General Councilor, to Amy Bowerman, Office of Chief Council, Securities and Exchange Commission, letter of Jan. 4, 1994. See also Sheila Minor Huff, Regional Environmental Officer, U.S. Department of the Interior, to Howard Druckenmiller, Director, Bureau of Environmental Analysis and Review, Wisconsin DNR, letter of July 31, 1986.

29. The resolution received 5.3% of the vote in 1995, falling short of the 6% necessary for the resolution to be automatically considered the following year. See "Exxon Asked to Disclose Public Opposition to Mines," *Forest Republican*, May 4, 1995.

30. *Isthmus Newsweekly* (Madison, WI, May 26, 1995).

31. Peter A. Geniesse, "Wolf Key to Mining Fortunes," *Appleton Post-Crescent*, April 24, 1994.

32. Nathan Seppa, "Old Foes Now Allies: Indians, Sports Fishermen Join to Oppose Mine," *Wisconsin State Journal*, Feb. 11, 1994.

33. Larry Van Goethem, "Exxon and the Wild Wolf River," *Wisconsin Sportsman*, 15:2 (March 1986, 39).

34. Dr. Arthur S. Brooks, "Comments on the DEIS's Description of Water Impacts of the Crandon Project," June 1986, p. 10.

35. Seppa, note 32.

36. James D. Patton, letter to Carroll D. Besadny, Secretary, Wisconsin Dept. of Natural Resources, May 20, 1988, p. 4.

37. Ron Seely, "Exxon's PR Man: J. Wiley Bragg," *Wisconsin State Journal*, April 25, 1994.

38. Wisconsin Public Intervenor's Comments on Notification of Intent, April 23, 1994.

39. Don Behm, "Proposed Giant Mine Raises Fears: State Official Questions Impact on Water Supply of Zinc, Copper Project," *Milwaukee Journal*, April 28, 1994; "Mining Mustn't Spoil the North" (editorial), May 8, 1994.

40. Jerry Goodrich, letter to Forest County residents, April 15, 1994.

41. WATER newspaper ad, *Forest Republican*, May 5, 1994.

42. Ron Seely, "Plan Changes for Mine Wastes," *Wisconsin State Journal*, April 19, 1995.

43. Bruce Selcraig, "Native Americans Join to Stop the Newest of the Indian Wars," *Sierra* 79:3 (May/June 1994, 47).

44. Cited in Peter A. Geniesse, "Fighting Exxon," *Post-Crescent* (Appleton, WI, June 19, 1994).

45. Testimony to the Wisconsin Review Commission, Mole Lake, June 18, 1994. Reprinted in *Report on the Track Records of Exxon and Rio Algom*, March 24, 1995, p. 11.

46. U.S. Department of the Interior, Minerals Management Service, "Social Indicators of Alaskan Coastal Villages," Part 1, Technical Report no. 155 (Anchorage: Feb. 1993, 207).

47. Minewatch, "Summary of Material about the El Cerrejòn Coal Mine and the Wayuu in the El Guajira Peninsula, Colombia." Materials collected by Survival International and summarized by Minewatch, London (Feb. 1994, 1).

48. George Vukelich, "Minding the Mine" (Interview with Armando Valbuena Gouriyù), *Isthmus Newsweekly* (Madison, WI, July 8, 1994).

49. Americas Watch and United Mine Workers of America, "Petition before the U.S. Trade Representative on Labor Rights in Colombia" (May 1990, 23).

50. Survival International, "Top Ten List" (London: Sept. 1992).

51. Roger Moody, *The Gulliver File: Mines, People, and Land: A Global Battleground* (London: Minewatch, 1992, 367).

52. Ron Seely, "Exxon Mine Plans Opposed," *Wisconsin State Journal,* March 24, 1995.

53. Dave Newbart, "Mining Firms' Past Hit," *The Madison Capital Times,* March 23, 1995.

54. Cited in "Mining Moratorium Challenges Mining Companies," *Pioneer Express* (Crandon, WI, Dec. 18, 1995).

55. Don Behm, "DNR Board Likely to Reject Petitions for Ore Mining Ban," *Milwaukee Journal,* 1994.

56. Tim J. Sheehan, "Judge's Ruling Sides with Mining Opponents," *Leader-Telegram* (Eau Claire, WI, Sept. 12, 1995).

57. Julie Wichman, "Elephants Leave Tailings Behind: State Republicans Stampede from Mining Bill," *Shepherd Express* (Milwaukee newsweekly), May 23, 1996.

58. Janet Smith, Dept. of the Interior, Fish and Wildlife Service, Green Bay, WI, Field Office, comments to the U.S. Army Corps of Engineers on a Section 404 permit application for the proposed Crandon mine, Nov. 18, 1994, p. 3.

59. Ibid., p. 2.

60. Ibid., p. 3.

61. Public hearing on Exxon's Crandon project, Sokaogon Chippewa Reservation, March 29, 1995.

62. Full-page advertisement in *Forest Republican* (Crandon, WI, Oct. 11, 1995).

63. U.S. Army Corps of Engineers, St. Paul District, "Evaluation of Groundwater Modeling at the Crandon Mining Site," Feb. 21, 1996, p. 1.

64. WATER Press Release, Jan. 26, 1996.

65. Steve Fox, "Taking Us Down to the River: An Indian Pueblo Challenges Upstream Polluters," *Workbook* 17:4 (Winter 1992, 153–54).

66. Steven Walters, "Tribe Seeks Air Pollution Protection within 60 Miles of Reservation," *Milwaukee Sentinel,* Dec. 13, 1994.

67. Don Behm, "2 Tribes Hope to Control Reservations' Water Quality," *Milwaukee Journal,* Feb. 5, 1995.

68. Mike Monte, "Indian Tribes: Our New Environmental Conscience?" *Wisconsin Outdoor News,* July 21, 1995.

69. James Buchen, "Delegation of Federal Clean Water Act," *Badger State Miner,* Oct./Nov. 1995.

70. Steven Walters, "Tribes Request Could Jeopardize Current, Future Jobs, Groups Say," *Milwaukee Journal/Sentinel,* April 27, 1995.

71. "Tribal Water Plan Supported," *Daily Journal* (Antigo, WI), Feb. 1, 1996.

72. "Indian Lawsuit Will Proceed," *Wisconsin State Journal,* April 5, 1996.

73. Ron Seely, "New Opposition Group to Crandon Mine Forms," *Wisconsin State Journal,* March 26, 1996.

74. "Company Starts Publicity Campaign to Support Mine," *Wisconsin State Journal,* April 30, 1996.

75. Robert Imrie, "More Crandon Mine Tests Ordered," *Wisconsin State Journal,* May 22, 1996.

76. Keith Schneider, "A Wisconsin Tribe Tries to Turn Back a Giant," *The New York Times,* Dec. 26, 1994.

77. Winona La Duke, "Indigenous Environmental Perspectives: A North American Primer," *Indigenous Economics: Toward a Natural World Order* (Ithaca, NY: Cornell University, Adwe:kon Journal, summer 1992, 57).

78. This essay is a condensed and revised version of material from Chapters 1 and 2 in my book *Dirty Gold: Indigenous Alliances to End Global Resource Colonialism* (South End Press, 2011).

79. This update draws heavily from Al Gedicks and Zoltan Grossman, "Defending a Common Home: Native/Non-Native Alliances against Mining Corporations in Wisconsin," in Mario Blaser, Harvey A. Feit, and Glenn McRae (Eds.) *In the Way of Development: Indigenous Peoples, Life Projects and Globalization* (London: Zed Books and the International Development Research Centre, Ottawa, 2004).

80. Ron Seely, "Firm, Town Trade Barbs," *Wisconsin State Journal,* June 18, 1999.

81. Robert Imrie, "New Concern Raised on Pollution," *Wisconsin State Journal,* August 5, 2002.

82. Winona La Duke, "Dams, Transmission Lines, and Mines," *Potawatomi Traveling Times,* December 1, 2000.

83. Jon Kamp, "Minnesota Aquarium Feud Fuels Power Line Dispute," *Dow Jones Energy Service,* December 8, 2000.

84. Nikki Kallio, "New Mine Owners Face Opposition," *Wausau Daily Herald,* October 18, 2000.

85. Chuck Sleeter, "Wolf River Headwaters Protection Purchase Proposed as Final End to Crandon Mine Controversy," press release, June 20, 2002.

86. WWEP letter to BHP Billiton, September 13, 2005.

87. Robert Imrie, "Indian Tribe Gets $8 Million Gift," *Wisconsin State Journal,* May 31, 2006.

88. Tracey Khanna, Editorial comment, *Mining Environmental Management Journal* 8:3, May 2000, p. 19.

89. Ted Worthington, "Investment Attractiveness Index," *Engineering and Mining Journal* 204:2, February, 2003. pp. 26–27.

90. Gavin Bridge, "Mapping the Bonanza: Geographies of Mining Investment in an Era of Neoliberal Reform," *The Professional Geographer* 56:3 (August 2004, 407).

91. Sweeting and Clark, note 79, p. 7.

92. Ibid., p. 6.

93. World Wide Fund for Nature, *Indigenous and Traditional Peoples of the World and Ecoregion Conservation* (Gland, Switzerland, 2000, 1).

94. Ibid., p. 8.

95. Bernard Nietschmann, *The Interdependence of Biological and Cultural Diversity.* Center for World Indigenous Studies, Occasional Paper #21 (1992, 3). Emphasis added.

96. Sweeting and Clark, note 79, p. 12.

97. Magnus Ericsson and Viktoriya Larsson, "E&MJ's Annual Survey of Global Mining Investment," *Engineering and Mining Journal* 211:1 (January/February 2010, 25).

98. Ibid., p. 9.

99. Payal Sampat, "Scrapping Mining Dependence," in Linda Starke, Ed., *State of the World 2003: A Worldwatch Institute Report on Progress Toward a Sustainable Society* (New York: W.W. Norton & Co., 2003, 111).

100. Kirk Johnson, "A Drier and Tainted Nevada May Be Legacy of a Gold Rush," *The New York Times*, December 30, 2005, p. A 1.

101. Christopher Sewall, *Digging Holes in the Spirit: Gold Mining and the Survival of the Western Shoshone Nation* (Berkeley, CA: Western Shoshone Defense Project and Project Underground June 1999).

102. Western Shoshone Defense Project, press release, 12/3/09.

103. U.S. Environmental Protection Agency. Toxic Release Inventory, 2004. Washington, D.C.

104. Note 91.

105. Susan Bass, Pooja Seth Parikh, Roman Czebiniak, and Meg Filbey, *Prior Informed Consent and Mining: Promoting the Sustainable Development of Local Communities* (Washington, D.C.: Environmental Law Institute, 2003, 2).

106. Ibid., p. 3.

107. Jose Aylwin, "Land and Resources," *Cultural Survival* 30:4 (Winter, 2006, 15).

108. Ibid.

109. Suhas Chakma, "Short-Circuiting Justice in the Name of Terror," *Indigenous Affairs* 3 (2003, 6).

110. Geoff Nettleton, Andy Whitmore, and Jonathan Glennie, *Breaking Promises, Making Profits: Mining in the Philippines* (London: A Christian Aid and Indigenous Peoples Links Report, 2004, 20).

111. Gustavo Gonzalez, "Latin America: 'War on Terror' Zeroes in on Indigenous People," www.finalcall.com (June 20, 2005), accessed 12/1/06.

112. National Intelligence Council, *Mapping the Global Future: Report of the National Intelligence Council's 2020 Project*. Pittsburgh, PA: Government Printing Office. ISBN 0-16-073-21 8-2 (2004, 78).

113. Gonzalez, note 111.

114. Sara Miles, "The Real War: Low Intensity Conflict in Central America," *NACLA Report on the Americas* 20:2 (April/May 1986, 19).

115. Larry Rohter, "Mapuche Indians in Chile Struggle to Take Back Forests," *The New York Times*, August 11, 2004.

116. Aylwin, note 111; Leslie Ray, *Language of the Land: The Mapuche in Argentina and Chile*. Copenhagen, Denmark: International Work Group for Indigenous Affairs, Document No. 119 (2007).

117. Kathrine Wessendorf, Ed., *The Indigenous World* (Denmark: International Work Group for Indigenous Affairs, 2008, p. 14).

118. John A. Wickham, "September 11and America's War on Terrorism: A New Manifest Destiny," *American Indian Quarterly* 26:1 (2002).

119. Robert D. Kaplan, "Indian Country," *The Wall Street Journal*, September 21, 2004, p. A22. Kaplan's most recent book, *Imperial Grunts: The American Military on the Ground*, was supposedly read by President George W. Bush (John Brown, "Our Indian Wars Are Not Over Yet," TomDispatch.com, (February 19, 2006), www.truthout.org/docs_2006/012006F.shtml.

120. Ibid.

121. Melinda Selverston-Scher, *Ethnopolitics in Ecuador: Indigenous Rights and the Strengthening of Democracy* (Coral Gables, FL: University of Miami Press, North-South Center Press, 2001, 127).

122. Alison Brysk, *From Tribal Village to Global Village: Indian Rights and International Relations in Latin America* (Stanford, CA: Stanford University Press, 2000, 287).

123. Donna Lee Van Cott, "Indigenous Peoples and Democracy: Issues for Policymakers," in Donna Lee Van Cott, Ed., *Indigenous Peoples and Democracy in Latin America* (New York: St. Martin's Press, 1995, 2–3).

124. Robert D. Kaplan, "Supremacy by Stealth: Ten Rules for Managing the World," *Atlantic Monthly* 292:1 (July/August 2003, 66).

125. Ibid.

126. Al Gedicks, *Resource Rebels: Native Challenges to Mining and Oil Corporations* (Cambridge, MA: South End Press, 2001, 55).

127. Al Gedicks, "Resource Wars against Native Peoples in Colombia," *Capitalism, Nature, Socialism* 14:2 (June 2003).

128. Anette Molbech, *The Indigenous World 2000–2001* (Copenhagen: International Work Group for Indigenous Affairs, 2001, 113).

129. Teo Ballvé, "The Dark Side of Plan Colombia," *The Nation* 288:23 (6/15/09), p. 22.

130. Kaplan, note 124, p. 68.

131. Kaplan, note 119, p. A22.

132. Kaplan, note 124, p. 83.

133. Simon Romero, "Plan to Increase U.S. Troop Presence in Colombia Worries Neighbors," *The New York Times* (7/23/09), p. A14.

134. John Lindsay-Poland, "Retreat to Colombia: The Pentagon Adapts Its Latin America Strategy," *NACLA Report on the Americas* 43:1 (January/February 2010, 23).

CHAPTER 8

Purity and Danger: Regulating Organic Farming

Valerie Wheeler and Peter Esainko[1]

SECTION I: The End of the Millennium

Without food, there is no life. Without human culture, there is no human food. But culture varies, as does food and how it comes to be, through access to resources and labor. Control of access to food defines social relations before any other need. Until 10,000 years ago resources were wild, and human social organization was small-scale. Even with localization of wild resources after the last glacial retreat, with sedentary living and the subsequent domestication of plants and animals, communities remained small. In some places on the planet, domestication of storable grains facilitated the rise of tribute-taking, nonproductive political elites, growing populations, cities, and the eventual emergence of states some 5,500 years ago.[2]

In the millennia since, history can be characterized as continually escalating patterns of production, leading to environmental decline, with subsequent conquest of farther geographical realms. New ways to organize labor, land, water, even new "foods" sustain in the short run otherwise threatened economies. Since the 16th century, the ever-faster engine of change has been commerce in search of profit, generating a global economy. The goal of food production is no longer to feed people but to turn food into money. The strategies employed to that end, especially industrialization in the last 200 years, carry heavy social and environmental costs that we are only beginning to comprehend.

American agriculture since its inception has been explicitly commercial, producing food to be sold to non-producers who benefited more than farmers themselves. Agriculture subsidized American development at great cost to the farmer and the countryside. Since the 18th century agriculture has been intensified scientifically: since 1850, chemically through fertilizers; since 1900, mechanically through planting and harvesting machines; since 1920, economically through consolidation and debt, turning farms into factories; and since 1950, petro-chemically. This model of development has become global, and the response to the resulting cycles of overproduction and falling prices has been to increase productivity still more. Large producers replace small ones, as large cultures replace small. And the landscape has become industrialized. Agricultural chemicals pollute surface and groundwater. Without the addition of organic matter, soils compact under heavy machinery and erode in wind and water. Irrigation depletes underground water sources, and salts build up in the soil. The toxic residues of fertilizers, pesticides, and herbicides compromise the food supplies and health of wildlife and humans.[3]

Yet, another theme of agriculture as a "way of life" has played counterpoint to the dominant commercial one—a counterpoint usually difficult to hear outside of sentimental and nostalgic contexts but periodically resonant, sounding out long-term costs of extractive agriculture and seeking reform.[4] One such contemporary counterpoint is the current organic farming movement, a production system that emerged in reaction to the problems of conventional agriculture and that is becoming institutionalized through U.S. federal regulations ("national organic standards").

The National Organic Standards Board (NOSB) has defined "organic agriculture" as

> an ecological production management system that promotes and enhances biodiversity, biological cycles, and soil biological activity . . . based on minimal use of off-farm inputs and on management practices that restore, maintain, and enhance ecological harmony. "Organic" is a labeling term that denotes products produced under the authority of the Organic Foods Production Act. The principle [sic] guidelines . . . are to use materials and practices that enhance the ecological balance of natural systems and that integrate the parts of the farming system into an ecological whole. Organic agriculture practices cannot ensure that products are completely free of residues; however, methods are used to minimize pollution from air, soil, and water. Organic food handlers, processors and retailers adhere to standards that maintain the integrity of organic agricultural products. The primary goal of organic agriculture is to optimize the health and productivity of interdependent communities of soil life, plants, animals, and people.[5]

Organic farmers maintain soil fertility and control moisture and pests primarily through crop rotation (biodiversity) and managing organic matter such as crop residues and both animal and green manures. They make supplements from unaugmented natural materials; for example, fish emulsion and rock phosphate are allowed, but not fortified fish emulsion or phosphate treated with sulfuric acid. Cultivation and crop rotation control weeds. These farmers use petroleum products only to run the machines. An established organic farm is an ecological system tuned by the timing decisions of a knowledgeable farmer who knows that farm and its history intimately. The farmer is an artisan who farms as a way of life—in sharp contrast to the "technicians" in industrial agriculture who work in outdoor factories producing a narrow inventory of homogeneous crops.

In this chapter we examine some problems in American agricultural production, the rise of an organic farming movement in response to these problems, and the social, symbolic, and economic difficulties in achieving a fundamental transformation of our food production system. Our discussion is based on research conducted over 13 years, including ethnographic research on organic farms in chemical-intensive counties in Ohio, participant observation research in agricultural extension and other agro-policy arenas, and comparative research on the organic movement in both California and Ohio. The questions we consider are these: What will be the effect of national standards on organic agriculture? Will it evolve to converge with conventional agriculture in the industrial model? Will the artisans become workers, if they remain on the land at all? What will happen to the right to livelihood of organic farming? And finally, why does it matter?

20th-Century "Farming"

Farmers are . . . helpless subjects of the corporate kingdoms of agripower. The lords of the manor in the feudal system of the Middle Ages . . . demanded no more of their subjects than modern suppliers of chemicals, machinery, and fuel demand of theirs.[6]

The United States is no longer an agricultural society. Less than 2% of the population are farmers, and the number is declining. The rest of us have little connection with food production, and agriculture is just another special interest dominated by multinational corporations. At the beginning of the century, however, most Americans were still on the farm or had just left it for new factories in the cities. The federal government, through land grant universities and the agricultural extension service, had spent four decades developing scientific (and commercial) agriculture. During the Progressive era (1900–17) those institutions further sought to tie rural populations to national development by supervising home life as well, promoting increased production to provide "cheap food" for urban factory workers, thus subsidizing industry. Knowing that commodity prices would fall with increased production, farmers resisted such appeals until World War I, when temporarily high international prices and wartime government control of farm supplies and equipment pulled and pushed farmers into greater production on increased acreage. In May 1920 prices collapsed to prewar levels, leaving farmers bankrupt, debt-ridden, and poorer than ever, since nonagricultural prices were 50% to 100% above prewar levels. The only relief offered farmers was expanded credit, the primary "solution" (and method of control) for the rest of the century. Low prices forced persistent high production, which, while not getting farmers out of their predicament, benefited urban populations. The Roaring Twenties were an urban phenomenon; in the countryside, the Great Depression reigned.[7]

In the 1930s the ecological bill for agricultural extraction came due; the result was a human-made ecological disaster, the Dust Bowl.[8] Although erosion had been a serious effect of European-style farming in the United States from colonial days, the scale of the Dust Bowl could not be ignored, and the federal government formed the Soil Conservation Service under Hugh H. Bennett in 1935. He was a founder of Friends of the Land, a citizen auxiliary to promote a "new agriculture" that included prominent intellectuals, scientists, ecologists, writers, and farmers such as Liberty Hyde Bailey, Paul B. Sears, Edward H. Faulkner, W. A. Albrecht, Gifford Pinchot, Aldo Leopold, and E. B. White. The organization's periodical *The Land* included art and poetry, as well as scientific, technical, and philosophical articles on conservation farming. Member-author Henry A. Wallace, Secretary of Agriculture from 1933 to 1940, transformed the Department of Agriculture's yearbooks from dry annual reports to detailed handbooks for farmers, providing state-of-the-art information for agricultural practice. The most famous member of the Friends of the Land was writer Louis Bromfield, owner of Malabar Farm in Ohio. Bromfield built a thousand-acre showcase of conservation farming from several small, worn-out farms. Tens of thousands of visitors came to his and other conservation farms; most of those visitors were farmers, eager to learn ways to save their soil.

The conservation movement was not necessarily organic, although many of its scientists wrote about organic processes and methods. The first use of the phrase "organic farming and gardening" in the United States may have been by J. I. Rodale, who founded a periodical by that name in 1942. He was concerned about the effects on human health of both chemical fertilizers and pesticides (such as arsenic, sulfur, and DDT). Rodale's inspiration and cofounder of the magazine was Sir Albert Howard, who beginning in 1905 observed, experimented with, and invented methods of producing compost to supply large commercial farm soils with the humus he considered essential for soil fertility and plant health. Howard argued that plant pests and diseases were symptoms of poor soil health; that healthy plants were not attacked significantly by pests and diseases; that chemicals poison "life in the soil," such as mycorrhiza, that make nutrients available to plants; that compost and green manures will put soil "in good heart" and thus make it suitable for healthy plant life. He was critical of the separation of agricultural science from practical farming, the methods of conventional scientific research, and large-scale commercial farming. He thought the profit motive was inappropriate in the production of food, which, like water and shelter, should not be expected to pay its way. "The people must be fed," he wrote; "the financial system is . . . but a secondary matter."[9]

Howard and Rodale gained followers but did meet criticism, even ridicule. Even those in the conservation movement were ambivalent about the organic argument. One important agronomist referred to "the organic cult and the chemical camp."

In the early 1950s, in the pages of *The Land,* a heated exchange took place over chemical fertilizer. Its defenders, although granting some benefits from humus, insisted that "organiculture" (another Rodale term) was a religion, and its adherents were "cockeyed cultists" who followed a "ridiculous dogma" and were therefore "organatics." In their mild replies the practitioners of composting, manuring, and the use of untreated minerals documented successful organic farmers and called repeatedly for testing of organic methods by experiment stations. *The Land's* editors preferred a middle ground with a tilt toward organics, but they endorsed the use of chemical fertilizers in cases of severely limited fertility.

The conservation movement was vital, exciting, and effective in its time—but was quickly forgotten with the petrochemical intensification of agriculture in the 1950s.[10] Just as the internal combustion engine became the profitable way to use gasoline, agricultural chemicals became the profitable way to use wartime inventions—nitrates and pesticides. Hybrid corn seed, mechanization, and industrial inputs from World War II spread rapidly, generating productivity that was "the envy of the world" while increasing the scale and concentration of agriculture and reducing the number of farmers. In 1962 Rachel Carson's classic *Silent Spring*[11] challenged the wisdom of this chemical age, but postwar social changes—the civil rights movement, the Vietnam war, and the Great Society—put agricultural and environmental issues on hold until the 1970s.

DDT was banned in the United States in 1972, although it is still manufactured for export, and residues are still found on agricultural land here. Hundreds of other chemicals replaced it in a new boom.[12] Cheered on by U.S. Secretary of Agriculture Earl Butz, farmers planted "fence row to fence row," tearing out conservation shelter belts and terraces and planting corn destined for the global market. They also greatly increased their consumption of machines, fertilizers, pesticides, and land, using loans urged on them by the federal government and financial institutions looking for a high rate of return on petrodollar deposits. Domestic investment in agricultural expansion was analogous to investment loans to third world countries, with a crucial difference: banks could not foreclose on Argentina or Peru if they failed to make their loan payments, but they could and *did* on farmers at home when prices fell with overproduction.

The postwar economic expansion ended in 1973, as did the rise in domestic real weekly wages, but this reality was obscured by inflation. After 25 years of increasing fertilizer and chemical use without conservation methods, the soil contained inadequate organic matter to keep it from eroding into watersheds already contaminated with chemical runoff. The scientific solution this time was "no-till" agriculture, or planting a new crop directly into the previous year's crop residue—a method even more dependent on herbicides and toxic chemicals.[13] By mid-decade, a new generation of philosopher-scientist-writer-farmers began to critique the environmental and social disaster: some of the most notable were Barry Commoner, Jim Hightower, Wendell Berry, Gene Logsdon, and Wes Jackson. Organic farms were rediscovered and found to be both economically viable and ecologically superior.[14] But chemical agriculturalists again defended their technology by raising the specter of starvation. Their solution to problems caused by technology was to apply more technology.

Organic Farming

In 1972 Rodale Press, publisher of *Organic Gardening,* converted 290 acres of its Pennsylvania farm into organic production and in four years had a stable and fully productive system in place (140 bushels of corn per acre—compared to the top county conventional yield of 157 bushels achieved with 190 pounds of nitrogen, 230 pounds of phosphorus, and 673 pounds of potassium).[15] In this case the organic system was obviously economically advantageous because of reduced input purchases. That year Rex and Glenn Spray put their 600-acre Ohio farm into an organic system, the state's most successful for the next 25 years, with 132% of county averages for corn in one five-year period.[16] Their father had begun using the herbicide atrazine in the late 1940s, but within a few years annual grasses were a serious pest, requiring more herbicides for control. After eliminating petrochemicals, the brothers used a local slaughterhouse product to fertilize the soil but then changed to a carbon-based product whose distributors also supplied advice. Thus began a structured program of crop rotations, tillage, and organic matter management that made this farm a stable, fertile, non-eroding, and ordered ecosystem—an example to this day to farmers of Ohio that it can be done. Public recognition of that example was a long time coming, however, as the social, institutional, and symbolic pressures against organic farming barred even neighbors from acknowledging what they saw driving by the verdant fields. The organic farmers confessed that they sometimes felt like pariahs.

In 1973, 50 farmers formed California Certified Organic Farmers (CCOF) to define, standardize, and regulate the term *organic.* In 1977 the Ohio Ecological Food and Farming Association (OEFFA) was organized. In 1979 Robert Rodale, J. I. Rodale's son, founded *New Farm* magazine, an important source of alternative information for working farmers throughout the United States. Then in 1979 U.S. Secretary of Agriculture Bob Bergland asked for research into the potential of organic farming for mitigating environmental and economic problems in American agriculture. After surveying 69 organic farms in 23 states, a multidisciplinary team produced a sympathetic report in 1980, the same year that land prices ended their inflationary spiral, leading farmers to bankruptcy as their equity fell below their debt.

This exposed "petrofarming" as both an ecological disaster and an economic and social one, and a new literature appeared on "saving the family farm."[17]

Organic advocates had hoped that the official and sympathetic USDA report would, at long last, give organic farming authority. Instead, the incoming Reagan administration eliminated the office that produced the report and announced that the solution to agriculture's problems was the free market, which meant eliminating price supports, subsidies, and thus, farmers. In the Congress, legislation introduced to support "organic" and "innovative" farming failed. Scientific, industrial, and policy personnel involved in conventional agriculture opposed change and resisted any loss of their domination of agricultural policy and practice. Finally, "organic" still had an image problem as a primitive, unproductive, and anti-science agriculture practiced by marginal people.[18]

The Purity Rule

> [University people] act as if contact with farmers would de-professionalize them; they avoid us peasants. —A young organic farmer, 1988

In human affairs, culture universally defines any relationship to conceptions of food. Humans also universally distinguish between "culture" and "nature," ranking culture above nature.

Where the organic of any sort contacts the social—birth, death, sex, sweat, and manure—it creates cognitive impurity, and rituals abound to separate the two again. Social anthropologist Mary Douglas explicated this principle most clearly:

> The purity rule is a control system to which communicating humans all submit. It imposes a scale of values which esteem formal relations more than intimate ones. The more the society is vested with power, the more it despises the organic processes on which it rests. The more hierarchised the social system, the stronger the control demanded. Social distance measures itself by distance from organic process.[19]

A profound effect of technology in industrialized agriculture, for example, has been to distance the farmer from what is farmed: a 12-row planter machine with air-conditioned cab equipped with a stereo and a cellular phone gives higher status and insulation from nature than do smaller tools.[20]

But the crops and animals produced are "food," and food is organic; without it, there is no life. The more "culturized" food production and processing are, the more that food's organic source is obscured. Occasionally, raw foods are culturally elaborated into a cuisine. In the 1970s the counterculture developed a "natural food" system as an alternative to mainstream corporate food processing and distribution. Although the concept of "natural" was quickly rendered meaningless by a retailing food industry, at least one cuisine from the period survived—California cuisine.[21] Its consumers are upper-middle class and high prices at such places insulate those of high status, allowing the use of normally status-lowering behavior to strengthen differentiation from lower orders who cannot afford to eat there. Organic foods in elite markets are incongruous but profitable, as farmers selling in those markets have observed.

Elites become so by distancing themselves from the organic processes of food production, leaving farmers intimately involved with organic processes and thereby assigned a lower position in the social hierarchy. Historically in the United States rural people are seen as ignorant hicks, comical hayseeds, and stupid yokels. In this century farmers' status has risen with increasing social distance from the organic realm, a distance created by machines and science. Professions create elite status, and beginning in the late 19th century, agriculture grew increasingly professionalized. Scientists in agricultural experiment stations, formed by the 1887 Hatch Act, sought to raise their own status by doing "basic" research, although their client farmers wanted applied studies. To mute this contradiction while continuing to lift their status, the scientists tried to professionalize farmers, using the simple agriculture criterion of per-acre productivity achieved through technology. (This is still the sole measure of farming success. The use of other measures, such as profit and efficiency would demonstrate the supremacy of lower-status farmers such as the Amish.[22])

In contemporary western science basic research has consistently had higher social status than applied research and is most cognitively and socially distant from everyday reality. Applied research, by definition immediate and intimate, has lower status and is therefore avoided or regarded with ambivalence. Furthermore, applied science means involvement with people, fields, and farms that the narrow hierarchical view considers disorderly—researchers complain that farmers cannot be controlled in valid experiments. On-farm research, which contradicts the "purity" rule, has low status, is avoided, and is even rejected as scientifically invalid. The ecological perspective on agriculture, however, requires looking at variables interacting in a whole system. Although it is less work to look at only one or two variables at a time with all others controlled by elimination, and although it is difficult to keep many concepts in mind at once, the "laws of nature" are inherently complex, evolving, and unpredictable. Organic farming research must be on-farm, even on-*a*-farm, because that is where the system is—diverse, site-specific, and intimately managed by humans. That such complex research has been limited is explained by greater costs in money and time, and lesser rewards (publications, credit, grant money) for such research. Symbolic barriers are not discussed.[23]

Sustainable Agriculture

In an interesting transference of the "purity" rule, organic agriculture was accused of being "too pure" because its rejection of chemical-intensive agriculture was unequivocal. It was explicit and uncompromising about practice and who did it: *farmers* did it, not scientists or manufacturers. This perception seemed to prevent dissemination of the ideas behind organic farming, and so new concepts were invented. Instead of organic, the new agriculture should be ecological, biological, or regenerative. The term that caught on was *sustainable agriculture*, coined by Wes Jackson in 1980 to describe an agricultural program run on solar energy that saved soil through perennial food crops.[24] The term, if not the specific meaning that Jackson gave it, quickly supplanted the problematic "o"-word. It sounded progressive, self-evident (who would want agriculture or development or the environment to be unsustainable?), broad, and sufficiently safe that diverse professional groups could at least start to talk to each other about real change.[25] And its agenda keeps getting bigger:

> What do we want to sustain—food production, food consumption, groundwater levels, profits, gender relations, current patterns of property ownership and income distribution? Who should benefit from sustainable agriculture—farm owners, agricultural workers,

consumers, transnational food industries, the hungry? How can we best work toward sustainability—technological development, policy changes, economic reforms, educational developments? Such questions have been obscured by the current emphasis on farming practices, which overlooks problems such as hunger, poverty, racial oppression, or gender subordination that many experience in current agrarian structures (for example, family farms, rural communities, and wage labor).[26]

The danger of such a broad goal of a radical social reorganization of the food production system explicit in these questions is that it marginalizes organic farming as a mere production method and niche market rather than exploring its potential for sustainability.[27]

Sustainable agriculture is a big concept—difficult to operationalize, an indefinable feel-good term that attracts everyone, neutralizes challenges, and so far has changed little. To correct the definitional weakness, it has been proposed that basic scientific research will provide the facts to make the concept real,[28] a rededication of the model of science as the source of authoritative knowledge that again excludes.[29] Finally, sustainability is an upper-middle-class movement of officials and academics,[30] an elite that seeks to construct its authority for top-down innovation through science on one hand and ambitious national policy initiatives on the other. Meanwhile, out in the countryside, symbolic barriers have not been removed; some conventional farmers, even if willing to experiment with change, do not like the term *sustainable* any more than they do *organic*. Both seem too far from the mainstream, although the first more closely adheres to forms of agriculture that have been found wanting. Its structural and cultural contradictions make its future look cloudy.

Meanwhile, farmers and their local organizations continued to develop the organic agriculture system. They rediscovered and invented nonchemical production methods, disseminated information and supported each other through conferences and field-day demonstrations, constructed local certification organizations to inspect and credential crops as "organically grown," developed markets, and built relationships with consumer and environmental groups concerned about the destructiveness of chemically dependent global agriculture.

In 1981 farmers, activists, faculty, and students from the University of California, Davis, and other interested persons established the Steering Committee for Sustainable Agriculture and held the first of what are now annual conferences on alternative agriculture. Now known as the Ecological Farming Conference, this is the largest annual gathering of the organic/sustainable community in the United States. By 1984 California Certified Organic Farmers annually certified 150 growers. In 1994 it certified 518 growers, 9 processors, and over 49,000 acres. Major crops in acres are wine grapes, rice, table grapes, apples, and cotton. Statewide standards were set in the Organic Foods Act of 1990, including mandatory registration of all organic producers and handlers.[31] By 1990, 22 states had certification standards. Initial pressure on farmers for national standards seems to have come from European organic groups concerned about international trade, but American producers seemed content with their local organizations.

During this period institutions promoting conventional agricultural science ignored the organic movement or warned off curious conventional farmers. Organic farmers continued to develop alternative extension systems and informal empirical research, periodically attempting to get the attention of the agricultural establishment but being rebuffed as unscientific, old-fashioned, regressive, uneconomic, and misguided. The clash of paradigms was physical as well as ideological: with few exceptions, agricultural scientists and extension agents would not set foot on organic farms.[32]

The Big Change

In 1989 everything changed. That spring, the Natural Resources Defense Council (NRDC) publicly charged that alar, a growth regulator used on apples, was a public health hazard that the federal government could no longer ignore. In a media extravaganza, the government insisted that foods were safe. Meanwhile, conventional apple growers, forced into bankruptcy as demand for their product disappeared, filed suit against the NRDC, and organic producers sold a normal year's supply of apples in three weeks. A family-owned supermarket chain in California introduced residue testing to market its produce as free of pesticides and tried marketing organically grown food. Other California supermarkets charged that the firm was engaging in unfair practices by implying that food in other stores was contaminated. The California Department of Agriculture insisted that its testing of 1% of fresh fruit and vegetables was sufficient to protect the public, which therefore did not need private residue testing. Other supermarkets tentatively offered organic produce to customers. Prices went up.

In the autumn of 1989, after four years of data collection and negotiation, the National Research Council's Board on Agriculture published an extensive report on "alternative" agriculture, calling for fundamental reforms and blaming federal commodity support programs for environmental and economic degradation. The report included case studies of 14 farms that fit the category "alternative," ranging from one certified organic (the Spray farm in Ohio) to one in subtropical Florida that was heavily dependent on chemicals but used less than recommended application rates. Response to the report varied. The sustainable agriculture movement began to congratulate itself for having won. The Fertilizer Institute claimed that starvation would result from following the report's recommendations, that animal manures could contaminate human food, and that, besides, consumers valued appearance and taste more than nutrition or purity. The Cooperative Extension in Ohio warned that without pesticides most crops would fail overnight, leaving Americans dependent on foreign food containing unknown dangers. Highly placed agricultural administrators warned the public against "emotion" in decisions about food and farming, and suggested that materials used in organic farming would make people sick.[33]

While Americans told household surveyors that they were willing to pay higher prices for organically grown produce, those who shopped in supermarkets did not, and prices dropped. In contrast, business increased dramatically in community-based natural food stores and cooperatives that sold mostly locally grown produce, at least in California. Organics had the most success nationally as processed non-staple foods: baby food, breakfast cereal, and snacks such as popcorn and chips, all of them value-added items that are still important in the processed organic foods inventory.

National Standards

Not wanting to see the term *organic* be made meaningless, as *natural* was in the 1970s, the "organic food industry"—retailers, processors, manufacturers, and farmers—sought to protect and develop the budding market by making a push to legislate a single national labeling standard. For example, a jar of organic pasta sauce may include tomatoes from California and Ohio, mushrooms and onions from other states, and herbs from yet another source. To be certified organic, the sauce must be made of ingredients from certified sources. If different states have different standards for labeling an item as organic, the status of the processed food could be compromised. The manufacturer must be able to document the source for each ingredient, and the farmer must be able to document the method of production. Handling, transport, and storage of both fresh and processed foods must also comply with standards that state that food cannot be contaminated by contact with forbidden substances, such as fungicides, during storage.

In early 1989 a proposed U.S. Senate farm conservation and water protection act included a two-sentence definition of organic food and instructed the Secretary of Agriculture to do a feasibility study of a national certification program. Alarmed by their exclusion in developing such a bill, representatives of 35 independent state and regional certification groups organized with consumer and environmental public interest groups to capture the move to include national organic standards in the 1990 Farm Bill, turning the focus of regulation from the purity of the product to how it is produced. They successfully lobbied Congress to include national certification in the bill. Organic supporters felt validated by the new regulations. Others thought the oppressive rules imposed by distant bureaucrats and big business would corrupt the organic philosophy.[34]

After the passage of the law the next step was to write federal regulations. The virtually all-volunteer grassroots organic farming and marketing organizations, having invented the production methods and enterprises, thought they had a good chance to influence the makeup of the National Organic Standards Board (NOSB), a body appointed in 1992 to advise the Secretary of Agriculture. But the initial board did not include any farmers with experience in vegetables, fruits, or nuts (major organic crops); any small farmers; or any farmer from California, which has the largest and most diverse group of organic growers in the United States. Instead, those with ties to conventional agricultural science and commodity groups and corporate food manufacturers dominated. Many in the organic movement felt co-opted: they had worked hard for the legislation but were then excluded from the formal regulation process. Some individuals were so disappointed with the outcome that they did not want to be part of regulation; others warned that organic practitioners must continue to be involved through lobbying and testimony, or risk the future altogether.

However, developing regulations for organic farming took so much more time than expected that the original board members' terms expired. Their replacements have tended to include more members and supporters of the organic community. The NOSB and volunteer technical support persons have put in thousands of hours to write standards for organic crop and livestock production, materials, processing, and certification. Severely limited budgetary support, the many steps required in drawing federal regulations of any kind, shifting political administrations, and institutional ambivalence on the part of the USDA has slowed the work. Hundreds of pages later, the proposed standards are not yet written into regulations, though they are on their way to having the force of law in 1997. The manager of the USDA's National Organic Program observed: "No program that the Department has put together has had as much public comment and public input as this one has . . . will have . . . will continue to have. . . . We think this is a model for how future regulations should be developed."[35]

Business or Way of Life?

> We are not an industry—we are a community with shared values that cannot be imposed by the regulatory process. We value stewardship of the land, cooperation, conservation of resources, and independence. We are a very diverse group . . . we are not in it for the money. There are very few organic farmers who could not make a lot more money at some other kind of work.[36]

For over half a century, organic farmers have been a rebuke to the dominant agricultural system. Today's organic farming value American agrarian ideals of community, self-help, and cooperation and have resisted alienation of their considerable labor. They are sophisticated about cooperation among themselves and exploitation by scientific, political, and economic elites. They farm for at least some profit but do so without subsidy, subject to the market's full effect—which may force them back toward specialization (as a "niche" market) or industrial methods (large-scale use of land, labor, and energy), about which they are profoundly ambivalent.

As long as organic agriculture was on the fringes of American consciousness and culture, it could be stigmatized as backward and uneconomic, and dismissed. Under the umbrella of more respectable sustainable agriculture in the 1980s, however, and aided by increasing public interest in the quality of food, organic agriculture became a voice in agricultural reform. The movement generated its own parallel farming, research, extension, and marketing functions, including local self-regulation to protect farmer and consumer from those who would violate organic principles and practices and fraudulently label their product "organic." Under pressure by some segments of the movement to develop national regulations to facilitate commerce, farmers managed to keep certification focused on the ecological purity of farming practice rather than on the dietary purity of food. If the consumer's desire for pesticide-free food could be met without altering farm practices, neither the organic farmer nor the environment would benefit.

Before national standards, contrasting visions of organic agriculture as a business or as a way of life could coexist. With national standards, business wins. Organic farmers and advocates worry about having to bear the full costs of implementing national regulation while losing local participation. Opportunists with no interest in organic philosophy or long-term practice are entering the market, maximizing production to take advantage of premium prices, which in turn will drive prices down, reproducing the conventional history of conventional agriculture. Those who support the goals of organic farming but want organic food to be "more affordable" for a mass market also reproduce cheap food policy, which did and will drive out small producers, and the industrial processes of specialization and routinization.[37]

The organic people have other reasons to worry. Under industrial capitalism, agricultural reform has been difficult and short-lived where it has happened at all. Attempts to change can revert to the original trend, and winning can turn into losing. For example, a recent citizen attempt in Michigan to control the nuisance of huge hog-containment operations that pollute air, water, and land was nullified by legislative extension of the state's "right to farm" laws to these operations rather than bringing them into the domain of industrial regulation.[38]

> Increasingly, the organic foods marketplace is beginning to look and feel much like the conventional marketplace. Price, rather than the total costs of production and stewardship, is once again reigning supreme. Overproduction . . . is depressing farm gate prices, while marketing efforts are inadequate to absorb the growing production. Investment bankers . . . now prowl organic trade shows eager to incorporate emerging organic manufacturers into larger food multinationals or venture capital driven marketing plays.[39]

> CCOF used to be made up of farmers and the cost was affordable; after all, we just wanted to make sure that the folks with the CCOF labels were in fact organic. The costs now are getting very high because as I see it the inspectors are charging way more for inspections. My last one was so high and I was so broke I thought I was going to have to quit myself. . . . I started getting a bill from the state . . . charging everyone that called themselves organic. . . . What did we do that is so wrong that we have to pay off the gov[ernment] to let us farm organic?[40]

Conventional agriculture has been insulated by subsidies for major crops since 1933. Organic agriculture, however, has always been subject to market forces, since the premium usually given organically grown crops is higher than the support price.

Classical economics developed the Iron Law of Wages, which states that wages tend to fall to subsistence levels in a free market.[41] This law has been neglected, not only because its implications were unpleasant but more likely because it was not understood that subsistence is defined within a culture and differs with social status and time. For example, an office worker must spend money for clothes that a factory worker need not consider; here "subsistence" must include what is expected in office dress.

Even less noted is the entrepreneur's corollary to this law: that any successful enterprise attracts competition that brings profits close to zero, unless new markets open or some noncompetitive advantage is gained, usually with government assistance or subsidy. Larger firms with better access to such advantages can delay their moment of truth for quite some time, but at last (as in the United States since 1970) are squeezed and must in turn squeeze and downsize their workers. The popular invocation of "supply and demand" obscures this law's action.

Both wages and profits thus yield their fruits, first to owners of land from which wealth is produced (who in practice may be the entrepreneurial firm), and after that to those in charge of assignment of rights. In the case of organic farming, landlords (or their proxies, banks) can reap only that part of profits that conventional farmers would also have to yield. This leaves a potential windfall for private or state agents selling rights to the name "organic." A national certifying agency, by extracting part or all of this surplus, can thus reduce the farmer to a subsistence livelihood.

The organic farmer also risks continued transfer of wealth to other nonfarmers: manufacturers of materials and knowledge for which the farmer has to pay. Will organic agriculture simply substitute expensive "natural" external inputs for petrochemical ones? Will the prohibition against synthetic materials be weakened? The centerpiece of concern over reproducing the very system the organic community has sought to reform is the materials list in the national standards, that is, substances approved for fertility and pest control. The latter class of materials also reintroduces the problem of food purity: plant-based pesticides, such as neem, pyrethrum, rotenone, and sabadilla, can be highly toxic, although biodegradable, in biological systems. Furthermore, inert ingredients in manufactured materials may themselves be toxic but are excluded from evaluation because of trade secret protections to business. Decisions regarding inclusion of such materials by NOSB have not been unanimous; specifically, the consumer representative on the board disassociated herself from the botanicals review because she thought other members did not sufficiently evaluate these substances before listing them as allowed materials.[42] Where fertility and pest control are achieved through crop rotations and cultivation, as on the Spray farm in Ohio, inputs are not an issue.

Conclusion

> It is clear to me that if we are to have any hope of creating an ecological food system, with anything like democratic control, that food system has to be local and organic.[43]

National standards for an agricultural production system are unique in American history. Their existence fills some farmers with dread, some with hope. As a method, organic farming successfully produces food; as an economy, however, it is vulnerable. A large question looms about the extent to which this institutionalization of alternative farming methods will actually change the structures of American agriculture as a whole or simply be absorbed by those structures as another market opportunity. In Ohio, for instance, more-conventional farmers are beginning to grow some of their soybeans organically, not because they are interested in the long-term practice of a less extractive agriculture but because of the $18 each bushel brings— far more than the mere $5 for conventionally grown beans. All such farmers want to know is the minimum they must do to be certified by an international organic trade organization; they are not interested in participating in the educational or certifying activities of the state organic farming community. Such opportunism repels established organic farmers, and the chronic worry of smaller farmers that they will be squeezed out economically as large producers drive down prices means that standards themselves will not create security. It is "business" as usual.

Is there an alternative?

Currently, organic growers may combine several economic strategies: selling wholesale to distributors and stores, direct selling in farmers' markets, and subscription farming. The last form is the least commercial and the most outside conventional economic institutions. Community-supported agriculture, realized in a voluntary association called a "CSA," links farmers directly with subscribing or member households, which give the farmer at the start of the growing season or monthly an estimated share of costs of production and livelihood for the farmer. In exchange each household receives a weekly portion of the production available that week or a market-defined portion equivalent to the money paid in. In some CSAs members are expected to contribute labor, and the idea of equitable sharing of both benefit and risk is established morally, not by the market. In others the CSA is a business enterprise with a "familiar face" created through newsletters and occasional visiting days to the farm. CSAs are not the answer for all farms; they seem to work best for small farms located in or near communities with a relatively tight social structure.

A CSA is an "imagined community" that urban dwellers may find attractive, but their commitment may be tenuous, no less self-interested than any other commercial transaction. Turnover in CSA membership forces the farmer to recruit replacements to keep the association alive. CSAs *can* exist outside the organic certification system. Where "organic" is a feature of membership, and the membership is large, participation in a certification system may be necessary.

Organic farming methods work. They have been successfully tested in the modern world for over half a century. The movement is too big to disappear or act as a mere niche market, and it is growing internationally. Austria, for example, has about 25,000 organic farms on 1 million acres; 12% of its land area is certified organic or in transition, probably 15% by the end of 1996. Although this case is unique, Germany, Greece, Italy, Portugal, Spain, and Switzerland have shown comparable or greater growth since 1990, and Switzerland and Sweden have nearly 4% of their agricultural areas being farmed with organic methods, the latter officially planning for 10% by the year 2000. This growth is occurring as a result of top-down and bottom-up efforts: farmers, communities, and consumers are actively seeking alternative food production strategies, and national governments are establishing policies that encourage organic food production. In the United States, if the national organic standards become law and are implemented, if the 1996 Congressional mandate to phase out all agricultural subsidies by the year 2003 is implemented, if Congress in the present period of relentless conservatism does not revoke the Organic Food Production Act, if farmers can and will pay the full cost of regulation, we can expect the organic movement to bifurcate. These changes at the national level will make organic production strategies much more attractive to conventional farmers, who may gradually come to adopt the holistic social as well as ecological values of organic food and farming. However, given the economic structure of conventional agriculture, the shift to organic production does not mean we will see a rise in the number of small, self-sufficient farms. Large growers will continue to be part of the hegemonic global food industry. The survival of small growers is dependent on their ability to make a living locally, and this depends on the willingness of their American customers to pay the full cost of food.

SECTION II: View from the 21st Century

National Organic Standards in the New Millennium

> [A]lternative agrifood movements have been most tolerated where they present little challenge to the institutional and ideological formulations of the dominant culture. —Patricia Allen, *Together at the Table: Sustainability and Sustenance in the American Agrifood System*.[44]

On December 21, 1997, seven years after Congress authorized creation of a national organic standard, the United States Department of Agriculture (USDA) released the first draft of the proposed Federal Rule for public comment. Reactions were negative, furious, and loud. Over four months, the USDA received 275,603 comments by telephone, mail, and e-mail. Although there were dozens of points of disagreement between the proposed Rule and what organic stakeholders expected, the public almost universally opposed inclusion of sewage sludge, irradiation, and genetically modified organisms (GMOs) as permitted inputs and practices. A revised Rule made public in March 2000 omitted the dreadful three and made other changes, eliciting another 40,774 comments. The final Rule, published in the Federal Register on December 21, 2000, became law on October 21, 2002. In the interim, certifying agents were certified, the materials list constantly revised, and livestock standards still a work in progress. After that October date, the word "organic" could be used on a product only if the producer, distributor, and processor were in full compliance with the Federal Rule, which could not be superseded by any other regulations.

Some of the people involved were appalled: "For those who identified with the organic *movement*, the federal law represented a huge symbolic loss. It effectively asked agencies that had been most hostile to organic farming to confer it legitimacy, and it forced organic farmers to do business with the very agricultural establishment they set out to oppose."[45] In contrast, the organic *industry*, those producers, processors, and distributors in interstate trade who had initiated the drive for national standards in the first place, benefited most from the Rule, despite producers' success in shifting the focus of regulation from product to production process. Those at greatest risk were small farmers and certifiers, for whom the cost of becoming certified under the USDA would be prohibitive.

In this postscript to the original essay we discuss the consequences of the absorption of organic farming into the dominant capitalist system. Imposition of federal standards has forced farmers and consumers to confront the integrity of the standards, effects of scale and corporate penetration, and GMO contamination.[46]

The Final Rule: Co-Option and Loss

Organic regulation grew out of an alternative agricultural movement. Farmers developed their own information networks, typically interacted face to face, and made decisions consensually. Consumers and other advocates joined with farmers in establishing state associations for support, information sharing, and certification of organically grown products. These early advocates identified themselves ecologically, agronomically, socially, and ethically in opposition to industrial chemical agriculture. The movement's members prefer to organize in egalitarian bounded groups whose way of knowing is critical and holistic and whose ideal system is sustainable, small scale, and harmless to the environment. They envision nature as vulnerable and depleted, and they reject and deflect risk, dreading "catastrophic, irreversible and inequitable developments."[47] Economics, however, has been the movement's Achilles' heel. Organic farmers are not subsistence farmers; they have taxes, rent, mortgages, and labor to pay, equipment and inputs to buy, and customers to seek. Organics is a *trade* growing out of a *movement* into an *industry*.

The National Organic Standards Board (NOSB), which includes representatives of the various stakeholders in organics and is the point of contact between government and interested parties, oversaw development of the regulations but has congressionally mandated authority only over which material inputs are permitted in certified systems. The USDA does not have to accept the NOSB's recommendations on other matters. The board's limited power allowed other federal agencies and the executive branch to insert irradiation, sewage sludge, and GMOs[48] into the first draft of the Rule, in an effort to prevent organic agriculture from getting "too far away from traditional paradigms and procedures that can be understood by the agencies."[49] The Organic Trade Association and the National Campaign for Sustainable Agriculture immediately organized some 500 groups to protest the draft rule, producing the 275,603 comments mentioned.

In the long run, however, the dominant cultural biases of the economic system have prevailed. While organic production systems value quality, true cost, rural life, raw foods, and aesthetics, conventional production systems prioritize quantity, low cost, urban life, and highly processed foods as fuel. Organic production is complex, multivariate, artisanal, and relationship-based, both ecologically and socially. Organic consumption, however, remains simple, univariate, industrial, and individualistic, without close relationships to nature and often within weakening social relationships, as when individual diets and "grazing" replace family dinners at home. The economic constraints of each party are also distinct. Farmers work to enhance fertility and reduce pest risk in long growing cycles; consumers work to reduce financial risk through low prices in short paycheck cycles. In economic recessions consumers reduce their financial risk by not buying high-priced foods. Consumers may also seek to reduce risk to health by eating certain foods, but high costs may obviate this choice. In the United States consumer food consciousness tends to be individualistic, medicinal, or spiritual, not social, aesthetic, or secular (as in France, for instance). Less and less often do consumers buy raw food to transform at home; instead they buy processed convenience food. An organic corn chip is still a corn chip.

The result is a dual but lopsided organic economy. On the artisanal side, the exemplary form is the subscription farm and the most common the farmers' market. Intermediate between these two is the community co-op. Industrial mainstreaming is the other side: shelf space in conventional supermarkets and prevalence in specialty groceries such as Whole Foods and Trader Joe's. Each of the artisanal outlets has its vulnerabilities. Some shoppers at farmers' markets may pay a price premium for food labeled as organically grown, but others may prefer to buy cheaper, conventionally grown ones sold a few feet away. The subscription farm may face financial instability if members drop out. Development may also imperil such farms, as in northern California, where some successful subscription farms are threatened by water shortages, traffic, and pollution from the conversion of a nearby Native American *ranchería* casino into a resort.[50] Community food co-ops may expand in response to perceived demand, risking their financial viability; or the social costs of scaling up may alienate workers and clientele as the business model becomes more visible.

Industrial mainstreaming also has its dangers. Although organic foods constitute just 2% of the national food market, the overall effect of growth in organic demand has been to attract opportunists to the watering hole, and the existence of national standards has facilitated their penetration of the organic. The larger players then seek to bend the standards to their own interests.

The Integrity of the Standards

The struggle did not end with the codification of national standards. Two especially vulnerable points have been production and processing inputs and livestock requirements. According to the NOSB, synthetic or toxic inputs are not to be used, except when nothing else is available—but that exception is the rub. Originally, the organic industry assumed that market demand would generate new materials that meet organic standards. Variances or exceptions would be granted only in extreme circumstances. Instead the trend has been to place synthetic materials permanently on the materials list and to increase the percentage of nonorganic materials allowed in a process or product, from 5% to 10% and even more. Such "adaptation" is consistent with an emphasis on "growing the market" by reducing entrance barriers and changing conventional agricultural practices primarily through substituting organic inputs for synthetic ones, such as fertilizers. In this model agronomic and industrial practices change minimally; practices such as crop rotation, on-farm composting, and increasing biodiversity are ignored. Organic production and processing are thus assimilated into conventional agricultural practices.

In 2002 Maine blueberry grower Arthur Harvey sued the USDA, arguing that the Final Rule was not consistent with the Organic Foods Production Act of 1990 prohibiting use of synthetics in organic production and manufacture. At issue was a broad exemption of nonorganic materials when organic substitutes were not available. The blueberries produced through this process continued to be labeled "organic" or "100% organic," despite the growers' use of nonorganic inputs. An appeals court agreed with Harvey that the regulations had to be clarified and brought into compliance with the law. Rather than change the regulations, however, the Organic Trade Association (OTA) convinced Congress to attach a rider to the 2006 Agriculture Appropriations Bill that rendered the Harvey decision moot.[51]

Out of 600 nonorganic ingredients that processors asked the National Organic Program (NOP) to include on the list of acceptable materials, 38 were allowed in the Interim Final Rule, such as food colorings, bovine intestine casings, and sweeteners. Some see this outcome as positive: "Instead of allowing any ingredient that cannot be found organically, the universe of potential nonorganic ingredients . . . has been radically reduced. The new rules strongly support the development of organic minor ingredients."[52]

Standards for livestock were contentious from the outset. The conventional livestock industry feared that organic livestock standards requiring lower stocking rates, higher quality feed, no antibiotics, and more humane treatment for animals might undermine or reflect poorly on their highly profitable industrialized practices, in which animals are machines in an assembly line. Hog production and dairy production are especially vulnerable to criticism.[53] Despite these concerns, the Final Rule on livestock mandated that to be organically certified, livestock must not be fed animal byproducts but instead organically certified feed; must not be treated with antibiotics or synthetic parasiticides if the animal is to remain in the herd or flock; and must be born of an organically raised mother or raised organically from the last third of gestation. Living conditions must be clean and sheltered, with fresh air and sunlight, and ruminants must have access to pasture.

Although conventional growers contested all these stipulations, access to pasture was the most contentious issue, because it affects stocking rates, the most important factor in the scale of production. In 2001 an estimated 5% of organic dairy operations did not have enough land to meet the pasture requirement—but these tend to be the largest dairies. For years the USDA would not allow the NOSB to vote on the pasture issue, even calling for more "study." Since the largest factory dairies are in the arid West, defenders of the Rule were convinced that the USDA was acting to benefit these large businesses and not the integrity of the National Organic Program.[54]

In 2005 Cornucopia Institute (CI) in Wisconsin, an advocate of smaller family farms, has been a persistent critic of industrial-scale dairies that claim to produce milk organically. In 2005 CI filed a formal complaint against the Aurora Dairy Corporation in Boulder, Colorado, for multiple violations of organic standards. The most egregious charges involved the absence of access to pasture and the introduction of conventional animals into the milking strings. The owner of Aurora is Marc Peperzak, the largest operator of conventional factory farms in the United States, including industrial-scale dairies. Peperzak was also invested in Horizon, an organic holding company founded in the mid-1990s that now controls 30% of the conventional and 55% of the organic milk market. The huge volume of milk is sold under the private labels of Walmart, Safeway, Giant, Wild Oats, and Costco. CI filed a fourth complaint with the USDA after discovering that a contract ranch it visited had

198 Ꮿ Part IV Agriculture and Agri-Conflict

never been certified. Aurora itself was certified by State of Colorado personnel who may not have had experience with organic inspections. Their interpretation of "access to pasture" excluded lactating animals who spent their days trudging between feed lot and milking parlor, a clear violation of the intent of the organic standards.

The USDA investigated the Aurora Organic Dairy and on August 29, 2007, announced that it had "willfully violated 14 provisions of regulations,"[55] but the agency imposed no fine and did not suspend the dairy's organic certification. Instead, it put Aurora on probation for a year: if it was not in compliance in a year's time, it would be decertified. The OCA responded: "It is unconscionable that the USDA allowed Aurora to continue, after making millions of dollars, in this 'ethics-based' industry, when they had concluded that Aurora willfully violated the law."[56] Aurora apparently "made a calculated bid to game the system while building a fast-growing venture-backed organic dairy business, only correcting things once the action got too hot."[57] But the USDA's decision was not the end of the story: in October 2007, class action lawsuits on behalf of consumers in 27 states were filed against Aurora, alleging "consumer fraud, negligence, and unjust enrichment."[58]

On February 12, 2010, the USDA issued the long-awaited Final Rule on access to pasture: animals must graze on pasture during grazing season at least 120 days each year, including during the finishing phase, and they must get a minimum of 30% of feed from that grazing; producers must manage pasture to meet feed and conservation requirements. The Rule becomes effective June 17, and certified organic operations have one year to come into compliance.[59] This is a major victory for organic livestock farming.

Predatory Capitalism and the Next New Thing

Once organic production proved profitable, it suddenly became fashionable. In 1997 M&M Mars Corporation, ranked seventh in 2002 in North American food sales, bought Seeds of Change, an important source of open-pollinated, heritage, and organic food seeds. In 1999 General Mills, ranked 18th, bought Cascadian Farms, one of the most prominent organic food processors and a pioneer in the movement. That year Heinz, ranked 10th, bought Hain Celestial, itself the owner of 13 brands of organic teas, canned goods, and baby foods. By 2002 Dean Foods, ranking 29th, owned Horizon Dairy, which already owned The Organic Cow of Vermont, Alta Dena Dairy, and White Wave/Silk organic soy milk products.[60] By mid-2007 Heinz, down to 24th in North American food, sold its shares in Hain Celestial, which had absorbed 21 organic firms, including Walnut Acres, another pioneer.[61] Eleven of the top conventional food processors in North America have absorbed dozens of organic processors, looking for profits in a sector that has been growing at 20% a year.

What has been called "stealth ownership" threatens to reduce "organic" to another feature of branding.[62] Organic has scaled up. The bagged mixed salad greens in nearly every American grocery store is likely labeled "Earthbound," owned by Natural Selection with headquarters in the Salinas Valley of California. The business began in a California kitchen 20 years ago when a New York couple, Drew and Myra Goodman, sought customers for ready-to-eat salad greens grown in their own market garden. Natural Selection moved into the mass market when it received orders from Costco in the early 1990s, then from Walmart and Albertson's. Quickly partnering with large-scale conventional growers in the Salinas Valley who learned to grow organically, the firm now has six partners and contracts with growers in

California, Arizona, and Mexico for tens of thousands of acres of organically grown baby greens.[63] Invited in 2002 to the annual California Eco-Farm conference to be featured as "successful organic farmers," the Goodmans gave their presentation between two other market gardening couples, one with 25 acres, the other with 12. The contrast only amplified, to a restive audience, the disproportionate character of the Goodmans' operation.

In 2006 Earthbound Farm/Natural Selection had to deal with undesirable publicity from a serious *E. coli* O157:H7 outbreak in spinach packaged in its facility, and scale became an issue again. When the name Earthbound Farm/Natural Selection was made public, many assumed that improperly processed manure had caused the contamination—a primal fear in conventional critiques of organic farming practices. Some in the organic community countered that industrial organic had brought this disaster on itself by being too big—such contamination would be less likely on small farms. Earthbound's response was to develop an intensive testing program and a food safety scientific advisory panel.[64]

Another side of Earthbound's success is the squeezing of small producers of salad greens out of the market, as they lost the price premiums that sustained their livelihood to market share obtained through volume.[65] Being forced out was bitter for pioneers: "a corporate organic farmer suggested to a family farmer struggling to survive in the competitive world of industrial organic agriculture that he 'should really try to develop a niche to distinguish yourself in the market.' The small farmer replied: 'I believe I developed that niche 20 years ago. It's called organic. And now you're sitting in it.'"[66]

The power of small producers in the market has eroded steadily. Only those who limited themselves to direct marketing through CSAs or farmers' markets have some insulation. Those primary producers remaining are subject to control from above by packers, handlers, shippers, processors, distributors, and retailers. Freedom to transact is eliminated through contract between unequal parties, and profit flows upward with primary producers on the bottom. Guthman calls this *oligopsony*: "a few players are able to set prices and effectively limit how production is carried out. . . . even those who are external to [organic] industry structure are being pushed into capitalist decision making as the industry grows and changes."[67]

As in other businesses the industrialization of organic agriculture has led to standardization, specialization, increasing size, centralization of command and control, and mass merchandizing.[68] Two national organic food retailers in the United States are Whole Foods and Trader Joe's. In 2007 Whole Foods, a publicly held company, having bought 13 natural food chains in the United States and Great Britain since 1991,[69] bought Wild Oats Markets, its largest competitor. In 2006 the chain had 270 stores and earned $5.6 billion. Employees are reported to be paid and treated well, although company policy is aggressively antiunion. The business has a checkered environmental and social record; journalist Michael Pollan has criticized its industrial scale and weakness in regional sourcing.[70] Whole Foods stores tend to be located in affluent neighborhoods, and its prices are high.

Trader Joe's, a 288-store chain privately owned by Albrecht Discounts (a German retailer) since 1979, rose from modest convenience-mart roots in Los Angeles. Offering only selected merchandise, it specializes in semiprepared fresh and frozen meal fixings and inexpensive wines. Also earning $5 billion in 2006 Trader Joe's sources internationally and attracts middle-class devotees to its semifine grocery mix, much of it packaged under its private label. It offers low prices and good quality most of the time, preferring small vendors to corporate sourcing. Organic foods are included, but the brand centers on international rather than organic chic. It offers good wages, benefits even to part-time employees, and advancement, although it is not unionized. Trader Joe's ranks second in customer satisfaction and Whole Foods fifth.[71]

Small Scale Co-Ops

Local retail cooperatives are more in line with the ideals of the organic founders—small and local, democratically governed, and involved with the larger community promoting health, education, and social justice. The Sacramento Natural Foods Co-op (SNFC), second largest in the United States (the largest is in Minneapolis) was founded in 1973 and evolved from a food-buying club to a retail business with sales of $23.2 million in 2009. Its 5,700 member-owners tend to be loyal shoppers, receiving periodic discounts of 5–10% as well as monthly senior and "anti-depression Friday" discounts open to the general public. Most members rarely exercise their voting rights, however, which may have affected the decision to build a second store that subsequently failed in the recent recession, financially endangering the whole structure. Members, employees, and management pulled together in the crisis, and the SNFC is rapidly paying down the long-term debt it incurred. Focus groups have reminded the new Board that co-op members are more risk-averse now.

Crisis reveals the structure of power in any institution or organization. In the Earthbound Farms case, although the E. coli contamination was eventually found to have come from the most obvious source, an adjacent cattle pasture, it opened the door to a wave of new regulations against possible wild animal sources of contamination that threaten organic conservation practices and small farm production of salad greens. Irradiation of all field-grown greens has been proposed, a violation of organic standards. Media exposure of Whole Food's founder and CEO John Mackey has revealed a confusion of contradictions around making money and doing good, competition, hostility to labor, and über-capitalist ideology that, along the with recession, reduced profits and capital, subjecting the firm to the demands of large investors and full corporatization.[72] Near-failure made the Sacramento Natural Foods Co-op stronger as an economic and democratic institution, and built closer ties through workshops, tours, and dinners between customers and local farmers.

GMO Contamination

The most serious threat to organic production is the potential catastrophe of genetic contamination of organic crops by genetically modified organisms in neighboring fields. In anticipation of "accidental contamination," the European Union set the permitted level of GMOs in a product at .9%.[73] Current standards in the United States and the United Kingdom ban any GMO content in organic products, offering consumers concerned about food safety an alternative to the widespread, unlabeled presence of GMO proteins in commercial food. In agriculture genetic engineering is merely the latest intensification in food-producing technology. Like other technologies before it, biological engineering would create jobs, feed the hungry, clothe the naked, cure the sick, and make enormous profits. Corporations saw new opportunity for economic growth and especially for further control of the food system—owning life itself, not just land, machines, and inputs.[74] Monsanto, the American chemical producer, began to shift from chemical to biochemical with the development of bovine growth hormone in the 1980s. The company sought to insulate itself from public outrage at the harm its products might cause by recruiting political backing and working its way into government agencies. A "revolving door" developed between corporations and government agencies during the Reagan-Bush administrations.

Despite continuing resistance in Europe and Asia, U.S. government officials and corporations pursued genetic engineering in the 1990s. Europeans were reluctant to risk their food system and had experienced bad science in the bovine spongiform encephalopathy (BSE) outbreak and 2000's catastrophic foot and mouth livestock epidemic. While American citizens are largely unaware of genetically modified organisms in the food supply, British and European consumers remain highly suspicious of them. In the United States biotech companies and their allies continue to oppose legislation that would require foods containing GMO ingredients to be so labeled.

American farmers, faced with perennial failure, were seduced by the promise of higher yields at lower input costs. (Monsanto has developed only two products that work even in the short term: crops resistant to their herbicide Round-Up so more can be used on a field, and *Bacillus thuringensis* genes in field corn to kill corn earworm.) If pollen from a stand of Monsanto GMO canola drifts into my non-GMO field, and Monsanto finds its patented protein in my crop, it will charge me royalties and fines for using that protein. Canadian canola breeder and farmer Percy Schmeiser challenged Monsanto in just such a case, lost in Provincial court and appeals court, but won, after seven years, in Federal appeals court. However, it is no longer possible to grow organic canola seed in Canada, because GMO pollen is ubiquitous. The Big Three genetically engineered food crops—corn, soy, and canola—are found in most non-organic packaged foods in the United States.

Monsanto has faced setbacks. American farmers rejected GMO wheat and rice because foreign markets were closed to them. Attempts to improve nutrition or generate medicinal properties in foods have foundered because of the scientific and regulatory difficulty of multigene engineering, the problem of taste, the high costs of bringing a product to market, and comingling of crops. Despite Monsanto's aggressive tactics, the genetic engineering of fruits and vegetables, the major organic sector, is not profitable. However, an important case involving alfalfa is pending and will be argued before the U.S. Supreme Court. An appeals court prohibited field trials of Round-Up Ready alfalfa, because no Environmental Impact Statement had been filed. Such a report, now in its comment period, came out of the USDA in December 2009, finding "no significant impact."[75] Alfalfa pollen, like canola pollen, can be carried great distances by wind and bees. GMO pollen will easily contaminate both organic and conventional non-GMO alfalfa stands, but the USDA said it was up to farmers to protect their crops from GMO contamination. Organic dairy farmers, heavily dependent on alfalfa hay, have great interest in this case. A major battle between proprietary GMO agriculture and organic agriculture may be shaping up. Coexistence is not an option.

What Does the Future Hold for Organic Agriculture?

The antidote to an upside-down world is the working world of organic farmers, but only if consumers value and defend it. Farmers and farm workers cannot do it alone. Organic farming is a special case that illuminates the global agricultural systems on which we depend for sustenance, health, livelihood, and life itself. The cornucopia of American supermarkets makes affluent consumers oblivious to the vulnerabilities of the whole system. Food insecurity is right there, under our noses. *Quality*—is any food we eat as good as it seems? Have the standards for producing food, organic or not, been weakened or not enforced? *Nutrition*—is food a source of health or disease? *Affordability*—can working people afford high quality, healthy food? *Availability*—what is there to eat that is available locally? *What* can we grow, *where* will we grow it, and *who* will grow it under conditions of rapid ecological change? Erosion in any one of these dimensions starts a cascade of increasing insecurity that even Alice's Red Queen cannot outpace. Practitioners and advocates of organic farming address these questions in exquisite detail, and only by heeding their answers can the American food system "get to somewhere else."

Notes

1. Our thanks to Richard N. L. Andrews and Laura B. DeLind for their helpful comments on an earlier draft of this paper.

2. John H. Bodley, *Anthropology and Contemporary Human Problems*, 3rd ed. (Mountain View, CA: Mayfield Publishing, 1996, 1–5).

3. National Research Council, *Alternative Agriculture* (Washington, D.C.: National Academy Press, 1989, 97–130); Ann Misch, "Assessing Environmental Health Risks," *State of the World 1994* (New York: W. W. Norton/Worldwatch Institute, 1994, 117–36).

4. Ralph Borsodi, "The Case against Farming as a Big Business," *The Land* 6:4 (1947–48, 446–51).

5. National Organic Standards Board, "Definition of Organic" drafted and passed in Orlando, Fla., April 1995. The U.S. Dept. of Agriculture estimates that in 1994 there were about 5,550 organic producers in the country (estimated to be 0.3% of all farms), 4,050 of them certified by at least one and sometimes more of the 33 private and 11 state organizations. Those organizations will continue to certify under the Organic Production Act to a single national standard that supersedes all others. Organic sales for 1994 were estimated at $2.3 billion, perhaps 1% of the total agricultural economy, up from $1.9 billion the previous year (Committee for Sustainable Agriculture, *Organic Food Still Matters*, summer 1995, p. 12).

6. Wes Jackson, *Altars of Unhewn Stone: Science and the Earth* (San Francisco: North Point Press, 1987, 97–98).

7. David B. Danbom, *The Resisted Revolution: Urban America and the Industrialization of Agriculture, 1900–1930* (Ames: Iowa State University Press, 1979). In 1900, 42% of Americans lived on 5.7 million farms averaging 147 acres; by 1992 the numbers had fallen to less than 1.8% on 1.9 million farms averaging 490 acres. Prices per bushel, measured in constant (1967) U.S. dollars, for wheat and corn in 1900 were $2.48 and $1.40; they peaked in 1919 ($4.17, $2.92, and $7.92, respectively) and by 1990 had dropped to $0.67, $0.58, and $1.47. Sources: *U.S. Bureau of the Census, Historical Statistics of the United States, Colonial Times to 1970*, Bicentennial Edition (Washington, D.C.: Government Printing Office, 1975); *U.S. Bureau of the Census, Statistical Abstracts of the United States* (Washington, D.C.: Government Printing Office, 1981, 1991, 1995); U.S. Dept. of Agriculture, National Agricultural Statistics Service, Agricultural Statistics (Washington, D.C.: Government Printing Office, 1967 to 1993).

8. Donald Worster, *The Dust Bowl: The Southern Plains in the 1930s* (New York: Oxford University Press, 1979).

9. Sir Albert Howard, *An Agricultural Testament* (London: Oxford University Press, 1940), 198.

10. See Worster, note 8, for a less enthusiastic assessment.

11. Rachel Carson, *Silent Spring* (Boston: Houghton Mifflin, 1962). The book was violently attacked, and Dow Chemical published a rebuttal, *Silent Autumn*, threatening world hunger without use of pesticides.

12. H. L. Boul et al., "Influence of Agricultural Practices on the Levels of DDT and Its Residues in the Soil," *Environmental Science and Technology* 28:8 (1994, 1397–1403). See also National Research Council, *Alternative Agriculture* (Washington, D.C.: National Academy Press, 1989) for a summary of productivity and chemical use in American agriculture from the 1960s to the 1980s. For data on soil loss and water quality, see National Research Council, *Alternative Agriculture* (Washington, D.C.: National Academy Press, 1989, 97–119).

13. National Research Council 1989, note 12. For a historical view of organic matter and erosion control, see James F. Parr and Sharon B. Hornick, "Agricultural Use of Organic Amendments: A Historical Perspective," *American Journal of Alternative Agriculture* 7 (1992, 181–89); for a case study of no-till use in the Midwest, see Michael Chibnik, "Saving Soil by Abandoning the Plow: Experimentation with No-Till Farming in an Iowa County," in Michael Chibnik, Ed., *Farm Work and Fieldwork: American Agriculture in Anthropological Perspective* (Ithaca, NY: Cornell University Press, 1987, 90–117).

14. R. Klepper et al., "Economic Performance and Energy Intensiveness on Organic and Conventional Farms in the Corn Belt: A Preliminary Comparison," *American Journal of Agricultural Economics* 59 (1977, 1–12); J. A. Langley et al., "The Macro Implications of a Complete Transformation of U.S. Agricultural Production to Organic Farming Practices," *Ecosystems and Environment* 10 (1983, 323–33) [of 10 areas, only Texas and the Southeast lost net income; gains elsewhere ranged from 14 to 80%]; T. Cacek and L. L. Langner, "The Economic Implications of Organic Farming," *American Journal of Alternative Agriculture* 1:1 (1986, 25–29).

15. Wendell Berry, *The Unsettling of America: Culture and Agriculture* (San Francisco: North Point Press, 1977, 196–97).

16. National Research Council, 1989, note 12, p. 262.

17. USDA Study Team on Organic Farming, *Report and Recommendations on Organic Farming* (Washington, D.C.: U.S. Dept. of Agriculture, July 1980). For discussion of the loss of family farms, see Gary Comstock, Ed., *Is There a Moral Obligation to Save the Family Farm?* (Ames: Iowa State University Press, 1987); Peggy F. Barlett, *American Dreams and Rural Realities: Family Farms in Crisis* (Chapel Hill: University of North Carolina Press, 1993); Amory B. Lovins et al., "Energy and Agriculture," *Meeting the Expectations of the Land*, Wes Jackson et al., Eds. (San Francisco: North Point Press, 1984, 68–86).

18. Garth Youngberg et al., "The Sustainable Policy Agenda in the United States: Politics and Prospects," in Patricia Allen, Ed., *Food for the Future: Conditions and Contradictions of Sustainability* (New York: John Wiley & Sons, 1993, 295–318).

19. Mary Douglas, "In the Nature of Things," *Implicit Meanings* (London: Routledge & Kegan Paul, 1975, 214, 216).

20. Marty Strange, *Family Farming: A New Economic Vision* (Lincoln: University of Nebraska Press, 1988).

21. Warren J. Belasco, *Appetite for Change: How the Counterculture Took on the Food Industry 1966–1988* (New York: Pantheon Books, 1989).

22. David B. Danbom, "The Agricultural Experiment Station and Professionalization: Scientists' Goals in Agriculture," *Agricultural History* 60:2 (1986, 246–55).

23. See also Lawrence Busch and William B. Lacy, *Science, Agriculture and the Politics of Research* (Boulder, CO: Westview Press, 1983). William Lockeretz, "Removing Applied

Agricultural Research from the Academy," *American Journal of Alternative Agriculture* 10:1 (1995, 19–24); Peter Esainko and Valerie Wheeler, "A Little More than Kin and Less than Kind: Organic Practice vs. Institutional Theory," paper given at the Varieties of Sustainability Conference, Agriculture, Food and Human Values Society, Asilomar, CA, 1991.

24. Wes Jackson, *New Roots for Agriculture* (Lincoln: University of Nebraska Press, 1981 and 1985).

25. Youngberg et al., note 18.

26. Patricia Allen, "The Challenges of Sustainability in Food and Agriculture," *Organic Farmer* 4:1 (1993, 20–21).

27. Youngberg et al., note 18, p. 310.

28. Youngberg et al., note 18, pp. 311–12.

29. Since 1988 the U.S. Dept. of Agriculture has spent some $6 to 7.5 million in a competitive grants program originally called LISA (Low Input Sustainable Agriculture), then SARE (Sustainable Agriculture Research and Education program). Small grants are given for research, demonstration, and extension projects by public- and private-sector professionals, farmers, and business persons. SARE funds on-farm research, though very few projects deal with organic systems. Profitability is a primary concern. SARE also has a sophisticated system for disseminating the results of its projects.

30. Frederick H. Buttel, "The Production of Agricultural Sustainability: Observations from the Sociology of Science and Technology," in Patricia Allen, Ed., *Food for the Future* (New York: John Wiley & Sons, 1993, 19–45).

31. *California Certified Organic Farmers*, Statewide Newsletter 11:4 (1995, 19); CCOF information brochure, 1994.

32. Valerie Wheeler and Peter Esainko, "Structural Power and Authoritative Knowledge in Alternative Agriculture," paper at the Society for Applied Anthropology, Charleston, SC, 1991.

33. National Research Council, 1989, note 3; Institute of Food Technologists, "Organically Grown Foods: A Scientific Status Summary," *Food Technology* 44:12 (1990, 123–30); Preston Smith, "Why Does Jack Hate LISA?" *New Farm* 11:7 (Nov.–Dec. 1989); Martha Carroll, "Organic Growing Still Has Many Drawbacks," press release, Ohio Cooperative Extension Service, Ohio State University, OARDC, Wooster, 1989; Charles Hess, "Sustainable Agriculture: The Power of Thought," *Sustainable Agriculture in California: A Research Symposium* (University of California, Davis: Sustainable Agriculture Research and Education Program, 1990, 1–20); Gerald W. Thomas, "Sustainability: Striking a Balance between Economic and Ecological Constraints," *Sustainable Agriculture in California: A Research Symposium* (University of California, Davis: Sustainable Agriculture Research and Education Program, 1990, 1–5); John E. Kinsella, Speech at the Student Farm Field Day, University of California, Davis, 1990.

34. Thomas Forster, "OFAC Lobbying Efforts Triumph," *Organic Farmer* 1:4 (1990, 26); Gene Logsdon, "Kiss of Death? Federal Organic Standards Are Not What the Doctor Ordered," *New Farm* 15:3 (1993, 12ff).

35. Harold Ricker, "National Organic Program Update," Eco-Farm Conference, Asilomar, CA, January 1996.

36. Elizabeth Henderson, "Some Comments and Concerns about the NOSB," *Organic Farming* (Fall 1992, 21).

37. Fred Kirschenmann, "The Organic Food Industry: Where We've Been, Where We Are, and Where We're Going," Speech delivered at the 10th Annual Organic Trade Association Dinner, Sept. 14, 1995, Baltimore.

38. Laura B. DeLind, "The State, Hog Hotels, and the 'Right to Farm': A Curious Relationship," *Agriculture and Human Values* 12:3 (1995, 34–44).

39. Frederick Kirschenmann et al., "Toward a Sustainable, Organic Food Marketing System," *Organic Farmer* 4:2 (1993, 19–20).

40. Sal Schettino (sals@rain.org), "Sustainable," Organic Gardening Discussion List GL@ UKCC.uky.edu, www.rain.org/~sals/my.html, accessed 02/11/96.

41. Named by Ferdinand Lassalle, this law was derived by David Ricardo from pioneer work by the French physiocrats. Other schools of thought favored the just wage, the wages fund, marginal productivity of labor, bargaining theory, purchasing power theory, and equal wages.

42. "The Special Review of Botanicals," *Farmer to Farmer* 3:10 (Jan. 1995, 7).

43. Bill Duesing, "Is Organic Enough?" The Natural Farmer (NOFA), Winter 1995–96; Bill Reichle, "Fairness in Certification—the Rules Have Changed," *Farmer to Farmer* 3:7 (Jan. 9, 1995, 12).

44. Patricia Allen, *Together at the Table: Sustainability and Sustenance in the American Agrifood System* (University Park: The Pennsylvania State University Press, 2004).

45. Julie Guthman, *Agrarian Dreams: The Paradox of Farming in California* (Berkeley and Los Angeles: University of California Press, 2004, 116).

46. This essay cannot address even larger issues of the underlying contradictions of radical agrarianism that include farming as a business, the mechanisms of land valuation, and the core American value of militant self-reliance. See Guthman 2004 for good discussions of the first three issues.

47. Schwarz and Thompson, pp. 66–67; Mary Douglas, *Natural Symbols: Explorations in Cosmology* (Harmondsworth: Penguin, 1970), *Implicit Meanings* (London: Routledge & Kegan Paul, 1975), *Cultural Bias*, Occasional Paper No. 35 (London: Royal Anthropological Institute of Great Britain and Ireland, 1978); Michiel Schwarz and Michael Thompson, *Divided We Stand: Redefining Politics, Technology, and Social Choice* (Philadelphia: University of Pennsylvania Press, 1990).

48. Tim Sullivan, "The New National Organic Regulations," workshop at the Ecological Farming Conference, Asilomar, CA, January 22, 1998.

49. Katherine DiMatteo, "The New National Organic Regulations," workshop at the Ecological Farming Conference, Asilomar, CA, January 22, 1998.

50. Hudson Sangree, "Truce in Capay Valley: Once-Hostile Neighbors Warming to Cache Creek Casino," *The Sacramento Bee*, September 15, 2007, A1, 16.

51. E. Melanie DuPuis and Sean Gillon, "The Dynamics of Alternative/Sustainable Economies: Modes of Governance as Everyday Forms of Collaboration," *Agrarian Studies*, Yale University, www.yale.edu/agrarianstudies/papers/01dupuis.pdf, accessed 9/15/07; Jack Kittredge, "Michael Sligh: Stay the Course on Organic Standards," *The Natural Farmer*, vol. 2, no. 68, Northeast Organic Farming Association, Spring 2006, www.organicconsumers.org/articles/article_417.cfm, 10/19/07.

52. "Status of Non-Organic Ingredient Commercial Availability Requirements," *Certified Organic* (Santa Cruz: California Certified Organic Farmers, Fall 2007, 22); Karen Berner, "What They Are, How They're Used, and Why They Made the List," *The Daily Green*, July 18, 2007, http://organicconsumers.org/articles/article_6154.cfm, accessed 9/15/07.

53. Laura DeLind, "Social Consequences of Intensive Swine Production: Some Effects of Community Conflict," *Culture & Agriculture*, vol. 26, no. 1, 2004, pp. 80–89; Valerie Wheeler and Peter Esainko, "'Access to Pasture' and Other Amenities: National Organic Standards," *Culture & Agriculture*, vol. 26, no. 1, 2004, pp. 90–101.

54. Mark Kastel, "Maintaining the Integrity of Organic Milk," report presented to the USDA National Organic Standards Board, April 19, 2006, State College, Pennsylvania, http://cornucopia.org, accessed 9/15/07.

55. Mark Kastel, "USDA Brings Enforcement Hammer Down Heavily on Nations Largest Organic Dairy (Aurora)," Cornucopia Institute, August 30, 2007, www.organicconsumers.org/articles/article_6869.cfm, accessed 9/15/07.

56. Mark Kastel, "Organic Consumers Launch Nationwide Lawsuit in 27 States against Aurora Organic Dairy for Violating Organic Standards," press release, Organic Consumers Association, October 17, 2007, www.organicconsumers.org/articles/article_7757.cfm, accessed 10/29/07.

57. Samuel Fromartz, "Organic System Mending: USDA Forces Boulder-Based Dairy Farm to Change Practices," *Rocky Mountain News—CO*, September 8, 2007, www.organicconsumers.org/articles_article7027.cfm, accessed 9/15/07.

58. Mark Kastel, note 56.

59. USDA News Release No. 0059.10, "USDA Issues Final Rule on Organic Access to Pasture," February 12, 2010, Washington, D.C.: United States Department of Agriculture, www.usda.gov, 2/16/10.

60. Philip Howard, "Organic Industry Structure: Top 30 Food Processors in North America," Dept. of Community, Agriculture, Recreation, and Resource Studies, Michigan State University, East Lansing, October 2002, www.organicconsumers.org/articles/article_6159.cfm, accessed 9/15/07.

61. Philip Howard, "Organic Industry Structure: Significant Acquisitions and Introductions," Dept. of Community, Agriculture, Recreation, and Resource Studies, Michigan State University, East Lansing, July 2007, www.msu.edu/~howardp and www.organicconsumers.org/articles/article_6159.cfm, accessed 9/15/07. (See the Howard website for several excellent organic food business graphics diagramming the relationships and concentrations in the organic industry.)

62. Rich Ganis, "Organic Goes Industrial," *Informed Eating*, vol. 1, no. 2, Nov./Dec., 2002 (Oakland, CA: Center for Informed Food Choices), www.informedeating.org, in Michael Sligh and Carolyn Christman, "Who Owns Organic? The Global Status, Prospects, and Challenges of a Changing Organic Market," (Pittsboro, NC: Rural Advancement Foundation International, 2003).

63. Michael Pollan, *The Omnivore's Dilemma* (New York: Penguin Press, 2006, 164).

64. Will Daniels, "Food Safety: Uncovering the Myths Surrounding the *E. Coli* Outbreak of 2006," *Certified Organic*, Santa Cruz: California Certified Organic Farmers (Fall 2007, 16:19, 24).

65. Julie Guthman, note 45, pp. 165–66.

66. Michael Pollan, note 63, p. 9.

67. Guthman, note 45, p. 60.

68. John Ikerd, "Organic Agriculture Faces the Specialization of Production Systems: Specialized Systems and the Economical States," conference paper presented at Organic Agriculture Faces the Specialization of Production Systems, Lyon, France, December 6–9, 1999, www.missouri.edu/~ikerdj/papers/FRANCE.html, accessed 9/28/07.

69. Philip Howard, "Organic Industry Structure: Retail Acquisitions and Mergers, 1984–2007," Dept. of Community, Agriculture, Recreation, and Resource Studies, Michigan State University, East Lansing, www.msu.edu/~howardp, accessed 11/03/07.

70. Michael Pollan, "My Letter to Whole Foods," *The New York Times*, June 12, 2006, http://pollan.blogs.nytimes.com, accessed 01/23/07; "My 2nd Letter to Whole Foods," September 15, 2006, www.michaelpollan.com/article.php?id=83, accessed 10/31/07; Bonnie Azab Powell, "Michael Pollan, Whole Foods' John Mackey Usher Berkeley Foodies into 'Ecological Era'," *UC Berkeley Web Feature*, News Center, February 28, 2007, www.berkeley.edu/news/media/releases/2007/02/28_pollanmackey.shtml, accessed 03/31/07.

71. "2007 Top 75 North American Food Retailers," *Supermarket News*, February 2007; "Win at the Grocery Game: How to Shop Smarter, Cheaper, and Faster," *Consumer Reports*, October 2006, 36–40.

72. Nick Paumgarten, "Food Fighter: Does Whole Foods' C.E.O. Know What's Best for You?" *The New Yorker*, January 4, 2010, pp. 36–47.

73. Peter Shield, "GMOs Threaten Organic Standards," *Natural Choices*, June 13, 2007, www.organicconsumers.org/articles/article_5649.cfm, accessed 11/06/07; Sybille de La Hamaide, "France Suspends Planting of GMO Crops," Reuters, October 26, 2007, http://organicconsumers.org/articles/article_7944.cfm, accessed 10/26/07.

74. Jeremy Rifkin, *The Biotech Century: Playing Ecological Roulette with Mother Nature's Design* (New York: Jeremy P. Tarcher/Putnam, 1998).

75. USDA, "Glyphosate-Tolerant Alfalfa Events J101 and J163: Request for Nonregulated Status," Draft Environmental Impact Statement—November 2009, www.aphis.usda.gov/biotechnology/downloads/alfalfa/gealfalfa_deis.pdf, accessed 02/16/10.

CHAPTER 9

Resource Access, Environmental Struggles, and Human Rights in Honduras

James Phillips

SECTION I: The End of the Millennium

On May 3, 1991, five peasants were shot and killed as they slept on a piece of land they had peacefully occupied in northern Honduras. The Honduran government had awarded them title to the land 15 years before, but an army colonel and other large landowners had continued to occupy it. The army colonel was later convicted in the 1991 peasants' murder, and he served two years in prison before being released. Known throughout Honduras as the El Astillero massacre, this incident and others like it gave rise to many popular songs in peasant communities, including one with these words: "The land is for sustaining life, not just for the powerful. The life of a peasant is worth the same as a rich man's."[1]

In Honduras today, the preservation and advancement of basic human rights, the equitable use of land and resources, and the preservation and sustainable use of the country's natural environment are three inextricably connected aspects of a single historical process. In the experience of many Hondurans, a powerful connection is being forged between environmental degradation, inequitable systems of land tenure and resource control, and the erosion of a variety of basic rights. This connection derives its power from the current sense of insecurity and crisis in Honduran society.

Control of Resources, Environmental Degradation, and the Crisis of Insecurity

Large landowners have existed alongside peasant farmers in Honduras for much of the country's history and especially since the arrival of the banana companies in the early 1900s. Typically, Honduran landowners who could afford to expand production of profitable export crops did so by expanding their own landholdings, often annexing the land of peasants.[2] The process of consolidating large holdings by eliminating small holdings or pushing peasants to marginal lands was quickened by the expansion of export markets for Honduran fruit, beef, and wood after World War II and into the present. In recent years, this process has been clearly documented in southern Honduras and the northern fruit-company areas.[3] The country's unequal land tenure patterns have successfully restricted access to natural resources for rural Hondurans, contributing to a growing sense of insecurity about resources and meeting needs basic. Insecurity has been sharpened by clear signs of accelerating environmental degradation and dwindling resources, especially for the poor majority.

Deforestation is generally cited as the most apparent environmental problem in Honduras.[4] Soil erosion and depletion, water contamination, and lack of urban waste management are other important concerns. Deforestation has continued at such a pace that in 1988 the director of COHDEFOR (the Honduran Forestry Department) warned of emerging and irreversible desertification.[5] The following year, a report issued by the Honduran Ecology Association calculated that 10 hectares of forest were being destroyed in the country every hour.[6] In sum, "rates of loss of forests, soils, fisheries, and other crucial natural resources exceed rates of regeneration and . . . ensuing consequences such as land degradation, watershed deterioration, and destruction of coastal resources have reached critical levels in many areas."[7]

Throughout the 1980s climatic symptoms of environmental deterioration became apparent. For example, peasant farmers in the northern department of Yoro endured such a drought that many were forced to replace their traditional diet of corn, which the drought destroyed, with the wheat flour sent as food aid from the United States.[8] Punctuating the drought were major floods. Floods in Choluteca in 1988 and the Aguan Valley in 1990, both agricultural centers, devastated poor residents whose homes or plots of cultivation perched precariously on marginal lands above rivers or on steep mountainsides. Floods also affected thousands of landless rural families who migrated to rapidly growing cities such as Tegucigalpa, the nation's capital, where they lived in flimsy shacks along riverbanks and canals or on mountainsides considered too steep for urban development.

During the past 30 years the availability of basic foods consumed by most of the population—maize, beans, sorghum—has declined, even as export agriculture has expanded. From 1952 to 1986 the number of kilograms of corn produced per person declined from 140 to 107, with similar declines in beans and sorghum. The number of hectares per person planted in these crops also declined.[9] Some of the effects of this declining production were clear by the 1970s: the local price of maize increased by 107%, and beans 117%, from 1972 to 1979.[10] Meanwhile, the level of per-person daily caloric consumption, already the lowest in the hemisphere, has declined further. As noted by anthropologist Susan Stonich, "despite 30 years of economic growth, a majority of Hondurans find themselves less able now than in the mid-1960s to obtain their basic food requirements."[11]

Environmental deterioration and limited access to land and resources, which were largely controlled by foreign corporations and local elites, had a major effect on the daily diet, income, physical security, and other life-quality indicators of many Hondurans, sharpening their sense of insecurity and crisis.

Forces Blamed for Environmental Deterioration

In Honduras, assigning blame for the country's environmental problems, deforestation in particular, is an exercise fraught with political implications.[12] During the past 30 years environmental degradation, especially deforestation, has intensified as a result of the interplay between the export-oriented market strategies of agro-industries and large landowners (fruit, sugar, cotton, beef, and wood) and the survival/subsistence strategies of hundreds of thousands of small-scale peasant farmers. Since the arrival of the Spaniards 500 years ago cattle ranching has been a significant aspect of life in Central America. Traditionally, the owners of large cattle ranches formed a politically powerful local and national elite in Honduras. In this century, as corporate fast-food chains in the United States and elsewhere expanded and the demand for beef grew, ranching expanded in Honduras and came under increasing foreign corporate control. Foreign fruit companies have been even more dominant landowners, clearing thousands of acres of forest and planting banana, pineapples, and other export crops.[13]

Aside from the initial deforestation involved in converting forest to agribusiness, the company plantations and cattle ranches have tried to take advantage of cycles of market expansion or higher consumer prices in the importing countries by further expanding production in Honduras, which has often meant expanding landholdings by displacing peasant farmers.

Logging has also contributed to peasant marginalization and deforestation.[14] Historically, Honduras has been a lumber-exporting country, but earlier logging for precious tropical hardwoods (mahogany) largely has been replaced by the growing demand of local elites and the export market for oak, highland pine, and other woods used in construction and fine furniture. With worldwide demand for paper and paper products burgeoning in the computer age, foreign companies have targeted forests of lowland pines in eastern Honduras for paper and pulp production.[15] Logging roads have opened access into previously remote regions, drawing marginalized peasants, ranchers, and others. Peasant farmers displaced by corporate agribusiness plantations and ranches often went to more marginal, forested areas, where they cleared land and farmed until the tropical soils gave out or they were displaced again by plantations and ranches. They continued to move on, tried to find work on the plantations or ranches, or migrated to the city. This process has shaped the current crisis in Honduras, and it continues today. Progressive marginalization of peasant farmers contributes to destruction of forests and depletion of topsoils not suited for farming; however, it is the poverty and landlessness of peasants that drives them into areas marginally suited for cultivation and pushes them to intensify cultivation beyond what the soil and resources might sustain. In addition, the poor rely on the forests for firewood, including charcoal. Gathering firewood in the forest is cheaper than having to buy energy for domestic use, and the availability of "free" firewood helps sustain many poor families.[16]

Two additional causes of environmental destruction in Honduras are forest fires from natural and human causes and war.[17] As the primary base for U.S. military presence in Central America during the 1980s Honduras had more miles per person of airstrip runway (most of it military) than any other country in the world. Peasant groups regularly complained that many peasants were displaced when military bases were built or expanded and that the joint war games and training maneuvers of the U.S. and Honduran armies resulted in forest damage, environmental pollution, and other physical and social disruptions. Church workers in southeastern Honduras estimated that 10,000 Honduran peasants and rural dwellers were displaced from their homes and lands by the presence of Nicaraguan Resistance forces (Contras) on Honduran soil during the 1980s.[18]

"Honduras Is an Occupied Country . . . Run by the U.S. Embassy"[19]

Most of the major causes of environmental destruction in Honduras can be understood in a context of national dependency within an international system—a perspective shared by many Hondurans. The impact of the U.S. military presence during the 1980s makes this clear, but Honduran peasants, to say nothing of the country's environmental resources, are also at the mercy of expansions and contractions in the foreign markets served by the fruit, beef, and logging companies. In times of market expansion these large companies become more aggressive about expanding into peasant lands. In times of foreign market contraction or economic downturn, however, peasants who own land are tempted to overexploit it to survive; those who rent land from others often see their rent raised; and poor urban dwellers return to rural areas seeking land to grow food in order to escape hunger in the cities. External economic cycles drive the environmentally destructive actions of both large-corporate and small-peasant land users.

The history of Honduras, with its intimate connection to and dependency on foreign economies and policies, has conditioned Hondurans to understand both internal repression and inequitable access to and control over resources as products of (or at least conditioned by) their external dependency. The dominance of foreign fruit companies and their involvement with local military and police power in quelling labor protests and dislodging peasants, for example, is a central experience in the country's popular history.[20] This understanding of basic rights violations as tied to external dependencies and external control of land and resources has also prompted a popular sense that the natural resources of the country are constantly in danger of being sold to foreigners by the country's own power elite.[21]

Responses to the Crisis

The two processes of increasing land and resource monopolization by a relative few and accelerating environmental degradation have acted in tandem to produce increasing insecurity for Honduran peasants, rural workers, and ultimately the entire society. Hondurans have responded to this history of rising insecurity, inequity, and environmental deterioration in ways that link social conditions, especially the abuse of fundamental human rights, to environmental integrity, as illustrated in the struggle over agrarian reform.

Agrarian reform in Honduras has been a slow process of considerable struggle since the 1950s. When a modern, full-scale agrarian reform law was passed in 1962, years of partial and temporary measures and conflict had preceded it, and more conflict and frustration were to follow.[22] Ironically, 1974 was the peak year for land distribution to Honduran peasants. In that year a total of 287 peasant groups and almost 10,000 peasant families received some 47,000 hectares. Distribution declined after 1974 and has never kept pace with peasant expectations or the government's own declared goals. Much of the land that government agencies—in particular the National Agrarian Institute, or INA—classifies as having been distributed to peasants in some years has involved no new land transfers, but only confirmation of title to land already worked by peasants.[23] Many plots are too small to enable self-reliance and many recipients get little or no credit or other support. The Law of Agrarian Modernization (1995) considerably weakened the 1962 Law.

Some analysts argue that the agrarian reform, weak as it is, has been chiefly responsible for sparing Honduras the bloody revolutions and civil wars experienced by other Central American countries in the 1970s and 1980s.[24] The fact that an agrarian reform law remains on the books and functions at a minimal level, together with some channels through which to apply political pressure, has provided peasant organizations with a legal standard against which to measure the inequities of land and resource access in Honduran society. This ongoing struggle is what Honduran peasants mean when they say, "*We* are the agrarian reform," and it highlights the importance of peasant unions and organizations.[25]

The peasant organizations have increasingly rejected colonization schemes and migration to "new" lands in forested areas as a solution to land hunger. Their opposition initially sprang from their desire to force government authorities and agencies to take seriously the responsibilities mandated by the agrarian reform laws and to protect the rights of peasants unjustly and illegally pushed off their lands by large landowners and corporations. In short, the unions chose to fight for what they believed was theirs rather than to support the flight of their members to marginal areas.[26] This approach amounts to an organized demand for accountability from government officials, large landowners, and agribusinesses.

Union leaders and members have become increasingly articulate about other reasons for their refusal to support peasant movement onto marginal lands. They want to avoid conflicts among peasant groups seeking the same lands. They also want to avoid supporting peasant invasions of lands claimed historically by indigenous tribal peoples, who are seen as natural allies in the struggle for land rights and resources. The unions also are increasingly aware of the environmental damage caused by unchecked land marginalization, for many of their own members have had bitter experiences of soil erosion and depletion, decreasing yields, and increasing poverty. Others have worked hard clearing and cultivating marginal forest areas only to see their land taken over by large landowners once the clearing is done. In addition, the policy of claiming land they have already been cultivating, rather than seeking marginal lands, keeps their actions within the scope of agrarian reform processes.

To exercise political pressure for continued agrarian reform and to dramatize and reverse the injustice that they believe is involved in the way peasants have been pushed off their lands, the unions support annual nonviolent land occupations by peasants throughout the country at the start of the planting season. They prefer to risk the hazards of open confrontation with large landowners who, from the peasants' perspective, have illegally seized peasant lands. For peasants the hazards of such confrontation are many and serious. In Honduran law land occupations have been classified as acts of terrorism, although harsh measures against peasant occupiers are not always enforced. They are like Russian roulette: you can succeed or you can die. And in the 1980s and early 1990s people did die. The El Astillero massacre of 1991, described at the beginning of this chapter, was only one of many such incidents.[27] Moreover, repression has not been confined to those directly involved in land occupations. Peasant union leaders and supporters have been threatened, imprisoned, tortured, "disappeared," and killed.[28]

The El Astillero killings were especially troubling to many Hondurans because the landowner in question was an army colonel, a man in a position of power and relative impunity in Honduran society. Although massive public pressure resulted in his conviction and imprisonment, he was released and returned to his rank in just two years. The case seemed to underscore the need for accountability from the nation's power elite in matters of land and resource control and fundamental human rights. All the survivors of the El Astillero massacre went into hiding—as far as possible. Two survivors eventually left Honduras and were granted asylum in the United States in 1995.

The El Astillero incident, and others like it, illustrate two other kinds of responses to the crisis of insecurity: repression and exile. Violent repression is perpetrated by private persons and public figures who can count on their own power and impunity. Exile is a response to the inaccessibility of resources (economic survival) but also to the threat of physical violence, for in Honduras the two are often closely related. Cases of asylum raise questions about the relevance of the distinction in U.S. immigration law and policy between economic immigrants and political refugees, as well as about the plight of those who may be called "environmental refugees."[29]

The response of some indigenous groups in Honduras provides an example of the indivisibility of rights and how people are beginning to articulate this unity. At least six major self-defined groups of indigenous peoples live in Honduras today, including about 18,000 Tol-speaking Xicaque people who live in villages and settlements in the mountains and hills of the northern department of Yoro.[30] The Xicaque hold forested lands in the mountains that they regard as theirs by reason of formal treaties with the Honduran government going back to the 1860s. Before 1974 individual caciques (local community leaders) granted permits to outsiders (non-Xicaques) to log areas of the tribal forests. After the 1974 establishment of COHDEFOR (the Honduran Forestry Development Corporation) the Xicaques found themselves increasingly at the mercy of bureaucrats who had to approve contracts and who were in a position to reward caciques whom they liked and punish caciques whom they regarded as too independent. This politicization from the outside was disruptive and destabilizing for the Xicaque.

In 1979, after a period of tensions, killings, and other problems, the Honduran government joined with the Xicaques in forming the Yoro Indigenous Cooperation Project (PROCOINY) to provide a vehicle for dialogue. While engaged in speaking and other activities through PROCOINY, Xicaque leaders came into dialogue with other organized groups, including labor and peasant unions, grassroots Church groups (Christian-based communities), foreign aid donors, indigenous groups outside Honduras, and many others. Eventually a movement among younger Xicaque to redefine their Indian identity and to become a clearly recognized political force led to the formation of the Federation of Xicaque Tribes of Yoro (FETRIXY) in the late 1980s. FETRIXY gradually assumed the functions of a pantribal governing council, replacing the local caciques as speakers for the Xicacque people. FETRIXY drafted a set of objectives and guidelines for the use and preservation of the tribal forests and prompted the search for new ways to combine traditional sustainable forest management and use with modern methods and markets for forest products.

But as they worked to redefine and strengthen their cultural, political, and economic identity, the Xicaque faced various external pressures and challenges, including threats, intimidations, and killings perpetrated by large landowners and occasionally Honduran army personnel, as well as land invasions by landless, marginalized peasants. In 1988, for example, the Xicaque formally complained to the National Agrarian Institute, which had permitted a group of non-Xicaque peasants calling themselves Los Invencibles to occupy one of the "best regions" of the Xicaque land.[31] In another incident peasants were accused of killing a Xicaque in a land dispute. In the period from 1988 to mid-1993 five tribal leaders were killed, including Vicente Matute, president of FETRIXY.[32] These incidents provoked the independent Committee for the Defense of Human Rights in Honduras (CODEH) to denounce what it perceived as a systematic campaign by large landowners and the military against fundamental rights of the Xicaque and other indigenous peoples of Honduras. CODEH defined those rights in terms of rights to life and physical security, rights to continued tenure and use of tribal lands, and rights to free expression of tribal cultural identity and lifeways. All these, CODEH declared, were inextricably related.[33]

In the context of these conflictive histories it is easier to understand the importance of massive popular protests such as those that greeted a proposed logging agreement in 1991. In that year agencies of the Honduran government entered into negotiations with a U.S.-based transnational corporation, one of the world's largest producers of cardboard. They were negotiating an agreement that would have given the cardboard-maker 40 years of logging rights to 320,000 hectares of tropical lowland pine forest in the Mosquitia region of eastern Honduras (about one-third of the country's territory and home to thousands of Miskito Indian people) as well as rights to log certain forested regions within a 150-mile radius of the northern Honduran Caribbean port of Puerto Castilla. The corporation promised to create 15,000 new jobs and pay Honduras U.S. $20 million.[34]

Most of the Honduran public, even members of the National Congress, knew little or nothing of the negotiations until a tentative agreement was announced in September 1991. Massive public protest demonstrations followed, with marches and rallies in several cities. Typical statements heard during the protests express the concerns, demands, and hopes of many Hondurans, while they provide insight into the evolution of environmental rights in that Central American country:

> The state bureaucracy which oversees forests in our country has grown while the forests have dwindled. Those who control forestry here are politicians and private interests instead of trained technicians and forestry professionals. Personal gain replaces national interest. —Member of Colegio de Profesionales Forestry de Honduras (Honduran Organization of Forestry Professionals)

> Once again, after a long silence, we students are speaking up to defend our rights. In Honduras, students have always been among the first to defend rights, and many have died for this. But we are defending the future as well as the present. So for me, this is really like a big celebration. —University student

> I am here protesting with these others because, once again, the government is trying to sell our country to foreigners. They want to sell the future of my children and the country for their own profit. I have struggled all my life to have enough land to grow my food, and things are still hard. I don't want my children and grandchildren to have the same, or worse, problems. —Peasant farmer

> We don't want to be left in the middle of a desert or without any natural resources which are the habitat of many animals and with which our people sustain themselves. . . . We don't like being treated like people who don't think. . . . Our people have never asked the government for our necessities. —President of Miskito Asia Tankana, an indigenous organization

Such protests are another form of response, one that unites various organizations representing different sectors of Honduran society. This fact, considered with many of the statements of participants, illustrates a process of identifying environmental sustainability, access to resources, and various basic rights as closely related aspects of a single historical process.

Conclusion

An integrated understanding of the connections between equitable access to land and resources, environmental sustainability, and human rights has been emerging in Honduras, together with an increasing sense of the indivisibility of rights. This integrative insight has been the product of a long history that has moved many Hondurans through successive levels of understanding about human rights in relation to the country's natural environmental resources. Different groups in Honduras have experienced these levels of human rights understanding in different ways.

The struggles of the peasant unions have moved them farther toward a wider sense of the connections among inequitable systems of land tenure, environmental degradation, and deterioration of human rights. Peasant marginalization is a result of both unjust and restricted control of land and resources. Marginalization is a cause of environmental deterioration from which the peasants themselves immediately suffer. Trying to end marginalization can precipitate gross violations of peasants' rights. In fact, the whole process is one of progressive violation of increasingly more fundamental rights. The violation of one type of right sets in motion a process for violation of other kinds of rights. One fruit of the Honduran situation over the past 20 years has been a clearer empirical recognition of this essential indivisibility, a recognition gradually articulated by wider sectors of Honduran society.

The history of human rights activism in Honduras began with denouncing gross violations of the rights of individual peasants, indigenous peoples, and environmental activists, usually violations involving killing, disappearance, or torture by large landowners, the military, and others. The right to life and physical security was the most fundamental issue, and it was at first incidental that those threatened were so threatened precisely because of their involvement, in some way, in struggles over natural resources.

But in the logic and dynamic of Honduran experience the centrality of the struggle over the land and its resources could not remain an incidental, secondary-rights consideration. Human rights groups—especially CODEH, the largest one, and the one with the highest public profile—increasingly understood the gross violations of life and physical safety as manifestations of systematic repression, itself a symptom of pervasive structural injustices—in particular, the system of inequitable and insecure access to land and other natural productive resources. Human rights extended to equitable access and reasonable use of these resources.

Finally, these rights were meaningless unless they were sustainable and could be exercised by future generations as well. It was necessary to safeguard the natural environment. Underlying the indivisibility of all these rights were both philosophical considerations about the integral nature of human life, and practical and historical experience of how they reinforce each other. One practical thread uniting them was accountability. The same impunity and lack of accountability that permitted some to control and use land and resources however they pleased also permitted them to eliminate or contain any possible threat to their control in whatever way was most effective.

In the context of Honduran history accountability raises questions about democratic process and national sovereignty. Government and military officials, politicians, and those with economic power in Honduran society may find it increasingly difficult to make decisions about environmental resources, to cede resource rights to foreigners, or to resort to violent repression—without accounting to other sectors of society in the future. The Honduran experience invites conclusions that parallel recent writings about the connection between sustainable development and levels of popular participation.[35] At a celebration after the suspension of the logging agreement discussed above, a leader of Fundacio Cuero y Salado, the country's largest environmental group, was quoted as saying: "This has been an incredible event in which all sectors of the Honduran people united against a government plan that was seriously flawed, justifying their position to the government to the point where the government accepted the voice of the people. This has been a great example of democracy working in the country."[36]

SECTION II: View from the 21st Century

On January 5, 1981, the Honduran daily *El Tiempo* interviewed Honduran Central Bank economist Edmundo Valladares about the state of the nation. Summarizing the economist's critical perspective, the headline read, "The misery financing the model of development" (*La miseria financiando el modelo de desarrollo*). The "model" was a free-market economy that invited foreign investment by deemphasizing the needs and demands of workers, peasant farmers, and the poor—a large portion of the population. In July 2003 almost 1,600 representatives from a variety of popular organizations across Central America met in Tegucigalpa, the Honduran capital, in the Fourth Mesoamerican Forum against Plan Puebla-Panama, a free-trade agreement intended to advance the "model" even further. The delegates condemned the erosion of labor rights, the repression of indigenous and Afro-Honduran communities, the privatization of public services, biopiracy, and threats to civil society that Plan Puebla-Panama seemed to represent. They called instead for a different model of economic integration that would promote the welfare of all sectors of society. What had changed in 22 years was not so much the model as the scope and nature of the response.

In 1997 I described a dual process of convergence in Honduran society: a growing awareness among Hondurans of the relatedness of different kinds of rights, and an increasing cooperation and articulation among various sectors of Honduran society to defend those rights. In the intervening years Hondurans broadened the meaning of basic rights and extended the social context of those rights, even as changes occurred in Honduras in the interval, especially the country's preparation for and entry into two regional free-trade agreements actively fashioned and promoted by the United States. This section describes some of the changes that have taken place in Honduras as it integrates into global free-trade systems.

Underlying the changes was a shift in the dominant discourse employed in defining issues, proposing solutions, and advancing popular struggles. The older discourse that framed issues in terms of security versus human rights was not entirely discarded but was mixed with the language of economic (market) development and that of human and community development. A particular dialect of this newer language of struggle evoked awareness of the environment. All sides began to use the language of environmental responsibility. Increased use of terms such as *property reform* and *land entitlement* reflected a sensitivity to the conflicting land and resource demands of the country's peasants and indigenous peoples on one side and its foreign investors on the other. Essentially, the new discourse continued the tradition of using ambivalent but highly charged terms to further a particular agenda and to confuse or blunt opposition.

Colonization to Globalization: Farm, Plantation, Maquiladora

The integration of Honduras into larger international and global economic systems is a process that has evolved over many years, gradually becoming more demanding and encompassing of the country's resources and society. Under Spanish colonial rule and later British influence, Honduras was an outpost of far-flung empires. Over the years colonial systems of *latifundia* as well as ranching, foreign resource extraction, foreign-owned plantations, land erosion and depletion, and population increase gradually restricted the available land base of the country's peasant farmers, forcing many to plantation or *hacienca* labor.[37] By the 1950s the dominance of North American fruit companies, the mixing of peasant subsistence and seasonal plantation labor in the north and peasant sharecropping and ranch work in the south, created a society that was both rural and proletarian.[38] The concerns of this "rural proletariat" were those of both peasants and workers.

The immense landholdings and labor force of the U.S.-owned fruit companies were seen variously as engines of economic growth, symbols of foreign intervention, signs of Honduran dependency and the weakness of national sovereignty, and a major force in peasant landlessness and the creation of a rural proletariat. The modern labor movement in Honduras grew out of workers' protests at the fruit companies in the 1950s. Peasant unions and labor unions became primary forms of organization, social security, and expression for the concerns and frustrations of many Hondurans. Despite repressive company and government opposition to union organizing, by the latter half of the 20th century Honduras had some of the oldest and most militant labor and peasant movements in Latin America.

In the 1980s the involvement of the United States in Honduran life became more intense. The country became the base of operations for U.S. efforts to intervene in two of Honduras's neighbors—to support the Salvadoran military and government in their war with the FMLN (*Farabundo Marti*) guerrillas and to support the Nicaraguan resistance (*contras*) in their attempts to topple the FSLN (Sandinista) government in Nicaragua. The Honduran military received much attention and aid from U.S. military and government agencies during the decade, although there were differences within the Honduran military over its role in internal order and national security and concerns about national sovereignty amid what seemed like U.S. occupation. Land was taken to construct military bases, joint military games were held, and U.S. military units conducted medical and other programs to win the hearts and minds of the Honduran people. But by 1990 the Central American wars had ended, and U.S. military attention had shifted elsewhere. Increasing land scarcity, landlessness, and food insecurity in the 1980s gave new urgency to peasant and rural labor organizing and protest. Repressive reaction to this militancy weakened some organizations, including peasant and labor movements, but it also promoted new kinds of awareness and struggle.

The next phase in United States involvement in Honduras began in the 1990s and focused on promoting the integration of Honduras and other Central American countries into regional free trade and globalization initiatives. In the decade between 1997 and 2007 Honduras engaged two different free-trade agreements—Plan

Puebla-Panama (PPP) and the Central American and Dominican Republic Free Trade Agreement (CAFTA-DR). Policies and practices intended to move the country farther down the road of globalization were increasingly adopted. These affected many areas of life and helped to shape some of the changes that are described in this chapter.

Free Trade, Human Rights, and the Environment

As part of the country's integration into free-trade agreements, Honduran governments since the early 1990s have promoted the establishment of assembly factories (*maquiladoras*). This was seen as a way to provide employment and exportable goods, but it also depended on a labor pool of landless families or those with insufficient land to support a rural farming way of life. Government plans also depended on large supplies of cheap energy to be produced by hydroelectric dam projects in different regions. But popular opposition to the dam projects was sparked by concerns over the forced removal of rural communities in the way of the dams, and the environmental and cultural destruction caused by such projects. In Honduras such opposition often raises issues of fundamental human rights, because defining community, environmental, and cultural rights can lead to the loss of even more fundamental rights. Leaders of popular protests against a hydroelectric dam project in the eastern department of Olancho were threatened and murdered.

Environmental discourse has not been confined to those protesting free trade. Honduran governments also began using the language of environmental concern. In 1998 the government announced its intent to promote more ecologically friendly farming, ecotourism, and ecoprospecting. In some major cities local governments planted trees in the main plazas, supporting official environmental rhetoric. When Honduras demanded an environmental impact statement before allowing work on the El Tigre Dam project to supply Honduran hydroelectric energy to neighboring El Salvador's maquiladora sector, El Salvador withdrew from the agreement. By 2002 Honduras had one of the largest maquiladora sectors in the world, where workers' daily wages averaged U.S. $3.50.

In much of Central America, including Honduras, national energy plans in preparation for entry into the free-trade agreements included privatization—foreign ownership and management of the country's energy system. Privatization transforms a basic public not-for-profit service into a profit making enterprise. The many popular protests against privatization of services usually declare access to basic services derived from national resources a human right, and denounce the commercialization of these services. Privatization of utilities was seen as a threat to the well being of the vulnerable poor and others who cannot afford rising costs.

From Agrarian Reform to Land Market

Access to land is perhaps the most pressing and conflictive issue in Honduran society. The 1962 agrarian reform law that would transfer unused arable land to peasants in need of land has not been vigorously or effectively implemented. Although the law never seemed to provide enough land to poor peasants through legal transfer, it was credited with providing a legal standard to which peasant groups may appeal in their demands for land. The law represented the principle that access to land for those who need it was a matter of importance, even duty, for government and society. Until recently other laws also affirmed the state's protection of land as a national resource and access to land for Honduran citizens as a social priority. Article 107 of the 1982 Honduran Constitution prohibited foreign companies from owning land within 40 km of the Caribbean coast. Article 346 of the Constitution recognized a limited right of indigenous people to their traditional territory. In addition, Honduras was a signatory to the 1969 International Labor Organization (ILO) Convention on Indigenous and Tribal Peoples that asserts the rights of indigenous people to their resources and cultures.

One of the requisites for Honduran integration into a free-market economy fully integrated into a global system has been the ability to transfer land and property in an orderly and secure fashion, allowing for rapid turnover of ownership as the market dictates. In essence this means treating land as a market commodity rather than a source of family livelihood, a basis for a community's culture and way of life, or a national resource as envisioned by most peasant, indigenous, and environmentalist organizations. Beginning in the early 1990s "property reform" became a high priority for the elite that controlled the Honduran government. The goal was to facilitate the process of entitlement that would create the conditions for a modern "land market" and investment and development in the tourist and maquiladora sectors. To this end the Honduran Congress passed the Agricultural Modernization Law in 1992, effectively neutralizing the 1962 Agrarian Reform Law. In the late 1990s Congress proposed reforms to Article 107 that would have opened the Caribbean coastal areas to foreign ownership. Organizations representing indigenous and autochthonous groups as well as peasant, labor, and environmental interests formed the Front for the Defense of National Sovereignty. They opposed changes to the law, arguing that the land belonged to the Honduran people, foreign development would jeopardize delicate and important ecological systems, and the Garifuna people who lived along the north (Caribbean) coast would see their territory—the basis of their culture—alienated and degraded and their cultural rights undermined. Congress abandoned the proposed changes, but only temporarily.[39]

Since the late 1990s the Honduran government and free-market proponents have employed several arguments to further the reform of land and property laws. These arguments attempt to reconcile the rhetoric of environmental preservation, free-market mobility, and secure entitlement to land. In the name of environmental protection, a law passed in 2001 (*Ley forestal de areas protegidas y de vida silvestre*) transferred to government control forested land that had long been in the care of indigenous groups. This allows government to decide the role these forests should play in the ongoing globalization of the Honduran economy.

In the late 1990s the Honduran government increasingly adopted the discourse of land entitlement. This approach allowed the promotion of the concept of secure land title as a basis for a free market in land while espousing the idea that access to land was the right of all. It seemed to hold out the promise that peasant farmers and the members of indigenous communities might now finally have secure title to their lands. To these ends, in 2004 the Honduran Congress passed a property law and initiated a state program funded by the World Bank, *Proyecto de Administracion de Tierras de Honduras* (PATH). The new law and PATH have been described as an example of neoliberal multiculturalism, "a contemporary mode of governance characterized by efforts to wed a restricted recognition of cultural difference and ethnic rights to the neoloberal principles of state decentralization, privatization, and the promotion of markets as the benevolent motor of development."[40] The law has been protested by a coalition of popular organizations on the grounds that it introduces a right of third parties to obtain traditional communal lands, and it undermines the traditional role of land in the life of peasant and indigenous communities. An example of such protest was the International Meeting of the Landless in San Pedro Sula in northern Honduras in July 2000. The delegates representing a variety of popular organizations claimed that agrarian policies carried out in the framework of neoliberalism were replacing the values of the 1974 land reform law with the mechanisms of a land market. The guarantee of land as a right for peasant farmers, a basis of the 1974 land reform, was undermined by the sale of land as a commodity for developers and investors.

The shift in government land policy described here represented a change in official ideas about the nature of rural peasant poverty and the policies to address it. "The redistributive land-reform project . . . [defined] unequal land distribution and the related power structure as the underlying cause of rural poverty. By contrast, the neoliberal defines poverty as an individual attribute to be alleviated by policies such as individual land title."[41]

Land as Battleground: Market Development, Human Development

Despite the new legal discourse emphasizing entitlement and land access for all, the land conflicts that have long plagued Honduras continued and seemed undiminished after 1997, as the land issue and the need for "property reform" became more urgent. The percentage of peasant farmers and rural people without land in this agrarian country continued to grow, even as demand for land by foreign and Honduran investors and companies grew.

Some conflict involved lands controlled by U.S. fruit companies or lands formerly used as bases for U.S. military units in Honduras during the 1980s. In May 2000 several hundred landless families occupied the land of a former U.S. military base. Many had lost homes and land in Hurricane Mitch, 18 months earlier. Their takeover was prompted by desperation. When the base was decommissioned in 1991 the government agreed to give the land to landless farmers, but several cattle ranchers bought it instead. In August 2007, in Comayagua near a former military base, 150 members of *the Union Nacional de Campesinos* (National Peasant Union) took over the offices of the National Agrarian Institute (INA), the government agency in charge of carrying out land distributions under the Agrarian Reform Law. They held the INA employees hostage and demanded the release of more than 100 peasants jailed for illegal land occupation[42] (*The New York Times*, August 1, 2007). Such examples reveal some of the themes that recur frequently in recent land conflicts in Honduras. These include the desperation of the landless, their determination to remain as farmers, and the weakness of government agencies in supporting peasant demands and upholding the intent of the 1974 agrarian reform law. Other recurring themes concern the monopolization of land by wealthier landowners, multiple conflicting claims to the same land, and the vestiges of a legal system that classified peasant land takeovers as acts of terrorism.

Ongoing conflict continued in the Aguan Valley, a major agricultural area in northern Honduras where U.S.-based fruit companies own thousands of acres. The area has long been the location of struggles between the fruit companies and peasant and indigenous communities. In May 2001 Amnesty International's Urgent Action Network reported that 25 indigenous leaders and several peasant leaders had been killed for their activism in the area since 1991. Amnesty denounced the killings and

the impunity that the killers apparently enjoyed and brought international attention to the case of a Catholic pastor in the area who was the target of death threats
because of his advocacy and leadership of local peasants in their land struggles and
his denunciation of human rights abuses. Large landowners were offering 500,000
lempiras (about U.S. $32,000) to have him killed. In 2007, 74 families (178 persons,
including 45 children) of the *Tierra Nuestra* (Our Land) peasant organization were
threatened with eviction from land they had occupied all their lives. The owner, a
major U.S. fruit company, wanted the land to plant African palms. These are a few
examples that illustrate the contrast between economic export market development
and human social development in the Aguan Valley.[43]

Deforestation: Robbing Resources, Ignoring Rights

Where there is land conflict in Honduras, there are human rights issues. In the eastern departments of Olancho and Gracias a Dios environmental and cultural concerns
are the central issues in land conflict. These two large departments contain large
stretches of tropical forest and diverse riparian and wetland ecosystems. During the
late 19th and early 20th centuries mahogany was logged and exported, but access
was limited. There were few roads and travel was by river, sea, or small plane. In recent decades the area has been increasingly opened with new roads and the logging
of less precious woods, especially pine, for inexpensive furniture, paper, and cardboard. U.S.-based corporations have tried to secure long-term leases to thousands
of acres, particularly in Olancho. Honduran entry into recent free-trade agreements
has only promoted the exploitation of Olancho's forests. Within regional free-trade
agreements, Honduras can position itself as one of the few remaining substantial
sources of wood for a burgeoning furniture, paper, and cardboard market.

National and local organizations of various kinds have denounced the foreign
exploitation of Olancho and Gracias a Dios and the killings of activists. *Movimiento
Ambientalista de Olancho* (Olancho Environmentalist Movement, MAO) has been
one of the more prominent and active of the new organizations. A chief demand of
MAO is that the Honduran government enact a 10-year moratorium on commercial
logging in Olancho while creating a sustainable forest policy. In 2003 MAO and
other groups organized and participated in a March for Life from local communities
in Olancho to the Honduran capital, Tegucigalpa, even as several MAO activists and
at least one of its most prominent leaders, a Catholic priest, received death threats.
The Committee of Families of People Detained/Disappeared in Honduras, one of the
country's major human rights groups, issued a communique stating that, "terrorism
in Olancho is placing at risk the lives of those defending the environment." The next
day MAO activist Carlos Arturo Reyes was killed.[44]

Much of the increased logging in the past decade was illegal—no official permit,
no taxes, and frequent recourse to bribing, threatening, or gaining the collusion of
local officials. The attraction of commercial logging in a time of free-trade agreements and burgeoning demand for cheap furniture and paper products provides
incentive to illegal logging. By some estimates as much as three-quarters of all the
hardwood logging done in Honduras and one-quarter of all the pine logging can be
considered illegal. Government agencies are responsible for regulating logging activity in Honduras. Illegal logging bypasses this and throws into disarray any forestry
planning the government may pursue. Because illegal logging enterprises do not pay
taxes and can sell in a clandestine market, the nation loses both its forest resources

and any wealth that would accrue to the national treasury from the exploitation of these resources.

By some definitions illegal logging includes the unregulated extraction of firewood by peasant families. Peasants are sometimes blamed for deforestation, both because of their removal of firewood and because many peasant farm plots are in marginal or forested areas where peasants can still find land. But legal and illegal logging operations often harm peasant and indigenous communities. In Honduras there are documented cases of rural communities that have experienced progressive desiccation, lowered rainfall, contaminated or silted water supplies, dwindling fish and wildlife populations, and other forms of environmental degradation due to the removal of nearby forest. One result is the collapse of small farming—a catastrophe for local peasant families. MAO was organized in part as a response to this situation.

Logging, especially illegal logging, has implications for human rights, sustainable community, democratic participation, and sovereignty in Honduras. Environmental activists that interfere with massive logging are threatened and killed. Future generations are robbed of the nation's wealth. Illegal logging also thrives in and promotes a context of corruption and impunity that may include members of the country's elite institutions, criminal drug enterprises, and the corruption of local and mid-level officials. This culture of crime and impunity encourages the powerful to violate the rights of the poor and, to some extent, all Hondurans. Some local communities demand greater input into decisions about logging and forest policy. They argue that they have the greatest and most immediate stake in ensuring the sustainability and well-being of their area, in contrast to foreign interests and external forces.[45]

Mining: "Honduras Is Worth More Than Gold"

Since the mid-1990s Honduras has experienced a major growth in gold-mining enterprises that have become another important source of conflict over land, resources, and environment. According to a study by the Association of Non-governmental Organizations in Honduras (ASONOG), more than 30% of Honduran territory was licensed to foreign mining companies between 1995 and 1998. Most of these companies were based in the United States, Canada, and Australia. A few weeks after Hurricane Mitch in 1998 Honduras passed a mining law that reduced taxes on foreign mining companies, offered nearly unlimited rights to water, provided few environmental regulations, and allowed companies freely to petition for removal of peasant and indigenous communities from land under company lease. Critics charged that the companies themselves wrote large portions of the law, taking advantage of the crisis in Honduran economy and society caused by the hurricane's devastation. In 2000 the International Monetary Fund urged Honduras to reduce further the taxes on foreign mining companies.

Human rights groups and international observers denounced mining companies for forced evictions and harassment of peasant and indigenous communities, and for several deaths. Environmental degradation, especially pollution of rivers and water sources due to mining and dredging operations, has undermined the sustainability of peasant farming and community life. In 2001 peasant and indigenous groups joined with environmentalist and human rights organizations to launch an international campaign with the slogan "Honduras is worth more than gold."[46]

One of the major consequences of unregulated logging and mining operations such as those described here is the displacement of rural peasant households and communities who become landless because the land is taken by the exploiters of natural resources or because the land of communities adjacent such operations becomes so polluted that it can no longer produce enough to sustain a way of life. It has been argued that this is not simply an unintended and unfortunate by-product of logging and mining in a global economy. Rather such development not only "produced severe ecological exploitation but also depended on it for the subsidized reproduction of semiproletarian labor and generation of a larger mass of surplus labor" (Faber 1992:27 quoted in Jansen 2007).[47] Thus environmental degradation is not only a result of mismanagement but is also an intrinsic part of the model of development that produces its own labor force by displacing rural communities from livelihood on the land.

The conflicts that such development generates today represent a widening of the struggles over land that characterized previous decades in Honduras. They are now carried on in a global context where processes of economic globalization are met with local resistance that knows how to develop and use national, regional, and global networks and media in its cause.

Profiting from Disaster: Tourist Developers, Garifuna, and Mitch

For many years the Bay Islands off the northern, Caribbean coast of Honduras have been a tourist destination. For several reasons the tourism industry remained low-key and relatively undeveloped on the adjacent mainland until the 1990s. As Honduras moved toward entrance into CAFTA, and perceptions and policy became more global and market-driven, the area was seen increasingly as an economic resource with potential for expanded development of a tourism infrastructure. Mitch provided an opportunity to further this vision.

In November 1998 Hurricane Mitch struck Honduras. According to some estimates, more than 6,000 people died and more than 600,000 (10% of the population) were left homeless. Sixty percent of the country's infrastructure was damaged or destroyed. Three-quarters of basic food crops in the field were lost (Phillips 1998; Paul Jeffrey, personal communication based on information gathered by Honduran Christian Commission for Development).[48] The degree of destruction caused by the hurricane was attributed to several factors. In Honduras per capita income was U.S. $900 per year, and an estimated two-thirds of the population lived in poverty, many in disaster prone areas with poor housing that left them vulnerable. The country had limited institutional capacity to prepare for and respond to a disaster of this magnitude. Short-term, politically expedient development decisions had damaged the environment and its natural defenses against widespread disaster. The relative lack of a strong civic culture made local and community defense and coordination more difficult because of social fragmentation, alienation, and mistrust among sectors of society—government officials, the military, social classes (Benitez Ramos et al. 2005).[49]

As often happens after such disasters, different interests took the opportunity to advance various agendas in the context of a daunting recovery and reconstruction process. The language of environmental concern became more prominent. Popular organizations demanded greater voice in decisions about environmental policy, natural resource use, and economic development schemes. The government formulated a policy and a process to accommodate more input from communities and social sectors about these issues, but it maintained control of the process. Jimmy Carter and the Catholic archbishop of Tegucigalpa called for dismissal of the Honduran foreign debt, then around U.S. $4 billion. Foreign and some Honduran investors and tourist enterprises advanced the idea that the best reconstruction plan would be promotion of tourist development along the country's northern, Caribbean coast. They argued that the profit from an expanded and thriving tourist industry would bring needed revenue to Honduras, turn the north coast into a development pole for the country, and bring employment to residents of the area. Honduran government agencies that saw an expanded tourism infrastructure as an integral part of Plan Puebla Panama and CAFTA-DC supported these plans. But this agenda brought the government and development interests into direct conflict with dozens of Garifuna communities whose traditional territory is the northern coastal area.

The estimated 80,000 or more Garifuna people living along the Caribbean coasts of four Central American countries claim descent from Carib Indians and run-away African slaves deported from the eastern Caribbean to Central America by the British in 1797. The coastal Garifuna communities in Honduras maintain some cultural traits that differentiate them from mainstream Honduran society. One of these is a tendency to see land and natural resources as communal and as tied to the ancestors over generations. Despite the spread of private landowning among Garifuna communities, the idea of privately owned land being sold and resold over a short period for gain is not highly compatible with this traditional perspective. Over many years Garifuna communities struggled to protect the environment that gives them basic food sources such as deer, wild pig, some species of fish, medicinal plants, and important water sources. These seemed increasingly threatened by private and government promotion of Caribbean coastal tourism. Popular Belizean singer and world music songwriter Andy Palacios decries this threat in "Miami," a song named for a Garifuna coastal community in Honduras.

The Importance of Being Indigenous: Ethnicity, Resources, and Rights

A 2001 census recognizes nine indigenous or autochthonous ethnic groupings in Honduras, making up about 10% of the country's population. Ethnic identity is complex. Creoles (*Negros ingleses*) are identified as primarily African/Caribbean in culture. Two other recognized ethnic groupings—Garifuna and Miskito—combine indigenous and African tribal cultural traditions. This is important especially for the Garifuna, because ethnic/cultural identity has been crucial in defining their rights. Their mixed Amerindian and African heritage and relatively recent arrival (c. 1800) in the territory that is now Honduras have created a double challenge in recent decades. In the 1950s and 1960s Garifuna organizations and activists emphasized their "blackness" and directed most of their efforts against racial discrimination. Garifuna activists founded the *Organizacion Fraternal Negra de Honduras* (OFRANEH) in 1977 as an outcome of anti-racist protests in the northern coastal town of Puerto Cortes. By the 1970s national policies designed to promote nationalism and tourism began to emphasize the "indigenous" and folkloric aspects of Garifuna identity. By the mid-1980s OFRANEH began to define its objectives more in terms of collective land and cultural rights and increasingly adopted an indigenous identity.[50] The shift was prompted in part because "indigenous" peoples seemed to be gaining recognition of certain limited rights, while black Afro-Hondurans seemed to be outsiders in a country that considered itself *mestizo*—recognizing its European and Amerindian, but not its African, heritage. It did not seem to matter that Garifuna indigenous identity derived not from Central America but from Carib-speaking peoples of the eastern Caribbean.

Despite such ethnic positioning indigenous identity has been no guarantee of rights. Since the mid-1990s conflict over control of indigenous lands has escalated. New challenges have emerged, such as the transfer of forested lands to government control in the name of environmental stewardship (for example, the aforementioned *Ley forestal de areas protegidas y de vida silvestre*). This transfer illustrates what Lu Holt describes as a catch-22 for indigenous peoples. Indigenous groups that have higher population densities, more modern technology, more developed subsistence economies, or are more engaged in the national economy than befits the traditional stereotype of indigenous people, are likely to be considered unsuitable forest stewards. But these groups are also more likely to understand the threats to the forest from "modern civilization" and to be most active in protecting forests. The use of a traditionalist/essentialist stereotype of indigenous culture allows others to portray modern indigenous communities as defective stewards of the land and to use the rhetoric of environmental protection against indigenous claims over traditional territories, especially negating the claims of the most environmentally activist communities.[51]

Indigenous communities have developed new ways to defend their claims to traditional lands and their reputation as environmentally responsible stewards. In 2003, after several years of collaboration, the Center for Native Lands (Washington, D.C.), indigenous organizations, independent researchers, and National Geographic produced a composite map that demonstrates both the effectiveness of indigenous stewardship of natural resources under their control, as well as the extent of the threats to these resources. The map shows the distribution of forest and marine resources from southern Mexico to Panama superimposed on a map that identifies indigenous communities whose names do not appear on conventional maps. The composite reveals a close correlation between indigenous communities and major areas of forest cover. The composite map was published in early 2003 in *National Geographic* (Central American edition) and WorldWatch. Members of the research team that produced the map saw it as a tool for indigenous communities in their struggles to ensure control over their lands and as a response to the failure of development projects and enterprises to consider indigenous communities or the impact on environments. An attempt to produce such a map in the early 1990s was hindered by the aftermath of recent civil conflicts in Central America.

Indigenous Emergence, Popular Convergence

With an apparently increasing series of threats to their rights and resources, indigenous organizations have emerged as a leading force in the struggles over land, environmental preservation, and human rights in Honduras. In the 1980s many indigenous and autochthonous communities had their own organizations, sometimes several, to advance their rights and interests. OFRANEH became the more confrontational of the organizations representing Garifuna concerns, while MOPAWE focused on preserving the environmental and cultural integrity and economic and political development of Miskito communities, and FETRIXY came to represent the interests of Xicaque people. But they were sometimes influenced by *mestizo* leadership and government restrictions. By the late 1980s some of these organizations were collaborating in a series of common demands including protection and communal titling of indigenous lands, recognition and protection of languages and cultures, and the right to make decisions about the use of their land and resources for traditional and commercial purposes. In 1992 indigenous ethnic groups formed the *Confederación de Pueblos Autoctonos de Honduras* (CONPAH). This represented an attempt to establish clear indigenous (rather than *mestizo*) leadership and control of the component organizations as well as recognition of common concerns.

During the 1990s indigenous people expanded their concerns, developing a more integral vision of human and cultural rights, environmental health, access to land, and issues of poverty and development, and building connections with other sectors of Honduran society. They began to emerge as a major force in national-level struggles over environment, resources, and human rights. In 1993 Lenca activists in southwestern Honduras were instrumental in forming a coordinating body to bring together for common cause various popular organizations in the southwestern Department of Intibuca. This coordinating committee eventually expanded into the *Consejo Civico de Organizaciones Populares e Indigenas de Honduras* (COPINH), representing popular organizations that tend toward direct action, political activism, and protest rather than less confrontational collaboration with government and foreign interests.[52]

COPINH tried to integrate land and cultural rights issues with environmental concerns, and deployed the language of diversity as a value for Honduran society. In 2003 COPINH hosted the Third Forum on Biological and Cultural Diversity in the town of Esperanza, in the middle of a poor and largely indigenous and peasant border region near El Salvador. The Forum addressed several of the issues discussed in this chapter, and identified logging, mining, and tourism expansion as problem areas for the preservation of environment, indigenous and peasant lands, and human rights.

Back to the Future?

In the early morning of June 28, 2009, soldiers from the Honduran army entered the home of President Manuel Zelaya and forced him to leave the country. A wealthy landowner and businessman, Zelaya had promoted ideas of lessening poverty, especially in rural areas, and had proposed a nonbinding referendum to gauge the mood of Hondurans about ways to open the political system to more popular participation. Both the Congress and the Supreme Court, long dominated by landowning and business interests, declared that Zelaya's proposed referendum would violate the Honduran Constitution. Relying on popular support Zelaya set June 28 as the date for the referendum. Armed with the Court's opinion, the army intervened to remove Zelaya and impose de facto martial law.

In the following days human rights groups and others reported many detentions, beatings, killings, and some disappearances. Known supporters of Zelaya and leaders of various popular organizations, students, academics, and Honduran staff members of some nongovernmental organizations working with poor communities reported harassment, threats, arrests, and violence by army and police units. Radio stations critical of these events or identified with promoting the interests of peasants, labor unions, popular and indigenous organizations were threatened and shut down. Large popular protests and marches were dispersed and people beaten.

Reports of human rights violations continued for months. In September Zelaya slipped back into Honduras and sought refuge in the Brazilian embassy. His return prompted large street demonstrations of support. In January 2010 the de facto government held a presidential election. Declaring that it was necessary for the country to heal its wounds and return to normal, the new president decreed a general amnesty to cover the violations of all those involved in the removal of Zelaya and the events that followed. Zelaya was to be given permanent exile in the Dominican Republic, thus removing a symbolic rallying point of popular mobilization.

For some people the events of June represented a return to the early 1980s, when Honduras suffered a particularly intense period of human rights abuses against popular organizations and their leaders. Many decades of social problems, landlessness, poverty, and weak human rights protections prompted severe repression that was exacerbated by a culture of impunity. Shortly after the events of June a leader of one of the country's leading human rights organizations said: "All this accumulated impunity and the human rights abusers who are calmly walking the streets of Honduras, this all has to do with what's happening now. When repression goes unpunished, it happens again."[53]

Contrary to attempts by the new government and some foreign media to cast Zelaya as the problem, members of popular organizations interpreted these events as another phase in the struggle to correct many unjust social conditions and widen the scope of popular participation in the politics and decision making of the country as a necessary way to protect gains in human rights—a theme illustrated throughout this chapter. Zelaya and his referendum were not the cause but only very visible symbols of this larger agenda. He had to be removed, popular protest had to be repressed, and normality had to be restored so that the agenda of globalization could proceed. But the discussion in this and an earlier chapter illustrates that normality in Honduras may be the continuation of popular struggle.

Conclusion

Honduran history has seen the gradual penetration of foreign international interests and global economic systems into local communities and the evolution of popular adaptation or resistance to this perceived threat to community. As the global (external, foreign) nature of the economic and cultural intervention has become more pronounced and seemed more disruptive, the popular response has become more "global," as well: uniting different sectors of Honduran society in common cause and developing a sense of the relatedness of the issues they confront. The incidents I described in 1997 were a moment in this evolution. This evolution was not simple or uniform. It developed alongside ongoing struggles that seemed to remain focused entirely on local concerns that were often exploited by foreign corporate, government, or elite interests. Divisions and conflicts within and between popular organizations became a feature of Honduran life that vied with broader and more inclusive visions of the struggle.

The "globalization" of the Honduran economy during the past decade may not represent a radical departure from the structures of exploitation of the recent past but rather, as the current chapter illustrates, a wider scope and intensity of exploitation. The nature of the popular response, however, has undergone a remarkable transformation. In fundamental ideological and practical ways, peasant localism, indigenous territory and culture, and the ethnic identity of autochthonous minorities represent significant challenges to the logic of economic globalization by presenting local identity, security, and self-determination as fundamental values. In Honduras today popular movements explore ways to transform these values into definable and defendable rights. Paradoxically, they defend the local by setting it in a much wider context, uniting groups across social sectors and even national boundaries and integrating environmental, resource, and human rights issues into a vision of the better life. Will what is happening in Honduras contribute to a new model of community that celebrates and enhances local and traditional community and culture by identifying with and defending the rights of other local and traditional communities in the region and the planet in a new form of global communitarian consciousness?

Notes

1. Elias Ruiz, *El Astillero: Masacre y Justicia* (Tegucigalpa: Editorial Guaymuras, 1992).

2. Centro de Documentacion de Honduras, *25 Años de Reform Agraria* (Tegucigalpa: Centra de Documentación de Honduras, 1988).

3. Susan Stonich, "The Political Economy of Environmental Destruction: Food Security in Southern Honduras," in *Harvest of Want: Hunger and Food Security in Central America and Mexico*, Scott Whiteford and Anne E. Ferguson, Eds. (Boulder, CO: Westview Press, 1991).

4. Deforestation can be assessed in various ways ranging from statistical measurements (for example, 40% conversion of forest to other uses) to assessments that emphasize "the reduction of the capacity of a forest to fulfill a particular (social, cultural, or economic) function," a perspective advocated by Miriam Schmink, "The Socioeconomic Matrix of Deforestation" (paper presented at Workshop on Population and Environment, Hacienda Cocoyoc, Morelos, Mexico, Jan. 1992). This latter approach raises issues of political control and accountability and implies that conflict is possible, even likely, among apparently divergent functions deemed important by different groups in a society.

5. Jorge Arevalo Carcamo, quoted in the Honduran daily *El Tiempo*, Sept. 7, 1988.

6. Mayra Lisset Funez Martinez, *Problematica ambiental en Honduras* (Tegucigalpa: Asociación de Ecología, 1989).

7. Susan Stonich, note 3, p. 46.

8. This aid occurred within the context of an ongoing campaign by U.S. businesses to develop in Honduras a market for imported wheat-based products as permanent replacements for locally grown corn.

9. Stonich, note 3, p. 52.

10. Economist and Central Bank advisor Edmundo Valladares, quoted in "La miseria financiando el modelo de desarrollo," *El Tiempo*, Jan. 5, 1981.

11. Stonich, note 3, p. 46.

12. Carcamo, note 5, reported that 811,000 hectares of forest were destroyed by fire in an 11-year period, 80,000 hectares were degraded through slash-and-burn agriculture, and 6,000,000 cubic feet of firewood taken. The three causes singled out in this report—forest fires, peasant farming methods, and collecting firewood for fuel—emphasize activities of peasant farmers and poor rural dwellers. Funez Martinez, note 6, provides more insight into the forces at work by mentioning the role of cattle ranching for beef export (creating pasture out of forest). Her list of factors contributing to environmental deterioration includes: overcultivation and overgrazing; indiscriminate cutting of trees for wood; inappropriate agricultural technologies; fires; firewood as the major energy source in households and small businesses (bakeries, for example); natural disasters; migratory agriculture (slash-and-burn and short-term colonization of forest areas); and urbanization. Such a list is still inadequate for understanding the causes of environmental degradation.

13. Walter LaFeber, *Inevitable Revolutions: The United States in Central America* (New York: Norton, 1983, 43–46).

14. James D. Nations and Daniel I. Komer, "Indians, Immigrants and Beef Exports: Deforestation in Central America," *Cultural Survival Quarterly* 6:2 (1982, 8–12); Mario Ponce Cambar, "Honduras: Politica agricola y perspectives," in *Honduras: Realidad National y Crisis Regional* (Tegucigalpa: Centro de Documentación de Honduras, 1986, 249–78).

15. Cambar, note 14.

16. Carcamo, note 5.

17. Carcamo, note 5; Funez Martinez, note 6.

18. Information about the environmental and other effects of war and military presence in Honduras was gathered by the author during three months of fieldwork in Honduras in 1988 and reported in James Phillips, "Deforestation as Symbolic Catalyst for Protest toward Change: Honduras," paper presented at the 13th International Congress of Anthropological and Ethnological Sciences, Mexico City, Aug. 1, 1993. See also Environmental Project on Latin America (EPOCA), *Militarization*, Green Paper No. 3 (San Francisco: EPOCA, 1989).

19. A comment by a prominent Honduran lawyer to the author in 1984. Foreign scholars also point to the country's foreign dependency as a cause of rural poverty. See, for example, Alison Acker, *Honduras: The Making of a Banana Republic* (Boston: South End Press, 1988, 11). Also LaFeber, note 13, pp. 9–10.

20. Mario Posas, *El Movimiento Campesino Hondureño* (Tegucigalpa: Editorial Guaymuras, 1981).

21. Phillips, note 18, pp. 13–15.

22. Douglas Kincaid, "'We Are the Agrarian Reform': Rural Politics and Agrarian Reform," in *Honduras: Portrait of a Captive Nation*, Nancy Peckenham and Annie Street, Eds. (New York: Praeger, 1985, 135).

23. Centro de Documentación de Honduras, note 2, pp. 3–5.

24. Kincaid, note 22, p. 135.

25. Kincaid, note 22, p. 136.

26. Elvia Alvarado, *Don't Be Afraid, Gringo: A Honduran Woman Speaks from the Heart,* Medea Benjamin, Trans. and Ed. (San Francisco: Institute for Food and Development Policy, 1987); "Land Takeovers Planned," *Latin America Daily Report,* July 16, 1991.

27. Ruiz, note 1; c.f., Committee for the Defense of Human Rights in Central America, "Massacre at Aguas Calientes," *Acción Urgente,* May 10, 1991.

28. There are many reports of killings of peasant leaders, detentions, tortures, and threats. Here are a few: Amnesty International Urgent Action, UA 298/87, Oct. 30, 1987; "Unequal Distribution of Land Is Social Time Bomb in Honduras Countryside," *Central America NewsPak* 6:8 (1991, 138, trans. of an article in the Mexican daily *Excelsior,* May 24, 1991, part 3:1); "Peasants Killed," *Latin America Daily Report,* July 16, 1991; Centro de Documentación de Honduras, *Conflictos Agrarios en Honduras: Cronología 1982–1986* (Tegucigalpa: Centro de Documentación de Honduras, 1986).

29. James Phillips, "Are There Environmental Refugees?" paper presented at the Annual Meeting of the Society for Applied Anthropology, Albuquerque, NM, April 1995.

30. Jose Maria Tojeira, *Los Hicaques de Yoro* (Tegucigalpa: Editorial Guaymuras, 1982).

31. Reported in the Honduran daily *La Prensa*, March 3, 1988.

32. Anthony Stock, "Land War," *Cultural Survival Quarterly* 16:4 (1992, 16–18); Comite para la Defensa de los Derechos Humanos en Honduras (CODEH), *Boletín* 80 (Sept. 1991, 2).

33. Comite para la Defensa de los Derechos Humanos en Honduras (CODEH), *Boletín* 80 (Sept. 1991, 8–9).

34. Comite para la Defensa de los Derechos Humanos en Honduras (CODEH), *Boletín* 85 (Feb. 1992, 8). Hannah C. Riley and James K. Sebenius, "Stakeholder Negotiations over Third World Resource Projects," *Cultural Survival Quarterly* 19:3 (1993, 39–43). Riley and Sebenius analyze the failure of communication and integration between the formal negotiations in this case and the "informal" popular expression discussed here. Their list of references chronicles the coverage accorded this incident by the *Chicago Tribune*.

35. Craig R. Kirkpatrick, "Ecology, Government Legitimacy, and a Changing World Order," *Bioscience* 42:11 (Dec. 1992, 867–69); Sharachandra M. Lei, "Sustainable Development: A Critical Review," *World Development* 19:6 (June 1991, 607–21); Riley and Sebenius, note 34, pp. 42–43.

36. Quoted in Greg Grigg, "Honduran People Say No to Stone," *Focus on Honduras* summer 1992, pp. 1–3.

37. Alison Acker, *Honduras: The Making of a Banana Republic* (Boston: South End Press, 1998); Mario Ponce Cambar, "Honduras: Politica agraria y perspectivas," in *Honduras: Realidad Nacional y Crisis Regional* (Tegucigalpa: Centro de Documentación de Honduras, 1986); Mario Posas, *El Movimiento Campesino Hondureño* (Tegucigalpa: Editorial Guaymuras, 1981).

38. Kees Jansen, "Structural Adjustment, Peasant Differentiation, and the Environment in Central America," in *Disappearing Peasantries? Rural Labor in Africa, Asia, and Latin America*, Deborah Bryceson, Cristobal Kay, and Jos Mooij, Eds. (London: Intermediate Technologies Publications, 2000); Susan Stonich and Billie R. DeWalt, "The Political Ecology of Deforestation in Honduras," in *Tropical Deforestation: The Human Dimension*, Leslie E. Sponsel, Ed. (New York: Columbia University Press, 1996).

39. Mark Anderson, "When Afro Becomes (Like) Indigenous: Garifuna and Afro-Indigenous Politics in Honduras," *Journal of Latin American and Caribbean Anthropology* 12:2 (2007).

40. Anderson, ibid.; Charles R. Hale, "Neoliberal Multiculturalism: The Remaking of Collective Rights and Racial Dominance in Central America," *PoLAR: Political and Legal Anthropology Review* 28:1 (2005, 10–28).

41. Jansen, note 38, p. 194.

42. *The New York Times*, August 1, 2007.

43. Many such incidents were reported by local residents and by staff members of international agencies in the region.

44. Bruna Genovese, "Marching for Life," *International Policy Report* (Washington, D.C.: Center for International Policy, June 2004); Suzanne York, "Honduras and Resistance to Globalization" (San Francisco: International Forum on Globalization, 2003), www.ifg.org/analysis/globalization/honduras2.htm.

45. Maria Fiallos, "Honduran Indigenous Community in Standing Forest Area," *Honduras This Week* (English language weekly) June 9, 2003.

46. Michael Marsh, "Honduras Is Worth More Than Gold" (Tegucigalpa: Asociación de Organismos No Gobernamentales, 2002), asonog@hondudata.com.

47. D. Faber, "Imperialism, Revolution, and the Ecological Crisis in Central America," *Latin American Perspectives* 19:1 (1992, 17–44), quoted in Jansen, note 38.

48. Information gathered from various news accounts and personal communication from colleagues in Honduras.

49. R. F. Benitez Ramos, A. Barrance, and H. Stewart, *Have the Lessons of Mitch Been Forgotten? The Critical Role of Sustainable Natural Resource Management for Poverty Reduction in Honduras* (Canadian International Development Agency and Poverty and Environment Partnership, 2005).

50. Anderson, note 39.

51. Flora Lu Holt, "The Catch-22 of Conservation: Indigenous Peoples, Biologists, and Cultural Change," *Human Ecology* 33:2 (2006, 199–215).

52. Anderson, note 39; Douglas Payne, "Honduras: Update on Human Rights," Perspective Series PS/HND/00.001 (Washington, D.C.: INS Resource Information Center, 2000).

53. Identity of speaker withheld for security reasons. However, much of the information in this section appeared in mainstream news media in the United States or in reports from nongovernmental agencies in Honduras.

SNAPSHOT: The Human Right to Eat: Agro-Profiteering and Predictable Food Scarcity

Joan P. Mencher

India is experiencing a shortage of staple foods for several reasons—water tables are sinking rapidly; there is inadequate government investment in agriculture, irrigation, and loans for farmers; agricultural land is being sold for residential use because agricultural profits have been so poor. Between 1968 and 1998 India's production of cereals doubled, but between 1998 and 2008 it contracted after the government, following the advice of the World Bank and U.S. economists, cancelled support prices.

In my field research over the last 50 years I have always been surprised by the disconnect between what farmers tell me and what I hear from economists—most of whom rarely visit many farms. Starting with the colonial occupation of India, the government's agricultural policies have focused on the accumulation of money by the well-do-do farmers and the government at the expense of those who tilled the land. Instead of promoting the production of multiple crops either through crop rotations or intercropping, it has focused increasingly on crops for export rather than on feeding its own population. The journal *Seedling*, published by the nongovernmental organization GRAIN, points out that all of the largest grain traders in the world have greatly increased their profits during the past two years. Cargill, for example, announced an 86% increase in profits from commodity trading for the first quarter of 2008 over the same period in 2007.[1] It is not surprising that the poor do not have enough to eat.

Many of us consider the right to food to be a fundamental human right. But the concept of "rights" paradoxically has been appropriated by multinational corporations and governments to expand the philosophy of neoliberalism. For example, recent changes in Mexican law have elevated the "right" of private ownership over traditional indigenous practices of communal ownership of land, water, and other resources. There are countless examples around the world in which individuals or corporations have asserted "rights" to ownership in order to steal products of nature from local traditional societies, both indigenous and non-indigenous, by patenting them in a slightly modified form. In response, argues a Canadian farmer: "Farmers all over the world need to start thinking once again of food as a source of nutrition and sustenance and to reconnect with old ideas about fertility, knowledge, labor, and community . . . awareness that the corporate strategy for world domination is unsustainable and ultimately self-defeating."[2] The world over, people are beginning to look to a new pattern of agriculture directed toward feeding people rather than profit.

By the late 1970s making India self-sufficient in food became a rallying call. But instead of attempting land reform, for political reasons the government emphasized monocropping, export for profit, and complex market chains, adopting the U.S.

model based on a limited number of commodities. This approach relied extensively on petrochemical-based fertilizers, pesticides, and large farms. The so-called liberalization of the economy in the last 10 years has relied on the views of economists who believed that it would be good for trade if India were to import many of its basic grains, taking advantage of what economists call "economies of scale," a concept borrowed from industry that ignores the realities of rural/agricultural life. As George Mombiot recently pointed out, we have known since the 1960s that small farms produce greater yields per acre than large farms, sometimes as much as 20 times greater.[3] Industrial agriculture is less a matter of efficiency (productivity, energy, or capital usage) than of political power.

Food is not simply a product, like a piece of cloth or a machine, although food companies have tried to turn it into one. The growth of plants and animals is part and parcel of local communal life, of the quality of rural day-to-day existence, and the local exchange of goods. The current policy makes people dependent on the transportation of food and food products over long distances (using large amounts of petrochemicals), as well as on petrochemicals for fertilizers, herbicides, and enormous quantities of pesticides that are destructive of the soil and human health. India's central and state governments have chosen to focus on larger dams and irrigation projects while neglecting local-level water conservation and water harvesting, small household level ponds, and local recycling of semicontaminated water (for example, bath water). They fail to employ the most ecologically sound methods of water use, which has inevitably had a negative impact on agriculture.

In 1995 an important conference organized by the International Food Policy Research Institute based in Washington, D.C., concluded that with existing technology and new methods, India would be able to feed itself for the next 25 or more years. Yet the significant increase in export farming, the continual neglect of small farmers, the belief held by the urban elite that nobody really wants to farm and the rapid increase in the price of oil and other petrochemical products have made it extremely difficult for poor and even mid-sized farmers. For example, various state governments in south India failed to support the use of (formerly) common lands by self-help groups of landless women who were producing vegetables both for their own consumption and the local market. This represents a broader failure to see sustainable agriculture by villagers as a meaningful alternative to so-called modern agriculture.

Elites, including many economists, tend to belittle small farmers who grow for the local community and perhaps the nearby city and encourage farm policies that make rural people more dependent on importing foods and fail to meet the needs of local farmers and consumers. The government's downplaying of procurement policies—buying of grains and basic foodstuffs at lower than market prices—only exacerbates food crises and may even create them. I have seen NGOs struggling to fund programs that assist small farmers who must fight both their local and central government policies. I have witnessed farm after farm produce high yields of multiple crops when they are given financial support, technical advice, and community support. The focus of these groups is clearly at odds with most government policies.

Some current trends in the United States also reflect a rejection of centralized agricultural policies and large corporate interests. More people are turning to Community Supported Agriculture associations (CSAs), farmers' markets, and small-scale urban agriculture, creating a significant though still small movement that may well transform the way we eat. Its origins are very different from motives for change in India. While the gap between urban elites and food cultivators is certainly as great in India as it is in the United States—and perhaps it is even greater in India because of the entrenched caste system—it is still possible for Indian farmers to be weaned from export crops and return to production for local and regional markets. For example, in Bangalore I have seen how organic food brought in to a city market usually sells out in a few hours, even in poorer neighborhoods. People want healthier foods. Urban people are beginning to grow their own vegetables and fruits (though not yet grains) and even keep a few hens to provide their families with fresh eggs.

For a number of reasons the increasing cost of food may expedite a return to local consumption. In India and elsewhere the poorest people—in rural areas the landless, in urban areas the homeless or slum dwellers—lack even tiny amounts of space to grow food, adopt innovations in water conservation, or take other progressive measures. At this moment in many countries, such people are barely able to afford the minimum nutrition their bodies need. This situation is fine for the commodity traders, who profit from other people's hunger. Is a trader's "right" to obscene levels of profit more sacred than a poor person's right to eat?

This dilemma brings us back to the question of human rights—the rights to land, housing, water, food, and a decent quality of life. When these rights are recognized, people will have the chance to gain more autonomy over their lives. The struggle for them is essential for human survival and the survival of all types of life on the planet.

Notes

1. www.grain.org, 06/06/08.
2. *Seedling*, Oct. 2007, 6–7.
3. George Monbiot, "These Objects of Contempt Are Now Our Best Chance of Feeding the World," *The Guardian*, June 10, 2008, 25.

CHAPTER 10

Mass Tourism on the Mexican Caribbean: Pervasive Changes, Profound Consequences[1]

Oriol Pi-Sunyer and R. Brooke Thomas

This chapter explores some of the consequences of rapid tourism development in Quintana Roo, the eastern portion of the Yucatán peninsula and Mexico's newest state. It is a place known for its beautiful beaches, reefs, Mayan pyramids, and tropical forests. In the course of the last 30 years, a massive influx of tourists has transformed what had been the most peripheral and lightly settled region of Mexico into one of the world's major tourist destinations.

We followed this change through three stages of fieldwork. Phase 1 (1993–94) examined the impact of different forms of tourism on Maya villages and resort service communities. Phase 2 (2000–01) shifted priorities to the town and tourist destination of Tulum. Here we sought out the principal actors effecting change and examined their roles in resource conflicts. Phase 3 (2008–09) took one of these conflict arenas, environmental protection versus intensified development, and explored the seriousness of environmental degradation. In essence, our research demonstrates how tourism alters everyday life, the complexity of rapid change in an increasingly diverse setting, and how these processes are influenced by national policy and global economy.

Our first article on Quintana Roo was published in 1990, and tourism and the profound changes that it can engender have been our central concern ever since. But tourism does not exist in a vacuum and, when we began our research, large-scale tourism was still largely limited to Cancún and other resort areas in the northeastern quadrant of the state. A major interest at that juncture was to understand how Maya communities coped with (or benefited from) not only tourism but also the myriad changes—from electricity to roads—that followed in its wake. We paid particular attention to the Maya for several reasons: there was an extensive literature on Maya life and communities, we had both worked in village-level societies, and we shared an interest in contemporary indigenous people. Much of our earlier research was conducted inland from the coast, but even in the early 1990s we were aware that the "Cancún model" was moving south—and fast. It seemed evident that major changes were in the making and that we needed to pay greater attention to the coast, its inhabitants, and its future. These different contexts required significantly different approaches. The scale was of a totally different order, as were many of the issues. Also, the 1990s witnessed major societal stresses throughout the country. By early 1995 Mexico had been confronted by a catastrophic financial crisis, an insurgency in Chiapas, and the spectacle of a former president hiding in exile. The reality of these political, social, and economic factors was bound to influence our research agenda.

The following section is a condensed version of the chapter published a decade ago. We retain most of the language and "voice" of the original essay and have made no attempt to "bring it up to date" by changing observations and statistics.

Is tourism a "life and death matter"? Perhaps not in a literal sense, but for many inhabitants of the so-called Third World, and especially for indigenous groups in such countries, tourism represents a particular face of both development and forced social change. Fundamentally, this process often works to dismantle collective identities and reduces the ability of individuals and communities to survive economically and culturally. Travel is now the single-largest item in international trade, and since the 1960s "hospitality" has grown at the rate of some 10% per year. A phenomenon of this magnitude—global in scope, touching societies of every type, manifesting itself in sundry forms and scales—is not inherently all good or all evil. The key analytical question—and not always an easy one to answer—is whether it improves the lives of local people or tends to reinforce and perpetuate relations of dependency and inequality.

Tourism in Mexico is a major source of foreign exchange, perhaps even a new kind of tropical export product. But it is also a highly competitive industry, since international hotel chains, tourists, and tour operators have numerous alternative sites and destinations at their disposal. Consequently, attracting foreign tourists and foreign capital is a difficult process that has often meant austerity (particularly for the poor), a labor force under increasingly tight discipline, and other "belt-tightening" measures. It is certainly true that tourism, particularly resort tourism, employs many people, but it does so in ways significantly different from most other industries. Specifically, the majority of tourism-related occupations calls for little formal education or specialized training. This reflects a wider reality. Not only have Mexican economic policies failed to narrow the gap between rich and poor, but also one can argue that the expansion of mass tourism further reinforces the dualistic structure of Mexican society.

Our position is not only that mass tourism is likely to reinforce preexisting socioeconomic structures but also that inequalities will affect most severely the lives and prospects of just those populations with whom tourists come into contact, people who are often characterized by extreme material poverty and minimal influence. Clifford Geertz, discussing economic development in Southeast Asia, comments that modernizing states "do not bring all their citizens equally with them when they join the contemporary world of capital flows, technology transfers, trade balances, and growth rates."[2] Fundamentally, when peripheral regions, such as Quintana Roo, are brought into the process of modernization, local populations (commonly regarded as "backward" by national elites) are assigned subordinate roles in the development process—sometimes to the point of invisibility.

Quintana Roo

The 1950 census shows the population of Quintana Roo as numbering 26,967, a figure that would increase to 50,169 by 1960. Not until the late 1960s did infrastructure begin to change significantly. First came the roads, then the airports, and with them an influx of new residents, both Mexican and foreign. Not long before, the region had barely registered on the mental maps of cosmopolitan Mexicans. When they thought about it at all, it was usually in terms of a backwater associated with the questionable activities of smugglers, chicle gatherers, and forest-dwelling Indians. With the expansion of tourism the region, and particularly its coast, rapidly became redefined as a tropical paradise. Tourism publicity often contrasts the modernity of Cancún and other resorts with a changeless natural world of "still crystal-clear waters and virgin beaches," a land "that still belongs to nature, where ocelots, kinkajous, and spider monkeys still roam wild in their native habitat."

The reality is rather different. Cancún is a city of some 500,000 inhabitants, and it attracts more than 2 million visitors a year. Furthermore, the coast from Cancún south is being converted into a string of resorts, theme parks, and hotels. Also, Cancún is very much a child of 1960s development thinking, a mega-project requiring massive investment. It has certainly become a major international tourist destination. But it would be wise to remember the cyclical and uncertain character of global tourism and particularly the decline of Acapulco, once the major Mexican playground for the rich and famous. Some observers believe that Cancún is already confronted by similar problems of degradation, image, and security.

It is perhaps the realization that Cancún's long and massive line of hotels no longer quite responds to contemporary needs and tastes that has helped to bring about some diversification of the market in the direction of environmental and cultural tourism. In Quintana Roo there is little in the way of village-based cultural tourism attracted by markets, crafts, and ceremonies. More than anything else, alternative tourism plays on the theme of the grandeur that was Maya civilization and the quest for the particular kind of dream world associated with jungles, exotic animal life, and Maya spirituality. Not surprisingly, one encounters many latter-day Indiana Joneses indulging their fantasies, as well as more serious ecological tourists. The impressive Maya sites of the area, particularly Tulum and Cobá, receive a large influx of visitors; Tulum is already showing signs of wear and tear.

A major problem related to all forms of tourism stems from the inherent fragility of the biogeographical system on which the touristic system has been erected. The tourist boom has had both anticipated and unforeseen consequences on environmental quality, consequences that, unless remedied, are bound to impinge on the profitability of the industry. At the same time the growing environmental awareness—as well as an emerging market for ecologically friendly tourism—has directed attention to the uniqueness of the peninsula and to the crisis it faces.

A Fragile, Living Rock

Generally unnoticed by the tourist, and certainly little heeded by developers, is the fragile nature of Quintana Roo's linked environments. The 16th-century Spanish bishop Diego de Landa described this land thus: "Yucatán is the country with the least earth I have ever known, since all is a living rock." Contemporary Maya farmers describe much of this terrain as *zekel*: "land very stony or full of stones." Precipitation from tropical storms falls on the interior forest percolating through thin pockets of topsoil; it then rapidly makes its way into the porous calcite bedrock that underlies the peninsula. From here it flows through a complex network of underground rivers to the coast where it surfaces in freshwater vents in the mangrove swamps behind the beaches, in lagoons, or beyond the beach itself. In many cases hotels along the tourist zone are built on a lens of beach between the swamp and the sea and are protected under calm conditions by the offshore barrier reef running the length of the peninsula's eastern coast. Connecting these terrestrial and marine ecosystems is the underground flow of water that makes its way across the limestone platform.

This fragile living rock supports a tourism industry built with little land-use planning or environmental impact analysis. As a result Cancún already suffers from problems of urban congestion, decline in air quality, and a substantial deterioration of its lagoon. The main highway south from Cancún is lined with an assortment of billboards advertising resorts with such alluring names as Secret Beach and Shangri-La. These supposedly remote and beautiful locations generate very tangible environmental problems, including the consumption of great quantities of underground water and the discharge of nutrient-rich waste materials that smother and degrade the fragile reefs. There is an obvious contradiction between the promoted theme of an unmarred nature and the reality of an increasingly impacted environment. A number of sincere and meaningful efforts are attempting to counteract these trends, but all too often ecology has been co-opted by the market.

All tourism, it has often been pointed out, is a form of play and fantasy. Surely, it will be argued, if tourists want to identify with jungle adventurers (ecological or otherwise), this is strictly their business. It would be that, except that the shift toward environmental and "adventure" tourism, as well as the transformation of archaeological sites into tourist attractions, carries material and cultural consequences for local people. Most obviously, whatever land and resources are taken out of local control reduces local economic options.

The not unreasonable fear of some Maya that their universe—including their spiritual world—is being drastically altered has a bearing on the general question of rights to land and resources. That Quintana Roo was a thinly settled territory is beyond argument, but this did not make it an "empty space" or its inhabitants incompetent guardians. Here, as in so many other locations with an indigenous population, the assertion by those in power that local people were not using their lands "properly" has been used to "redefine" resources—specifically, beaches, extensive archaeological sites, and forest—as state or private property. Now the Maya find themselves in the middle of an international debate on ecological preservation. Everyone seems to talk about "the Maya," but what was evident from our conversations with both managers in the tourist industry and long-established residents is how little most of them knew about their Maya neighbors. We were told that the Maya were "happy"; happy by nature but also happy to find work as maids and gardeners. Not a few non-Maya residents saw Maya people as exotic archetypes with "admirable qualities."

Our initial aim in Quintana Roo was to study a set of communities that were experiencing tourism in significantly different ways and varying degrees of intensity.

We recognized that "tourism" was a kind of shorthand, part of a more general process of incorporation into national life and national economy. Yet people *did* discuss tourism and clearly recognized it as an important element in their lives. Specifically we looked at the structure of group relations, ongoing changes in diet and health, natural resource use, and general cultural perceptions—in sum, how villagers saw themselves and the increasingly complex world they inhabit. Two of our sites were predominantly Maya, the other two were mixed in population.

Our sample consisted of two service communities, Akumal and Ciudad Chemuyil, attached to beach resorts; Cobá, a village adjoining a major inland archaeological site; and Punta Laguna, a hamlet deep in the interior that supplements traditional agriculture with ecotourism. The four sites differ in size and composition of population, resources under their control, degree of articulation with tourism, and their isolation from state institutions and market forces. We use "community" with caution, not only because the term often implies a high degree of boundedness but also because populations in Quintana Roo fluctuate in response to many factors, including the availability of work, agricultural prospects, security of tenancy, and government plans and policies. We collected community aggregate data and used an extensive household questionnaire to sample some 25% of the population of these settlements. We also undertook in-depth interviews, carried out dietary and store inventory surveys, and conducted nutritional and anthropometric surveys in two elementary schools.

Differing Faces of Tourism

As sun-and-sea resorts spread down the coast, service communities developed in their wake. These draw people from towns and villages across the Yucatán peninsula, and increasingly from other parts of Mexico. Akumal was such a settlement. We selected it because of its dependency on resort employment and the pressures faced by its residents. The 400 villagers lived directly outside the boundaries of a resort and recreation complex of the same name, and the contrast between the resort and service community could not be starker. The resort is pleasant, spacious, and well maintained, and it faces a sandy beach. It is filled with contented visitors and the owners of holiday properties. The houses of the service community were built of scavenged forest materials, scrap or cinder block—more shantytown than tropical hamlet. Although electricity was available, the community lacked garbage collection, sewage system, and potable water. The main water line to the resort passed through the village, but residents were forced to rely on a series of shallow and unsanitary wells.

Already in 1993 pressure was mounting to evict the people of Akumal. The resort management and condo owners declared it an eyesore and a health hazard. By the summer of 1994 approximately half the homes had been razed. Finally, in the summer of 1996, assisted by a hurricane that damaged many structures, the government ordered all houses and small businesses (there were several) vacated. Why did the people of this dilapidated settlement have such an attachment to it? Chiefly because housing was cheap, if often inadequate. Also, it was close to employment, and it offered a space of autonomy from the controls of industry and the demands of government.

Ciudad Chemuyil, the second service community that we looked at, is a new development that, at the time of the study, contained 250 houses. It was established by a consortium of hotels and the government in order to concentrate, and presumably the better to control, a growing labor force attracted by expanding tourism. Promotional literature describes it as a "new Maya city," and plans call for an eventual growth to 250,000 inhabitants. Even if this target is not reached, a massive population increase will transform the human geography of the coast and may reinforce class and ethnic separation. The new settlement (presented as superior, healthier, and more modern) consists of small, poorly ventilated, cement block houses—all identical—on minimal lots. Company minibuses pick up maids, gardeners, and cooks in the morning, take them to their places of work, and return them in the evening. This is essentially a company town, totally dependent on resort employment, and with a population tied to 30-year mortgages underwritten by employers.

Unlike Akumal and Ciudad Chemuyil the village of Cobá did not come into being as a result of tourism. Settled some 50 years ago by a small group of Yucatecan farmers, Cobá has grown over the years to approximately 900 inhabitants. What makes it a tourist destination is its location at the edge of one of the largest archaeological complexes in Mesoamerica: the Classic Maya site from which the community takes its name.

The development of the ruins into an attraction for the "adventurous" tourist followed the completion in the 1970s of a road connecting Cobá to the coastal highway. This link brought tourists and, in due course, electricity, easy delivery of commercial goods, potable water, a health clinic, and a school. By the time of our study the men and women of Cobá were increasingly dependent on different types of wage work, including resort construction. As our colleague Ellen Kintz notes, this dependence on wage labor "provides cash but strains social ties."[3] Some 60,000 annual visitors, mostly foreigners, make their way to the archaeological site and the protected forest trails that surround it. Tourists arrive by car and bus and generally leave by the end of the day. Although tourism has stimulated the sale of handicrafts and the establishment of a handful of stores and restaurants, most townspeople complain that the tourist trade leaves them nothing.

From the very beginning tourism was contentious because the newly designated archaeological zone contained some of the community's prime agricultural land. Other destabilizing changes included a heightened awareness of class and ethnic inequalities, plus pressures to privatize the *ejido* communal holdings (this tends to split the community generationally). The strains also manifest themselves in the religious sphere. A generation ago religious practice was a variant of folk syncretism that joined features of Catholic ritual to a Mayan cosmology. Elements of this system remain, but Cobá has become an arena for competing creeds, and some two-thirds of the population identify with different Protestant and Evangelical denominations. The new beliefs tend to privilege the individual over the community.

At the opposite pole of dependency typical of the communities along the Cancún-Tulum corridor is the hamlet of Punta Laguna. This is a forest community composed of a handful of interrelated families and subsisting almost entirely from its fields, kitchen gardens, and the products of the surrounding forest. Unlike the situation in nearby Cobá, ritual practices remain largely intact, and community bonds, essentially links of kinship, are strong. Honey represents one of the few cash crops, and this fact helps explain why the residents have long protected a large stand of the canopy forest. The forest, in turn, offers food and shelter to a colony of spider monkeys.

Tourists come in small numbers to see the monkeys and are escorted by teenage boys who act as guides. These youths speak with enthusiasm about the local flora and fauna and use tracking skills to locate the monkeys. Most tourists are fascinated by the experience and its homespun nature. However, such tourism does not contribute much to the local economy. The gratuities collected by guides put a little extra money into circulation, and the guest waiting in the entrance shed is invited to buy postcards and honey. Even if income is not high, the fact that protecting the environment can help support the community is a valuable lesson. In brief, this little hamlet is about as self-sufficient in basic needs as any place in the state, but people feel poor, and youth is beginning to search for work on the coast.

Surviving in a Changing World

What is happening to the Maya (and to other residents) as they confront the spectrum of changes and challenges that has engulfed them? One of the most visible changes is in food consumption patterns, especially in the high dependence on commercial soft drinks and sugar-fortified fruit juices. Mexico has one of the highest Coca-Cola consumption rates in the world, about 16 ounces of soft drinks daily. As one teenager remarked, "We drink it for breakfast, lunch, and dinner, and when we're hot or cold." Soft-drink consumption is often associated with snacking, and the snacks in question tend to be high in fats, salt, and sugar.

Coke and junk foods constitute merely a part of a more general pattern. As people, particularly those on the coast, become removed from their *milpas* (agricultural plots) and kitchen gardens, they find access to a variety of fruits and vegetables to be problematic. The consequences of this changing diet are most apparent in the ubiquity of dental caries. These are pervasive throughout all age groups, and dental rot and missing teeth are pronounced in the service communities. Some babies are given Coke in a bottle as early as six months of age and come to prefer it to mothers' milk.

Another, more positive, cultural modification is in household demographics. A pattern of early marriage and large families has been typical of the Quintana Roo Maya, who, until recently, lived in a region where agricultural land was readily available. In surveys some isolated communities still showed a preference for teenage marriage. But an increasing number of respondents, particularly on the coast, thought that marriage and childbirth should be delayed and that "waiting beyond [the age of] 20 was best."

Younger and older households unanimously expressed a desire for smaller families in all communities except Punta Laguna. Also, there was a general agreement that young couples wanted to live separately from their parents. These opinions no doubt reflect idealized situations, but they also have a bearing on how people act. Education, for example, is increasingly seen as necessary for employment and advancement, and this view includes the education of girls (who nevertheless trail boys in years of school attendance). Cost is another factor. In the service communities a high number of young householders responded that two children constituted the ideal complement, a clear departure from the household structures they had grown up in. This pattern is still emerging, but its direction is unmistakable, reflecting comparable demographic shifts in other societies experiencing the processes of modernization. Also, it demonstrates that when Maya people (often depicted as highly "traditional") are in a position to make decisions that influence their lives, they are not averse to doing so.

Other changes and adaptations are linked to strategies of subsistence. Historically Maya farming communities were essentially self-sufficient and needed few outside items. Until recent times, most goods were acquired from itinerant merchants who carried their merchandise on muleback. Loss of access to land and forest, together with the growth of population, has brought pressure on local resources and increased the purchase of commercial products. When we asked what forest resources were becoming most scarce, people consistently drew attention to the difficulty of obtaining the hardwood upright posts and the palm thatch needed to make traditional houses. In Cobá, for instance, one must go at least 4 km from town to find these materials. Nor surprisingly the scarcity of wood and thatch has led to an increase in the use of cinder blocks for house building. But the shift to industrial goods requires more money, money that usually can be earned only by outside employment.

In a less direct manner the search for outside employment has reduced the number of households that maintain kitchen gardens. These relatively small plots adjacent to dwellings are tended and controlled by women. They produce an array of valuable foodstuffs including vegetables, herbs, fruits, and medicinal plants; it is not unusual to find chickens, even a household pig. Kitchen gardens should be seen as part of a larger agricultural complex—a complement to *milpa* agriculture—and it is very significant that they fall within women's sphere of control. Also, the exchange of produce from these gardens helps to underpin the ethos of reciprocity. But women who find outside employment have little time to maintain them.

At another level tourism, together with the political, ideological, and economic restructuring of the region, has brought about the penetration of national and international values and of models of self and society that are not always internally consistent and that may conflict with customary Maya forms. Now numerous religions compete for the Maya soul, a national educational system fosters a societal model based on assimilation, and clinics undermine the legitimacy of curers and, by extension, the validity of the Mayan worldview. The most powerful pressures derive from changing economic relations.

As tourism has grown, consumption norms (and expectations) have soared. Televisions and appliances are seen as virtual necessities, and younger people have become particularly concerned with style. There is certainly a generational gap, especially in the service communities where contact with tourists is common. Laborers returning to inland villages following a stint on the coast are likely to arrive with new clothes and hairstyles, electronic gadgets, and Mexicanized mannerisms. Yet the vast majority of respondents agreed that there was really no alternative to nonagricultural employment, preferably in town but if necessary in a more distant location. Talking to dedicated farmers—and there are still a number of them around—we learned that farming continues to offer a satisfaction, a deep sense of belonging, that they could not find elsewhere. But there is a catch. Consistently these same farmers remarked that although *milpa* generally provided all the food the family needed, even in the best years it brought in little cash.

The outside world is internalized in different ways, from an increasingly cash-based economy, to new forms of identity, to an expanded sense of national and global spheres. A very important contributor to this process is television. Television is omnipresent, and almost 90% of the households have television sets. A black-and-white set costs U.S. $200, equivalent to a well-paid waiter's monthly wage. For a minimum-wage or part-time laborer, the cost of a set and installation may well represent half the annual cash income—and yet television has almost become a necessity.

Attitudes toward television are decidedly ambivalent. Many people report the TV is on six hours a day, all day on weekends. Parents complained that their children do not do their homework, and many adults readily admit that they watch too much television and it interferes with their work. Nevertheless, the whole family watches the nightly soap operas, whose plots and incidents seem to be known to everyone, and parents commonly use the television as a handy babysitter.

The programming depicts a world that is often the antithesis of the values, social roles, and patterns of behavior typical of established Maya culture—a metropolitan world of consumption inhabited by well-to-do, light-complexioned (often blond) individuals. The implicit message is that those who are portrayed are the legitimate representatives of the national culture.

Mexican television is no more a mirror of actual Mexican life than is television elsewhere, but Maya viewers are seldom in a position to make such informed judgments. Our impression is that the message of consumption and its relationship to modernity does get through clearly. What of the underlying ideological premises? When asked about specific settings depicted in programs, several of our informants placed them "very far away" in a world that we gathered was not quite real, or connected to their own tangentially if at all. This "distancing" may help protect the Maya from the sense of cultural marginality that has been so destructive to many small-scale societies; while the "outside" world of televised images is invited to enter the house, history and experience have also taught the Maya to be very cautious. As with numerous aspects of modern life, television is not rejected but incorporated through a prism that allows for a variety of options or meanings.

Change and Consequences

The intersection of Mexican public policy with the forces of global capitalism continues to evolve. In 1994 Mexico, under pressure from the United States, signed the NAFTA free trade agreement. The treaty was designed to deregulate the Mexican economy, including the *ejido* system of collective property. Many other resources have been privatized, and Mexican industry has had to compete with that of the United States and Canada. As much as 25% of the Mexican economy has been "dollarized," which means that it is tied very directly to the U.S. economy. The two most important economic sectors (oil production is declining) are the *maquiladora* plants, many close to the U.S.-Mexican border, and tourism.

Like many developing nations involved in modernization, Mexico has opted for tourism as a key development strategy, and tourism has become an increasingly important source of foreign exchange. Quintana Roo contributes more than a third of Mexico's tourism income, and this industry has come to influence, perhaps even define, most spheres of local life.

That tourism is "an agent of change" has by now become conventional wisdom. Change in Quintana Roo has long been rapid and omnipresent. We began our fieldwork with the assumption that change would come in multiple forms and could either challenge or reinforce long-established inequalities. Tourism is a labor-intensive industry and employs a large number of low-paid, and initially unskilled, people. In Quintana Roo much of this workforce comes from the poorest parts of the country and from closer-in Maya communities. Given this reality we doubted that change in and of itself would greatly alter longstanding ethnic, racial, and class divisions, although it might open opportunities for some poor people.

The outside world depicted on television was now much closer and was often represented in the form of Maya-like motifs, particularly in architecture and the naming of new urban zones. We assumed that change—especially when it comes from the outside—not only has a material dimension but also can influence cultural meanings and belief systems. What does it mean to be Maya today?

In Mexico, as elsewhere in the Americas, the latter part of the 20th century witnessed an upsurge in native activism, especially with respects to human rights and control of ancestral lands. A political movement in Chiapas, for example, called not only for the recognition of indigenous cultures as unique and autonomous entities but also for a new deal from the state. How are Maya people—the majority still rural—managing a rapidly changing social and political environment? The issue is much less a matter of "culture change" in the traditional anthropological sense than it is one of handling forms of modernity that were in the process of rapidly remapping all of southern Mexico, not just Indian villages. The Maya had survived some four centuries of Spanish rule and almost two centuries of postcolonial Mexican authority. How would these skills work in a much-changed political, social, and economic setting where for most people wage labor is the main source of income?

Our research found a transformation of spatial relations, cultural meanings, and environmental issues accompanying the drive to make over Quintana Roo into Mexico's fastest growing tourist destination. We should remember that much of Quintana Roo remained under armed indigenous control well into the 20th century and that this fact precluded significant influence by external agents, national or otherwise.[4] The most crucial change, and certainly the most measurable, has been demographic. It has transformed the Maya into a minority people.[5] Even in 1960 Quintana Roo was essentially Indian country. Recent figures (2005) show the total population of the state as just over one million—a 20-fold increase, chiefly due to migration, in a span of 50 years.

During our 1990s research we were probably insufficiently sensitive to the consequences of this change. Initially we believed that this steep rise would begin to abate as the growing number of job seekers saturated the labor market. We failed to predict the degree to which the search for employment would become the nation's central social and economic concern. Even depressed wages did not stem the movement of people to one of the relatively few places where at least *some* jobs could be found.

Strangely, the macroeconomics of Mexico's southern border began to resemble conditions on the northern frontier. It was not a *maquiladora*-based economy of assembly plants but one equally tied to transnational demands, in this case those of tourists. At both geographic poles most people lived by selling their low-skilled labor. However, the full picture is more complex: within a context of generalized poverty, extreme, and growing, economic inequality became the norm.[6]

Besides some of the obvious consequences of mass tourism, such as the impact on an environment that had experienced relatively little stress before the advent of modern development practices, the tourist industry transformed social relations to a degree that would have been hard to imagine when we began our research. At that time Maya villagers, in particular young men, looked for work in the tourist sector that was primarily temporary, to supplement family income.[7] Such employment is a mechanism that helps to support small-scale agriculturalists and their families. Although outside work brought elements of an outside world, it seemed to us that Mayans had made adaptations and adjustments, material and conceptual, that generally allowed them to maintain what an earlier generation of anthropologists would have termed a viable folk culture.

Shifts in demography signaled changes in other spheres—social, ideological, and environmental. For example, our study of village agriculture and the use of forest resources concluded that one can reasonably speak of an indigenous ecology, or of indigenous ecological knowledge, but the way of life that such knowledge systems supported was under considerable pressure from several directions. Locally village populations expanded on limited common land. As people lived longer and fewer children died, pressure on forest resources was likely to increase; concurrently, the need to find work beyond the community would similarly grow. At the micro level of the village and family we could follow these permutations and examine what strategies were being deployed. But our Maya villagers lived mostly in the interior, and the critical changes were taking place along the coast, an area with relatively few peasants, Indian or otherwise.

The master model we had used to understand village society was drawn from political economy backed by an ethnographic methodology reflecting what Clifford Geertz called "the understanding of understanding," or of how people make sense of their conceptual universe. Maya households were, indeed, trying to make sense of a world that had changed spectacularly. Sometimes it was hard for our friends to find the words or concepts to adequately express their thoughts and fears. Witnessing people wrestle with modernity allowed us to collect narratives of how life had changed, and particularly of the erosion of personal and collective self-sufficiency. The only reasonable option on the horizon to help meet increasing material needs was an augmentation in outside employment. But this route also had its own set of problems, including possible generational alienation and racial discrimination.[8]

The world of the coast, and Tulum in particular, was very different: dynamic, often chaotic, and certainly multifaceted and exciting. It was also a social environment undergoing exceptionally rapid change, physical and sociocultural. At the heart of this change was a profound transformation in tourism itself. On our first exploratory visits to the coast in the late 1980s and early 1990s the typical tourists were young adventurers: global backpackers seeking a transformative experience. The very concept of traveling "off the beaten track" implied a readiness to take risks and to live—it was assumed—"like the natives." In the process this international cohort developed an identity reinforced by tales of adventure and risk, a status, it was assumed, far superior to that of the pampered tourist. For many backpackers travel of this type can best be thought of as a rite of passage separating youth from the more serious responsibilities of adulthood, and the very act of going to the far corners of the earth was what mattered most, not what might be found once there. Also, the backpacker world was, and remains, heavily English-speaking and very much geared to the advice and admonitions offered by the *Lonely Planet* guidebooks, so much so that Beth Notar, who has studied tourism in the Chinese borderlands, refers to the phenomenon as "The Lonely Planet Empire."[9]

This backpacker search for adventure and authenticity had local repercussions. It began to transform the economy, especially where small-scale enterprises, such as inexpensive accommodation (ideally on the town beach) and modest restaurants or cafes, were concerned. Since group ethos stressed the virtues of frugality, the direct economic consequences, while difficult to measure, were probably relatively limited, at least initially. Nevertheless, this early cohort of foreign visitors brought local people in contact with different styles of life and hence helped to make tourism in general more acceptable. Also, backpacking and adventure tourists travel light and must survive on what is locally available. As Stroma Cole, an anthropologist with previous experience as a tourist guide in remote parts of Indonesia points out, "back-packer tourism creates a demand for cheap accommodation and a parallel structure of transport, restaurant, and support services."[10]

But backpack travel was not the only new social phenomenon. Economic and political stresses in Mexico had in part been responsible for a significant migration of middle-class Mexicans (chiefly from central Mexico) to peripheral localities such as Quintana Roo. We can think of this as a type of counterculture displacement, the outcome of a search by young Mexicans for a more "natural," and certainly less money-driven, style of life. Beginning in the 1970s there was also a movement—again, initially not large—of relatively well-to-do North American and European visitors, some of whom would decide to stay in the area. Motivations varied, but among younger people they often included a certain alienation from mainstream so-ciety. A major attraction was a landscape of luxuriant mangroves, coral beaches, and sparkling lagoons. At this juncture the Mexican landscape represented a space of the imagination—even a tropical dreamscape—made possible by improved transpor-tation, low population density, and a still limited disruption of seafront and forest.

This relative isolation began to recede in the early 1990s, and the process has continued at an accelerated pace. In very short order a settlement that had been not much more than a crossroads truck stop close to a Maya hamlet began to tap an emergent mass tourist market, particularly the busloads of day-trippers from the Cancún hotels. Although at first there was not much contact between residents and visitors to the archaeological site, some tourists did venture into Tulum *pueblo* and this, in due course, led to the establishment or expansion of restaurants, shops sell-ing Mexican crafts, and various other businesses, all of which made the burgeoning township more attractive to tourists. The stores, for their part, began to reflect the needs and tastes of a clientele that was increasingly post-backpacker but not looking for a typical resort hotel vacation. Interestingly, a good number of the new entre-preneurs were drawn from the pool of national and international talent that, some years earlier, had settled in Tulum. What they shared was an understanding of the changing clientele and its consumer tastes.

We are not suggesting that Tulum was in the process of being transformed into a mini metropolis, or a tropical Greenwich Village, but rather that it was becoming a convergence zone for different people with distinct (as well as overlapping) hopes and aspirations. Although we were struck by the extent to which it seemed to offer a space for personal expression and the remaking of self, most inhabitants were nei-ther particularly spiritual nor very much given to cultural pursuits. The majority of new residents, it should be remembered, were of working class or peasant origin, and if they were seeking something, it was economic security and a degree of stabil-ity. At the same time, as the community grew, it also attracted its quota of investors, developers, bureaucrats, and entrepreneurs.

The most recent change in Tulum has involved the reconfiguration of the town—and by now it most certainly is a town—into a service and bedroom community of some 20,000 inhabitants supporting beachfront resort hotels. Concomitantly devel-opers and authorities plan to lure well-to-do foreign and Mexican residents. From what we understand—the script changes every few years—the Mexican government, in collaboration with major hotel chains, intends to greatly increase hotel density and urban construction. The pressure is already being felt. The huge resort town Cancún should be the cautionary tale. Today it has more than 30,000 hotel rooms and receives some 8 million visitors a year (it is the tourism portal for the whole coast), and it must manage an average of 190 daily flights.[11] When it was inaugurated more than 30 years ago, it was touted as a tropical resort, modern and comfortable, but still very much in harmony with the environment.

True, even in the Cancún tourist zone, environmental voices may be heard, but as the phenomenon has spread down the coast, the state's interest is much more on rapid growth and job creation than on ecological protection, although the government claims it can achieve both. As for the tourists themselves, given that tourism is usually a break from humdrum reality, it is not surprising that environmental consciousness typically plays a minor role in most travel planning.[12] However, the central issue is not what tourists think but the ecological and social impact of the current development cycle. In our earlier writing we drew attention to the fragility of the Yucatecan environment, and we were certainly not the only voices. In 2000 Alberto Pereira Corona explained how the high impact of "low-impact" beach tourism seriously disturbed turtle hatcheries and degraded reefs that accounted for much of Quintana Roo's coastal biodiversity.[13] There is absolutely no doubt that the pressure on the environment will grow and that every new development, every new hotel, adds to the problem. If the past is any guide, the call for serious environmental impact studies will come after, perhaps long after, much damage has been done. Yet, as Deborah McLaren explains: "Tourism has provided us with fantasies. At the same time, it provided potentially free public relations that may help to encourage rethinking of the industry and create alternatives."[14]

Tulum Today

Interior Quintana Roo now forms part of Tulum's vast "catchment area." One example of this situation is the growing labor migration from the interior to the coastal zone, another is the plan to build an international airport close to one of the Maya communities we studied several years ago. Also, the interior is being changed by land speculation and the building of luxury homes in villages close to Tulum. In short, town and hinterland are increasingly interconnected.[15] This process is not only economic but also political: Tulum is now the center (*cabecera*) of a new municipality, and several of these interior villages fall within its administrative orbit. The town and its expanding hinterland mirror the shifts, dislocations, and the search for greater cohesion and security typical of frontier areas and border zones. For those who have moved there to find work, it is a place of hope and expectation, but in interviews many people also complained of violence and a general sense of insecurity. This was not a class-specific worry: both poor and well-to-do residents complained of a similar vulnerability.[16]

It is also a particular kind of melting pot. Much like the cities of the Industrial Revolution (or some present-day urban areas in Latin America), its population is increasing at an unprecedented annual rate, in this case a remarkable 14.8%, which probably makes it Mexico's fastest growing urban zone. The population, as we have noted, is highly diverse, both in terms of national/cultural composition and class position. Although it clearly is home to people with a mix of backgrounds and experiences, its inhabitants less evidently share a common system of meaning or compatible social concepts. There are many ideas and notions regarding what life in Tulum means or what the future should look like, but although the town is clearly influenced by global culture, it is difficult to detect much in the way of a collective sense of citizenship or belonging. What characterizes Tulum at this juncture is that in social and cultural terms it essentially lacks the cultural myths, beliefs, conditions, and institutions that in other, more stable, contexts help to weave the standard "ties of marriage, work, business, and leisure" into relatively cohesive neighborhoods and towns.[17]

Friction

The lack of "cohesion" and the difficulty of finding "shared meanings" is an often-described dimension of societies undergoing comparable changes. A useful way of conceptualizing such tensions is offered by Ana Tsing's, concept of "friction." Friction, she writes, aids us in understanding the apparently contradictory: "how emergent cultural forms—including forest destruction and environmental advocacy—are persistent but unpredictable effects of global encounters across difference."[18]

Encountering and managing the novel and the fearful is hardly a new experience in Quintana Roo. Five centuries ago, the Maya people gave their own highly distinct set of meanings to the doctrine and the ritual of a universal creed as disseminated by Spanish friars; many continue to practice it this way. However, they generally had the choice of moving deeper into the forest, an option that no longer exists. Until a generation or so ago most Maya people in Quintana Roo were village dwellers and subsistence agriculturalists. They had been so for centuries and had made their home in what environmental scholars now often call "The Maya Forest."[19] This is not to imply that they all perceived or made use of the forest environment in an identical manner. For some—and at an earlier time almost all—individuals and communities, the forest and its products were closely linked to religious ritual and Maya identity. For others, particularly a generation or more ago, the forest was associated with autonomy and self-sufficiency; and of late, some villagers have come to view the forest as a commodity to be managed with reference to market forces. Until recently, however, "forest knowledge" was local knowledge gained through experience and passed on from one generation to the next.

Consequently one can say that in a variety of ways Maya villagers understood the need for conservation and sustainability, even if they did not use such terms. Nowadays this localized ecology is confronted by a new ideology: a powerful (and well financed) cultural-environmental movement that speaks of "biological diversity," "sustainable development," and the preservation of global resources. These discourses often come into conflict with the attitudes and perceptions of those who may have used and cared for the land for generations. Sometimes what happens is that the owners of forest property, in attempting to satisfy the perceived needs of a new clientele, apply their distinct interpretation of ecology. For example, a couple of years ago we visited what was being laid out as eco-park and found that the owners kept cages of unhappy-looking forest creatures plus several monkeys tethered to long chains. All this, we were told, was done in the interests of ecology and so that visitors might have the opportunity to know the local fauna. More recently, we went to another local eco-project and found that the family had pooled their resources to build a large and costly bullring, although it was stressed that boys and young men would simply chase the bulls, nor hurt or kill them. It seemed to us that both these projects evidenced a considerable difficulty in comprehending the mentality, the conceptual world, of would-be clients.

In discussing these episodes we are trying to illustrate how friction looks on the ground. We are in no sense suggesting that Maya farmers or former farmers represent a significant risk to the environment, and we reject the notion, sometimes referred to as "environmental racism," that the natural world must be protected from indigenous people. The Maya are few, and the developers numerous and powerful. How many square miles of forest will be cut down to build the new airport?

In and around Tulum, a clear indication of friction is how the commoditization of land, and the transformation of communal ownership into private, has led to the massive sale of rural properties.[20] As might be expected, the result is a sharp decline in farming and a notable increase in the number of newly affluent former cultivators. It is hard to predict how long this new wealth will last, but currently it is reflected in the new houses being built by former cultivators and the shiny SUVs and pickups that they or their children are driving. Such conspicuous consumption is in sharp contrast to the abject poverty of Tulum's most recent migrants, traditional Maya Indians from Chiapas who may be found living in tarpaper shacks half a block from the dwellings of the newly wealthy and their longer established neighbors.

The cityscape itself makes for other contrasts: the town lacks a sewage system, the quality of the municipal water supply is always under suspicion, and garbage pickup is unpredictable. In the street where we leased our apartment, one of our neighbors (an extended Maya family), periodically released two very large pigs to forage at will, a process that included ripping into such garbage bags that had not been suspended beyond their considerable reach. We should add that our apartment was not located in some sparsely inhabited, village-like, district but a mere three blocks from the town's main avenue with its foreign-owned restaurants, craft shops, and trendy cafes. Basically, the pig-owning family behaved very much as if they were still living in the country, where barnyard animals are allowed to roam the streets. This behavior upset their urbane next-door neighbors who tried to keep the pigs away from their homes and garbage bags by throwing small stones and making "shoo" noises, tactics that hardly disturbed the foragers. There was certainly a good deal of tension. We discuss the "pig story" for a reason: at the "sidewalk level" it tells us something important about social and cultural dissonance, and the stress of everyday life.

At the same time almost everyone talks of Tulum as a remarkable locality, but can it be a genuinely shared space vested with a set of common meanings? Such expectations run into serious problems, some local, others more general. The type of society we are discussing—a place in flux, a virtual "no place" a generation ago—is bound to raise questions of community and identity. Newness is part of the reality, but it has not resulted in a collective "pioneer" experience. Equally important are the dynamics: Tulum is a place whose inhabitants must by necessity face the consequences of an integrated world economy engaged in the production and distribution of discourses and representations related to the very place where they live.

Cohesion, Articulation

Many people are in agreement that Tulum matters because of its location, its special meaning, its possibilities—so can this agreement make for a commonality of interests, perhaps even an element of social cohesion? Surely the possibilities are there, but much more will need to be done to bring about the greater social solidity that many people claim they desire. Writing in a report that we distributed to the community and the authorities in 2005, we pointed out several social-civic weaknesses and stressed the need for a more robust degree of community involvement. Initially, it seemed almost incredible to us that people who again and again insisted on their strong attachment to Tulum often failed to convert words and feelings into action. In the report we noted that many people with deep affection for the town were aware of serious problems:

> Many are highly conscious of the civic problems that face the town, including those of political representation and citizen participation. However, we have noted a great reluctance on the part of these knowledgeable and articulate people to run for public office, or even to be too visible in the political process. Political exposure makes people vulnerable to enemies, old and new, and to accusations of self-promotion and corruption.[21]

At the beginning of the decade such issues did not appear to merit a great deal of official concern. Tulum's 2001 Master Plan for Development is detailed with respect to infrastructural needs but exceedingly vague regarding matters of governance and citizen participation. It does mention identity and place, the need to reinforce the quality of life of all residents, and the goal of "socioeconomic integration of the different sectors of the population."[22]

The general weakness of civic engagement is in part due to the reasons noted above; there are also other factors that have to be taken into consideration, which we did not discuss in the Tulum Report. Returning to the issue of insecurity and fear of violence, we stress that these trends are growing not declining. Everyday life in an insecure environment makes people anxious and exacts a psychological toll. It may also limit social interaction: people turn inward, reduce the density of their networks, and certainly live a less pleasant life. "Everyday" and "routinized" violence seldom make the headlines, but it is these "mundane" problems that are particularly significant in influencing social conditions.[23]

Two recent articles address these matters in the context of Mexico. In *Days of the Dead*, the journalist Alma Guillermoprieto[24] discusses what she calls "Mexico's war on drugs" and how the deployment of Mexican troops across the country may well have resulted in serious problems. These include mounting tension between local security forces and federal troops, and the weird sense of being "occupied" by your own army, in your own country. We have witnessed this in Tulum, and it is by no means self-evident that a military convoy with mounted machine guns and soldiers at the ready produces a sense of security.

Not long before this piece appeared, Amnesty International published a report, *Women's Struggle for Safety and Justice: Violence in the Family in Mexico*.[25] It details the situation in two Mexican states and finds that in several instances the authorities failed to follow the measures and regulations required by Mexican law. In Mexico as a whole there has been a spike in all manner of killings, whether of government officials, drug traffickers, or less well-defined victims. The carnage has filled the press with stories (and lurid photographs) of murders, kidnappings, and torture.

We need to stress that Quintana Roo is *not* in the same category of violent places as some parts of northern Mexico, where killings are common and the military are deployed in force. Still, the sense of fear and uncertainty has important social consequences. For example, in the course of our interviews, a considerable number of female respondents explained that violence against women was common and growing and that it had lasting consequences. Many who talked about the situation claimed that the authorities showed little interest in the well-being of abused women or in other forms of everyday violence. Our point in discussing these responses and publications is to incorporate into our analysis a phenomenon that makes dynamic civic discourse difficult and undermines a people's confidence in society. In a recent public opinion survey of "satisfaction" with the way democracy works in some nations, Mexico is third from the bottom of the 18 Latin American countries polled.[26] In Quintana Roo it must be particularly difficult to be "satisfied" given that the former governor is serving a long drug-trafficking sentence in an American prison.[27]

Much of the "friction" in the system can be linked to major changes in Mexican politics—shall we say, changes in how power is exercised and who benefits from the political order. Situating Tulum and Quintana Roo in national political and economic context makes it far easier to understand why the people of this town respond in the manner described. Although many factors are involved, a critically important one is the result of a political reordering—from the top—of Mexican society. The Mexican political model, consolidated in the 1930s, survived with minor changes well into the 1990s. It was a particular kind of one-party state with the PRI (Institutional Revolutionary Party) acting as the vehicle for the state's social remodeling and modernization programs. Cooptation was more common than repression, and perhaps the guiding political principle was that every squeaky wheel merited some grease. The system concentrated authority and influence in the person and office of the president but limited it to a single six-year term. While it was not democracy in the liberal sense, this system did offer some benefits. Predictability was one, and it also made possible significant social and economic changes, including land reform, industrialization, and investment in education.

From the 1990s to the present Mexico has witnessed what some term a "democratic opening" that, together with greater options at the ballot box, has also permitted the dismantling of much of the state apparatus and a massive increase in the role and power of foreign and national capital. There was certainly ample corruption in the old PRI system, and typically it took the form of somewhat regulated bribery and considerable access to the public purse by well-situated politicians. As explained by John Gledhill, this form of enrichment has changed considerably:

> Mexican politicians appear to have become increasingly tied into the world of drug-trafficking and money laundering. The purchase of banks and currency exchange houses for the latter purpose ties in well with the "legitimate" activities that free trade policies have promoted, through the privatization of state enterprises and encouragement of investment in tourism, transport and consumerism.[28]

He notes that there are other phenomena that warrant concern, including the persistence of *caciquismo* (the power and influence of local political bosses), a model of capitalist development imposed by the global north, growing paramilitary violence, and the increasing militarization of national security. He also takes his anthropological colleagues to task for the little attention they pay to such developments; a critique that we believe is warranted.

Tourism and the Politics of Greed

In this subsection we discuss two related aspects of contemporary tourism: tourists' fantasies and their effects and the cultural, economic, and environmental consequences of the current model of tourism development. Tourists to Quintana Roo come chiefly from the developed West, many from the United States. The modern longing for the authentic—the "real thing"—is powerfully linked to international tourism, and the tourist industry meets such needs by producing or concocting appropriate objects or spaces of desire. In Quintana Roo two commodities are commonly "packaged" in this manner: the Maya archaeological heritage and the natural environment. With respect to archaeology, the result is sometimes a virtual disconnect between the average tourist and the places visited.

A *New York Times* piece on visitors to the ruins of Palenque in Chiapas captures the phenomenon in an extreme form: "On this solstice, the temples and tombs of Palenque were towers of Babel, with English, Spanish, Italian, German, Dutch, Japanese, and many other tongues spoken by travelers clutching Lonely Planet guides." For a considerable number of visitors the importance of Palenque is based on the perception that it is a "power place." As one visitor explains: "I'm here today because of the power of this place. This power could have been made by the Maya. Or it could have been here since the beginning of time."[29] Granted that there are plenty of serious visitors, a common attitude is to treat Maya sites as privileged playgrounds, more places of fantasy than historical monuments. Both economically and culturally our point is a serious one. The Tulum site is one of the most visited in Mexico. A large number of tourists visit Tulum, yet they leave remarkably little money in local pockets. Also, it is paradoxical that the Maya community, who used the site for religious purposes until they were expelled by the government in 1938, play no role in its management and receive no benefits from it.

The problem of limited economic benefit is a general one, and a key factor is the growth—one could say the dominance—of all-inclusive resort hotels along Mexico's Caribbean coast. This type of destination influences tourism as a whole, since a growing number of tourists experience the region as guests in such hotels. Clients are expected to select from an extensive list of activities, most within the confines of the resort, others in the form of guided visits to local sites and attractions. As one hotel website puts it: "So many choices . . . indulge." But "the wide variety of beach, land and water activities" that are advertised have minimal connection to local society. As for "the action of eco-adventure sports," one fears that the "eco" is more show than substance. This and comparable resorts (a term that has undergone a significant semantic shift) are designed to be self-contained beachfront complexes catering to a public that consumes fantasies of Otherness but that is hardly encouraged to engage in genuine cultural encounters. Guests may choose from a variety of themed restaurants within the compound or perhaps ponder the "Ultimate Wedding" package that can be arranged for just $2,650—minister and hair-stylist included. What seems to matter is a location of appropriate tropical splendor.

Interpreting phenomena of this type calls for some stepping back, some distancing, from the front stage of day-to-day tourist activity. As Dean MacCannell pointed out in his significantly titled book, *Empty Meeting Grounds*:

> In the name of tourism, capital and modernized peoples have been deployed to the most remote regions of the world, further than any army was ever sent. Institutions have been established to support this development, not just hotels, restaurants, and transportation systems, but restorations of ancient shrines, development of local handicrafts to sell to tourists, and rituals performed for tourists.

He proceeds to explain: "In short, tourism is not just an aggregate of merely commercial activities, it is also an ideological framing of history, nature, and tradition; a framing that has the power to reshape culture and nature to its needs."[30]

MacCannell was writing in the early 1990s, and it is interesting to see the degree to which much the same argument is used in a recent study of ecotourism, that privileged sphere of the hospitality business. Rosaleen Duffy in *A Trip Too Far* looks at the situation in Belize and addresses issues pertinent to both visitors and industry:

> Individual ecotourists are part of the process of ecotourism development, which brings economic, social, cultural, environmental and political transformations. This is because ecotourism relies on the same broader market structures as conventional tourism development. The question of profitability is central, because ecotourism is a blue-green strategy based on making conservation pay its way. This can directly undermine attempts to ensure that ecotourism is socially and politically acceptable, let alone beneficial.[31]

What Duffy suggests is that beneath an ecological veneer there can be more than a little "green greed," especially in societies and businesses that have recently opted for the "eco" label. For instance, one of the supposed benefits of ecotourism, compared to the conventional sort, is that it is meant to be culturally and socially aware, and too often this simply does not happen.

These circumstances and conditions are of particular relevance, because a prime attraction of Quintana Roo is the environment itself, and, as we have stressed, this environment is exceedingly fragile. The whole Yucatán peninsula can be conceptualized as a platform of carbonate and soluble rocks jutting into the Caribbean. There are no rivers and few natural lakes, and until a generation or so ago, *cenotes* (natural wells) were the major source of water for drinking and cooking. Topsoil is scant, and Maya subsistence was based on slash-and-burn agriculture, a system of land rotation that is ecologically sound only when the population is small and forest land plentiful.

Along the coast the environment is undergoing a series of massive alterations that are likely to make anything close to "sustainable development" unsustainable. We have a combination of urban development, infrastructure expansion, habitat loss and the increasing degradation and fragmentation of previously relatively undeveloped natural areas. These changes are ominous, because forest, mangrove, beach, and reef ecosystems are so closely interlinked. Rainfall rapidly makes its way through the porous rock to feed a series of underground streams and rivers, a veritable web of channels leading to the sea. All water, and much particulate matter, follows the same route, and no single pollutant causes more damage than nitrogen, highly concentrated in human and animal fecal matter. But every town dump, every golf course, every hotel, every landscaped area in an upscale development, causes environmental problems in the form of sewage and run-off. In one form or another, much of this ends up in the sea and in the process damages aquatic life.

If the danger is so clear, how should blame be apportioned for lack of foresight or limited concern? Undoubtedly, there can be no tourism without tourists, and it is eminently true that in the north-south interchange tourists and their predecessors have often behaved in ways that reflect a sense of privilege and entitlement. For example, Rosaleen Duffy cites a well-known Belizean environmentalist's opinion that many visitors come to "party and take drugs"; also, she takes note of "the heavily intertwined subjects of race and sex."[32] What we suggest is that in much of the developing world tourism of all sorts and kinds is implicated in new forms of domination that many tourists easily adjust to, because it all feels so "natural" to them. Inequality is certainly very much part of the picture in Quintana Roo. To use a recent example from a travel magazine, the Sian Ka'an Biosphere Reserve, whose main entrance is less than half an hour from Tulum, is described as an ideal location "where birds perch on mangrove roots and pumas roam the jungle beyond." Here is an eco complex "of modern buildings and tents with thatch roofs" where local workers cook for an on-site restaurant and "guide travelers on adventures." These eco-tourists might "have lunch with locals or volunteer to assist with a community education program,"[33] but they hardly live with locals, nor do locals run the show.

Much like the situation at Sian Ka'an, other "nature" destinations in Quintana Roo have geared up to attract an affluent, and largely foreign, clientele. One of these is Xel-Há, which a decade ago was little more than a large lagoon opening to the sea in a zone where salt water mixes with water from subterranean rivers. Facilities were limited, and many visitors brought their own lunch along with their diving equipment. Today it is a large operation with numerous attractions including beaches, restaurants, caves, forests, an "adventure cenote," and the now almost mandatory captive dolphins. It is operated by a private eco-park, and much of the advertising is in English. Visitors are urged to "explore the magic and adventure of nature at its fullest."[34] As Torres and Momsen write, this process of Disneyfication appropriates the area's pre-Hispanic heritage, while "the local environment [is] commoditized, reproduced, and packaged for global mass tourism consumption."[35]

If ecotourism often fails to live up to its gentler, kinder, expectations, the standard sea, sand, and sun product along the Riviera Maya north of Tulum poses serious environmental issues. Fundamentally, over the last decade the coast has undergone a massive buildup as resort complex after resort complex occupies the shore. Satellite photos show what looks like a coastline with a string of elongated emplacements. A sense of scale is provided by a recent advertisement in *The New York Times* for one of these hotels, part of a chain "known for its all-inclusive Unlimited Luxury vacations, which offer adults an extra measure of romance and sensuality in beautiful settings." The aerial view shows a very large structure between three and five stories high fronting a beach adorned with numerous large thatch parasols. The structure straddles the mangroves that mediate between land and sea.[36]

The ecological problem can be approached from two different but closely related levels. The first asks us to consider the use that is made of resources and has been well articulated by Alex S. MacClean: "When you're looking at using a limited resource [water] for purposes of golf in the middle of the desert, it raises questions about how resources, finite resources, are used and who gets to use them."[37] The allocation of the same limited resource is no less important in Quintana Roo and many other parts of Mexico. June Nash, who conducts much of her research in Chiapas, has studied how groundwater has been diverted to commercial enterprises including irrigation agriculture and beverage production. In her words, a "natural resource once considered a blessing for all people granted by the rain gods is now a contested commodity exacerbating the growing divide between classes." As she notes, the change has been drastic:

> The transformation of water from a deified resource to a commodified multibillion dollar industry reveals how public interest can be distorted by unregulated privatized expropriation. It is a morality tale that applies equally to other resources such as gold, silver, oil, and tin. Unlike these other resources, however, water has a human dimension; without water, humans cannot live.[38]

If the first issue involves resource allocation and its consequences, the second is more bluntly one of competition between human and non-human populations. The Galapagos can serve as a model. Much is at stake. In 1959 the Ecuadorian government established the Galapagos National Park. This highly protected zone comprised 97% of the land area of the islands. The remaining 3% included areas where human settlement dated back some time, and many of the residents were employed in administering the park. The 1959 partition has become increasingly problematic over the past decade. Much as in Quintana Roo, the number of tourists increased dramatically, and new hotels and other facilities were built to accommodate a wealthier class of visitor. Although the government had the authority to regulate the tourist flow, it was not feasible politically to set firm limits on the number of nationals wishing to resettle in what is, after all, an Ecuadorian province. The government is looking for a formula that may increase the allotted space for human habitation to perhaps 15% of land area. What stands out in the Galapagos case is the degree to which tourism can put indirect but substantial pressure on programs of protection, even in such a unique location. In short, it is particularly difficult for poor countries such as Ecuador and Mexico to restrict tourism, even indirectly, or limit the impact of human activities.[39]

Toward Environmental Consciousness

Much of this essay has been devoted to understanding how a previously unscarred land has felt the heavy hand of tourism. One might hope that the very process of environmental degradation would mobilize local people, perhaps even visitors. After all, what we are discussing is a straightforward matter: a once untrammeled place can simply be loved to death. There is evidence that mobilization along these lines can, in fact, take place. One of the most impressive displays of unity among environmentalists and advocates of social justice occurred at a hearing that coincided with our second field season in 2001. Two adjacent beaches that were major turtle hatcheries were slated for resort development, and the owners had already obtained the necessary permits. The meeting, organized by state environmental officials, was held in a large sports stadium. Forty-seven different groups attended, including representatives from hotels, labor unions, student groups, and an array of environmental and grassroots NGOs. The stadium was packed, and the audience was overwhelmingly in favor of keeping these beaches free of construction; also, these were the last beaches still open to local people. The debates and discussions were peppered with environmental key words such as "sustainability" and "biodiversity"; meanings, however, differed markedly. The most important outcome of the hearing was that in spite of testimony by hired biologists that the impact of the hotel complex would have a negligible effect on turtle reproduction, overwhelming evidence to the contrary, plus strong public support, won the day. Not long after the event, the licenses were revoked.

A theme that emerged during this debate—one that we had often heard before— was that nature itself was out of balance, or even "sick." Whether it was Maya farmers commenting on unreliable rainfall or fishermen discussing the decline in catches, the conception was very similar: something was awfully wrong. The environmental historian Carolyn Merchant, in "The Theoretical Structure of Ecological Revolutions,"[40] proposes a model that emphasizes the role of growing ecological contradictions and discontinuities in achieving environmental consciousness. This awareness does not happen all at once and is mediated and influenced by human culture and human activities. But mounting dissonance, she believes, can bring about a reordering of the relationship between societies and their environment. The model meshes well with the concept of "friction" we have used to discuss the complexity and the dissonance of the social world in and around Tulum. Most certainly, there is a sense that things can't go on as they are. Less clear is how to proceed to a better and more hopeful future.

In the Mexican context a major part of the problem has to do with issues of management and governance. As noted, the Mexican political system has undergone a shift from a centralized political order to one that must make room for other actors, other interests. Much of the pressure for this shift is external, and many Mexicans, disturbed by troubles at home and growing foreign influence, decry an erosion of national sovereignty.[41] These matters may appear far removed from tourism and ecology, but the link is direct and important. To understand this we need to recognize how radically the political landscape has changed, and not just in Mexico. In recent decades many Western societies have implemented policies to bring about a more collaborative approach to statecraft, one with room for NGOs, the private sector, and other entities. This shift is also reflected in United Nations initiatives, including several United Nations Environment Program summits.

The change is part of a broader ideological turn, one that stresses "responsibilizing" designated "stakeholders." This approach does not make government disappear, since "it is the state that takes it upon itself to define and grant legitimacy to a broad range of groups and associations and to establish rules according to which these entities may operate."[42] However, the ability to exercise a controlling role is influenced by a variety of factors. One of these is the power and authority of the state itself, what is often called its "legitimacy." In the case of Mexico few would argue that the prestige of the state has declined significantly since the 1990s, owing to numerous reasons, several of which we have mentioned. This decline is bound to erode confidence, and many of our interviews document how everyday life has deteriorated for reasons that range from insecurity to the rising cost of groceries. If the state has declined, the influence of the private sector has more than filled the vacuum.

This brings us to our final point. The new models of governance and participation mesh pretty well with life in the relatively affluent societies of the developed West. One does not have to make reference to "empowering" local actors at face value in order to recognize that a reasonably secure and reasonably educated public is likely to have time and incentive to become involved in local-level politics. For the same reasons, such people are well situated to critique the prevailing socioeconomic model. Perhaps the greatest loss that Mexico has suffered since it "opened up" is in the middle class, a demographic that had been growing since at least the 1920s but is now in considerable difficulties. Although this is not the only entity that makes for a good fit with environmental activism, it is certainly an important one.

There are lessons to be learned. The most hopeful and satisfying is that even in an environment so dominated by tourism interests it remains possible to bring people together when the last stretch of coast is about to be sold to developers. There is less to cheer about in the development plans, since both government and the private sector are pressing for more construction, more infrastructure. What is sorely needed is a strong and visible local environmental platform that does not depend on crisis situations or well-heeled foreign institutions.

Notes

1. The research for this paper was supported by grants from the Wenner-Gren Foundation for Anthropological Research (Research Grants #5618, # 6627, and #GR. ICRG-74) and several Faculty Research Grants from the University of Massachusetts at Amherst.

2. Clifford Geertz, "Life on the Edge," *New York Review of Books,* April 7, 1994, 3–4.

3. Ellen Kintz, *Life under the Tropical Canopy* (Fort Worth, TX: Holt, Reinhart and Winston, 1980, 80).

4. Guillermo Goñi, *De cómo los mayas perdieron Tulum* (México, DF: Instituto Nacional de Antropología e Historia, 1999). Text and photographs document how important foreign visitors were regularly escorted by armed Maya guides.

5. *VIII Censo General de Población* (Mexico, DF: Secretaría de Industría y Commercio, 1962, Table 5, p. 64; Table 39, p. 652). This population inhabited a space of 19,438 square miles, about twice the size of Maryland or New Hampshire.

6. Guillermo Bonfil Batalla, *México Profundo: Reclaiming a Civilization,* Philip A. Dennis, Tran. (Austin: University of Texas Press, 1996). See especially Chapters 8 and 9; *Democracy in Latin America* (New York: United Nations Development Program, Table 45, p. 127, Social Citizen: Inequality and Poverty, 2002).

7. This type of arrangement is discussed in the classic Maya ethnographies and also in much more recent studies. Robert Redfield, *The Village That Chose Progress* (Chicago: University of Chicago Press, 1962 [1950], 62–63); Alicia Re Cruz, *The Two Milpas of Chan Kom* (Albany: State University of New York Press, 1996).

8. The core problem was, and remains, poverty. The majority of the population in every one of Mexico's 100 poorest municipalities is indigenous, and most of these *municipios* are in the south of the country. "A Tale of Two Mexicos: North and South," *The Economist,* April 26, 2008, 53–54. Racism takes different forms in different places. In Mexico it is related to a national ideology of *mestizaje,* race mixture, that tends to view *indios* as backward. For extensive coverage of contemporary discourses on race in Latin America, see Anani Dzidzienyo and Suzanne Oboler, Eds., *Neither Enemies nor Friends: Latinos, Blacks, Afro-Latinos* (New York: Palgrave Macmillan, 2005).

9. Beth E. Notar, *Displacing Desire: Travel and Popular Culture in China* (Honolulu: University of Hawai'i Press, 2006); see especially Chapter 2, "Lonely Planeteers and a Transnational Authentic."

10. Stroma Cole, *Tourism, Culture and Development* (Clevedon: Channel View Publications, 2007, 44).

11. "Asia, Beware Benidorm." *The Economist,* May 17, 2008, 24; see also http://datatur.gob. mx/jsp/consulta.

12. This is not to deny that environmental tourism is a growing segment of the global market, and it does play a significant role in the Tulum area. Nevertheless, mass tourism and an ecological agenda are generally incompatible. Martin Mowforth and Ian Munt, *Tourism and Sustainability* (London: Routledge, 1998); see especially Chapter 4, "Tourism and Sustainability," and box 6.5 (p. 182), where some of our early work is discussed.

13. Alberto Pereira Corona, "El gran impacto del turismo de bajo impacto: El caso de Xcacel, Quintana Roo," in Johannes Maerk and Ian Boxill, Eds., *Turismo en el Caribe* (Mexico: Plaza y Valdés, 2000).

14. Deborah McLaren, *Rethinking Tourism and Ecotravel* (West Hartford, CT: Kumarian Press, 1998, 118).

15. Needless to say, the social consequences of building a major airport next to a peasant village are likely to be enormous. In all likelihood land for this project will be acquired through eminent domain. The airport is designed to supersede the one in Cancún for visitors to Tulum and the Riviera Maya.

16. In an extensive household survey of Tulum conducted by our Mexican colleagues, insecurity and vandalism topped the list of the town's perceived major problems. The next most important issue was abuse of drugs and alcohol.

260 ∞ Part V Development, Degradation, and Conflict

17. No doubt this situation reflects the growing importance of tourism and the fact that tourism is a transnational process. But Tulum is also home to long-established residents and retired people, not to mention people from the immediate region. The quotation is from Arjun Appadurai, *Modernity at Large: Cultural Dimensions of Globalization* (Minneapolis: University of Minnesota Press, 1996, 192).

18. Ana Lowenhaupt Tsing, *Friction* (Princeton, NJ: Princeton University Press, 2005, 3).

19. See, for example, David Manuel-Navarrete, "Challenges and Opportunities of Multi-Disciplinary Place-Based Research: The Case of the Maya Forest," *Environments: A Journal of Interdisciplinary Studies* 33:1 (2005, 215–29).

20. Much of this land, including Maya holdings, was held in *ejido* (communal) title and could not be disposed of as private property. Changes in the law—and in the Constitution—have allowed *ejidos* to operate not unlike real estate trusts.

21. Henry Geddes Gonzales, Oriol Pi-Sunyer, and R. Brooke Thomas, English-language version of *Reporte Tulum*, (Amherst, MA: 2005, 10).

22. *Programa Director de Desarrollo Urbano, 2001–2026* (H. Ayuntamiento Solidaridad and Gobierno del Estado de Quintana Roo, 2001). We are making reference to II Objectivos, pp. 22–23.

23. See Nancy Scheper-Hughes, *Death without Weeping: The Violence of Everyday Life in Brazil* (Berkeley and Los Angeles: University of California Press, 1993) and Stephen C. Lubkemann, *Culture in Chaos* (Chicago: Chicago University Press, 2008),

24. Alma Guillermoprieto, "Days of the Dead." *The New Yorker* (November 10, 2008, pp. 44–51).

25. Amnesty International, "Women's Struggle for Safety and Justice: Violence in the Family in Mexico," AI Index AMR/41/035/2008 (2008).

26. *Latinobarómetro*, October 11, 2008. Reported in *The Economist*, November 15, 2008, p. 46.

27. The ex-governor, Mario Villanueva Madrid, is reported to have been paid millions of dollars by drug cartels and allowed traffickers to hide some 200 tons of cocaine in Cancún. James C. McKinley, Jr., "Mexico Moves to Send Ex-Governor to U.S. on Drug Charges." *The New York Times*, June 22, 2007, p. A6.

28. John Gledhill, *Power and Its Disguises: Anthropological Perspectives on Politics*, (Sidmouth: Pluto Press, 2000, 116).

29. Tim Weiner, "Palenque Journal," *The New York Times*, December 23, 2002, p. A4.

30. Dean MacCannell, *Empty Meeting Grounds* (New York: Routledge, 1992, 1).

31. Rosaleen Duffy, *A Trip Too Far* (London: Earthscan Publications, 2002, 47).

32. Ibid.

33. Stephen Regenold, "Travel Goes Green," *World Traveler*, November 2008, pp. 57–59.

34. This material is taken from an undated (ca. 2007) glossy brochure, *Xel-Há, Siente la Naturaleza, Feel Nature*. No publisher listed.

35. Patricia Maria Torres and Janet D. Momsen, "Gringolandia: The Construction of a New Tourist Space in Mexico," *Annals of the Association of American Geographers* 95:2 (2005, 314–35, quote from p. 323).

36. Material (text and photograph) taken from "Escape to the Caribbean and Bermuda," special advertising supplement, *The New York Times*, December 9, 2008, p. ZS1.

37. Paul Gleason, "Montage," *Harvard Magazine*, January-February 2009, pp. 17–23, McLean quotation p.18. See also Alex S. McLean, *Over: The American Landscape at the Tipping Point* (New York: Abrams, 2008).

38. June Nash, "Consuming Interests: Water, Rum, and Coca-Cola from Ritual Propitiation to Corporate Expropriation in Highland Chiapas," *Cultural Anthropology* 22:4 (2007, 621–22).

39. Paul D. Stewart et. al., *Galápagos: The Islands That Changed the World* (New Haven, CT: Yale University Press, 1980).

40. Carolyn Merchant, "The Theoretical Structure of Ecological Evolutions," *Environmental Review* 11:4 (1987).

41. As recently as the 1960s the Mexican Constitution declared: "Under no circumstances may foreigners acquire direct ownership of lands or waters within a zone of 100 km along the frontiers and 50 km along the shores of the country." Gerald E. Fitzgerald, *The Constitutions of Latin America* (Chicago: Gateway Press, 1968, 152).

42. Oriol Pi-Sunyer, "The Anatomy of Conflict in a Catalan Maritime Community," in J. B. Aceves, E. C. Hansen, and G. Levitas, Eds., *Economic Transformation and Steady-State Values: Essays in the Ethnodgraphy of Spain* (Flushing, NY: Queen's College Press, 1976, 66).

CHAPTER 11

Mexico's Second Institutionalized Revolution: Origins and Impacts of the Chiapas Declarations

David Stea, Camilo Perez Bustillo, Betse Davies, and Silvia Elguea

SECTION I: The End of the Millennium

Prologue: Observations of a Human Rights Observer in Chiapas
(Camilo Perez Bustillo)

I traveled to Chiapas as a human rights observer for the National Lawyers' Guild on five occasions in the two years after the Zapatista uprising began in January 1994 (January 21–23 and August 23–28, 1994; March 7–9, 1995; and April and July/August 1996). During these trips, my colleagues and I visited four of the six highlands towns seized by the Zapatista Army of National Liberation (Ejército Zapatista de Liberación Nacional or EZLN), earlier the same month (San Cristóbal, Ocosingo, Oxchuc, and Huixtán), interviewed eyewitnesses of combat in Ocosingo's marketplace, and visited sites of combat along the highway outside San Cristóbal near Rancho Nuevo military base, including the site of an apparent mass grave in the forest near the base. I also participated in the first Mission Civil de Información (Citizen's Information Mission) organized by Bishop Samuel Ruiz as part of his mediation role at the head of CONAI, the nongovernmental mediation body in the on-again, off-again negotiation process between the government and EZLN. This trip took place following the government's February 8–9, 1995, military offensive (the first military offensive since the January 12, 1994, cease-fire). Finally, I attended the "Intercontinental Encounter for Humanity" held in Zapatista territory between July 27 and August 3, 1996.

The EZLN uprising and the Mexican military's counteroffensive campaigns in 1994 and 1995 displaced thousands of indigenous and mestizo peasants and deeply divided communities. Most of the territory that had been under EZLN control since the January 1994 uprising was retaken in the February 1995 offensive, driving the EZLN leadership and thousands of its unarmed supporters even deeper into the

Lacandon jungle and up against the Guatemalan border. The Mexican military offensive was matched by a military buildup on the Guatemalan side of the border, with the evident intent of catching EZLN in between. Thousands of indigenous and mestizo peasants who had fled Zapatista territory during the initial January 1994 military offensive (with its indiscriminate bombardment of civilian populations) were escorted back to their communities by the military's advance in February 1995.[1]

The most significant impact of the military's occupation was fear—terrorizing everyone, especially the women and children. The main complaints about the soldiers, beside the generalized fear they engendered, was that they were disrespectful, failing to ask permission for things they took, entering into and ransacking houses at will, "grabbing what they want." Other complaints included rifle barrels being jammed under people's doors, soldiers taking villagers' chickens, other soldiers taking photographs. Those taking photos of suspected Zapatistas warned that still more soldiers would arrive the next day and would make things unpleasant for them, causing more people to flee.

But for some, such experiences only strengthened their convictions and desire to resist. Many refugees identified themselves as supporters of the center-left Party of the Democratic Revolution (PRD) and found EZLN better to work with than the state or federal governments. Other refugees were members of the Indigenous People's Organization of Sierra Madre of Motozintla (ISAAM), who reported that EZLN—by contrast with some "outside" religious groups—"respected the traditional authorities in our community." These refugees' concern was that those being resettled by the Army "want to take our lands back."

The Monte Flor *ejido* (collective farm) members asked us to be their spokespersons "to Mexico and to the world . . . and to Bishop Ruiz," and each person present signed a formally sealed petition that a human rights observer mission be permanently established in the community (Monte Flor) to assure its safety if and when the Army came. Without revealing the communities' identities, we raised an issue that communities had raised: a pattern of reprisals by the Army against communities of political refuge and of human rights violations in the region. We raised this issue with Bishop Ruiz and members of CONAI in the form of a private, detailed briefing about the situation in Monte Flor and its neighboring communities, and gave them the original signed copy of Monte Flor's petition that a civilian encampment be established there.

Before the promised peace camp could be installed, however, the Army occupied the Monte Flor sector. By August 1995 there were 800 troops around Monte Flor, another 1,500 in nearby Flor de Café, and 2,000 still in Amatitlán—but troops had finally left Maravilla Tenejapa.[2] This meant a ratio of about five soldiers per resident in Flor de Café. The average ratio in the rest of Chiapas was one soldier for every three inhabitants, a total of between 36,000 and 40,500 troops concentrated among 37 communities. As of April 1996 a peace camp of observers from nongovernmental groups (both Mexican and foreign) had been established there, and the community was at least no longer alone in its fears and hopes.

Why did the uprising in the Chiapas region of Mexico—which began on New Year's Day, 1994—receive so much attention in world media? It was significant for several reasons:

1. It was the first major indigenous uprising in the Western Hemisphere since the collapse of the socialist states of Eastern Europe.

2. The Zapatista uprising began the day the North American Free Trade Agreement (NAFTA) took effect—it explicitly targeted the structural readjustment policies represented in neoliberal economics, in the form of "free trade" agreements.

3. The uprising was intimately linked to environmental degradation throughout the forested regions of Chiapas, especially in the Lacandon Biosphere Reserve.

4. Unlike most other Latin American struggles, this revolt was bottom-up rather than top-down—not a cause looking for a constituency, but a constituency that had found its cause.

5. The revolt espoused no traditional ideology. The discourse of the movement in its communiqués and public statements was unusually creative and literary in character, with pronounced indigenous content.

6. It was the first "online" revolution, linking EZLN with support networks around the globe.[3]

7. It was not just another uprising in a poor country beset by turmoil. Mexico is one of the wealthier and more developed members of what was once called Third World and until 1994 had been marked by incredible political stability with uninterrupted rule by a single party (the Institutional Revolutionary Party, or PRI) since 1929.

8. It was the first in a series of social tremors shaking Mexico's self-image of placidity and stability, ushering in a period of unprecedented violence and socioeconomic upheaval. Newly elected President Ernesto Zedillo used the Chiapas conflict as a scapegoat for Mexico's catastrophic economic collapse of December 1994—a collapse precipitated primarily by the rapid, ill-considered, and badly planned "neoliberal" restructuring set into motion during the previous administration of President Carlos Salinas de Gortari.

This chapter places the Chiapas revolt in broader context, examining the origins of human and environmental crises in Chiapas, the historical patterns of abuses, and the cumulative effect of these problems.

Neoliberalism, Indigenous Peoples, and the Environment

The proportions of urbanized population in the United States and Mexico are virtually identical, about 75%. Yet, although less than 1% of Americans are engaged in agriculture, almost 20% of Mexicans are so employed. In Mexico few rural farmers represent agribusiness: most mestizos and indigenous people eke out an existence by producing a combination of subsistence and market crops.

Confronted with the post–Cold War world and new hemispheric orders, Mexico has not fared well. After a half-century of import substitution policies, once well-protected domestic industries are now unable to compete in the neoliberal free market spawned in North America by NAFTA and globally by the World Trade Organization (WTO; GATT's successor). Devaluation and inflation severely diminished the purchasing power of Mexican workers in the mid-1990s, while millions lost their jobs. The shrinking Mexican middle class provides few customers for the products of the growing number of multinationals in Mexico, companies that increasingly produce only for export, fueling fears that all Mexico may become a huge maquiladora.

The negative impacts of structural readjustment (galloping privatization and deci-mated public spending) have been heaviest in the poorest areas of Mexico—areas with the greatest indigenous population. Mexico has the largest indigenous popu-lation in Latin America: up to 40% of the 40 million or more indigenous peoples who live in the Americas, depending on who's counting, and how. Who is considered indigenous depends on governmental definition. Despite Mexico's public veneration of ancient indigenous peoples, Mexico does not see itself as a pluralist country and does not value its living indigenes. The government has found it disturbingly easy to blame the devastation of the Chiapaneco tropical forest on the Mayans rather than on cattle ranching, commercial forestry, large-scale hydroelectric projects, and extractive industries such as mining and petroleum.[4] Environmental issues are of relatively low official priority in Mexico, despite the fact that its capital city boasts some of the world's worst air quality and significant increases in amebic dysentery (caused principally by polluted water) and infections.[5]

The Mexican government claims to have some of the toughest environmental laws in the world. President Carlos Salinas de Gortari (1988–94) received the 1991 Earth Prize, jointly conferred by the Nobel family and the United Nations for outstand-ing environmental statesmanship. Mexico was the first country to ratify the Vienna Convention and Montreal Protocol agreements for the protection of the ozone layer and, at the 1992 Earth Summit, was a signatory to the Treaties on Climate Change and Biological Diversity. Mexico has also claimed considerable success in its wildlife programs, including the protection of marine turtles (of the world's seven species of marine turtles, six nest on Mexico's beaches),[6] creation of breeding sanctuaries for gray whales, reduction of dolphin mortality in tuna fishing, and establishment of world-renowned monarch butterfly reserves.

Despite these initiatives, however, Mexico tends to ignore its environmen-tal laws. The forest cover of the Reserva de la Biosfera de la Mariposa Monarca has been reduced some 40% by incursions of local farmers.[7] The Secretaría del Medio Ambiente, Recursos Naturales y Pesca (Secretariat of Environment, Natural Resources, and Fisheries) gave Mexico the dubious distinction of having the highest rate of deforestation in the world.[8] More than 50% of Mexico's largely coniferous northern temperate forests are gone, and 95% of its tropical rain forests especially montane forests, many once covering large portions of Chiapas, no longer exist. Wetlands have been lost; most notably, the mangroves of Tabasco, Veracruz, and Chiapas, seriously damaging a once-thriving fishing industry.[9]

Chiapas: The Place, the People, and the Problems

Chiapas, the southernmost and most biodiverse of Mexico's states, is culturally and ecologically a part of Central America. The predominant cultural groups are Mayan-speaking Mayans, many communities contiguous with those of Guatemala. The highland and lowland flora and fauna, including the rain forests, are mainly tropical. The Mexican Republic, with 12 of the world's 14 ecosystems, is fourth among the countries of the globe in the number of species within its frontiers, first or second in the number of species per square kilometer of land area, and the most ecologically diverse area in the world that borders on an industrialized nation.[10]

The highest density of plant and animal species in Chiapas is found in the Lacandon rain forest, in and around which are located a large portion of Chiapas's highland Mayan communities. Part of a rainforest that once extended continuously from Campeche and the Yucatán to the Gran Peten of Guatemala, the Lacandon originally constituted more than 20% of Chiapas, over 5,000 square miles in extent. About 70% of the Mexican Lacandon has been destroyed since 1950 by highway construction, timber harvesting, oil drilling, cattle grazing, export-oriented agriculture, population resettlement projects, and, most recently, plowing airstrips for illegal drug and arms traffic.

In addition to its rich biodiversity, Chiapas is rich in energy resources. Accounting for less than 1/25 of Mexico's land area, Chiapas receives more than 10% of the nation's rainfall and generates some 45% of Mexico's hydroelectric resources and overlays or is adjacent to a large portion of Mexico's oil reserves, from which Mexico's national petroleum company extracts 92,000 barrels of oil and 516 million cubic feet of natural gas daily. Although environmental conservation efforts in Chiapas have thus far been limited largely to the Lacandon rain forest, Mexico and its Central American neighbors have hatched a grand—but as of 1996, largely unrealized—scheme for eco-cultural tourism called La Ruta Maya. Its business counterpart, El Mundo Maya, much less environmentally concerned, promotes other forms of tourism, together with neoliberal economic development.[11]

Chiapas is also Mexico's most culturally diverse region. Between one-third and one-half of the indigenous languages of Mexico are spoken here. Many of Chiapas's 3.2 million people are immigrants (many of whom are mixed-race mestizos). Of the remaining population, the one-third who are indigenous Maya are concentrated in the state's two poorest regions, Los Altos and the Lacandon. They were for many years the "forgotten people" of Chiapas, bypassed by national land reform policies and subject to the whims of large landowners. The ranks of the Zapatista Army of National Liberation (EZLN) are composed primarily of those who now dwell in and around the Lacandon: the Tzotzil, Tzeltal, Chol, Tojolabal, Mam, and Zoque Mayans. Not all of these groups are indigenous to the area. Many Chol arrived from Palenque; some Tzotziles are from Chamula; others were driven out of their traditional villages when they converted to evangelical Protestantism. Many other present-day Lacandones are the descendants of Mayan rebels from Campeche and Yucatán who arrived in the second half of the 19th century.[12]

Refugees, notably Mayans from Guatemala, also are a significant force in the social and environmental landscape. According to nongovernmental agencies, some 45,000 Guatemalan refugees have established residency in Mexico (not all in Chiapas), fleeing a series of repressive governments (backed by the United States) and genocidal acts.[13] They are denied permanent asylum, and their Mexican-born children are refused citizenship. The more than 20,000 Guatemalan refugees in Chiapas were less concerned with future-oriented sustainable agriculture and forestry practices than with feeding themselves, toward which end they cleared even more of the Lacandon forest.[14] After a failed effort to improve conditions in Chiapas in 1983, the Mexican government responded to an incursion by the Guatemalan military with tightened security, abandoning efforts at environmental protection and reduced conflict. A "strategic highway" almost 450 km long was cut through the Lacandon forest, also opening the area to oil exploration and eventually hydroelectric dams[15]—thus facilitating additional immigration into the state.

Chiapas has the highest illiteracy rate (30–50%) in Mexico, and many residents, particularly women, are monolingual (speak little or no Spanish).[16] Wages in the mid-1990s were one-third the national average,[17] and a large number of working Mayans receive no wages at all. Small-scale coffee and corn farmers were decimated by falling prices and competition from U.S. growers under NAFTA. Chiapas also has the highest death rates in Mexico, it has an infant mortality rate at least twice the national average and the highest maternal mortality rate in the nation. One-third of adult deaths are due to curable infectious diseases.

In a sense Chiapas has been operated as an internal colony. With 4% of Mexico's land area and population, Chiapas is the source of 20% of national income. Although the state generates nearly one-half of Mexico's energy, 63–70% of its homes have no electricity and 70–90% have no access to potable water (accounting in part for the high number of infant deaths due to dysentery). Chiapas produces nearly one-third of Mexico's meat supply, but 90% of indigenes rarely eat meat. In the past, protein needs were partially met through a subsistence diet of corn, beans, and squash.[18]

Health conditions reflect chronic problems with food security as well as an inadequate health care delivery system. In turn these problems derive from inequitable and insecure land tenure. The Constitution of 1917 initiated, through Article 27, a program of land redistribution establishing a system of collective farms called *ejidos*. This land redistribution program was never completed, but where land reform has occurred, it proved to be a mixed blessing, since much of western Chiapas was in the hands of ranchers and other large-scale landowners and the only land available to settle claims was in the forested eastern part of the state. In 1992 the much-publicized "reform" to Article 27 of the Constitution of 1917 actually brought an end to land reform, ending redistribution and, for the most part, collective ownership.[19] The government replaced large landowners as the hated enemy by taking over their role in three ways.

First, the state came to act as a self-interested proprietor of national lands rather than as a facilitator of peasant needs. Locals saw the creation and administration of biosphere reserves as completely arbitrary. Local populations were involved neither in decision making concerning these reserves nor in their subsequent management. Bioreserves were deemed off-limits to peasants, exacerbating the pressures on remaining lands. Second, by rewarding peasants loyal to the ruling party, the government set peasants against peasants, just as landlords had once done.[20] Finally, the government played a significant role in the demise of sustainable agricultural practice. Before 1982 the male members of many Chiapaneco families had become accustomed to spending time elsewhere as laborers in the public sector. After 1982, when the government slashed employment, many Chiapaneco families faced severe hardships, while others who lived near the Pan American highway were able to find non-farm work that enabled them to purchase herbicides and artificial fertilizers. As a result, in some areas preexisting systems of sustainable agriculture simply disappeared as the poorer families became even worse off and often had to rent their *ejido* plots to their richer neighbors.

The Zapatista Uprising[21]

The origins of the Zapatista rebellion predate the 20th century. The Yucatán peninsula and Chiapas have been the site of chronic warfare since at least the early 18th century.[22] However, the recent environmental crises that catalyzed the Zapatista rebellion are rooted in two phenomena stemming from suburbanization in the post–World War II United States: the housing boom and demand for furniture increased demand for tropical hardwoods, and the growing fast-food industry increased demand for cheap beef.

These pressures encouraged the informal invasion of the Lacandon even before governmental decrees of 1957 and 1960 officially opened the area to colonization. In 1972 the government announced grand plans for development of Mexico's northern and southern frontiers, subsequently "giving" almost two-thirds of a million hectares of the forest to the indigenous heads of 66 local families, its supposed "original owners," expelling thousands of Tzeltal and Chol settlers. Shortly thereafter these new large-scale landowners signed long-term contracts giving widespread timber-cutting rights to concessionaires such as the Castellanos Dominguez family. In an extraordinary about-face, Echeverria then canceled most private contracts, turning over forestry rights to a quasi-governmental logging corporation. The evicted settlers, under the leadership of priests and volunteer laity sent by Bishop Samuel Ruiz, began to organize in the Lacandon. A guerrilla organization called Las Fuerzas Populares de la Liberación Nacional, formed in Ocosingo, was effectively destroyed by federal troops in 1974. But the torch had been lit.

In 1978 the government created the Montes Azules Biosphere Reserve, carving 1,250 square miles out of the heart of the Lacandon forest without consultation with the Mexican public. *Ejidatarios* in the cañadas bordering the reserve, prevented for a time from expanding *ejido* lands into the forest, soon learned to move the boundary posts when no one was looking. As few funds had been allocated to patrolling the area, nocturnal boundary shifting posed no great problem. Then in the Mexican economic malaise of the 1980s the southern states slipped into invisibility and even greater poverty. The pace of deforestation increased. Cattle ranchers in Chiapas continued to expand into forest lands earlier cleared for farming by neighboring Mayans who were forced to move onto increasingly steep, less fertile, and more erosion-prone mountain slopes. At the beginning of the decade, just 19 families controlled more than 70,000 sq km of Chiapas's best land. General Absalón Castellanos, who was appointed governor of the state in 1982, worsened the cultural and environmental damage by cheating indigenous farmers out of their land, diverting public funds to enrich his own family, and encouraging lumbering in the Lacandon forest. Selected to deal with Guatemalan refugees fleeing the genocidal regime of Efrain Rios Montt, he allowed many well-documented acts of terrorism—torture, murder, and "disappearances."

Meanwhile a resistance force was beginning to organize in the inner reaches of the Lacandon, aided by groups of volunteers from northern Mexico. In August 1989 newly inaugurated President Carlos Salinas de Gortari, in a symbolic act designed as much as anything to reduce more than a century of hostility between Guatemala and Mexico, embraced Guatemalan President Vinicio Cerezo on the Suchiate bridge connecting the two countries. The occasion was the signing of a cooperative agreement on the management of borderlands, environmental planning, and the possible establishment of international parks called La Ruta Maya. It was intended to call attention to Mexican efforts at cultural and environmental preservation in the southern states of Yucatán, Quintana Roo, Tabasco, and Chiapas. The business community, beginning to recognize the tourist potential of areas away from Mexico's traditional beach resorts, organized their counterpart organization, El Mundo Maya. The existing beach resorts in Yucatán and Quintana Roo had employed Mayan labor only at the lowest levels: nothing different was anticipated for the new developments.

Not long thereafter then-U.S. President George H. W. Bush expanded his promotion of "the new hemispheric order" to include what has come to be called the North American Free Trade Agreement (NAFTA) or, in Mexico, Tratado de Libre

Comercio (TLC). He persuaded President Salinas de Gortari to support the idea, which, because of its "fast-track" provisions, would mean initiating radical structural readjustment in Mexico in an incredibly short period of time.[23]

Armed uprising was only one point in a broad spectrum of struggles aimed at fashioning sustainable survival. Mayan community groups initiated, organized, staffed, and implemented a variety of sustainability projects. Small-scale Mayan forestry cooperatives, by processing lumber on site, reduced the damage normally caused by extensive road construction. Small local factories then make the finished lumber into furniture. Other sustainability projects modified indigenous agricultural practices, combined subsistence and cash cropping, and encouraged animal husbandry and small-game hunting. Some coffee growers have turned to producing and exporting organically grown and processed coffee.[24]

Several nongovernmental organizations are now cooperating closely with one another as members of the Consorcio para la Conservación y el Desarrollo Sostenible del Sureste de México (Consortium for the Conservation and Sustainable Development of the Southeast of Mexico) and with the Mayan communities. These include Centro de Estudios para la Conservación de los Recursos Naturales (Center of Studies for the Conservation of Natural Resources), Centro de Investigaciones en Salud de Comitán (Center of Studies in the Health of Comitan), and Programa de Colaboración en Medicina Tradicional Herbolaria (Program of Collaboration in Traditional Herbal Medicine). Programs include managing and conserving natural resources in the most biodiverse region of the Republic; educating communities about the environment; protecting migratory birds; engaging in reforestation; providing agricultural, reproductive, and psychosocial healthcare; and identifying and classifying Mayan traditional herbal and medical knowledge for non-indigenes. Traditional Mayan forest management practices are more efficient and have a smaller ecological impact than do conventional ones. Moreover, some Mayan initiatives in the sustainable, commercial production of organic crops have the kind of bottom-up administration that the Zapatistas also instituted.

Neither the Mexican government nor local caciques and cattle ranchers looked very favorably on these initiatives, and the government has used the National Solidarity Program to assert control over local resource allocation. In some cases cooperatives found their water cut off or their food, tools, medicines, and documents proving their land title destroyed by the army.[25]

At the end of 1992 the newly formed EZLN decided to go to war. On May 22, 1993, the army clashed with the Zapatistas, then withdrew four days later. In December rumors reached the Zapatistas that the army was ready to strike again, with the excuse of eliminating drug traffickers in the area. Neither unexpected nor welcome, this news probably contributed to the decision to rise up in force on January 1, 1993, the day NAFTA was to take effect. In the one-and-a-half weeks that followed between 150 (official estimate) and 500 people (based on reliable, unofficial sources) died. The 10 days of war in Chiapas made the front pages of newspapers around the world and shook the official image of calm, passive, serene, obedient Mexico.

Initially there appeared to be considerable public support for the Zapatistas in Mexico as a whole. Many saw the Zapatista movement as a national call for social justice. A string of assassinations that began in March 1994 reduced EZLN visibility, however, and the devaluation of the peso in December 1993 undermined public support. The incoming president, Ernesto Zedillo, accused the Zapatistas of driving away foreign investment and thus causing Mexico's economic collapse. The

Zapatistas chose to demonstrate how little the army controlled the Lacandon by seizing 38 municipalities in December 1994, and then they melted back into the forest. In January 1995 Zedillo moved military forces into the areas of the Lacandon forest openly controlled by EZLN since the January 1994 uprising and then withdrew the troops in mid-February.

During this brief period between 20,000 and 30,000 peasants and indigenous Chiapanecos withdrew into the forest, putting further pressure on the battle-scarred Lacandon to provide them with firewood and land for cultivation. The environment appears to have been a prime victim of this undeclared war, despite the fact that the government seemed to have reached the beginnings of an accord with EZLN in early 1996.

Epilogue to the First Two Zapatista Years

Prolonged and often-interrupted dialogue between the Mexican government and EZLN resulted, on February 13, 1996, in the signing of accords on indigenous rights and culture. Yet these accords represented only one aspect of the Zapatistas' call for reform, which consistently links human rights to questions of environmental justice.[26] By contrast the Mexican government confronted by the country's worst economic crisis in half a century, has deprioritized environmental issues and social justice. As of late September 1996 no further substantive agreements had been reached, and even the February accords have not been translated into binding Mexican law as promised. EZLN's greatest success during the last half of the decade of the 1990s has been to turn the deadlocked peace talks into an ongoing national seminar bringing together the best and brightest of Mexico's "civil society." It has also organized and utilized input from hundreds of grassroots Comités Civiles de Diálogo (Citizen's Committees for Dialogue) and sponsored a successful series of regional gatherings around the world. The latter effort culminated in the first Intercontinental Congress for Humanity and Against Neo-Liberalism held in five different Zapatista communities between July 27 and August 3, 1996, with more than 3,000 attendees from 43 countries.

Sixteen "presumed" Zapatistas continued to be imprisoned, with 7 sentenced to prison terms of 6 years and 9 months as of August 1996. The appointment of military commanders in charge of "public security" in 19 of Mexico's 33 political entities in response to the June 28, 1996, emergence in Guerrero State of a new armed revolutionary insurgent group known as the People's Revolutionary Army (EPR) indicates a return to a hard-line approach. EZLN unilaterally suspended peace talks on September 4, 1996, an action precipitated by divisions within the ruling party that undercut the government's willingness to negotiate, the EPR's emergence, and the continuing militarization of Chiapas. Because U.S. funds for the Mexican military's campaign against drug trafficking can also be used in counterinsurgency efforts, the popular impression is that in the late 1990s, more than ever, U.S. tax dollars are buying death and repression for Mexico's popular movements and organizations.

SECTION II: View from the 21st Century

Prologue: Incidents of Travel in Zapatista (Betse Davies)

On July 16, 2007, I arrived in the new airport in Tuxtla Gutiérrez, the capital of Chiapas, and was whisked to San Cristóbal de las Casas on a brand new highway in a new and pricey airport cab. I suspected that this highway was created to move armed forces at a moment's notice. This was my second visit to San Cristóbal; my first was as a tourist several years earlier. The city was exactly the same—completely charming and full of European tourists. But now I was to experience the struggle for power between the government and the indigenous peoples—the world of which the average tourist knows nothing. I was part of an 11-member delegation under the umbrella of the Marin Interfaith Task Force. Our purpose was to learn about the government's current effort to retake the land that the Zapatistas seized in 1994 and to attend the opening of the Intergalactic Meeting between the Zapatistas and the World. We attended three meetings in San Cristóbal. The first stop was the campus of the Centro Indígena de Capacitación Integral Fray Bartolomé de las Casas (CIDECI). For almost 20 years CIDECI has worked to open autonomous training spaces for young indigenous people. The short-term goal is to provide career opportunities; the broader objective to create a new Chiapas. Labeled subversive and forced to move out of San Cristóbal, the organization bought land outside of town and began building the campus in 2004. There are spartan dormitories and areas set aside for technical training, food preparation, and agriculture. Water pumped from wells and a generator make the campus independent of government-provided supplies.

Our next visit was to Servicio Internacional Para la Paz, or International Service for Peace (SIPAZ), an international observation program created after the Zapatista uprising in 1994 to monitor the conflict in Chiapas. We met four of the young staff members and the priest who works with them. The latter is constantly being criticized by his superiors for his active liberal stance, but because he is so popular with the Catholics in the rural areas, he is not removed from his post. Inside their modest office, the staff described Chiapas as a state rich in natural resources, such as oil and timber, with great inequality and extreme poverty. They described politically divided communities whose divisions partially resulted from the government's "divide and conquer" strategy.

Finally, we visited Centro de Investigaciones Económicas y Políticas de Acción Comunitaria (CIEPAC, or Center of Economic and Political Research for Community Action), which produces educational materials and provides economic and political information and analysis for grassroots communities and popular movements in Chiapas. Miguel Pickard, the dynamic and knowledgeable director, laid out the recent history of the Zapatistas for us. In 2003 they transformed their scattered communities into five *caracoles*, or "snail shells," so named because they spiral inward and because of the use of a shell to call meetings. This move returned power and authority from EZLN to its civilian base.

When the conservative Felipe Calderón became president in 2006, repression of popular movements increased significantly, society became increasingly militarized, and even rape was used as a tool of control. As peaceful protest was suppressed, more armed groups began to emerge. The left is divided and demoralized. Even Pickard had received death threats. In his view it was unclear where the Zapatistas or the left in general should turn and what the future might hold. The next day we drove into the mountains, green with tropical foliage that obscured the scattered communities, to the Caracol of Morelia headquarters to request permission from the Zapatista authorities to visit the autonomous Zapatista municipality of Olga Isabel. We warily surrendered our passports at the gate—we were, after all, entering an area controlled by a different government—and waited for permission to enter. Then we waited for hours under a tree for the Junta de Buen Gobierno (Good Government juntas; the local Mexican authorities are the "bad government") of this *caracol* to receive us. In our short meeting with the three men and three women of the Junta, we heard about their history and the struggles they still face as they try to hold on to the lands they recaptured from surrounding haciendas. Although the government is trying to provoke confrontations among indigenous political communities, they have vowed not to give up. Tanja, our guide, explained that in an effort to control corruption, Junta officers move from one position to another at least once a month. Unfortunately, these constant transfers mean that they bring little experience to each new position.

Eventually, our passports were returned to us and we received our visas to visit Olga Isabel. We talked first to two health promoters and saw the meager supply of drugs available for the people within 5 miles of the town, all of whom can get medical care here. The healthcare workers do not charge for consultations at the clinic but do charge a bit for medicine. They emphasize preventative measures: boiling water, sterilizing it with chlorine, using a latrine, eliminating garbage, emptying puddles where insects can breed, and fencing off animals.

We also visited two communities in which the *abeja*—the bee—philosophy of peace prevailed. This philosophy has its roots in a 1992 land conflict with PRIistas (members of the Partido Revolucionario Institucional), who are still in power in Chiapas. Conflict between the PRIistas and the locals left one of the PRI leaders dead and led to the government's arrest of five locals without an investigation. The community organized and marched on San Cristóbal to demand that these men be freed. Initially nameless, the marchers eventually settled on *las abejas*, because bees have a queen, produce honey, look for flowers and water, and always come back to the hive. "We also work like this," the director told us. Through the march, pilgrimage, and prayer, they were able to gain the men's freedom, and the civil society organization Las Abejas was born. Although the paramilitary troops who perpetrated the conflict are still at large, the Bees are determined to continue in peaceful struggle and refuse to use arms. They have asked the government to demilitarize the area, but the government has not done so. Both military and paramilitary groups come through here on a daily basis. The group gains strength from the thousands of visitors to the community.

Both the communities that we visited have suffered tragedies. The brutal massacre at Acteal in 1997 was the most devastating: 45 women, children, and older men were killed while the younger men were working in the fields. The attackers ripped unborn babies from the wombs of four of the women and hacked the fetuses to death. Today at Acteal photos, crosses, murals, and paintings in the underground room built over the graves of the 45 memorialize their lives. Every year since the massacre the community commemorates the terrible event on December 22. The year 2007 marked the 10th anniversary of the massacre and also the 15th anniversary of the founding of Las Abejas. The president of the board of directors of Las Abejas invited us to return for that ceremony.

This encounter was a powerful experience for me. What would we *Norteamericanos* do if we faced a situation like this? The determination of this group to persevere is something to admire and support. Next we went to Nuevo Paraiso (New Paradise), now home to 13 families with 120 people. This group of Abejas had been displaced from their own farmlands. With the help of a French church group, they were able to buy 8.5 hectares of land for a new village in April 2007. They are fortunate to have a natural leader in their midst. Manuel guided the conversation and translated other community members' stories from their native Tzotzil into Spanish. First he coaxed the story out of the men, and then barefoot women surrounded by babies and tiny children and wearing traditional dress took their turn. It was obviously painful for the community members to recall their difficult history: two of the men sobbed as they spoke. Early on the community joined the peaceful Las Abejas when the latter faced arrest on undisclosed charges. The Abejas weren't guilty, but they were afraid. Then Juan Jiménez, an outsider, came into the area and began to extort payment from the families. His thugs somehow worked with the police, so the community members had no recourse. At first the community paid the 850 pesos demanded per family, borrowing the money against their coffee harvest. But soon Jiménez demanded more money, and one man was severely beaten when he could not pay. Community members were forced to leave for the village of Pantelho, where the 18 families lived in 10 small houses, but at least they could earn a living in that village.

When the women spoke they told of asking for justice from the government but receiving no help. The Zapatistas helped them leave their land and move to Pantelho. They do not receive further help from the Zapatistas, because they are engaged in different struggles. They say: "We are pacifists. We ask for justice only with words." With funds from Europe they bought the land, but the gunfire they still hear at night makes them uneasy. They like having observers, because they feel safer: maybe Juan will stay away if outsiders are watching. Whereas the Zapatista communities we met were determined to break all bonds of dependency and remain autonomous from the Mexican government, those at Nuevo Paraiso seemed at home with external assistance; in fact, not being under the umbrella of a large, powerful group, they seemed dependent on such aid. That evening we went back to the CIDECI campus in San Cristóbal for the Zapatista Round Table Meeting with Campesinas of the World. ("Intergalactic" turned out to be a PR word used to attract attention—and it did!).

Hundreds of people from all over the world were present. The simultaneous English translation devices that were provided enabled us to understand representatives from organizations engaged in the struggle for land and justice in India, Brazil, South Korea, and Mexico. No one I asked was sure of what Subcomandante Marcos was talking about: he seemed to combine myth and folk legend into a strange story. We also visited Caracol 2 in the town of Oventic for a two-day meeting of the Zapatistas with the international representatives. Here we found a cement walkway lined with booths selling educational materials, colorful books, clothes produced by cooperatives, local fruits, and food for the hordes of people present. A sign on the ambulance at the First Aid section said it had been donated by a town in Italy. People wore colorful costumes: many had donned ski masks, the local people wore their traditional white, and government officials sported hats covered with ribbons of every hue. Speakers and other officials sat in a large covered area facing the audience. There were plenary sessions on women's cooperatives, community organization, and autonomy. The popular media largely ignored the major Zapatista meetings; only one newspaper in Chiapas covered the events.

I have touched only briefly on the horrifying stories of the difficulties, oppression, and armed attacks suffered by the indigenous people struggling to make a living on their land. As of 1997 paramilitary organizations were still terrorizing the Zapatista communities with the support and complicity of the state and federal governments, the police, and the armed forces, according to Zapatista authorities. Paramilitary actions are designed to provoke violence to justify a military incursion that would be both tragic and disastrous. Behind all this is the desire of the multinational corporations to extract the natural wealth of Chiapas.

"Soon you will be able to buy land anywhere in Mexico as the likelihood is that it will all be privatized by the present government," said a knowledgeable Mexican professional well acquainted with Chiapas. I think one reason for the international nature of the Zapatista meetings the year in which I participated was to bring the foreign acquisition of Mexican land to the attention of the world.

The Big Picture

This section places recent events in Chiapas in global and national context, outlines significant environmental developments in Mexico and Chiapas, and projects future related North American and hemispheric trends. Seven years before the Zapatista uprising of 1994, Nietschmann (also Stea and Wisner)[27] warned of a coming Third World War that world leaders would never explicitly acknowledge. Such a war, he suggested, was already in progress and was occurring within nations, between the governments and indigenous nations encapsulated within internationally recognized states:

> Nations without a state make up the Fourth World of internationally unrecognized nations. This Fourth World comprises the peoples and their nations that exist beneath the imposed states of the West . . . and the Third World. To defend their nations from being annihilated, many peoples have taken up arms and are carrying out what are the world's longest wars. . . . The vast majority of individual wars today—which together make up the Third World War—are between states and nations.[28]

The Zapatista rebellion epitomizes this kind of war.

La Otra Campaña

The Zapatista Army of National Liberation launched La Otra Campaña (The Other Campaign) in San Cristóbal de las Casas on January 1, 2006. It had been announced in July 2005 as the action arm of the Sixth Declaration of the Lacandon Jungle,[29] which emphasized the centrality of control over their own resources, particularly the land they live on, for the Zapatistas. The two prongs of activity in La Otra Campaña involve, first, travels by Subcomandante Marcos (renamed Delegado Zero) around Mexico to add additional supporters to the cause and to organize dissent against Mexico's neoliberal policies. The second part of the campaign, begun in 2007, seeks to establish political units of the EZLN (CCRI, or Comité Clandestina Revolucionario Indígena [Clandestine Indigenous Revolutionary Committee]) in selected areas of Mexico. To date, La Otra Campaña has spread to Quintana Roo, Yucatán, Campeche, Veracruz, Oaxaca, Puebla, Tlaxcala, Hidalgo, Querétaro, and Mexico City, with rumblings in Michoacán. The local emphases vary but have most often stressed resistance to the forcible evacuation of indigenous lands, opposition to the privatization of land and water, and resistance to globalization in general. La Otra Campaña is a response, above all, to the intensification of land privatization in recent years. Begun with the so-called reform of Article 27 of the Mexican Constitution, described earlier in this chapter, privatization continued as part of the "structural readjustments" demanded by international organizations, starting in the late 1990s, as a condition for extending additional loans to Mexico.

The U.S. press has largely ignored Mexico—and, in fact, has ignored most of Latin America[30] over the past six years, except for news involving the drug trade or undocumented immigration. A rare exception was the Los Angeles Times coverage of La Otra Campaña, but it was limited and misleading, casting Delegado Zero's organizing effort as a "speaking tour" while offering no quotations from any speakers. Perhaps part of the problem was, as Gibler has written: "The social change proposed by the Other Campaign is so sweeping it pushes, uncomfortably, at the boundaries of our political imagination, our ability to think of different ways of doing politics."[31]

Plan Puebla Panama

Plan Puebla Panama (PPP, also known as Mesoamerican Integration and Development Project, or Project Mesoamerica), authored in large part by the United States with Mexican cooperation, considerably antedates La Otra Campaña. It calls for massive infrastructure improvements to facilitate transportation and development in an area ranging from the Mexican state of Puebla south to Panama and home to more than 60 million people, many indigenous and almost all very poor. In the center of this region is Chiapas. In part PPP was conceived as a response to transportation problems posed by the overloaded, antiquated Panama Canal and an alternative to proposals for a second canal across Honduras or Nicaragua. U.S. export companies will occupy the Atlantic side, and a maquiladora zone will be constructed on the Pacific coast.

Thus, PPP is much more than a transportation corridor running from Panama north through Mexico to the USA and Canada. It is also much more than a mere extension of NAFTA. In particular, as indicated above, the Plan projects a vast expansion in the number of maquiladoras in Mexico.[32] Financed by the Interamerican Development Bank and other such international institutions, the PPP is projected to cost billions of dollars. Tom Hayden succinctly summarizes the factors shaping the plan: "the Plan Puebla Panama . . . must be seen in several contexts: the long conflict over the rights of indigenous people, who are the majority in the path of el Plan; the hyperexpansion of NAFTA; the militarizing of Mexico's southern border against immigrants; and the low-intensity war against the Zapatistas."

The PPP is also an attempt to revive the failed jobs promise of NAFTA. Few would argue, the Los Angeles Times said, "that NAFTA has been anything but devastating for Mexican farm families, which account for 23% of Mexico's 100 million people." Relocating the crisis-ridden maquiladora industry to southern Mexico, where wages are half those of workers in the Mexican maquilas on the U.S. border, is a desperate effort to prevent the hemorrhage of jobs to China, where "nimble Chinese hands," in the words of the Los Angeles Times, sew and stitch for 40 cents an hour, only one-sixth of the Mexican maquiladora wage.[33]

Even if the promised jobs materialize, critics claim that the PPP will hasten the privatization of land, public services, and the water supply. The plan would transfer control over these resources and services to interests in the capital or in foreign countries. Although the PPP will certainly benefit multinational corporations, it will damage and perhaps destroy the cultural and environmental bases of the region's indigenous peoples.

Consider the environmental impact. Under PPP, the Usumacinta River, the largest river between Texas and Venezuela, will be dammed to produce electricity on a scale similar to that of the Aswan Dam in Egypt. Thousands of people will be displaced and nearly 20 ancient Mayan sites flooded. Located at the eastern edge of

Zapatista-controlled territory, the proposed "development" will facilitate military control over the river and the border between Mexico and Guatemala.

Another resource consideration is oil. Huge deposits of oil and natural gas, perhaps the equivalent of almost four billion barrels,[34] are believed to be spread out among thousands of square miles in montane and tropical forests of Chiapas—in both Zapatista-controlled territory and current locations of Mexican army units.[35]

Technology's Triumph over the Natural World

The development envisioned under the PPP could cause severe environmental damage. The Mesoamerican Biological Corridor, ostensibly intended to link various biologically rich and diverse patches of territory throughout the PPP region, is in fact a pet project of the World Bank. Although the argument is that the corridor will protect both gene pools and territory needed to preserve the region's biodiversity, as well as endangered fauna and flora, the unsurprising truth is that the corridor will be available for exploitation by seed companies and the pharmaceutical industry, which propose to patent any new biological entities they "discover." One of these companies, Pulsar, is involved with Conservation International (CI), an environmental NGO among whose directors are the CEOs of at least five megacorporations. The possibility that such biological entities may have been "discovered" much earlier by resident indigenous peoples has been ignored. Local indigenes condemn genetic-engineering projects as "biopiracy."

Indeed, the patenting of seeds has a negative effect on peasant farmers: "In Mexico, thousands of peasant farmers protested against an American company that patented an indigenous bean variety that had long been grown by local farmers; the community is now asked to pay the patent holder $69 million annually to grow this traditional local bean!"[36] The forms of "development" being touted by Plan Puebla Panama seem to have little to do with local people: they concern energy development and resource extraction. PPP will almost certainly destroy fragile rain forests and displace indigenes of the corridor who have never been consulted about any aspect of the development plan.

PPP Ecotourism: Environmental and Heritage Tourist Development

As if to throw a bone to the environmentally conscious, PPP incorporates the tourist-friendly Ruta Maya, proposed more than a decade ago but only partially implemented in Guatemala during the civil war as a "sanitized" corridor. This part of the Ruta Maya links major archeological sites and excludes them from any possible action by indigenous groups—ironically, preventing the descendants of the builders of these ancient Mayan complexes from access to their own heritage. As with the PPP, local people have not been consulted at all in decision making concerning the Ruta Maya or its possible effect on their natural environment.

Despite extensive deforestation, which in recent decades has reduced Chiapaneco forest cover by more than 75%,[37] Chiapas remains an ecotourist's paradise: it includes 40% of the plant varieties in the entire country, some 80% of its butterfly species, and—as relevant to tourism as to Mexico's survival—some 40% of Mexico's fresh water supply.[38] "Ecotourism hotels" sponsored by such multinationals as the Ford Motor Company dot the Lacandon forest. Ecotourism has been put forth as an ideal solution to economic development in remote areas. However, "ecotourism" is regrettably often confused with "low-impact tourism." The latter minimizes the so-cial, cultural, and economic impacts on host communities; the former offers no such assurances. Indigenous Chiapaneco communities have expressed negative feelings about ecotourism projects, because they have led to the privatization of *ejido* land, the displacement of communities, the commodification of natural resources, the de-struction of forests, the pollution of water, and the violation of social and cultural norms.[39] (See also Chapter 9.)

In addition to the Lacandon, Chiapas has 37 protected natural areas, more areas than any other Mexican state, covering 20% of its territory. Among the largest of these protected areas is the Comprehensive Biosphere Reserve of Montes Azules (REBIMA).[40]

Environment and Social Justice: REBIMA Evictions from Montes Azules

REBIMA is a centerpiece of *La Selva Lacandona*. This high-altitude ecosphere is part of 340,000 hectares of rainforest located in montane Chiapas, near the Guatemalan border. Lacking any other options, the populations living around the reserve utilize the forest for unsustainable subsistence purposes such as slash and burn agriculture and timber harvesting. An organization called Montes Azules has dedicated itself to providing local residents with environmentally sensitive jobs in the "buffer region" between the Biosphere Reserve and the border, enabling them to utilize the rainforest in a sustainable manner.

That's the good news. Unfortunately, the bad news is that Montes Azules also lies in the PPP "development corridor," which means displacement of as many as 110 communities to make room for projects that, far from providing local people with viable livelihoods, would force them to leave the area. Under this plan communities inside the Reserve would be the first to be relocated, followed by those within the greater Lacandon Area. Also, communities in the buffer and forest protection zones would be reordered into so-called Strategic Development Centers (CED). These could be more correctly labeled "development concentration centers," their purpose being to concentrate development aid in a few centers. The goal is to restrict or eliminate subsistence opportunities, thus gradually forcing *campesinos* to leave their commu-nities. Once concentrated, *campesinos* would have no alternative than to abandon their traditional culture and search for employment in *maquilas* and tourism.

Even more unfortunately, the process of displacement is not peaceful. On November 13, 2006, armed men presumed to be members of a paramilitary force massacred nine indigenous women and men and two children in the Montes Azules region. On August 18, 2007, after other incidents, residents of the towns of San Manuel and Buen Samaritano were accused of damaging the Montes Azules UNESCO-MAB biosphere reserve in the Lacandona forest and were forcibly evacu-ated on helicopters. Less than two weeks later, on August 31, Amnesty International requested "immediate suspension" of evictions from the Reserve. In the interim the Lacandon community of Ricardo Flores Magón declared itself an "Autonomous Municipality in Rebellion."[41]

The 2006 Election and Beyond

Felipe Calderón was sworn in as President of Mexico on December 1, 2006, after a bitterly and tightly contested election whose results his rival, Andres Manuel Lopez

Obrador (popularly known as "AMLO") of the center-left Partido de la Revolución Democratica, refused to accept for a considerable period.

Although the previous administration of Vicente Fox Quesada had no official policy toward Zapatista-occupied parts of Chiapas and took little action against the Zapatista communities, Calderón stated from the beginning that he would employ a "stronger hand." As of the end of 2009, however, most of the activity has been rhetorical, with the events in the Montes Azules region and several recent deaths in the *municipio* of Ocosingo[42] suggesting that unreported violence continues.

In his presidential campaign Calderón also pledged to reduce poverty (as did Fox before him), but the first half of his administration has not been promising, at least in cost-of-living terms. Consider corn, the major food product of Chiapas as well as much of the rest of Mexico. Mexico has reportedly lost as much as 75% of its indigenous maze varieties in recent years.[43] Those who must buy tortillas saw the price of this basic product increase from 6 to 8.5 pesos a kilo as the presidency of Calderón began (2007) (an increase of almost 42%), and then to 10 pesos by autumn,[44] an overall rise of 67% in just nine months. During the same nine months the federal government raised the price of basic subsistence products by 34%, vastly exceeding general inflation and more than seven times greater than increases in wages.[45]

The proportion of people in extreme poverty in Mexico's southern states, especially Chiapas, greatly exceeds the national average of 19%.[46] The situation has been exacerbated in the past few years by a reduction in remittances from Mexican workers in the United States because of three pair of factors: tightened immigration restrictions in the United States since 2001, making employers more fearful of hiring undocumented immigrants; a crisis in the U.S. housing market, reducing construction, which was a major source of work for immigrant labor;[47] and the catastrophic recession that has characterized the 2008–09 period globally. As a result of the paucity of work north of the border, some Mexican immigrants have begun heading south again.

Despite these grim circumstances the Zapatista rebellion has had a number of indirect positive results over the past decade. NGOs now run certification programs for the benefit of coffee cultivators who can demonstrate that they are engaged in environmental protection, community investment, and fair treatment of workers.[48] As for those corn farmers still struggling to keep their land and to sell their surplus in the face of a flood of cheap U.S. corn, there is some vague hope on the horizon as, with more U.S. farmers turning to the production of biofuels, the price of U.S.-raised hybrid varieties soars. Increased prices of northern corn may make Mexican maize competitive once more, at least within Mexico itself, perhaps providing a little relief for the remaining small farms in Chiapas and for those who work them.

Whither the Zapatistas? Some view Subcomandante Marcos as more prolific in the production of words than acts. Moreover, conflicts have occurred between the rebels and villagers angry about unfulfilled promises of increased prosperity and security or behaviors outside of or contrary to traditional norms.[49] As indicated in Prologue II, NGOs may in certain *caracoles* have effected more real change than has the EZLN.

A Continuation (with No Conclusion)

The spirit of revolutionary change has spread beyond Chiapas, and beyond early *Zapatismo*, to more of southern Mexico, thanks as much to the atmosphere engendered by the Zapatistas as to specific EZLN actions. The emergence of the EPR in Guerrero is a good example. Beginning with a teachers' strike in May 2006 the movement spread over Oaxaca, and its members, now the APPO (Asamblea Popular de los Pueblos de Oaxaca) occupied the state capital, a city of more than a million inhabitants, a short time later. Many of the same economic and social grievances that motivated the Zapatistas also provoked action in Oaxaca.

Most important, the waves of Chiapas revolt, although largely ignored in the United States, have reached shores far beyond Mexico. Writers such as Berger[50] have likened the effects of the events that fired Chiapas during and since 1994 to the storm or protest that deluged parts of many nations in 1968, a rejuvenation and revitalization of the idealistic left that spread from southern Mexico to the rest of Latin America, and engulfing much of Western Europe.[51]

> During the Reform, the Center spoke; during the Revolution, the North spoke. When will the South speak?[52] —José López Portillo, former President of Mexico
>
> The land belongs to those who work it. —Emiliano Zapata

Notes

1. Twenty-five "presumed" Zapatistas of various alleged ranks were rounded up in the simultaneous early morning raids in February 1995. Meanwhile, it was widely rumored that Marcos's capture was imminent or had already taken place and was being kept secret until his initial questioning had been completed. A witch-hunt atmosphere was quickly generated by press reports of arrest warrants being sought for an "enemies" list of over 2,000 names developed by Mexican military intelligence, including Bishop Ruiz. Other names included leftist leaders, people involved in trade union movements, and people who were supportive of the EZLN's demands, such as the radical lawyer-activists Ricardo Barco and Benito Mirón. The March Citizen's Information Mission was intended to provide a representative cross section of Mexico's nongovernmental organizations and citizens' groups with an unmediated look at the situation in Chiapas—at first hand—in order to assess the impact of the military's February crackdown.

2. *La Jornada*, Aug. 11, 1995, pp. 1, 9.

3. For example, one of the authors was receiving complete daily online reports about EZLN while in New Zealand in mid-1994.

4. For example, the sentiments of former President Carlos Salinas de Gortari, quoted in *International Wildlife Magazine*: "It's not automatic that with growth the environment will improve, but it is automatic that with poverty the environment will worsen." It has been equally easy to deny that such assumedly simple, docile people could launch their own revolution, and thus to assert that it must have been fomented by outsiders.

5. By contrast, Cruz Ecológica Mexicana, an informational clearing house based in Mexico City, listed in the mid-1990s more than 300 Mexico-based environmental NGOs. Remarkably, so many organizations have had little apparent effect.

6. Tom Barry, *Mexico: A Country Guide* (Albuquerque, NM: Interhemispheric Education Resource Center, 1992).

7. David Barkin, personal communication, 1996.

8. Claudia Ramos, "Preocupa Deforestación: Es la Más Alta del Mundo," *Reforma*, March 28, 1996, p. 1A. A view of the social conflicts involved in the deforestation specifically of the Lacandon is provided by Lourdes Arizpe, Fernanda Paz, and Margarita Velázquez, *Cultura y Cambio Global: Percepciones Sociales sobre la Deforestación en la Selva Lacandona* (México: Centro Regional de Investigaciones Multidisciplinarias, 1993).

9. Indeed, deforestation and wetlands destruction are two prime examples—albeit negative examples, in the Mexican case of the needed interaction between environmental preservation and economic development. The solution proposed by the Mexican government to deforestation, similar to that already tried in other parts of the developing world, is plantation forestry (see, for example, Miguel Perez and Andres Resillas, "Presenta Zedillo Programa Sectoral: Impulsan Inversión el Sector Forestal," *Reforma*, March 28, 1996, p. 3A). This approach will certainly increase wood product but will have little or no effect on restoring biodiversity, the centerpiece of the deforestation controversy.

10. Only 2.5% of Mexico's land area is protected in its natural form, in 44 national parks, 22 biosphere reserves of one form or another, as well as several specially designated areas. Although new areas are currently coming under protection, it is unlikely that Mexico will ever rank with Costa Rica, where by 1988 27% of the land area had been placed under some formal protection.

11. For a critical look at the effects of La Ruta Maya tourism on the Mayan peoples in Quintana Roo, see Chapter 9 in this volume. A more popular (and more positive, if somewhat questionable) view is provided by Wilbur D. Garrett, "La Ruta Maya," *National Geographic* 176:4 (Oct. 1989, 424–79).

12. One positive effect of the Zapatista movement has been to unite previously disparate Mayan groups under a single cause. Another has been to empower women. Unquestionably, with few exceptions, Mayan women have been subservient to men, in reproduction and other spheres, over the half-millennium since the Conquest. The Zapatistas, through the promulgation of the "Revolutionary Law of Women" as its first act on January 1, 1994, are attempting to change this situation, and it is thus not very surprising that one-third of Zapatista fighters are female, as well as several of their most prominent leaders.

13. Beatriz Manz, *Refugees of a Hidden War: The Aftermath of Counterinsurgency in Guatemala* (Albany: SUNY Press, 1988). This figure excludes those seeking asylum who have not registered with the United Nations High Commissioner for Refugees, Guatemalans en route to the United States, and Guatemalans who enter Mexico as seasonal workers in the coffee harvest. Some estimates suggest that the number of Guatemalan refugees in Mexico may be as high as 200,000.

14. Duncan Earle, personal communication at the annual meeting of the Association of Borderlands Scholars, 1996.

15. Alan Riding, *Distant Neighbors: A Portrait of the Mexicans* (New York: Vintage Books, 1989, 293–4).

16. *Reforma*, June 4, 1995.

17. Ibid. The Mexican minimum wage varies slightly by region, but was under U.S. $60 per month at the turn of the century in most parts of the country. Unlike the U.S. minimum wage, however, the Mexican *salario minimo* is more a base for wage computations—that is, so-and-so earns X *salarios minimos*.

18. John Ross, *Rebellion from the Roots* (Monroe, ME: Common Courage Press, 1995, 263).

19. George A. Collier and Elizabeth Q. Lowery, *Basta! Land and the Zapatista Rebellion in Chiapas* (Oakland, CA: Food First Books, 1994, 45).

20. Ibid., p. 51.

21. Some popular accounts have appeared in nonacademic journals of the dramatic events in Mexico's southernmost state. These include Medea Benjamin, "On the Road with the Zapatistas," *Progressive* May (1995, 28–31); Marc Cooper, *The Zapatistas* (Westfield, NJ: Open Magazine Pamphlet Series, 1994); and Saul Landau, "The Challenge of the Chiapas," *Progressive* April (1995, 41–43).

22. Many argue that the roots of the Zapatista revolt can be traced back to the Spanish Conquest, almost 500 years ago. The monuments that have been erected, such as those

to Mendoza in Yucatán and Mazariegos in Chiapas, commemorate the crudest of the conquistadores. To celebrate the Columbian Quincentennial in 1992 local Mayans pulled down and destroyed the statue of Mazariegos in the center of San Cristóbal de las Casas, as the culmination of a march in which over 50,000 indigenous activists participated— this is considered to have been the largest demonstration in southern Mexico in recent history and a key forerunner to the 1994 uprising.

23. President Salinas, a tiny man, threw himself into this task with such enormous zeal that he acquired the nickname *"La hormiga atomica"* ("the atomic ant").

24. Barry, note 6.

25. In other words, solidarity efforts have typically been concentrated in those areas in which the PRI is most interested in getting votes. See Wayne Cornelius, "Mexico's Delayed Democratization," *Foreign Policy 95*: summer (1994, 53–71).

26. Ross, note 18, p. 265.

27. Bernard Nietschmann, "Third World War: The Global Conflicts over the Rights of Indigenous Nations," *Utne Reader*, Nov./Dec. (1988, 84–91) [reprinted from *Cultural Survival Quarterly*, Dec., 1987]; D. Stea, and B. Wisner, Eds., "The Fourth World: The Geography of Indigenous Struggles," special issue of *Antipode*, 16:2 (1984).

28. Nietschmann, note 27, pp. 186–88.

29. Subcomandante Marcos, *La Otra Campaña* (San Francisco: City Lights Bookstore, 2006).

30. Jorge Castañeda, "Latin America: The Forgotten Relative," *Foreign Affairs*, 2003 (May-June), 82(3), 67–81.

31. John Gibler, "Who's Not Listening: The L.A. Times and the Failure of Political Imagination," *ZNet*, 2006 (February 13).

32. Tom Hayden, "Seeking a New Globalism in Chiapas," *The Nation*, 2003 (April 7).

33. Hayden, ibid.

34. Hayden, note 32. Note that five billion barrels are regarded by the petroleum industry as a "mega-deposit."

35. Hayden, note 32.

36. International Forum on Globalization, *Alternatives to Economic Globalization: A Better World is Possible* (San Francisco: Berrett-Loehler Publishers, 2002, p. 180).

37. Jan de Vos, *Oro Verde: La Conquista de la Selva Lacandona por los Madereros Tabasqueños, 1822–1949* (Mexico: Fondo de Cultura Economica, 1988).

38. Hayden, note 32.

39. *"Protected Natural Areas,"* Government of Chiapas 2001, CIEPAC 2002, COMPITCH, 2005; also *SIPAZ Report*, Oct. 17, 2008.

40. Ibid.

41. Al Giordano, "The Other Journalism with the Other Campaign in Chiapas," 2006 (November 13). Ricardo Flores Magón founded the Mexican Liberal Party (PLM) in 1905 in opposition to the excesses of the Porfirio Díaz dictatorship. The PLM's motto "Land and Liberty" was taken over by Emiliano Zapata, who was inspired by and shared Flores Magón's ideals. Declared a "bandit" by the United States government, repeatedly arrested and imprisoned in the United States, Flores Magón died, apparently of a severe beating, in Leavenworth Prison, Kansas, in 1922.

42. The most violent conflict in the last few months occurred in the county [*municipio*] of Ocosingo when hundreds of persons (including peasants of the Lacandon Community and uniformed persons) attacked 17 families installed in the village Viejo Velasco Suarez, in the Lacandon Jungle. This aggression, in the middle of a huge confusion about the number of victims and the possibility of their belonging to EZLN, resulted in 4 persons dead,

among them a pregnant woman, and 4 missing persons, presumably executed. Amnesty International has strongly criticized the governmental response to this situation.(*SIPAZ Report*, 2007, March, p. 5).

43. *International Forum*, note 35, p. 27.

44. *SIPAZ Report*, note 41.

45. Christian Gutierrez, "México: !Cada vez más pobre!" *Atención*, 33:41 (2007, 73).

46. "Mexico: New Governments, Old Issues," *SIPAZ Report*, 12:1 (2007, 1–5); "Oventik: Encounter of the Zapatista People with the Peoples of the World," *SIPAZ Report*, 12:1 (2007, 6–7).

47. Elizabeth Malkin, "Mexicans Miss Money from Relatives up North, *The New York Times (World Business)*, 2007 (October 26).

48. Elisabeth Malkin, "Certifying Coffee Aids Farmers and Forests in Chiapas," *The New York Times (International)*, 2007 (April 22).

49. "Zapatistas: After Conflict, Rebel Allies Leave Village," *Herald Tribune, International Edition*, 2004, 4A.

50. John Berger, "Entre los dos Colmar," *Mirar* (Buenos Aires: Ediciones de la Flor, 1998).

51. José Seoane, "Rebelión, dignidad, autonomía, y democracia: Voces compartidas desde el sur, *Chiapas 16*, 2004, 107–16.

52. Luis Hernández Navarro, quoted in *La Otra Campana*, note 29.

CHAPTER 12

Life and Death Matters in Eritrean Repatriation

Lucia Ann McSpadden

SECTION I: The End of the Millennium

On the road to Mendefara, South of Asmara, Eritrea, May 1995

"I used to play in the woods here when I was a child," Woldemichael said in a soft, sad voice.[1] Surprised at the apparent impossibility, I ask him, "How could this be true?" The land stretches out around us in undulating open plains, mostly dirt and scrub grass. It is "open sky" country; one can see far in all directions except where the view is jarred by a rusting tank left by the retreating Ethiopian army in 1991, making graphic the presence of 30 years of village-to-village warfare.

Woldemichael's angry response, shocking in its truth, brought home the deep wounds to the earth, to the people, and to the future of Eritrea. "The land has been destroyed by the war—the Ethiopians bombed the countryside; they cut down the trees—for construction, for fuel, to remove cover for the liberation fighters, to destroy us, I think. People were not able to farm, to care for the land. People needed fuel; they cut trees and shrubs, too—anything they could find. Now you see what we must work with, what we must rebuild. Now you see that we are beggars! We will not allow you to treat us like beggars!"

Repatriation, Peace, and Human Rights: A Question of Power and Control[2]

"First, we are dealing with people. There is an attachment, a closeness. This is the most important. Repatriation is not just statistics. It is to give back to people who have been denied their universal rights, people who have been ousted from their home because they are from a certain area—nothing else."[3]

The longest-standing armed conflict in Africa, the Eritrean struggle for liberation from Ethiopia, produced hundreds of thousands of refugees between 1961 and 1991. Over one quarter of Eritrea's population fled to save their lives. Although these Eritrean refugees ended up in many different countries, the majority, over 500,000, have been in asylum in neighboring Sudan—some for up to 20 years.[4]

The retreat of the Ethiopian army from Eritrea in May 1991 brought this war to an end. The April 1993 referendum established Eritrea as a sovereign nation, and its government was formed from the liberation fighters. The return of 450,000 to 500,000 refugees from Sudan to Eritrea quickly was a salient issue for the new government of Eritrea, for the United Nations High Commissioner for Refugees (UNHCR), and for international donors. The negotiations for this repatriation were particularly prolonged and difficult, revealing the international and national complexities of repatriation and the contradictions within the international refugee system itself.

In the context of a country as devastated as Eritrea, these negotiations make painfully clear the vulnerability of the refugees, of the environment, of the people and the nation. Care for the earth, care for the people who stayed behind, care for people who fled and now will return—these are all intertwined with and affected by the system of international response to refugees and their repatriation to their country of origin, a system in which power and control are central concerns. Repatriation is embedded within political, economic, environmental, and social realities. How refugees are repatriated provides the foundation for the challenge to build and sustain true peace with justice.

As a Ghanaian theologian has said: "True peace is inseparable from dignity, honour, righteousness and justice, in short right relationships and honourable conditions."[5] Peace is not limited to the absence of war, although surely it requires the absence of armed conflict. It is not "peace at any price." Its critical conditions are grounded in the basic human rights of an individual and of the community. Peace has many aspects: safety, the lack of fear, the availability of basic life necessities, the overcoming of hostilities and/or dehumanization, the elimination of barriers between peoples and between communities and nations, and the balancing of power.[6]

Repatriation, the spontaneous or organized returning of refugees from countries of asylum and resettlement back to their native land, is at once a "peace issue" and a "power issue." This is especially true when the numbers are large, the groups of refugees identifiable, the physical and social environment fragile, and the populations economically vulnerable. Repatriation is about the insertion of groups of vulnerable persons into populations that often are also living a precarious existence. Repatriation is about rebuilding a nation after armed, usually long-term, conflict. Repatriation is typically about bringing together peoples who frequently represent opposing forces. Repatriation is about allocating scarce resources and reinserting people into the life of the land. Repatriation is about economics, politics, and social conditions. Honor, dignity, justice, reconciliation, righteousness, and rights are not abstractions: they are the results of specific policies, specific decisions. Repatriation negotiated and implemented without concern for honor, dignity, justice, and right relations lays the conditions for future conflict and even war. Repatriation is a challenge for building peace with justice.

In organized, large-scale repatriations, humanitarian intervention in the processes of reintegration and reconciliation is negotiated by a complex array of governmental, intergovernmental, and nongovernmental actors. These actors must "address the question of how short-term considerations of relief (food, shelter, water, and medicine) link up with issues of human rights protection, demilitarization, reconciliation, political reform, containment of ethnic conflict, regional reconstruction, and the wide range of development issues."[7]

One of the defining qualities of "refugeeness" is that of being controlled by state powers and authorities. Refugees are subject to specific measures and restrictions, because, in fleeing, they have crossed national borders.[8] Power is central to effective repatriation and reconstruction in what is frequently a devastated environment: "Since assistance to processes of repatriation involves questions of 'reinsertion' of people, 'reactivation' of local and regional economies, and (re)construction of civil administration, assistance becomes deeply engaged in the development of technologies and *distribution of power*" (emphasis added).[9]

Repatriation involves the question of the reinsertion of people, the rebuilding of the economy, the reconstruction of political structures—all issues of power and the allocation of and access to social, economic, and political resources. If the agreements on entitlements and obligations are not well worked out, the process of repatriation will be inadequate to the challenge of reinserting large groups of people into a devastated environment.

Eritrean Colonialism and Liberation[10]

The history of the Eritrean liberation struggle sets the context and shapes the approach of the government of Eritrea to the repatriation negotiations. Eritrea became a colony of Italy in 1889 and thus is distinct from Ethiopia in important ways. After Italy's defeat in World War II, Eritrea was placed under British trusteeship. The UN General Assembly recommended the federation of Eritrea with Ethiopia in which Eritrea was to be in control of its domestic affairs. Basic human rights for Eritreans were granted. However, in 1962 Ethiopia unilaterally dissolved the federation and made Eritrea its subordinate province. The United Nations, in spite of its unique responsibility for Eritrea, did not intervene.[11] "Eritrea, therefore, still hosts bitterness against the United Nations and does not have faith in UN integrity."[12]

In 1961 the Eritrean Liberation Front (ELF) launched an armed resistance with the goal of independence, thus beginning 30 years of brutal trench warfare. The battle was waged in the rural areas, with Ethiopian offensives especially aimed at civilians. In the 1970s a second liberation front, the Eritrean People's Liberation Front (EPLF), split from the ELF and in 1980 drove the ELF out of Eritrea into neighboring Sudan. The ruthlessness of the Ethiopian attacks sent hundreds of thousands into Sudan as refugees.

In May 1991 Eritrea achieved the goal of its struggle, liberation. There is a clear and pervasive sense on the part of the former fighters, government officials, and Eritreans generally that Eritrea won its independence alone, without help from any other nation or international body.[13] The EPLF became the Provisional Government of Eritrea (PGE). In 1993 Eritreans—in diaspora and those within the newly independent Eritrea—voted, via a referendum, to confirm Eritrea's independence from Ethiopia and, thus, its government.

Eritrea and the Repatriation Context

Politically Eritrea is at peace, and its government, a one-party state, by all accounts is legitimate[14] and has widespread, although not unanimous, support in the country. It has broad ethnic and religious representation at the official levels. The leaders and most of the civil servants are drawn from the ranks of the EPLF. The government of Eritrea has proven itself, according to western governments and nongovernmental (NGO) sources, to be honest and "clean" in its governing. Confidence in the integrity of the leadership is widespread and high. This confidence is strengthened by the fact that since liberation, thousands of former fighters have been working in the government without salary, including those at the highest level. Thus the political factors that caused the refugees to flee no longer exist. Peace is also a social and community reality: one can safely walk the streets day and night. Armed soldiers or police no longer hover on every street corner. The government's human rights record has not been seriously questioned.[15]

Environmentally and socially, however, Eritrea is a devastated country. The physical infrastructure has been almost totally destroyed: churches, mosques, schools, hospitals are gone; roads and railroads were ripped up by the Ethiopian forces. The natural resource base is fragile and degraded. The countryside was severely bombed, hundreds of tons of steel, including tanks, litter the land, and mines remain a significant problem.[16] The highlands, where the majority of the population lives, have been severely deforested.[17] Deforestation increases erosion and drought in areas dependent on rainfall for agriculture. The lowlands, historically populated by nomads, are drought-prone. The capacity of the land to absorb 500,000 refugees (15% of the population) from Sudan is doubtful. Before the war Eritrea was basically self-sufficient in food;[18] after the war approximately 80% of the population is dependent on food aid.

The population of Eritrea—approximately 50% Muslim and 50% Christian—represents nine ethnic groups. The Christians live mainly in the more prosperous highlands, whereas the Muslims live predominately in the lowlands. In the process of developing the constitution[19] as well as in the government structures, there is an intention to include the various ethnic groups as well as both Muslims and Christians. However, some people expressed concern that government officials come predominately from the highlands while most of the returnees will be resettled in the lowlands. The fact that the majority of refugees in Sudan are Muslims, many with a previous relationship to the ELF, poses a significant challenge to the goal of nation building based on ethnic/religious inclusion. There are reports of anti-Eritrean government activities by the National Islamic Front (NIF) in the camps in Sudan.[20]

Thus the Eritrean political, economic, and social context provides a unique and remarkable reality in which the international community must refine repatriation processes and procedures. The government has no financial capacity for absorbing large-scale loans, but there is a high level of *esprit de corps* and commitment to the future of the nation. According to several UNHCR officials Eritrea was the one ray of hope in Horn of Africa. However, as a Swedish government official also remarked: "We were eager to get going with the repatriation. We had supported the Eritrean people,[21] and now this was an excellent situation in which to really do repatriation quickly and well. But it didn't happen. It got all bogged down in misunderstandings."

How did the negotiations get "bogged down," and what happened to the concerns for the rights of people and for the sustainability of the environment—natural, physical, and social?

Repatriation Negotiations

After liberation in May 1991 the PGE Commission for Eritrean Refugee Affairs (CERA) began formal contacts with UNHCR. UNHCR opened a permanent office in Asmara in November 1991. Right away considerable difficulties emerged regarding the negotiations for the repatriation. Misunderstandings were embedded in the Eritrean government's historical distrust of the United Nations. Also, the Eritrean government, formerly a liberation movement, had little exposure to international agencies, their mandates, their established methods, their expectations, their limitations. These misperceptions and misunderstandings, as well as contradictions within the international repatriation system, influenced negotiations for several years.

As the government presented its repatriation budget of $600 million for a comprehensive program of return and reinsertion, it became clear that UNHCR and CERA were divided over the amount of funding and what was to be included within repatriation. From the government perspective, refugees were languishing in camps and not able to return owing to the lack of development in Eritrea. The PGE insisted on placing repatriation within a total development approach for the entire country. UNHCR stated that its donors would not fund development: UNHCR would not build a hospital but would dig a small number of tube wells.[22]

The relevant standard for UNHCR was that refugees could not be given a higher standard than those who stayed behind—that is, given a "prize for leaving." For example, the government offered a plan for concrete block houses with an estimated price tag of U.S. $900–$1,200 each. But the UNHCR perceived that the donors would question such a high amount of funding going to shelter and asked why the returnees needed concrete block houses when the rest of the Eritrean people lived in huts, both in Sudan and in Eritrea.[23]

The strategies and trends of their international donors fundamentally shaped UNHCR's strategies, and in December 1991–January 1992, its first international appeal for Eritrea went out. Recognizing that they had moved beyond the old days of "seeds, tools, and a handshake," UNHCR noted that donors now expect UNHCR to prepare for the return but won't fund development through UNHCR.[24] Therefore, their advice was to implement a small and specific project, show donors how the money was spent, then solicit more money for additional projects. Financial resources follow successful repatriation, not the other way around. They also noted, "If we can't spend it, it gets taken away either by the donor or in-house for other emergencies."[25]

This approach was unacceptable to CERA/PGE, which insisted that repatriation must not begin until sufficient funds were guaranteed for reintegration *and* reconstruction. CERA also stressed the social consequences of the proposed repatriation scheme: "Eritrea would be drowned in a sea of returnees who had no suitable accommodation . . . this would cause major social and economic upheaval as the country did not have the necessary resources for assimilating the returnees."[26] The basic dilemma was, "One has to see the refugees as part of the community. They are in the same area with those who remained, former fighters, former displaced. We have to target the community, not target the refugees as a separate group. It is a matter of community development not group development."[27] They refused to allow UNHCR to begin discrete projects and insisted that the entire country had suffered in the liberation struggle; one area should not receive assistance while another did not.[28] Meanwhile, the UNHCR argued that specific projects that were sound, useful, and funded would have to be put on hold.[29]

The issue of how to determine the amount of funding was also a critical disagreement throughout the negotiations. The PGE, citing the very high cost per head for certain repatriations, such as South Africa and Namibia, perceived that UNHCR was discriminating against Eritrea. UNHCR responded that repatriation funding was not solicited on a cost per head basis but admitted that it was a "bedeviling argument."

Increasingly, the Eritrean government stated that an *issue of principle* was involved, that UNHCR was proposing inadequate reintegration funds and clearly wanted to "dump refugees."

Throughout, both UNHCR and the PGE insisted that their aim was to get the refugees in Sudan back to Eritrea in safety, honor, and dignity, and to enable them to become self-sufficient and contribute to the development of Eritrea. However, by 1992 the relationship between UNHCR and the Eritrean government had so deteriorated that the PGE suspended talks with UNHCR, and the UNHCR office in Asmara was downsized to a one-person administration. Patience had worn thin within the agencies and among the populace, and public attacks had damaged the confidence of donors and international agencies.[30] Meanwhile, the vast majority of refugees remained in Sudan, the most vulnerable were dependent on the decisions of the powerful.

Both parties did continue their efforts toward the organized return of refugees. The UN Department of Humanitarian Affairs (DHA) took over the up-front intergovernmental efforts and developed a planning process, including the UN, NGOs, and international donors, for an organized repatriation program. The resulting Joint Government of Eritrea and United Nations Appeal for Eritrea was presented to an international donors pledging conference in Geneva on July 6, 1993. The planning process resulted in an 11-component repatriation and reintegration program, PROFERI (Programme for Refugee Reintegration and Rehabilitation of Resettlement Areas in Eritrea), to return 430,000 refugees during three years and seven months at a cost of U.S. $262.2 million. A specific objective of PROFERI was to link repatriation of refugees to the rehabilitation of the country, avoiding the creation of a privileged class of returnees within a deprived local population so that the total population would be able to sustain itself after PROFERI ends.[31]

Despite the fact that PROFERI "seemed to present an ideal example of a coordinated response between governmental and nongovernmental agencies to bridge the gap between rehabilitation and development," the results of the donors' conference were extremely disappointing, some would say disastrous. Pledges amounted to $32.4 million; of this only $11 million was "new money," and the remainder was food aid that would have been available in any case. Tension rose again: "We were misled by DHA and UNHCR. If they had known that donors would not fund such a big project, why did they work with us to develop it? It was not intentional, but it happened. . . . It was a bitter lesson."[32]

Several explanations were offered as to why donor response was so unenthusiastic:

1. The program isn't a "pure" repatriation; it is rural development plus repatriation. It is too big and will take 50 years; refugees need to be returned now.

2. Being a partner in development means long-term involvement, which donors do not want.

3. Interest in Eritrea (media pressure) was not there.

4. There was an uncertainty about the capacity of a dedicated but inexperienced Eritrean administration to manage such a large and varied program.

5. The government (GOE) was insisting on national project management and execution.

6. The government won't permit international NGOs to work there; this is a great inhibition to getting money.[33] More and more international donors are funneling their money through NGOs.

The last two points highlight a basic principle of the government of Eritrea that the program would be largely coordinated and executed nationally by the GOE, which restricted international NGOs. Donations were welcomed, but only as long as they were consistent with the goal of building up national capacities, not substituting for them.[34]

Pilot Phase of PROFERI: January 1994–May 1995

With the failure of the PROFERI appeal of July 1993, the government of Eritrea, UNDP, DHA, and UNHCR came back together to plan on the basis of the limited funds available. However, the larger donors refused to release money unless the government made an arrangement with UNHCR.[35]

In March 1994 UNHCR began to function locally in the repatriation process. The new Chief of Mission stated his intention to work closely with the government:

> I could say "You are a sovereign government. You decide." . . . The government credibility is based on having liberated the country on their own; it is their own achievement. They are legitimate and that creates credibility. However, winning the peace is much more difficult. The real fight is ahead. They are starting below zero. The government will have to deliver . . . back to the people. . . . I did not come to tell the Eritreans this or that. We have a common goal, to get the refugees back.[36]

In this more positive climate the government allocated nearly U.S. $7 million for a pilot phase to repatriate approximately 25,000 returnees (some 4,500 households) from Sudan.[37] It was underfunded but was a commitment by GOE and UNHCR to "get the show on the road."[38] Approximately 20,000 persons were repatriated and received initial reintegration support.[39]

The next stage of PROFERI, Phase One, aimed to repatriate some 135,000 Eritreans from Sudan with a budget of approximately U.S. $111 million.[40] At a planning and evaluation workshop, UNHCR stated its support and emphasized that the problems between it and GOE "were of the past."[41] However, tensions and contradictions were still clear. The UNHCR Chief of Mission stated, *"The real task for the Eritrean Government and all international partners is the reintegration process,* to give the returnees the tools and means to help themselves, their families, and their communities. . . . Initial relief and infrastructure like water, health, shelter, basic education, land distribution, and agricultural and livestock support are all key elements for a real reintegration process which should be planned for and started immediately" (emphasis added).[42]

The PROFERI programme found itself in a contradictory position. Clearly, donors would not continue to support relief to Eritrean refugees in the Sudan forever. Yet, limited finances contributed to the inability to implement fully the comprehensive pilot phase, thus making it difficult to meet donor expectations as to quality and preparation of settlement sites. Delays between pledges and the actual time of payment exacerbated this problem.

Transparency was an additional concern. CERA officials consistently stated that the PROFERI programme was transparent: donors could come to inspect and evaluate sites and offices. However, donor representatives stated that the government was *not* transparent, because it did not provide adequate written records regarding the use of funds. In response CERA officials noted the detailed planning including issues previously raised by donors.

Two issues were central: funding by and relationships to international donors, and the effect of the environmental conditions on the total planning and process. These were shaped by and embedded in the two overarching and unanswered questions: whether donors would fund development within repatriation, and who controls the process.

A Development Solution to a Humanitarian Problem[43]

PROFERI's mandate includes rehabilitating the region affected by the return and resettlement of the refugees. It is community development, not group relief; it promotes basic services that will benefit all the people in a region.[44]

Environmental Challenges and Resource Access

The devastated and ecologically fragile environment in Eritrea sets the basic conditions and challenges for the return. Appropriate shelter is a problem, because depleted "woody biomass resources in the lowlands of Eritrea cannot be expected to meet the shelter needs of [the returnees]."[45] Nor could it meet fuel needs for cooking and heating. Plans for fuel-saving alternative stoves and the planting of tree seedlings were recommended by GOE to combat the problem.

With 80% of the population dependent on food aid, land availability, adequate tools and materials, and access to water are critical basic needs. As subsistence, settled agriculture is expanded in an area historically utilized by agro-pastoralists, there is a direct effect on the environment, which may not be able to sustain such a rapid and marked population increase. There is also competition for scarce or threatened resources.[46] Given the low amount of rainfall in the lowlands, sanitation and providing safe drinking water for the returnees are also huge challenges.

In such a context, environmental concerns (for example, the governments support for tree conservation[47]) were in tension with concern for humane, livable conditions in extraordinarily hot climates (many donors and NGOs preferred wood roofs to the corrugated metal roofs suggested by the GOE). Additional issues under debate included experience with alternative construction materials, funding, fuel needs, environmental protection, the need to prepare sites quickly, and the involvement of the community (bottom up vs. top down) in planning for shelter. And once again, the opinions of donors influenced the funding of any proposal.

Competition for scarce or fragile resources not only increases tensions directly related to such resources but also sets in motion conflict that can be orchestrated along ethnic and religious lines. Aware of this danger, the government is committed to preventing the linkage between resource competition and ethnic/religious issues, a commitment that underlies the government's insistence on linking national and community development to repatriation. Reports about the activities of Islamic fundamentalists in the refugee camps in Sudan are particularly worrisome in this context.

Who Controls Repatriation?

These issues point to the hard choices and contradictions within repatriation—for example, time constraints, money limits, differing donor and government perspectives, ecological realities, resource availability. Although there were no questions as to the immensity of the development needs, there were concerns about the capacity of the GOE to carry out such an extensive program, as well as concerns about plans for and funding of capacity building. The most basic question of whether donors were willing to fund development connected to repatriation was compounded by disagreements regarding control of the process.

Donors were clearly uncomfortable with the national execution approach, which may be one reason for the sluggish donor response to PROFERI.[48] Capacity building is closely tied to the approach of national execution. Donors queried the GOE's capacity to carry out PROFERI plans. CERA responded with an interest in capacity-building linked to national execution. It was aware, for instance, of the need to improve its record-keeping. Additionally it was cautious about becoming dependent on "experts:" "We don't want 'lend me your watch, and I will tell you the time.'"[49]

The issue of control was critical in the early negotiations; for example, early proposals to develop alternative fuel projects, initially accepted and shaped by Eritrean women's groups, were later rejected and not implemented, apparently because they came with funding from UNHCR. Control continued to be pervasive in the donors' workshop before Phase One of PROFERI. Arguments about building materials were framed in environmental terms, but the underlying issue became trust and control. Importantly, environmental concerns are inherently development issues not encompassed within "traditional repatriation."

The government expressed control through emphases on self-determination, independence, and reserving implementation for the government. International donors expressed control through restrictions on funds, emphasis on particular procedures of reporting, and/or by the actual withholding of funds. UNHCR expressed control through an emphasis on operational mandates and procedural limitations.

Will the International System Lead to a Sustainable Peace?

> How can countries, scarred by the effects of war, insecurity, land mines and poverty, burdened with the problem of demobilized soldiers [combatants] and displaced civilians, be realistically expected to reabsorb those who return, when they are hardly able to sustain those who remained? The Horn of Africa is but one example of many. Are we not simply creating new and more tragic emergencies? And at what cost to the peace process in these countries? As conflicts are resolved, countries must be rebuilt, so that they can begin to support once again their own population, including the returning refugees and displaced persons. . . . The link between the reintegration of refugees and national post-conflict reconstruction is thus of paramount importance.[50]

Madame Ogata's impassioned statement shows how the Eritrean case described in this chapter exposes *essential challenges within the international refugee system.* These challenges are embedded in the contradictions within the institutionalized international response to refugees. The linking of repatriation to development conceptualizes repatriation as part of the nation-building challenge that joins diverse and vulnerable groups of people within a devastated reality. Without reconstruction of the country, there is no sustainability—and likely no lasting peace. Development, however, is a long-term process necessitating a long-term commitment with donors.

For countries that are primarily agricultural, issues of land availability, basic resources, and (re)developing cooperative communities are central. Economic and social sustainability is directly related to land and environmental issues. Eritrea is illustrative of the common situation in which returnees are being resettled in the same areas with former fighters, areas already inhabited by agro-pastoralists who, as nomads, must have access to large tracts of land for their animals. The land is fragile. Returnees, who have been sustained in Sudan by the cooperation of the Sudanese government and international donors, are obviously weighing the comparative costs and benefits of that existence against the challenges of starting a new life in Eritrea. The potential for dissatisfaction, and subsequent political instability, is real: "The only way voluntary repatriation can be an attractive and a lasting solution under such conditions is by creating a stable socio-economic base in the areas of return."[51] The failure to achieve such a stable base can have dire consequences: "Unless the capacity of communities and areas of return to absorb additional populations is addressed, mass repatriation may spur new forms of human deprivation, social tensions and migratory movements."[52]

Yet, there is a "wide gap" separating relief assistance and longer-term development programs.[53]

As we have seen in Eritrea this gap is due to several factors: (1) donors understand repatriation as moving refugees from "here to there," not as development; (2) donors' repatriation money comes out of different budgets than development money;[54] and (3) the legendary "mandate dilemma" within the UN system prevents integration.[55] UNHCR has been struggling for years with the mandate dilemma and its own limited responsibility "to register refugees, transport them . . . and provide initial relief."[56] UNHCR's Quick Impact Projects—community-focused, one-time, small budget projects intended to be a bridge to longer-term development done by other UN agencies or NGOs—require close coordination between UNHCR and such agencies. However, this coordination has not usually been successful:[57] "The humanitarian 'Market of Mercy' is a hard market, everyone is struggling for their share. . . . We all define our own small little sectors. That is more important than helping people!"[58]

Funding—and competition for it—is a basic contradiction within the international refugee system. Donors, the United Nations, and governments all insist that their goal is self-reliance and independence for the returnees. However, this goal can be subordinated when donors put conditions on their aid and attach "strings" to funds. Typically, "whoever pays the bill calls the tune."[59]

As we have seen, funding contributed to conflicts in the Eritrean repatriation negotiations. UNHCR, which receives over 90% of its funds from donor governments, is totally dependent on a small group of western nations. At the Summit for Social Development in 1995, President Isaias Afwerki insisted: "certain assumptions and relationships must change . . . donor-recipient relationships based on dictation of unsuitable antidotes will just not do. . . . Symmetry should be the linchpin of relationships between rich and poor countries." And while donors should insist on rigorous monitoring of their funds, "our independence of decision should not be encroached by conditionalities of aid."[60] Eritrean government officials noted the presence of approximately 250 NGOs in Ethiopia (in contrast to the 10-plus in Eritrea) and emphasized that they did not intend to turn the development of Eritrea over to outside forces, even humanitarian ones. "The expectation [is to have] an Eritrean working alongside . . . so that when the expert leaves, there is an Eritrean who is now knowledgeable to carry on. We want to increase our own capacity . . . not empower international NGOs."[61]

Quite often the donor governments have a political agenda tied to their contributions so that particular situations fade out of interest for them. An NGO staff noted that although development funding is hard to come by, money for Bosnia comes quickly. A donor country representative asserted that they were sitting on funds for Croatia, Bosnia, and Somalia. They knew things were going to "blow up" there. Meanwhile, preventive work such as reconciliation and confidence building gets no attention. Money is given for symptoms—for visible and graphic crises—not to address causes, not to prevent future destabilization: "Now things are quiet and stable here [in Eritrea]. What you are doing is conflict prevention. This needs significant support from the international community. Unfortunately, the international community only responds when there are guns and blood."[62] Development as part of the total repatriation process is an expensive, long-term process that requires considerable political will on the part of the entire international community.[63]

In my discussions with donor representatives several key issues surfaced that are typically present in the broader international context: (1) the political agenda of donor countries; (2) the linking of aid to the utilization of services from the donor country;[64] (3) linking continued aid to careful reporting as a measure of government accountability and transparency; (4) a general distrust of Third World governments and failure to make distinctions between them;[65] (5) donor-specific reporting requirements that can be overwhelming and nonproductive for the recipient.

In the midst of the negotiation, planning, and execution of repatriation programs, it is easy to lose sight of the human dimension, of the need for effective working partnerships. "True partnership is based on equality. There is no equality when there is disparity in possessions. But I have possessions—my experience and my skills. Recipients have possessions and know how to use them. We want to be in a situation of mutual responsibility."[66] Paying attention to the human dimension means addressing the hard questions of repatriation in a context of patience, dignity, and respect.

Implications and Recommendations

A government that is truly the legitimate government of the people, as Eritrea's government is, can only maintain that legitimacy by providing for the basic needs of its people. To do that, there must be sufficient resources within a reasonable length of time, a willingness of the government to listen to and respond to the people, and a cooperative, problem-solving relationship between the local people and the government. When the people experience meaningful progress, they will likely be patient, will cooperate with the government toward common goals, and will work intently and intentionally toward the development of their own country.

If the government is not able to deliver such services after a reasonable length of time, a likely outcome is increasing discontent, the turning of one group against another group (seeing "the other" as a threat), and eventually antigovernment organizing. In such a context not only are the people deprived of their basic needs, threatened, and dispossessed, but the likely response of a government is to become oppressive, to attempt to stifle dissent, to be a government against the people rather than for the people. Human rights come under attack and people become victims.

The international community must move quickly to bring Eritrean refugees back from Sudan. It is morally and politically time to act, and is in the best interests of the donors and the UN. The fundamental challenge is for the international community to work together to combine returning refugees—repatriation—with community and national development—reintegration. These are opportunities to work proactively for peace. "If voluntary repatriation is to become a truly durable solution to refugee problems, *peace and an opportunity to return home are not enough.* Unless the capacity of communities and areas of return to absorb additional populations is addressed, mass repatriation may spur new forms of human deprivation, social tensions and migratory movements" (emphasis added).[67]

UNHCR, caught between governments, donors, and its own mandates, guards against an expansion of its mandate. The government of Eritrea, sensitive to the danger of outside control and of losing that for which so many have struggled and sacrificed, refuses to allow others to dictate conditions and guards against being overwhelmed while working toward the outside limits of possibilities. The donors, facing multiple and increasing demands as crisis follows crisis and wanting to ensure the responsible use of funds, fall back on rules, regulations, and procedures. They guard against being pulled in beyond their normal limits.

There is a need for new mechanisms and greater flexibility. There is a need to raise funds faster, for the UNHCR to have access to adequate and sufficient funds to negotiate from a position of being able to act. There is an urgent need for effective coordination between UN agencies, as well as among those agencies, donors, NGOs, and recipient governments.

The government of Eritrea is moving from a liberation movement to a constitutional government. After 30 years of war, the challenge of winning the peace is complex. The military style of decision making that was necessary and effective during the liberation struggle is being challenged to shift to a more participatory, delegatory style in response to the demands of building a nation at peace.[68]

There is a pressing need for donors to be open to new ways of doing repatriation, to be aware of and responsive to the specific realities of particular situations, to find creative ways to release and combine funds for relief as well as for development for repatriation. There is a need for more funds: the international donor community had, as of spring 1995, pledged less than 30% of the requested budget for PROFERI.

Analyzing the Eritrean repatriation negotiation, we can make some recommendations for the UN, national governments, and international donors.

Repatriation and the UN Family

1. The "mandate dilemma" urgently needs attention. There must be close coordination and cooperation between UNHCR and other UN agencies as well as between these agencies and governments. Flexibility on the ground in order to respond quickly is necessary. *UNHCR cannot do repatriation alone.* There is a need (a) to define who in the UN should be working with UNHCR in the country of origin and in what capacities, and (b) to equip them with appropriate mandates, with necessary funds, with on-the-ground support.

2. Ongoing mechanisms of consultation should be developed between UN agencies, as well as among UN agencies, the government, the donors, and the NGOs. A structured format in which the government and NGOs can discuss and dialogue about repatriation with the donors as observers might increase the intentionality of dialogue and the insights of the donors.[69]

3. Trusted intermediaries can be extraordinarily helpful in mediating conflicts between agencies and governments. Mechanisms to identify, to train if necessary, and to utilize such intermediaries would be an important contribution.

4. Capacity building is a central feature of long-term sustainability in development-based repatriation. UNHCR and UNDP should support and encourage this with donors to develop flexible funding and program plans for capacity building.

Government of Eritrea   To meet the demands of carrying out successful repatriation of such a large number of refugees in a short time, structures of cooperation and coordination are needed at various levels: with the UN agencies and international donors, both of whom have a wealth of knowledge about repatriation and about development; with local communities and leadership as they face the incorporation of such large numbers of returnees; with refugee/returnee leadership as they struggle to develop a hopeful life; and with international and indigenous NGOs that can link the local communities to the national structures.

International Donors: The Main Actors   Repatriation clearly must combine return with reintegration, immediate aid with long-term development. This requires a more expanded approach to funding by international donors, an approach that addresses the following challenges: (1) Accepting and supporting the legitimacy of the government of Eritrea; (2) welcoming the government's direct and active role in development, including PROFERI; (3) recognizing the real time pressures, funds appropriate to the needs should be contributed and released in a timely manner; (4) given the unquestioned importance of adequate reporting, recommending that all the donors and the government of Eritrea agree together on one format and one procedure for reporting that would be acceptable to all parties and that would serve the program needs through ongoing program evaluation aimed at increased competency; (5) since the separation of short-term relief/aid funds from longer-term development funds within governments' administration is a block to effective funding of repatriation, seeking more internal cooperation in funding projects that include both relief/aid and development; (6) welcoming the GOE's commitment to develop national capacity through local staffing and building capacity within funding packages; (7) separating the funding of technical support (often provided by expatriate experts) from the provision of direct aid.

Over and above these specific concerns and recommendations, we face the very real need to develop cooperative partnerships in response to an important opportunity to empower people at the grass-roots level and undergird the conditions for peace. The words of the Eritrean Ambassador to Sweden and the UNHCR Chief of Mission Asmara capture the essence of this challenge: "We are asking for so little. We are asking for stability. We are asking for a contribution to stability. Protective measures is the approach that is needed rather than waiting for a disaster."[70]

> For decades, we have seen the Horn of Africa as a theater of war, violence, famine and death. Not only have suffering and destruction been the order of the day, but political instability has threatened the whole region. Today, we have a historic possibility to create the basis for lasting peace and prosperity, not only in Eritrea, but in the region. For the first time in 30 years, people return home. Let us not miss this opportunity. The efforts we witness in Eritrea for creating a sustainable peace will be to the advantage of the whole Horn. I know of no better investment.[71]

SECTION II: View from the 21st Century

I am saddened to write this section. Following extensive work with Eritrean refugees resettled in the United States, refugees who hoped to return to Eritrea after the end of the 30 years of armed struggle, I went to Eritrea in 1995 to research the repatriation of refugees from Sudan. I happened to be there at the fourth anniversary of the end of the war with Ethiopia. Eritrea was at peace. As the UNHCR Chief of Mission aptly said, there was "a historic possibility to create the basis for lasting peace and prosperity." There was such energy and hope.

During the celebrations in Asmara, music of the various Eritrean ethnic groups filled the air; people walked arm in arm in the streets talking and laughing; everywhere people gathered. Eritrea was independent and, in spite of the devastation from the war, the fragile economy, the deforestation and environmental degradation that especially affected the subsistence communities, the future in freedom made the challenges worthwhile. I, too, had such hope for Eritrea and its people. Today, over 10 years later, that hope seems to be gone.

Background

The political economic situation in Eritrea today must be understood in the context of the 30-year liberation struggle. Eritrea is led by ex-guerrilla fighters; their experiences shape their vision and their memories are long and deep.[72] These government leaders are highly suspicious of the international community, and not without reason. Their suspicions are based on a history of betrayal; the outside world supported the Ethiopian colonial rule of Eritrea and, during the liberation struggle, supported Ethiopia in various ways. For example, the United States and the Soviet Union both gave significant military aid and other support to Ethiopia but not to Eritrea. There was and continues to be deep suspicion regarding the intentions of the UN, western nations, and even international NGOs.[73] Today the international community continues to give support to Ethiopia—diplomatic, developmental, and military and, on the whole, is suspicious or nonsupportive of Eritrea politically.

It is still common practice for only a portion of the aid to get to the recipient country. The majority of the funds are typically used for salaries, materials, and consultations.[74] Eritrean government leaders, headed by President Isaias Afewerki, continue to insist on a policy of self-reliance, asserting that the GOE must decide what projects need to be done and in what manner. At the Summit for Social Development, March 1995, President Afewerki stated, "donor-recipient relationships based on dictation of unsuitable antidotes will just not do . . . our independence of decision should not be encroached by conditionalities of aid."[75]

The German Development Institute (GDI) in 1995 summarized the GOE's approach as follows:

> In general, Eritrea is seeking external assistance to solve its outstanding problems. However, the government emphasizes that assistance may not encroach on Eritrean sovereignty and its independent decision making. . . . The country being assisted . . . [prioritizes] the problems and [designs and implements] their solutions; . . . funds earmarked for technical assistance should be directly transferred to the concerned country as budgetary support for it to decide how to spend it to build its capacity.[76]

Several persons whom I interviewed commented that the Eritrean government's emphasis on self-reliance is a commendable and basically sound approach. However, they also asserted that in the current political climate of Eritrea, with its "the international community is our enemy" sensibilities and its repression of internal dissent, self-reliance has been shaped into a harsh tool that wounds the people and the nation.

Perhaps surprisingly, Ethiopia was the first to recognize Eritrea after independence. However, after 1996 tensions increased. Eritrea stopped using the Ethiopian currency and issued its own, the *Naqfa*. For Ethiopia, access to the port of Assab was and is a major issue. In 1998 there was a plane attack on Mekele, the capital of Tigray in Ethiopia. A bloody border war ensued and lasted until 2000, an apparently senseless conflict about territory with no economic value.

Regional Instability

The border war was conducted at a horrific loss of life; tens of thousands of persons were killed, civilians as well as soldiers.[77] Today large numbers of troops—Ethiopian and Eritrean—remain along the border and tensions are acute. Under the auspices of the United Nations the border was fixed using satellite images. The outcome favored the Eritrean position. Ethiopia has not implemented the decision of the border commission, and Eritrea is accusing the international community of not putting enough pressure on Ethiopia. In March 2008 the Government of Eritrea (GOE) put restrictions on diesel fuel supplies, causing the United Nations Mission for Ethiopia and Eritrea (UNMEE) detachments to withdraw from the Temporary Security Zone.[78] No international observers are now monitoring the border. Ed Harris, reporting for the BBC from Eritrea, reflects that "these tensions can seem very convenient for both governments. 'They can blame anything—from lack of flour to [military] mobilization—on the border issue,' one young Eritrean said of his government."[79]

Since April 2008 Djiboutian and Eritrean troops have been deployed along the northeastern border of Djibouti. Djibouti claims that Eritrean troops have crossed into its territory, a claim which the Eritrean government denies. In addition, the Eritrean government is entwined with the situations in Somalia and Sudan. African Union leaders recently condemned Eritrea for "its negative activities in destabilizing regional peace and security."[80] Some sources assert that President Afewerki is supporting the Oromo Liberation Front in Ethiopia and Somali opposition groups.

The GOE restricts the travel of all foreign nationals, including resident diplomats and international nongovernmental personnel. All visitors and residents must apply for permission to travel outside of Asmara. "Travelers should be aware that the [GOE] does not inform the U.S. Embassy when American citizens have been arrested or detained."[81]

Food, Hunger, and Self-reliance[82]

After independence 80% of the population was on food aid. The economic progress Eritrea experienced since independence in 1991 has been reversed by the 1998–2000 border war and aggravated by consecutive years of drought/crop failure beginning in 2000. Retail prices of basic food items have steadily increased. According to the World Food Programme, more than 2 million persons in this country of approximately 4 million experience food insecurity.

International nongovernmental organizations (INGOs) have had a major role in food security and agricultural support. There were 36 INGOs in the country when the GOE required them to register and subjected them to strict regulation. Sixteen registered; some left; some were effectively expelled. Currently there are five

INGOs registered and operating in Eritrea: Catholic Relief Services; Lutheran World Federation; Norwegian Church Aid; Oxfam UK; Registry Trust International. There is one local NGO: Vision Eritrea. INGOs are restricted to hardware components of projects, not software such as civil society and community development. Capacity building and working with farmers are still accepted; community organizing is not. The lack of fuel allocations makes it difficult for INGOs to do their work. As the GOE has consistently stated, INGOs are not expected to implement a project but to do monitoring and funding.

The World Food Programme and international agencies involved in food aid fear that hunger and malnutrition are at dangerous levels in Eritrea. President Afewerki responded to this international concern by writing a hostile letter to the UN Secretary General accusing the UN of "portraying a humanitarian crisis in Eritrea that did not exist."[83] The 2008 Global Hunger Index, which ranks 88 countries on undernourishment, prevalence of child malnutrition, and rates of child mortality, ranked Eritrea 87—second to worst, just above the Democratic Republic of the Congo.[84] No official data on last year's harvest or health indicators in Eritrea have been released by the GOE, and, because foreigners—including staff of humanitarian aid organizations—are forbidden from traveling outside Asmara, it is difficult to get a more accurate assessment.

Signals from President Afewerki suggest that the government will not be asking for emergency food assistance. The GOE states that the food issues should be dealt with internally through an increase of production. In 2008 in response to the question of "Are you food sufficient?" Afewerki forcefully asserted:

> If we are food self-sufficient is not the issue. We are not food sufficient. Anyone who wants to provide food aid, give to Somalia. We are not in the position to talk about food aid. Food aid as politics. We are not interested getting food aid. We don't want to be spoon fed. We want to live on our soil. We don't want to be crippled by food aid which is linked to an agenda that makes us dependent.

> R. KHAN: "However, there are food shortages in Asmara."
> I. AFEWERKI: "Who told you that?"
> R. KHAN: "We've been told that there is a black market in food supplies."
> I. AFEWERKI: "This is another fabrication. Go to Egypt and USA and find food shortages. Address these issues."[85]

Exacerbating the food vulnerability, in 2005 the GOE "seized more than 100 aid vehicles, demanded tax on relief items, expelled several key nongovernmental organizations (NGOs) and stopped the distribution of food aid."[86] More than one million Eritreans were affected, especially those in rural areas. The government took over all the food stores, most from the United States, without any agreement with donors. The World Food Programme is closed. No crop assessments are being done. There is no free market for the farmers; only the GOE buys the produce at the government's own price. Ed Harris of the BBC reports that with the stoppage of food distribution in 2005 the rate of malnutrition was rising. The GOE has instituted a cash-for-work policy. Eritreans will receive cash in exchange for working on food security projects such as irrigation and road building. Although it is not clear how this will alleviate the lack of food security and attendant malnutrition, the GOE asserts that this policy is working toward a long-term solution.

The border demarcation hammered out in 2000 by the UN as part of a comprehensive peace agreement has stalled. Significant human and economic resources have been diverted to mobilization and militarization and away from farming. According to one report up to 70,000 internally displaced persons have been living in makeshift camps for over five years.[87] Some grain-producing areas in the western lowlands cannot be cultivated, owing to unexploded land mines. The 2003 Livelihood Systems Measurement Survey found 66% of the population living below the poverty line, with rates as high as 80% in rural areas. As a result of the war up to 40% of households are female-headed and thus especially vulnerable to food insecurity.

The World Food Programme lists the following impediments to food security in Eritrea: drought; the stalemated peace process with Ethiopia; unexploded ordnance and mines, especially in the Temporary Security Zone [TSZ], which stretches over the formerly grain producing areas; internal displacement;[88] continued military mobilization leading to lack of labor for agriculture; high inflation and a sharp increase in the prices of basic food; and increasing fuel prices and rationing of fuel.

As a number of concerned observers noted, the GOE's principles are right in many ways, especially regarding dependency and self-reliance. They are pursuing appropriate policies given what is happening on the world market. They are trying to build their own capacities, especially through national service and using the army to build infrastructure and hospitals. However, they cannot do everything by themselves. For example, the special UN envoy for Africa came to talk about the food—given by donors, especially the United States—which the government took without permission from the donors. Then, Eritrea gets into a very difficult situation with those same donors when there is a food security crisis, which there is right now.

Political Representation and Repression

A remarkable, countrywide participatory process for developing a constitution was held in the mid-1990s, headed by Dr. Bereket Habte Selassie. The resulting constitution was approved by a referendum in 1997 but has not been implemented. No national elections have been held; an interim parliament has not met since 2002. Gaim Kibreab asserts that the "guiding concept of the EPLF/PFDJ's philosophy of governing is that the Eritrean national political arena cannot accommodate more than one political organization."[89] President Afewerki explains this by saying that Eritrea must remain on a "war footing" until the boundary dispute with Ethiopia is resolved.[90] In the 2008 interview [above] Afewerki asserted:

> What election? We will see what the election in the US will bring about. We will wait 3 to 4 decades before we hold elections. Maybe more; who knows. Depending upon what you mean by elections. Such as Jordan, Ethiopia, Iraq. . . . It may never happen. May take decades. What do you mean by democracy? Genuine elections? That is another issue. If you mean elections promoted by USA, separate agenda, is not elections for us.[91]

Political Repression

Political repression is widespread. According to Amnesty International: "Torture has routinely been used as a punishment for critics of the government and members of minority faiths, as well as for offences committed by military conscripts. Arbitrary incommunicado detention 'without charge or trial' is widespread and long-lasting—several prisoners of conscience have been held thus for over a decade—with many detainees held in secret and their whereabouts not known."[92]

In September 2001, 11 government leaders were arrested, because they publically questioned Afewerki's leadership especially in regard to the border conflict with Ethiopia and the lack of implementation of the constitution.[93] These political leaders as well as journalists arrested during the same period remain, without charge or trial, in solitary confinement in a secret detention center. According to Human Rights Watch, by January 2008 nine of the 31 prisoners reportedly had died.[94] Human Rights Watch estimates that there are additionally "between sixty and eighty persons in detention apparently because of their criticism of the government," including University of Asmara students, prominent businessmen, and military officers.[95] Amnesty International estimates a much higher number of political prisoners stating that there are several thousand prisoners of conscience who have been held incommunicado for many years, often in secret locations or military prisons. It is asserted that some have died of illness and injuries sustained from torture.[96] Again, President Afewerki denies these allegations: "What kind of opposition do you mean? Agents sponsored by Langley, by Israel. . . . There has never been opposition in Eritrea. This has been manufactured by Langley . . . Freedom of the press? If you mean press financed by corporations, by the military industry . . . like special interests, CNN, we are not party of this kind of freedom of the press."[97]

Eritrea is the only African country without privately owned news media. In 2005 the U.S.-based Committee to Protect Journalists [CPJ] described it as one of the world's leading jailers of journalists. Another press watchdog, Reporters Without Borders, notes that there is "no freedom of expression:" "The government closed the private press in 2001 for 'endangering national security' and arrested many journalists after several publications printed the dissenting views of some National Assembly members. There are no private radio or TV stations. The only press allowed is the government-related press."[98] In 2007 Reporters Without Borders ranked Eritrea last of 169 countries on its Press Freedom Index.[99] No civil society organizations or media exist other than those controlled by the ruling People's Front for Democracy and Justice.

Religious persecution has also escalated. In 1995 the Proclamation Religious Organizations no. 73/1995 prohibited all faiths from receiving international funds or engaging in political activities. All religious organizations were required to register with the GOE and provide membership and funding details. Since 2002 only four religious groups have been officially recognized and allowed to operate in Eritrea: Orthodox, Catholic, Lutheran Christian churches, and Islam. Minority faith groups are banned, and house worship and bible study are not allowed.

Over 2,000 persons have been arrested because of their religious affiliations and/ or beliefs.[100] Evangelical Christians who have been arrested face severe pressure to recant their religious beliefs. Reports of torture and terrible conditions are routine.[101] Although the Orthodox church is legally recognized, the GOE in 2006 stripped Abune Antonios, the Patriarch of the Eritrean Orthodox Church, of his ecclesiastical authority. In 2006 he was reported to be under house arrest without visitors because of his protest regarding the arrest of three Orthodox priests and for refusing to close down their church.[102] The reasons for the repression of minority faiths have not been given by the GOE. Several informants asserted that it was related to military conscription, particularly regarding the Jehovah's Witnesses.

Since October 1995 6 months of military training and 12 months of active military service have been required of all Eritreans, men and women, between the ages of 18 and 40. Later the upper age limit for women was lowered to 27. Because of the border conflict with Ethiopia the length of required military service is typically extended indefinitely, causing great stress among families and rupturing traditional social networks of support. Conscription is carried out by round-ups. In November 2004 thousands of military-age persons, including over 500 relatives of persons accused of evading conscription, were rounded up and arrested in Asmara and taken to a prison.[103] Persons of at least 17 years of age are refused exit permits to leave Eritrea. Many do try to flee, and the rate of desertion is reportedly high. Many have fled to Egypt and Libya and requested asylum, but routinely have been denied. UNHCR reports that in two years the number of asylum applications to Western countries by Eritreans has increased by 57% and describes the exodus as "one of the world's most protracted refugee situations."[104]

Education has also been militarized. Diplomas are issued only after completion of military service. Students spend their final year of high school at the Sawa military training center and undergo military training along with their regular studies. As of 2003 no high school graduates are allowed to attend the University of Asmara—a site of previous political dissent. They are either conscripted into the military or sent to technical schools. Obviously, such conscription, removing strong young persons from rural communities, has a serious negative effect on agricultural production and every other aspect of socioeconomic development.

Since independence and liberation from Ethiopian rule the Eritrean diaspora has been a major source of support for the GOE. They send funds to families, have begun businesses with relatives still in Eritrea, and had been taxed by the GOE at a preferential finance rate. Recently the GOE removed that preferential rate for the diaspora, reducing the amount of money coming in to Eritrea from Eritreans living abroad. Eritreans who returned to invest have left and gone back to "developed" countries. Some diasporic groups have begun to organize to protest the political repression in Eritrea, and the GOE asserts that such groups are actively fomenting rebellion against the government. Groups in Western countries often link with nongovernmental organizations such as Amnesty International in order to strengthen their protests.

The "Big Picture"

This chapter has depicted a nation that experienced the struggles for liberation in the longest-standing war in Africa and began to chart a new road to the future. The beginning of that road was shaped by a participatory process for developing a constitution, a commitment to independence, and a reliance on the commitment of its people—both civilians and former fighters—to a strong, independent Eritrea. Although many donors were hesitant and even negative, many INGOs that had supported Eritrea during its struggle for freedom lauded this new, refreshing approach to nationhood through self-reliance and commitment.

Today that road seems deformed by both external forces and internal responses. The internal commitment to nation building has been compromised and attacked. Dissent by loyal leadership has been brutally squashed; "unable to govern by democratic means, the Eritrean state has fully deployed coercion as an instrument of control."[105] Human Rights Watch graphically describes Eritrea as "a country in shackles."[106] The rhetoric of nation-building through the efforts of committed people and their leaders continues, but money and action have shifted to the military defense of borders and ports, fueled by the suspicion and nonsupport of significant parts of the international community. Ethiopia continues, albeit defying the UN border decision, to be the country in the Horn of Africa favored by the international community. Eritrea clearly interprets this as being politically/diplomatically attacked and responds with hostility.

After independence, peace through national security focused on providing and building the capacity to insure critical humanitarian needs, linking, for example, the return of the refugees from Sudan to the development of the country, especially agriculture and infrastructure. With an unwavering insistence on self-reliance, Eritrea shaped its national security around meeting the pressing needs of its people—the returnees, the former fighters, and the civilians. The vision of a nation in which all were involved was actualized through the complex participatory constitution-building process—a first-ever experience in Africa. This was the "ray of hope" to which the UN Head of Station referred.

Today the meaning and the mechanisms to achieve security have shifted to securing borders, squashing dissent, and backing away from negotiations on cooperative use of ports. The free expressions of religion, of opinions, of different life paths are blocked. There is no true civil society in the typical use of the concept; "both civil society and state in Eritrea are structured on the military model."[107] Employment is either in the military or through other government avenues. Some even refer to Eritrea as having moved to being a prison of its own—of becoming a totalitarian state.

Though Eritrea's leaders are responsible for their own actions, these actions do not occur in isolation. As I stated at the beginning of the chapter, one cannot understand Eritrea today without taking into account the history—the struggle for liberation, development, and international cooperation shaped by self-reliance, but also the unequal political and economic support of the international community for Ethiopia relative to Eritrea, which lends credence to Eritrea's suspicions and hostility. The geopolitics of the Horn of Africa vis-à-vis the Middle East is an ever-present reality that also plays out in the Eritrean border states of Somalia, Djbouti, and Sudan.

The Ray of Hope Has Disappeared

As I conclude this chapter my sadness and discouragement are profound. There are no more words to add except to hope, perhaps without reason, that international pressure on one hand and support for the people of Eritrea on the other hand might alleviate what is reported here. My closing image is back to the hundreds of people walking the streets of Asmara, hand in hand, listening to music, laughing and soaking in the wonder of an independent country where they could build a hopeful future. The ray of hope that glimmered in this Horn of Africa country has disappeared. As one young woman said "dreams don't come true in Eritrea."[108] People suffer. Where do they turn?

Under stress from grinding poverty and horrific human rights violations, Eritrea's able-bodied citizens are today voting on their feet. In the hope of making it to Ethiopia or Sudan and beyond and at huge risk to their lives, Eritreans are again on the road in ever larger numbers.[109]

Notes

1. The name has been changed; the statement is accurate. Woldemichael is a former fighter and refugee to Germany who returned to Eritrea to help rebuild his country.

2. This study is based primarily on personal interviews with Eritrean government officials, representatives of donor countries and international NGOs, Eritrean former fighters, Eritrean civilians, UNHCR, Geneva staff and UNHCR, Eritrea staff, other UN agency staff (UNDP and DHA), and participants in the earlier Cross Border operations. The interviews were conducted in Eritrea, Sweden, the United States, Ethiopia, and Geneva, in November and December 1994; January 1995; May and June 1995. Documentation was graciously provided by the Refugee Studies Programme, Oxford University; the UNHCR Documentation Centre; the Commission for Eritrean Refugee Affairs (CERA); the Eritrea Relief and Rehabilitation Agency (ERRA); the Eritrean Embassy, Stockholm, Sweden; the Swedish Foreign Ministry; the German Development Institute (GDI); and UNHCR Asmara and UNHCR Geneva. Various international NGOs provided background material.

3. Ambassador Tseggai Tesfazion, Stockholm, Sweden.

4. The exact number of Eritrean refugees in Sudan is not possible to obtain. The Sudanese government Committee on Refugees (COR) figures, 450,000 to 500,000 at the time of liberation, May 1991, are used by UNHCR and the government of Eritrea.

5. J. Pobee, "'Peace, with Justice and Honour, Fairest and Most Profitable of Possessions'," *Power and Peace* (Uppsala, Sweden: Life & Peace Institute, 1992, 93).

6. See Pobee, ibid., for a fuller discussion of these points within the African context.

7. F. Stepputat, "National Conflict and Repatriation: An Analysis of Relief, Power and Reconciliation," *CDR Project Proposal 93.4* (Copenhagen: Centre for Development Research, Oct. 1993, 5).

8. See J. Clifford, "Traveling Cultures," in *Cultural Studies*, L. Grossberg et al., Eds. (New York: Routledge, 1992) and H. Moussa, *Storm and Sanctuary: The Journey of Ethiopian and Eritrean Women Refugees* (Dundas, Ontario: Artemis Enterprises, 1993), for further discussions of this point.

9. Stepputat, note 7, p. 5.

10. The history of Eritrea's liberation struggle is long and complex. I focus here on factors that have a contemporary relationship to the negotiations for repatriation.

11. UN Resolution 390-A(V) explicitly stated that the provisions of the federation would not be amended or violated by anybody other than the General Assembly. The autonomy of the Eritrean government was guaranteed by the United Nations.

12. M. Fahlen, *UNHCR Mission Report, Eritrea*, 1995–05–26, p. 2.

13. From 1976 to 1991 "unofficial" food aid funded by northern European countries was channeled into the liberated areas of Eritrea through the efforts of Swedish Church Relief, Norwegian Church Aid, and the Sudan Council of Churches—the Emergency Relief Desk in Khartoum. See M. Duffield and J. Prendergast, *Without Troops and Tanks: Humanitarian Intervention in Ethiopia and Eritrea* (Lawrenceville, NJ: Red Sea Press, 1994) for a description of the Cross-Border Operation.

14. Chief of Mission, UNHCR Asmara, May 1995.

15. "Countries of the Horn: 3—Eritrea," *New Internationalist* 238 (Dec. 1992, 17).

16. John McCallin, UNHCR Horn of Africa Desk, Geneva, Switzerland, Jan. 1995.

17. As discussed in "Environmental Aspects of Resettlements," Naigzy Gebremedhin, Coordinator of Eritrea's National Environmental Management Plan, May 1995, only 0.40% of Eritrea is now forested. Thirty years ago it was 15% forested. According to an FAO report (*Environment Eritrea*, 1:3 [Feb. 1995]), fuel wood demand in Eritrea exceeds supply by 150%.

18. M. Fahlen, *UNHCR Mission Report, Eritrea*, p. 3.

19. A Constitutional Commission, officially independent of the government and committed to the protection of citizens' rights and a pluralistic form of governance, is implementing a

two-year participatory process to involve all regions and sectors of Eritrean society in the development of the constitution. If this process is successful, Eritrea has a good chance of becoming a peaceful model in the Horn of Africa.

20. E. Habte Selassie, UNDP/UNDO, Nairobi, Kenya, May 1995; G. Kibreab, 1995, UNHCR officials.

21. The Swedish government had provided funds for food aid delivered through the Cross-Border Operation from Sudan during the liberation struggle.

22. UNHCR Geneva staff, Jan. 1995.

23. UNHCR Geneva staff and "Eritrea," *World Refugee Survey* (Washington, D.C.: U.S. Committee for Refugees, 56).

24. This point was also made in interviews by representatives of several international donor countries. They stressed that repatriation (humanitarian emergency relief) funds are administered separately from development money.

25. Karin Landgren, UNHCR, Jan. 1995, Geneva, Switzerland.

26. Ahmed Tahir Badouri, *Eritrea Profile*, Jan. 7, 1995, p. 7.

27. Elias Habte Selassie, May 1995, Nairobi, Kenya.

28. Elias Habte Selassie, UNDP May 1995, Nairobi, Kenya.

29. UNHCR, Geneva, Jan. 1995.

30. Nils Arne-Kastberg, Swedish Mission to the UN, October 1994.

31. "Joint Government of Eritrea and United Nations Appeal for Eritrea," vol. 1, PROFERI, Executive Summary, June 1993, p. i.

32. Dr. Nerayo Teklemichael, Director of ERRA/GOE, May 1995, Asmara, Eritrea.

33. "Eritrea," *World Refugee Survey*, p. 56.

34. GOE, "Joint, Government of Eritrea and United Nations Appeal for Eritrea," vol. 1, PROFERI, June 1993, pp. i–ii.

35. Arnulv Thornbjornsen, UNHCR Chief of Mission, May 1995, Asmara, Eritrea.

36. Asmara, Eritrea, May 1995.

37. CERA/GOE, "Progress Report on Repatriation and Initial Relief and Food Aid Components of the Pilot Project and Statistical Information on Returnees," May 1995, p. 1.

38. Norwegian Church Aid staff, Nov. 1994, Asmara, Eritrea.

39. M. Fahlen, *UNHCR Mission Report, Eritrea,* May 15–23, 1995, p. 1. Spontaneous returnees receive less material support than those who return under the organized repatriation program.

40. UNHCR, *Country Operations Plan,* State of Eritrea, May 29, 1995, notes that the actual number able to be repatriated depended in part on truck availability.

41. This was also the message I received in individual interviews with UNHCR, CERA, ERRA, and various NGOs.

42. Arnulv Torbjornsen, Chief of Mission, UNHCR, Asmara, May 19, 1995, presentation at Donor Workshop, Asmara, Eritrea.

43. Herbert R M'Cleod, UNDP Resident Representative, May 20, 1995, statement at PROFERI Workshop, Asmara, Eritrea.

44. The PROFERI development and integration approach is similar to the national Recovery and Rehabilitation Programme for Eritrea (RRPE) of ERRA but is targeted solely to returnees. RRPE is targeted to the broad population. There are plans to combine CERA and ERRA into one agency, although that had not occurred at the time of the Donors Workshop, May 1995.

45. N. Gebremedhin, "Environmental Aspects of Resettlements," GOE, report to Donors Workshop, Asmara, Eritrea, May 19–20, 1995.

46. See A. Hansen, *Current Conditions in Returnee Camps in Gash & Setit Province*, report prepared for GTZ Integrated Food Security Programme (IFSP), Gash & Setit, Tessenei, Eritrea, March 1995, for an elaboration of these concerns.

47. The GOE's environmental report, "Environmental Aspects of Resettlements," estimated that approximately 42,000 housing units—five persons per household—will be required to house 420,000 returnees. A traditional *Hidmo* would require 100 fully grown trees, an impossibility in Eritrea. There was concern that even the materials for ordinary huts would not be available.

48. As an example, FINIDA negotiated over a year with the GOE regarding cooperation with the university. FINIDA agreed to a lot of give-and-take but would not give in regarding having two Finns at the university to sign checks. When the GOE would not agree to this, FINIDA pulled out.

49. Gerense Kelati, Commissioner of CERA, May 19, 1995, Donors Workshop, Asmara, Eritrea.

50. Madame Sadako Ogata, UN High Commissioner for Refugees, June 8, 1994, Washington, D.C.

51. G. Kibreab, *Ready, Willing, and Waiting* (Uppsala, Sweden: Life & Peace Institute, 1995).

52. UNHCR, "Policy & Methodological Framework for Quick Impact Projects (QIPs) as a Means of Facilitating Durable Solutions through Integration," June 30, 1994, pp. 1–2.

53. UNHCR, 1993, 173.

54. H. Bjuremalm, Swedish Foreign Ministry, Oct. 1994.

55. See E. G. Ferris, *Beyond Borders: Refugees, Migrants and Human Rights in the Post Cold-War Era* (Geneva: World Council of Churches, 1993) for a detailed exploration of the international refugee response system.

56. UNHCR Chief of Mission, Asmara, Eritrea, May 1995.

57. See also Kibreab, note 51.

58. UNHCR Chief of Mission, Asmara, Eritrea, May 1995.

59. U.S. refugee resettlement agency staff.

60. International Peace Service, n.d.

61. Elias Habte Selassie, May 1995, Nairobi, Kenya.

62. Member of the German parliament speaking at the Donors Workshop, May 19, 1995, Asmara, Eritrea.

63. Helene Bjuremalm, Swedish Foreign Ministry, Oct. 1994. Also, see Ferris, note 55.

64. A German representative recalled that when Germany gave DM 3 million to a particular Eritrean project it was likely that only DM 1 million would finally be available for the direct implementation of the project. The remainder would be used for salaries, materials, and consultations from Germany. Frequently technical support was included within direct aid.

65. This is especially ironic in the Eritrean context, since all the donors informally agreed that the Eritrean government was an honest, legitimate government—in clear contrast to a government such as that of Nigeria.

66. Dr. Nerayo Teklemichael, Head of ERRA, government of Eritrea, May 1995, Asmara, Eritrea.

67. UNHCR, note 52.

68. Part of the responsibility of the Constitutional Committee is to structure mechanisms for such participation into the governance of the country.

69. I am grateful to Nils-Arne Kastberg, Swedish Mission to the UN, Geneva, for this suggestion.

70. Ambassador Tessegai Tesfazion, Nov. 1994, Stockholm.

71. Arnulv Torbjornsen, UNHCR Chief of Mission Asmara, presentation to Donors Workshop, May 19, 1995, Asmara, Eritrea.

72. See Gaim Kibreab, *Critical Reflections on the Eritrean War of Independence: Social Capital, Associational Life, Religion, Ethnicity and Sowing Seeds of Dictatorship* (Trenton, NJ: The Red Sea Press: Trenton, 2008) for a detailed and nuanced analysis of the political/historical background and processes leading up to the current political situation in Eritrea.

73. For example, Jacques Willemse of Dutch Interchurch Aid, one of the INGOs cooperating in delivering aid to the Emergency Relief Desk, stated: "The UN and even major sectors of the NGO community kept their distance, if not being openly hostile. As late as 1988 a donor representative responded to my pleas for more food aid for ERA by claiming that 'you are asking us to feed the enemies of our friend [Ethiopia]. We don't do that.'" Quoted in Lucia Ann McSpadden, *Negotiating Return: Conflict and Control in the Repatriation of Eritrean Refugees* (Uppsala: Life & Peace Institute, 2000, 32).

74. For example, see a statement from a German government representative in Lucia Ann McSpadden, *Negotiating Return: Conflict and Control in the Repatriation of Eritrean Refugees* (Uppsala: Life & Peace Institute, 2000, 124–5).

75. International Peace Service, n.d. See also the reports from the Donors' Conference held in Geneva, July 6, 1993, pp. 86–87 and the Donor Workshop, 19–20 May, 1995, Asmara, Eritrea, pp. 98–102, as presented in Lucia Ann McSpadden, *Negotiating Return: Conflict and Control in the Repatriation of Eritrean Refugees* (Uppsala: Life & Peace Institute, 2000).

76. Government of Eritrea, "Partnership in Development," Asmara, 1994, cited in Gärke et al., *Promoting the Reintegration of Former Female and Female Combatants in Eritrea: Possible Contributions of Development Co-operation to the Reintegration Programme*, Final Report, German Development Institute (GDI), Berlin April, 1995, p. 21, cited in Lucia Ann McSpadden, note 75, pp. 100–01.

77. See Lucia Ann McSpadden, "The Eritreans and Ethiopians," *Endangered Peoples of Africa and the Middle East: Struggles to Survive and Thrive*, Robert K. Hitchcock and Alan J. Osborn, Eds. (Westport, CT: Greenwood Press, 2002, 79) for more detailed figures.

78. This fuel restriction was also imposed on all international NGOs. This effectively makes it impossible for the INGO staff to visit projects regularly. Typically the staff must ask for the fuel and are allowed to visit the projects at the beginning, in the middle, and at the end of the project in question.

79. "Self-reliance could cost Eritrea dear," BBC News, http://news.bbc.co.uk/go/pr/fr/-/2/hi/business/5121212.stvn, published 07/05/06.

80. *Horn of African Bulletin*, Vol. 22, No. 2, p. 7, February 2010.

81. Travel Warning: U.S. Department of State, *Bureau of Consular Affairs*, Washington, D.C., November 24, 2008.

82. See Lucia Ann McSpadden, note 77, pp. 87–90, for a summary background of issues that provide a current context for food security challenges.

83. "Self-reliance could cost Eritrea dear," BBC News, http://news.bbc.co.uk/go/pr/fr/-/2/hi/business/5121212.stvn, published 2006/07/05.

84. BBC News, "Global Hunger Index in Full," http://newsvote.bbc.co.uk/mpapps/pagetools/print/news.bbc.co.uk/2/hi/in_depth/7670229..., 11/25/08.

85. May 23, 2008 interview by Riz Khan (Aljazera), accessed February 24, 2010 www.youtube.com/watch?v=UAXKsZ8OsWo&feature=related.

86. "Self-reliance could cost Eritrea dear," BBC News, http://news.bbc.co.uk/go/pr/fr/-/2/hi/business/5121212.stvn, published 07/05/2006.

87. World Food Programme, www.wfp.org/country_brief/indexcountry.asp?country/Eritrea 2008.

88. Only recently the GOE, with support from the international community, has launched a resettlement campaign to move approximately 75,000 IDPs back to their places of origin, where they will continue to receive support until they are able to reestablish their livelihoods. An estimated 10,000 IDPs still remain to be resettled.

89. Gaim Kibreab, *Critical Reflections on the Eritrean War of Independence: Social Capital, Associational Life, Religion, Ethnicity, and Sowing Seeds of Dictatorship* (Trenton, NJ: The Red Sea Press, 2008, 413).

90. Human Rights Watch, January 2008.

91. May 23, 2008 interview by Aljazera with R. Khan shown on the Awate website.

92. www.amnestyusa.org/print.php, 12/29/08.

93. See Dan Connell, *Conversations with Eritrean Political Prisoners* (Trenton, NJ: The Red Sea Press, 2005) for verbatim interviews with five of these men who became political prisoners.

94. Human Rights Watch country report, January 2008.

95. Ibid.

96. www.amnestyusa.org/print.php, 12/29/08.

97. May 23, 2008 interview by Aljazera with R. Khan shown on the Awate website.

98. http://news.bbc.co.uk/2/hi/africa/country_profiles/1070813.stm#overview.

99. Human Rights Watch, note 94. The GOE dismisses reports by RWB, because it is based in the United States.

100. Amnesty International, www.amnestyusa.org/print.php, 12/20/08.

101. "Eritrean Christians Tell of Torture," Tanya Datta, BBC News, northern Ethiopia, 09/27/09, http://newsvote.bbc.co.uk/mpapps/pagetools/print/news.bbc.co.uk/2/hi/africa/7015033,stm. Personal accounts of religious persecution are also poignantly reported in "Religious Persecution in Eritrea," Jonah Fisher, Former BBC correspondent in Asmara. BBC News, http://news.bbc.co.uk/go/pr/fr/-/2/hi/africa/3663654.stm, 09/17/04.

102. Letter of petition by Amnesty International to the General Secretary of the Holy Synod in Asmara, Eritrea.

103. "Eritrea: Over 500 Parents of Conscripts Arrested," Amnesty International Public Statement, December 21, 2006.

104. "Eritrean Christians Tell of Torture," Tanya Datta, BBC News, northern Ethiopia, 09/27/09, http://newsvote.bbc.co.uk/mpapps/pagetools/print/news.bbc.co.uk/2/hi/africa/7015033,stm.

105. Kidane Mengisteab and Okbazghi Yohannes, *Anatomy of an African Tragedy: Political, Economic, and Foreign Policy Crisis in Post-Independence Eritrea* (Trenton, NJ: The Red Sea Press, 2005, 273).

106. Human Rights Watch, January 2009. "Eritrea Country Summary," in Human Rights Watch World Report 2010, www.hrw.org/en/world-report-2010/eritrea.

107. Kidane Mengisteab and Okbazghi Yohannes, *Anatomy of an African Tragedy: Political, Economic, and Foreign Policy Crisis in Post-Independence Eritrea* (Trenton, NJ: The Red Sea Press, 2005, 272).

108. Nicole Hirt, *"Dreams Don't Come True in Eritrea": Anomie and Family Disintegration due to the Structural Militarization of Society,* Working Paper 119, German Institute of

Global and Area Studies, Hamburg, Germany, January 2010, p. 5, www.giga-hamburg. de/workingpapers.

109. Kidane Mengisteab and Okbazghi Yohannes, *Anatomy of an African Tragedy: Political, Economic, and Foreign Policy Crisis in Post-Independence Eritrea* (Trenton, NJ: The Red Sea Press, 2005, 273).

CHAPTER 13

Environmental Justice, Health, and Safety in Urban South Africa: Alexandra Township Revisited

Ben Wisner[1]

Elsewhere in this volume the concept of environmental rights is equated with the human right to a healthful environment and to sustainable livelihood. In the context of urban South Africa in the postapartheid era, this definition is useful. It focuses attention on the activism of township dwellers in struggling for such rights. It also highlights the limitation of reform and incrementalism in situations that have been rendered nonviable by spatial logic of racial separation and the control of labor power.

In May 2009 South African President Jacob Zuma opened a shopping mall in Alexandra Township, the focus of much resistance against apartheid where black residents have suffered grave environmental threats for decades. He said: "Alexandra is home to many leaders of the ANC. We can count leaders like Kgalema Motlanthe, Alfred Nzo, Thomas Nkobi and many more who were residents of this township. [It] has given this country expertise and talent." The township has been well-known for resistance actions like the Alexandra bus boycott, but, he continued, "from today, Alex must be known for development and progress."[2] Do these words and this symbolic act mark the successful end of protest and final attainment of a healthful environment and sustainable livelihoods for the residents of Alex, as it is called?

This chapter is a detailed study of one of South Africa's best-known black townships, Alexandra. The context for the study was a review of South Africa's four largest metropolitan areas, first at the end of the first year of the new Government of National Unity (GNU) and again in April 2009, precisely 15 years after the historic elections that ended apartheid. Urban policy in South Africa since the National Party came to power in 1948 was designed to control "nonwhite" access to and residence in urban areas. In the course of implementing this plan for racial separation and the control of the nonwhite labor power needed in cities, the apartheid regime was in nearly constant conflict with African, colored, and Asian communities. Attempts to

311

"clear black spots" from "white" cities by resettlement were resisted by the residents. Other groups of migrants from rural areas or outlying peri-urban zones set up illegal shack communities on vacant land as near to jobs as they could get. The regime often fought back by further rounds of forced removal and resettlement.

In the course of nearly 50 years of such urban struggle, many lives were lost in violent confrontation. In addition, a far greater price was paid by the affected communities because of increased health and safety hazards to which its peoples had been subjected. The demographic and spatial instability of nonwhite urban areas has made community assessment and mitigation of hazards difficult. Always short of economic means for investment in infrastructure, the locus of planning control was always outside these communities. Squatters and shack dwellers especially, fell outside even the meager attempts by townships to supply water, sanitation, electricity, drainage, roads, traffic regulation, and health services.[3] Spatial apartheid produced extreme densities and hence subdivision of structures for relatives or renters. This spatial pattern of extremely dense urban settlement with insufficient services has led to critical health and safety hazards. In addition to public health, fire, and traffic hazards, these areas often became the site of illegal dumping of hazardous waste. Other common hazards are flooding, mass erosion of slopes, and air pollution caused by mineral coal fires used for warmth and cooking where electricity is commonly absent or unaffordable.

Resistance to apartheid gave rise in the 1980s to campaigns of ungovernability. Residents were urged by political organizers to refuse to pay for utilities and/or for rent owed to the townships, because these forms of local government were seen as nonrepresentative and the services they provided were poor. In the period of reconstruction following the April 1994 national elections, which produced a government of national unity led by the African National Congress (ANC), the ripples of ungovernability are still to be seen. Local governments were not elected until October 1995. Provisional arrangements remain ad hoc, the product of ongoing negotiations between civic organizations and the adjacent white municipalities that often provided a caretaker role in the absence of effective township councils.[4]

Research into the hazard vulnerability of Alexandra suggests that health, safety, and sustainable livelihoods had been blocked—hence environmental rights violated—through the complex spatial and social consequences of struggle over urban occupancy. However, this chapter attempts to go beyond describing the hazardous situation thus caused and laying blame to address the question of reconstruction and healing. A review of efforts by citizens and evolving nongovernmental organizations and a consideration of the policies of the new government provide some room for guarded hope.

However, the challenge to both government and citizen-based organizations is not to minimize the extent of the problem. A dual strategy of immediate increase in services and mitigation of the worst hazards must be coupled with two longer-term processes: (1) de-densification through land acquisition and provision of affordable housing, or at least building loans and site and service, and (2) investment in people through neighborhood- and community-based capacity building for locally initiated work on what people agree are priority hazards. Although by 2009 there had been some progress in both these areas, it has come as the result of the forced removals of thousands of people judged "vulnerable to floods." This is ironic. Having resisted apartheid's removals for decades and developed pride and, indeed, fame for its culture of resistance, Alexandra Township finally succumbed. The relationship between a large class of persistently poor urban dwellers and the state remains complex and characterized by mistrust.

Urban and Rural Settlement Ecology under Apartheid

For the majority of people in South Africa, both urban and rural, the system of racial separation distorted relations with nature in a profound way. By allowing residence and land use in only certain places demarcated for "nonwhites," apartheid created overcrowding and made dangerous and environmentally destructive practices necessary for ordinary people trying to satisfy their basic needs for shelter, water, sanitation, and income. In rural areas this took place in two principal ways. As tenants and workers on white-owned farms and ranches, insecurity of tenure for nonwhites and low incomes precluded all but the most modest self-built or self-financed improvements in housing, sanitation, landscaping, and dooryard gardening. In the many small fragments of territory collectively known as the *homelands*, where South Africa maintained the legal fiction that all black citizens belonged and were (in principle) required to return when not formally employed, sheer population density usually interfered with sustainable land management. Pastures in these former homeland areas are today overgrazed, forests are denuded, stream flow is reduced, soil erosion is extreme.[5]

In urban South Africa, conditions are similar, and for related reasons. Under apartheid only certain so-called townships were designated as residential zones for nonwhites. Even before the campaign of ungovernability and final wave of resistance against "pass laws" (which formally regulated the movement and residence of nonwhites) in the 1980s, houses and home compounds in these townships were subdivided to allow space for relatives coming to the city to work or to rent. Infrastructure and services in the townships was always rudimentary—one of the causes of the "rent and rate" boycotts in the 1980s—but such subdivision made the burden even greater on existing facilities such as water, drainage, sanitation, fire protection, markets, and open space. In addition, attempts by apartheid planners to "rationalize" nonwhite settlement meant that numerous established nonwhite neighborhoods were rezoned and their inhabitants forcefully relocated, usually to sites with only minimal services (water points and pit latrines) at distant locations on the ever-widening periphery of urban areas. Many nonwhite urban dwellers resisted relocation, and their resulting struggle with the authorities resulted in even less access to lifeline infrastructure and even more physical damage to the urban ecology because of arson, erection of road blocks, and creation of squatter camps—sometimes overnight—in open space being contested.

Relations between humans and nature in such urban areas were just as distorted as in the homelands and in "white" farm areas. Urban waterways were polluted and often narrowed by the disposal of solid waste. Housing was closely packed, blocking natural drainage lines and precluding the conservation of trees. Open space was rare; even heroic efforts to maintain vegetation were usually thwarted by sheer weight of usage. Wastewater rutted roads and collected where insects and other disease vectors could breed. The air was often polluted with the smoke of thousands of mineral coal braziers, the principal source of heat for cooking and warmth in the winter. The density of dwellings and narrow and poorly aligned and maintained streets and lanes both created conditions for frequent injuries of pedestrians—often children—from passing vehicles and increased the danger of fires.

In both urban and rural areas under apartheid, there was, and there remains, a gross imbalance between human needs and activities and geographical and ecological conditions such as topography, drainage, surface and ground water, microclimate, and soil fertility. A crisis of environmental health and safety resulted at both the rural and urban end of the settlement continuum. As conditions became progressively worse in rural areas, even more pressure was put on available "nonwhite" space in cities. Then with the lead-up to the elections in April 1994 and the period of the "new South Africa" afterward, a tidal wave of immigrants from the countryside began to reappropriate urban space from which they or their parents had been removed by apartheid. Residential densities soared, and attempts to introduce planned land use and service provision in the new political situation seemed meager, by comparison.

Urban Health and Safety Crisis and Environmental Rights

The introduction to this volume discusses the connections between human rights as conventionally recognized in international law and the notion of environmental rights. The two principal bases for claiming environmental rights are the right to health and the right to a livelihood or, more broadly, the right to development. By restricting nonwhites in South Africa—some 87% of the population—to only 13% of the land, the apartheid system clearly violated the rights of millions of people to health and livelihood. The degradation of rural homelands has made the population of roughly 10 million people living there highly vulnerable to any additional stress, such as the drought in 1992. In keeping with the racial bias governing access to land, employment, housing, and other key material and social resources under apartheid, drought aid during this recent crisis was highly skewed—the government allocated R703 (South African rand) per rural white resident and only R13 per rural African.[6] The unsustainability of rural livelihoods is mirrored in health statistics. Mortality by the fifth year of life, generally thought to be a sensitive indicator of the overall nutritional situation, is around 50% in the homelands.[7] Access to improved water supplies in the 10 homelands in 1990 was enjoyed by only 46% of the people, whereas only 13% had access to adequate sanitation.[8] Violation of the right to livelihood and to health in rural South Africa has steadily increased the numbers migrating to African townships, as described earlier. The result is a housing shortage estimated at between 2 and 3 million units.[9] In 1993, 5–7.7 million people were living in shacks.[10]

The new South Africa is attempting to deal with the human and environmental consequences of its land and housing policies of the past. Its constitution recognizes citizens' right to basic human needs, including water and shelter.[11] If, indeed, its citizens are considered to have environmental rights that include healthy and secure shelter, water, sanitation, drainage, clean air, and so forth, then credible and accountable elected authorities should either provide the resources to satisfy claims against these rights, or—in the absence of sufficient resources for direct and immediate delivery—the affected people must be encouraged to become part of a self-help process that will contribute toward satisfying their own needs. This chapter argues that *both* "top-down" and "bottom-up" approaches are necessary. Active citizen participation in improving the health and security of urban areas is necessary in the short term, but it is also desirable in the long term, because it empowers participants, builds local nongovernmental institutions, and strengthens democracy.

Both top-down and bottom-up efforts exist in urban South Africa. In Alexandra Township a political consensus was made official in 2001 around a renewal program that has injected considerable public and private investment, job training, and master planning. Nevertheless, the poorest of the poor have also been forcefully relocated, and some of the plans and investments have been directed at upscale shopping and tourist facilities of questionable value to the working poor.

Urbanization in South Africa

In 1993 the South African population was estimated to be 40 million.[12] Urban growth rates ranged between 3% and 5% during the 1980s and 1990s, accelerating rapidly after 1986.[13] The African population in cities grew from 8.5 million in 1985 to 14 million in 1993.[14] In 1990 the proportion of people living in urban areas totaled 18 million and was 49% of the national total. By 2001 this number was 25 million, and the proportion had grown to 58%.[15] These urbanized rates are not high by the standards of an industrialized country, but the pressures discussed above have resulted in increasing rates of urbanization, especially by poor Africans moving in from rural areas. For example, the African population of Greater Cape Town grew from 200,000 in 1982 to more than 900,000 in 1992.[16] According to one estimate, the urban population is expected to double between 1990 and 2010.[17] Johannesburg gained 500,000 migrants during 2001–6 alone and is projected to attract a similar number during 2006–11, with no end in sight.[18]

Not only is the rate of urbanization increasing, but also the spatial pattern of this growth is highly concentrated. In 1990 some 37% of South Africans lived in the country's four largest urban regions:[19] Greater Cape Town (Cape Peninsula, 2.5 million), Greater Durban (3.4 million), Greater Port Elizabeth (.9 million), and the PWV[20] (7.5 million). According to current estimates, within a decade three-quarters of the entire urban population could live in the PWV, Greater Durban, and the Cape Peninsula.[21]

Urban Health and Safety: Typical Patterns

Conditions in the townships and more peripheral squatter communities in these major urban regions have much in common: congestion, poor sanitation and drainage, inadequate access to services such as health care, fire fighting,[22] refuse collection and telecommunications, and high rates of crime. In addition, these communities are often located near heavy industry, because industrial belts were used by apartheid planners as a means to buffer racial groups from one another. Air and water pollution from these industries adds to the insults on environmental health and safety, as does illegal dumping of waste.

Particular physical characteristics give rise to special problems in many areas within these urban regions. For example, in the Cape Flats southeast of Cape Town, a large aquifer creates rising damp that weakens structures and combines with the cold, wet winter weather brought by the southeastern gales, creating much respiratory disease. Similarly, some communities in the PWV are built on dolomitic geological formations that are prone to the rapid creation of sinkholes, a unique physical hazard. Local topography and regional climate combines in some places, such as Soweto and Alexandra in the PWV, to create conditions in which smoke produced by burning coal is only very slowly dispersed. The resulting concentration is another cause of respiratory disease in the winter. Greater Durban's squatter communities are exposed to cyclones and hilly topography in some areas accelerates erosion and mudslides. Overlying these peculiarities, all African urban inhabitants face a general pattern of combined risk from geophysical, biological, social, and technological hazards.

Megacities and Disaster: The Broader Context

The pattern of exposure to risk and vulnerability to hazards in South African cities should be seen in the global context of worldwide experience with the hazardousness of increasingly large, complex urban areas. Within the last few decades we have witnessed the growth worldwide of a number urban regions with many millions of inhabitants in each of them. Despite confusion produced by differing methods for classifying cities and counting people, there is no doubt that the so-called megacity is one of the most interesting and troubling phenomena of the late-20th century. These urban regions—whether they be Cairo, São Paulo, Manila, Los Angeles, or Greater Johannesburg (the PWV)—share a number of morphological, socioeconomic, political, and environmental characteristics. They spread and sprawl over very large areas spatially, incorporating smaller preexisting urban places, peri-urban settlements, and newer "edge cities."[23] They are the sites of very diverse economic activities and employment patterns ranging from "high-tech" white collar to the semi-proletarian, subterranean, "parallel" economies of large homeless and street populations. There is an ever-increasing income and social distance between the rich and the poor in these urban regions. They are politically fragmented into sometimes hundreds of different administrations and jurisdictions. Environmentally, they import great quantities of energy, food, and water—often from hundreds or even thousands of kilometers away. Their waste stream pollutes the air, soil, and water within the megacity region and sometimes far beyond. Motorized transport—energy inefficient and air polluting—knits these large urban regions together.[24]

Because of the great polarization of wealth in the megacity, its benefits (economic, cultural, environmental) tend to accrue to the rich, while the poor tend to bear the costs of such concentration. In Los Angeles, for example, the predominantly poor Hispanic population lives in the zone of highest air pollution, and it is their housing stock that is least protected against earthquake.[25] To the extent that urban population density is a rough indicator of stress on lifeline services, quality of life, and the potential for disasters, disparities *within* megacities also reveal socioeconomic polarity. Thus, for instance, in the predominantly African Alexandra Township, Johannesburg, the density is 688 persons per hectare, while in predominantly white areas the density is only 44 per hectare.[26]

Studies of megacities in many parts of the world suggest that they are the sites where people are vulnerable to a wide range of hazards—precisely the range seen in South Africa (see Table 13.1).[27]

These hazards interact with one another in complex ways. For example, floods have washed drums of toxic chemicals out of storage yards into residential areas. There are often "cascades" of secondary and tertiary hazards produced by the primary event. Vulnerability to these hazards in large cities is not evenly distributed. Exposure and the ability to cope and recover economically are distributed unevenly according to a person's class, gender, age, ethnicity, and whether or not she/he is disabled.

Table 13.1   Megacity Hazards

Geophysical/climatic hazards	Floods, drought, wildfires, storms, landslides, earthquakes . . .
Technological hazards	Industrial explosions and fires, air pollution, waste exposure, reservoir failure, nuclear accidents . . .
Biological hazards	HIV infection, drug overdose, childhood cancer, heat exhaustion, water-borne disease . . .
Social hazards	Violent crime, child poverty, homelessness . . .

Protecting communities, especially the most vulnerable communities, from such hazards should be one of the major priorities of both environmental and health policies. Disaster prevention, mitigation, and preparedness are activities where the concerns of environmental and health policy overlap greatly. Work on disasters falls squarely into both areas: into the field of urban and peri-urban environmental management and restoration and health interventions focused on preventing disease, injury, premature death, and loss of livelihood. There are, of course, other areas where environmental policy and health policy interact strongly—for example, in shop-floor occupational health and safety practices as well as in such disease-prevention activities as vector control, water supply, and sanitation.

There is, in short, a crisis with multiple dimensions affecting the South Africans, who, for specific historical reasons, are swelling the degraded urban environments discussed. Alexandra Township is a case in point.

Alexandra Township: An Extreme Case

Alexandra Township presents an extreme case of the violation of environmental rights. It historically has been one of the chief entry points into the urban system for environmental refugees from rural areas. It has also suffered in an extreme way the spatial vise grip of apartheid planning. In addition, political struggles over land use and local government have created a culture of ungovernability and violence that continues to threatens the ability of community-based organizations to engage in reconstruction and development.

Alexandra is a small area (4 km²) lying on the northeast edge of central Johannesburg, wedged between affluent white suburbs, such as the extremely upscale Sandton, within a "buffer" zone of light industry. It is an old, well-established African township, officially established in 1905, when it had been possible for Africans to own urban property—an unusual privilege. It has been and remains an important transit point for young people coming to Johannesburg to seek work. Alexandra is thus a mixture of more established households, many of them earning rents from shack dwellers living in tin and wooden shelters built in the "yards" of formerly privately owned homes and in the town council's brick houses, and a more transient population. In 1990, 56% of Alexandra adult residents had been living there for more than 21 years, 22% for 11–20 years, 13% for 4–10 years, and 9% for 1–3 years.[28] Alexandra contains great ethnic and national diversity—including a considerable number of former Mozambican war refugees and other immigrant Africans.

People have resisted repeated attempts to remove them since the National Party came to power in 1948. During the early 1950s several African residential areas were destroyed and their inhabitants moved further out into the periphery surrounding Johannesburg. For example, hundreds of thousands of Africans were forcefully removed from Sophiatown to an area some 20 km to the southwest of central Johannesburg, across open land dominated by huge mountains of mine tailings. This settlement subsequently grew into present-day Soweto, with a population of nearly 4 million.[29] Informal settlements grew up in and around many of these new peripheral townships.

From 1960 to 1980 some 3.5 million nonwhite South Africans were removed or relocated as a result of the "logic" of racial separation.[30] In that spirit, in the 1960s apartheid planners invalidated existing freehold rights held by residents of Alexandra in preparation for reconstructing the entire area as a site for high-rise single-sex dormitories (called hostels) for workers. Much housing was destroyed, and thousands of people were forced to move to Soweto.[31] However, there was great community resistance and protest, and only a few of the hostels were ever built. Alexandra continued to exist as officially a "temporary" township throughout the 1960s and 1970s.

Beginning in 1979 a series of "upgrading" projects were conceived, though with little community participation.[32] These included work on roads and drainage, provision of water taps and bucket latrines, and expansion of the township house rental stock. Following the mass protests that began in 1986, further "upgrading" took place, including tarring roads, providing some waterborne sewage and storm drains, and some electrification. In addition, approximately 900 homes for middle-income residents were built across the Jukskei River in the East Bank area. Under the "Alexandra Renewal Project" initiated in 2001, more affordable housing was built across the river on the East Bank as well as self-help multiple occupancy flats (apartment houses) in Alex proper. Unlike Soweto and other townships Alexandra is very close to the center of Johannesburg and closely borders some of the richest white residential areas, such as Sandton and Kew. Numerous attempts have been made, with the support of township councilors suspected of having personal financial interests, to seize land for lucrative projects such as a convention center.[33] Thus the distance between ordinary residents and their town council widened, eventually leading to a rent and utility fee boycott beginning in the late 1980s.

African townships in the midst of major urban regions did not share a common tax base with the white municipalities that are adjacent neighbors in the urban mosaic.[34] For example, the Johannesburg City Council (serving white municipalities) received 30% of its income from the central business district and 70% from industry and commerce in the city as a whole.[35] Yet townships such as Soweto and Alexandra received virtually no tax revenue from industry and commerce because they were (and still are) located outside their borders. Labor power commuted from these townships to work in those industries, creating wealth and making purchases in white businesses whose profits also did not provide tax revenue for the residential home areas of the workers and shoppers.

The late 1980s and 1990s were a period of confrontation and violence. That era also saw the consolidation of popular power through the activities of the Alexandra Civic Organization (ACO), founded in 1986. Negotiation with surrounding white municipalities and the Johannesburg City Council continued; the parties discussed services and the future of local government after the official end of apartheid. Housing, roads, refuse removal, lack of electricity, and street lighting headed the list of residents' concerns.[36] Controversy swirled around a proposed "site and service" scheme offered by the mainstream Independent Development Trust (IDT) that provided 80-meter houseplots, water and electricity connections, and latrines in an area known as the Far East Bank in the former racial buffer zone of vacant land between Alexandra and a major national motorway.[37] The township was increasingly racked by violent attacks by militant factions as the national elections drew near. For example, in 1991 Zulu migrant workers supporting the Inkatha Freedom Party attacked homes adjacent to their hostel, burning a large area subsequently referred to as "Beirut." In August 1994 refugees from this area were still living in church halls and doubling up with relatives, increasing congestion in the township.

Having generated effective forms of grassroots organization over the years (manifesting such institutions as the Ministers' Fraternal and Alexandra Civic Organization), boycotts of rents, utility fees, and the Johannesburg bus system were effective. The politics of protest culminated in the call by both the ANC and the ACO for the campaign of ungovernability in the late 1980s. In addition to the boycotts, the call went out to the rural areas for as many people as possible to come to settle in Alexandra, whose population grew rapidly from approximately 75,000 in 1979 to 180,000 in 1986, then 360,000 in 1992, and roughly 400,000 in 1994.[38] Residential density is 160 accommodation units (mostly backyard and freestanding shacks) per hectare. It is this incredibly high urban density that presented a great challenge to the process of "reconstruction and development" launched by the Government of National Unity (GNU) in 1994.

In 1996 postponed nationwide municipal elections were finally held and boundaries redrawn. Alexandra became part of a swath of greater Johannesburg that now included its upscale counterpart, Sandton.[39] The resulting local council had to learn to negotiate across a seemingly unbridgeable gap in levels of living, perceived needs, and priorities. However, unlike many similar blighted areas in urban South Africa, Alex had a high political profile. It was well known for decades of resistance against apartheid, music and cultural production, and famous residents—including Nelson Mandela, Samora Machel (the former President of Mozambique), the wife of Thabo Mbeki (South Africa's president in 2007), and many other politicians, poets, musicians, and sports stars. After several years of piece meal redevelopment attempts, in 2001 following a mandate from the President, Thabo Mbeki, a consensus was achieved among many civil society organizations, private sector, and local government on a master plan to renew Alexandra. Considerable financial support was pledged directly from the president's office, and other resources were offered by the Johannesburg Metropolitan Council and the provincial government of Gauteng.

Hazard Profile: Risk, Exposure, Vulnerability, and Response   Alexandra's area is about 1.5 square miles, or roughly 4 square km. A population of 400,000 (the high estimate) works out to a density of 100,000 per sq km, or 1,000 persons on every hectare.[40] It lies on a hillside that slopes into the Jukskei River valley. Virtually every square meter of open space has been settled by squatters or otherwise built over. This includes the areas on and near the three major storm drains that run down the hillside into the river. Shacks (*mekhukhu*) fill the backyards of more substantial brick houses, and there are four extensive areas of shack development.[41] In 1989 approximately 70% of Alexandra residents were living in informal housing. Some 14,000 families lived in single rooms attached to houses; 11,000 in freestanding shacks; 6,100 in backyard shacks; 400 in council houses; 1,500 in high-rise apartments; and 1,700 in private houses. There were 8,400 hostel beds.[42]

Such density exposes the population to a wide variety of hazards. Fires are common. With light shack construction and no firewalls, disastrous fires spread quickly. At present the nearest fire department is in the white community of Randburg several kilometers away, so response time is slow, and given the density of shack development, there are few points of access. Minibus taxis are the main form of transportation to and from work for township residents. Drivers are highly competitive, and traffic is a major hazard to pedestrians, especially children, who have little play space other than the road.

Flood Hazard in Alexandra: Using aerial photographs and household sampling, a team at Pretoria University calculated that a One study calculated that a flood of the Jukskei River with a recurrence interval of 50 years could destroy nearly 900 shacks, endangering 4,400–10,500 people,[43] depending on one's estimate of family size per shack. Another found 1,235 shacks below the 50-year floodline[44] and a total of from 4,940 to 7,410 people exposed to this risk (more conservatively assuming only four to six persons per family, respectively). The catchment of the Jukskei has been rapidly urbanized since 1940 with the consequence that runoff from intense summer rainfall very rapidly finds its way into the main channel. This rapidly peaking storm hydrograph provides little warning to people at risk of impending flood. In addition, illegal dumping of garbage has narrowed the Jukskei, increasing the risk of flood. The people living in shacks in the river flood plain are among the poorest in the township, with few options, little income to facilitate a move, or few resources to help them recover after a flood. They are also some of the most recent arrivals, many of them foreign nationals—including war refugees from Mozambique. Therefore they are highly vulnerable to flood, as their poverty, minority status, and lack of social networks lock them into their present exposed locations and makes recovery from flood damage difficult.

A 20-year flood would presently affect 575 shacks (2,800–6,900 persons). Even relatively common 5-year flood could destroy (and, indeed, has destroyed) as many as 220 shacks (1,100–2,600 persons).[45] These calculations do not take into account the shack dwellers adjacent to the three major storm drainage lines: local runoff associated with a 10-year flood could flatten the shacks of 3,000 people near these culverts that drain into the river.[46] Several hundred more families live in shacks on the west bank of the river above the floodline but precariously near the edge of a steep 15–20 m escarpment. In flood, the Jukskei River undercuts this area, which is highly erodable, because it is made up of landfill. The stability of the slope is further compromised by constant seepage of domestic wastewater.

Earlier response to the flood hazard took the form of an early-warning system based on gauges monitoring river heights and rainfall in the river catchment, together with warning sirens and pre-established assembly points. However, the long history of hostile relations between Alexandra residents and officials has made it difficult to generate public support for this system. Under the 2001 master plan a more proactive, direct, and controversial approach was taken by authorities. That year some 11,000 people were forced from their homes in the zones most exposed to flooding—roughly twice the number of flood-exposed residents calculated not so many years earlier from air photo data. The displaced were rehoused in Braamfischerville in Soweto and Diepsloot, north of Randburg.[47] Both these locations are very long distances from the employment and livelihood opportunities as well as social networks of the people removed. Meanwhile, others were cleared from homes near major roadways within Alex, all part of a commitment to providing security and open space. So thorough were the planners that obstacles were erected in the newly grassed over area near the west bank of the Jukskei River to keep children from playing football and turning the area back into a dust bowl.[48]

Health Hazards in Alexandra Many residents burn coal in open braziers for heat in the winter. A pall of smoke settles in the river valley in the evening and in the early morning. Density, poverty, lack of accessible and affordable electricity,[49] and topography combine to create a major risk to the respiratory health of Alexandra's residents, especially those living in the valley (who tend to be the poorest) and especially to the very young, the very old, and those, such as retired miners, who may already suffer from lung disorders or tuberculosis.[50] Also related to cold winter weather is the risk of hypothermia among newborn children.[51]

In the context of such day-to-day privations, it should come as no surprise that privatization of electricity and utility rate increases have sparked a new round of urban social movement protest.[52] Roughly 25% of Alexandra residents use a bucket system for defecation. These bucket latrines provided by the township council. The buckets are, in principle, emptied and cleaned every week and the buckets cleaned at a facility near the cemetery on the northern edge of the township. The system is unsanitary, and, given the long financial and administrative crisis in the township council, maintenance can lapse.[53] The same washing blocks used to clean buckets serve as an informal site for township laundry. This site is just 10 m from the Jukskei River, adding to health risks.

Piles of refuse are a well-known trademark of Alexandra. The extremely high population density and paucity of government services have created enormous problems of household waste disposal. Vermin abound, providing disease vectors. Stray dogs and rats are a safety and health hazard to children. The response to these and other health problems has been intermittent cleanup campaigns by various citizen-based organizations, political demands by the ACO for the provision of skips (dumpsites) for refuse and a schedule of refuse removal, and small amounts of extension work by health educators and environmental health workers from the Alexandra Health Center.

Adding to the confusion and complexity of the decision to displace shack dwellers near the Jukskei, was public fear of cholera, endemic in South Africa, where as many as 50,000 cases have been reported in recent years. Environmentalists and government officials worried that contamination of the Jukskei could endanger downstream areas.

"The move to relocate the Jukskei shack dwellers was absolutely environmentally correct," said Mary Metcalfe, Gauteng's MEC for Agriculture, Conservation, Environment and Land Affairs. "Cholera is a growing problem, and in any case, the riverbanks are not suitable for housing because of their flood attenuation function. The banks are going to be reclaimed as part of a broader regeneration of Alexandra in which environmental components including public open space, sanitation, and solid waste removal will be central."[54]

Given the terrible sanitary conditions throughout urban South Africa, such sentiments might also be seen to play on irrational fears or at least to be a disproportionate attribution of blame. One's suspicions that urban "renewal" amounts to "removal" of the poor and powerless (many Mozambican war refugees among them) are heightened by announcement of a plan to turn a nearby disused water treatment plant into a water park and tourist center.[55]

The situation is highly vexed with strong opinions on both sides. Some see little change in Alexandra despite forced removals and considerable construction and greening activity:

> What relationship do Alexandrans have with their wealthy neighbours? Sandton's financial firms, hotels and exclusive retail outlets draw in workers for long, low-paid shifts in the security, cleaning and clerical trades. Once they clock out, Alexandra workers are quickly repelled from consumption due to high prices, blatant class hostility and intensive surveillance. They return to shacks and broken sewage systems. For many tens of thousands, a single yard watertap sometimes serves forty families surviving amidst overcrowding and filth. Materially, very little had changed since democracy arrived in 1994, aside from new but tiny houses on the township's eastern hill, and a slum-clearance programme which began in earnest in 2001, along the filthy Jukskei River, a stream coursing through Alexandra, which during the summer rainy season often suffers fatal floods.[56]

Yet promoters of the Alex Renewal Project (ARP) see it as aiming to "upgrade fundamentally living conditions and human development potential within Alexandra" and as "an integrated development programme . . . designed to deliver housing, roads, water, sanitation, schools, clinics, magistrates' offices and police stations."[57] The ARP ran from 2001 to 2010. During this period de-densification has been accomplished by relocating people, beginning with those living in the most flood-prone areas. Some 15,000 housing units were built, more than 30,000 households connected to the electricity grid, and commercial development such as the Pan Africa mall have established. It included innovative pilot projects such as the use of solar electricity in new homes built on the Far East Bank.[58] These are considerable accomplishments. However, a fundamental remains. Has such top down investment and planning brought the poorest people in Alexandra healthy and living conditions and sustainable livelihoods?

Composite Urban Risk: In a township like Alexandra, daily life is carried on under the threat of a variety of simultaneous risks. Violence, sexually transmitted diseases (including HIV-AIDS), hepatitis, and other diseases associated with poor sanitation coexist with the threats of fire, flood, traffic accidents, and chronic or acute illness from a variety of hazardous substances in the air and waters. This simultaneity and coincidence in the lives of individuals means that risk perception and self-protective behavior can be quite complicated. Parents may rank risks affecting their children higher than those more generally pervasive in the urban environment. Women suffering domestic violence may not recognize it as a risk they can do anything about until they begin to confide in friends or neighboring women. Disabled people will view risks in terms of the limitations created by their limited mobility, sight, or hearing.

Just as vulnerability is stratified by age, class, gender, ethnicity, and subculture, so are risk perception and behavior modified by these human differences. So numerous are the risks, and so great the number of people exposed to them in a township like Alexandra, that South Africa has given rise to a new term: the *situational disaster.*[59] Alexandra itself is a disaster. Therefore, the approach to reconstruction has to be holistic. Given that numerous threats exist at any given time and place in the township— plus a shifting kaleidoscope of risk that, changing with small variations in physical topography and political topography, is contingent on the previous night's illegal dumping or a "taxi war" as well as changes in the seasons—one must ask, Who is best placed to prioritize and to coordinate efforts to prevent or limit disasters?

Since February 2001, when President Thabo Mbeki launched the top-down Alexandra Renewal Project, the answer seems to be "experts" and "officials" in consultation with private sector investors. By contrast, experience from cities all over the world shows that priorities should be set by neighborhood groups that are small and homogeneous enough to experience a similar constellations of risks, yet large enough to have a strong voice in municipal allocation of resources. While the current Alexandra Renewal Project has a veneer of "participation" by civil society, it is questionable how deep that "participation" and trust goes. Another question mark over the social basis for participatory planning was raised by deadly rioting in 2008 that targeted foreign African migrants, both legal and illegal, many of whom live in Alexandra Township.[60] Are there more participatory process of community-based hazard identification and mitigation?

Reclaiming Urban Environmental Rights

Community-Based Hazard Identification and Mitigation   The literature on megacities and disasters, primary health care, self-help housing, community-based environmental management, and related fields is unanimous in finding that community participation is essential in dealing with such complex, changing, and growing hazards for several reasons: (1) local knowledge of the environment is often more detailed and accurate, especially in rapidly growing and changing peri-urban situations; (2) participation leads to endorsement and support for action by the community; and (3) the cost of surveys and mitigating action in so many neighborhoods and townships would be prohibitive without the assistance of the citizens themselves. Under apartheid, consultation with communities was rare, and a thoroughgoing participatory planning approach even rarer: "upgrading is not being undertaken in consultation with residents and priorities appear to be determined by military officers in consultation with township officials."[61]

Major partners in the Government of National Unity such as the African National Congress (ANC) are committed to preventive health action, affordable housing, and accelerated enhancement of township environments. Community participation is seen as a means to these ends. According to the ANC's *Policy Guidelines,*

> Health and lack of health are rooted in the economic and social fabric of any society. Socio-economic circumstances are more important than medical services in ensuring good health. . . . The primary health care approach is essentially that of community development. It aims to reduce inequalities in access to health services . . . and integrates the many sectors of modern life such as education and housing. Further, it is based on full community participation.[62]

Counter-disaster planners worldwide recognize what might be called a "disaster management cycle" with the following phases:[63]

- *Prevention*—when the physical cause of the disaster can be eliminated or the potentially affected populations can move out of its range;
- *Mitigation*—when the physical cause or risk cannot be eliminated, but the potential for loss, injury, and death can be reduced;
- *Preparedness*—when people can take specific actions in advance in order to increase their personal protection or contribute to mitigation and prevention and to be ready to respond to an emergency or disaster;[64]
- *Response*—actions taken by the community and by authorities to save life and property in the event of a disaster;
- *Rehabilitation*—actions taken by the community and by authorities to reestablish essential services, as well as social and economic activity;
- *Recovery*—actions taken by the community and authorities to reconstruct housing and facilities and to reestablish livelihoods.

Residents are not only *capable* of contributing considerably to each of these phases but in many cases *are the primary actors*, by default. For example, after the major earthquakes of the past decade (for example, Armenia, Mexico City) 90% of those rescued were dug out by their neighbors, not emergency crews or trained rescue experts.

Preliminary discussions in Alexandra in August 1994 and January 1995 revealed that there is widespread knowledge of the full range of hazards affecting life in the township and that its people are taking initiatives to cope, according to their capacities. For example, parents had built their own speed bumps to slow down the minibus taxis. Groups exist to spread awareness of the hazard about AIDS virus and to clean up rubbish. Numerous initiatives are taken by church-based groups. In general, the community is active on its own behalf, but efforts are fragmented and not often recognized or supported by official agencies.

Again, community participation is not a "second-best" arrangement. Citizens have local knowledge and intense motivation to improve their lives and environments. Since they are on the ground, they provide vital continuity and the ability to monitor and evaluate actions that have been taken, ensuring the vital links between recovery, prevention, and mitigation. Ideally, the vulnerability of people in a community is reduced by actions taken in the aftermath of an emergency or disaster so that they are *less vulnerable* to the next extreme event or exposure to the next hazard. By contrast, vulnerability actually increases in many cases in which top-down actions have been taken, for example in the re-housing of disaster victims without their participation in choosing the site.

Obstacles to Participatory Hazard Reduction   In counter-disaster planning, as in other kinds of field-based, applied research, the attempt is often made to "tap" or utilize something called "local knowledge." Usually this effort is confined to asking local residents to name or identify hazards, locate them in space and time, and relate their past experiences with, and responses to, these hazards. This has been a fruitful line of applied research,[65] but it is important to recognize the limitations of this kind of knowledge.

All human beings exist within a dense world of meanings. To gain the confidence of a local community and to forge collaboration between local residents and outside "experts," it is necessary for both sides to become conscious of many more dimensions of their worldviews and life worlds than they do at present. So-called participatory research has tended to focus too narrowly on *indigenous technical knowledge* (or ITK). There are, however, many other forms of knowledge.[66] Technical knowledge answers questions such as When?, Where?, and How? For example, discussing the danger of flood along the storm drainage system in Alexandra township in Johannesburg, outside experts and community residents can usefully exchange views on answers to these questions. But there is much more than just these questions. To understand the flood hazard, one must also juxtapose outsider and insider views of *who* it is who lives on or near these storm drains. This involves *social knowledge.* Also included in this category of knowledge are answers to questions concerning agency: Who is it that wants to deal with this "problem"? In whose interest is activity focused around the storm drain problem? In addition, there arise questions about fundamental social and historical causation. This requires *critical knowledge.* Why do people live on and near these drainage lines? Why have "experts" decided to try to help with this situation at this moment and not before?

In the cases of both social knowledge and critical knowledge the outsiders and the insiders may well have divergent views. These divergences must be made explicit and discussed, if mutual respect and confidence between outsider experts and local residents are to be established. Such an exchange can increase the probability of adequate and lasting solutions.

The context of these forms of knowledge is broader shared understandings concerning the place of an individual, family, or group in a community, of communities in society, of people in organic nature. These understandings, more often than not, are unconscious or implicit. This is true of groups of local residents as well as groups of "experts." Here, too, it can be fruitful for outsiders and insiders to *make explicit* and exchange views on their understandings. For example, in Alexandra township the definition of "the community" is very difficult. There are many sets of interests and identities differing by national origin (for example, Mozambican war refugees, Nigerians, South African citizens); ethnic origin (for instance, Sotho, Xosa, Zulu); gender, age, socioeconomic class, degree of mobility, acuity of sight, hearing, and so on (for example, the disabled versus the able-bodied). Before effective, long-lasting use can be made of even technical knowledge, it may be necessary to clarify and reach consensus on *minimum common needs and goals* that can provide the basis for common action. Practically speaking, divergent views of the meaning of "community" appear in some people's failing to support flood warning and evacuation plans in their own area—justifiably, because they are afraid that in their absence their meager belongings will be looted by thieves.

In a similar way Alexandra illustrates numerous possibilities to understand the nature of the society surrounding this little area of 5 square km. What is "government"? Should it be trusted? Should business interests from the outside be trusted? What, if any, relevance does outside consultants' experience in dealing with flood hazards in Brazil or in greater Durban have for people in *Alexandra?* These are questions that point toward an understanding of the place of Alexandra in a wider social world. The fear of looting that blocks acceptance of a flood evacuation plan proposed by outside experts is partially based on a perception of inability or unwillingness of the greater society surrounding Alexandra to provide police protection for the property of shack dwellers. A difference in the understanding of the place of community in society, of the "resources" of that broader society (such as police protection) that are available, is at issue. During 1996 hundreds of squatters began to build in the area called the Far East Bank. Former members of the militant local civic organization who have, since November 1995, been elected to the local government are in the position of trying to evict them. Meanwhile, some consensus needs to be reached concerning options for re-housing those most exposed to flood hazards. Another change in that wider social environment further complicates the "dialogue" between community and outside agents. In May 1996 the administration of the Reconstruction and Development Program (RDP) was moved from its own ministry to the office of the deputy president. Plans for RDP implementation in urban areas—not unlike trends in many of the world's cities—are placing more and more emphasis on "law and order" in the face of rising crime rates. How will this reorganization of the RDP affect the ability of community members to channel RDP funding into areas of health and safety that are locally defined as priorities?

Finally, there are understandings of the place of humans in the realm of organic nature. Although it doesn't look very "natural" and drains an urban catchment, the Jukskei River is still a river. What is the understanding of "river" and the relation of people-to-river that is common among the people who live in Alexandra? What is the *range* of understandings? How do these differ from such understandings held by outside "experts"?

Discussion and clarification of these kinds of understanding and knowledge can facilitate a much richer and more effective collaboration between outside and inside actors in the effort to identify and mitigate hazards. However, this process takes time, political will, and trust. The mass removal of 11,000 shack dwellers in operations reminiscent of the apartheid regime's attacks on squatters suggests that the ANC-led elite did not have the patience, the political will, or the trust required to take the more difficult and complex approach of dialogue and participatory planning.

Disaster and Development: Mainstreaming Prevention

Hazardous urbanization in South Africa has been driven by the collapse of sustainable livelihoods in rural areas, coupled with constraints on Africans' urban residence and employment in the cities to which they have migrated. The key to unlocking this trap is not to pick in a fragmented, piecemeal way at one or another hazard (flood, or air pollution, or fire). Rather, the way forward is to utilize the opportunities offered by dismantling the apartheid order to draw communities into a systematic process of reconstruction and development.

In South Africa in the 1990s that process was said to have a number of elements.[67] It was to be integrated, people-driven, focused on promoting peace and security, inclusive of disenfranchised groups, democratic in its methods of decision making; it also should link reconstruction and development by focusing on critical infrastructure. In early 1995 the national office for this three-year reconstruction and development program (RDP) began to allocate financial resources to eight provinces of South Africa. The provinces, in turn, created "local development forums" in the newly formed metropolitan substructures and the remaining transitional metropolitan councils. This included the substructure into which Alexandra had been absorbed. As accountable and inclusive development forums arose, funds were passed along for urban infrastructure projects (fire protection, sanitation, water supply, drainage, slope stabilization, electrification, and the like). Such was the beginning of urban reconstruction. However, the results were piecemeal and did not keep pace with enormous, pent-up demand for housing and other serviced. Meanwhile, more and more migrants arrived in the major cities.

In addition to investment in urban infrastructure, there was a massive plan to provide loans and grants for affordable housing.[68] The ANC's 1994 campaign promise was one million units nationwide over five years (1995–2000). "The total number of houses built from 1 April 1994 to 31 March 2000 was 997,552. By September 2002 the houses completed or under construction had risen to 1,444,932."[69] Despite this impressive housing growth the number of slum dwellers has actually grown— according to the government's *State of the South African Environment*: "The proportion of South Africa's urban slum households declined from 32% in 1996 to 28% in 2001. Similarly, the proportion of the urban population living in slums declined from 27% to 25%. The percentages of slum households are larger than the percentages of the slum population, because slum households are generally smaller than other households. In absolute terms, however, over the same period, the numbers of slum households increased by 361,000, and the size of the slum population increased by 395,000."[70]

Where and how are new houses built? Here, too, community-based hazard assessment can help to avoid costly or dangerous mistakes. For example, in principle it is possible to find land on which to site thousands of homes within 10 km of the central business district. However, much of this land is owned by mining companies.[71] Even were these companies willing to provide land for housing, what long-term health and safety hazards might exist on or near old mine sites? In the rush to deliver housing, careful assessment may not be done. The existence of community groups sensitized to their rights and ability to call for and participate in hazard assessment makes it more likely that environmental health will be considered.

Writing for the first edition of this book, I argued that localized identification of priority hazards by development forums in partnership with smaller neighborhood groups could prove to be a way to kick-start the urban RDP process in the most difficult and degraded environments, such as Alexandra. The *reverse* is also likely. Linking RDP funding for urban infrastructure to such a participatory process could bring disaster prevention and mitigation into the mainstream of the development process. That link between active participation, risk reduction, and development is still possible. Yet events over the past 10 years make it more unlikely. In 1996 the RDP was replaced as a guiding national strategy by a fully neoliberal framework called the Growth, Employment and Redistribution strategy (GEAR).[72] In common with so-called Poverty Reduction Strategy Plans (PRSPs) put in motion throughout Africa according to the World Bank play book, GEAR prioritized economic growth and assumes that the poor will "catch up" and that market relations will guide and promote social well-being. It is not surprising, then, that the more radical remnants of civil organizations have been frozen out of the process of Alexandra Renewal or that the projects that cause more excitement on the city's website are those involving shopping malls (such as the one recently opened in Soweto) and tourist facilities.

Conclusions

Government officials blame the poor in Alexandra for potentially polluting a river but turn a blind eye to massive contamination of soil and water by the South African mining industry. Especially in greater Johannesburg, South Africa's industrial hub, how will such disasters as the Bhopal gas tragedy in India (1984) or Love Canal (1978 in New York) be avoided? How can the precarious environmental health and safety of urban neighborhoods be improved rapidly?

This chapter has not answered these important questions, but it has suggested how to approach them and indicated some obstacles. First, consultation with urban residents and respect for their local knowledge must be central to the function of development forums and their relations to new forms of government engaged in implementing the reconstruction and development program. Second, a healthy range of nongovernmental organizations and citizen-based institutions such as the "civics" (ACO in Alexandra, for example) and the Group for Environmental Monitoring (GEM) need to be maintained and strengthened as watchdogs monitoring reconstruction. This is problematic because of a serious decline in funding for NGOs since the elections. Third, new forms of technical assistance need to be devised to assist the processes of reconstruction and monitoring. There are a number of excellent nongovernmental organizations dedicated to planning and design under a national umbrella called the Urban Sector Network. In addition there are organizations such as the Group for Environmental Monitoring and the Environmental and Development Agency that need support for innovation in bringing skills and technology to the service of the emerging development forums and other citizen-based organizations.

Finally, the de facto hegemony of the ANC needs to be questioned in order to make space for some deviations from the neoliberal agenda of privatization and market mania. The national trade union congress, COSATU, has done just that, questioning greater Johannesburg's reliance on the private sector for its housing master plan.[73] It realistically take decades to bridge the enormous disparities created by apartheid, but one should not forget that apartheid, while unique and extreme, was nevertheless a species of capitalism—some called it racial capitalism. And capitalism, too, creates and widens disparities unless strictly regulated. Again hear the trade union congress: "The 1.8 million-member Congress of South African Trade Unions (Cosatu), although politically allied with the ANC, criticizes the government's economic policy emphasis on market liberalization and tight government spending. 'Society as a whole, particularly the working class and the poor, bear the cost of conservative economic policy,' the union federation said of the government's budget for fiscal year 2000/01."[74]

Notes

1. As a newcomer to South Africa, I was helped in my preliminary research by a very large number of extremely generous people. At Planact there were Graeme Reid, Barbara Schreiner, Wendy Ovens, Mpumi Nxumalo-Nhlapo, Jenny Evans, Chris Benner, Aso Balan, Mzwanele Mayekiso, Patrick Bond, Pat Ramela, Ahmedi Vawda, Cheryl Abrahams, and Penelope Mayson. At University of the Witwatersrand I must thank William Pick, Coleen Vogel, Khosi Xaba, Laetitia Rispel, Alan Mabin, and Chris Rogerson, as well as Prof. W. J. R. Alexander at Pretoria University. I must also thank Toffee Mokonyama and Hans Meeske of the South African Disaster Relief Agency (SADRA), David Fig of the Group for

Environmental Monitoring (GEM), Cedric de Beer at the Johannesburg City Council, and Ernest Maganya at the Institute for African Alternatives (IFAA). In Alexandra, I am most grateful to Beyers and Johann Naude, Kim Goodman, Emanuelle Daviaud, and Queen Cebekulu at the Institute for Urban Primary Health Care. In and around Phambili Books, I was stimulated by discussions with Dale McKinley and Langa Zita. In Durban I learned a great deal from Dhiru Soni, Brij Mahal, Vadi Moodley, Astrid and Ari Sitas, and in Cape Town I benefited from a conversation with Brett Myrdal. In Pietermaritzburg, Cecil Seethal was my host and guide, and in Ladysmith, Indran Naidoo. Finally, I owe Ken Mitchell a great debt for drawing me out of my rural retreat into the world of megacities (circa 1994).

2. "Shoppingmall Opens in Alexandra Township," www.sagoodnews.co.za/infrastructure/shopping_mall_opens_in_alexandra_township.html, 5/29/09.

3. A. Vallie, R. Motale, and L. Rispel, "Informal Settlements: Health Priorities and Policy Implications," *Critical Health* 46 (1994, 28–32).

4. J. Beall, "Decentralizing Government and Centralizing Gender in Southern Africa: Lessons from the South African Experience." Occasional paper 8 (Geneva: UNRISD, 2005); J. Beall, "Decentralizing Government and Decentering Gender: Lessons from Local Government Reform in South Africa," *Politics and Society* 33:2 (2005, 253–76).

5. F. Wilson and M. Ramphele, Eds., *Uprooting Poverty: The South African Challenge* (New York: Norton, 1989); D. Cooper, "From Soil Erosion to Sustainability: Land Use in South Africa," in *Going Green: People, Politics and the Environment in South Africa*, J. Cock and E. Koch, Eds. (Cape Town: Oxford University Press, 1991, 176–92); D. Cooper, "Apartheid in South African Agriculture," in *Transforming Southern African Agriculture*, A. Seidman et al., Eds. (Trenton, NJ: Africa World Press, 1992, 199–216); D. Weiner and R. Levin, "Land and Agrarian Transition in South Africa," *Antipode* 23:1 (1991, 92–120).

6. Love, 1993, cited by C. Cooper et al., *Race Relations Survey 1993/94* (Johannesburg: South African Institute of Race Relations, 1994, 251).

7. B. Wisner, "Commodity Relations and Nutrition under Apartheid," *Social Science and Medicine* 28:5 (1989, 445).

8. Cooper et al., note 6, p. 354.

9. Cooper et al., note 6, pp. 319, 322–23.

10. Cooper et al., note 6, pp. 319, 328.

11. Right to Water, "Legislation," www.righttowater.info/code/Legislation_5.asp.

12. Cooper et al., note 6, p. 82.

13. B. Schreiner, "Urban Planning and Development and the Environment," *in ANCICOSATUISANCOISACP Environmental Policy Mission*, Group for Environmental Monitoring and the Environmental and Development Agency (Johannesburg: Unpublished report, unpaginated, 1994).

14. Cooper et al., note 6, p. 96.

15. UN-Habitat, Statistics, www.unhabitat.org/list.asp?typeid=44&catid=234.

16. Cooper et al., note 6, p. 101.

17. Schreiner, note 13.

18. Statistics South Africa. Mid-Year Population Estimates, 2007. Population Release 0302, www.statssa.gov.za/publications/P0302/P03022007.pdf.

19. Cooper et al., note 6, p. 95.

20. PWV stands for the urban region encompassing Pretoria, Greater Johannesburg (Witwatersrand), and Vereeniging. It is more or less identical to the provincial boundaries of Gauteng, South Africa's smallest and most populous province, and the country's industrial heartland.

21. Schreiner, note 13.

22. For example, during the first two weeks of January 1995, fires destroyed 600 homes in informal settlements in Greater Cape Town alone, including a large fire that razed 500 houses in the community of Marconi Beam. See W. Smook, "50 Fires Each Day," *Peninsula Times*, South Edition, Jan. 18, 1995, p. 1. See also R. Pharoah, "Fire Risk in Informal Settlements in Cape Town, South Africa," in *Disaster Risk Reduction: Cases from Urban Africa*, M. Pelling and B. Wisner, Eds. (London: Earthscan, 2009, 105–26).

23. See Alan Mabin, "Suburbs on the Veld, Modern and Post-Modern," University of Witwatersrand South Africa, 2005, http://wiserweb.wits.ac.za/pdf%20files/wirsmabin.pdf.

24. R. Fuchs et al., Eds., *Mega City Growth and the Future* (Tokyo: United Nations University Press, 1994).

25. B. Wisner, "There Are Worse Things Than Earthquakes: Hazard Vulnerability and Mitigation Capacity in the Greater Los Angeles Region," paper presented at the UN University International Conference on Natural Disasters in Megacities, Tokyo, Jan. 10–11, 1994.

26. Mabin, 2005:19. In fact, 688 persons per hectare turns out to be at the low end of a range of estimates. Others are discussed later in this chapter.

27. J. Mitchell, "Natural Disasters in the Context of Megacities," paper presented at the UN University International Conference on Disasters in Megacities, Tokyo, Jan. 10–11, 1994.

28. M. Mayekiso, *Civic Struggles for a New South Africa* (unpublished manuscript, 1994, later published as *Township Politics: Civic Struggles for a New South Africa*. New York: Monthly Review Press). This may be an underestimation of the transient component of the population. Another study conducted by the Alexandra Health Centre in 1992 found 43% to have arrived within the past five years. See G. Rex and A. Fernandes, "Urbanization and Planning of the Health Services of Alexandra Township," *Critical Health* 46 (1994, 34).

29. Other famous cases of wholesale destruction of vibrant nonwhite communities include District 6 in Cape Town and Cato Manor in Durban. See I. Edwards, "Cato Manor: Cruel Past, Pivotal Future," *Review of African Political Economy* 61 (1994, 415–27).

30. D. Smith, *Geography and Social Justice* (Oxford: Blackwell, 1994, 227).

31. L. Lawson, "The Ghetto and the Green Belt," in *Going Green: People, Politics, and the Environment in South Africa*, J. Cock and E. Koch, Eds. (Cape Town: Oxford University Press, 1991, 48).

32. Lawson, note 31; Mayekiso, note 28.

33. Mayekiso, note 28.

34. In January 1995 new "municipal substructures" were created that cut across former racial boundaries, providing a larger tax base for these new, larger urban units and the possibility of cross-subsidies from wealthier to poorer communities. In November 1995 local elections were held to fill executive positions in these new substructures.

35. Schreiner, note 13.

36. Mayekiso, note 28, cites a survey conducted by the Alexandra Civic Organization in the early 1990s that found that 95% of respondents listed housing in their lists of the "five worst problems," 70% said bad roads, 66% indicated refuse removal, 65% lack of electricity, and 55% said street lighting.

37. Mayekiso, note 28.

38. Mayekiso, note 28. No complete census exists. Various surveys, using sampling to give average family size and aerial photography to count shacks, yield different results. There is considerable flux among family members in some parts of the township.

39. J. Beall, O. Crankshaw, and S. Parnell, *Uniting a Divided City: Governance and Social Exclusion in Johannesburg* (London: Earthscan, 2002); P. Bond, *Cities of Gold, Townships of Coal* (Trenton, NJ: Africa World Press, 2000).

40. Mayekiso, note 28; Lawson, note 31, p. 48.

41. H. Mashabela, *Mekhukhu: Urban African Cities of the Future* (Johannesburg: South African Institute of Race Relations, 1990, 13).

42. Lawson, note 31, pp. 49–50.

43. Y. Goosen, "Threat of Future Floods to Life and Property along the Upper Juskei River," unpublished paper, Dept. of Geography and Environmental Studies, University of Witwatersrand, Johannesburg, 1994, p. 11.

44. W. Alexander, "Flood Risks in Informal Settlements in Soweto and Alexandra," unpublished research note, Dept. of Civil Engineering, University of Pretoria, Pretoria, 1993, p. 1.

45. Goosen, note 43, p. 11.

46. J. Naudé, personal communication, Aug. 1994, from the engineer and contractor responsible for recent cleaning out of the storm drains.

47. Ndaba Dlamini, "Alex Counts Its Losses and Gains," www.joburgnews.co.za/2004/dec/dec8_alex.stm.

48. Michelle Nel, "Mondi Wetlands Project," www.wetland.org.za/.

49. In 1991 only 25% of Alexandra had access to electricity; see Lawson, note 31, p. 51. More of a problem is the high connection fee and a system of prepayment that, some argue, works out to a rate higher than that paid in more affluent parts of the urban region. See Mayekiso, note 28; c.f. E. Kgomo, "Smoke over Soweto," in *Restoring the Land: Environment and Change in Post-Apartheid South Africa*, M. Ramphele, Ed. (London: Panos, 1991, 117–23) on the affordability of coal vs. electricity in Soweto.

50. C. Vogel, "The South African Environment: Horizons for Integrating Physical and Human Geography," in *Geography in a Changing South Africa: Progress and Prospects*, C. Rogerson and J. McCarthy, Eds. (Cape Town: Oxford University Press, 1992, 174–75).

51. K. Goodman, personal communication from the director of the Institute of Urban Primary Health Care at the Alexandra Health Centre, 1994.

52. P. Bond, "Resurgent Urban Social Movements: Case of Johannesburg 1984, 1994, 2004," Centre for Civil Society Research, University of Kwazulu-Natal www.ukzn.ac.za/ccs/files/Bond-sm.pdf ; T. Ngwane, "Sparks in Soweto," Interview, *New Left Review*, July-August, 2003.

53. Lawson, note 31, p. 50.

54. Michelle Nel, note 48.

55. Ibid.

56. P. Bond, note 52.

57. Ndaba Dlamini, "Alex Renewal Is on Course," www.joburgnews.co.za/2005/nov/nov28_renewal.stm.

58. Ndaba Dlamini, "More Work Lies Ahead for ARP," www.alexandra.co.za/10_media/jonews_100205.htm, 02/05/10.

59. H. Meeske, personal communication from the coordinator of the South African Disaster Relief Agency, Jan. 1995.

60. International Federation of Social Workers (IFSW), "Xenophobia and Anti-Immigrant Riots in South Africa," www.ifsw.org/en/p38001361.html?force_folder=038000059.

61. H. Mashabela, *Townships of the PWV* (Braamfontein: South African Institute of Race Relations, 1988, 10).

62. J. MacDonald, "South Africa's Future Health Care Policy: Selective or Comprehensive Primary Health Care?," in *Sustainable Development for a Democratic South Africa*, K. Cole, Ed. (London: Earthscan, 1994, 140), citing ANC, *Ready to Govern*, ANC Policy Guidelines, 1992.

63. Panafrican Centre for Emergency Preparedness and Response (PCEPR), *The Challenge of African Disasters* (Geneva and New York: World Health Organization and UN Institute for Training and Research, 1991); Office of the UN Disaster Relief Co-ordinator (UNDRO), *Mitigating Natural Disasters* (New York: United Nations, 1991); W. Carter, *Disaster Management: A Disaster Manager's Handbook* (Manila: Asian Development Bank, 1992); A. Kreimer and M. Munasignhe, Eds., *Managing Natural Disasters and the Environment* (Washington, D.C.: World Bank, 1991); A. Kreimer and M. Munasignhe, Eds., *Environmental Management and Urban Vulnerability* (Washington, D.C.: World Bank, 1992).

64. The term *emergency* is generally used to describe a situation or hazard that threatens lives, lifelines such as power and water supply and the like, or livelihoods, and demands that actions be taken immediately to avoid a disaster. *Disaster* refers to the situation in which lifelines and livelihoods have been damaged (without loss of life and injury).

65. G. White, Ed., *Natural Hazards: Local, National, Global* (New York: Oxford University Press, 1974); I. Burton et al., *The Environment as Hazard*, 2nd ed. (New York: Guilford, 1993); A. von Kotze and A. Holloway, *Reducing Risk: Participatory Learning Activities for Disaster Mitigation in Southern Africa* (Durban: International Federation of Red Cross and Red Crescent Societies and Dept. of Adult and Community Education at the University of Natal, distributed by Oxfam UK and Humanities Press in the United States, 1996).

66. I am grateful to Peter Park, Emeritus Professor of Education at University of Massachusetts, for the threefold typology of knowledge. Also see B. Wisner et al., "Participatory and Action Research Methods," in E. Zube and G. Moore, Eds., *Advances in Environment, Behavior and Design* (New York: Plenum, 1991, 271–96); and B. Wisner, "Teaching African Science," in E. Allen et al., Eds., *African Studies and the Undergraduate Curriculum* (Boulder, CO: Lynne Reinner Publishers, 1994, 173–208).

67. African National Congress (ANC), *The Reconstruction and Development Programme* (Johannesburg: African National Congress, 1994, 4–7).

68. R. Hartley, "White Paper on Housing," *Sunday Times*, Johannesburg, Dec. 11, 1994.

69. William Rowland, "South Africa: Houses and Bombs," *Disability World* 16 (November-December, 2002), www.disabilityworld.org/11-12_02/access/southafrica.shtml.

70. Republic of South Africa, "Slum Housing," in *State of the Environment*, http://soer.deat. gov.za/indicator.aspx?m=588, 2005.

71. Smith, note 30, p. 240.

72. Growth, Employment, and Redistribution: A Macroeconomic Strategy, Republic of South Africa, www.stanford.edu/class/history48q/Documents/GEAR.pdf.

73. COSATU, COSATU Submission to the Greater Johannesburg Metropolitan Housing, www.cosatu.org.za/docs/2000/gjmchous.htm, 08/04/2000.

74. Ernest Harsch, "South Africa Tackles Social Inequalities," *Africa Recovery* 14:4 (January, 2001, 12); www.un.org/ecosocdev/geninfo/afrec/subjindx/144soafr.htm.

CHAPTER 14

Health, Human Rights, and War: Structural Violence, Armed Conflict, and Human Health in the Andes[1]

Tom Leatherman

pproximately 236 armed conflicts have been recorded since WWII, and in 2007 alone there were 34 active conflicts in 25 countries.[2] These conflicts have claimed millions of lives and have left many millions more prone to hunger, malnutrition, disease, psychological trauma, and the long-term effects of living displaced and disrupted lives in disrupted environments, economies, and social structures. Armed conflict is a major political-economic, environmental, and public health issue.

Over the past several decades there has been a steady increase in studies of the health effects of armed conflicts.[3] Much of the published research is in the form of case studies using country-wide or regional survey data. In a recent analysis of postwar health effects of civil conflicts, Ghobarah and colleagues argue for the need to move beyond country and regional case studies to comparative analyses since the immediate and long-term health impacts of conflict vary across wars, environments, and populations.[4] While comparative analyses *are* essential, there is also a need for more ethnographically informed longitudinal analyses that can link historical antecedents of conflict to postconflict conditions and can better understand people's vulnerability and resilience to political violence in local sociocultural, political-economic, and environmental contexts.[5] Such analyses might better capture the complex interrelationship between "structural violence" and "political violence" and how this affects health and well-being now and in the future.

In this chapter I offer observations on the contexts and consequences of armed conflicts particularly in relationship to structural violence, livelihoods, and health. I begin by briefly outlining the nature of this relationship and review public health impacts of armed conflict. I then provide local-level and longitudinal observations on the 20-year civil war in Peru initiated by the PCP-SL, Communist Party of Peru-Sendero Luminoso (Shining Path), and how it affected lives and livelihoods of people in the District of Nuñoa (Department of Puno), in the southern Andean highlands. I conducted research into the relationships between poverty and poor health in Nuñoa in the early 1980s before the widespread presence of Sendero Luminoso and have recently returned to begin collecting information on the years of conflict. My observations are based on preliminary information gleaned from archival research and 20 interviews carried out during four trips between 2003 and 2009. I interviewed public officials, health professionals, human rights advocates, schoolteachers, priests, store owners, and members of farming-herding communities.[6]

Based on the Peruvian case study, as well as a review of literature on conflict and health, I argue that (1) manifestations of structural violence in terms of extreme poverty and inequalities, food insecurity, malnutrition, and illness, were important catalysts for violent conflict, and that conflict, in turn, re-shapes the contexts and conditions of inequalities and poor health; (2) in assessing the health and human costs of conflict and postconflict environments, broader social and economic impacts that might alter food security, social cohesiveness, and political power are relevant measures of health, along with mortality, morbidity, and psychosocial stress; and (3) violent conflict has significant and deleterious effects on individuals and the social environment but that individuals and communities experience conflict differently, with different degrees of vulnerability and resilience, depending in part on their position within larger society and economy. Hence, the effects of conflict are uneven in short- and long-term implications for livelihoods, food security, and health.

Structural Violence and the Political Violence of Armed Conflict

Most conflicts would appear to have their roots in the structural violence of poverty, social and political marginalization, racism, sexism, and other forms of structured inequalities, and how they deny access to resources, constrain agency, and limit human potential.[7] Structural violence is embedded in ubiquitous social structures and normalized by stable institutions and regular experience. This *normalization* and *regularization* can make it appear less invisible, more natural, and silent; part of the social machinery of oppression.[8] To render the invisible visible, an analysis of structural violence and health must combine history, political economy, and biology.[9]

In studies of health, structural violence is often used to denote the ways inequalities promote malnutrition and disease, and increase the vulnerabilities to their effects. It can manifest as chronic hunger and poverty, pollution and environmental degradation, military and police brutality, and unequal and inadequate housing, education, and health care. These are lived dimensions of inequalities that provide part of the contexts for political violence, the "targeted physical violence and terror administered by official authorities and those opposing it, such as military repression, police torture, and armed resistance."[10]

An analysis of structural violence in armed conflicts that pays attention to history, political economy, and biology, illustrates that the histories of regions in conflict have deep roots in colonial and postcolonial exploitation, contemporary politics, racial or religious exclusion, and socioeconomic discrimination, as well as struggles over strategic resources such as land, water, trade routes, and petroleum.[11] At the local level these contexts create conditions of poverty, social and political marginalization, environmental scarcities and degradation, food insecurity and poor health, and severely constrained agency to operate under these conditions. They can heighten vulnerabilities and rob people of hope. In these contexts armed struggle may appear to be a rational response. As Cohen and Pinstrup-Anderson discuss in relationship to severe food insecurity: "Tensions ripen into violent conflict especially where economic conditions deteriorate and people face subsistence crises. Hunger causes conflict when people feel they have nothing more to lose and so are willing to fight for resources, political power, and cultural respect."[12] In turn: "Conflict is one of the most common causes of food insecurity. The displacement of people and disruption of agricultural production and food distribution leave tens of millions of people at risk of hunger and famine."[13] This synergistic relationship then shapes the lives, livelihood, and health of people living in environments shaped by war.

Public Health Costs of War

The public health costs of war can and should be viewed broadly.[14] Following The Declaration of Alma-Ata (WHO 1978), I view health as "a state of complete physical, mental, and social well-being, not merely the absence of disease of infirmity" and review public health costs of conflict in terms of physical health, infrastructure, social and psychosocial well-being, and environments and food security.[15]

Physical Costs: Morbidity and Mortality

One of the most obvious costs of war is in human life; of military participants but especially, and increasingly, of civilian lives. Mortality estimates can range widely over different conflicts and even within single conflicts, but all are equally devastating. Between 1998 and 2001 an estimated 2.5 million civilians died in war-torn Democratic Republic of Congo—between 50,000 and 200,000 in Bosnia and perhaps 500,000–800,000 during the 1994 Rwandan genocide.[16] Ghobara and colleagues, using WHO data, report that about 269,000 people died as casualties of civil war in 1999 alone, and this amounted to a loss of 8.44 million years of healthy life (DALYs).[17] Moreover, they estimate that as many as 15 million additional lives were lost in 1999, people whose death was attributed to disability, disease, and the chronic effects of previous years of civil war.

Most of the victims in mortality estimates (perhaps 90%) were civilians, and most of the death occurred away from the battlefield.[18] The majority were refugees and the internally displaced, especially women and children, and the elderly, who are particularly vulnerable to the psychological trauma, malnutrition and disease, violence and sexual abuse in crowded, unhygienic, and often unsafe conditions of emergency camps.[19] Those living in refugee camps are prone to disease outbreaks from relatively common problems such a diarrhea, to more severe infectious diseases such as cholera, dysentery, acute respiratory infections, measles, and new and re-emergent diseases, such as HIV-AIDS and TB.[20] The ubiquitous presence of landmines in conflict areas extends the risk of death and disability for years into the future. There are between 60 and 119 million mines in 70 countries, and land mines kill or maim 2,000 people every month, mostly women and children. One in every 236 persons in Cambodia is an amputee due to mine related injury.[21]

Social and Psychosocial Costs

The long-term mental health costs of the social and psychological trauma experienced during violent conflict is perhaps the area of health and conflict most frequently studied. Levels of depression, suicide, and interpersonal violence often increase in postwar societies, and PTSD (posttraumatic stress disorder) is a common diagnosis based on the presence of anxiety, sleep disorder, nightmares, symptoms of depression, dissociation, alcoholism, and a range of other psychological and physical symptoms.[22] Yet, trauma is experienced and somaticized unevenly. Pedersen notes that although PTSD has become synonymous with "trauma," most individuals in conflict situations (75%) do not develop PTSD, and show varying degrees of resistance and resilience.[23]

Conventional means of assessing trauma based on PTSD scales may be far from adequate when applied across the multiple cultural and social contexts in which conflicts occur.[24] The application of traditional western notions of psychosis, which is heavily personalized, misses the very important point that trauma is interpreted within cultural frameworks and is experienced and felt socially as much as personally in many cultural settings.[25] Thus, for the victims of war, we should study trauma in local cultural contexts, as opposed to the more common practice of interviewing victims far removed from the environments, communities, and social contexts in which trauma occurred.[26]

It is also clear that levels of trust, cooperation, and social support are all diminished during and following conflict. In a recent review of *Anthropology and Militarism*, Gusterson discusses how "fear as a way of life" leads to uncertainties over when one might be killed, trust of friends and neighbors, hope for a better future, and citing Green, how "routinization allows people to live in a chronic state of fear with a facade of normalcy, while the terror, at the same time, permeates and shreds the social fabric."[27] The insidious nature of terror as a psychosocial force that undermines and assaults community cohesion is an understudied though important dimension of public health. An intact social fabric is critical for resilience and hope in the future, both of which not only directly affect individual and community health outcomes but also contribute to rebuilding of social structures and infrastructures that promote food security and health.

Environments and Food Security

Armed conflicts not only take a toll in lives and property and promote massive population displacement but also degrade environments and disrupt food production and the distribution of food and medicine.[28] Conflicts were cited as major causes in one-third of the 44 countries that suffered extreme food emergencies in 2001 and 2002, and comparative analyses across multiple countries and wars have found average reductions in food production of 10–12% during years of conflict.[29]

The most obvious way in which conflict leads to food insecurity and hunger is through the deliberate use of hunger as a weapon.[30] Armies starve opponents; steal produce; destroy food supplies, livestock, and other means of production; cut off markets; and impede or divert food relief. Decline in farming populations, and hence production, result from attacks, terror, enslavement, forced recruitment, malnutrition, illness, and death. Livestock raiding often increases during conflicts, is potentially devastating to livelihoods, and slows the recovery from conflicts and other disasters such as droughts and famines.[31] Moreover, combat destroys environments and in the case of landmines makes them dangerous for years to come (a buried landmine can stay active for 50 years).

Disrupted food security leads to hunger and malnutrition and significantly increases the risk to mortality and morbidity for displaced populations. In such contexts even relatively rare micronutritional diseases have occurred; scurvy (vitamin C deficiency) in Afghanistan, pellagra (niacin deficiency) among Mozambican refugees in Malawi, and beriberi (riboflavin deficiency) among Bhutanese refugees in Nepal.[32]

Infrastructure Costs

Destruction to health care infrastructures and reduced government support of social, education, and health sectors during conflicts constitutes another sort of attack on health.[33] In many instances health centers and health workers are directly targeted,[34] but in other cases, health programs might be allowed to continue and health indicators might even improve. For example, during war years of the 1980s and early 1990s in El Salvador infant mortality, rates of immunization, and some other common health indicators remained steady or improved slightly. The ability to maintain or improve this dimension of public health during a time of war was in part due to relief efforts from the World Food Program and others, as well as apparent efforts by warring factions to spare hospitals and to allow immunization campaigns to proceed.[35]

In most countries experiencing armed conflict increased military spending is necessarily paired with a concurrent reduction in expenditures in health, education, food, and other basic needs. Between 1960 and 1994 the developing world imported U.S. $775 billion worth of military supplies. According to Martin Donahue, "three hours of worldwide military spending is equal to the WHO's annual budget. Three weeks of world arms spending could provide primary health care for all individuals in poor countries including water and hygiene."[36] Health systems are also affected by structural adjustment programs of the IMF and World Bank that link much needed international loans to open markets and reductions in the public sector, price subsidies, assistance programs, and other safety nets. Debt and structural adjustment burdens correlate with conflict. Smith found that 50 of 71 countries receiving structural adjustment loans were experiencing conflict and that 22 of the top 25 developing country debtors were in conflict, including Argentina, Honduras, Mexico, Peru, the Philippines, and many African countries.[37]

Summary: Reproducing Contexts and Consequences of Conflict

Armed conflict directly and indirectly heightens mortality and morbidity, promotes psychosocial distress and social disruption, degrades environments, diminishes food security, and reduces infrastructures and investments critical to public health. These multiple effects do not occur in isolation but carry the added likelihood that each might synergistically worsen the effects of the other. The effects of political violence, in turn, may well reproduce and intensify the negative effects of structural violence and negatively affect livelihoods and health into the future. In the remainder of the chapter I examine how these interrelationships play out in one conflict, the recent civil war in Peru (1980–2000), and in one region, the District of Nuñoa in the southern Peruvian highlands (1986–92).

Armed Conflict in Peru: The Case of Sendero Luminoso

Over the 20-year period 1980–2000 the Communist Party of Peru Sendero Luminoso (Shining Path) waged war against the Peruvian state and all factions who threatened their potential control of the countryside, including leftist groups advocating peasant rights. The war began in the impoverished Department of Ayacucho in the Andean highlands, under the leadership of a university philosophy professor, Abimael Guzman, and his followers, and from this epicenter expanded into areas where poverty and vulnerability provided an opportunity for gaining recruits, such as in peasant communities of the southern sierra of Puno.[38]

There is a consensus that the seeds of revolt were sown in deep poverty, neglect, political marginalization, and little hope that future generations would fare any better.[39] The history of the highlands is one of repeated exploitation, from the Spanish conquest and colonization, postcolonial domination of rural highland populations by a landed oligarchy, and a failed agrarian reform to a series of more recent economic shocks and crises in the decades leading up to the revolution. Between 1970 and 1990 the Peruvian population grew by 60%, but the economy did not. In 1980 the rate of growth in GDP was negative.[40] Salaries dropped, unemployment and underemployment rose, inflation reached triple digits, and the poor became even poorer.[41]

In poor, rural, and largely indigenous communities in the central and southern highlands, levels of poverty, hunger, and illness were profound and were important contexts for the revolution. Infant mortality rates in the southern Andes of the early 1980s were between 110 and 129 per thousand live births, more than twice as high as Lima.[42] Sixty percent of the population was in extreme poverty, and levels of stunted growth, indicative of chronic malnutrition, were equally high. There was less than 1 physician per 10,000 residents in the central and southern highlands, and illiteracy rates were 5 to 9 times greater than in Lima.[43] Moreover, government economic policies that favored urban industrial growth and neglected the rural sector, as well as a severe and sustained drought, led to the stagnation of agriculture in rural highlands. An ineffective agrarian reform implemented by the early 1970s that placed control of much of the land in the hands of large state-controlled cooperatives, and not indigenous communities, further deepened the sense of hopelessness and anger at the state and its agents.

These same conditions were evident in the District of Nuñoa, where infant mortality was 128 per 1,000, one of the highest rates in the rural sierra. Sixty percent of the children in the district were chronically malnourished, and 20% severely malnourished. In one extremely poor community the infant mortality rate was about 200 per 1,000; 70% of the children were chronically malnourished and 34% severely malnourished.[44] Before the implementation of the agrarian reform in Nuñoa in the early 1970s, 2% of the landholders controlled 61% of the land base, yet after the reform, three large cooperatives controlled 60% of the best land and employed only about 25% of the rural population.[45] As many said, "we just traded one owner for another." Throughout the district the poorest households experienced a significant negative impact of illness on agricultural production, and this further diminished food security, nutrition, and health.[46] This reproduction of poverty and illness was part of a sense of hopelessness felt by many families.

The Costs of Conflict in Peru

Clearly the revolution had far-reaching impacts in Peru. A report of the Truth and Reconciliation Committee estimated that 70,000 died and one million people were displaced during the 20 years of internal conflict. Material losses were estimated at U.S. $21 billion, a figure equivalent to the entire foreign debt. In addition, Peru experienced a hyperinflation of over 7,000% in the late 1980s and early 1990s.

Levels of poverty increased between 1985 and 1991, and chronic malnutrition in 1991 was estimated by FAO at 40%; 12% higher than in 1980.[47]

The vast majority of those who died, and an estimated 70% of those displaced, were from rural indigenous communities, especially those in the southern highlands from Ayacucho to Puno. In the Department of Ayucucho an estimated 10,000 were killed or disappeared, and another 180,000 (36% of the population) displaced in the 10-year period of intense conflict between 1983 and 1992. Massive displacement depopulated the countryside, left communities and households without support networks, diminished local food production and other means of livelihood, and led to severe food insecurity. Even after the end of the conflict, in some areas 80% of the displaced populations suffered from malnutrition, and cholera, TB, and other infectious diseases have persisted or increased.[48]

Social and psychological trauma (for example, depression, nightmares, fear, distrust) may be the most widespread but unmeasured effect in rural areas. Duncan Pedersen and colleagues who have conducted one of the few systematic surveys of trauma related disorder in the central highlands, found that 50% of adults reported symptoms of psychosocial traumas and 1 in 4 adults met the criteria of PTSD.[49] In addition, reports from the displaced and returnee communities note that poverty and landlessness are increasingly associated with alcoholism and interpersonal and domestic violence, as well as the "extremely aggressive" behavior of minors who had been forcibly recruited by *Sendero* or the *Rondas campesinos*.[50]

View from Nuñoa

Nuñoa presents a somewhat different picture as it experienced what might be termed "low-intensity conflict," typified by sporadic acts of violence but constant fear. The district felt the presence of Sendero Luminoso and the civil war from 1986 to 1993. In an early event in 1986 Sendero Luminoso instigated a raid (*saqueo*) against cooperatives and larger landowners, stealing perhaps a thousand animals (mostly sheep and cattle), and vandalizing and looting buildings and homes. Over the next three to five years repeated raids significantly diminished cattle and sheep herds and decimated most of the prime breeding stock. Soon after this first attack Sendero Luminoso made their presence very clear by a public assassination in the town square—torturing and killing a veterinarian from the largest cooperative in the District. In subsequent attacks over the next five years, peaking in 1989–92, the town hall was burned, elected officials were assassinated, and police stations were attacked and robbed of their weapons. By 1990 there was no permanent police force or local government authorities, and the district was declared by Sendero Luminoso a "liberated zone." Retaliation by counterinsurgency government forces (*Sinchis*) put the area under siege by a second force, leaving most of the population caught in the middle. Finally in 1991, following a visit by newly elected president Alberto Fujimori, a permanent army force came to the district. In 1992 Abimael Guzman was captured in Lima, and by the end of 1992 most of the overt violence had abated.

Impacts of Conflict in Nuñoa

The real and potential health impacts of conflict I see based on very preliminary interview data are linked to issues of livelihood and food security, psychosocial distress, and shifting social relations in the region. Yet, these impacts were unevenly felt by different segments of the population and may have very different short and long-term consequences.

Livelihood and Food Security

By all accounts the Sendero years were a time of greater food insecurity in Nuñoa. People report that less food was available and at higher prices. Constant rustling had decimated herds and led many large landowners to sell their animals to meat buyers at a considerable loss. Farmers limited the amount of land put into cultivation in fear that crops might be destroyed or stolen. Regional production data for the early 1990s suggest that almost 37% less land was put into potato cultivation and that there were 34% fewer cattle than in the mid-1990s. Markets were disrupted because the roads were considered unsafe for travel. Many *tiendas* shut down or were abandoned out of fear of being robbed by Sendero (or counterterrorist forces) and because there were few products to sell and even fewer customers with money to spend. Moreover, inflation led to higher prices for those goods available, which further accentuated food insecurity in the region. People remember food lines for meat, cheese, and other products—there was never enough food to meet people's needs.

During the late 1980s and early 1990s a major reallocation of land occurred in the region with minimal short-term effects on regional food security but perhaps very important long-term effects. By the mid-1990s all but one cooperative was abandoned and replaced by 10 new farming-herding communities (*communidades campesinos*). This was due in part to government policies to reallocate more land to indigenous communities but was also due to fear of attack by Sendero. For the most part these new communities produce food only for their own consumption and thus have not provided foods for the local market, although presumably their own food security has improved.

The short- and long-term nutritional and health effects of the combination of these events in Nuñoa is unclear. The infant mortality rate in 1993 at the end of violence was 111.9, down somewhat from the early 1980s but still among the highest rates in Puno and in all of Peru. By 1996 infant mortality was down to 104 deaths per 1,000, although still higher than surrounding areas, where it had dropped another 10–20%. Levels of chronic malnutrition (as indicated by stunted growth or low height for age) remained unchanged through the late 1990s, while other regions showed significant improvements in child growth.[51] Records from clinics and health posts in 2005 suggest that malnutrition remains a leading cause of morbidity for children aged 5–15 years.[52]

Yet there is a sense of optimism in the newly formed indigenous communities. What members of the new rural communities say is that economic conditions have not improved much "but now we have means of survival, where before we had nothing." The best example comes from the poorest community in which we worked in the 1980s. Members of this community were widely suspected to have been leaders of raids on cooperatives and landowners and to have collaborated with Sendero Luminoso. Their role in these events is uncertain, but most households have doubled their landholdings, and, more important, their pastures for herding. The former cooperative land they now occupy is the site of a thriving cheese industry supplying mozzarella to pizzerias in Cusco's tourist economy. They also have a secondary school and one of the better rural health clinics. So here is at least one community that has substantially improved its economic situation in the past 20 years, which should translate into greater food security and improved nutrition and health.

Psychosocial Impacts of Trauma

The period 1989–92 was clearly a time of fear in Nuñoa. Common practice was to lock the doors and turn off the lights in one's home as soon as night fell—and hope for no knocks at the door or other disturbances. Many fled the area and haven't returned. No systematic surveys of the sort carried out by Pedersen and colleagues (2001) in the central highlands have been attempted in Nuñoa, but reports from mental health teams working in the District and interviews with a sample of 12 informants suggest a range of social and psychosocial effects, and the unevenness of these effects on individuals and communities.

As part of the truth, reconciliation, and reparations process small teams of public health workers are traveling to communities affected by violence and conducting talks about recognizing signs of social and psychological effects of trauma. One goal is to work with health centers and town committees to combat and prevent violence in the community. Another is to educate the population about signs of depression and other mental health problems that could be products of violence. They estimate that up to 20% of the 3,000 people they have spoken with have been directly affected by the violence of years of conflict, and 70% indirectly affected. Anxiety, depression, interpersonal and domestic violence, and alcoholism are the primary effects of the war on the population mental health.

In interviews I heard accounts of persistent nightmares, *ataques de nervios* ("intense anxiety") and of youths now in their late teens and 20s who still are disturbed by the sounds of gunfire on TV. One informant told us people became afraid, many became quiet, almost mute, and others became agitated and even violent in their interpersonal interactions—especially teens and young adults. The son of a relatively wealthy rancher talked about how his entire family turned inward, stopped communicating with one another, and easily became angry and argued.

Yet, even in Nuñoa, effects were uneven, and it was hard to predict who would be most vulnerable or most resilient in response to traumatic events—as exemplified by two friends from the 1980s. The first friend, Ramiro, took pride in his classically stoic nature. He recounted how in late 1980s a letter was nailed to his door ordering him to leave his teaching post and town or be killed. He slept in hiding and on guard most nights, but after additional threats and almost being caught on the streets by Sendero, he left town for good. Fifteen years later, he spoke of these events with an emotional combination of sadness and bitterness, and at the time of the interview in 2004 felt that he could never return to his birth home.

The other friend, Antonio, was a timid man with an almost subservient manner. He had a low-paying but steady job working in the town hall and served as a secretary to several peasant organizations. First he was forced to quit his job with the town government after three death threats by Sendero. But later he was detained, interrogated, beaten, and almost killed by counterinsurgency forces suspicious of his work with peasant communities. He also recounted sleeping in different houses or out in countryside most nights over a three-year period. The ultimate event for him was a battle between Sendero Luminoso and the police outside the door of the house he rented, during which four police officers were killed, and he and a friend dragged the bodies from the street to his house. After this, he said, he was no longer afraid of anyone. "I was quiet and timid, but now I am assertive, even rebellious." He currently works to organize his barrio and seems to take pleasure in being an occasional thorn in the side of local officials.

Although analysis of these two examples is premature, it would appear that economic position, social status, and ethnicity might have worked to shape each individual's sense of fear and loss. Ramiro had a respected position as a teacher and was linked through family ties to former landowners who still commanded positions of elevated status and respect. Antonio had somewhat less to lose economically and socially and now has permanent holdings in a newly formed farming-herding community. He feels that indigenous groups have more respect than before. He had every reason to be more traumatized but emerged, in his words, a stronger more confident person. What is clear is that the psychosocial (and other) effects of conflict are felt unevenly and that a host of social, psychological, and economic factors underlie this variation.

Impact on Local Social Relations

All informants have told us that the social structure and broader social relations have shifted in Nuñoa, again in uneven ways and with ambiguous consequences. For many townspeople the period of Sendero's dominance from 1989 to 1992 established a kind of fear and uncertainty that is still felt. Informants spoke of the "1,000 eyes and ears" of Sendero that disciplined their speech and activities then and, to a lesser degree, now. The consensus is that people are moving on with their lives, but with a heightened distrust of their neighbors and less interest in engaging in the sorts of cooperative social relations that have been historically important in Andean society. This loss of trust and cooperation could present real barriers to the collective futures in the region.

Yet the most radical shift in social relations over the past 20 years is an increased access to land and social and political power among indigenous groups that were previously marginalized and disenfranchised. The economy and politics of Nuñoa in the 1980s were dominated by the legacy of the hacienda system. Now elected leaders are middle class but indigenous, and more land is under the control of peasant communities. One individual, formerly landless but now part of a newly formed community, put it in modest terms: "it's not like conditions have improved much, and there is still a lack of equality and justice, but at least now we are treated with a little respect—not like animals as before." There is a greater sense of empowerment among at least some rural producers in newly formed communities, and this feeling can only contribute to a greater sense of hope and well-being, and perhaps ultimately to improved food security, nutrition, and health.

Discussion: Contexts and Consequences of Conflict

In this example from Peru I have argued that the preconflict structural violence of extreme marginalization, poverty and poor health, frustration, and hopelessness were important precursors to the civil war instigated by the PCP-SL. The effects of conflict in Nuñoa are perhaps most acute for food security and social and psychological distress and disruption, although both await systematic study. The experience of violence and loss during the civil war negatively affected lives, livelihoods, security, health, and sense of well-being. However, the effects were uneven. Food insecurity persists, but those who were the most disadvantaged and food insecure (that is, landless or near-landless peasants and members of poor indigenous communities) now control more land, which could lead to greater food security in the future. All our informants communicated a clear expression of the various ways the civil war produced a sense of loss, regret, and diminished lives. Yet some emerged empowered and others more deeply disturbed. This situation appears to reflect results in other zones of conflict, where residents prove to be more or less vulnerable and resilient to the experience of conflict.[53] To begin to understand why and how this continuum of response takes place, we need more local-level ethnography using idioms of distress that are culturally salient, and in locales where there is a sense of preconflict structures of violence as well as postconflict assessments.

Para Que No Se Repita: Truth, Reconciliation, and Reparations in Peru

The civil war in Peru was one of many worldwide at the end of the 20th century. A key concern for anthropologists and public health workers expressed here is how armed conflict shapes health and well-being into the future. A key concern for all involved is to make sure that the conflict and violence of the last two decades of the 20th century are not repeated in the 21st. That these events are not repeated is one the missions of the truth and reconciliation process that began in 2001 in Peru and continues today. Peru's Truth and Reconciliation Commission (TRC) presented a comprehensive and far-reaching report in 2003 that documented abuses by both Sendero Luminoso and the state's military, police, and antiterrorist forces.[54] In the process of collecting 17,000 testimonies and documenting abuses from all sides, it made attempts to be inclusive of those historically marginalized by the state and to be gender sensitive.[55] An important aspect of the TRC was that its mission included reconciliation as well as truth gathering and that it provided recommendations for victim reparations and institutional, legal, and educational reforms that could help prevent large-scale internal conflict in the future.[56]

Implementing the recommendations of the TRC has fallen to a number of governmental and nongovernmental agencies and human rights groups that are woefully understaffed and underfunded, and this situation presents problems for achieving the goals of the commission. As a result many who suffered violence and loss have begun to question the commitment of the government to reconciliation and reparations.[57] These perceptions are not unfounded, particularly under the second presidential administration of Alan García, given that his first administration (1985–90) has been accused of human rights abuses. There is resentment among some that the TRC held the military responsible for human rights abuses. It is also reported that the current government does not prioritize reparations for victims of abuses by the armed forces but only for those who suffered at the hands of Sendero.[58]

Laplante outlines the ambitious framework for reparations included in the final report of the TRC and how efforts to achieve these goals have unraveled in practice. Several of the problems include: (1) that the recommendations were not legally binding; (2) that the process of registering victims has proved to be inadequate and caused delays in paying reparations; (3) that victims are often reluctant to provide details and thus relive their traumatic experience (for example, sexual violence) and in some cases to name perpetrators still living in their community; (4) that preference is given to acknowledging abuses by Sendero Luminoso but not the state; and (5) that the very idea of reparations has been redefined as community development.[59] In the following sections I briefly discuss how several of these problems are limiting the efforts of reconciliation and reparation processes in the Department of Puno.

One area of recommendations made by the TRC was to better address the health and education needs of the population. There has been a shift in the health sector in recent years toward a more integrative, holistic framework in addressing health needs of the population. A specific change has been a new attention to mental health. Earlier I described the outreach provided by mental health teams in zones affected by armed conflict. Yet a major obstacle they face is that there are only three teams for the entire Department of Puno and the over 200 communities affected by violence. In addition, there is only one physician to move among the three teams. One aspect of this program is to register victims for expedited enrollment in a state health plan, but to date only about 1,500 of an estimated 30,000 eligible individuals have been registered. Many do not want to come forward as victims, but the bigger problem is the limited opportunity to register.

Laplante notes how money for reparations is increasingly prioritized as support for community-based development projects.[60] In the Department of Puno, basically all reparations are targeted for community development and not individual victims. Eligible communities deemed "impacted" based on earlier government surveys can present a plan for development and if accepted receive up to 100,000 soles (about U.S. $33,000). An estimated 200 communities (out of 1,800 communities in the department) are considered eligible, but only about 35 communities are expected to receive any help through 2009. One problem is that only about half of the eligible communities are registered, a first step before presenting development plan for funding. This is because there are only 10 offices to register affected communities in the entire Department. Moreover, when communities do receive aid, new conflicts arise when nearby groups not deemed eligible, or whose plan was not accepted, question why them and not us. There is a perception in some communities that reparations are politicized, favoring those who support the ruling APRA party of president Alan García.

When reparations are framed in terms of community development, there is an additional problem with how eligible communities are prioritized for assistance. Priority is given to communities with individuals who have experienced death, displacement, detentions, and sexual abuse. Yet communities affected less directly by violence but who have suffered the loss of their entire livestock, which in the Andes is tantamount to economic disaster, are not considered a priority for receiving development aid.

Thus obtaining development help is extremely difficult for poor communities and individuals not directly affected by violence. It is also difficult under the current system for individuals to register titles for their land. Most land is registered in the name of communities. But government-based micro-credit programs are minimal in the region, and small bank loans are not possible without collateral, such as a land deed. Thus much of the development support in the region comes through foreign NGOs.

Conclusion

In the introduction to this volume, Barbara Rose Johnston quotes anthropologist Eric Wolf, who argued that "the arrangements of a society become most visible when they are challenged by crisis."[61] It is hard to imagine situations in which the "arrangements of a society," or the manifestations of structural violence, are more visible than for people living with the violence and devastation of armed conflict. Those who suffer the most are typically those with the least power in society, who are the most vulnerable to the effects of structural violence, and who live with the most constrained agency though which they might protect themselves against threats, be resilient in the face of violence, and rebuild their lives afterward.

The political violence of armed conflict is underlain by structural violence that robs people of access to resources, creates food insecurities, and strengthens the reciprocal synergism of poverty and poor health. The costs of conflict, in turn, help reproduce and intensify the very conditions that create crisis and desperation and prompt violence as an option for social change. Thus to begin to grapple with the complexities of civil war in Peru or elsewhere entails knowledge of both preexisting contexts and myriad responses to conflict at both local and national levels. It requires a sense of the lived histories of individuals and communities that shape their vulnerability and resilience when faced with violent conflicts so that the uneven effects of conflict can be better understood. In this sense the need for longitudinal and community-based ethnographic research on the contexts and consequences of conflicts emerges as a challenge for anthropology, public health, and human rights advocates, as well as all who hope to ameliorate long-term effects of armed conflict and prevent future violence.

Notes

1. This chapter is an abstracted and updated version of Thomas Leatherman and R. Brooke Thomas, "Structural Violence, Political Violence, and the Health Costs of Civil Conflict: A Case Study from Peru," *Anthropology and Public Health: Bridging Differences in Culture and Society*, 2nd ed., Robert A. Hahn and Marcia C. Inhorn, Eds. (Oxford: Oxford University Press, 2008, 196–220).

2. Lotta Harbom, Erik Melander, and Peter Wallensteen, "Dyadic Dimensions of Armed Conflict, 1946–2000," *Journal of Peace Research* 45(5): 2008, 697–710.

3. For example, M. C. Inhorn and L. Kobeissi, "The Public Health Costs of War in Iraq: Lessons from Post-War Lebanon," *Journal of Social Affairs* 23: 2006, 13–47; H. A. Ghobarah, P. Huth, and B. Russett, "The Postwar Public Health Effects of Civil Conflict," *Social Science and Medicine* 59: 2004, 869–84; B. S. Levy and V. W. Sidel, *War and Public Health* (New York: Oxford University Press, 1997); D. Pedersen, "Political Violence, Ethnic Conflict, and Contemporary Wars: Broad Implications for Health and Social Well-Being," *Social Science and Medicine* 55(2): 2002, 175–90; A. Zwi, and A. Ugalde, "Towards an Epidemiology of Political Violence in the Third World," *Social Science and Medicine* 28: 1989, 633–42.

4. Ghobarah et al., note 3.

5. Pedersen, note 3; D. Summerfield, "A Critique of Seven Assumptions behind Psychological Trauma Programmes in War-Affected Areas," *Social Science & Medicine* 48:1999, 1449–62.

6. Leatherman and Thomas, note 1; T. L. Leatherman, "A Biocultural Perspective on Health and Household Economy in Southern Peru," *Medical Anthropology Quarterly* 10(4):1996, 476–95; T. L. Leatherman, "A Space of Vulnerability in Poverty and Health: Political Ecology and Biocultural Analyses," *Ethos* 33(1):2005, 46–70.

7. P. Farmer, *Pathologies of Power: Health, Human Rights, and the New War on the Poor* (Berkeley and Los Angeles: University of California Press, 2003); P. Farmer, "Sidney W. Mintz Lecture for 2001: An Anthropology of Structural Violence," *Current Anthropology* 45(3): 2004, 305–25.

8. Ibid., p. 307.

9. Ibid.

10. P. Bourgois, "The Power of Violence in War and Peace: Post–Cold-War Lessons from El Salvador," *Ethnography* 2(1): 2001, 5–34.

11. E. Messer, M. J. Cohen, and J. D'Costa, "Food from Peace: Breaking the Links between Conflict and Hunger," Food, Agriculture, and the Environment, Discussion Paper 24 (Washington: IFPRI, 1998). See also M. J. Cohen and P. Pinstrup-Andersen, "Food Security and Conflict," *Social Research* 66(1):1999; S. Teodosijevic, "Armed Conflicts and Food Security," ESA Working Paper No. 03-11, Agricultural and Development Economics Division (Rome: FAO, 2003); WHO, "Collective Violence," World Report on Violence and Health, WHO, Ed. (Geneva: WHO, 2002, 214–39).

12. Cohen and Pinstrup-Anderson 1999, ibid., p. 6.

13. FAO, *The State of Food Insecurity in the World* (Rome: FAO, 2002).

14. See Ghobarah et al., note 3; Inhorn and Kobeissi, note XX; Pedersen, note 3; WHO, note 11.

15. Declaration of Alma-Ata. International Conference on Primary Health Care, Alma-Ata, USSR, September 6–12, 1978, www.who.int/hpr/NPH/docs/declaration_almaata.pdf, accessed 5/15/10.

16. R. Waldman, "Public Health in War," *International Health* 27(1): 2005, 1–4.

17. Ghobara, note 3.

18. SIPRI, *SIPRI Yearbook 2002* (Stockholm: Stockholm International Peace Research Institute).

19. D. Guha-Sapir and W Gijsbert, "Conflict-Related Mortality: An Analysis of 37 Datasets," *Disasters* 28(4): 2004, 418–28; Pedersen, note 3; S. Pieterse and S. Ismali, "Nutritional Risk Factors for Older Refugees," *Disasters* 27(1): 2003, 16–36; A. Ager, Ed., *Refugees: Perspectives on the Experience of Forced Migration* (New York: Pinter, 1999); Messer et al., note 11; E. Kalipeni and J. Oppong, "The Refugee Crisis in Africa and Implications for Health and Disease: A Political Ecology Approach," *Social Science & Medicine* 46(12): 1998, 1637–53.

20. Ghobarah et al., note 3; Kalipeni and Oppong, ibid. Pedersen, note 3; Waldman, note 16.

21. Messer et al., note 11.

22. For example, R. C. Cervantes, V. N. Salgado, and A. M. Padilla, "Posttraumatic Stress in Immigrants from Central America and Mexico," *Hospital and Community Psychiatry* 40(6): 1989, 615–19; M. Hollifield, T. D. Warner, N. Lian, B. Krakow, J. H. Jenkins, J. Kesler, J. Stevenson, and J. Westermeyer, "Review: Measuring Trauma and Health Status in Refugees," *Journal of the American Medical Association* 288(5): 2002, 611–21.

23. Pedersen, note 3.

24. P. Bracken, J. Giller, and D. Summerfield, "Psychological Responses to War and Atrocity: The Limitations of Current Concepts," *Social Science and Medicine* 40(8):1995, 1073–82; Pedersen, note 3; Summerfield, note 3.

25. Summerfield, note 3.

26. D. Pedersen, J. Gamarra, M. Planas, and C. Errazuriz, "Violencia political y salud en las comunidades alto-andinas de Ayucucho, Peru," *Memorias del VI Congreso Latinoamericano de Ciencias Sociales y Salud* (Lima, Peru), June 10–13, 2001; D. Summerfield and L. Toser, "'Low-Intensity' War and Mental Trauma in Nicaragua: A Study in a Rural Community," *Medicine and War* 7: 1991, 84–99; and, for example, in the work of Kimberly Theidon, "Gender in Transition: Common Sense, Women, and War," *Journal of Human Rights* 6: 2007, 453–78.

27. H. Gusterson, "Militarism and Anthropology," *Annual Review of Anthropology* 36: 2007, 161–62; L. Green, "Fear as a Way of Life," *Cultural Anthropology* 9(2):1994, 227–56. See

also N. Scheper-Hughes and P. Bourgois, Eds., *Violence in War and Peace: An Anthology* (Oxford: Blackwell Publishing, 2004).

28. Cohen and Pinstrup-Anderson, 1999; FAO, note 12; Messer et al., note 11; Teodosijevic, note 11; WHO, note 11.

29. FAO, note 13; Messer et al., note 11; Teodosejivic, note 11.

30. J. Macrae and A. Zwi, "Famine, Complex Emergencies, and International Policy in Africa," *War and Hunger: Rethinking International Responses to Complex Emergencies*, J. Macrae, A. Zwi, Eds. (London: Zed Books, 1994, 6–36); Messer et al., note 11.

31. D. J. Hendrickson, J. Armon, and R. Mearns, "The Changing Nature of Conflict and Famine Vulnerability: The Case of Livestock Raiding in Turkana District, Kenya," *Disasters* 22(3):1998, 185–99.

32. Waldman, note 16.

33. Zwi and Ugalde, note 3; R. I. Lundgren and R. Lang, "'There Is No Sea, Only Fish': Effects of United States Policy on the Health of the Displaced in El Salvador," *Social Science and Medicine* 28(7):1989, 697–706; Cervantes et al., note 22.

34. Summerfield and Toser, note 26; Pedersen, note 3.

35. A. Ugalde, E. Selva-Sutter, C. Castillo, C. Paz, and S. Canas, "The Health Costs of War: Can They Be Measured? Lessons from El Salvador," *British Medical Journal* 321: 2000, 169–72.

36. M. Donahue, "Causes and Health Consequences of Environmental Degradation and Social Injustice," *Social Science & Medicine* 56: 2003, 573–87.

37. Cited in Messer, note 11, p. 13.

38. D. Poole and G. Rénique, *Peru: Time of Fear* (London: Latin American Bureau Limited, 1992); Jose Luis Rénique, *La Batalla por Puno: Conflicto Agrario y Nación en los Andes Peruanos 1866–1995* (Lima: IEP, 2004); S. Stern, Ed., *Shining and Other Paths: War and Society in Peru, 1980–1995* (Durham, NC: Duke University Press, 1998).

39. C. McClintock, "Why Peasants Rebel: The Case of Peru's Sendero Luminoso," *World Politics* 37:1984, 48–84; Poole and Rénique, ibid.

40. UN, *Profiles in Displacement: Peru*, Report to Commission on Human Rights (Geneva: UN Commission on Human Rights, 1996).

41. M. Reid, *Peru: Paths to Poverty* (London: Latin American Bureau Limited, 1985).

42. J. Sheahan, *Searching for a Better Society: The Peruvian Economy from 1950* (University Park: University of Pennsylvania Press, 1999).

43. Poole and Rénique, note 38; Sheahan, ibid.

44. Leatherman, note 6.

45. S. Luerssen, "Landlessness, Health, and the Failures of Reform in the Peruvian Highlands," *Human Organization* 53(4):1994, 380–87.

46. Leatherman, note 6.

47. Truth and Reconciliation Commission (TRC), *Final Report* (Lima: Peru, 2003); UN, note 40; Poole and Rénique, note 38; FAO, note 13.

48. Pedersen et al., note 26; UN, note 40.

49. Pedersen et al., note 16.

50. UN, note 40.

51. I. G. Pawson, L. Huicho, M. Muro, and A. Pacheco, "Growth of Children in Two Economically Diverse Peruvian High-Altitude Communities," *American Journal of Human Biology* 13: 2001, 323–40.

52. Centro de Salud Nuñoa, "Reporte annual de actividades: Micro red Nuñoa. Ministerio de Salud," 2005.

53. Pedersen et al., note 26; Summerfield and Toser, note 26.

54. TRC, note 47.

55. Theidon, note 26.

56. Lisa J. Laplante, "From Theory to Practice: Implementing Reparations in Post-Truth Commission Peru," *Waging War, Making Peace—Reparations and Human Rights*, Barbara Rose Johnston and Susan Slyomovics, Eds. (Walnut Creek, CA: Left Coast Press, 2009, 76–95); TRC, note 47.

57. Laplante, ibid.

58. Laplante, note 56.

59. Ibid.

60. Ibid.

61. See Barbara Rose Johnston's discussion of Eric Wolf comments on crisis in "Human Rights, Environmental Quality, and Social Justice," in Chapter 1 of this book; and Eric Wolf, "Facing Power: Old Insights, New Questions," *American Anthropologist* (92):1990, 586–96.

SNAPSHOT: War and Political Violence Are Destructive to Life and Health

Ellen Gruenbaum

Wars and violent conflict constitute the one of the greatest human rights and public health challenges of our time, not only because of the greater numbers of civilian casualties in contemporary wars and the massive destructive power of today's military technologies but also because increasingly civilians and ordinary life are deliberately targeted. Violent political conflicts create conditions of social misery in which deprivation, illness, economic loss, bereavement, mental anguish, and suffering are rampant and traumatizing, infecting people's futures with enduring injury and animosity.

In the Darfur region of Sudan conflict has raged since 2003. More than 200,000 people have lost their lives to violence and the related disruptions of people's abilities to provide themselves with food, water, homes, and safety. More than 2 million people have fled before the destruction wrought by Janjaweed militias who attacked and burned of villages with the support of aerial bombardments by the Sudanese military. These displaced people sought refuge in humanitarian camps, and about 240,000 fled across the border to Chad. International outcry against what has been labeled ethnic cleansing or genocide slowly gathered momentum, generated humanitarian assistance—insufficient though it has been—and led a stronger United Nations peacekeeping presence since 2007. In March 2009 the International Criminal Court in Hague issued an arrest warrant for Sudan's President Omar El Bashir for his role in war crimes related to the Darfur conflict. The arrest led to a political backlash against humanitarian organizations delivering aid to the displaced.

Although ethnic cleavages have been used to fuel the conflict, ethnic animosity does not explain this situation, nor is it accurate to describe ethnicity in the region as a simple dichotomy of Arab and African, as international pundits commonly do. The conflict is rooted in something more complex: the heritage of human rights abuse and environmental disasters. These include decades of Sahelian droughts, development-induced population displacement, and subsequent competition for critical and scarce resources. It is further fueled by ideologies of prior claim on land use combined with political and economic neglect of the region by the central government. The conflict in 2003 was sparked by specific grievances consequent to the long war between the central government and the southern Sudanese People's Liberation Movement (SPLM) as well as the terms of the peace negotiations—terms that were intended to benefit the south and central regions of the country but not Darfur in the West. Rebel groups sought to share in Sudan's potential wealth from oil and the national development it was expected to generate. The current peace agreement is tenuous and the coalition government with SPLM raised unrealized hope for a just resolution to the Darfur crisis. Meanwhile the international community has failed to develop a coherent approach to resolving the conflict.

Specific statistics on mortality, injuries, illnesses, and other casualties and atrocities have been difficult to track—and counts are contentious—since 2003. Mamdani, for example, critiques the "racialization" of the conflict by outside political organizations seeking to distract Americans from the war in Iraq and vilify Arabs in order to focus attention on the "war on terror."[1] He notes that deaths in the region in 2008 were due to grazing land competition, rebel groups' activities, and government-organized counterinsurgency, not merely victimization of "Africans" by "Arabs," as some of the would-be support groups portray it. Has the world's humanitarian impulse been drafted into the vision of the war on terror, casting the Darfurians as new victims in the new world security scenario?

Whatever the political uses of the conflict for international consumption, the world community, with its recent memories of the unanswered tragedies such as Rwanda, has been horrified by the scope of the suffering in Darfur. The civilian population had experienced aerial bombardment of homes, farms, schools, and markets.[2] Thousands have been displaced from their homes and farms by raids, burning of villages, destruction of crops and livestock, poisoning of wells, intimidation, and terror, including rapes, murders, violence, capture, and enslavement. The civilian population has experienced hunger, malnutrition, exposure, and starvation. For residents in displaced and refugee camps there has been a lack of security as both government forces and government-aligned militias continue to attack, or fail to protect, humanitarian and medical relief operations. For example, in 2006 six UN World Food Program warehouses were destroyed in Northern Darfur, and, following El Bashir's indictment in 2009, relief operations were blocked altogether in some areas. For civilians in areas targeted for ethnic cleansing as well as for vulnerable displaced populations struggling to collect firewood and water around the camps, rape has been used as a weapon of terror to dishonor women and their families, driving residents from their homes, from camps, and from the regions. There are reports that ethnic identity has been used as a basis for racism, genocide, "ethnic cleansing," and repopulation with people from favored ethnic groups, creating "facts on the ground" to permanently expropriate the recent inhabitants.

Notes

1. M. Mahmood, *Saviors and Survivors: Darfur, Politics, and the War on Terror* (New York: Random House, 2009).

2. Human Rights Watch, "Darfur 2007: Chaos by Design: Peacekeeping Challenges for AMIS and UNAMID," *Human Rights Watch*, Vol. 19, No. 15(A), Sept. 2007, http://hrw.org/reports/2007/sudan0907/sudan0907web.pdf.

SNAPSHOT: Considering the Human Health Consequences of War in Iraq[1]

Marcia C. Inhorn

War and Empire

In November 2007 there were 30 violent conflicts going on around the world.[2] Are they "wars"? Definitions of war, conflict, armed struggle, and revolution are imprecise and depend heavily on the vantage point of those doing the fighting. Violent conflict is called war only when an official declaration of war exists. If we use this narrow definition there are currently eight wars being fought in the world, in Sri Lanka, Somalia, Chechnya, Afghanistan, Iraq, Waziristan (Pakistan), Chad, and Mexico (a "drug war"). Interestingly, the extensive political violence occurring in such places as Kashmir, Kurdistan, the Gaza Strip, Darfur, and Lebanon is defined as "conflict" not war—even though the six-week conflict between Lebanon and Israel in the summer of 2006, which left nearly 2,000 people dead, was called "war."

Of the eight wars and five conflicts that I have just mentioned, 10 are occurring in the Middle East and the broader Muslim world. The United States is fighting wars in Afghanistan and Iraq, and over the last 50 years has intervened militarily in the Middle East region 10 times. This record, along with military interventions in other parts of the world, bespeaks the increasingly imperial aspirations of the United States as the world's economic and military superpower.[3] Middle East scholar Laurie Brand puts it this way: "What word but 'empire' describes the awesome thing that America is becoming? It is the only nation that polices the world through five global military commands; maintains more than a million men and women at arms on four continents; deploys carrier battle groups on watch in every ocean; guarantees the survival of countries from Israel to South Korea; drives wheels of global trade and commerce." Brand concludes that this imperial expansion is being justified by "the exigencies of prosecuting a war against terrorism, a battle that is portrayed as existential in nature and global in scope."[4]

War in Iraq

Iraq has suffered an undue share of war and death during the past 50 years. The Baath Party rose to power in 1963, and Saddam Hussein became president in 1979. In his first year of office Hussein invaded Iran, pitching his country into a bloody eight-year war that cost more than a million lives and represents the longest conventional war between two countries in the 20th century. In 1990 he invaded Kuwait, this time incurring the wrath of Kuwait's Western allies. The United States and a coalition force of approximately 30 nations invaded Iraq in January 1991 in a six-week war that led to Hussein's surrender in February 1991.[5]

The costs to Iraq lasted much longer. Iraq was economically sanctioned by the UN Security Council; from 1990 to 2003, Iraq faced restrictions on importation of all items except medicine.[6] Not until December 1996 was the UN Oil-for-Food Program initiated to attempt to alleviate major sanction-induced food shortages and malnutrition. The sanctions ended only when the United States declared war on Iraq on March 19, 2003. During this ongoing war in Iraq—which grew into an uncontrollable intersectarian civil war—the health of the population is deteriorating on multiple levels.

Body Counts and Health Costs

No one can say precisely how many Iraqis, including civilians, have been killed. The U.S. military reportedly has not kept records of Iraqi casualties. Body counts have become a major rallying cry for some human rights organizations, which demand U.S. coalition accountability. A major study of Iraqi casualties was carried out twice, in 2003 and 2006, by a research team affiliated with Johns Hopkins Bloomberg School of Public Health, Columbia, and MIT universities, in collaboration with a brave team of physician-epidemiologists in Baghdad.[7] Both studies have been published in the prominent medical journal *Lancet* to a great deal of fanfare, criticism, and outright denial by the U.S. government. In the 2006 restudy the estimated body count of Iraqi civilians who had died violently was increased to more than 655,000.[8] In comparison, as of April 2009, 4,270 U.S. military casualties have been confirmed by the Department of Defense—an unacceptable number but a mere fraction of the Iraqi death toll.[9]

Iraq is in the midst of a mental health crisis.[10] Since the U.S. invasion, cases of post-traumatic stress disorder (PTSD) have increased by 35%, precipitated particularly by the major battles and explosions that have devastated urban neighborhoods.[11] The vast majority of Iraq's 13 million children are likely affected by psychological trauma in addition to the "grave risk of starvation, disease [and] death."[12] At least a half million of these children are in serious need of psychological treatment.[13] The number of Iraq and Afghanistan veterans diagnosed with PTSD is also rising rapidly, from nearly 30,000 in 2006 to nearly 50,000 only one year later, according to a Veterans Administration study.[14] But few of these are counted in the Pentagon's official tally of approximately 30,000 wounded in Iraq.

Almost half the Iraqi population consists of children. Once child malnutrition was rare in the country. Now UN agencies estimate that one out of every eight children in Iraq dies before the age of five, one-third are malnourished, one-quarter are born underweight, and one-quarter do not have access to safe drinking water.[15] These devastating figures reflect the fact that about 75% of Iraqis currently lack secure access to food; thus, child malnutrition rates are now high in a country where malnutrition among children was once rare.

The refugee crisis also has been devastating to human health. Many of those Iraqis able to leave the country have fled. During the First Gulf War, those encouraged by the U.S. government to revolt against the regime of Saddam Hussein, mostly Shia Muslims, were subsequently forced to flee. After living for up to six years in deplorable conditions in Saudi Arabian refugee camps the Shia refugees were largely resettled in the United States, where they are now an impoverished and unassimilated ethnic enclave of nearly 80,000 in Detroit, Michigan.[16] The U.S. Patriot Act makes it unlikely that additional Iraqi refugees will be allowed into the United States. To date only a trickle of Iraqi refugees from the current war have been given asylum; even many of the brave Iraqi interpreters who risked their lives to work with U.S. forces have been callously denied asylum,[17] as have Iraqi Fulbright scholars.[18] The majority of the refugee population of 2.2 million has fled to Syria and Jordan, resource-poor countries whose infrastructure is being overwhelmed. An additional 2.7 million people are internally displaced within Iraq; they can neither return to their homes nor safely emigrate.[19]

Environmental Costs

The war has taken a great toll on the environment, especially as a result of the contaminant depleted uranium, or DU. DU is the waste product of uranium enrichment and is about 60% more radioactive than natural uranium. Like other heavy metals DU is chemically toxic to humans. It has been used since 1959 in the U.S. munitions industry because of its high density, melting point, and tensile strength, and because it ignites when it fragments. The U.S. military has called it the "silver bullet" for destroying enemy tanks and uses it as armor on tanks. It has been used extensively in both U.S. wars in Iraq.

When DU explodes, it creates "a fine, respirable size dust that contaminates an impact site and presents a hazard to combat troops and civilians." DU dust in the environment has a radioactive decay chain lasting 4.5 billion years, posing long-term health risks to exposed populations. Because only a few dozen U.S. Gulf War veterans who are the victims of DU "friendly fire" have been studied, evidence of DU's immediate and long-term health effects remains inconclusive. In laboratory rats, DU causes cancer, kidney damage, central nervous system damage, negative reproductive effects, and other health problems.[20] Already, according to WHO, there are reports of increased rates of cancers, congenital malformations, and renal diseases among the Iraqi population since the First Gulf War.[21] Some environmental activists and Gulf War veterans groups have attributed so-called Gulf War Syndrome to DU exposure.[22] Convinced of a link between health problems and DU exposure, the Italian government has agreed to a precedent-setting DU compensation package.[23] By contrast, the U.S. Department of Defense has been accused of gross negligence in failing to assess the health and environmental costs of its use of DU in Iraq.

Medical Anthropology in the Warzone

I have never been to Iraq, but I have worked with Iraqi Shia refugees of the First Gulf War living in Dearborn, Michigan.[24] To my knowledge, no medical anthropologist has worked in Iraq in the past 50 years. One reason is Iraq's turbulent and dangerous history. But another reason is our failure as a profession.

Why is there so little research on the medical anthropology of war? First, I would argue that we are scared of studying war, and rightly so. Doing fieldwork in a warzone is life threatening. Yet journalists—whom anthropologists often criticize for their lack of language training and cultural immersion—risk their lives in pursuit of knowledge about the effects of war. To date nearly 190 journalists and media assistants have lost their lives in Iraq—the highest toll in the history of journalism.[25] How many anthropologists have been so brave?

Second, it is extremely difficult for scholars to enter war zones—our universities and their institutional review boards will not allow it, nor will the host country at war.[26] But it is not impossible, strictly speaking. The National Science Foundation (NSF), for example, has had a separate source of funding for anthropological research in "high-risk situations" where immediate response and research is needed. The NSF Cultural Anthropology program is not beholden to host country politics in the way that some other funding agencies are, including the U.S. State Department's Fulbright program. NSF has funded several anthropologists doing fieldwork in contemporary Iraq and Afghanistan, as well as in Sri Lanka, Congo, and Tajikistan.[27] As a discipline, we have been faint of heart and lacking in moral courage in this arena. We have turned away from the brutal realities, the embodied suffering, the psychological devastation, the sexual violence, and the refugee aftermath of war. It is not enough to study "structural violence"—as important as the violence of poverty and powerlessness may be.[28] War creates poverty, but it also creates many other forms of embodied suffering that require our anthropological attention and our concern.[29] It creates trails of human misery that take generations to overcome. War is bad for human health and well-being on multiple levels. The health effects of war are immediate and long term, direct and indirect.[30] War precludes the possibility of Health for All, the utopian goal of the Declaration of Alma-Ata.[31] If global health is to become a worldwide aspiration in the 21st century, then medical anthropologists must assess the health costs—as well as the political costs—of war and agitate for peace in the new millennium.

Notes

1. I am both a medical anthropologist and an area studies scholar. Since September 11, 2001, I have been involved in directing various centers for Middle Eastern and North African Studies and I spent much of 2007 on research leave in the Middle East. An earlier version of this essay was published as Marcia C. Inhorn, "Medical Anthropology Against War," *Medical Anthropology Quarterly* 22(4) 2008:216–24.

2. Wikipedia, "List of Ongoing Conflicts," http://en.wikipedia.org/wiki/Ongoing_wars, 11/22/07.

3. Marcia C. Inhorn and Carolyn F. Sargent, "Medical Anthropology in the Muslim World: Ethnographic Reflections on Reproductive and Child Health," *Medical Anthropology Quarterly* 20(1) 2006:1–11; Johns Hopkins Bloomberg School of Public Health, "Updated Iraq Survey Affirms Earlier Mortality Estimates," www.jhsph.edu/publichealthnews/press_releases/2006/burnham_iraq_2006.html, 11/22/07.

4. Laurie Brand, "Scholarship in the Shadow of Empire," *Middle East Studies Association Bulletin* 39(1) 2005:3–18.

5. Wikipedia, "Iran–Iraq War," http://en.wikipedia.org/wiki/Iran-Iraq_War, 11/22/07; Wikipedia, "Gulf War," http://en.wikipedia.org/wiki/Gulf_War, 11/22/07.

6. World Health Organization (WHO), "Potential Impact of Conflict on Health in Iraq," 2003, www.who.int/features/2003/iraq/briefings/iraq_briefing_note/en/, 11/22/07.

7. G. Burnham, R. Lafta, S. Doocy, and L. Roberts, "Mortality after the 2003 Invasion of Iraq: A Cross-Sectional Cluster Sample Survey," *Lancet* (368) 2006:1421–28; Les Roberts, Riyadh Lafta,

Richard Garfield, Jamal Khudhairi, and Gilbert Burnham, "Mortality before and after the 2003 Invasion of Iraq: Cluster Sample Survey," *Lancet* (29) 2004:1–8.

8. Johns Hopkins Bloomberg School of Public Health, note 3.

9. Michael Ewens, "Casualties in Iraq: The Human Cost of Occupation," www.antiwar.com/casualties/, 04/13/09.

10. Fiona Fleck, "Mental Health a Major Priority in Reconstruction of Iraq's Health System," *Bulletin of the World Health Organization* (82) 2004:555.

11. Jamie Tarabay, "Iraq Mental Health Deteriorates with Violence," *National Public Radio*, www.npr.org/, 05/03/06.

12. Jocalyn Clark, "Threat of War Is Affecting Mental Health of Iraqi Children, Says Report," *British Medical Journal* (326) 2003:356.

13. Medical Aid for Iraqi Children, "About Us," 2003, www.maic.org.uk/aboutus.htm, 11/22/07.

14. Michael Isikoff and Jamie Reno, "How Do You Fund a War, but Not the Casualties?" *Newsweek*, October 29, 2007:10.

15. WHO, note 6.

16. Linda S. Walbridge and T. M. Aziz, "After Karbala: Iraqi Refugees in Detroit," in *Arab Detroit: From Margin to Mainstream*, Nabeel Abraham and Andrew Shryock, Eds. (Detroit, MI: Wayne State University Press, 2000, 321–42).

17. Sam Knight, "In the Face of Death," *Newsweek*, September 24, 2007:34–37.

18. Anthropology News, "Iraqi Fulbright Scholars Seek Asylum in U.S. Washington Wire," *Anthropology News* 48(8) 2007:26.

19. UN High Commission for Refugees (UNHCR), "The Iraq Situation," www.unhcr.org/iraq.html, 04/13/09.

20. Factual detail in the first two paragraphs of this section are from Dan Fahey, "The Emergence and Decline of the Debate over Depleted Uranium Munitions, 1991–2004," 2004, www.danfahey.com/2004-DanFahey.pdf, 11/22/07. For additional detail on human health costs of radioactivity and militarism, see *Half-Lives and Half-Truths: Confronting the Radioactive Legacies of the Cold War*, Barbara Rose Johnston, Ed. (Santa Fe, NM: School for Advanced Research Press, 2007).

21. WHO, note 6.

22. Dan Fahey, "Summary of Government Data on Testing of Veterans for Depleted Uranium Exposure during Service in Iraq," 2005, www.danfahey.com/2005-DanFahey.pdf, 11/22/07.

23. International Coalition to Ban Depleted Uranium, "€30m Veterans' DU Compensation Package Approved by Italian Cabinet," 2009, www.bandepleteduranium.org/en/a/230.html, 05/18/10.

24. Marcia C. Inhorn and Michael Hassan Fakih, "Arab Americans, African Americans, and Infertility: Barriers to Reproduction and Medical Care," *Fertility and Sterility* 85(4) 2006:844–52.

25. Committee to Protect Journalists, "Iraq: Journalists in Danger: A Statistical Profile of Media Deaths and Abductions in Iraq 2003–09," http://cpj.org/reports/2008/07/journalists-killed-in-iraq.php, 05/18/10.

26. For criticisms of the ethical implications of anthropological work in war zones, see Catherine Besteman, Andrew Bickford, Greg Feldman, Roberto Gonzalez, Hugh Gusterson, Gustaaf Houtman, Kanhong Lin, Catherine Lutz, David Price, and David Vine, "US Intelligence and Anthropology," *Anthropology News* 48(8) 2007:3–4; David Rohde, "Army Enlists Anthropology in War Zones," *The New York Times*, October 5, 2007, www.nytimes.com/2007/10/05/world/asia/05afghan.html, 11/22/07.

27. Deborah Winslow, personal communication, December 6, 2007. For notable new work in this area, see Barbara Rylko-Bauer, Linda Whiteford, and Paul Farmer, Eds., *Global Health in Times of Violence* (Santa Fe: SAR Press, 2009).

28. Paul Farmer, *Pathologies of Power: Health, Human Rights, and the New War on the Poor* (Berkeley and Los Angeles: University of California Press, 2003); Paul Farmer, "Sidney W. Mintz Lecture for 2001: An Anthropology of Structural Violence," *Current Anthropology* 45 (2004):305–25.

29. To consider health consequences of multiple forms of violence, from conquest and colonialism to the aftermaths of war, see Nancy Scheper-Hughes and Philippe Bourgois, Eds., *Violence in War and Peace: An Anthology* (Malden, MA: Blackwell, 2007).

30. Hazem Adam Ghobarah, Paul Huth, and Bruce Russett, "The Post-War Public Health Effects of Civil Conflict," *Social Science and Medicine* (59) 2004:869–84.

31. World Health Organization (WHO), "The Declaration of Alma-Ata," 1978, www.who.int/hpr/NPH/docs/declaration_almaata, 11/22/07.

CHAPTER 15

Radiation Communities: Fighting for Justice for the Marshall Islands

Holly M. Barker

SECTION I: The End of the Millennium

I was watching the evening news on my television which told of a person receiving some two million dollars from McDonald's fast food to compensate for the pain and anguish of being scalded by a cup of coffee. Tell me, can that be compared to the pain of watching your first child die of leukemia or your wife giving birth to some monstrous horror?[1]
—Kaleman Gideon, Likiep Atoll

They failed to warn and inform the people about the nuclear tests, and also how they used us as guinea pigs to learn how our bodies could resist or absorb the poison from the tests. Just like when they are about to send a rocket into space they put many kinds of animals (in the rockets) for their experiments. That's exactly what they did with us.[2]
—Tempo Alfred, Ailuk Atoll

Some of the fish that we used to eat are now poisonous. We cannot eat them anymore. And some fruits of the breadfruit tree that shouldn't bear seeds according to the laws of nature, strangely enough, seeds grow in them. Pigs also have defective bodies. Some have twisted legs. Sometimes the (supply) ships wouldn't come for a long time so we had to kill and eat them. What could we do? We were hungry and we needed something to eat.[3]
—Jalel John, Ailuk Atoll

We never had any of these illnesses, these grotesque deformities, these grape-like things (we give birth to) that do not resemble a human being at all. And you ask me what I think! I think that if it were not for the United States and their all-consuming desire for superiority over the Russians, we, the people of Rongelap, would not have to turn our head in shame for fear of being considered freaks of nature. And to add insult to injury, they have heartlessly coined the term "nuclear nomad" to describe our plight, . . . the deaths of our children and the destruction of the islands our forefathers shed their blood for.[4]
—Aruko Bobo, Rongelap Atoll

I first heard about the Marshall Islands when the United States Peace Corps accepted my application to volunteer and assigned me to the infant nation. Like many westerners, I envisioned a tropical paradise with idyllic beaches and happy people. My dreams were quickly shattered: Instead of joining me in celebration, my mother shrieked: "You can't go there!" My parents schooled me about the Marshall Islands and their history as a nuclear test site, explaining that the United States had conducted above-ground nuclear weapons tests on its Bikini and Enewetak atolls.

Despite concerns about lingering radiation in the Marshall Islands, I received assurances from the U.S. government that the islands to which Peace Corps volunteers are assigned are safe for human habitation.[5] Nonetheless, on arrival in the Marshall Islands, I purposefully asked to be stationed in the southernmost village—a location farthest from the "ground-zero" sites. From 1988 to 1990 I lived and worked in a remote island village as a schoolteacher. At the end of my Peace Corps assignment I found it difficult to simply walk away from the Marshallese. Fortunately, I returned to the United States at precisely the time the Embassy of the Republic of the Marshall Islands (RMI) in Washington, D.C., was looking for assistance.

As the Senior Political Advisor at the Embassy, I work with the RMI national government in its continued effort to secure assistance from the U.S. government for radiation problems associated with the nuclear weapons testing program. For the past two years I have gathered historical documents and ethnographic data about Marshallese people in communities that were exposed to radiation yet, because of a series of bureaucratic obstacles, remain ineligible for assistance from the U.S. government. In this chapter I present some of this ethnographic and historical data, and describe how the process of compiling and using this information has been empowering both victims and the newly formed government. I also describe some of the RMI efforts to seek redress from the U.S. government and the effects of this process on the RMI-U.S. bilateral relationship.

Nuclear Weapons Testing in the Marshall Islands

More than 50 years ago, the Marshall Islands—an island group in Micronesia, the west central Pacific—was selected as the testing site for the U.S. atomic and hydrogen weapons program because of their geographic isolation.[6] Between 1946 and 1958 the U.S. government conducted 67 nuclear tests above, on, and in the seas surrounding the islands. Many of these tests, including the infamous 1954 Bravo shot, equivalent to more than 1,000 "Hiroshima" bombs, were designed to produce as much local fallout as possible.[7] In this era there was an international outcry over worldwide radiation levels tied to U.S. nuclear weapons testing. The United States deflated international protests by decreasing upper atmospheric fallout—in turn increasing local fallout. The isolation of the islands provided U.S. scientists with the perfect laboratory conditions for studying the effects of radiation on human beings and the environment.

From the end of World War II until 1986 the Marshall Islands was a United Nations Trust Territory administered by the United States. Under the terms of the Trusteeship the United States had direct responsibility for the health and safety of the Marshallese people. Paradoxically, it was this colonial relationship that allowed the United States to justify the detonation of thermonuclear devices deemed too dangerous for testing in the continental United States. The U.S. government thought of the Marshallese as an "expendable population" whose interests were usurped by U.S. national security interests.[8] Even when the Marshallese were legitimately concerned about their safety and welfare, the colonial nature of the Trusteeship prevented them from effectively voicing their concerns. In 1954 the Marshallese people submitted a petition to the UN expressing their concerns about radiation hazards. The Director of the Medical Division of Biology and Medicine in the Marshall Islands, Dr. John C. Bugher, convinced both the U.S. ambassador to the UN and the UN Secretary General to delay submission of the petition until the testing series under way in 1954 was complete.[9]

The Trusteeship arrangement allowed the selective victimization of the Marshallese to take place: without their knowledge or approval, the Marshallese relinquished their rights to a healthy life and a clean environment to the U.S. government and its nuclear weapons testing program. The Marshallese people, not the United States, continue to pay the price for the government's Cold War weapons testing agenda. The testing program has meant exile, death, illness, and suffering for the Marshallese population. Lingering radiation has caused unquantifiable economic and cultural loss as well. In a nation with just 70 square miles of land, some entire islands were vaporized, and others remain too radioactive for inhabitation or use.

Although radioactive fallout from the tests moved across each of the 29 populated atolls in the country, the U.S. government considers only four atolls in the Marshall Islands to have been "exposed." As a result, only these four receive compensation or participate in a U.S. Department of Energy medical and environmental monitoring program: the two ground-zero atolls of Bikini and Enewetak and the two that received heavy fallout from the Bravo test, Rongelap and Uterik. The specific nature of the assistance is spelled out in the treaty that governs bilateral relations between the United States and the Marshall Islands, the Compact of Free Association. When the Compact came into force in 1986 the Trusteeship terminated, and the RMI became a sovereign nation for the first time in more than 400 years.

From the beginning of the testing period until termination of the Trusteeship, the Marshall Islands' government was forced to rely on the U.S. government to explain the extent of damage. Because it controlled and limited the Marshallese negotiators' access to information, the U.S. determined which atolls were defined as "exposed" and eligible to receive assistance under the Compact, which establishes the responsibilities of the U.S. to mitigate the adverse human and environmental effects of the nuclear weapons testing program. Of course, the U.S. government also determined which communities to ignore.

In December 1993 U.S. Secretary of Energy Hazel O'Leary announced an "openness initiative" for her department. As the Cold War waned, this initiative made thousands of previously declassified documents available to the public for the first time. Approximately 20,000 pages of information pertaining to the nuclear testing program were delivered to the former RMI Minister of Foreign Affairs, Tom D. Kijiner. The RMI government assigned its former Ambassador to the United States, Wilfred I. Kendall, responsibility for reviewing the documents. This newly released evidence clearly demonstrates that the atoll environment and surrounding seas were contaminated to a much greater degree than the RMI government realized. This information has enormous implications for a government struggling to provide for the healthcare needs of all exposed populations—both the Marshallese who were alive during the testing period and those born and raised on contaminated atolls where they ate and drank from an irradiated food chain. The true exposed population in the Marshall Islands cannot be neatly corralled into temporal and physical categories that the United States has previously used.

The documents also demonstrate that the Marshallese people and the environment were unnecessarily contaminated during the Bravo shot. Although residents were evacuated for smaller tests to protect them from fallout, Marshallese living in communities directly downwind from ground zero were not evacuated before the Bravo shot despite the fact that the Bravo test was designed to produce more radioactive fallout than any previously detonated weapon. Moreover, U.S. government planners knew it was impossible to guarantee that radioactive fallout would not expose inhabited atolls and that weather patterns in the northern Pacific are unpredictable.[10] A meteorological report submitted before the detonation of Bravo concluded that a high-yield detonation could trigger a cloud of radiation that would expand as it became self-sustained by energy derived from condensation. After considering the recommendations of this report, Major General P. W. Clarkson, Commander of Joint Task Force Seven, proposed to "treat the report the same as I would a report from any other member of my staff when I do not agree with him. In short, we will kill it and stick it in the file."[11]

Just six hours before the detonation of Bravo on March 1, 1954 the joint task force responsible for detonation of the thermonuclear weapon held a briefing during which weather forecasters confirmed that the wind was blowing in the direction of inhabited atolls. Despite this dire forecast a decision was made to detonate Bravo. Precisely as the weather reports predicted radioactive fallout from Bravo was carried downwind to populated communities in the Marshall Islands.

In the hours and days after Bravo's detonation, the U.S. government instructed airplane pilots to monitor the path of the radioactive cloud. Pilots confirmed that Rongelap Atoll, less than 100 miles away from ground zero, received near-fatal doses of radiation. Aruko Bobo, a Rongelapese woman, remembers the reaction of her community the morning the U.S. government detonated Bravo:

> We were in the middle of the reef between the two islands when the whole of the western skies lit up so brilliantly that it seemed as if it were noon instead of 5:00 o'clock in the morning. The color went from bright white to deep red and then a mixture of both along with hues of yellow. We cowered among the large boulders on the reef, too frightened to decide whether to flee back to the islet or to dash across the reef to the main island. It was the boy who finally galvanized us to make a mad rush towards the main island. Just as we reached the last sand bank, the air around us was split by a most horrendous noise. I cannot describe what it was like. Perhaps like thunder but the force given off by the sound was so great we could actually feel wave after wave of vibrations. As if the very air had become a living thing. We made the last hundred or so yards to the main island in total pandemonium.[12]

Information recorded by U.S. military planes also confirmed that atolls where U.S. servicemen and Marshallese resided were exposed to dangerous levels of radiation. Evacuation teams were sent first to Rongerik Atoll, where 27 U.S. servicemen were stationed. The military's final report of radiological safety for the Bravo shot shows that the government viewed the Marshallese as an expendable population: "In the decision to authorize the Rongerik evacuation, consideration was given to the fact that only the US troops were being removed, whereas native populated atolls were also undoubtedly contaminated to the same or higher degree."[13] It was not until 52 hours after Rongelap's exposure that the military evacuated the Rongelapese. Shortly thereafter, another populated atoll to the west, Uterik, was evacuated. Both communities were brought to Kwajalein Atoll where they were involuntarily placed in a biomedical program entitled "Project 4.1: The Study of the Response of Human Beings Exposed to Significant Fallout Radiation."

Those evacuated from the two atolls were not the only communities exposed to Bravo's fallout. Records from U.S. military flights over the area after Bravo test, declassified in 1993, confirmed that other communities were also exposed to dangerous amounts of radioactivity. In 1954 the U.S. military considered a 10-roentgen exposure as the dividing line between dangerous and harmless levels of radiation, and 3.9 roentgens was the maximum permissible exposure for U.S. servicemen for an entire year.[14] Rongelap's dose was originally estimated at 175 roentgens; this figure was later adjusted to upward of 200 roentgens. Uterik's exposure was estimated at 17 roentgens—substantially less than Rongelap's exposure, yet far in excess of a dangerous dose. The RMI government has evidence from the newly released Department of Energy (DOE) documents confirming that Ailuk Atoll, approximately 20 miles southeast of Uterik, was exposed to 20 roentgens of radiation. When radioactive fallout began to settle on Ailuk and nearby Likiep Atoll, there was no communication system to report the fallout and no military ships came to evacuate residents. Said one local man: "Even though we knew and felt that Ailuk was poisoned, we couldn't do anything because we were ignored all along."[15] Despite the fact that the population of Ailuk was exposed to twice the "dangerous" dose and more than quadruple the maximum permissible exposure of U.S. servicemen for one year, the U.S. government clearly decided not to evacuate the Ailukese, using the rationale that Ailuk was too difficult to evacuate because of its "sizable" population. In fact, in 1954 there were only 401 residents on Ailuk.[16]

From 1954 until the present the U.S. government has continued to monitor and study the effects of radiation on the people of Rongelap and Uterik. This medical care contains a research component, but until quite recently, radiation victims had not been informed that some aspects of their medical care were not done for their personal health but rather for the benefit of scientific knowledge. Although the subjects have moved to different locations in the nation, the biomedical program that began on Kwajalein after Bravo continues. The U.S. government resettled four communities onto irradiated lands to study the human absorption of radionuclides from an irradiated environment (people from Uterik, Rongelap, Bikini, and Enewetak). Two months after Bravo, the Uterikese were resettled to their home atoll, and more than two years after Bravo, the Rongelapese were told their atoll was safe for resettlement. The Bikinians and the Enewetakese who were removed from their ground-zero homes during the actual testing were resettled in subsequent years and have been subjected to the biomedical program at different times.

Although researchers monitored the increased body burdens of the four resettled populations, the Marshallese were never told about their increased risk. In the case of the Rongelapese, the U.S. government was aware of high radionuclide concentrations in all of the major foods of the Rongelapese (including coconut crabs, arrowroot, pandanus, bananas, fish, and clams). According to Dr. Esra Riklon, a Marshallese medical officer who accompanied Atomic Energy Commission (AEC, predecessor to the DOE) and DOE teams to the resettled atolls:

> the common complaint—because I was the one who translated—was that after they eat arrowroot, they always developed a burning sensation in their throats, and constriction of the throat which caused them to have difficulty in breathing . . . some of them developed rashes, nausea, and vomiting. . . . (The U.S. said) this was an allergic reaction to food. . . . I didn't believe it was allergic. . . . I began to question the integrity of my job. I began to

realize that answers given to me to translate regarding important questions were often ambiguous or outright lies.[17]

Incremental increases in the radioactivity of food sources were also monitored by U.S. researchers as radiation from several weapons detonated after Rongelap's resettlement continued to expose the environment and the people.

Coconut crabs on Rongelap were identified as the most dangerous food source, because the crabs primarily eat contaminated coconuts and concentrate the radionuclides from coconuts in their bodies. Despite the obvious danger associated with coconut crab consumption, the food restrictions that the government suggested to the Rongelapese vacillated: at times they were told coconut crabs were safe to eat and at other times they were considered off limits. During each phase of the changing restrictions, the U.S. government monitored the body burdens of the Rongelapese and acknowledged in internal reports that the coconut crabs were increasing the internal radiation exposure of the Rongelapese. These increases were monitored despite an internal policy that the Rongelapese who were already exposed to near lethal levels of external radiation in 1954 should receive no additional radiation exposure for at least 12 years.

How did the U.S. government respond to the increased body burdens of the resettled Marshallese? In 1974 the AEC relaxed the restrictions for Marshallese radiation ingestion at precisely when an increase was needed, because people were returning to their islands and ingesting contaminated foods. At the same time the maximum exposure levels for the U.S. population were significantly lowered. This loosening up of the exposure levels for Marshall Islanders occurred in spite of an Environmental Protection Agency report recommendation that U.S. standards for radiation exposure be applied to U.S. activities in the Marshall Islands. As a result of the larger "acceptable" levels of radiation ingestion, the body burden measurements of the monitored populations showed that Cesium-137 was increasing in the populations living on contaminated lands. For example, the Department of Energy reported that over a one-year period (in 1982) scientists had documented dramatic increases of radionuclides in the Rongelapese, with the "body burdens for females less than 11 years of age "increasing by 82%, and adult male burdens up 56%.[18]

The Bikinians were also ingesting dangerous amounts of radionuclides, having returned to their home in 1972 after the United States completed its "cleanup" efforts. Unfortunately, methods used to define exposure dose and risk (and establish "habitability") did not include the cumulative and synergistic effects of drinking water, growing food, eating shellfish, and so forth—of day-to-day life on the island. By 1978 medical researchers found significant increase in exposure levels and the Bikini islanders were again evacuated.[19] By this time Bikinians had ingested more radioactive cesium from their environment than any known human population.[20] Even within the DOE, certain individuals recognized that the U.S. failure to provide information on the total radiation exposure of the population constituted a "cover-up." Negotiations are still under way with the U.S. government to engineer a safe resettlement of Bikini; 1996 marks the 50th year that the Bikinians have lived in diaspora.

Evidently, Bikini, Enewetak, Rongelap, and Uterik were adequate for the U.S. government's research purposes. Despite the fact that Ailuk received more radiation than Uterik the U.S. government excluded Ailuk from medical care and environmental monitoring programs. Unlike the four atolls the U.S. monitors closely, populations from Ailuk Atoll, plus other atolls in the northern and central parts of the country, were not removed when the atolls were at their "hottest." (Many of the most dangerous radionuclides attenuate relatively quickly, as their half-lives are often just a matter of weeks.)

Marshall Islands Government Response

> As we are in the same family with America, then America should look after its own people. . . . Help us![21]

Recently, the RMI government has stopped relying on the U.S. government to define the parameters of radiation exposure in the Marshall Islands. The RMI government is conducting its own research of historical documents pertaining to the testing period and is collecting ethnographic data from Marshallese radiation victims. These efforts are part of its quest for a complete and true understanding of the events that took place within its boundaries. It is clear that the U.S. government blatantly concealed information about the degree of destruction to the environment and the health of the people caused by such testing. Furthermore, there is evidence of repeated exposures, increased harm to the Marshallese, and the failure of the U.S. government to provide for peoples it knew were exposed to radiation.

Now that the RMI government is beginning to understand for itself the full impact of the testing program on the environment and its people, it is using this new information in bilateral and multilateral forums to demand that the United States, as well as the international community that sanctioned the U.S. testing program under the auspices of the UN Trusteeship Council, address the persistent radiological problems in the Marshall Islands. For each statement pertaining to the effects of the weapons testing that the Marshall Islands makes at international and bilateral gatherings, RMI government officials can substantiate their claims with reams of documentary evidence. Unfortunately, however, this documentary evidence alone does not compel the United States to change its policies toward the radiation communities. In order to secure assistance for the neglected radiation victims, the RMI government knows it must demonstrate that the persistent, adverse implications of radiation exposure continue today. To compile this evidence, the RMI government initiated a project to collect ethnographic data from the neglected communities spearheaded by the RMI Embassy in Washington, D.C. As an anthropologist employed at the Embassy, I was asked to collect ethnographies from Ailuk Atoll and Likiep Atoll. Although scientists now consider both Ailuk and Likiep safe for human habitation, the RMI government believed ethnographic research would illuminate existing environmental and health implications on those atolls resulting from radiation exposure. Ethnographic data could help the RMI government identify the aspects of the radiation problem that are actionable[22] and to provide sufficient justification for the U.S. Congress to broaden its definition of "exposed" spatially and temporally. The currently limited definition is the major obstacle in securing assistance for the neglected communities because it excludes entire populations, such as all individuals born after 1954. Although the generation born after 1954 was not exposed to external fallout from the tests, it was raised on contaminated atolls and consequently exposed to internal sources of radiation through the food chain.

The neglected communities of Ailuk and Likiep were extremely amenable to the project, since they immediately understood the importance of data ownership. Instead of acting as research subjects for the U.S. government, documentation of their experiences will help their own government—the Republic of the Marshall Islands—request U.S. policy changes aimed at providing tangible assistance to the neglected communities.

Human Environmental Impacts: The People's Point of View

This never happened prior to the nuclear explosions.[23]

As anticipated, there is both observable and ethnographic evidence of acute harm and changes to the environment and health of the populations on Ailuk and Likiep atolls. The people have many stories about the horribly deformed trees, animals, and people in the years following the nuclear testing. Most of these severely deformed plants or people did not survive. But survivors can describe these losses clearly; they remember the animals and children born with two heads or missing limbs. Kajitok and Kiora, an elderly couple from Likiep, distinctly remember one of their children born after the testing period. Kajitok, the husband, recalls:

> After the testing . . . (my wife) got pregnant. When the baby was born, it had two heads. . . . Two heads. Two heads. One was on top of the other. . . . (The bottom head was) ripped open here [touches his forehead to show where the second head emerged from]. . . . It looked like the child's head had dents. The baby lived for a moment. . . . It breathed for just a short time when it was born. Maybe not an hour, only some minutes. It was alive, but it wasn't doing well.[24]

Deformed animals were born as well. Typhoon, a man from Ailuk Atoll, remembers

> sudden changes that we never experienced before the nuclear testings. It happens to trees and even animals and people. . . . A cat for instance. A cat gave birth to a single kitten with what seems like two bodies combined. We might say a "twin" with one body. Eight legs and eight paws.[25]

The trees and food crops on Ailuk and Likiep, like the animals, were affected by radiation. A woman from Likiep named Alian remembers changes in the food crops:

> One thing which stands out in my mind was the quick and total destruction of all the arrowroot plants on the atoll. Since arrowroot is one of our staple foods, we were astonished to find the arrowroot had been destroyed along with such things as breadfruit, coconut trees, and pandanus. We assumed that whatever caused this was poisonous because it was not only our vegetation at ground level that was destroyed, but also those (crops) growing in the soil.[26]

It is not difficult to ascertain from communities such as Ailuk and Likiep, where people depend on their local environment for their subsistence, that radionuclides deposited from testing fallout worked their way into the environment, through the food crops, and eventually into the people themselves. There are observable effects of health problems induced by environmental contamination. Perhaps the most poignant example is Mimi, an 8-year old girl from Ailuk. Mimi is missing half of her left arm. She has no knees, and her stunted legs have only three toes on each foot. Mimi's family made a small crutch for her to drag herself from place to place. Mentally, Mimi is normal, but she is embarrassed to leave her family's compound or attend school. She cowers from nonfamily members on the atoll, who are quick to point out that Mimi "ebaam!," which literally means "She is bombed." Mimi is suffering as a direct result of the U.S. nuclear weapons testing program, yet she is ineligible for assistance. Mimi's grandmother recalls how U.S. officials explained Mimi's deformities to her and the 420 other residents of Ailuk:

> (The U.S. government) told us that approximately 100 newborns will have visible abnormalities on their bodies within the next 30 years. Just this island, 100 newborns. . . . (Mimi is) within the 30 years range predicted by the scientists in 1978 that many babies will be born with abnormalities.

To the casual observer it is obvious that the frequency of disability in Ailuk is not "normal." Yet, compensation for nuclear damage throughout the Marshall Islands is based on the erroneous assumption that Ailuk represents a normal background level of radiation. Because Ailuk was never evacuated after the Bravo travesty, Ailuk was labeled "unexposed" by the U.S. government. Ailuk became representative of a *normal* background level of radiation despite earlier reports confirming radiation doses in excess of 20 roentgens. The U.S. government was able to define "exposed" as simply those four atolls that were evacuated because it had absolute control of the information about the exposure of all atolls. This information was never shared with the RMI government. For Mimi's family on Ailuk, the U.S. manipulation of definitions allowed DOE to justify Mimi's disabilities and deny medical care or assistance to Mimi and other neglected radiation victims.

Gender Dimensions

> Four (of my) children were born prematurely. . . . One of them died after his first birthday. Another one was still-born. . . . I have yet to see any doctors.[27]

Marshallese women have a particular need for medical care to address the severe reproductive problems that are ignored by the U.S. government and that were never fully understood by the RMI government. Medical anthropologist Glenn Alcalay found a direct correlation between the distance between ground zero and where women reside, and their incidence of miscarriages, still-births, and birth anomalies.[28] Data I gathered on Ailuk and Likiep for the RMI government confirms Alcalay's findings. Marshallese women who were exposed to radiation are suffering silently and differently from their male counterparts because of cultural taboos as well as the refusal of the U.S. government to acknowledge the multigenerational implications of radiation. Marshallese women are extremely concerned about their children who were born after the testing:

> You know my children—they say we adults are the only ones who are exposed today— but they are exposed too. If everyone here is exposed, how can they not be? . . . I am one of the poisoned ones. . . . Aren't they contaminated since their mothers and fathers were exposed?[29]

Female radiation victims often do not discuss their birth anomalies with even their husbands, because the missionaries taught the Marshallese that birthing problems are an indication that women are unfaithful to their husbands. There is, however, little doubt that the reproductive problems women are experiencing are connected to their exposure to radiation in their environment. Catherine, for example, moved to Rongelap in 1957 when the U.S. government resettled the Rongelapese who were evacuated after the Bravo incident. Because she did not live on Rongelap in 1954, she was not exposed to Bravo's radioactive fallout. Yet, Catherine lived on Rongelap for several years:

> I returned to Rongelap ... in 1957, and I saw friends and relatives who were afflicted with illnesses unknown to us. Their eyesight deteriorated, their bodies were covered with burn-like blisters, and their hair fell out by the handful. It was around this time that I had my first pregnancy. My baby had a very high fever when he was delivered, and the attending health assistant conveyed his doubts as to whether my son would survive the night. He was so dehydrated from the fever that his skin actually peeled as I clasped him to me to nurse. The only thing we knew to do was to wrap him in wet towels. And so it was that I held him to my body throughout the night, changing the towels and willing him to fight for his life. He lost the fight just as dawn broke.
>
> My second son, born in 1960, was delivered live but missing the whole back of his skull— as if it had been sawed off. So the back part of the brain and the spinal cord were fully exposed. After a week, the spinal cord became detached and he, too, developed a high fever and died the following day. Aside from the cranial deformity, my son was also miss-ing both testicles and a penis. He passed water through a stump-like apparatus measuring less than an inch. The doctors who examined him told me that he would not survive. And sure enough, he was dead within a week. You know, it was heart wrenching having to nurse my son, all the while taking care his brain didn't fall into my lap. For in spite of his severe handicaps, he was healthy in every respect. It was good he died, because I do not think he would have wanted to live a life as something less than a human.
>
> The health assistant who delivered the child sent a message to Kwajalein, and I am cer-tain those [U.S.] doctors came for the express purpose of seeing first-hand a live "nuclear baby." In fact, they flew in the very same day the message was sent. . . . They were very impersonal, almost casual, when telling me that my baby was not unique and that they had seen other babies like mine in other countries. . . . They did a complete physical (of the baby), took blood samples, and lots and lots of photographs.[30]

Dr. Esra Riklon, the Marshallese doctor working with AEC/DOE, verified that he and an American doctor were immediately dispatched to Rongelap to examine the "monster baby."

The vocabulary of Marshallese women also indicates that their birth anom-alies are recent and therefore could not have existed prior to the weapons testing program. When women describe the deformed, unsuccessful pregnancies they ex-perience, they refer to the children as "monsters," "jellyfish," "grapes," "apples," "octopuses," "clams," and other nonhuman words taken from objects of familiarity or from their local environment. If these reproductive problems existed before the nuclear weapons tests, the Marshallese would have more precise names for these conditions. Nonradiation-induced illnesses have their own labels in the Marshallese language, not names based on comparison to other living objects.

Implications

> Exposure will never again be defined in terms of fallout from BRAVO alone, but will now incorporate the cumulative effects of all tests, and the effects of residual contamination in the environment.[31]

In addition to complementing the historical research conducted by the Embassy, the ethnographies served several other important functions. For example, Marshallese at the local and national levels are better informed about the extent of radiation problems in the undocumented communities, and, more specifically, among women. Understanding the nature of the problem is essential if the affected communities or the national government are going to increase their ability to solve their own health care and environmental restoration needs.[32]

The neglected communities are putting pressure on their national government to take action, and the national government is responding. This is a clear indication of how the project is empowering both the local and national governments. The historical and ethnographic data justifies the RMI government's demands for the U.S. government to remedy the human environmental abuses immediately, and the ethnographic data demonstrates that the need for action is immediate. Although the RMI government inherited persistent and acute radiation problems from the United States, it is not realistic to expect the RMI to finance mitigation measures.

Because the U.S. government is failing to assume its full responsibility for the lingering radiation problems at the bilateral level, the RMI government is seeking assistance from the international community. The RMI is speaking out about its new information at numerous multilateral forums, such as the UN General Assembly and the UN Conference on Women in Beijing (September 4–15, 1995). The RMI delegation successfully convinced the international community to refer to the continued need for environmental restoration and health care for the radiation communities in the former UN Trust Territory in the report accompanying the extension of the Nuclear Non-Proliferation Treaty and the Platform for Action from the Women's Conference. The RMI government also appeared before the International Court of Justice on November 14, 1995, to explain to the Court why nuclear weapons are a crime against humanity that deny basic human rights to a safe and clean environment.

The RMI government is actively pursuing bilateral remedies for its radiation problems. On January 15, 1994, in the midst of the RMI government's document review, the Clinton Administration formally acknowledged that the U.S. government supported radiation experiments on human beings during the Cold War. Then it established an Advisory Committee on Human Radiation Experiments to investigate the extent of U.S. involvement in human experiments and to make recommendations to the White House about how to respond to biomedical violations. On four separate occasions the RMI government presented its research to this committee and, as a direct result of this lobbying effort, the Advisory Committee acknowledged in its final report that more than four communities in the RMI were exposed to radiation and that it was not merely the Bravo shot that contaminated the environment and exposed the people.[33] These conclusions from an independent, nonbiased committee are crucial, because the Marshallese lack the political and economic clout to have their viewpoints seriously considered by the U.S. government. The Marshallese are not considered U.S. constituents, and it is difficult for the RMI to secure funds from U.S. government policy makers who do not want to appropriate funds or change policies if it is avoidable.[34]

After reviewing the case of the Marshall Islands, the Advisory Committee concluded that significant efforts need to be made to address the shortcomings of the U.S. government's care for the exposed population. Specifically, it recommended that the U.S. government:

1. Review the present U.S. medical monitoring program "to determine if it is appropriate to add to the program the populations of other atolls to the south and east of the blast whose inhabitants may have received exposures sufficient to cause excess thyroid abnormalities;"

2. Involve Marshallese "in the design of any further medical research to be conducted upon them;"

3. Establish a panel to "review the status and adequacy of the current program of medical monitoring and medical care provided by the United States to the exposed population of the Marshall Islands."[35]

While these recommendations represent an important step forward in forcing the U.S. government to acknowledge that it failed to care for all exposed populations in the Marshall Islands, extensive lobbying and political pressure are still necessary to secure policy changes that will provide tangible assistance to all radiation victims. Although the committee failed to address the comprehensive needs of the radiation victims, the RMI government endorses these recommendations and is working with the Congress and agencies in the U.S. government to implement them.

Changes in U.S. public policy must occur to make the neglected communities eligible to participate in U.S. health care and environmental monitoring programs. An adequate response to the persistent radiation problems in the Marshall Islands requires:

1. A new definition of "exposed" that is not restricted temporally or geographically;

2. Medical care for *all* victims of external and internal radiation exposure;

3. Environmental restoration of all contaminated islands to a level that is safe for human habitation in the United States;

4. Safe storage of all radioactive materials;

5. Increased capacity for the Marshallese to determine what does and doesn't constitute a radiation threat. This includes the training of Marshallese doctors, scientists, and radiation technicians and proper diagnostic facilities for professionals;

6. A nationwide epidemiological study that will identify all types of illnesses associated with radiation, such as women's reproductive health problems;

7. An independent review of all past and present U.S. medical and environmental programs resulting from the nuclear weapons testing;

8. Increased transparency and communication of results to the Marshallese recipients of U.S. programs.

Conclusion

The Marshall Islands case is a grave example of the way in which U.S. colonialist policy and national security interests culminated in basic human environmental rights violations. The U.S. exploited the Trusteeship arrangement in order to establish the world's most superior nuclear arsenal. The U.S. government established a massive weapons testing program thousands of miles from the continental United States, preserving a high quality of life for some American citizens and showing a complete disregard for other Americans (the Marshallese were ostensibly U.S. citizens under the Trusteeship). The Marshallese were of secondary importance to U.S. national security interests. The illness and death of marginalized people and the environmental contamination of their land were justifiable in order to better understand the destructive capacity of nuclear weapons.

It is painful to come to terms with the U.S. government's view of the Marshallese during the Cold War and to ponder what these attitudes reflect about the values of American society. The Marshallese were powerless victims subject to the whims of a superpower that controlled what information the people had access to, when citizens could petition the United Nations, what populations of people would receive (or be denied) compensation or care, and what the international community and American citizens knew about the events that took place in the Marshall Islands. Now that the truth is out, American and Marshallese leaders are compelled to act. The U.S. government has incredible resources that can be used to address many of these problems. As a sovereign nation, the Republic of the Marshall Islands will no longer tolerate the subordination it endured for decades. RMI government-initiated research into past events legitimizes its request for remedies from the United States and the international community, requests that require the parties to come to terms with the hegemonies allowing these injustices to occur. The simple act of asking questions, listening, and recording the experiences of its citizens has been an empowering experience, both for the island residents and the government that serves them. Compiling a comprehensive understanding of historical events and their current consequences validates and acknowledges the painful past, as well as provides the tools to fight for a better future.

SECTION II: View from the 21st Century

Political history involves, at very fundamental levels, personal histories. Comments by John Anjain, Jr., the son and namesake of the former mayor of Rongelap illustrate this fact:

> My family suffered the consequences deeply from the nuclear testing program. No one family should lose this many loved ones in their lifetime. They have sacrificed, given so much, and paid the price with their lives for a peaceful world, a world they didn't even know and owed nothing to. My father, John Anjain [Sr.] died from stomach cancer, my brother Lekoj died from leukemia, my mother had thyroid cancer and died from yet another form of cancer. Two other brothers, George and Zach, died from other complications linked to radiation. My youngest brother, Fred, born on Rongelap, was diagnosed with polio. All these illnesses and deaths I strongly believe resulted from the nuclear testing program.

> Knowing how dangerous it would be, and as a father, it would be very irresponsible of me even to think about sending any members of my family back to Rongelap to live in a poisonous environment, or any other family for that matter. Don't get me wrong, we know these remaining families will do anything to find a way to go home. It is their home, that's where they belong, and that's the bottom line.

> Destruction was forced upon us, our land, and our way of life. I can take this one step further and say our LIVES were taken away from us. The impacted people have been in bondage for many years, let them go home to get their life back. This is the very reason why we must continue to fight and push hard for the C(hanged) C(ircumstances) P(etition) to get done.

> The Changed Circumstances Petition needs to get done because our impacted people are still suffering severe adverse health effect directly related to the United States' nuclear testing program. Our lands are still off-limits because of radiation poisoning. If the Petition is approved, we will be able to continue to do cleaning up on contaminated portion of

these lands, and return the people to their homes where they belong. They have sacrificed so much and have been away from home for too long.

I join forces with my late father, late brothers, uncles, all the brave men and women who came before us to fight for the cause. We celebrate their resiliency and their courage. I feel the CCP must be re-told over and over again, we much re-educate our new counterparts in this new administration, along with the new Congress. Our objective must be firm and steady as we tell our story. We must make it clear WHY and the REASON this government must respond positively to the CCP. Compassionately, we must tell the story of our once-called-Island-PARADISE, now contaminated and barren, resulting from the U.S. nuclear testing program. The impacted generation is desperately in need of proper medical care today, not tomorrow. I feel very strongly that if the CCP goes through and is approved by this Government, it will give us hope for the future. It will surely secure and protect the future well being of our children and their children. To me, failure is not an option when it comes to the well being of our people. If we fail, we would have failed the legacy of all the hard working people who came before us, and those who are no longer with us today. By the grace of God, we must not let it happen. —John Anjain, Jr., March 29, 2009[36]

In the 21st century our generation may not feel responsible for the decisions made by leaders during the Cold War of the 20th. But we do have an obligation to stop the structural violence against contemporary Marshallese, a violence that continues to destroy the lives of families like John Anjain Jr.'s.

In this update for a new millennium I review Marshallese struggles to secure from the United States assistance in fully addressing the ulcerating conditions resulting from the nuclear weapons testing program. Although the Marshallese no longer endure nuclear detonations, they suffer from the structural violence of an impoverished nation unable to care for the radiogenic diseases of its population. Cancer in the Marshall Islands is essentially a death sentence. The failure of the United States to provide adequate healthcare means that the violence against the Marshallese continues. Structural violence is also mobile, following Marshallese immigrants to the United States: because they are not U.S. citizens, they frequently cannot access the healthcare they need.

Compensation through the Nuclear Claims Tribunal

In the past decade the Marshallese continued their attempts to address the U.S. legacy of nuclear militarism. One major effort involves the assessment of health and efforts to secure compensation and medical assistance through the Nuclear Claims Tribunal (NCT). Established in 1986 as a result of the Compact of Free Association the NCT is the result of a Reagan-era agreement between the United States and the Marshall Islands. In this Agreement, the Government of the United States accepted responsibility for compensating citizens of the Marshall Islands for loss or damage to property and person resulting from the nuclear testing conducted in the northern islands (June 30, 1946–August 18, 1958). A separate agreement established a $150 million trust fund that was expected to cover all property and personal injury claims. The NCT was set up as an administrative court to adjudicate claims and make awards from this trust fund outside the United States.

The documents declassified in 1993, discussed in Section I of this chapter, suggest that Marshall Islanders can expect thyroid cancers and other radiogenic diseases on a nationwide scale, not just in the four atolls immediately downwind from ground zero. The NCT Public Advocate worked to help develop personal injury claims as well as advocate for compensation and health care for a broader array of radiogenic disease. By 2008 the NCT had recognized some 37 radiogenic cancers and other diseases resulting from exposure to nuclear weapons testing and fallout still persistent in the environment. In their 2008 report, the Tribunal reported partial payment on personal injury awards to 2,127 individuals totaling $96,658,250, with $23,131,552 still owed. Half of Marshallese claimants who demonstrate to the judges that they contracted radiogenic illnesses after exposure to radiation have already died without receiving full compensation.

Declassified documents also supported efforts to fully identify property damage and determine appropriate remedy. With real estate appraisals and scientific expert reports on historic and current radiological contamination and remediation alternatives, the Tribunal issued judgments in claims from four atolls, Bikini, Enewetak, Rongelap and Utrik. The total amount awarded for loss of use, cleanup, and consequential damages is more than 2.25 billion ($2,284,100,000). Partial payments of $1.6 million for Enewetak and $2.3 million for Bikini were awarded in 2002 and 2003. The Tribunal ran out of funds before it was able to consider and issue a ruling on claims from other atolls. Additional funding from the U.S Congress is needed before the Tribunal can pay these claims and is critical for reducing soil contamination, improving healthcare, and helping communities to improve their well-being in the post-testing era.[37]

Deteriorating Health and Healthcare

The RMI government launched a second major bilateral effort to get the United States to fund the Tribunal fully and to address the full scope of damages and injuries resulting from the testing program. Under the terms of the original Compact, the RMI Government has the right to petition the U.S. Congress for assistance if it can demonstrate that new and additional information exists—information it did not know when it negotiated the first settlement and that renders existing funding manifestly inadequate. The RMI Government submitted a Changed Circumstances Petition on September 11, 2000, a key initiative of President Imata Kabua's administration (1997–2000). This petition required drafting the language and rationale for additional assistance, generating the political will within Congress to consider the petition, and participating in Congressional hearings. Much of this work occurred through the RMI Embassy in Washington, D.C., where Ambassador Banny de Brum chaired regular meetings with elected leaders from affected atoll communities, elders, the Nuclear Claims Tribunal, lawyers, a physician, a health scientist, an anthropologist and RMI government representatives. These participants articulated the ongoing needs related to the testing program.[38] The petition asked Congress to authorize and appropriate additional funds to cover unpaid personal injury compensation; unpaid property claims; improve medical infrastructure to provide necessary primary and secondary medical care to "exposed" populations; improve a Section 177 Health Care Program; and extend monitoring programs for exposed populations to any group that can demonstrate high levels of radiation exposure.

Congress took no action in 2000. It did not act in 2001. Finally, in 2003 U.S. Attorney General Richard Thornburgh conducted an independent review of the Nuclear Claims Tribunal performance and legal validity of its awards. The Thornburgh Report found that NCT proceedings adhered to procedures consistent with U.S. judicial practices and standards and that the compensation provided to date for personal injury and property damage was "manifestly inadequate," especially when compared to federal compensation for U.S. citizens affected by mainland tests that resulted in lower levels of exposure to people and less contamination to once-inhabited lands.[39]

As the United States became consumed in the events of September 11, 2001 and the invasion of Iraq in 2003, the CCP remained in the distant background. In 2004, in an effort to bring new attention to the petition, the RMI Government resubmitted it along with the Thornburgh Report. This move succeeded in prompting the first formal response from the U.S. government. The Bush Administration issued a report to Congress rejecting the merits of the petition, arguing that the new information from declassified documents and scientific research was not relevant and claiming that all obligations of the United States have been met in full. Congressional hearings were held in 2004 and again in 2005.

Changes in Governance

All around the world, the political fortunes of the powerful rise and fall with the ability of governments to provide for the basic needs of its citizens. Since the first edition of this book, the entire political landscape of the United States and Marshall Islands has changed not once, but four times. The Bush and Clinton administrations came and went, as did Marshallese presidents Kessai Note and Litokwa Tomeing. Each time there is an election—even an off-year election—politicians become too busy running campaigns to devote time and energy to complicated issues. When new administrations and congressional representatives are sworn into office, there is a long period of inactivity as department heads are appointed and new staffers actually assume responsibility for specific issues. And these newcomers are anxious to demonstrate their relevance to pressing current issues. In this context historical issues, such as addressing the long legacy of U.S. nuclear weapons testing, are difficult to keep at the top of the political priority list. The turnover in government staffers with every new administration translates into a profound loss for the Marshallese who spend years cultivating relationships and educating people to the point where they can effectively understand and critique existing programs and policies.

The Marshallese also have had to wait patiently while U.S. leaders respond to immediate priorities, such as Hurricane Katrina or the economic crisis. But these events, while important, do not negate the validity of historical obligations. For the nearly two decades that I worked as a staff advisor at the RMI Embassy, U.S. government officials and congress people offered a litany of excuses for their lack of political or economic will to provide meaningful assistance to the Marshallese. In this context, and with scant financial resources, it is difficult to imagine that the RMI will ever convince Congress to address the true consequences of Cold War nuclear militarism.

Redefining Bilateral Relationships in a Time of Resurgent Militarism

Just as the Changed Circumstances Petition was the central initiative of the Imata Presidency, the administration of Kessai H. Note, which began in 2000, had one goal that superseded all others—to renegotiate and extend the initial bilateral Compact of Free Association that was set to expire in 2003. Under this agreement, the United States provides economic and financial aid to RMI and defends its territorial integrity; in return, the RMI provides the United States with unlimited and exclusive access to its land and waterways for strategic purposes. Because of its dependent position, the RMI had no leverage in the negotiations, and the United States rejected requests by the Kabua and Note administrations to include nuclear issues in these negotiations. President Bush signed the amended Compact, known as P.L. 108-188, after three years of negotiation and Congressional scrutiny. The new agreement includes, until at least 2066, the Military Use and Operating Rights Agreement for defense sites on Kwajalein Atoll that are central to U.S. missile defense and space operations programs. The United States retains the responsibility to defend the RMI as it would U.S. territory—a commitment the United States makes to no other foreign country outside the Freely Associated States. Although the final agreement does not address needs stemming from the nuclear testing program, the RMI believes it secured the best deal it could, given the political and economic realities of post–9/11 militarism. Other new provisions include: focused economic grant assistance for the next 20 years; a trust fund that is expected to supplant U.S grant assistance in FY 2023; continued access to important federal programs such as the National Weather Service, Pell Grants and, with certain qualifications, FEMA; a discretionary Supplemental Education Grant in lieu of other education-related federal programs; the establishment of a Joint Economic Management and Financial Accountability Committee to ensure accountability and effective management of Compact grant assistance; improved "homeland security" for the United States and, at the same time, continued visa-free access for RMI citizens entering the United States; and a requirement that the U.S. presidential administration review and report to the Congress at five-year intervals on progress made under the Compact.

The ways in which the militarized political climate that erupted after September 11, 2001, affected efforts of the RMI government and other human rights initiatives. Members of Congress, their staff, and lobbyists hired by the RMI government all indicated that it was essential for the RMI government to publicly support U.S. militarism if the RMI wanted the United States to consider its petition. Indeed, the RMI issued public statements in support of U.S. actions and continued to align itself with the United States at the United Nations (where the RMI votes with the United States more than does any other nation).[40] Popular support of US foreign policy is also widespread in the Marshall Islands, as is support of the military's continued use of RMI land, sea and airspace, and Marshallese citizens increasingly volunteer in the U.S. armed forces.

In many ways the RMI was paralyzed between the contradictory needs of demonstrating continuing injuries and unmet obligations associated with Cold War militarism, on the one hand, and demonstrating RMI support for an expansive new phase of US militarism—the war on terror—on the other. The RMI suspended work on the Changed Circumstances Petition in order to pass a nonbinding House Concurrent Resolution 410. Adopted by both houses of Congress in 2004 this resolution was crafted to remind lawmakers of the RMI's role in helping the United States achieve its military objectives and states that the United States has no closer ally in the world than the RMI.[41] This nonbinding resolution required an incredible investment in time and massaging of political contacts on Capitol Hill. But Republican advisors to the Embassy staff argued that that the resolution would help educate Congress about the historical strategic partnership and, thus, build support for the RMI's Changed Circumstances Petition.

In 2005 the U.S. House and Senate held hearings on the petition. The state of the health care delivery system in the RMI and the many unmet needs of the Marshallese is characterized in the testimony of Dr. Neal Palafox to the joint hearing of the

House Committee on Natural Resources and the Subcommittee on Asia and Pacific of the House International Relations Committee:

> There is no mammography unit to detect breast cancer or colonoscopy to detect colon cancer in Ebeye [one of two urban centers], no operational CT scanner in the RMI, and no operational dermatome in the lab to process cancer specimens. When there is no medical oxygen in the hospital due to medical equipment problems, major surgery, which many cancer patients require, is not an option. . . . Comprehensive cancer care requires local health systems to address prevention, screening, biopsies, pathology services, surgical expertise, intensive unit care, chemotherapy expertise, scanners, lab support, palliative care, and issues of survivorship and quality of life. None of these systems are fully operational, and some are non-existent. In 2003 only 9% of women who were in the age category to receive cervical PAP smears (to screen for cervical cancer) actually received a PAP smear. There is neither an oncologist nor a cancer registry in the RMI.[42]

Andre Bouville of the National Cancer Institute (NCI), in his testimony, reported the findings of a study conducted to discern how much cancer in the RMI would normally occur in the population, as it would anywhere else in the world, and how many cancers are the result of the testing program:

> About 5,600 baseline cancer cases [those expected to occur in the absence of exposure to fallout] may develop within the lifetime of the cohort alive during the test years 1946–1957, with an estimated population size of 13,940. About half of those baseline cases, approximately 2,800, have already occurred.

> In addition, about 500 cancers may develop as a result of exposure to fallout radiation. Hence, exposure to fallout could result in about a 9% increase—to about 6,100—in the total number of fatal and nonfatal cancers expected.

> We estimate that the thyroid gland was the most heavily exposed organ because it is the target organ for radioactive iodine, a major component of fallout. Of the estimated additional 500 fallout-related cancers, approximately 260 cases are expected to be thyroid cancer. We expect that about 400 out of the estimated additional 500 radiation-related cancer cases will occur in the 35% of the population who were under 10 years old when exposed to fallout. Since members of this age group are now 3 between ages 50–60, almost all of those cancers are likely to have occurred by the end of the next few decades. Higher excess cancer rates are expected in the populations exposed to the highest doses that lived in the northern atolls.[43]

This was significant testimony. One of the reasons that Congressional staffers balked at the RMI's earlier petitions, especially the request to provide cancer care in the RMI, is that the United States did not want to pay for cancer care for people who contract the disease for reasons other than exposure to radiation. Thus, the Senate directed the NCI to assess the data and advise. Not only does the NCI study predict that an additional 500 people will develop radiogenic cancers in years to come, but the total number of people who developed cancers from their radiation-exposure far exceeds the number of people whom the United States recognizes as affected and thus eligible for healthcare assistance.

Other testimony at the May 25, 2005, hearing acknowledged that the cost of addressing Marshallese radiological damages and injuries is expensive but not without precedent, as they are based on the level of care, protection and compensation that U.S. citizens receive under similar circumstances. Downwinders and DOE workers exposed to radiation in the United States receive a much higher standard of healthcare for their radiation exposure than do the Marshallese. Clean-up activities at Hanford, Washington, provide a similar comparison for restoration of contaminated lands in the United States and the RMI. Some 8,500 times more radioactive iodine was released in the RMI than at Hanford. In response to the environmental contamination caused by Hanford, the U.S. government appropriates $2 billion and employs approximately 11,000 workers annually to assist with the cleanup. From the FY05 budget the Department of Energy is estimating a total life-cycle cost of $56 billion and a completion date in 2035. In contrast, the Nuclear Claims Tribunal estimated the cost to repair the much more significant damage and contamination of Enewetak and Bikini atolls to be $1.1 billion ($454 million and $629 million, respectively) or just over 50% of an annual clean-up appropriation to Hanford. And then there is the inequity in applying cleanup standards. The RMI government believes that Marshallese citizens have a right to the same cleanup standard as the United States maintains for its own citizens. The goal for cleanup at Hanford is 15 mrem, yet the U.S. government maintains that the RMI should settle for the less rigorous international or outdated standard sometimes as high as 150 mrem, despite the fact that Marshallese citizens were wards of the U.S. government when their exposure to radiation occurred.

In addition to a call for parity Marshallese testimony argued for Congressional attention to the unique human costs endured by their citizens, emphasizing the point that the U.S. government conducted its nuclear weapons testing program in the Marshall Islands because it recognized the hazards of these activities for its own citizens and ecosystems. Such an abusive history not only presents a special obligation for the United States that it has long ignored, it also creates uniquely difficult realities for families, communities, and the Marshallese nation:

> we are sitting here talking about numbers, policies, and science, yet for all of us in the Marshall Islands, the U.S. Nuclear Weapons Testing Program is a profoundly human experience—we experience the broad-reaching effects of the testing program on the most intimate and personal levels: from our home islands that we can no longer inhabit, to the sickness and death of our friends and family. Again, to put this into human terms, the National Cancer Institute estimates hundreds of cancers related to the U.S. Nuclear Weapons Testing Program have yet to appear. This means that hundreds more of the people who we talk to, sleep next to, eat with, love, and work with will endure tremendous physical hardships and possible death. We can do our best to prepare our health system to deal with this burden, but we can never remedy the human and emotional toll that this takes on us as individuals, families, communities and a nation.[44]

Minister Zackios's testimony on the ways that the testing program profoundly altered human relationships in the RMI offered compelling yet all-too-brief attention to the day-to-day human sufferings that rarely factor into U.S. policy making. With just five minutes of public testimony time per speaker, there is no chance the Minister or any other representative from the RMI could adequately convey to Congress the complexity of these issues.

Two months later the Minister and other Marshallese tried again, this time with the July 2005 Senate Committee on Energy and Natural Resources hearing on the RMI's Changed Circumstances Petition. Perhaps the most stunning contribution to the House hearing came from the Chairman of the House Subcommittee on Asia and the Pacific of the House International Relations Committee, who asked his Senate colleagues for permission to address the Committee. In his remarks Congressman

Eni Faleomaveaga from American Samoa unleashed his anger over the inequitable treatment of Marshallese radiation survivors and showed pictures of a deformed Marshallese baby. Chairman Faleomaveaga told his Senate colleagues that it is unethical to provide the Marshallese any services below the standard that the U.S. Government provides to its own citizens exposed to radiation either through military service or living downwind from U.S. testing locations:

> the State Department fails to explain how the declassified documents, released a decade after the agreement was reached, indicating a wider extent of radioactive fallout than previously disclosed, or a National Cancer Institute study indicating that more cancers will surface, do not constitute a legal basis for Congress to consider their circumstances.
>
> Mr. Chairman, I submit this is much larger than a legal issue—this is a moral issue. The fact is, the people of the Marshall Islands are still suffering severe, adverse health effects directly related to our nuclear testing program and they are still unable to use their own lands because of the radiation poisoning. We have a moral obligation to provide for health care, environmental monitoring, personal injury claims, and land and property damage in the Marshall Islands. This is the least we can do, considering the historic contribution the people of the Marshall Islands have made in the Cold War struggle to preserve international peace and promote nuclear disarmament.
>
> The people of the Marshall Islands have brought their ongoing health, environmental, and loss of land issues to Congress for our consideration. While we may find that we cannot provide the amount of money requested, . . . I believe we do have an obligation to examine carefully the application they have submitted, to ensure that we live up to the responsibility we embraced over 50 years ago when we began nuclear testing in the Pacific. We should not be looking for ways to sidestep this responsibility. We should ask ourselves if we have done everything we can possibly do to make things right for the people of the Marshall Islands who have sacrificed their lives, their health and their lands for the benefit of the United States.
>
> I have reviewed the petition. I have researched this issue extensively, and I believe enough evidence exists to justify a thorough review of the changed circumstances in the petition.[45]

These hearings demonstrated that although the RMI achieves small political successes from time-to-time, such as the extension of food programs, bilateral efforts to improve the healthcare system have failed.

After these Congressional hearings the Senate Committee on Natural Resources drafted S. 1756, a bill to "provide supplemental ex gratia payments to the Marshall Islands for the impacts of the nuclear testing program (S. 1756)." This bill instructs the Secretary of the Department of Energy to monitor the nuclear waste storage facility on Runit Island and the surrounding groundwater; requires the Secretary of Energy to report to the Senate and House committees with jurisdiction over the Marshall Islands and the nuclear testing program about its monitoring activities; clarifies the eligibility of Marshallese citizens employed by DOE to assist with the clean-up of Enewetak and Bikini atolls to participate in a U.S. Department of Labor (DOL) compensation and healthcare program for DOE workers exposed to radiation; and instructs the Department of Interior to provide $4.5 million annually, with inflation adjustments to:

> provide enhanced primary health care, with an emphasis on providing regular screenings for radiogenic illnesses by upgrading existing services or by providing quarterly medical field team visits, as appropriate, in each of Enewetak, Bikini, Rongelap, Utrik, Ailuk, Mejit, Likiep, Wotho, Wotje, and Ujelang Atolls, . . . [and] to enhance the capabilities of the Marshall Islands to provide secondary treatment for radiogenic illness.[46]

This provision in S. 1756 represents a major departure from previous U.S. policy because, for the first time in more than 50 years, the U.S. Congress acknowledges that communities beyond Bikini, Enewetak, Rongelap, and Utrik were adversely affected by the U.S. nuclear weapons testing program. The tradeoff in for this admission? The U.S. insisted that the RMI Government accept vastly lower levels of financial assistance than requested in the Changed Circumstances Petition.

In 2008 the Marshallese voted no confidence in Kessai Note and President Litokwa Tomeing came to power. With this development Ambassador de Brum and his staff, me included, were relieved of duty. President Litokwa Tomeing's administration took seven months to express its support for S. 1756 to Senator Jeff Bingaman, Chairman of the Senate Energy and Natural Resources Committee. The major concern with S. 1756 was one sentence: "This legislation constitutes the Committee's response to the RMI's 'Changed Circumstances' petition and any claim for further compensation is an issue that is now up to the courts to resolve."[47] In other words, S. 1756 would extinguish Congressional responsibility for nuclear damages and additional assistance, limiting future petitions to the courts. The Tomeing administration was faced with the unenviable choice of accepting more assistance—knowing that it was far too little to address the RMI's expensive, complex, and multigenerational problems—or rejecting S. 1756. The delay did not stop action on the bill, and the Senate Energy Committee unanimously voted S. 1756 out of committee on September 11, 2008, exactly eight years to the day after the RMI first submitted the petition.

President Tomeing's presidency ended in a vote of no confidence in April 2009. The new president, Jurelang Zedkaia, reappointed Banny de Brum as the RMI Ambassador to the United States. Senate Bill 1756 still sits with the Senate Energy and Natural Resources Committee, and many argue that the U.S. obligation to the Marshallese has been met. The political struggle continues.

Conclusion

Given the institutional failures to address the human consequence of hosting nuclear militarism, it is not surprising that Marshallese are increasingly leaving their home islands to seek healthcare in Hawai'i and the continental United States. Census data from Micronesians living in Hawai'i in 1997 and 2003 reveal a 20% increase in the Marshallese population during that six-year period. By 2008 some 15,000 Marshallese, or a quarter of the total population, immigrated to the United States, many to Hawai'i.[48]

Washington State is now home to approximately 1,000 Marshallese residents. Interviews with the Marshallese community in Seattle indicate that access to Seattle's healthcare services for indigent populations, including cancer care, is a major factor in their move to this area. Many moved from Hawai'i, where the escalating costs of providing public health care for Pacific Islanders, and especially the high-cost health services required by the Marshallese, are creating an increasingly tense and stigmatized social environment. Marshallese citizens, as former U.S. Territorial citizens, are able to enter the country without visas. Given the relative ease of migration, poor health care at home, and current meltdowns of both the global economy and the Arctic ice shield, additional increases in immigration rates are likely.

Nuclear issues in the Marshall Islands are not confined by time or place. Similarly, the nuclear legacy spans political parties and administrations in both the United States and the Marshall Islands. Generations of politicians before us have taken a piecemeal approach to addressing smaller parts of the large, complex issues that emerged from the weapons tests and their aftermath. But the sum total of our collective efforts is inadequate. The violence of the weapons tests continues each day that a Marshallese man, woman, or child cannot get adequate healthcare for conditions that result from their exposure to radiation or their inability to live on their home islands and cultivate radiation-free resources for survival from their environment.

The United States owes the people of the Marshall Islands equity in healthcare, clean-up standards, and compensation. In failing to provide equity it sends the signal that a Marshallese life and Marshallese land do not have the same value as those of U.S. citizens. If the United States truly values the historical allegiance of the Marshall Islands, as enshrined in House Concurrent Resolution 440, or intends to take responsibility for the damages and injuries resulting from U.S. activities, then its response must be equitable and immediate. Marshallese do not have the luxury of time—the seas are rising, and the Marshallese are once again being forced to relocate because of U.S. activities. It is time for the U.S. to make the Marshallese our political and financial priority.

Notes

1. G. Kaleman, Sept. 2, 1994. Interview conducted by Holly M. Barker, Newton Lajuan, Trans. Majuro Atoll, Republic of the Marshall Islands.

2. A. Tempo, Sept. 8, 1994. Interview conducted by Holly M. Barker, Newton Lajuan, Trans. Ailuk Atoll, Marshall Islands.

3. J. John, Sept. 5, 1994. Interview conducted by Holly M. Barker, Newton Lajuan, Trans. Ailuk Atoll, Marshall Islands.

4. A. Bobo, Aug. 27, 1994. Interview conducted by Holly M. Barker, Newton Lajuan, Trans. Kwajalein Atoll, Marshall Islands.

5. In Dec. 1995 the Peace Corps informed the government of the Republic of the Marshall Islands that it is suspending the Peace Corps program in the Marshall Islands indefinitely, owing to budget constraints.

6. Barbara Johnston, *Who Pays the Price?: The Sociocultural Context of Crisis* (Washington, D.C.: Island Press, 1994).

7. Atomic Energy Commission, Nov. 11, 1954. Memo from Brigadier General Alfred D. Starbird to Major General A. R. Luedecke, Chief of the Armed Forces Special Weapons Project.

8. Johnston, note 6, p. 10.

9. Dr. John C. Bugher, May 11, 1954, Report of meeting with Ambassador Lodge, UN, May 10, 1954.

10. Joint Task Force Seven, *Operation Castle: Radiological Safety, Final Report,* Vol. 1 (Washington, D.C.: Spring 1954, F-11).

11. P. W. Clarkson, Dec. 21, 1953. Letter to Dr. Alvin C. Graves regarding the Pate-Palmer Weather Report.

12. Bobo, note 4.

13. Joint Task Force Seven, note 10, p. K-8.

14. Ibid., p. D-11.

15. A. Koju, Sept. 2, 1994. Interview conducted by Holly M. Barker, Newton Lajuan, Trans. Ailuk Atoll, Marshall Islands.

16. Joint Task Force Seven, note 10, p. K-64.

17. E. Riklon, Aug. 18, 1994. Interview conducted and translated by Holly M. Barker, Majuro Atoll, Marshall Islands.

18. Dept. of Energy, Dec. 16, 1982. Internal memorandum concerning presentation of DOE survey results from the northern Marshall Islands to the government of the Republic of the Marshall Islands.

19. See International Physicians for the Prevention of Nuclear War, *Radioactive Heaven and Earth: The Health and Environmental Effects of Nuclear Weapons Testing in, on, and above the Earth* (New York: Apex Press, 1991, 80).

20. H. Balos, Feb. 15, 1995. Statement to the White House Advisory Committee on Human Radiation Experiments on behalf of the Bikini Local Government, Washington, D.C.

21. T. Rellong, interview.

22. W. Leap, "Tribally Controlled Culture Change: The Northern Ute Language Renewal Project," in *Anthropological Praxis: Translating Knowledge into Action,* Robert M. Wulff and Shirley J. Fiske, Eds. (Boulder, CO: Westview Press, 1987).

23. D. Jilo, Sept. 2, 1994. Interview conducted by Holly M. Barker, Newton Lajuan, Trans. Ailuk Atoll, Marshall Islands.

24. K. Lokeijak, Aug. 14, 1994. Interview conducted and translated by Holly M. Barker, Likiep Atoll, Marshall Islands.

25. Rellong, note 21.

26. A. Alik, Aug. 14, 1995. Interview conducted by Holly M. Barker, Newton Lajuan, Trans. Likiep Atoll, Marshall Islands.

27. R. River, Sept. 8, 1994. Interview conducted by Holly M. Barker, Newton Lajuan, Trans. Ailuk Atoll, Marshall Islands.

28. G. Alcalay, March 15, 1995. Statement to the White House Advisory Committee on Human Radiation Experiments, Washington, D.C.

29. E. Boaz, Aug. 26, 1994. Interview conducted by Holly M. Barker, Holly M. Barker and Elizabeth Cruz, Trans. Kwajalein Atoll, Marshall Islands.

30. C. Jibas, Aug. 23, 1994. Interview conducted by Holly M. Barker, Newton Lajuan, Trans. Majuro Atoll, Marshall Islands.

31. B. de Brum, "Reaction of the Government of the Republic of the Marshall Islands to the Final Report of the White House Advisory Committee on Human Radiation Experiments" (Washington, D.C., Oct. 3, 1995).

32. E. C. Green, "The Integration of Modern and Traditional Health Sectors in Swaziland," *Anthropological Praxis: Translating Knowledge into Action,* Robert M. Wulff and Shirley J. Fiske, Eds. (Boulder, CO: Westview Press, 1987).

33. Advisory Committee on Human Radiation Experiments, *Final Report* (Washington, D.C.: Government Printing Office, Oct. 1995).

34. L. Gill, "Examining Power, Serving the State: Anthropology, Congress and the Invasion of Panama," *Human Organizations* 54:3 (Fall 1995).

35. Advisory Committee, note 33.

36. J. Anjain, Jr., March 29, 2009. Email conversation with the author.

37. See B. R. Johnston and Holly M. Barker, *Consequential Damages of Nuclear War: The Rongelap Report* (Walnut Creek, CA: Left Coast Press, 2008).

38. H. M. Barker, *Bravo for the Marshallese: Regaining Control in a Post-Nuclear, Post-Colonial World* (Belmont, CA: Wadsworth, 2003).

39. D. Thornburgh, G. Reichardt, and J. Stanley, *The Nuclear Claims Tribunal of the Republic of the Marshall Islands: An Independent Examination and Assessment of its*

Decision-Making Processes (Washington, D.C.: Kirkpatrick & Lockhart LLP, January 2003).

40. See, for example, Office of the President, press release regarding President Note's acceptance of the credentials of Clyde Bishop as the new U.S. Ambassador to the RMI. Majuro, 2006.

41. United States House of Representatives. H. Con. Res. 440, April 30, 2004, recognizing the 25th anniversary of the adoption of the Constitution of the Republic of the Marshall Islands and recognizing the Marshall Islands as a staunch ally of the United States, committed to principles of democracy and freedom for the Pacific region and throughout the world: Washington, D.C.

42. N. Palafox, testimony by the physician contracted by the Department of Energy to operate the healthcare program for "exposed" Marshallese to the Senate Energy and Natural Resources Committee regarding the RMI's Changed Circumstances Petition, July 19, 2005.

43. A. Bouville, National Cancer Institute testimony to the Joint Hearing of the House Resources Committee and the House Subcommittee on Asia and the Pacific of the House International Relations Committee, May 25, 2005.

44. G. Zackios, testimony by the RMI Minister of Foreign Affairs to the Joint Hearing of the House Resources Committee and the House Subcommittee on Asia and the Pacific of the House International Relations Committee, May 25, 2005.

45. E. Faleomavaega, testimony by the Chairman of the House Subcommittee on Asia and the Pacific of the House International Relations Committee to the Senate Energy and Natural Resources Committee regarding the RMI's Changed Circumstances Petition, July 19, 2007.

46. United States Senate. S. 1756, "Republic of the Marshall Islands Supplemental Nuclear Compensation Act of 2007," Senate Energy and Natural Resources Committee: Washington, D.C.

47. A. Stayman, personal email regarding Report Language to accompany S. 1756 (2008).

48. B. Graham, "Determinants and Dynamics of Micronesian Emigration," a resource document for participants in the "Micronesian Voices in Hawaii" conference (April 3–4, 2008), Honolulu.

CHAPTER 16

Complex Problems and No Clear Solutions: Radiation Victimization in Russia

Paula Garb

SECTION I: The End of the Millennium

The development of nuclear technologies brings the potential for catastrophic and long-lasting damage to the earth and life. Nuclear accidents have warned us about these hazards, most notably at Chernobyl. Other serious incidents include radiation releases from nuclear weapons complexes in both the United States and Russia. Sociocultural studies of populations that have been exposed to radiation from such accidents suggest ways to assist people coping with nuclear-age hazards. With this aim I have studied communities in Russia that have been exposed to radiation from nuclear weapons facilities,[1] examining divergent perceptions of how the people's health and lifestyles were affected by the radiation, whom they blame, and what strategies they have devised both to ameliorate the problems and to preserve their cultures in these contaminated environments. I grapple with issues of environmental human rights and environmental racism and analyze the responses from and discourses of scientists and officials in the nuclear community.

The weapons facility known as Mayak Chemical Combine is located in the Chelyabinsk region in the Urals in Chelyabinsk-65, a closed city that was not on the map until 1989. Mayak was the Soviet Union's first weapons-grade plutonium production center. Throughout the Cold War, Mayak produced nuclear materials for the country's nuclear weapons, causing severe environmental contamination to the Chelyabinsk region and its population of 3.6 million. As a result of accidents, more than 146 million curies of radiation were released over time. By comparison, Three Mile Island, in the United States, released only 14–20 curies. Chernobyl, in the former Soviet Union, released 50–80 million curies. Most of the radioactive elements released from Chelyabinsk were strontium-90 and cesium-137, but small amounts of plutonium were also lost. About 120 million curies are trapped in Lake Karachay inside the facility; some 120 million were released in a storage tank explosion in 1957; 3 million are trapped in Lake Staroe Boloto; 2.75 million were dumped in the Techa River from the late 1940s until 1956; 600 were disbursed by a 1967 dust storm; and 6,000 curies are in groundwater creeping from the complex toward the city of Chelyabinsk, the region's administrative center with a population of over 1 million.[2]

I also include relevant information from Russia's two other plutonium production sites at Krasnoyarsk and Tomsk, which have released radioactive elements in the environment.[3] For comparative purposes I cite experiences around U.S. nuclear weapons sites, including conversations with officials at the former plutonium production site in Hanford, Washington, and with U.S. representatives (environmental activists, medical researchers, social scientists) at international conferences that I attended in Chelyabinsk (1992), Krasnoyarsk (1994), and Kaluga (1994).[4]

The People of Chelyabinsk

The people living in the Chelyabinsk region include Russians, Tatars, Bashkirs, Chuvash, Mari, Ukrainians, Byelorussians, Kazakhs, Jews, and Germans. Russians form the majority, followed by the Tatars and Bashkirs. Of these groups the earliest settlers were the Turkic-speaking Bashkirs, whose history in the area dates back to the 14th century. Traditionally, they were nomads and many aspects of this heritage are still evident today even though they have been sedentary agriculturalists since the early 18th century. Most Bashkirs in the Chelyabinsk region live in the Argayash and Kunashak districts, both of which are heavily populated with Bashkirs and Tatars and experienced severe radiation exposure from Mayak. Tatars, who speak a related Turkic-language, appeared in the region in the late 17th century. They have a centuries-long history of farming and urban development. Tatars did not settle in compact communities but were dispersed throughout Chelyabinsk. Despite the cultural differences between Tatars and Bashkirs, due mainly to the differences in their traditional nomadic and farming backgrounds, they share more in common with each other than with the non-Turkic and non-Muslim ethnic groups who are their neighbors. Intermarriage between the two groups is much more common than it is with other nationalities.

Of the towns and villages in the sample, Muslyumovo (population 4,022) has the largest percentage of Tatars and Bashkirs (Tatars number 3,302, Bashkirs 379, Russians 341). The main occupations in Muslyumovo are related to the operation of the local state farm, which focuses on stock breeding and grain growing, and servicing the local railway station. The village is situated along the Techa River approximately 30 miles from Mayak, and is contaminated both from the dumping of plutonium waste from Mayak in the early 1950s and from the 1957 explosion.

Kyshtym, another town in our sample, is about 7 miles from Mayak. It has a total population of 42,283 (of which 38,432 are Russians, 1,365 Tatars, and 931 Bashkirs). Other minorities include small numbers of Byelorussians, Ukrainians, Kazakhs, Germans, Chuvash, Jews, Mordvinians, and Mari. Most of the population works in radio, copper, and machine-tool building. Other important sources of employment are the local railway station, the truck and bus depot, and services industry. Over the decades, employment in the closed cities of Chelyabinsk-65 and Chelyabinsk-70 (focused mainly on weapons research) has been an especially coveted opportunity for people in Kyshtym.

The third town in our study, Dal'naya Dacha, is a community on the outskirts of Kyshtym, and it is closest to the Mayak complex. It was established in the early

1950s to service a health resort built there for the employees of Chelyabinsk-65. Most of the population is Russian, but there are also some Tatars and Bashkirs. The majority of the residents work for the health resort as service personnel. Through their work they enjoy, more than residents in the rest of Kyshtym do, better access to the relatively abundant food and consumer goods available to Chelyabinsk-65. Like the people of Kyshtym, many families in Dal'naya Dacha also have relatives who work and live inside the city of Chelyabinsk-65, and through them they have an additional dependence on the facilities.

A History of the Contamination and the Evolution of Perceptions about Mayak

During the construction of the Mayak nuclear weapons facility (1945–49) the people in and around Kyshtym were not told what the facility would be used for—only that it was an important postwar construction site. It was a welcomed project, since it provided many unskilled jobs to local residents, especially in the nearest town of Kyshtym. Then in 1949, when the plant began operation, abundant unskilled labor from the local communities was no longer needed and the site was closed to all outsiders. The large numbers of soldiers coming in and out of the gates and the general secrecy that shrouded the plant's activities led local people to conclude that the facility had something to do with the military, although this was never confirmed officially.

By 1952–53 signs warning residents that it was dangerous to use the water began appearing along the Techa River near the plant. People periodically noticed what they described as "pink pieces of fluff" floating in the water, and anglers brought home 3-feet long fish that were blind.[5] Officials did not explain why it was dangerous to swim in or use the water in the Techa River. Rumors began to circulate about radiation contamination, but if people even knew the term they understood it simplistically, equating its effects with those of an X ray. Inhabitants claim that officials never explained to them either the scope of the radiation contamination or its health and environmental consequences. About 28,000 people along the Techa depended on the river for drinking and irrigation water.

In the early 1950s, 22 villages along the river in its most contaminated areas were evacuated after a marked increase in disease and deaths were observed among the inhabitants.[6] People were moved to noncontaminated areas, leaving ghost villages. The vast majority was settled in what were to be temporary houses that became substandard in time. These evacuations did not seem to stir any local public protest, no doubt because heads of households had to sign papers swearing themselves to secrecy and because, even though the plant was hiring fewer locals, it was still regarded as a potential source of privileged employment. If a son or daughter was hired by Mayak and moved to the closed city, he or she could share the benefits of their high standard of living with relatives on the outside.

In the late afternoon of September 29, 1957, one of the facility's 80,000-gallon storage tanks exploded after its cooling system failed. About 20 million curies of radioactive debris were released over a territory about the size of New Jersey and approximately 10,700 people were permanently evacuated. However, over half of these people were not evacuated until eight months after the accident: they consumed contaminated food for three to six months without restriction and continued to eat some contaminated food until their evacuation. The entire population of the region ate the 1957 harvest, which was heavily contaminated with radionuclides.[7]

According to Mikhail Gladyshev, former director of Mayak's plutonium facility:

> The day after the explosion it was clear that northeast winds were spreading radioactive materials over population centers and waterways, so we began evacuating the population from their native villages. We had to arrange for the issuing of new clothes and other necessities for the evacuees, their decontamination in showers, and resettlement. It took major organizational efforts and expenditures. The overwhelming majority of the evacuees were Bashkirs. It's amazing that the whole evacuation was completed in a relatively short period and without any resistance from the population. The job was finished so rapidly that very soon the people adapted to their new conditions and new life.[8]

Evacuees we interviewed confirm that the population did not put up any resistance. The people were conditioned by the strong Soviet government to obey orders and to believe that their leaders knew what was best for them. For the Bashkirs the tradition of military discipline had an even longer history, going back to the period between 1798 and 1865 when the Bashkirs served en masse as rank and file soldiers in the czarist army guarding Russia's eastern borders. The harsh military discipline imposed on the Bashkirs by their Russian commanders apparently helped to mold an obedient population.

Even though the evacuation met with no resistance and went more smoothly than officials expected, the evacuees suffered deep emotional and cultural trauma from their sudden uprooting from ancestral villages. I talked to people in Dal'naya Dacha who worked at one of the health resorts where evacuees were housed from October of 1957 to May of 1958. They recall caring solely for evacuees from neighboring villages and doing this job without the assistance of Mayak officials or physicians. Aleftina Fisko, who worked in the cafeteria of the Chelyabinsk-65 resort, told me that throughout the period evacuees were at her resort, no doctors or managers from Mayak even visited the site, "as if they were afraid of being contaminated."[9] Fisko recalled that in early October 1957 several hundred Bashkirs and Tatars, whole families with children and elders, were brought to the resort:

> Most of them did not speak any Russian; they chattered to each other in their own language. They lived in buildings that were only used in summer so they weren't heated, and were given free food for only two months. Afterward they had to find their own food until they left in May, I have no idea where to. All the belongings they brought with them from home were confiscated and burned. The Bashkir women tried to sneak into the building where they had been forced to leave all their clothing, including their ethnic attire. As soon as they were seen in these clothes they were made to give them up for burning. Some of them were so desperate they even managed to go back to their villages before they were burned down in order to retrieve food and clothing. The women did all the housekeeping and hunting for food, while the men roamed around town and drank vodka.[9]

One evacuee from the 1957 disaster told me that when the soldiers came from Mayak to inform his fellow villagers that they had to leave their homes forever the very next morning, they advised the men to drink up whatever vodka they had in stock to protect themselves from the exposure. Some men were apparently delighted by this officially sanctioned drinking spree, which may have led to increased alcoholism among this population.

Men and women informants recalled their resettlement with tears in their eyes as they described how they had to slaughter their own animals the night before they left, prepare their homes for burning, and part with family heirlooms. They were loaded onto army trucks that took them to barracks or unheated resort facilities, herded into showers, issued military clothing, and left to rebuild their lives without any government assistance. Some were eventually offered other housing, but many were forced to find shelter and jobs on their own. One major obstacle to rebuilding their lives was that when they were forced to leave their homes they also had to sign a paper promising not to tell anyone why they had moved and where they had moved from. This made the process of applying for new homes or work extremely difficult, because the secrecy agreement meant they were unable to offer any references in support of an application. The people who wept in front of me said that for years they had pushed all thoughts about their past from memory and refrained from talking to anyone about what happened. Some said that I was the first to hear their stories.

Despite the 1957 accident Chelyabinsk-65, with its Mayak production facility, remained the ideal city of the future to the local people, especially in Kyshtym. Those who worked there boasted to their friends and relatives about the high wages, their interesting and prestigious work, excellent infrastructure, and consumer goods. For young people it was a desirable job. Those who could not get jobs at the closed facilities were envious and, perhaps, somewhat hostile to those who could. It is as though the people of Kyshtym had a love-hate relationship with the facilities. A man who was in his late 50s said that when he was in his 20s (in the 1960s) the people of Kyshtym started calling the residents of Chelyabinsk-65 "chocolate people" for the chocolate bars (symbols of the good life) available in abundance inside the gates and absent outside. He remembers that teenagers in Kyshtym would get into fistfights with visiting boys from Chelyabinsk-65.[10]

The people gradually began to understand the effects of radiation on the environment and health as information was released after the 1986 disaster at Chernobyl. However, it was not until 1989, when the government officially acknowledged the Mayak disasters, that the Chelyabinsk population became fully aware of the implications of their proximity to the nuclear weapons facility. Of course, they knew of their own health problems but did not relate them to Mayak until these relatively recent revelations. In Muslyumovo, for instance, the people were told by officials since 1953 that the river was "dirty," but not that the source of the "dirt" was Mayak. The local Bashkirs and Tatars called their "strange" illnesses the "river disease," whose symptoms were periodic, and in some cases constant, numbness in their extremities, aching joints, frequent and severe headaches, bleeding of the nose and gums, and fatigue. People even died of the "river disease."

In Muslyumovo they did not know the name of the river until 1953 when they were told by local officials that it was "dirty" and that they must not use the water for anything. After 1989, when they learned that the "dirt" in the river was radiation and how dangerous it was, the young people of the village renamed the Techa the "atomka," which is a slang derivative from the Russian word "atomic." The people did not draw a connection between the river and Mayak. Mayak was not allowed to be part of their consciousness, because it was a defense plant, completely hidden from view and public discussion. Another factor was that the very inadequate infrastructure (that is, bad roads, no phone lines) in Russian rural areas keeps population centers fairly isolated from one another. Therefore, people did not and do not really know much about what is going on even in their own region. However, the official status of this off-the-map secret facility was the main reason for the lack of information. People did not discuss such matters, they pretended that such places did not exist for fear of thinking or saying something that would get them in trouble. It was as if the Mayak and the secret cities were truly invisible.

The first published information about the health effects of Mayak was released in December 1991. The publication of study findings had the impact of a bombshell on the entire population. The public learned that since 1950 the incidence of leukemia among the population exposed to radiation along the Techa River had increased by 41%. From 1980 to 1990 all cancers among this population had risen by 21%, and all diseases of the circulatory system by 31%.[11] The raw data are not available to confirm the results of this study, and it is likely to be incomplete. Local doctors say it is impossible to obtain completely dependable health data, because physicians were supposed to limit the number of death certificates they issued with diagnoses of cancer or other radiation-related illnesses. It was general Soviet practice to control health statistics so that rates of certain illnesses would not be embarrassingly high. My Russian colleague was told by a rural physician in Chelyabinsk that once a certain number of illnesses had been reached, no more were to be reported. Another problem is that the Muslim Bashkirs and Tatars, due to religious considerations, would not always permit an autopsy to establish cause of death. When they did allow an autopsy they were angered to see that a whole team of physicians were at the side of the deceased within hours after death, whereas during the illness the doctors did not appear once to offer the patient aid.

Perceptions of Health Risks

According to a 1992 public opinion survey of residents in the Chelyabinsk Region, among the combined populations of Muslyumovo and Kyshtym, 86% feel that their family's health has been affected by Mayak.[12] Approximately half the residents of Chelyabinsk City and Chelyabinsk-70 also say their families have been affected.[13] In the village of Muslyumovo Dr. Gulfarida Galimova has been keeping records in lieu of reliable official statistics. Although hers may also be flawed, they reflect the depth of the fear so palpable in Muslyumovo. Dr. Galimova claims that every family has someone with the "river disease." She has determined that the average lifespan of the women of Muslyumovo is 47 (72 is the average for the nation) and of the men is 45 (69 for the nation). The death rate in Muslyumovo is 24% greater than it is for the noncontaminated villages in the same Kunashak region. The mortality rate at birth is 10 times higher. Galimova maintains that sterility and infertility have become commonplace among her patients, especially those who went through puberty in the late 1940s and early 1950s, when Mayak was dumping its radioactive waste into the river. Since 1950 the cases of leukemia have increased by 41% and are double those in the noncontaminated areas of the region. The number of asthma cases is four times greater.[14]

Another independent health researcher who worked in the area in the early 1990s was geneticist Nina Solovyova from the Institute of Cytology and Genetics in the Siberian Branch of the Russian Academy of Sciences. She also identified the "river disease" among the subjects of her study and named it the Muslyumovo Syndrome. In addition to the symptoms of the Muslyumovo Syndrome, increasing numbers of children, according to the village schoolteachers, are lethargic and slow learners. Solovyova revealed through DNA and chromosome analyses conducted in 1993–94 that 30% of Muslyumovo residents show genetic deformation. When she proposed her DNA and chromosome study to the local government, she was promised funding from FIB-4 (a branch of the Institute of Biophysics managed by a classified division of the Ministry of Public Health), a government institution that has monitored the health of the Chelyabinsk victims for decades. Doctors working there signed sworn statements that they would tell patients neither what they were being examined for nor their diagnosis. The data collected are still unavailable to outside researchers. The U.S. Department of Energy is trying to pry loose the information in a major joint project to analyze the data together, but the Russians have made that task very difficult. As Solovyova's preliminary data began to show higher-than-average aberrations, FIB-4 canceled its contract with her, because it doubted the Validity of her data, which did not correspond to FIB's data.

When a team of UCI researchers tried to replicate Solovyova's study independently, the project was called to the attention of the local counterintelligence agency (successor of the KGB), which halted the collection of blood samples. In a conversation with the Muslyumovo physician who had asked the Americans to do this study, a counterintelligence officer told her that Muslyumovo blood was worth millions of dollars, and therefore she had no right to give it away to anyone. Apparently some local authorities would like to profit from giving foreigners access to such data. This incident and Dr. Galimova's related advocacy for her patients' rights to independent medical opinions have cost the doctor her job. This is perhaps one reason why I was only able to find a few physicians in the region who are active in the antinuclear movement and align themselves politically with their activist patients.

Living with Radiation Contamination: Effects on Lifestyle

It is difficult scientifically to draw a direct link between the above-mentioned health problems and exposure to radiation. To do so requires long-term research by diverse independent scholars who test and retest the data. However, it is already evident that local people are modifying their everyday behavior in an attempt to avoid or mitigate what they perceive to be the health risks involved in living near or on contaminated territory.

The Muslim Bashkirs and Tatars who live right next to the contaminated Techa River believe they are at greater risk than non-Muslims from radiation exposure because of their special relationship to water. Practicing Muslims must wash their hands before they say their prayers several times a day. Women, whether they are worshipers or not, must bathe and wash carefully their genitals many times a day. They told me that because of these strict rules of hygiene both for women and men, in noncontaminated areas Bashkir and Tatar women have lower than average incidences of gynecological cancer, but that the reverse is true in contaminated regions because of the abundant use of water in personal hygiene. For instance, a woman in Muslyumovo who suffers from Muslyumovo Syndrome said that when living in her husband's home as a young newlywed in the late 1950s and 1960s, she wanted to convince her mother-in-law of her commitment to cleanliness in the Muslim Tatar tradition, so she bathed and washed clothes daily in the Techa River right by their home. Had she known about the river's radiation contamination and the health risks, she would have been more cautious, as are today's young village women. Other individuals said they are trying to reduce the amounts of water they use, particularly from the river. Adults rarely swim in the river now, because of their awareness of the "river disease," but it is still hard to control the children, especially on hot summer days. Even during the winter it is not uncommon to see teenage boys ice fishing on the frozen waters. Many adults and children alike cross the river daily at its narrowest site to get from one part of the village to another. Many children could not get to school every day without this convenient crossing.

The food chain is, of course, another important means by which the population is exposed to radioactive elements. Most of the food families consume is grown on their homesteads. Some families who live in close proximity to the river try to sell their garden produce (mainly potatoes), meat, and milk at farmers' markets in the city of Chelyabinsk or the nearby town of Kunashak; they purchase for their own consumption produce from what they hope are noncontaminated areas. But most families in Muslyumovo consume their own homegrown food, including the beef and milk from their livestock that is central to the diet of the relatively recently nomadic Bashkirs and even their traditionally sedentary Tatar neighbors. Since the livestock grazes and drinks at the river, the people perceive these products to be the most damaging to their health.

Milk that is fermented, however, is regarded as an antidote to the "radiation" illnesses. Bashkirs and Tatars traditionally have believed that fermented mare's milk, called *koumiss*, cures all illnesses. *Koumiss* contains vitamins, especially vitamin C, and antibiotic elements, all of which, Russian researchers say, have strong healing qualities.[15] *Koumiss* and other fermented dairy products in the traditional Tatar and Bashkir diet are seeing a comeback in the past couple of years in connection with the population's heightened awareness of radiation exposure and the possible consequences. Also seeing a comeback are herbal and other folk medicines. Traditionally people have used the skin or mold from fermented products (cheese, buttermilk, farmers' cheese) to heal wounds. Contemporary homemakers maintain that products that have grown mold lose their radioactivity, as though the mold somehow devours the radioactive elements in the milk. They think that the healing qualities of pressed geese and horse dung are also useful in treating cancers. Local people are reviving the use of many herbs to prevent and cure all illnesses, and particularly those they associate with the radiation contamination. Some of the more common ones thought to remove radionuclides and intoxicants from the body are *Gledidomium majus*, *Acorus calamus*, *Aloe arborescent*, honey, pumpkin, and *Allium cepa*. Gynecological illnesses are treated with *Allium sepa*, *Arctium lappu*, *Pinus sp.*, *Linum mitatissimuni*, *Origanum vulgares*, and *Aloe arborescent*. At least two women claimed to have cured themselves of cancer by drinking herbal teas made from hempseed and burdock root.

Women tend to put their faith in folk medicine to prevent and cure illnesses that they regard to be related to radiation. The men rely on alcohol, particularly vodka. Many informants noted that alcoholism has increased in recent years among the male population. They cannot say what the main cause of this alarming phenomenon is but indicate that the alcoholics believe they are protected from the consequences of radiation exposure.

People have introduced some dietary changes as well. For instance, even practicing Muslims who do not eat pork themselves do not prevent other members of their families from eating pork, because it is believed to be less contaminated than beef. They believe that pork absorbs less radiation because of its greater ratio of fat and meat to bones and because pigs stay in their yards and do not drink from the river. Local residents are taking other measures recommended throughout the country to lessen the general risk of cancer. They are growing more vegetables and eating them more regularly—"like the Russians"—as a means of cutting beef consumption and adding vitamins to the diet. Finally, they are giving up some of their traditional ethnic delicacies that require extensive frying in large quantities of grease, as well as smoked meat, which doctors say is carcinogenic. The Russian population has also looked to the Bashkirs and Tatars for ways to cut their risks of cancer. They now tend to brew their tea in Bashkir and Tatar traditions, which means they try not to drink tea that has been steeped for more than five to seven minutes and do not use old brew because they have heard from medical researchers that tea can be carcinogenic if it is not freshly brewed.

Cultural attitudes toward pathology have influenced the way locals express concerns for their families' health and their decision making about seeking medical care. Muslims in this area, especially the elders, feel it is wrong to call attention to personal misfortune. They are particular about their privacy when it comes to a deformity, pathology, or illness in the family. For instance, a child born with a deformity is regarded as punishment from Allah, and therefore any abnormality should be hidden from others and suffered alone. By contrast, Russian families *demand* public attention to their ailing children and demand special considerations and benefits. Muslim women condemn such behavior, maintaining that a sick or deformed child should not be used as a means to improve a family's living conditions or income.

Another problem is that Muslim women are much more reluctant than other ethnic groups to have gynecological examinations, so such illnesses are often not diagnosed early. Muslim men are more likely not to see a doctor for any ailment. If they are religious they claim that their recovery is in the hands of Allah, and if they are not they say either that they don't have time to see a doctor or that it won't do any good. Men tend to want to be kept in the dark about the risks of radiation more than women. "Better not to know anything. What will be, will be," was a typical male response. Women were more likely than men in Muslyumovo to favor moving out of the contaminated area.

As this section has shown, people may not know the exact risks they face living in Chelyabinsk, though they are certain that their health and lives are in danger and they are creatively helping themselves and finding ways to minimize the threat, making dietary and other lifestyle changes. Another solution, particularly for the people of Muslyumovo, is to leave the area by any means possible. Since it seems unlikely that the government will finance their relocation, individuals are trying to "evacuate" their own families. One local schoolteacher who has three of her own children, and is looking for a way to move out, constantly gives her students these three pieces of advice: don't have anything to do with the river; get away from Muslyumovo as soon as possible; and don't marry each other.

Assigning Culpability

When people are asked who is to blame for their predicament, they commonly point to Moscow, to the national government that dictated the production policies in civilian and military industry. They recognize that local plant officials did not make decisions independently of Moscow, particularly in the Stalin period when Lavrenty Beria, head of the NKVD (predecessor of the KGB) until 1953, was personally in control of all the military facilities. However, they are particularly bitter about what they feel was the betrayal by local officials and doctors who knew about the contamination and its health effects and yet did not inform the public so that they could take effective measures to protect themselves.

Special anger also is focused on FIB-4, which for decades conducted elaborate tests on thousands of Chelyabinsk residents to study but not treat the health effects of radiation after the accidents. "If they had only told me how much radiation I had accumulated I never would have had children," was a common refrain I heard from patients who were periodically summoned for testing by FIB-4. It was only in April 1990 that the public was told about the real focus of the institute's research work, although little of the data has been released either to the patients or to outside researchers. Another common complaint about Chelyabinsk doctors was that while a loved one was dying of an illness suspected of being related to radiation exposure, family members sat by the bedside alone. As soon as the patient died, it was common for a whole team of doctors to come at once to do tests: "When these teams come out they are so cold, they do not seem to even notice our anguish. Where were they when we needed them?"

There are also bitter words for Mayak. A speaker at a public rally in Muslyumovo on September 26, 1993, poignantly sums up the sentiment of her neighbors: "We curse Mayak, which robbed us of our parents and our health." I often heard people say that Mayak produced weapons for a cold war during which time no bomb was ever dropped—except on the people of Chelyabinsk! These expressions of anger do not seem to reflect sentiments against strong defense capabilities. On the contrary, often the same people who were most critical of the facilities also voiced concerns about maintaining Russia's national security. For instance, Gosman Kabirov, a local environmental activist and a Tatar who blames Mayak for his inability to have children and for the illnesses of his parents, brothers, and sisters, has wondered aloud whether western organizations are funding the Russian environmental movement with the goal of using the antinuclear movement to undermine Russia's security. In March 1993, at a conference of antinuclear organizations in the Socio-Ecological Union, he praised Mayak's accomplishments in defense and civilian industry:

> Mayak is a unique complex, not only in our country, but in the world. Indeed, it has brought our country enormous benefit, and made it among the best in the world. The isotope plant that opened in 1962 produces fiber optics, devices for radiation control, batteries for artificial hearts, new materials and reinforced plastics, and new technology for storing nuclear waste (vitrification). All this brings the state hundreds of millions of dollars in profits. And we should not underestimate the fact that Mayak had Americans worried about the Russian bomb. It's no wonder that Chelyabinsk was one of the main targets for a nuclear weapons attack on our country. But at what price? That's what we have to talk about.[16]

While some are concerned with national security, others express sentiments tied to the growing nationalist movements of Tatars and Bashkirs throughout Russia—movements that raise claims of genocide and promise to help the people get the justice that so far has not been forthcoming from the national or local governments. The following is representative of statements used to incite ethnic indignation:

> What is the reason for the selective policies in evacuating people from the villages contaminated in 1957 in the Chelyabinsk region after the sudden nuclear explosion of radioactive materials in the storage tank? ... Tatar and Bashkir villagers were left without help, they were not evacuated to safe places. Meanwhile the population of Russian villages were taken away immediately from the explosion site and their villages were bulldozed.[17]

These charges cannot be confirmed: there are no studies in Russia equivalent to the works of Bullard, Wenz, Johnston, and others who have identified and analyzed

environmental injustices against U.S. minority communities and Third World populations.[18] There are local Tatars and Bashkirs who claim that their population was
singled out to be the guinea pigs of Russian scientists researching the effects of radiation on humans. They cite doctors who were asked by secret research facilities to
identify patients for studies according to their ethnic background.[19] Activists from
Bashkiria and Tataria try to incite anger over such accusations of "genocidal" politics. So far the population resists, telling these outside activists not to put a wedge
between the different nationalities of Chelyabinsk.[20] Local environmental activists in
Chelyabinsk tend to either deny or play down the possibility that the health and lives
of Bashkirs and Tatars were undervalued when decisions were made about evacuations. They fear that raising such issues will generate ethnic tensions that could erupt
in violence, which has been (and continues to be) so destructive in other parts of the
former Soviet Union.

Activists in Muslyumovo's antinuclear organization, known as the White Mice
(Russian equivalent for "guinea pigs"), hesitate to charge officials with environmental racism, though they are not hesitant to charge them with human rights violations
because the government has not been responsive to their demands that the village
be moved to a site farther away from the river. They have written to the UN Human
Rights Commission stating their grievances of environmental injustice, but have not
framed their complaints as a case of environmental racism. How do plant officials
respond to accusations against them? Yevgeny Ryzhkov, director of public relations
for Chelyabinsk-65, focuses blame on past production procedures and past policies
of not informing the public. "Now," he says, "my policy is to be available to answer any questions from the public so that rumors won't abound." He claims that
mistakes were made in the past, but now they are much less likely because of the
knowledge and experience accumulated over the years. The population outside the
plant continues to mistrust him and other officials, and he says he can't blame them,
because they were lied to before.

Another common remark I heard from officials, scientists, and members of their
families who have lived inside Chelyabinsk-65 and Chelyabinsk-70 since before the
1957 explosion is that they as individuals are very healthy and therefore are living
proof that even the accidents of the 1950s and 1960s were not as damaging to the
people's health as claimed. Some of these informants appear genuinely to believe
what they say. However, a couple of them, speaking to me off the record and away
from their fellow residents, have said just the opposite. This view was also reflected
in the results of a UCI public opinion survey conducted inside Chelyabinsk-70 where
roughly half the population claims that their families' health has been affected by
operations at the facilities in nearby Chelyabinsk-65.[21] Reliable health data are next
to impossible to obtain, so none of these claims can be proven right or wrong.

Officials in local government at the region and district levels seem to talk out of
both sides of their mouths. On the one hand, they have fought hard to get the terms
of the Chernobyl law, which ensures generous government allocations to areas affected by the Chernobyl accident, expanded to the Chelyabinsk region. In doing so
they have cited the tremendous health and related social problems caused by the
1957 accident, which released far more curies than Chernobyl. On the other hand,
when they are talking to their own constituents and to inquiring guests such as I,
they tend to maintain that the environmentalists should be focused on industrial
pollutants and low living standards as the main culprits in the region's health problems, not the military complex. At a meeting of several region leaders (September

1992) I heard one of them maintain that the "greens" had done more damage to the country than Chernobyl because they generated *radiophobia*, the term used in Russia to denote excessive fear of radiation among the population. They claimed that radiophobia was far more debilitating than the actual objective problems they faced. Furthermore, the situation was worsened by visiting foreigners (such as I) asking people questions about how they were affected by radiation. Another official at the same meeting, a physician, claimed that he had gone door-to-door in communities like Muslyumovo where people were convinced that all their ailments were due to radiation, and that he concluded that their illnesses were caused by their low standard of living, not by radiation. None of the officials at this "roundtable" meeting argued against these statements.

Galina Plokhikh, a member of Optima, which is a group of environmentalists in Chelyabinsk secondary schools, is familiar with these attitudes. Speaking at a conference in Krasnoyarsk in September 1994, she said: "We are told that the main source of illnesses and short life is not Mayak but low living standards and general environmental damage. Our officials say, Do not bother protesting because they will help us."

Proposing Solutions

Most of the people I talked to in the vicinity of Mayak, particularly in Muslyumovo, do not see assistance on the horizon or immediate solutions forthcoming—either from their national leaders or from the local government. Most believe that Mayak is an eternal reality, an inescapable evil that no one knows how to fight. They expressed an overwhelming feeling of doom that has been reinforced by a series of disappointments. Just before Russian President Boris Yeltsin visited Muslyumovo in September 1991, the residents unanimously voted for resettlement and hoped that their problems would be solved by the money allocated by the Russian government to compensate for the damage done by Mayak. Instead, the 1 million rubles they received was used in part to pave a road in the center of town where Yeltsin's car would drive and build a small hospital that has not significantly improved their health care. People are convinced that the rest of the money, also intended for general improvements to the community (not compensation to individuals), was pocketed by their local officials (Bashkirs and Tatars).

In the summer and fall of 1994 they were told that financial compensation would be allotted to anyone who could show that they were victims of excessive radiation exposure. So people began bringing doctors' certificates to a special commission set up to review the applications for benefits, only to find that the fine print of the ruling excluded almost everyone who made a claim. Anyone who no longer resided in Muslyumovo, even if the person had moved away the day before but lived their whole life in Muslyumovo up to that point, was not eligible. And anyone born after 1958—that is, a child or grandchild of victims who may show genetic aberrations—was also ineligible.

The remaining handful of activists in and around Muslyumovo who refuse to be discouraged by these setbacks maintain that they will continue to work toward two goals:

1. An end to the bureaucratic obstacles to individual compensation to radiation victims and their offspring based on health certificates showing high whole

body counts of strontium-90 and cesium-137, related health problems, and DNA or chromosome changes in offspring; and

2. An end to government obstacles to independent scientists from Russia and other countries who want to collect and analyze health data. Residents in Kyshtym differ in their approach in that some still harbor hope that Mayak will come through with some general assistance by sharing its economic benefits with the surrounding community outside the closed cities. The people of Kyshtym think there is a chance that Chelyabinsk-65 will incorporate Kyshtym, especially since the town of Novogorny (right next to Chelyabinsk-65) was incorporated in February 1993. The advantage to the people of Kyshtym is that they hope they will then also enjoy the better city funding and consumer goods supply system. Igor Gul', deputy of a district council in Kyshtym told us in March 1993 that "Our whole struggle for the environment in Kyshtym has been reduced to a fight with Mayak for land and benefits."[22]

Officials at national and local level, especially at Mayak, argue for economic revitalization based on reprocessing spent fuel from Soviet-type reactors in the former republics, Finland, and Germany, and storage at Soviet sites (not in vitrified form). Their argument is that the hard currency earned by handling hazardous waste can be used for environmental cleanup programs. Decree No. 472, signed by President Yeltsin on April 21, 1993, enables the region to keep 25% of the profits gained from reprocessing operations to be used by the local governments for "implementation of radiation monitoring, improvement of environmental conditions, and socioeconomic development programs in the above-mentioned regions, and also to carry out scientific research and practical work on enhancing safety in the management of spent nuclear fuel and its waste from reprocessing." This prospect of increased revenues for the ailing region budget is held out to the public as a means by which Mayak can justify its existence to its antinuclear neighbors who are told that they are suffering not from radiation exposure but from a very low standard of living. No guarantees, however, are made about how the extra money will be spent by the local government. Thus, other than government officials, few people support the idea of more money in the budget in exchange for more nuclear wastes in the region.

Some Russian and U.S. Comparisons

Perceptions of serious health problems, whether real or imagined, are common to all communities studied. As noted earlier, according to the results of our public opinion survey of residents in the Chelyabinsk region, among the combined populations of Muslyumovo and Kyshtym, 86% feel that their family's health has been affected by Mayak. Moreover, approximately half the residents of Chelyabinsk City and Chelyabinsk-70 also say their families have been affected. Contrasting this information with data from a parallel survey of Washington State residents living in contaminated regions near the Hanford weapons facility in late 1993, only 5% of the surveyed Americans fear that Hanford has affected their health or safety, although a third worry about future damage from the facility (these concerns are much greater among residents of Spokane and the towns on the Yakima Indian reservation).[23]

Krasnoyarsk and Tomsk, where plutonium is still being produced, also have their own "Muslyumovos." Lyudmila Fatianova is a high school physics teacher from the village of Atamanovo, about half a mile away from the Krasnoyarsk-26 facility and populated largely by ethnic Russians but also by Ukrainians and Byelorussians. She claims that out of her village's population of 2,500, the number of patients with cancer is abnormally high: 35 diagnosed as of January 1994, 9 of whom had passed away by September 1994. She is also alarmed that many of her friends are sterile or infertile, and increasingly more of her students show marked learning disabilities. As a physicist she admires the work of her colleagues at Krasnoyarsk-26, but as a mother, woman, and teacher she is totally against it.[24]

A study conducted by Dr. Vladimir Mazharev and fellow research physicians at a nongovernmental research center in Krasnoyarsk shows that the number of adults with psychological disturbances in the contaminated areas of Krasnoyarsk is higher than in noncontaminated areas and higher than among children. Even more persuasive are his data showing that population centers farthest away from the contaminated areas have fewer incidences of leukemia in men and women; lower morbidity among adults due to malignant tumors and leukemia; dramatically fewer incidences of illnesses among children of the respiratory, nervous, or cardiovascular systems; and lower infant mortality due to life-threatening birth defects.[25]

Research physician Tamara Matkovskaya reports alarming symptoms among children exposed to radiation releases from the Tomsk accident at its plutonium facility on April 6, 1993. She found that within a couple of hours after the accident most of the children in her sample experienced nausea, vomiting, diarrhea, headaches, and drowsiness. Diarrhea in many of them continued for several months. She maintains that the more long-lasting effects are chronic lethargy, a marked decrease in memorization abilities, less positive emotions than usual, an absence of imagination, and poor motor development.[26]

The United States also has sites with similar health concerns. For instance, for Hanford downwinders, their Muslyumovo is known as Death Mile. It is 11 miles from Hanford's Purex plant, which formerly manufactured weapons grade plutonium. The downwinders claim abnormally high rates of cancer, deformed lambs, hairless cattle, and cancer in their pets.[27] Residents in the vicinity of the Livermore National Laboratories, in California, maintain excessive numbers of people with melanomas, while around the Los Alamos National Laboratories in New Mexico there are claims of high numbers of brain tumors. These are but a couple of the several sites in the United States where citizens voice serious concerns about their health because of the environmental consequences of nuclear weapons development.

In all these cases the populations that have only relatively recently learned bits and pieces about the activities of the secret operations of these facilities feel that the authorities were not concerned about public health and in some cases deliberately used these civilians as guinea pigs to better understand the long-term effects of low-dose radiation on humans. In Chelyabinsk the ethnic groups most affected were the minority Tatars and Bashkirs because of the large numbers of their populations in the vicinity. At the notorious test sites of Semipalatinsk in Kazakhstan and Novaya Zemlya in Russia, most of the victims were minority indigenous peoples. However, in Krasnoyarsk and Tomsk the vast majority of the population is Russian. It appears as though there has been a general disregard for *all* humans that crosses every ethnic and socioeconomic boundary. Even the elites who were perpetrators of these accidents and experiments and who worked in the closed facilities were also victims, because they were not free to leave their jobs or their own contaminated communities. This was not the case with the employees at nuclear weapons facilities, who were free to leave their jobs. However, few of them, especially in the early years of the industry, were aware of the health risks.

In both the United States and Russia, the victim populations are angry, because officials did not inform the people of the hazards. Farmers at Hanford's "Death Mile" were not warned of the possible dangers of the routine releases of nuclear materials and accidents of the 1950s and 1960s. Fatianova in Krasnoyarsk said that it was not until 1988–89 that they heard anything about a contaminated zone that they should avoid. She feels that her infertile friends were the ones who spent the most time swimming in the Yenisei River in that very zone they now know is contaminated.

The common response of plant officials to these claims is that the people should put this in the past. Leonard Lazarev, a prominent nuclear physicist from St. Petersburg, and Russia's main ideologue for reprocessing spent fuel, speaking at a plenary session of the Krasnoyarsk conference, said: "We shouldn't be so emotional about the former accidents. During the Cold War we made mistakes in our haste, but we won't do that anymore." I have heard these arguments from U.S. nuclear weapons physicists as well. I find that the approach does not pacify such people as Fatianova, Galimova, Matkovskaya, and others, who believe that their fellow citizens are suffering from present-day problems at these facilities.

It seems as though the nuclear physicists who are convinced that their work does not put populations at risk are not always patient with the accusations; leveled against them. At the conferences I have attended on these subjects in Moscow, Chelyabinsk, and Krasnoyarsk I could see on numerous occasions that representatives from the Russian nuclear establishment smirked and even laughed while testimony of health problems were presented from grassroots activists. I am told by a colleague, Hugh Gusterson, who has studied the culture at the Livermore labs in California,[28] that public relations officers there usually respond to public claims of health problems with sympathy but at the same time explain that the facility is not responsible. Clearly, there must be Russian public relations officers who would also follow this path, but I have been struck by the frequency with which I observe an openly unsympathetic manner on the part of public representatives of the Russian defense complexes.

Even some sympathetic observers of radiation victimization believe the people would be better off if they did not know about their exposure to radiation or the consequences. They encourage denial. For instance, V. N. Abramova, a psychologist at the Prognosis Research Center in Obninsk, Russia, the home of a nuclear weapons research facility, speaking at the Kaluga International Seminar "Ecological Consciousness—Ecological Security," argued that the less said, the better, since the government cannot provide adequate compensation to people living in high-risk areas and cannot afford to relocate them. She has observed that it is easier for people to cope when they are doomed to live with radiation if they are not constantly reminded by interviewers and the media, or by discussions of compensation (which she believes are unrealistic because of the state of the economy).

In the discourse surrounding actually trying to tackle the problems of environmental damage, economics is a common theme. In Russia today, while a fierce struggle for power is being waged at all levels of government, while the economy is on the verge of collapse, unemployment is rising, and living standards are plummeting, the people around the weapons sites are truly bewildered as they seek solutions to their plight. They all feel desperate and powerless in the face of the formidable problems posed by their secretive neighbors. Apparently many officials across Russia feel the same way. As nuclear physicist Lazarev said at the Krasnoyarsk conference: "Russia's bank is empty. If Americans don't have enough money to meet their technological challenges, what can we expect from our government? What we need money for is to build roads, homes, make a better life for the population. This is what the people are lacking. The problem is not radiation exposure."

The debate over the real causes of health problems in these areas will not be resolved until data collected by government agencies in secrecy and new data produced by independent investigators are carefully analyzed. Meanwhile, it is necessary to facilitate the process of releasing secret data and allowing new data to be accessed and analyzed. V. G. Khizhnyak, an inspector from the Krasnoyarsk Gosatomnadzor (the equivalent of the U.S. Nuclear Regulatory Commission), maintains that obstacles to this process are still a big problem in Russia, where he charges that research outside the facilities is either discounted or impeded. Just a few examples are Solovyova and Galimova, who have tripped over many obstacles in Chelyabinsk to collect independent data; also interesting, the original data for the study by Tamara Matkovskaya (cited earlier) were stolen from her Tomsk office, while the kind of valuables one would expect a common burglar to covet, such as her computer, were left untouched. Matkovskaya has also had to live with the fear caused by threatening phone calls to her home.

Russia, however, does not have a monopoly on secrecy. Much comparable U.S. data still remain to be revealed. The secrecy often borders on the absurd. For instance, when a photographer tried to take a picture of anthropologist Hugh Gusterson to accompany a magazine article, he posed Gusterson standing against the background of the Livermore labs. A public relations officer was on the spot in a minute to stop the effort. He explained that the blackened windows in the background might give some information to the KGB about what goes on inside. Tongue in cheek, Gusterson suggested: "Maybe guards of both countries could be trained together to save money."[29]

Not only did the Soviets wait until 1989 to publicly admit the explosion at Mayak in 1957, but the United States kept its knowledge of the explosion a secret as well. The CIA and U.S. weapons researchers knew about the explosion not long after it occurred. Presumably the United States chose not to point a finger at the Soviet weapons manufacturers in order not to raise questions among the U.S. public about safety matters at home. A special commission of International Physicians for the Prevention of Nuclear War and the Institute for Energy and Environmental Research, writing in *Plutonium: Deadly Gold of the Nuclear Age,* made the following assessment of this secrecy:

> As mentioned, the government of the United States discovered soon after the accident that there had been some kind of large radiation disaster in the Urals. However, it chose not to publicize this issue, despite the intense hostilities of the Cold War, presumably because questions would have been raised about the prospect of similar explosions in the U.S. nuclear weapons complex. Eventually such questions, among others, were instrumental in stopping plutonium production at Hanford at the end of the 1980s, just as the Chernobyl accident was instrumental in stopping the operation of the N-reactor of similar design at Hanford.
>
> A complete disclosure of the Chelyabinsk-65 explosion data, along with site-specific data from other centers where high-level waste tanks exist, would allow assessments for other

locations regarding the force of possible explosions, the quantities of radionuclides which might be spread in fallout, the potential cancers in surrounding communities, and the health dangers to workers during such an accident and in on- and off-site cleanup. Lack of adequate data from the former Soviet Union about the explosion and from most countries about the exact nature of the contents of their tanks, has prevented us from engaging in such assessments here.[30]

Valery Menshikov, a senior aide for Alexei Yablokov, who is a prominent government critic of the Russian nuclear establishment, is also aware of secrecy problems among the U.S. nuclear establishment. He pointed out at the Krasnoyarsk conference that the U.S. Department of Energy never gave up any data without constant public pressure and that this will also be necessary for the Russian environmental movement to accomplish. "This is the way it works," he said, "in a democratic society."[31]

The solution that the Russian Ministry of Atomic Power has devised to help Chelyabinsk overcome its environmental legacy is a plan to reprocess and resume construction of a new reactor as a way to bring in revenues, especially hard currency. There is an equivalent approach for Krasnoyarsk and Tomsk, where similar projects are the object of public controversy. Valery Lebedev, General Director of the Chemical-Mining Plant at Krasnoyarsk-26, speaking at the Krasnoyarsk conference, made this explanation for their production operations: "We are continuing to produce plutonium not because we are hawks but because our region needs energy and the money." So building more reactors is presented by industry officials as a way to improve the situation. As Yury Fedotov, of the Chemical-Mining Plant, said at the Krasnoyarsk conference, "RT-2 has to be seen as a nature protection plant which will help solve the problem of spent fuel and will be economically beneficial. The economy and ecology are inseparable. No ecological measure is possible without money. We have to make our own money which will also help us solve our environmental problems. All our previous problems were from not having purification installations and from the big rush. Now our work will be safe."

As Russia grapples to resolve these problems, it must contend with a phenomenon unknown in the United States: its unique, closed cities. These cities are unique both in terms of the way in which they are not accountable to the local public, only to Moscow (not even to the local KGB and local government), and in terms of the problems they pose for conversion, for reemploying these huge populations and reintegrating them in the larger society (if that's the decision to be made). As Menshikov pointed out at the Krasnoyarsk conference, a special conceptual framework is needed for Russia to conduct conversion, to find alternative ways for these cities to continue developing.

Conclusions

It is clear from this study that environmental disasters around Russia's three weapons-grade plutonium facilities have affected populations both inside and outside the closed nuclear weapons cities, prompting citizen organizations to make charges of environmental human rights violations. Even if it were to be proven someday that the health effects from the actual releases of nuclear materials have been insignificant or nil, we can already assert that these populations have certainly been traumatized by their fears of radiation exposure. In the case of Muslyumovo, people are adapting to the predicament in ways that are threatening to long-standing cultural traditions.

Further anthropological studies of other population centers at these sites and the areas near similar facilities in the United States could show equivalent modification of culture related specifically to a perception of nuclear victimization.

Bashkirs and Tatars make accusations that their minority populations in Chelyabinsk were targets for selective human rights violations. They make this claim because they believe that Muslyumovo and a few other predominantly Bashkir-Tatar villages were not evacuated from the Techa River deliberately so that the people could be used as guinea pigs to study the long-term effects of low-dose radiation. However, no such minority populations exist at Krasnoyarsk and Tomsk, where Russian and other Slavic villagers have also been subjected to nuclear victimization. Thus it is difficult to make unequivocal claims of environmental racism, since it appears as though the leaders of the Soviet defense industry showed a general disregard for the health of *all* civilians. Further studies of this and other environmental disaster areas in Russia may or may not show a clearer pattern of environmental racism.

Representatives of Russia's nuclear establishment argue that all these problems should be put in the past, that the most damaging health risks are from other forms of industrial pollution, or from a low standard of living or from radiophobia. The solutions they offer involve seeking money from the national government for clean-up and economic development and urging the reprocessing of imported spent fuel for hard currency. Citizen groups oppose these approaches and maintain that the victims never see the money from national and local budgets and that reprocessing fuel or plans for more reactors will only further the environmental damage. What complicates the resolution of these problems is that whether we look at sites in Russia or the United States, a common pattern is that of withholding information from the public. Both the Russian (formerly Soviet) and American weapons facilities have been allowed to work in secrecy in the name of national defense.

In view of all this populations around these sites have been traumatized. Their lives have been significantly altered by the predicament they have found themselves in; not by the knowledge they have about radiation exposure, but rather by the absence of information that can help them make rational choices about the care of their health and the health of future generations, information that can empower them to control their own environments.

Several policy recommendations for both countries can be made based on what we know about the environmental situation around such weapons facilities:

1. Ensure access to all related environmental and health information, historical and contemporary, so that it can be processed and comprehended by government and independent researchers, as well as nongovernmental organizations and individual citizens. No longer can national security considerations serve as an excuse for continued secrecy in analyzing existing data and collecting new data.

2. Remove all obstacles to independent research so that carefully reasoned decisions can be made by all interested parties. Experience in both countries shows that it requires strong public and international pressure to pry loose such data.

3. Guarantee complete freedom of citizen action and joint problem-solving between citizen groups and representatives of the nuclear community. While more studies are under way to confirm or disprove linkage between radiation exposure and illness, it is necessary for communication between citizens and officials

in the nuclear community to remain open. These officials must acknowledge and accept that residents in these controversial areas deserve respect as human beings and sympathy as possible victims of the Cold War, and should take seriously the concerns of these populations. Populations that believe their human environmental rights have been violated should not be impeded in their efforts to appeal to the United Nations and other international organizations concerned with human rights.

4. Devise a fair and meaningful system of compensation to the victims of environmental disasters.

5. Guarantee full participation of citizens in decisions about new reactors and nuclear production processes. Until greater understanding has been reached on the effects of past releases of nuclear materials, great caution should be taken in proceeding with new projects.

As an anthropologist, I see a real need for research that focuses on the sociocultural experience of radiation victimization—studying changes brought about by environmental damage and deterioration of health, changes including lifestyle change, environmental consciousness, environmental justice, and environmental racism. All too often the national and international agencies assigned the difficult task of assessing the damage of the nuclear weapons industry compile reports replete with numbers that measure curies and proffer involved explanations of technological problems, while descriptions of the predicament of the humans, animals, and plants that live in these environments are virtually absent. These reports provide the basis for policy formation, and their gaps produce significant shortcomings in responding to the needs of nuclear-age disasters. The human environmental dimension needs to be strongly inserted into this debate, and this dimension includes both real and perceived predicaments, response to disastrous conditions, and the biocultural implications of such response.

SECTION II: View from the 21st Century[32]

On my first visit to Chelyabinsk, in December 1991, a television journalist who had covered environmental stories for 20 years made this prophetic comment: "It will take more than one generation to improve the environment. We will have ample food and clothing long before the environment is cleaned up." Indeed, economic conditions in Russia have improved dramatically since the early nineties when I began this research. Russians no longer wait in long lines for goods in short supply. Unfortunately, the same kind of progress has not taken place in terms of environmental cleanup, financial compensation to radiation victims, and improved living conditions, economic status, and medical care in the contaminated areas of Chelyabinsk. This situation is largely due to Russia's lack of resources and lack of determination to right the wrongs committed by the nuclear weapons industry against its own people during the Cold War. The resistance of local and national officials to face these daunting issues has not changed in the past decade.

In recent years some of the region's villagers have sued the Russian government for damage to their health. An account in the *Seattle Times* by Mark McDonald describes a conversation he had with one such defendant, an ethnic Tatar named Glasha Ismagilova. She was 11 at the time of the 1957 Kyshtym explosion and, like hundreds of other children her age, she was taken by her school into the fields to dig up and dispose of contaminated crops. McDonald writes: "Week after week they dug up contaminated potatoes and carrots with their bare hands, then buried them in pits. They filled poisoned wells, cleaned bricks covered in radioactive soot, buried dead cattle, dismantled houses." It was not until the mid-1980s that she and others were told the nature of the contamination. Ismagilova, according to McDonald, "spoke calmly about her own illnesses—about the new three-inch tumor on her liver, the painful crumbling of her knees and hips. Tears started to come only when she remembered borrowing her mother's orange sundress on that morning 47 years ago when the Mayak cleanup began. She wanted to look nice, because she thought her fourth-grade class was headed off on a field trip."[33]

The ethnic Tatars and Bashkirs who constitute the majority of villagers most affected by the Mayak disasters also charge environmental racism. Controversy still rages about why the ethnic Russian side of the village that Ismagilova comes from was evacuated and the ethnic Tatar and Bashkir side was not. An official cited in McDonald's article claims that no one knows why some were resettled and others were not. According to McDonald: "Ismagilova does not accept the government's explanation that the Tatar side of her village was safe enough while the Russian side had been contaminated. She said this was genocide . . . 'our families were not well-educated, so it was easier for the authorities to keep us in the dark. . . . Almost all the people here were liquidators, but they're too old and sick to press their claims,' Ismagilov said, the tears coming again. 'They did the state's dirty work 45 years ago, and now they have no money. Not even enough for bread. They have no future.'"

There are indications that the minority Bashkir and Tatar populations in the Chelyabinsk region may have been a target of selective human rights violations, mainly because Muslyumovo and a few other predominantly Bashkir–Tatar villages were not evacuated from the Techa River, perhaps deliberately so the people could be used as guinea pigs to study the long-term effects of low-dose radiation. However, no such minority populations exist at nuclear weapons facilities in Krasnoyarsk and Tomsk, where Russian and other Slavic villagers were subjected to similar nuclear victimization. This fact makes it more difficult to assert unequivocal claims of environmental racism, because it appears as though the leaders of the Soviet defense industry showed a general disregard for the health of all people, no matter what ethnic background, including employees at the plants.

For the reasons stated above, activists in the White Mice (the Russian equivalent of "guinea pigs"), Muslyumovo'a antinuclear organization, hesitate to charge officials with environmental racism. But they do charge human rights violations, because the government has not taken adequate measures to move the villagers to a site farther from the river. They have written to international human rights organizations about their grievances over environmental injustice but have not framed their complaints as charges of environmental racism.

In any case, medical evidence abounds that these villagers are at a very high risk for lethal exposure to radiation. Svetlana Kostina, a researcher at the Chelyabinsk regional government's department for environment and radiation, reports that "the current dose of radiation absorbed by Muslyumovo residents is 10 times higher than internationally acceptable levels. . . . Only 18% of the village children aged 6 to 14 can be called healthy, while the rest of the children suffer from acute memory loss, attention deficit disorders, and exhaustion."[34]

Galina Komarova observed in the four most contaminated villages along the Techa River that households that let their cattle graze on the banks of the Techa were polluted with radionuclides to a significant degree. Her onsite surveys showed that children spent an average of half an hour a day by the river and teenagers about an hour and a half a day. In spite of prohibitions issued by adults, and even though all residents knew that proximity to the river was directly related to higher exposure to radiation, Komarova saw children and teenagers daily playing by and in the Techa. Village shepherds spent up to 11 hours a day by the river. Komarova found that over the five years she studied lifestyles in Muslyumovo, from 1993 to 1998, use of the Techa grew more intensive, and not simply for leisure-time activities. Having lost their former sources of income because of the collapse of the collective-farm system and local industry, the Techa villagers had to resort to using natural resources for their livelihoods more than in the past.[35]

Ann Imse interviewed several patients at the Urals Center for Radiation Medicine in Chelyabinsk and observed the same ailments and psychological trauma that I had encountered 10 years earlier. For instance, 56-year-old Nadezhda Nikolskaya, who grew up along the Techa River near Muslyumovo and was hospitalized for radiation sickness, told Imse that she had lost two of her three sons to what she believes was radiation illness. She complained to Imse: "People still live there, and they don't do anything!" According to Imse, "Ivanov [the doctor in the hospital where Nikolskaya was interviewed] enters to give her a sedative. She meekly drinks it down." Vera Kazantseva, 76, another patient, said, "Our children are sick, our grandchildren are sick." Her four children and two grandchildren have ulcers, and Kazantseva is sure they come from radiation exposure.[36]

Nurislan Gubaidullin, 62, said his wife had died of stomach cancer several years earlier; his wife's mother, brother, sister, and niece had also died of cancer. He was told that the constant pain in his legs was caused by the high dose of radiation he received during cleanup after the 1957 Kyshtym explosion, when he plowed polluted lands on his tractor. "We've got a bad environment here. That's why we are all ill," he asserted.[37]

Officials at Mayak continue to deny the validity of accusations that link the serious health problems in the region to the activities of Mayak. Their quotes in articles by more recent visitors are nearly identical to those I heard from officials 10 years earlier. Here is an excerpt from Ann Imse's conversation with Yevgeny Ryzhkov (who was still Mayak's spokesman a decade after my own interviews with him) and another Ozersk employee:

> Mayak spokesman Ryzhkov insists the bad health among the plant's neighbors has nothing to do with radiation. He and fellow Mayak worker Vadim Borodin, now 75, cite themselves as proof, saying they're not suffering from radiation, despite higher contamination than these complaining civilians. "I'm 64 years old, and of course I have illnesses," Ryzhkov said. But he blames them on his genes, on smoking, on drinking. "The civilians should be blaming their unhealthy lifestyle, not radiation," he said. "People think they are receiving high doses, but it's stress. They think they are victims, and they need medical and psychological care."[38]

Not all of Russian officialdom has denied the terrible predicament of the Chelyabinsk radiation victims. The Chernobyl law, which mandated the relocation of all victims of the Chernobyl accident, as well as monetary compensation, applies also to all victims of the Chelyabinsk disasters, thanks to many years of tireless efforts by Chelyabinsk environmental activists. Implementation of that law in regard to Chelyabinsk victims, however, has required the environmentalists' constant vigilance and struggle, but without much success. In 1994, in the spirit of the law, the administration of the Chelyabinsk region passed a resolution to build a new village farther away from the Techa River, where Muslyumovo victims living in the most contaminated areas of the village could relocate. However, 11 years later the resolution still has not been implemented fully. For instance, as of February 2006, at the time of this writing, the 444 families in Muslyumovo who lived in the most contaminated areas of the village and who agreed to move to safer territory still awaited the necessary funding.

In December 2003 Grigory Yavlinsky and Sergei Mitrokhin, leaders of the opposition political party most closely associated with Russia's environmental activists, brought this issue to the attention of the highest authority in Russia, President Vladimir Putin, in a private meeting. As a result, Putin delegated the minister of atomic energy, Alexander Rumyantsev, to allocate funding for relocation. The problem is that ultimately relocation is contingent on the Chelyabinsk regional government developing and implementing a plan of action, which it has not done so far.[39]

In Russia today we hear controversy over the prospect of further contamination from the importation of foreign nuclear waste for reprocessing and storage. Arguments abound for and against this new trend: a potential source of huge revenues as well as further contamination. This is a major issue for environmental activists, who refer to this trend as "transforming plutonium bombs into a plutonium economy." On this issue, according to opinion polls conducted by ROMIR Monitoring, a market research company, the environmentalists have the support of 90% of the Russian population who are against the import of foreign nuclear waste.[40]

The importation of nuclear waste attracts billions of dollars to Russia's nuclear weapons sites and their closed townships, once enclaves of prosperity but now financially struggling communities, not much better off than the nearby historically poor towns and villages. Vladimir Slivyak, cochair of Ecoprotection in Russia, maintains that the importation of nuclear waste is "for the benefit of a small group in the nuclear power industry to the detriment of future Russian generations."[41]

This is how the spokesman for Ozersk's nuclear facilities, Yevgeny Ryzhkov, frames the issue: "'Our reprocessing techniques have been polished to perfection. . . . We have been doing this for 30 years with no negative effect on the environment.' Besides, he says that Mayak can afford the costly procedures of environmental cleanup only by reprocessing more spent nuclear fuel. 'As soon as we get more spent nuclear fuel to reprocess, we will thrive.'"[42] Furthermore, Ryzhkov claims that Mayak will never completely shut down. It is the only Russian factory making "certain nuclear parts for the military," making radioactive isotopes, reprocessing spent nuclear fuel, and "diluting uranium from Russian bombs to less-enriched uranium for power plants."[43]

Some locals believe they see evidence that Mayak continues to contaminate the area. Imse quotes Garifulle Khabibullin, an ailing villager from the Techa and a tractor driver at the time of the 1957 explosion who helped with the cleanup. He claims: "Sometimes, the river rises in the morning even when it has not rained, and by noon, it's back to normal level. . . . I'm sure they're dumping."[44]

In Russia's contemporary political climate it is much harder than it was more than a decade ago to investigate such claims. As Imse notes: "Reports of the death toll have disappeared. Doctors who spoke openly during the 1990s have stopped talking. Mayak officials deny that the plant's neighbors are being contaminated." A Tatar village mullah reflects the sentiments of those in Chelyabinsk, who have no reliable source of accurate information about their health risks as the neighbors of nuclear weapons facilities but have deduced from their life experiences that they are victims: "The government and authorities of the Chelyabinsk region are trying to forget this. But we in the villages will never forget this hell. Our sicknesses and daily funerals don't let us forget it!" [45]

Conclusion

There are no hopeful signs that anytime soon the people of Chelyabinsk will penetrate the culture of secrecy and denial in Russia's nuclear weapons industry to understand the full extent of the environmental and health consequences of the arms race, let alone mitigate the damage.

During the brief period of unprecedented openness about these problems right before and after the breakup of the Soviet Union, we learned that huge nuclear accidents had taken place in the 1950s and 1960s, that they were far bigger than the Chernobyl explosion in 1986, and that they affected a much larger population. When that secret was exposed, people began thinking of themselves as the victims of friendly fire—of Soviet bombs meant for the enemy but turned on the nation's own citizens. When they realized that other nuclear powers knew about the 1957 Kyshtym explosion long before it was revealed to the Soviet people, antinuclear environmental activists lamented that, if not for the culture of secrecy maintained by all nuclear powers, international pressure might have prevented subsequent accidents, including Chernobyl. In the period of openness officials were cooperative in sharing information and opening doors to more data.

Just a few years later it became impossible for me and others to predict official responses to fact-finding research in this area. One day you thought you had permission for research, but by the end of the day you did not. In the past decade, the anti-Western sentiments have increased and become a significant aspect of the political terrain in Russia, especially in relation to the issues covered in this chapter.

That said, I do not predict that the secrecy will return to what it was in the Soviet era, at least not as long as it is possible to take officials to court for violating safety rules. For instance, in March 2006 a Russian court ordered the dismissal of the director of Mayak, Vitaly Sadovnikov, for having authorized the dumping of "tens of millions of cubic meters of liquid radioactive waste into the Techa river in 2001–2004, even though the facility had enough money to prevent it. . . . Instead of preventing the damage to the environment, Sadovnikov had spent the money on maintaining a representative office in the Russian capital and lump payments to himself."[46] Nevertheless, I see no signs of a return to the openness that Gorbachev promoted just before the fall of the USSR.

As long as secrecy and denial prevail, it will be extremely difficult to conduct independent studies to verify the extent of health hazards that can be directly related to past and current activities at the Chelyabinsk nuclear facilities. What we do know, however, is that the attitudes of survivors with regard to their predicament range from complete denial of any health risks to a heightened state of anxiety that all health problems they and their families suffer are due to significant radiation doses in the water and food chain over long periods of time. This level of anxiety, illustrated in the poignant statements conveyed in this chapter, is sufficient to warrant further research and action that can give the population credible information to help them make better choices about where to live and how to adapt their lifestyles.

Notes

1. This multidisciplinary project with colleagues at University of California–Irvine (UCI) and Washington State University was called Citizen Responses to the Environmental Consequences of Nuclear Weapons Production in the United States and Russia. Material presented in this chapter derives primarily from survey data and in-depth interviews conducted by colleagues and me, mostly in the fall and winter of 1992, in towns and villages in close proximity (from 3 to 30 miles) Mayak Chemical Combine. We surveyed 1,500 people from five sites—Chelyabinsk, Kyshtym, Muslyumovo, the closed city of Chelyabinsk-65, and Chebarkul, a noncontaminated city that was intended as a control site. A random sample was drawn from local electoral lists, which are essentially complete lists of residents in Russian population centers. Interviews were done face to face and conducted by local people specially trained for the project. Interviewers had no restricted access to informants. In Muslyumovo a local official confiscated a few of the completed questionnaires when the survey was finished. I did follow-up in-depth interviews with about 20 people in each site.

2. See Thomas B. Cochran et al., "Radioactive Contamination at Chelyabinsk-65, Russia," *Annual Review of Energy Environment* 18 (1993) 507–28; Alina Tugend, "Victims of Silence," *Orange County Register,* Close-up, June 6, 1993, pp. 1–8.

3. This information is drawn from a trip I made to this Siberian area in September 1994 when I interviewed environmental activists and officials attending a conference on post-Cold War disarmament, conversion, and security issues.

4. First International Radiological Conference, "The Environmental Consequences of Nuclear Weapons Development in the Southern Urals," Chelyabinsk, Russia, May 20–22, 1992; Second International Radiological Conference, "After the Cold War: Disarmament, Conversion and Security," Krasnoyarsk-Tomsk, Russia, Sept. 12–18, 1994; International Seminar, "Ecological Consciousness—Ecological Security," Kaluga, Russia, Sept. 23–25, 1994.

5. Gosman Kabirov, March 1993, conversation with Paula Garb, Muslyumovo.

6. Cochran et al., note 2, p. 513.

7. Cochran et al., note 2, pp. 521–22.

8. Mikhail Gladyshev, *Memoirs* (recorded by Pyotr Tryakin, 1990), unpublished manuscript.

9. Aleftina Fisko, April 1993, conversation with author, Dal'naya Dacha.

10. Sergei Lolovich, March 1993, conversation with Galina Komarova, Kyshtym.

11. Government Report on the Health of the Population of Russia in 1991, *Zelyony mir,* No. 48, Dec. 1992.

12. I participated in this as part of the UCI-Washington State University project mentioned in the introduction.

13. Russell Dalton, Paula Garb, Nicholas Lovrich, John Pierce, John Whiteley, "Chelyabinsk-Hanford Environmental Survey: Survey Highlights," press release, May 5, 1994.

14. Gulfarida Galimova, March 1993, conversation with Galina Komarova, Muslyumovo.

15. *Zelyony mir,* Dec. 1992.

16. Gosman Kabirov, presentation made to a conference of the antinuclear groups in the Socio-Ecological Union, Moscow, March 12–14, 1993.

17. A. Kabirov, "Tyomnye zakoulki rossiiskoi istorii: prestupleniya imperil" ("Dark Alleys of Russian History: Crimes of the Empire") (Kamaz: Naberezhnyi Chelny, 1993, 60).

18. See Peter S. Wenz, *Environmental Justice* (Albany: State University of New York Press, 1988); Robert D. Bullard, Ed., *Confronting Environmental Racism: Voices from the Grassroots* (Boston: South End Press, 1993); Barbara R. Johnston, *Human Rights and the Environment: Examining the Sociocultural Context of Environmental Crisis* (Society for Applied Anthropology, 1993).

19. Anonymous physician in Chelyabinsk, Sept. 1994, conversation with Galina Komarova.

20. Yevgeny Ryzhkov, Dec. 1992, conversation with author, Chelyabinsk-65.

21. Chelyabinsk-Hanford Environmental Survey, University of California–Irvine/Washington State University, May 5, 1994.

22. Igor Gul', March 1993, conversation with Galina Komarova, Kyshtym.

23. Survey Highlights, note 1.

24. Lyudmila Fatianova, presentation at the Second International Radiological Conference, Krasnoyarsk-Tomsk, Sept. 14, 1994.

25. V. F. Mazharov et al., "Some Indicators of Health among the Rural Population on Territories with Possible Critical Radiation Exposure," *Abstracts,* Second International Radiological Conference, Krasnoyarsk-Tomsk, Sept. 12–18, 1994, p. 107.

26. T. M. Matkovskaya, "Children's Health in a Radiation Zone," *Abstracts,* Second International Radiological Conference, Krasnoyarsk-Tomsk, Sept. 12–18, 1994, p. 109.

27. Karen Dorn Steele, "Downwinders—Living with Fear," *Spokesman-Review,* Spokane, WA, July 28, 1985.

28. Hugh Gusterson, *Testing Times: A Nuclear Weapons Laboratory at the End of the Cold War* (Berkeley and Los Angeles: University of California Press, 1995).

29. Hugh Gusterson, Sept. 13, 1994, conversation with author, Krasnoyarsk.

30. *Plutonium: Deadly Gold of the Nuclear Age* (Cambridge, MA: International Physicians Press, 1992, 92–94).

31. Valery Menshikov, presentation at the Second International Radiological Conference, Krasnoyarsk-Tomsk, Sept. 14, 1994.

32. This postscript is abstracted from "Russia's Radiation Victims of Cold War Weapons Production Surviving in a Culture of Secrecy and Denial," Paula Garb, in *Half-Lives and Half-Truths: Confronting the Radioactive Legacies of the Cold War,* Barbara Rose Johnston, Ed. (Santa Fe, NM: SAR, 2006).

33. Mark McDonald, 2004, "Russia Finally Acknowledging '57 Nuclear Disaster," *Seattle Times,* April 7, www.mindfully.org/Nucs/2004/Karabolka-Nuclear-Disaster23apr04.htm, 10/25/2006.

34. Anna Badkhen, 2001, "Wasting Away," www.eng.yabloko.ru/Publ/2001/Agency/tol-waste.html, 05/12/2006.

35. Galina Komarova, "Ethnic and Confessional Aspects of the 'Maiak' Accident," CIS Environment and Disarmament Yearbook (Jerusalem: Marjorie Mayrock Center for Russian, Eurasian, and East European Research, Hebrew University of Jerusalem, 2003, 1–33).

36. Ann Imse, 2003, "Legacy of Agony, Disability," http://rockymountainnews.com/drmn/world/article/0,1299,DRMN_32_1768363,00.html, 4/15/2005.

37. Badkhen, note 34.

38. Ann Imse, 2003, "Radiation Hell," www.rockymountainnews.com/drmn/world/article/0, 1299,DRMN_32_1761420,00.html, 4/15/2005.

39. Yabloko News Agency, 2005, "The Issue of Muslyumovo Discussed in the Ministry of Atomic Energy," www.chel.yabloko.ru/news/print.phtml?id=470, 10/25/2006.

40. Natalia Mironova, "Danger Links between Plutonium Bombs and Plutonium Economy: Transparency and Openness Help Society to Make a Choice," paper presented at the 2000 World Conference against the Atomic and Hydrogen Bombs, August 9, 2000, Nagasaki, Japan.

41. *Pravda*, 2003, "Hungary to Export Spent Fuel to Russia Illegally," September 11, 2003, http://english.pravda.ru/russia/economics/11-09-2003/3699-spent-0, 10/26/2006.

42. Badkhen, note 38.

43. Ann Imse, 2003, "Nuclear Cesspool," http://rockymountainnews.com/drmn/world/article/ 0,1299,DRMN_32_1768364,00.html, 4/15/2005.

44. Imse, note 38.

45. Imse, note 38.

46. Bellona, 2006, "Mayak Plant's General Director Dismissed from His Post," www.bellona. org/news/Mayak_plant_%20general_director_dismissed_from_his_post, 3/10/2006.

SNAPSHOT: Building a Clean, Green Nuclear Machine?

Barbara Rose Johnston

Most people agree that the development of clean, green energies is urgently need-ed to address climate change, solve our economic woes, and reduce our oil de-pendencies and related militarism. Many people, including many environmentalists, believe that nuclear power is one important way to achieve these goals.

In 2009 Italy and Sweden repealed a national moratorium against building new nuclear plants, a pronuclear government was voted into power in Germany, and Bangladesh, Belarus, Egypt, Indonesia, Iran, Israel, Italy, North Korea, Lithuania, Poland, Thailand, Turkey, and the United Arab Emirates all announced their intent to build their first nuclear power plants. These nations will be joining a nuclear club that generates 15% of the world's power, with plants in Argentina, Armenia, Belgium, Brazil, Bulgaria, Canada, China, Croatia, Czech Republic, Finland, France, Germany, Hungary, India, Japan, South Korea, Mexico, Netherlands, Pakistan, Romania, Russia, Slovakia, Slovenia, South Africa, Spain, Sweden, Switzerland, Taiwan, Ukraine, United Kingdom, and the United States. Some 434 commercial nuclear facilities are currently generating power, with another 54 facilities under construction, 151 in the planning stage, and another 354 being proposed. To fuel this massive expansion of the nu-clear power industry, long-abandoned uranium mines are being reopened, tailing piles are being reworked, and new mining rights contracts have been awarded to firms operating in the United States, Canada, Australia, Guatemala, Argentina, Brazil, India, Armenia, the Czech Republic, Slovakia, Finland, Russia, Ukraine, Kazakhstan, Kyrgyzstan, Mongolia, Uzbekistan, Pakistan, China, Saudi Arabia, Niger, Namibia, Malawi, Zambia, and South Africa.[1]

Is nuclear energy truly the clean, green machine that its proponents make it out to be? Is it truly cost effective? Will nuclear power finally prove to be a safe source of sustaining energy? Or will we be lured into what many see as a dance with the devil? The answer to these questions depends on how you define "clean" and what you define as an acceptable "cost."

The average cost to build a nuclear power plant in the United States is report-edly some 2 billion dollars, though a 2007 estimate by Lew Hay, chairman and CEO of Florida Power and Light, suggests, "the cost of a two-unit plant will be on the order of magnitude of $13 to $14 billion." Energy will not actually begin to flow for years—some 7–12 years after plans are approved.[2] The average cost to host nuclear power is much more difficult to quantify, especially when we factor in degenerative health and other impacts over the entire nuclear fuel chain. For the communities and workers that host the links in this chain—uranium mining, milling, enrichment, energy and military use, and storage of wastes—the notion that nuclear power is clean and cost effective is, simply and sadly, ludicrous. The label "no-emissions carbon footprint" ignores significant environmental effects of mining, transporta-tion, processing, using water as energy and coolant, and building, operating, and decommissioning nuclear power facilities. The label becomes even more problematic when we factor in the short- and long-term health consequences of absorbing toxic heavy metals and the radioactive nature of these exposures, and the health care costs of treating such illness and disease. There are also stewardship costs of protecting, storing, and, perhaps someday, remediating nuclear waste.

Consider, for example, Navajo uranium miners who were exposed to low-level emissions of uranium and its radioisotopes and subsequently developed of acute and chronic health problems, including lung cancer, nonmalignant respiratory diseases, lymphatic and hematopoietic cancers other than leukemia, kidney disease, miscarriage, and cleft palate and other birth defects.[3] Consider the cleanup of the 680-acre site of the Uravan uranium and vanadium mine and processing facility in Colorado, completed in September 2008, reportedly cost $120 million. The eventual decommissioning of an aged nuclear power plant is currently priced at $300 million or more per plant. Cleanup costs from mining, milling, and inevitable spills and releases associated with Manhattan Project research and Cold War militarism at 17 nuclear weapons plants have been projected in reports to Congress to be between $100 billion to $200 billion dollars—not including cleanup costs associated with nuclear weapons detonation or waste from nuclear submarines.

There are even broader costs to nuclear waste, especially considering the long-term consequences of the commercialization of waste for use in military and police actions. Depleted uranium, the uranium remaining after its use as nuclear reactor fuel, is a low-level emitting heavy metal that is used as counterweight in aircraft and radiation shields in medical radiation therapy machines. It is also used by the military and police in as defensive armor and armor-penetrating ordnance. According to the World Health Organization the behavior of depleted uranium in the body is identical to that of natural uranium. Many of the world's citizens and soldiers have absorbed through inhalation or penetration fragments of depleted uranium, which can damage lymph tissues and thus the immune system, kidneys, and developing fetuses. It can affect bones, reproductive organs, and the function of the brain and neurological system.[4]

When these kinds of concerns are used to question the wisdom of a societal dependence on nuclear power, industries and governments typically urge the public to trust science, technological innovation in nuclear power, and occupational health and safety procedures. If Tritium, strontium-90, cesium-137, radioiodine, radon, and other radiogenic materials find their way into the rivers, aquifers, soils, the atmosphere, the food chain, and the human body, they argue, "science has shown" that relatively low-level exposures pose no deadly threat.[5] But contrary evidence has emerged from declassified Cold War-era research in the United States and former Soviet Union and from the immense number of studies published in the years following the Chernobyl nuclear power plant meltdown. For example, findings from human radiation experimentation have been long buried in the classified archives of the U.S. Atomic Bomb Casualty Commission, the Department of Defense, the Department of the Interior and the Indian Public Health Services, the Department of Energy and its predecessor the Atomic Energy Commission, and other U.S. agencies.[6] Some of this research documented nuclear weapons test fallout and the movement of radionuclides through marine and terrestrial environments, the food chain, and the human body.

A few of the many health problems identified by studies conducted on the effects of nuclear weapons testing in the Marshall Islands include changes in fertility, increased rates of birth defect, increased rates of cancers, physical and mental retardation, metabolic disorders, premature aging, and an array of cancers.[7]

The Marshallese medical studies were first conducted in 1954 and classified up through 1994. Declassified documents demonstrate that Atomic Energy Commission scientists fully expected adverse health effects to not only occur in the first generation of people exposed to fallout, but in the subsequent generations of people who live in a contaminated setting. The Marshallese health records bear out these expectations. Radiogenic disease in acute and chronic forms not only occur from acute exposure to ionizing radiation, but also develop following repeated exposure to low-level radiation, and are evident in the subsequent generations who inherit mutations resulting from parental exposures. Had the devastating findings of these studies been public in the 1950s, 1960s, 1970s, or even the 1980s, they would have threatened nuclear weapons development and testing programs with data that demonstrates the many adverse health effects from exposure to fallout almost certainly would have taken a different course. Furthermore, these findings, had they been public, they would have threatened a nascent nuclear power industry with evidence that low-level exposure can produce degenerative health outcomes, thus, standing in sharp contradiction to the U.S. Atomic Energy Commission's arguments that radiation is not only natural, low-level exposures are safe and perhaps beneficial to human health—and they should threaten the revival of the nuclear power industry today.

The Cold War-era pursuit of the "peaceful use of the atom" was abruptly halted following the 1986 Chernobyl catastrophe. The industry struggled for than a decade to repackage nuclear power as a social good, as economically necessary, and environmentally progressive. At the turn of the millennium, with a supportive U.S. government, the agenda of the nuclear power industry was gaining traction again. In 2001 the Nuclear Energy Institute, a lobbying organization, served as a key participant in Vice President Dick Cheney's Energy Task Force. Its policy recommendations included declaring energy a matter of national security, circumventing the environmental and social safeguards contained in the National Environmental Protection Act; increasing federal support for new nuclear power, including decreased liability in the event of accidents and public health disasters; and declaring nuclear power a carbon-free source, allowing it to earn carbon-credits. These and other goals favored by industry were included in the Bush Administration's 2005 Advanced Energy Initiative and the 2006 Energy Act. In 2007, as a result of U.S. advocacy, the European Union formally recognized new nuclear development as means to reduce greenhouse gas emissions, making the industry eligible under the carbon-credit system. Such actions created the political architecture necessary to insure the will and the fiscal means for a rebirth in the nuclear power industry.

To address public concern for the risks of nuclear power, concerted effort was made to characterize the Chernobyl catastrophe as a unique event, the result of flawed reactor designs and poorly trained workers.[8] The 2005 Chernobyl Forum report, the product of an initiative sponsored by the International Atomic Energy Commission and World Health Organization, suggests that the Chernobyl event added about 2% to the global radioactive background. Worldwide, 500,000–930,000 people received enough additional irradiation to be considered adversely affected; 9,000 died or developed radiogenic cancers, 4,000 children were operated on for thyroid cancer. Crucially, restoring confidence in the nuclear power industry, the report concluded that the degenerative public health conditions in the contaminated regions may be more closely tied to socioeconomic factors than the adverse consequences of Chernobyl exposure per se, and the catastrophe, in terms of human health, was not as significant as previously thought.

Declassification, greater transparency, and new research efforts and methodologies has produced revised assessments for the volume and nature of radionuclides released, recognized additional impacts from continued emissions, and generated new findings on the extent and impact of other isotopes in the fallout. These findings include the recognition that 3 billion people live in regions contaminated by Chernobyl's radionuclides. More than half the surface area of 13 European countries and 30% of eight other countries have been contaminated by Chernobyl fallout. The health of some 50 million people worldwide has been adversely affected—for every case of thyroid cancer there are about 1,000 other cases of thyroid gland pathology that causes multiple endocrine illness. Post-Chernobyl studies confirm increased morbidity, impairment, and disability; oncological disease; accelerated aging; and increased nonmalignant disease (blood, lymph, cardiovascular, metabolic, endocrine, immune, respiratory, urogenital, bone and muscle, nervous system, ocular, digestive, and skin). In their 2009 review of findings from post-Chernobyl research on genetic change, increased rates of genetic disorders, and increased congenital abnormalities conducted by Ukranian, Belarussian, and Russian National Academy of Science members, scientists and physicians concluded:

> The genetic consequences of the Chernobyl catastrophe will impact hundreds of millions of people, including: (a) those who were exposed to the first release of short-lived radionuclides in 1986 (an estimated 50 million people worldwide); (b) those who live and will continue to live in the territories contaminated by Stronium-90 and Cesium-137, as it will take no fewer than 300 years for the radioactive level to decrease to background; (c) those who will live in the territories contaminated by PU [plutonium] and Am [Americum], as millennia will pass before that deadly radioactivity decays; and (d) children of irradiated parents for as many as seven generations (even if they live in areas free from Chernobyl radionuclide fallout).[9]

Science, in its funding, production, and public policy application, is the product of social desire, cultural beliefs, and political-economic aspirations. On the question of whether nuclear power is truly "green" energy, science is easily manipulated. If green is defined as low-carbon and the temporal frame is limited to the operating life of the power plant, we get one answer. If green is defined as healthy for people and their planet now and in the future, we get a very different answer.

When we consider the cost of energy transitions, we need to ask, what is the cost of degenerative health that extends across generations? Such costs are not simple matters of money, nor even of ill health. Consider the Marshallese experience. Extremely high rates of cancer, degenerative conditions, miscarriage and infertility, congenitally deformed children—such conditions have societal costs as families struggle with raising physically disabled children, caring for increasingly feeble elderly, suffer from the fear and anxiety of additional exposures, and confront the reality of intergenerational effects. What are the social, economic, and cultural costs of living with radiogenic illnesses? Of the loss of access to radioactive lands and foods that sustained life and cultural traditions? What are the costs of a nation that cannot fully develop, constrained and stigmatized by its nuclear past? What are costs of failure for future generations when our reliance upon human ingenuity proves woefully misplaced and we fail to develop the medical care, cleanup strategies, and new technologies for transmutation and detoxification of medium and high-level wastes?

Can we truly afford this clean, green new nuclear industry?

Notes

1. See World Information Service on Energy—Uranium Project website reports, especially the maps that depict mining and expansion of the nuclear power industry, www.wise-uranium.org/index.html, 05/31/10.

2. Reported in "How Much Will New Nuclear Power Plants Cost?" Benjamin K. Sovacool, *Scitizen*, November 2, 2008, http://scitizen.com/future-energies/how-much-will-new-nuclear-power-plants-cost-_a-14-2287.html, 05/31/10.

3. See D. Brugge, T. Benally, E. Yazzie-Lewis, *The Navajo People and Uranium Mining* (Albuquerque, NM: University of New Mexico, 2007).

4. W. Briner, "The Toxity of Depleted Uranium," *International Journal of Environmental Research and Public Health*, 2010, January; 7(1): 303–13; M. S. Peragalloa, F. Listab, G. Sarnicolac, F. Marmod, A. Vecchionea, "Cancer Surveillance in Italian Army Peacekeeping Troops Deployed in Bosnia and Kosovo, 1996–2007: Preliminary Results," *Cancer Epidemiology*, 2010, February; 34(1): 47–54.

5. The Nuclear Energy Institute, for example, proudly proclaims on its website that "Nuclear energy is America's largest source of clean-air, carbon-free electricity, producing no greenhouse gases or air pollutants." Nuclear energy and the environment fact sheet, www.nei.org/resourcesandstats/documentlibrary/protectingtheenvironment/factsheet/nuclearenergyandtheenvironment, 05/31/10. See also the U.S. Department of Energy's "Low-Dose Radiation Research Program: Frequently Asked Questions," http://lowdose.energy.gov/faqs.aspx, 05/31/10.

6. Advisory Commission on Human Radiation Experimentation (ACHRE), *Final Report of the Advisory Committee on Human Radiation Experiments* (New York: Oxford University Press, 1996).

7. Summarized in Barbara Rose Johnston, ". . . More Like Us Than Mice: Radiation Experiments with Indigenous Peoples," *Half-lives and Half-truths—Confronting the Radioactive Legacies of the Cold War*, B. R. Johnston, Ed. (Santa Fe, NM: SAR Press, 2007, 25–54); see also Barbara Rose

Johnston and Holly M. Barker, *Consequential Damages of Nuclear War: The Rongelap Report* (Walnut Creek, CA: Left Coast Press, 2008). Holly Barker chronicles the legacy of the Marshall Islands in Chapter 15 of this book.

8. See, for example, World Nuclear Association "Chernobyl Accident," www.world-nuclear.org/info/chernobyl/inf07.html, 05/31/10.

9. Citing Alexy V. Yablokov, Vassily B. Nesterenko, and Alexy V. Nesterenko, *Chernobyl— Consequences of the Catastrophe for People and the Environment* (Boston: Blackwell Publishing and the New York Academy of Sciences, 2009, 77).

CHAPTER 17

Climate Change, Culture Change, and Human Rights in Northeastern Siberia[1]

Susan A. Crate

The Viliui Sakha are native agropastoralist horse and cattle breeders inhabiting the Viliui River regions of northwestern Sakha Republic, northeastern Siberia, Russia. It was in the summer of 2003, well into my second decade of study and research with Viliui Sakha, that I first heard my research partners testify to the local effects of global climate change.[2] Since that time, then, Sakha have continued to speak about the "softening"[3] of their climate and increasing summer precipitation, both of which are affecting their ability during the brief window of summer to harvest enough hay to winter their herds. As a researcher who works with indigenous[4] communities[5] dependent on the natural environment in their day-to-day livelihoods I find myself increasingly questioning my role in facilitating adaptive responses.[6] Questions of my complicity arise in the midst of witnessing and recording testimonies of the differential consequences of global climate change that is largely fueled by consumer-driven lifestyles. Increasingly, my response has been to shape and voice my field experiences in Arctic and sub-Arctic communities with a dual purpose: to convince home audiences to move toward a carbon-free, sustainable society[7] and to strengthen non-Western and indigenous voices in the broader effort to affect political action and bring attention to climate justice and human rights.

My own "ethnographic moment"[8] occurred when I heard a Sakha elder[9] recount the age-old story of *Jyl Oghuha* (Bull of Winter), which explains the extreme 100°C annual temperature range of Sakhas's subarctic habitat.[10] Sakha personify winter in the form of the *Jyl Oghuha*, a white bull with blue spots, huge horns, and frosty breath. In early December the *Jyl Oghuha* arrives from the Arctic Ocean to hold temperatures at their coldest (−60° to −65°C; −76° to −85°F) for two months. Although I had heard the story many times before, this time it had an unexpected ending:

> The bull of winter is a legendary Sakha creature whose presence explains the turning from the frigid winter to the warming spring. The legend tells that the bull of winter, who keeps the cold in winter, loses his first horn at the end of January as the cold begins to let

go to warmth, then his second horn melts off at the end of February and finally, by the end of March, he loses his head as spring is sure to have arrived. It seems that now with the warming, perhaps the bull of winter will no longer be. (Male Sakha elder, b. 1935)[11]

Both the transformation of their symbolic culture[12] (represented here by *Jyl Oghuha*) and of their subsistence culture (the increasing challenge of maintaining their herds as warming continues) reframe the implications of unprecedented global climate change. Global climate change, its causes, effects, and amelioration are intimately and ultimately about culture—climate change is caused by the multiple drivers of Western consumer culture, transforms symbolic and subsistence cultures, and will be forestalled only via a cultural transformation from degenerative to regenerative consumer behavior.

Encountering Global Climate Change in Viliui Sakha Communities

Sakha are a Turkic-speaking people whose ancestors migrated from Central Asia to southern Siberia around 900, then migrated northward, along the Lena River, to their present homeland beginning in the 1200s. They inhabit a subarctic region character-ized by continuous permafrost with annual temperature fluctuations of 100° Celsius from −60°C (−76°F) in winter to +40°C (104°F) in summer.[13] Viliui Sakha show a high level of adaptive capacity. With their northern move Sakha adapted their horse and cattle breeding subsistence to the subarctic climate by keeping their cows in barns nine months of the year and harvesting winter fodder for their herds in the brief summer. Russians began colonizing the Viliui regions in the mid-1600s, annexing indigenous lands, taking resources, and demanding *iasak* or fur tribute from all local inhabitants, which increased pressure on their already energy-intensive subsistence practices.

Far greater challenges for Viliui Sakha came in the last century of Soviet and now post-Soviet regimes. Sovietization involved both regional industrial exploitation and the transformation of kin-based, household-level production systems first into col-lectives and then into agro-industrial state farms by the mid-1950s. Collectivization concentrated settlement patterns[14] and brought changed subsistence practices from indigenous, time-tested, and ecologically based methods to an agro-industrial pro-duction system. Other effects of collectivization and state farm consolidation include: (1) the loss of indigenous ecological knowledge; (2) the loss of use of vast areas of land, rendered too distant from farm centers; (3) dependence on modern transpor-tation to reach necessary resources; (4) environmental stress in populated areas due to the concentration of wastes; (5) the radial depletion of adjacent resources; and (6) the dissolution of family/clan interdependence in the redirection of labor to the state farm, whose sole objective was producing meat and milk for the diamond industry.

For Viliui Sakha, Sovietization also meant diamond mining, which, like all Soviet-period industrialization, was not confined by environmental laws and regulations.[15] It contaminated local drinking water with heavy metals and phenols and local air with nuclear fallout.[16] Because large amounts of electric energy were needed for the mining industry the government built the Viliui GES (hydroelectric station), the reservoir of which flooded 356,000 acres of prime fields and woodlands contain-ing haying, pasturing, and hunting areas and economically valuable timberlands. The government imported workers from western parts of the USSR, mostly from Ukraine, Byelorussia, and European Russia, to supply the manpower. This increased the overall population of the Viliui regions and diversified their ethnic make-up.

In the early 1990s, with the collapse of the Soviet Union, the majority of local and regional state farm directors in the Viliui regions agreed to disband their farms. Overnight, village populations went from conditions of near-full employment and ample larders to unemployment and empty shelves. In response Viliui Sakha communities reinstated household-level food production via a system termed "cows-and-kin," which focused on keeping cows and exchanging labor and products with kin.[17] A typical cows-and-kin arrangement involves the interdependence of an elderly parental household that keeps cows and performs all daily tasks with one or several young households, usually the elders' childrens', who receive all their needed meat and milk products in exchange for performing the labor-intensive work of harvesting annual forage for the herd. Cows-and-kin, in some ways a return to pre-Soviet subsistence, represents a unique adaptation that is historically founded, environmentally sustainable, and culturally resilient and offers a sound mode of household-level food production for contemporary rural Viliui Sakha.

Today households continue to rely heavily on subsistence production, supplementing a mainstay diet of meat and milk products with gardens and greenhouses, forage (hunting, fishing and gathering), and other domesticates including horses, pigs, and chickens. Village households depend on a mixed cash economy with most of their cash originating from state transfer payments in the form of state subsidies and pensions. Monetary resources are freely shared, most often elder pensions shared freely with young kin households. Since the 1991 fall of the Soviet Union inhabitants have had more or less open access to Western media sources and a full array of consumer goods. Sakha in both urban and rural communities partake increasingly of a "consumer lifestyle." Consumption has become a means to asserting one's identity and status within the community.

Global Climate Change Encounters

From 2003 to 2006 I facilitated a community sustainability project with Viliui Sakha aimed to define sustainability on a local level and then identify barriers preventing communities from realizing those definitions. Barriers were many, but the local effects of global climate change proved to be the most difficult set of problems confronting local communities. In our 2004 survey a full 90% of all participants expressed their concern about local changes in weather and climate patterns.[18] Many offered their observations on dramatic and often unheard of changes in their local environment and voiced fears that these changes threaten subsistence strategies and survival.

The research included an elder knowledge project that brought youth together with elders to explore local ecological knowledge and to bolster understandings of sustainability.[19] Owing to the overwhelming concern about climate change, in our final year this project turned to focus on elder observations of climate change and its impact on lives and livelihood, thoughts about causality, and visions for the future.[20] Findings demonstrated that elders possess in-depth knowledge about the climate and how it is changing. Given the absence of any regular scientific monitoring of local climatic indicators,[21] village elders' knowledge represents a vital and nuanced source of on-the-ground conditions in the region. For example:

> The climate is definitely different from before. When I was little, the winters were very cold, minus 50–60 degrees. When we spit, it froze before it hit the ground and flying birds sometimes would freeze and die. The summer was a wonderful hot temperature and the

hay you just cut would dry very quickly. In the last few years the climate has changed. We have rain, rain, rain all the time and winter comes late and so does spring. For people who live with a short summer when there needs to be the right weather to accomplish all for the winter and there is cool rainy times so that the hay does not dry and has to sit and sit and the quality is bad because of that. It is the right time for haying but the conditions are all wrong. (Male Sakha elder, b. 1938)

What changes are people observing? First, Sakha elders reported that they can't read the weather anymore:

From long ago we could read the weather and know what weather would come according to our "Sier-Tuom" [Sakha sacred belief system]. But we can't do that anymore. Before we could tell from the star constellations, from the direction that the moon rose, where the moon is in constellation patterns. Now if you try and read based on that old way, you cannot predict the weather. It does not follow the old patterns. It used to explain everything for us but now it can't tell anything. (Female Sakha elder, b. 1942)

Second, the timing of the seasons had changed, jeopardizing winter survival. Spring and fall now come several weeks late:

When I was little, we finished school on the 18th of May. It was 1949–50 and on 18th May, there was already new grass and the cows were grazing. Since then spring has been later and later and later. Back then on the ninth of May the river ice would flow. Now it doesn't flow until the end of May or early June. (Female Sakha elder, b. 1939)

Third, elders said that climate variations are less extreme. It was during these testimonies that they referred again and again to the legendary Bull of Winter:

The climate has softened. Winters have warmed and summers are not so warm. All is softer. The north is especially warming I think. Then it will be cold in the winter and suddenly get warm in the winter. It was never like that when I was a child. Strong cold held for months. We have the legend about the bull of winter losing it horns. (Male Sakha elder, b. 1925)

Finally, elders reported a tendency toward long periods of calm and a relative lack of humidity:

The weather changes very very suddenly. For example, this year it was hot in June then very cold and windy. Fall is also sudden. Snow will suddenly fall and then there will be very warm days. Then, in winter it was −40 degrees and the next day, very suddenly, it was +3 or +4 degrees. (Male Sakha elder, b. 1938)

In other words, the heat is no longer dry but laden with moisture that is stifling: "Before it got very hot also, like it does now, but there was air—now it gets hot and you can't breathe [humidity]." Both the lack of calms and of humidity make the Viliui Sakhas's environment that much more challenging. Although these barriers are still surmountable, elders report that their family members are spending more time in cyclical work due to the increased challenge that these climate changes pose.

Several elders also commented on the arrival of new species from the South and the loss of familiar species. The new species include a variety of insects that prey on many of the garden and forage plants that Sakha depend on. Other common observations of local change included increased rain during the haying season, too much winter snow, more thunder, a change in the quality of sunlight and many new insects.

Many elders correlated these changes with their people's declining health and an increase in human diseases.

How is changing climate affecting people's daily lives? First and foremost, elders described the effects on harvesting forage for their animals:

> It ruins the hay harvesting when it rains for two months solidly. There is no winter forage for our cows and horses. If you keep animals you have to find food for them, and for us that is hay. And even if you plan to work every day at the hay, the weather keeps you from it. Every day it is raining. . . . The land is going under water and the hay lands are smaller and smaller and if you keep a lot of animals, it is very hard. So tied with the climate change, the most challenging moment is the hay lands shrinking, going under the water. The first problem is that the land areas are shrinking and the second problem is that the quality of the hay is worse. The hay itself has less nutrition and then when it is cut and lays and gets wet and dries many times, it also loses its nutritious quality. (Male Sakha elder, b. 1932)

They described the effects on their gardens and the negative impact that climate change has had on their ability to raise enough food to see them through the long winter:

> Potatoes rot in the ground and because there are many new insects that you can't get rid of, the greenhouse vegetables grown very poorly with the cold nights and too much water. The garden was very late. The water and cold kept us from planting potatoes until mid-June and we usually plant then by Nicole (May 22).[22] Other people had lots of water in their field and didn't plant the potatoes until July. (Female Sakha elder, b. 1930)

They described how difficult it has become for their horses spend all winter outside and to dig through the snow to find winter fodder. In the last decade elders have witnessed increasing amounts of snow (a result of warmer winter temperatures)[23] and an impervious ice layer beneath the snow (from a freeze/thaw that occurs commonly in the fall with warming):

> Then in the fall, the snow falls early and then it melts and makes a layer of ice under the snow and the horses cannot feed. They can't get through the ice. It also affects them in mid-winter when they have just foaled and they can't find food. This year there was so much snow that lots of animals died. Horses especially who could not get through the deep deep snow to find their food. It is warming. (male Sakha elder, b. 1935)

Many elders also raised concern about a decline in wildlife, especially hunting stock, a supplemental food source for many contemporary households that largely depend on household food production in the post-Soviet context:

> We hunters can't hunt. There were about the same amount of rabbits as in other years this winter. I hunt them and we eat them, I share with neighbors, send them to Suntar and to the capital. I caught over 50 this year. I go trapping in January when the snow is thinner. But as the snow is deeper I can't go and the deep snow is bad because dogs can't run and horses can't walk. Then in spring and fall, before the snow, hunters also can't hunt when there is so much mud and boggy land. (Male Sakha elder, b. 1933)

Not only are hay, hunting, and foraging areas diminished because of flooding, all land areas are threatened. In one of our four research villages there is deep concern about how water in inundating the grazing and gardening areas in the village center: "all the water ruins the usable areas near our homes—it diminishes all our land—with all the water, no one has any land anymore." We heard many accounts of land sinking, including this one of an island near the village of Kuukei:

> There is one strange thing I want to mention. We have an island on the lake, but now it has fallen. My deceased husband used to say the island will start to have all those depressions as the ice melts and go under water. And then a few years later the island will cease to be. I have been watching that island for the last 10 years, and I see this happening. (Female Sakha elder, b. 1933)

Beyond the question of whether the sinking is because of permafrost melting, and whether the melting is in fact due to climate change,[24] we want to understand how the *perception* of the sinking is affecting how Viliui Sakha orient themselves to their environment. Their sense of place and their understanding of "homeland" are both directly tied to an ecosystem dependent on water in its solid state. Although feeling at home in such icy confines is foreign to many of us, it is the familiar and the understood territory of comfort for northern inhabitants. This was clear when we asked: "Isn't it good that it is not so cold in winter and not so hot in summer?" In response, elders unanimously argued the opposite:[25]

> It seems that it would be for people's comfort and for using less wood in the winter and not getting so hot in the summer. It is not bad to have warm winters, being an old person, it is great! But as Sakha people, we need strong cold here. It is how our lives are organized and how the nature works here. The big cold is good. The diseases are gone. When it is warm it snows too much and it is not warm or cold. The winter warmth affects people's blood pressure. And the heat in the summer is different, humid and very hard for people to go. It is bad for the way of life here and for survival, the nature, people, animals and plants here are supposed to have very cold winters and very hot dry summers. That is the best for all life here. (Female Sakha elder, b. 1929)

One of the arguments of misinformed critics, who defy any urgency to action against global warming, is that northern peoples will probably be happy that their home temperatures are not so cold. This view is naive. Humans live and thereby learn a sense of place and homeland regardless of physical conditions. They may grow to prefer different conditions, but their sense of place and perception of home is bound in where they spent their formative years. Viliui Sakha elders often joke that the softening climate will bring them relief, but in fact they are fully aware that the climate regime their ancestors were used to is key to perpetuation of their people and the survival of local flora and fauna.

All the elders we talked to felt that conditions would progressively get worse. Many made a connection between warming and health: "The worst part is that diseases will multiply in the future if it continues to get warmer and warmer. People's lives will get shorter with all the disease, and no one will be able to keep animals here anymore" (Female Sakha elder, b. 1944).

Some linked local effects of global warming to the breakdown of their contemporary social fabric:

> People's attitudes will get worse and worse and things will go crazy. People's character is already changing. The way they relate to others has changed and I think it is because of the climate change. When I was young, Sakha didn't kill each other and when people beat each other up it was big news. The way people are so violent these days I think is connected to the change in air and climate. (Female Sakha elder, b. 1930)

Such connections is not unfounded. Similar cases of contextualization—the ways in which people associate changes in the natural environment with changes in their social environment—exist in other settings in northern Russia.[26] Studies in biometeorology are making such correlations in other cultural contexts.[27]

We also solicited elders' perceptions of the causes of global climate change. Many cited the reservoir of the Viliui hydroelectric station; however, studies have shown that the presence of the reservoir only results in a microclimatic change that would not include the extent of changes observed by the elders. Most elders agreed that the climate is changing owing to a host of other reasons: "Maybe from the mining activity and the electricity makers, the hydro-stations, it all affects. They say the Sea [hydro-station reservoir] affects us but I don't agree. The natural climate is all mixed up" (Male Sakha elder, b. 1933).

When Viliui Sakha experience detrimental environmental phenomena they blame either nature or humans, but more often the latter. When elders talk about the human causes, it is important to remember that in their lifetimes they have seen the introduction and the widespread use of technology. They were born and raised on remote homesteads without electricity and now live surrounded by most varieties of technology. It is an easy step to relate the changes in their physical environment with the entry and advancement of this technology. Explaining the changes as "caused by nature" also makes sense given that they live in a highly variable climate to begin with and know there have been climatic changes in the past. Some commented that climate change is occurring because of both natural and human-induced causes.

Natural causes elders talked about included changes from nature itself; the changing direction of the earth and all planets, each with a magnetic pull that is affecting us; changing sky and clouds; and the melting of Arctic Ocean ice, bringing lots of clouds and rain. Human-induced causes elders mentioned included the "breaking" of the atmosphere by rockets and bombs that go up into the sky; humans going into the cosmos too much and mixing up the sky; the changing of the atmosphere by something in the atmosphere that makes it all very warm; all the "technika" people are using that fouls the air; the holes in the ozone and the other wreckage done with all our technology; and too many atom bombs.

At first these elders' ideas may seem irrelevant to western scientific thought on the subject, but they are tangentially relevant and culturally provocative. Some elders provided, for example, explanations that related to phenomena other than global climate change. One elder commented: "The elders said it was like this last century also, and they say that every century the same conditions come around—100 years ago also the land was under water." Sakha also understand that there have been dry and wet years:

> They said that we would be having dry years now, but it is the opposite. Very wet years have come, lots of rain. Not in the spring when we need it, but in the summer when it gets in the way. There are many times as much water as there should be in the wet years, and if it continues like this, we will all go under water. We had the wet years, and so it should be dry by now. (Male Sakha elder, b. 1932)

Several elders explained that the waterlogged fields had more to do with Sakhas' negligence to work the land as they did in centuries past: "Before—in the Soviet time and before that—since our ancestors first came to these parts, we would make the fields so they were free of water, but not now." However, the inundation of fields by water in the context of all the other observed changes owing to climate change refute these explanations.

Many of the elders' testimonies reveal that they are understanding local climate change not only based on personal observations but also by integrating knowledge from other sources. One source was an ancient Sakha proverb: "Tiiiekhtere ool uieghe, khachchagha Buus baiaghal irieghe," meaning "They will survive until the day when the Arctic Ocean melts." Several elders recollected this proverb when they heard of the catastrophic flooding of the Yana River in the north of the Sakha Republic in summer 2005. Residents of three villages had to relocate permanently. Reports of this incident characterized it not as an isolated phenomenon but as directly related to the fact that the Arctic Ocean is no longer freezing up completely in the winters.

In the summer that flood, I identified only two media sources specifically addressing global climate change that reached the villages. One was the British Broadcasting Company's (BBC) airing of *The Day after Tomorrow*, an action/adventure, science fiction/fantasy thriller, aired several times on local television. It is likely that many of the elders' comments about the global implications of local climate change were based on images and sound bytes from this film.

The second was an article in the republic-wide *Komsomolskaia Pravda v Yakutii* by a Dr. Trofim Maksimov, a biologist and climate scientist in the capital city, Yakutsk.[28] Maksimov has worked for several decades on climate change in the Sakha Republic. His research shows that average temperatures are warming—that in the Sakha Republic average temperatures have risen by 2–3.5°C in the last 100 years and that average winter temperatures for the same time period are 10°C warmer. This correlates directly with the elders' observations of warming. His findings also document the movement of floral species northward: Dahurian larch, the common tree species of the Sakha taiga, is moving toward the tundra, and more temperate species are coming into the Republic from the south. Again, elders have observed similar movements. Maksimov is outspoken in arguing that this warming is irreversible and demands everyone's immediate attention. Despite the comprehensive treatment and information that Maksimov offers, only a handful of Viliui inhabitants subscribe to this newspaper. The paucity of Western scientific knowledge about global climate change among the Viliui Sakha in the context of such a rapidly changing environment gives cause for concern.

Elders' testimonies to the local effects of global climate change reveal no debate about *whether* climate change is occurring. Like most indigenous cultures practicing subsistence, they are, by default, ethnoclimatologists. With a continuous stream of experiential data, they know things are changing. However, their adaptive strategies could be bolstered by more information about how and why such unprecedented change is occurring. Through our collaborations with in-country climate scientists, we know there is data that corroborates local observations with which we could conduct an information exchange in the communities. Studies show, for example, the increases in annual temperatures and precipitation, the extent and pace of permafrost degradation, an unprecedented increase of water on the land, and the preponderance of permafrost ice wedges in the Viliui regions, making these areas one of the most susceptible to permafrost degradation.

Before we can share these data in the affected communities, we need to know our audience. This is not a simple process. People's perceptions of and responses to the local effects of unprecedented global climate change are framed by their past and evolving experiences and narratives. It follows that. to be most effective in providing information, we need to "take into account a people's belief system and cosmology in addition to understanding the[ir] more mechanical adaptive strategies."[29] If we hope to find ways to strengthen local understandings about unprecedented climate change, one starting point is to develop a solid background in the community's perceptions and understandings of that change. We need to be concerned first and foremost with Viliui Sakhas's perceptions and framing of global climate change. We need to diligently explore what they are seeing these climate perturbations *with*—how they are framing these changes.[30] This is where we must begin if we hope that our research and policy can play a facilitative role in adaptation.

The Human Rights Implications of Global Climate Change

> [I]ndigenous peoples maintain special ties with their traditional lands, and a close dependence upon the natural resources provided therein—respect for which is essential to their physical and cultural survival. . . . [D]amage to these land invariably leads to serious loss of life and health and damage to the cultural integrity of indigenous peoples. (Inter-American Commission on Human Rights)

The effects of global climate change are not just about communities' or populations' capacity to adapt and exercise their resilience in the face of unprecedented change. Human, animal, and plant populations are also relocated, as in the resent resettlements of indigenous refugees to safer ground in Tuvalu, Shishmaref, and other places. Lost with those relocations are the intimate human-environment relationships that not only ground and substantiate indigenous worldviews but also work to maintain and steward local landscapes. In some cases moves also result in the loss of mythological symbols, meteorological orientations, and even the very totem and mainstay plants and animals that ground a culture.

On a temporal scale the effects of climate change are the indirect costs of imperialism and colonization—the "non-point" fallout for peoples who have been largely ignored. These are the same peoples whose territories that have long been a dumping ground for uranium, industrial trash heaps, and transboundary pollutants. Climate change is environmental colonialism at its fullest development—its ultimate scale—with far-reaching social and cultural implications. Climate change is the result of global processes that were neither caused nor can be mitigated by the inhabitants of the majority of the most climate-sensitive world regions. Thus indigenous peoples and other place-based peoples find themselves at the mercy of—and having to adapt to—changes far beyond their control.

To what extent can resilient cultures adapt to unprecedented climate change? Indigenous peoples are not passive victims but have been actively advocating for themselves. In 2007 the Inuit Circumpolar Council (ICC) petitioned the United States to consider the human rights issues of climate change in the Arctic and the role the United States must play in reducing greenhouse gases. ICC Chair Sheila Watt-Cloutier explicitly posits climate change as a human rights issue:

> Inuit are taking the bold step of seeking accountability for a problem in which it is difficult to pin responsibility on any one actor. However, Inuit believe there is sufficient evidence to demonstrate that the failure to take remedial action by those nations most responsible for the problem does constitute a violation of their human rights—specifically the rights to life, health, culture, means of subsistence, and property.[31]

There are places such as northern Russia, however, where self-government and self-determination have no legacy and communities are not proactive on these issues.

Climate change raises moral and ethical questions about vulnerability, inequality, and fairness.[32] In international negotiations, power relations between the rich and powerful and the marginalized are played out, and these issues of justice desperately need to be centralized. Fairness in adaptation is key in the developing world, where the most vulnerable—the old, young, poor, and those dependent on climate-sensitive resources—can either benefit from or become more vulnerable as a result of international action. Although there is a significant role for social capital in adaptation, various social conditions and relationships present distinct risks of vulnerability.[33] Thus, we must not be over confident about the structural strength of traditional knowledge and cultural capacity to adapt.

Conclusion

Ironically, climate change offers humanity an opportunity for a quantum leap in sustainable development and peace making.[34]

Whether we are field researchers encountering social justice and human rights issues with our field collaborators, policymakers struggling to build political will, or graduate students dipping our toes in the vast issue of climate change that stretches far into our collective future, we need to take a positive, productive approach to creating change. If international cooperation is strengthened in response to the threats to human security and human rights posted by climate change, then international stability, governance, and development can also benefit.[35] The changes I am encountering with Viliui Sakha are the same sorts of changes being experienced by indigenous groups inhabiting climate-sensitive ecosystems and depending on subsistence resources worldwide. We must work rigorously, side by side with communities on local scales, to address this immense threat to culture and human rights.

Notes

1. I wish to acknowledge the Viliui Sakha communities and specialists with whom I have worked since 1991 and without whom this work would not be possible. The research for this chapter is based on ongoing support from the National Science Foundation, and most immediately from two three-year projects, #0710935 (2007–2010) and #0532993 (2003–2006) Office of Polar Programs, Arctic Social Science division. I acknowledge and thank NSF for this support. This chapter is based on previously published materials, in large part, an amalgamation of two pieces: Susan Crate, "Gone the Bull of Winter: Grappling with the Cultural Implications of and Anthropology's Role(s) in Global Climate Change," *Current Anthropology*, 2008, 49(4) and Susan Crate and Mark Nuttall, Eds., *Anthropology and Climate Change: From Encounters to Actions* (Walnut Creek, CA: Left Coast Press, 2009).

2. Three clarifications here and throughout: (1) I use "research partners" in the text to refer to the people and communities I conduct research with. (2) In this chapter I am referring to anthropogenic climate change, attributed directly or indirectly to human activity in accordance with the Framework Convention on Climate Change's use of the term (IPCC 2007: 20). Global climate change is a complex, changing phenomenon. It is beyond this chapter's scope to detail the science and recent findings. I will, however, provide a brief overview, based on the Arctic Climate Impact Assessment (ACIA 2005). Scientists studying ice cores and other evidence have ascertained the correlation between concentrations of CO_2 in the atmosphere and temperature. Since the industrial

revolution, global CO_2 concentrations have risen 35%. Average global temperature have increased 0.6°C, and added CO_2 at present rates will result in temperature of 1.4–5.8°C in the next century. Climatic changes are expected to result in a dramatic change in air and ocean currents, sea level rise, and unpredictable precipitation events. These changes will significantly affect human, animal, and plant communities. (3) I recognize that for some of my readers, using the term *global climate change* may be misleading, because it suggests a single phenomenon when global climate change is a complex of multiple processes, dimensions, influences, feedbacks, and impacts. However, it is beyond the scope of this chapter to define the exact combination of processes involved each time I use the term.

3. *Softening* refers to a lessening of the extremes of the climate, most often referring to temperature highs and lows.

4. I use the term *indigenous* as defined in Article 1 of the International Labor Organization's "Convention Concerning Indigenous and Tribal Peoples in Independent Countries" (ILO No. 169),

> People who are regarded as indigenous on account of their descent from the populations which inhabited the country, or a geographical region to which the country belongs, at the time of conquest or colonization or the establishment of present State boundaries and who, irrespective of their legal status, retain some or all of their own social, economic, cultural and political institutions.

Also, I use the terms *indigenous, aboriginal,* and *native* interchangeably (Michael Brown, *Who Owns Native Culture?* [Cambridge, MA: Harvard University Press, 2003].

5. I use *community/communities* in a general way to refer to a population that correlates to a specific ethnicity or geographic location, that is, "indigenous community" or "village community." These are not necessarily communities that are unanimously united in their interests and speak with one voice. Different inhabitants have different opinions, conflicting agendas, and different connections to the centers of power.

6. My intent here is not to create a polar contrast between indigenous peoples on the one hand and Western peoples on the other. On the contrary, my aim is to show the complex and multisited ways that indigenous peoples shape and are shaped by being within the world system in order to highlight both the tenacity and the susceptibility of their cultural survival—which itself depends on an intimate knowledge of and connection to the natural world—the very relationship that substantiates their utility for adaptation and resilience.

7. I use *consumer culture* generically to refer to any culture that is founded on consumption, the incessant attachment to materialistic values and/or possessions.

8. A term I use based on Stuart Kirsch's use ("Anthropology and Advocacy: A Case Study of the Campaign against the Ok Tedi Mine," *Critical Anthropology* 2002, 22:175–200) and for which he gives credit to Marilyn Strathern, "The Ethnographic Effect II," *Property, Substance, and Effect: Anthropological Essays on Persons and Things*, pp. 229–61 (London: Athlone, 1999).

9. I use *elders* differently from the popular use in the body of anthropological literature on North American First Nations and indigenous peoples. In the post-Soviet context elders do not enjoy a degree of authority within their community that corresponds to that, for example, of Inuit elders. Sakha elders belong to a specific age cohort (55+). Only in recent years, with conscious efforts to recall and revive their knowledge, are elders gaining some degree of authority in their settlements; Susan Crate, "Elder Knowledge and Sustainable Livelihoods in Post-Soviet Russia: Finding Dialogue across the Generations," *Arctic Anthropology*, 2006, 43(1): 40–51.

10. There are several portrayals of the Bull of Winter in classic Sakha ethnographic texts: "Winter, the hardest time for working people, Sakha personify in the form of a white bull

with blue spots which has huge horns and frosty breath. When this bull traveled to the spacious Sakha homeland, all in nature froze and the people and animals suffered from the cold. At the end of January, winter reached its peak. The day before the end of January, a mighty eagle arrived from the south, child of the warm sky, he scooped up snow in his nest and let out a loud cry. From the eagle's cry, the bull of winter stepped back and his horns, one by one, fell off, then, as spring approached, his head rolled off. During the ice flows, the trunk of the bull of winter swims at the bottom of the Lena to the Arctic Ocean, and the ice flow takes away the spirits of dead people and herds"; G. U. Ergis, *Ocherki pa Yakutskomy Folklory* [Essays on Yakut Folklore] (Moscow: Science Publishers, 1974).

"Jil Bull is the personification of winter in the form of a bull. Sakha believe that he comes every year from the Arctic Ocean and brings with himself cold, starvation, need, and etc. In spring, near Afanasii Day, he loses one horn, then near the second Afanasii day, he loses the other. Whether he dies in the spring or returns to the Arctic Ocean—the Sakha either forgot or did not know"; A. E. Kulakovskii, *Nauchni Trude* [Scientific Works] (Yakutsk: Yakutskoe Knizhnoe Izdatel'stvo, 1979).

"The freeze is definitely a bull and he has 2 horns—the first falls off on the first Afanasii Day (5 March), the second on the second Afanasii Day (24 April), and on the third Afanasii (14 May) the whole body falls." These dates are according to the old calendar, so in our calendar would be 19 February, 10 April, 30 April, respectively; V. L. Seroshevskii, *Yakuti* [The Yakut] (Moscow: ROSSPEN, 1993 [1896]).

"The Bull of Winter: Creating the world, the Gods asked humans: 'Do you want winter to be longer or summer?' The humans answered: 'Ask our friends—the horse and bull.' The horse wanted summer longer, because in winter its legs and hooves felt very cold. But the bull wanted winter longer, because in summer heat its nose got wet. Then the Gods made winter longer and summer shorter. Having got angry, the horse kicked the bull in the nose and knocked out its upper teeth. The bull butted the horse into its side and pierced through its bile. Since that time horse have not bile and horned cattle no upper teeth"; D. K. Sivtsev, *Sakha Fol'klora: Khomyyrynn'yk* [Sakha Folklore Collection] (Novosibirsk: Nauka, 1996 [1947]).

11. All quotes are anonymous, except for birth year and gender.

12. In this article I use the term *culture* to refer to both the series of prescribed human activities and the prescribed symbols that give those activities significance; both the specific way a given people classify, codify, and communicate experience symbolically and the way that people live in accordance to beliefs, language, and history. Culture includes technology, art, science, and moral and ethical systems. All humans possess culture, and the world is made up of a diversity of cultures. Accordingly, I use the term in both its singular and plural forms.

13. In the early Tertiary period, 50 million years BP, Eurasia's climate was warm, and Europe was home to a diverse flora and fauna; A. P. Okladnikov, Yakutia (Montreal: McGill-Queens, 1970). Southern Eurasia was moist and tropical with species such as laurel, palm, eucalyptus, fig, sequoia, and a broad range of evergreen tropical plants. Fossilized remains, found in the tundra of northern Sakha, of beech, hornbeam, alder, birch, elm, maple, oak, and walnut show the former deciduous forests. In the late Tertiary/early Quaternary the climate grew markedly colder and more humid across the earth. The northern fossil record shows a shift from deciduous forest to cold-thriving species. This climatic change was partly due to tectonic transformations that produced extensive mountain ranges and the submersion of the Bering land bridge; ibid.; S. P. Suslov, *Physical Geography of Asiatic Russia* (San Francisco: Freeman, 1961).

Increased precipitation brought heavy accumulations of ice and snow in formerly temperate areas, destroying formerly rich flora and fauna. Many parts of Eurasia were covered with ice, which reached 2 km (1.24 m) in some places.

Siberia was the exception. With its protection from oceanic humidity and precipitation by high mountains to the east and south and by the cold Arctic Ocean to the north, glaciation of northeastern and central Siberia during the last ice age lagged behind Europe. Most of eastern Siberia remained free from above-ground ice shields and provided refuge for many plant and animal species that were "iced out" elsewhere. Siberia was affected by underground ice or permafrost. Mammoth, wooly rhinoceros, wild horse, and musk ox remains date the permafrost formation to that time; ibid. The eastern Siberian permafrost is a relic of the last ice age—a surrogate of the massive ice covers that were characteristic of adjacent high latitude areas. This protection also explains why Siberian permafrost extends farther south—in some cases to the same latitudes as Kiev, Paris, and Vienna—than permafrost in other parts of the contemporary world; W. Jochelson, "The Yakut: Anthropological Papers of the American Museum of Natural History," 1933, 33(2), New York.

14. This was a collaborative project involving me, one research assistant from the United States, a research assistant in each of the four villages, and the direct involvement of the communities themselves. Hence, my use of the pronoun "we."

15. D. J. Peterson, *Troubled Lands: The Legacy of Soviet Environmental Destruction* (Boulder, CO: Westview Press, 1993, 175).

16. Susan Crate, "Co-Option in Siberia: The Case of Diamonds and the Vilyuy Sakha," *Polar Geography*, 26(4) (2003): 289–307.

17. Susan Crate, *Cows, Kin, and Globalization: An Ethnography of Sustainability.* (Walnut Creek, CA: AltaMira Press, 2006) and "Viliui Sakha Post-Soviet Adaptation: A Subarctic Test of Netting's Smallholder Theory," *Human Ecology*, 2003, 31(4): 499–528.

18. We administered surveys to a stratified sample of 30% (Elgeeii: n = 63, Kutana: n = 24) of all households surveyed by Crate in 1999–2000 (Elgeeii: n = 210, Kutana: n = 79). We completed surveys in an interview context to gather demographic, economic, and employment data and to track the past decade of post-Soviet cow-keeping activity, soliciting information concerning access to land, time input for daily cow-keeping and seasonal bottlenecks, kin networks and dependence on them for labor, land, and resources, changes in herd size, cash inputs, and annual production amounts of meat, milk, and other products. The survey instrument was developed based on both the communities' definitions of sustainability generated during the first field season of the project and standardized questions used in the Survey of Living Conditions in the Arctic project (www.arcticliving conditions.org/).

19. In each of our four research villages we worked with a village research assistant who identified and invited elders in their village to participate in the project. The village research assistant was also tasked with working over the winter months with 7th- through 11th-grade students to interview, transcribe, and present the elders' stories within their communities; Susan Crate, "Elder Knowledge and Sustainable Livelihoods in Post-Soviet Russia: Finding Dialogue across the Generations," *Arctic Anthropology*, 2006, 43(1): 40–51.

20. I worked with village youth in the Kutana village and on my own in the other three villages. We approached every elder in the original elder knowledge project (n = 43), and with 10 either unavailable or declining, we interviewed 33.

21. There are regional stations that provide data on a Republic-wide level. However, these data are not translated into public information specific to the villages where these elders live.

22. May 22 (new style) is St. Nicholas Chudotvorets/ Thaumaturge. Actually there are two holidays devoted to this saint; see www.calend.ru/holidays/0/0/1354/.

23. Typically it snows in these areas from mid-September to mid-November and then again from mid-February to mid-March. In the deep winter it is too cold to snow. In the last decade or so, as winter temperatures are milder, it tends to snow for longer periods in both the fall and spring, and the cold period of no snow is increasingly briefer.

24. Many of the pastures of the Viliui Sakha communities are located in thermokarst depressions known under the local name *alaas*; Susan Crate, *Cows, Kin and Globalization: An*

Ethnography of Sustainability (Walnut Creek, CA: AltaMira Press, 2006, 9–11). *Alaas* are characterized by very specific processes of freezing and thawing, permafrost degradation but also permafrost build-up.

25. Granted shorter winters may actually be beneficial for cattle and horse breeding. Horses and cattle will spend less time in the stables and barns (and more time on the pastures) if the annual average temperature increases. However, more precipitation (snow) and a higher frequency of freezing/thawing events will have an adverse effect.

26. Timo Pauli Karjalainen and Joachim Otto Habeck, "When 'the Environment' Comes to Visit: Local Environmental Knowledge in the Far North of Russia," *Environmental Values,* 2004, 13(2): 167–86; Jussi Simpura and Galina Eremitcheva, "Dirt: Symbolic and Practical Dimensions of Social Problems in St. Petersburg," *International Journal of Urban and Regional Research,* 1997, 21(3): 476–80.

27. For a broader context for the influences of climate on psychological factors, see *International Journal of Biometeorology* and http://biometeorology.org/.

28. The *Suntaar Sonunnaar,* the regional paper that most inhabitants subscribe to if they get a paper, was lacking in information on climate change from 2003–05; Ekaterina Ivanova, "Khvatit Gasovat" [Enough Gassing], *Komsolovkaia Pravda v Yakutii,* 28 July–4 August, 2005.

29. Arlene Rosen, *Civilizing Climate* (Lanham, MD: AltaMira Press, 2007, 117).

30. See Naomi Quinn and Dorothy Holland, Eds., *Cultural Models in Language and Thought* (New York: Cambridge University Press, 1987).

31. Sheila Watt-Cloutier, "Climate Change and Human Rights," in Carnegie Institute's Human Rights Dialogue special issue on Environmental Rights, 2004, www.cceia.org/viewMedia.php/prmTemplateID/8/prmID/4445.

32. See W. Neil Adger, Jouni Paavola, Saleemul Huq, and M. J. Mace, Eds., *Fairness in Adaptation to Climate Change* (Cambridge, MA: MIT Press, 2006).

33. For example, Susan Crate, "Gone the Bull of Winter: Grappling with the Cultural Implications of and Anthropology's Role(s) in Global Climate Change," *Current Anthropology,* 2008, 49(4); Susan Crate and Mark Nuttall, Eds., *Anthropology and Climate Change: From Encounters to Actions* (Walnut Creek, CA: Left Coast Press, 2009); M. Vásquez-León, C. T. West, and T. J. Finan, "A Comparative Assessment of Climate Vulnerability: Agriculture and Ranching on Both Sides of the U.S.-Mexico Border," *Global Environmental Change,* 2003, 13: 159–73; G. Ziervogel, S. Bharwani, and T. E. Downing, "Adapting to Climate Variability: Pumpkins, People, and Policy," *Natural Resources Forum,* 2006, 30: 294–305.

34. Ben Wisner, Maureen Fordham, Ilan Kelman, Barbara Rose Johnston, David Simon, Allan Lavell, Hans Günter Brauch, Ursula Oswald Spring, Gustavo Wilches-Chaux, Marcus Moench, and Daniel Weiner, "Climate Change and Human Security," *Radix,* www.radix-online.org/cchs.html, 2007.

35. Ibid.

SNAPSHOT: Climate Change and the Small Island Experience

Holly M. Barker

Islands. The word conjures up images of warm water, the bright white sands of pristine beaches, and blissful escape from our crowded, fast-paced lives. But for many island residents, this tourist imagery of secluded enclave is an imposed ideal that for many island residents provokes an exaggerated sense of isolation and abandonment. Island nations, which the United Nations calls Small Island Developing States (SIDS), are extremely vulnerable to the impacts of climate change, especially rising sea levels and the increased incidence of hurricanes and other violent storms. When storms wreak havoc—when island coastlines erode and fresh water aquifers are tainted with saltwater intrusion—tourists simply change their travel plans. The day-to-day reality of climate change for island nations is muted or invisible to those whose distant homes and fossil fuel consumption patterns are largely responsible for this increasing chaos and degradation.

There are 47 island nations scattered across the Pacific, Atlantic, and Indian oceans and some 52 island territories such as Puerto Rico, French Polynesia, and the Falkland Islands. Some are large, continental islands, such as Greenland and the Philippines, that broke away from larger landmasses. Others result from underwater eruptions or coral reefs. Island species, languages, and cultures are unique, because they evolved in isolation. The adaptation of plants, animals, and people to their environment is highly specialized, visible, and exquisite. Islands are home to unique forms of life, and because of their obvious limitations—there is only so much land, water, and soil—human impacts on fragile and highly specialized ecosystems are amplified. These miniature worlds serve as our canary in the coal mine for climate change, warning of the degenerative ecosystemic changes that are well underway. However, global crises are many and our global attention is easily diverted. No one is checking on the canary.

One of the most remarkable features about ocean water is the critical role it plays in moderating our climate. In warmer weather oceans cool the air; when the temperature drops, they warm the air. Historically, oceans have had a stabilizing effect on the earth's climate. Today, carbon emissions are creating a warming, or greenhouse, effect, causing the oceans to expand, water temperatures to rise, polar ice to melt at a faster rate, and sea levels to rise. Oceans now play a major role in *de*stabilizing local weather patterns and the global climate.

Those most responsible for climate change are largely sheltered from its extreme impacts. The 4% of the world's population that resides in the United States is responsible for one-quarter of the world's carbon emissions from burning fossil fuels. Island nations are responsible for three one-hundredths of 1% of global emissions. Wealthy nations and people—the major consumers of fossil fuels—are better able to insulate themselves and their families from drought, desertification, extreme weather, crop failure, tropical illness, and sea-level rise. For poor nations and people, climate change creates incremental burdens to existing vulnerabilities and diminishes their ability to adapt. According to the World Health Organization, SIDS are acutely vulnerable to climate change because of their small size, isolation, limited fresh water and other natural resources, fragile economies, often dense populations, poorly developed infrastructures, limited financial and human resources, and exposure to extreme weather events. Every acre is precious. Island populations do not have the luxury of moving or evading the impacts of climate change. New Zealand, for example, allows 17 people a year from Tuvalu to emigrate.

The experience of the Marshall Islands, a group 24 atolls in the northern Pacific, offers further insight on the difficulties that climate change presents for island nations. The people Marshallese are quintessential survivors. For centuries they have endured on tiny pieces of land, some 77 square miles in a vast ocean area the size of Mexico. The highest elevation on these spits of coral and sand is just 7 feet above sea level. As with many island nations, the soil is poor and agricultural resources are limited. The Marshallese people have survived every peril nature can conjure—tidal waves, typhoons, drought, crop failure, and disease. They have also suffered from the most extreme perils devised by humans, enduring some 12 years of nuclear war conditions as the United States detonated atomic and thermonuclear weapons, exposing the entire population and every island to dangerous levels of radiation, and lingering contamination, producing severe health consequences.

Because of climate change, the islands are now experiencing an increase in extreme weather events, including droughts and storms, rising tides, ocean acidification, coral bleaching and disease, surging tides, and erosion. Each event affects the ecology and culture of the Marshall Islands; the entire culture revolves around vital connections to land and family, and it is difficult for outsiders to comprehend what it means from a Marshallese perspective to see the graves of your ancestors and traditional leaders succumb to the seas. Another new phenomenon in the Marshall Islands and other coral atolls nations is that the increase in sea level pressurizes the fresh water lens underneath the islands and literally causes the water to burst through the land and flood the land. Neither Western science nor the Marshallese language has developed a term to describe this.

Western scientists offer only a dismal forecast for the future of the Marshall Islands, arguing that if there are no changes in carbon emissions, sea level rise, ocean warming and acidification, and changes in rainfall patterns force the abandonment of the atolls. The predictions of scientists are particularly problematic given that most of the political will to meaningfully address climate change must come from the major carbon emitters, not the island states. The adverse consequences of climate change become increasingly acute during each year of our global paralysis on the issue. Our failure to take action threatens the ability of species to survive on their islands.

Although island populations are not in a position to control the fossil fuel addictions of developed nations, they are not passive victims without agency on the climate change issue. Island leaders have banded together as the Alliance of Small Island States (AOSIS) at the United Nations and created a political bloc to advocate for their unique needs related to climate change. Regional organizations, such as the Pacific Regional Environment Programme (SPREP) and Caricom, the Caribbean region's equivalent, work with the United Nations and island governments to strengthen adaptations to climate change and reduce vulnerability. SIDS are also exploring an alliance with Arctic communities as part of a recent venture called Many Strong Voices, a five-year action plan to link research and advocacy and to support the most vulnerable.

In the Marshall Islands the government and business community are examining local opportunities to help mitigate the impacts of climate change, including dredging policy, waste management, coastal construction, and community outreach and education. Island leaders are vocal; they want their perspectives on climate change heard and are demanding that the world come to terms with the thousands of years of island history and culture that the behavior of industrialized countries now imperils. Island leaders are putting a human face on a concept that remains abstract to continent dwellers:

> (t)he Marshall Islands is a country on the frontline of climate change. Our difficult situation is made more precarious for the future by the lack of progress in dealing with greenhouse gas emissions. We see little evidence that there will be a concerted effort by the countries primarily responsible for climate change— the industrialized and rich countries—. . .[1] will not do anything serious until they feel the effects of climate change on their own bodies. The tragic results of the recent hurricanes of death and destruction are just appetizers for what is to come.
>
> Good preparation and disaster reduction strategies are crucial but in the end there is only so much a small island state can do to protect itself from the catastrophic impact of a hurricane, cyclone, typhoon or tropical storm. . . . Crop damage can wipe out an entire year of agricultural production; damage to productive lands can hamper development for years afterward. Critical funding earmarked for social or infrastructural investment must be redirected to meet emergency and medium term rehabilitation requirements. Potential investors will think twice before putting their money into ventures. (Aliioiaga Feturi Elisaia, in a statement to the United Nations General Assembly 2004)

Climate change has thrown thousands of years of history on its head. The same isolation of the islands that brought creativity, adaptability, and unique species, languages and diverse cultures now serves as an impediment, because the chaos of climate change is invisible to distant, developed countries. The world needs to protect and draw on the depths of its cultural, linguistic, and bio- diversity, because a deep arsenal is required to respond to this complex and immense problem. There is hope and potential in the traditional ecological knowledge and ingenuity of island peoples, but we need to find ways to incorporate their finely honed adaptation skills into the international arena. Although islands may be distant in our psyches, we need to remember that our planet is also a remote island in the universe, and so the planet's future is ultimately one and the same as that of the Marshall Islands.

Note

1. Hiroshi Yamamura, Minister of Internal Affairs of the Republic of the Marshall Islands, in a statement to the 22nd Special Session of the United Nations, 1999.

SNAPSHOT: Beset by Offsets: Carbon Offset Chains and Human Rights Abuses[1]

Melissa Checker

Scenario 1. On the East Coast of Scotland one of Europe's largest oil refineries flares excess gas into the sky, sending sulfur dioxide, nitrogen dioxide and other particles into the nearby town of Grangemouth.[2] Six thousand miles away in eastern Brazil the villagers of Sao Jose do Buriti struggle as their water sources dry up and the plants they have subsisted on for generations disappear.

Scenario 2. In a small Appalachian town nestled in a mountain hollow tap water runs grey and oily. Children who bathe in this water develop scabs. They often need caps on their teeth, because the water is laced with lead, nickel, and other heavy metals.[3] The groundwater in this West Virginia community is contaminated by nearly 2 billion gallons of mining waste pumped into the area's streams and rivers by coal companies. Halfway across the world members of the indigenous Benet community live in caves and under trees after being evicted from the Mount Elgon National Park by the Ugandan Wildlife Authority (UWA) and the state military.[4]

The residents of these far-flung communities are linked through carbon offsetting,[5] a mechanism for reducing greenhouse gas emissions that accelerated exponentially in the late 2000s. For instance, in the scenarios mentioned above, carbon-absorbing forests in Brazil and Uganda are meant to counteract carbon emitted by the Grangemouth refinery and coal-fired power plants. In this chapter I trace two carbon "chains" from offset producer to offset consumer to demonstrate that rather than balancing out carbon emissions, carbon offset projects create equal measures of human injustice for the communities that host them and for the communities surrounding the facilities that buy them. Moreover, I argue that offsets and other market-based "fixes" to climate change create more harms than they resolve, both to human beings and to the environment. Ultimately, the chain reaction catalyzed by these false solutions endangers all of us.

Carbon Offsets Come of Age

Carbon offsets were conceived as part of the Kyoto Protocol's Clean Development Mechanism (CDM) in the late 1990s. Industrialized Kyoto nations were issued "emissions credits" equivalent to any amount of emissions reductions over and above the 1990 levels set by the protocol. These countries then allocated their quota of credits to polluting industries, most often using a grandfathering scheme in which the dirtiest industries received the largest quota. Polluters who used up their allowance had two options: they could either buy credits from another polluter who had not exceeded their quota, or they could invest in pollution-reduction projects in developing countries, thereby "earning" credits that they could bank or sell. Carbon offset promoters describe this as a win-win scenario. Carbon-producing industries can make up for their emissions by investing in activities that reduce greenhouse gases, and at the same time those greenhouse gas-reducing activities stimulate sustainable development.[6] Purchasing credits (known as Carbon Emission Reductions, or CERs) quickly became the option of choice, and by 2009 the market for carbon credits reached $136 billion, according to leading carbon market analysts at Point Carbon.

Those not obligated by Kyoto could partake in the emerging, self-regulated voluntary carbon market. This market included individuals wishing to assuage their guilt over carbon intensive activities such as airplane travel, who purchased offsets for their flights, home energy use, weddings, and so on. Another aspect included eco-conscious entertainers such as Leonardo DiCaprio, the band Coldplay, and makers of the film *Syriana*, all of whom famously offset airline travel and other carbon emissions generated by their professional projects or pursuits. But the bulk of the voluntary market comprised business entities in non-Kyoto countries that wished to bolster and "green" their image.[7]

However, many contended that the premises behind carbon offsets were inherently flawed.[8] On a scientific level, emissions equivalences are difficult to measure at best. Economically, incentives to generate carbon credits depend on their market value. In the midst of 2009's fiscal crisis EU carbon prices fell by nearly half,[9] and prices on the Chicago Climate Exchange plummeted to 10 cents/ton in late 2009 after peaking at $7/ton in May 2008.[10] But perhaps the most questionable aspect of offsets is additionality, or whether offset monies fund *new* emissions reductions or projects that would have been done anyway. For instance, a November 2008 report by the U.S. General Accountability Office (GAO) examined the CDM and found that its effects on greenhouse gas emissions are uncertain, largely because it is "nearly impossible" to determine the level of emissions that would have occurred in the absence of each project.[11] A report by Germany's Institute for Applied Ecology found that 40% of CDM projects registered by 2007 represented "unlikely or at least questionable" emissions cuts, partly because many offset projects would happen even without offset funding.[12] The additionality question and the complexity of carbon financing make the market ripe for corruption. Throughout 2009 the carbon market was hit by scandal. By the end of that year the European Law Enforcement Agency found that 27% of the market was fraudulent.[13]

This kind of rampant corruption may become critical to the longevity of the plant. EU countries include offsets in their accountings of greenhouse gas reductions. For instance, a recent study by law professor and energy expert at Stanford University's Program on Energy and Sustainable Development, Michael Wara estimated that European-based polluters bought so many carbon credits that they emitted approximately 1% more in 2008 than they did in 1990.[14] But the European Commission reported that emission levels fell 3.6% between 2007 and 2008.[15]

This essay critiques offsets on yet another level by using "on the ground" case studies to demonstrate the immediate and dire consequences of offset projects for local communities. From a human rights perspective, carbon offsetting creates a double-jeopardy situation, exacerbating poor environmental, economic, political, and/or social conditions for local communities in the global south as well as the global north. Yet this critical review also offers a note of hope, as the connections between carbon offset producers and consumer communities create opportunities for transnational alliance-building and climate justice.

Mount Elgon, Uganda/Appalachian Mountains, United States

Mount Elgon, Uganda, offers one of the most well-documented and most violent examples of an offset project gone awry. In 1990 the Dutch Electricity Generating Board vowed to surpass Kyoto Treaty goals and reduce its carbon emissions to 1989 levels by 1994–95, with a further 3–5% reduction by the year 2000. The board aimed to accomplish its goals by improving energy efficiency at its plants, developing new technologies, and compensating for emissions through "cost effective" measures.[16] To implement the last of these strategies, the power board established the Forests Absorbing Carbon Dioxide Emissions (Face) Foundation, a nonprofit corporation dedicated to "establish[ing], maintain[ing], and/or enhance[ing], forest vegetation" in order to absorb carbon dioxide.[17] The forests also earn carbon credits for the CO_2 they ostensibly sequester.[18] The foundation (which in 2002 spun off from the power companies) could then sell the credits and reinvest the proceeds in further forest projects. In 1994 Face partnered with the Uganda Wildlife Authority (UWA) to plant 25,000 hectares of trees inside Mount Elgon National Park. In exchange for financing the planting of the trees Face received the rights to the carbon sequestered by those trees—estimated at 2.11 tons of CO_2 over 100 years.[19] While the trees thrived (especially in areas where agriculture had been encroaching on them), a number of research reports found that the people surrounding the tree plantations had the opposite experience.

A year before the Face-UWA project began, the Ugandan government declared Mount Elgon a National Park. In so doing it evicted approximately 6,000 people (some of whom had been living there for 40 years), giving them nine days to vacate their homes.[20] A year later UWA took over management of the Park, which entailed protecting the biodiversity of the area, managing the carbon plantations and securing the park's borders.[21] Evicted villagers, who were left homeless and without access to land to graze their cattle or grow subsistence crops, attempted to continue using park land. When UWA rangers responded with violence, local villagers organized to regain their land. In 1998 they filed land claims against the UWA and the Ugandan government. Several NGOs and universities heard about the situation on Mount Elgon and launched their own investigations, which corroborated villagers' claims. For instance, a 2006 World Rainforest Movement (WRM) report details villagers' descriptions of UWA rangers committing rape, arson, shootings, and other violent acts. According to the report villagers retaliated by throwing stones, burning trees, and sabotaging rangers' vehicles.[22]

Villagers also claimed that the forest project did not live up to its promises of sustainable development. Initially project leaders agreed to employ local people to work in the national park and tree nurseries and as tree planters. However, the WRM reported contended that the project employed very few people, and most of the jobs were available only during the planting period.[23] In 2005 the Benet's legal strategies led a Justice to rule that an area of the national park should be set aside for the Benet to live on and continue farming. Yet villagers claimed that the UWA flaunted the ruling and continued to prevent them from using the land. Thus violence and retaliations persisted.[24] To be fair, we note that land disputes on Mount Elgon predated the Face Foundation's offset project. At the same time the funding generated by the project provided the UWA with additional incentives and justifications to administer evictions and violently patrol the area.

Following this chain to its next link, we discover a complex and opaque web of financial instruments designed to maximize investors' profits.[25] Although the Face Foundation is a nonprofit organization, the offsets generated by its projects were marketed by a Dutch for-profit partner organization known as the Climate Neutral Group (CNG). CNG then sold the credits to over 500 businesses. It also partnered with another for-profit company, Green Seat, which sold offsets (including those created on Mt. Elgon) exclusively to individuals and corporations wishing to balance out emissions from airline travel.

After several major news outlets reported on the violence on Mt. Elgon in 2007, Green Seat posted a notice on its website claiming that neither it nor CNG used offsets from Uganda forestry projects any longer. The Face Foundation also claimed to have stopped planting trees in the park and to be disengaging from the project. "At this stage we don't get any carbon credits for this project," Denis Slieker, director of the Face Foundation, told the LA Times in 2007: "We do not plan to expand anymore in Mount Elgon before these matters are resolved."[26] But the Face Foundation's website continued to describe the Mount Elgon project as "ongoing."

What is certain is that the Face Foundation was initially established to offset emissions from two coal-fired power stations in the Netherlands. Although I was unable to track the precise owners of these projects, I did find that one of Climate Neutral Group's prominent customers is Enesco, one of the Netherlands top-three energy companies. Enesco is considered to be a particularly "green" energy company—in 2008 Greenpeace ranked it the "cleanest" power company in the Netherlands.[27] On January 1, 2008, the company proclaimed that its internal business operations were "100% climate-neutral,"[28] thanks in large part to offsets. Approximately 81% of ENESCO's energy supply comes from fossil fuels—61.2% is natural gas, and 19.7%— nearly one-fifth—comes from coal.[29]

Although Mount Elgon cannot be directly connected to ENESCO, the forests of the former very possibly offset the coal plants of the latter. Indeed, although in 1974 the Netherlands closed all its coal mines because of their dangerous conditions in 2008, the country imported 3.6 million short tons of coal from the United States, making it one of the world's top coal importers.[30]

One-quarter to one-third of all carbon dioxide emissions worldwide come from burning coal,[31] but even if the Ugandan project were able offset the climate harm generated by coal-fired power plants, it would not be able to offset their human costs. In addition to high levels of carbon dioxide, these plants emit sulfur dioxide, nitrogen oxide, carbon monoxide, mercury, and arsenic (among other pollutants), often into surrounding communities.[32] Moreover, beginning in the late 1970s a controversial method of coal extraction, known as mountaintop removal, expanded in the U.S. Appalachian states. The process uses explosives to blast away a mountain peak and expose coal seams. Although coal companies claim the practice is safer and more efficient than traditional shaft mining, critics contend that it scars the landscape and dumps tons of waste, some of it toxic, into streams and valleys. A 2005 U.S. Environmental Protection Agency (EPA) study estimated that by 2012, mountaintop removal projects in Appalachia would have destroyed or seriously damaged an area larger than Delaware and buried more than 1,000 miles of mountain streams.[33]

In addition, without foliage and natural layers of soil, the land cannot retain water. This causes floods increase, with waters that carry highly toxic debris. For instance, West Virginia resident Maria Gunnoe's home sat directly below a 10-story valley fill that contains two toxic ponds of coal-mine waste. Before mining began Gunnoe's property was not prone to flooding, but since the mine became operational, her property flooded seven times, covering her land with toxic coal sludge. In 2007 Gunnoe and her colleagues at the Ohio Valley Environmental Coalition (OVEC) won a federal lawsuit against the U.S. Army Corps of Engineers that repealed mountaintop removal valley fill permits in southern West Virginia granted without adequate environmental consideration and that banned the issuance of new permits. But the Corps defied the federal judge's orders and granted permits to construct two new valley fills above Gunnoe's community.[34]

During his 2008 campaign U.S. President Barack Obama expressed concern about mountaintop removal projects. However, in late May 2009 the (EPA) stated that it would not block 42 of 48 mine projects under review, including some of the most controversial mountaintop mines.[35] Obama also enthusiastically supported so-called clean coal technology, which captures the carbon released by coal-fired power plants. However, this technology does not address the immediate dangers of the mining process, itself.[36] In part, because offsets have enabled the production of coal-fired power plants, the coal industry remains strong. In fact, in January 2010 the UNFCC certified its first "clean coal" plant, enabling it to generate certified offset credits.[37]

The ramifications of this carbon chain are clear—in Uganda, the offset forest intensified existing land disputes and accelerated displacement, violence, and impoverishment among local villagers. The offset credits generated by the project facilitated the development of Dutch coal-fired power plants. Pursuing the path of the credits even farther, we can follow the coal supplying those plants to the Appalachian region of the United States, where coal extraction comes at great cost to local communities. In sum, this example demonstrates that the trail of carbon offsets—from Uganda to Appalachia—is lined with threats to human rights to health, safety, and well-being.

Grangemouth, Scotland/Sao do Buriti, Brazil

My second case depicts a similarly disturbing example of a carbon chain. But it also shows that part of the offset chain includes opportunities for new kinds of transnational alliances, which can challenge world leaders to find more sustainable solutions to climate change.

In the late 1990s British Petroleum (BP), then owners of the Grangemouth refinery, launched a major effort to "green" their image, in part by offsetting their carbon emissions through investments in projects that reduce the production of greenhouse gases. Around the same time a foundry near Sao Jose do Buriti publicized its plan to switch from using charcoal to carbon-intensive coal, due to a dwindling supply of charcoal-producing eucalyptus trees. Enter the World Bank. Through its Carbon Fund the Bank gathered funding from various sources, including BP, and initiated a project to expand the foundry's eucalyptus forest and generate carbon offsets. In addition to providing a renewable raw material, the trees would absorb carbon in the atmosphere. Each ton of carbon absorbed would then offset, or neutralize, a ton of carbon dioxide produced in Scotland.

But the formula left out the rights and interests of local Brazilians. A 2008 report by the Sustainable Energy and Economy Network's co-director, Janet Redman, states that the eucalyptus trees' enormous roots almost immediately began to soak up vast amounts water in and around its environs. A rapidly dropping water table meant that local people had to travel increasingly far to find water. Ironically, even though the tree-planting project was meant to reduce greenhouse gas emissions, it relied on herbicides and pesticides that local farmers' claim killed subsistence crops and poisoned streams. Furthermore, the water shortage destroyed certain kinds of micro enterprise and diminished biodiversity and medicinal plants. Finally, Redman writes: "Perhaps more seriously, groups allege that Plantar pressured local residents to sign letters of support for the project or forfeit employment at the plantations."[38] Those residents who did publicly oppose Plantar claim that they and their family members were threatened and/or hired to work at the plantation.[39]

Meanwhile, as one of Europe's largest oil refineries Grangemouth spewed sulfur dioxide, nitrogen dioxide, and small particulate matter. In addition, officials at the Scottish Environment Protection Agency (SEPA) cited the refinery as "one confirmed source" of an oil slick covering several square miles of the Firth of Forth.[40] For many years Grangemouth residents complained about high rates of asthma, as well as the smells and noise coming from the plant.

The refinery's social track record is similarly noxious. In 2005 BP sold Grangemouth to INEOS, the third largest chemicals firm in the world. In late April 2008, Unite (the Grangemouth's workers' union) became embroiled in a dispute with INEOS over pension policies. The union accused the company of buying assets and then cutting costs through the introduction of new working practices, lower wages, and terminating pension schemes.[41]

INEOS has also come under fire for its involvement in another carbon offset project, with its own set of human rights violations. Briefly, in 2005, INEOS partnered with GFL, which produces HCFC 22, a refrigerant gas for air conditioning units and refrigerators. GFL wanted to institute a program to capture and recycle HFC 23, a potent greenhouse gas that is a byproduct of producing HCFC 22. INEOS supplied the technology for the program, and both companies received the right to claim the carbon offsets. However, residents of Gujarat, where the GFL factory is located, claim that the factory has made them sick with joint aches, bone pains, unexplained swellings, throat and nerve problems, and temporary paralysis. An investigation by the UK's *Daily Mail* found "dangerously high levels of fluoride and chloride—fluoride in the water was more than twice the international acceptable limit. All the water fell well below any safe drinking standards and the soil had worryingly high levels of these chemicals."[42] Although the UN closely monitors the emission of HFC 23, it does not monitor the release of non-greenhouse gas pollutants. Thus, the program was deemed successful in terms of greenhouse gases. Indeed, in 2005 the Executive Board for the Clean Development Mechanism (CDM) of the Kyoto Protocol approved the GFL site as a CDM project and certified INEOS and GFL's carbon credits.

Both companies were then free to sell those credits to industries falling short of their national emissions caps. For instance, in 2006, GFL made news for doubling its sales revenue by selling a record number of carbon credits to Noble Carbon Credits group of Singapore, Rabobank Nederlands, and Sumitomo Corporation.[43] Noble Carbon Credits group sells carbon credits mainly to large industries needing to comply with Kyoto Protocols, including power and oil companies.[44] Both companies also won the ability to promote a "green" image, which is particularly confounding, given both companies' records for emitting other kinds of environmental pollutants. For instance, some of the proceeds from GFL's sales went to build a Teflon and caustic soda manufacturing facility that relies on processes known to be massively polluting.[45]

This example thus illustrates another way in which carbon credit schemes violate human rights by creating dangerously perverse incentives for polluters to continue to pollute. First, Plantar's threat to switch from charcoal to coal was a way for the company to "game" the carbon credit system and finance a project that it ought to have undertaken anyway.[46] Second, carbon offset schemes reward corporations for lowering greenhouse gas emissions, but they ignore—and thus enable—other highly toxic emissions that endanger the lives of local communities. Third, GFL's handsome profits from capturing HFC-23 have encouraged similar projects. This lowered the cost of producing HCFC-22, which in turn created an over-reliance on the chemical, itself a powerful greenhouse gas. For instance, a 2004 report by INFRAS, a German-based policy analysis and research group estimated that if the UNFCC certified HFC-23 capture projects, HCFC-22 emissions could account for 6% of the Chinese total greenhouse gas emissions by 2010.[47] Despite the report's urging the UNFCC agreed to certify projects, a trend that portends an increase in questionable climate reduction projects, as well as life-threatening situations for local communities such as those in Gujarat.

To combat that trend and to raise awareness about the consequences of carbon offset projects, Carbon Trade Watch (a project of the Transnational Institute) initiated a project to connect residents of Sao Jose do Buriti and Grangemouth through the exchange of video diaries. As the resulting documentary film depicts, residents of both communities reacted powerfully to their new awareness of their connected plights and many spoke of newfound determination to continue their local struggles. One of the Scottish participants even became an activist with Friends of the Earth and then ran for local office. I conclude with this case, because it demonstrates that, although carbon offsets connect local communities by creating and perpetuating conditions of poor health and environments, once elucidated those connections can also launch new opportunities for activism on local and transnational levels.

Conclusions

The future of carbon offsets appears murky. The failure of world leaders to achieve a solid agreement in Copenhagen's 2009 summit and the United State's failure to pass climate change legislation (which relied heavily on offsetting), combined with the 2009 recession and growing certification scandals, set the global carbon market tumbling. Around this time Australian, Japanese, and U.S. lawmakers began to pull away from offset schemes, which set the markets into further chaos.[48] Yet, while industry insiders debated whether the offset market would die or be reborn, thousands of CDM projects were already underway. And with Chinese officials currently discussing how to include carbon-trading programs in their next policy-setting Five-Year Plan, resurgent life for this scheme in other nations may again emerge.

As this essay has shown, much damage to humans and their environments had already been done. Demonstrating the urgency of that damage, the immediate consequences of offsets for human rights has been the main aim of this essay. For offsets do not represent the first time that economically and socially marginalized communities have faced such violations. Whether in industrialized or developing countries, these communities have borne the brunt of industrial pollution for decades. These are also the people to be first and worst affected by climate change. Indeed, they have truly been sacrificed to the needs of industrialization and capitalism. The fact that offsets did not represent any kind of real solution to climate change thus came as no surprise.

Their collective histories position such communities to be among those leading a transnational movement for real and meaningful climate change solutions. As the cases of Grangemouth and Sao Jose du Buriti show, linking the lived experiences of those beset by offsets powerfully strips the veneer from the greenwash covering many popular climate change solutions and reveals the ecological and social tarnish hidden beneath. Ultimately, carbon offset chains reach far and wide, and the climate fate of those living in sacrifice zones is linked to even the most affluent and "green" elites. In short, the stakes are high, and the time to abandon quick, capitalistic fixes in favor of nontoxic and holistic solutions is nigh.

Notes

1. Much of the research presented in this essay is also presented in Melissa Checker, "Double Jeopardy: Pursuing the Path of Carbon Offsets and Human Rights Abuses," *Upsetting the Offset: The Political Economy of Carbon Markets*, Steffen Bohm and Siddartha Dabhi, Eds. (Essex: MayFly Books, 2009).

2. For more information from "The Carbon Connection," a documentary produced by Carbon Trade Watch, see www.carbontradewatch.org/carbonconnection/index.html.

3. Charles Duhigg, "Clean Water Laws Are Neglected, at a Cost in Suffering," *The New York Times* (September 13, 2009), www.nytimes.com/2009/09/13/us/13water.html, 9/21/09.

4. Chris Lang, "Uganda: Thousands of Indigenous People Evicted from FSC-Certified Mount Elgon National Park," *World Rainforest Movement Bulletin* 131, June 2008, www.wrm.org.uy/bulletin/131/Uganda.html, 09/21/09.

5. For the purposes of this article I define *carbon offsets* as emissions reductions that are claimed to result in less greenhouse gases accumulating in the atmosphere, such as tree plantations (which are supposed to absorb carbon dioxide emissions) or fuel switches, wind farms, and hydroelectric dams, which are argued to reduce or displace fossil energy (Larry Lohmann, "Uncertainty Markets and Carbon Markets: Variations on Polanyian Themes," *New Political Economy* 2009, 12).

6. See Larry Lohmann, "Carbon Trading, Climate Justice, and the Production of Ignorance: Ten Examples," *Development*, 2008, 51:359–65; and Simon Bullock, Mike Childs, and Tom Picken, "A Dangerous Distraction," Friends of the Earth, 2009, www.foe.co.uk/resource/briefing_notes/dangerous_distraction.pdf.

7. David Fahrenthold, "There's a Gold Mine in Environmental Guilt," *The Washington Post*, October 6, 2008: A1.

8. As mentioned, these critiques are plentiful. For some particularly comprehensive examples, see Larry Lohmann, Ed., "Carbon Trading: A Critical Conversation on Climate Change, Privatization, and Power," *Development Dialogue* (Uppsala: Dag Hammarskjold Foundation, 2006); Kevin Smith, Steffen Bohm, and Siddartha Dabhi, Eds., *The Carbon Neutral Myth: Offset Indulgences for Your Climate Sins* (Amsterdam: Transnational Institute, 2007); *Upsetting the Offset: The Political Economy of Carbon Markets* (Essex: MayFlyBooks, 2009); Fahrenthold, note 7; Lohmann, notes 5 and 6; Stephan Faris, "The Other Side of Carbon Trading," *Fortune Magazine*, August 30, 2007. See also white papers from organizations such as Carbon Trade Watch, Corner House, and World Rainforest Movement.

9. "Hopes for $2 Trillion Global Carbon Market Fade," *Reuters.com*, March 3, 2010, www.reuters.com/article/idUSTRE6223KZ20100303.

10. See www.pointcarbon.com.

11. U.S. GAO, "Carbon Offsets: The U.S. Voluntary Market Is Growing, but Quality Assurance Poses Challenges for Market Participants," August 28, 2008, www.gao.gov/products/GAO-08-1048.

12. Lambert Schneider, "Is the CDM Fulfilling Its Environmental and Sustainable Development Objectives? An Evaluation of the CDM and Options for Improvement" (Berlin: Institute for Applied Ecology, November 5, 2007), www.oeko.de/oekodoc/622/2007-162-en.pdf.

13. See Europol's website, www.europol.europa.eu/index.asp?page=news&news=pr091209.htm.

14. James Kanter, "Do Carbon Offsets Cause Emissions to Rise?" May 8, 2009, http://greeninc.blogs.nytimes.com/2009/05/08/do-carbon-offsets-cause-emissions-to-rise/.

15. The EU did attribute a portion of these reductions to the economic downturn. European Environment Authority, "Greenhouse Gas Emission Trends and Projections in Europe 2008," eea.europa.eu, 3/18/2010.

16. W. Stibbe, J. Van der Kooij, J. Verweij, and Pedro Moura Costa, "Response to Global Warming: Strategies of the Dutch Electricity Generating Board," report to the 16th Congress of the World Energy Council, 1995, www.ecosecurities.com/Assets/3170/Pubs_Response%20to%20global%20warming%20Strategies%20of%20the%20Dutch%20Electricity%20Generating%20Board.pdf.

17. This quotation is taken from the Face Foundation's website, www.stitchingface.org.

18. Whether and to what degree the carbon absorbed by trees is equivalent to carbon emitted by the burning of fossil fuels is a subject of great debate. See, for instance, recent editorials by journalist Fred Pearce, www.guardian.co.uk/environment/2008/dec/17/carbonoffsetprojects-carbonemissions, and Stanford University climate scientist Ken Caldeira, www.nytimes.com/2007/01/16/opinion/16caldeira.htm.

19. House of Commons, Environmental Audit Committee, "The Voluntary Carbon Offset Market: Sixth Report of Session 2006–07" (London: TSO, 30).

20. Dabid Himmelfarb, "Moving People, Moving Boundaries: The Socio-Economic Effects of Protectionist Conservation, Involuntary Resettlement and Tenure Insecurity on the Edge of

Mt. Elgon National Park, Uganda," Agroforestry in Landscape Mosaics Working Paper Series, World Agroforestry Centre, Tropical Resources Institute of Yale University, and The University of Georgia, 2006, 16, www.yale.edu/tri/wkppragrofor.html. According to Himmelfarb, "the exact number of people left homeless varies depending on the source. In October 2003, *New Vision* reported that 561 families were left without land as a result of the re-drawn boundary at the Benet Resettlement Area"; Gerald Businge, "The Benet to Sue Gov't over Land," *New Vision*, October 2003, www.newvision.co.ug/D/8/26/309690.

21. Great Britain House of Commons Environmental Audit Committee 2007:30.

22. Chris Lang, "Uganda: Notes from a Visit to Mount Elgon," *World Rainforest Movement Bulletin* No. 115, February 2006, www.wrm.org.uy/bulletin/115/Uganda.html.

23. Ibid.

24. Chris Lang and Timothy Byakola, "A Funny Place to Store Carbon": UWA-FACE Foundation's tree planting project in Mount Elgon National Park, Uganda, World Rainforest Movement, December 2006.

25. See Lohmann, note 6.

26. Faris, note 8.

27. See http://somo.nl/news-en/greenpeace-awards-red-and-green-thermometers-to-e-on-and-eneco/.

28. See http://corporateuk.eneco.nl/outlook_and_strategy/Business_Operations/Pages/Default.aspx.

29. Joseph Wilde-Ramsing, Tim Steinweg, and Maaike Kokke, "Sustainability in the Dutch Power Sector" (Amsterdam: Center for Research on Multinational Corporations, 2008).

30. *U.S. Coal Supply and Demand 2008 Review*, U.S. Energy Information Administration, April 14, 2009, www.eia.doe.gov/cneaf/coal/page/special/exports_imports.html. The Netherlands also buys 11% of the world's offsets, making it the third largest buyer (tied with Japan). See "A Dangerous Distraction," note 6.

31. These numbers are disputed. See Jeff Goodell, *Big Coal: The Dirty Secret behind America's Energy Future* (New York: Mariner Books, 2007) for justification of the former and www.worldcoal.org/coal-the-environment/climate-change/index.php for justification of the latter.

32. U.S. EPA, 2005.

33. U.S. EPA Region 3, 2005.

34. For more details, see www.goldmanprize.org/2009/northamerica.

35. Tom Hamburger and Peter Wallsten, "Controversial Coal Mining Method Gets Obama's OK: Environmentalists Decry 'Mountaintop Removal,'" *Chicago Tribune* June 1, 2009, www.chicagotribune.com/news/nationworld/chi-tc-nw-mountaintop-mining-053jun01,0,3998035.story.

36. Many environmentalists also contend that coal can never be clean enough to become a workable climate change strategy.

37. Perhaps unsurprisingly, this plant is located in Gurujat, India.

38. Janet Redman, "World Bank: Climate Profiteer" (Washington, D.C.: Institute for Policy Studies, 2008, 24), www.ips-dc.org/getfile.php?id=181.

39. More information can be found in the documentary "The Carbon Connection," produced by Carbon Trade Watch, www.carbontradewatch.org/carbonconnection/index.html.

40. Ian Johnston, "A Gift from Scotland to Brazil: Drought and Despair," *The Scotsman*, July 7, 2007, http://thescotsman.scotsman.com/world/A-gift-from-Scotland-to.3302061.jp.

41. *The Economist,* "Running on Empty," 387(8577):46, 2008.

42. Nadine Ghouri, "The Great Carbon Credit Con: Why Are We Paying the Third World to Poison Its Environment?" Mail online, June 1, 2009, www.dailymail.co.uk/home/moslive/article-1188937/The-great-carbon-credit-eco-companies-causing-pollution.html.

43. Baiju Kalesh, "Gujarat Fluro Sets Record on Carbon Credit Sale," *The Times of India*, August 10, 2006, www.articlearchives.com/law-legal-system/environmental-law-air-quality-regulation/1765101-1.html.

44. The United Nations Development Programme, "The Clean Development Mechanism: A Users Guide," www.undp.org/energy/docs/cdmchapter7.pdf.

45. Ghouri, note 42.

46. For a further discussion of this type of "gaming" the carbon credit system, see Lohmann, note 5.

47. Othmar Schwank, "Concerns about CDM Projects Based on Decomposition of HFC-23 Emissions from 22-HCFC Production Sites," October, 2004, http://cdm.unfccc.int/public_inputs/inputam0001/Comment_AM0001_Schwank_081004.pdf.

48. Nathanial Gronewold, "The Stakes of Carbon Trading Are Losing Their Sizzle," *The New York Times*, March 12, 2010, www.nytimes.com/cwire/2010/03/12/12climatewire-the-stakes-of-carbon-trading-are-losing-their-2213.html, 3/18/10.

CHAPTER 18

Water and Human Rights

Barbara Rose Johnston

If gold drove the dreams that led to far flung migration in the 1800s, and oil was the "black gold" driving wealth and war in the 20th century, is water the new "blue gold" of the 21st? With growing population, climate change, and other demands on fresh water supplies, will scarcity generate a new era of water wars?

The Earth's fresh water supply is affected by changes in the hydrologic cycle: changes in the amount of water entering the system; the volume of water captured and stored in surface and subsurface reservoirs; the amount that runs off land and enters rivers, streams, and is eventually lost to the oceans; and the amount held by vegetation and released into the atmosphere through evapotranspiration. Supplies are also affected by human activity. Some 69% of the world's fresh water budget is used for irrigated agriculture, which, in turn, is responsible for 70% of the world's water pollution. Fresh water may be abundant, but safe drinking water may be scarce as a result of biological and chemical contamination from agriculture, industry, and urban life.

Scarcity is relative. Water demand is also a relative construct. Demand is sometimes a simple question of numbers—more people require greater amounts of water to meet basic needs. However, even as population increases, changes in water use behavior and technology can decrease total water consumption. The perception of water scarcity due to an inadequate supply of irrigation water, for example, may dissipate if water demands are reduced with a change in the type of crops grown and the kinds of technology employed.

Water scarcity is a relative concept influenced not only by supply and demand but also by how water is valued in cultural and economic terms, levels of access and patterns of use, and degrees of control over water resource management and distribution. Thus scarcity might reflect the economic ability to pay for water or the customs, social conditions, and relationships that privilege access for some and not others.

The insight that an environmental resource must be understood in terms of culture and power is nothing new.[1] Nevertheless, it bears repeating, especially in these times when environmental issues are driving the national and foreign policy agendas in many of the world's nations, and the spin cycle is working overtime as interest groups push and promote one interpretation or another of the problem and the solution. The public perceptions and actual experiences of scarcity are manipulated, and at times, even manufactured by nations, industry, and international agencies and financiers to legitimize the energy, water, and other critical resource development schemes, often pursued in the name of national security.

The Decline, Repackaging, and Resurgence of Hydropower

A case in point can be seen in the resurgent strength of the hydropower industry. The hydroindustry went into serious decline in the late 1980s. In that period exposés such as Catherine Caufield's *In the Rainforest*, a critique of Brazil's Tucuruí Dam Amazonian dam, and Marc Reisner's *Cadillac Desert: The American West and Its Disappearing Water* helped generate public awareness of the profound consequences of large dams and water diversions. Such work generated widespread anger over the destruction of natural resources, communities, cultures, and ways of life to sustain evergreen lawns, fill swimming pools, grow water-intensive crops in the desert, and generate electricity for distant urban centers.[2] In this climate controversy erupted over the financing and construction of China's Three Gorges Dam. Environmental activists, working in new local, national, and international coalitions, pressured international financiers with a campaign so successful that the World Bank was unable to locate experts to shape the resettlement action plan.[3] The World Bank, U.S. Export Bank, and Asian Development Bank, ended up withdrawing their financing commitments. Many activists thought they had seen the end of that dam. A naive and ethnocentric assumption, it turns out, that failed to consider the power of project culture, nationalist culture, determination and political will, and the many needs of a 1990s China, not to mention the greed of western investors.[4]

Outside China, the hydroindustry plunged into a tailspin in the 1990s. The international financial institutions that had fueled the industry's growth came under increasing pressure from both national governments and civil society to strengthen environmental and social safeguards and prove the value of development projects. Evidence mounted of the critical linkage between free-flowing rivers and healthy fisheries—and the salmon runs and other anadromous fisheries of the world were in serious and steep decline. Dam-displaced communities—especially the tens of thousands affected by large dam projects in India and Thailand—with access to computers, cell phones, video, and the internet, could not only challenge specific projects but also communicate to a global audience the data they collected and positions they advocated.[5]

Financiers not only began to employ social and environmental safeguards, they also began to do the math. A decade of environmental and social impact analyses and post-project audits revealed some dismal bottom lines; costs far outweighed benefits in many a large dam and water diversion projects. Thus, in April 1998, when 160 NGOs from 46 countries issued a resolution calling on the nations of the G-7 and the OECD to establish strong common standards to ensure that their export credit agencies withdraw or refrain from involvement in projects that harm the environment and local communities, the U.S. Overseas Private Investment Corporation set a benchmark for such standards. It revised its environmental policies and agreed (for the time being) to refrain from insuring or financing projects involving the construction of large dams that significantly and irreversibly disrupt natural ecosystems and projects that require the resettlement of more than 5,000 people.[6] Other institutions followed suit.

Many in the environmental and human rights arena saw the large dam industry outside China in terminal decline, especially in the days leading up to and following the release of the final report of the World Commission on Dams (WCD) in November 2000. Launched by Nelson Mandela, the WCD report seemed to be the last word on question of whether this form of massive hydroengineering was truly sustainable in human environmental terms.

The WCD's review of the 20th century boom in dam building produced a sobering set of conclusions.[7] Many large dams failed to meet projected energy and economic goals. Siltation and sedimentation reduced their operating life. By the year 1999, 60% of the world's rivers were dammed. Environmental impacts included endangerment or extinction of 30% of the world's freshwater fish. The construction of some 45,000 large dams caused displacement and severe poverty for an estimated 40 to 80 million people, the majority of whom were indigenous peoples and ethnic minorities. The WCD also assessed efforts to mitigate the human environmental costs of large dam development in 200 specific cases and found widespread overwhelming evidence that development failed to improve affected-community lives and protect the environment. The findings were accompanied by a set of recommendations for best practices that did not rule out large dam development but certainly made environmental and social sustainability key and decisive indicators of the feasibility of proposed projects, plans for management of operations, and distribution of the benefits of existing facilities. In addition to its recommendations for new hydrodevelopment, the WCD called for governments, industry, and financial institutions to accept responsibility for social issues associated with existing large dams and develop remedies, including reparation, restitution, the restoration of livelihoods, and land compensation for relocated communities. These recommendations reflect WCD's recognition that hydrodevelopment has, at times, involved the abuse of fundamental human rights and that the international community is obligated to provide just compensation, reparation, and the right to remedy.[8]

For a time, the WCD was cited as the authoritative source on the question of the adverse impacts of large dams. The activist community, national governments, and the sponsoring NGOs and agencies, such as IUCN and UNEP, began focusing on the implementation of WCD recommendations—briefing nations, encouraging the adoption of WCD guidelines, educating affected communities in a congress attended by representatives from 61 countries, translating recommendations into community-action guides, and developing and supporting reparation campaigns to address the many lingering problems from past dam development. By 2003 infrastructure lending at the World Bank hit an all-time low.[9]

Still, large infrastructure projects featuring hydroelectric dams and water diversions were being shaped. For example, Plan Puebla-Panama, initiated in 2001 and retitled the Mesoamerican Integration and Development Project in 2008, is a multibillion dollar development plan developed from decades-old templates of modernization: build highways, 381 hydroelectric dams, and new utility grids in the rural hinterlands from Guatemala to Panama to create the infrastructure that attracts foreign investment and accesses the untapped mineral and energy wealth of Central

America. Put the rural peasantry to work in manufacturing, export agriculture, and biofuel production. Move people off and privatize communal lands to allow the financing of large-scale agricultural loans and the production of boutique crops destined for the wealthy consumers of the United States and Canada. Bring the region (Southern Mexico, Central America, and Colombia) into modernity.[10]

Turkey's Southeast Anatolia Project (located in the basins of the Euphrates and Tigris and in Upper Mesopotamia) deploys a similar 1970s-era, neoliberal development template, this time with an overt "security" spin. Dams are being built to generate electricity for the European Union, which Turkey hopes to join. Water is contained and stored as a critical resource to be piped to thirsty nations in the Middle East. The mountainous terrain is tamed and frames broad reservoirs that allow an easily patrolled border. The troublesome residents of those mountain valleys are flooded out, divested of their claims to Kurdistan.[11]

The point here: with a resurgent security state pushed on the world by pre-9/11 Bush/Cheney energy and resource development agendas and post-9/11 Patriot Act security-through-militarism actions, the relative costs and benefits of hydroengineering were recalculated. Governments devalued biocultural diversity while prioritizing the defense of the national economy, resulting in the strategic enclosure of water to meet human, industry, and agricultural needs and to decrease reliance on foreign sources of oil. Water became more than an element, and more than an economic good. Water became a national security resource to be managed and defended with all the powers and force of the state, a framing encouraged by scholars such as Thomas Homer-Dixon and Michael Klare, who popularize the equation "resource scarcity leads to violent conflict."[12]

A further spin was achieved by capitalizing on "inconvenient truths." The global concern about climate change and the focus on carbon as the primary culprit provided another opportunity to repackage the hydrodevelopment industry. The European Union, following the lead of the United States, ignoring evidence that dam construction often involves major deforestation and that the reservoirs created by dams emit considerable greenhouse gasses, declared hydroelectric energy a low-carbon renewable source. New hydroelectric development is now considered to be an environmentally friendly endeavor and is promoted by governments as a carbon-offset project that generates official carbon credit that can be used in emission trading schemes, such as the European Union Emission Trading Scheme and the Kyoto Protocol, as Certified Emission Reductions.

It is perhaps no surprise that large water infrastructure development is again in favor. As the World Bank notes in a 2009 report justifying resurgent large dam building:

> Hydropower currently accounts for about 20% of the world's electricity supply and over 80% of the supply from (nonbiomass) renewable resources. Scaling up hydropower is not limited by physical or engineering potential: OECD countries have exploited over 70% of economically feasible potential. Yet only 23% of hydropower potential in developing countries has been exploited. Indeed, 91% of unexploited economically feasible potential worldwide is located in developing countries, with one quarter in China. . . .

> A decade of learning about environmental and social risks has shifted the definition of sustainable hydropower infrastructure. The World Commission on Dams, the follow-up work of the UN Dams and Development Program, sustainability initiatives of both industry and nonindustry organizations, and the requirements of financing institutions have

redefined the standards for environmental and social management. On this basis, there is a growing openness in the NGO community to consider hydropower a tool in a low-carbon future.[13]

The nations of the world, their bankers, and their builders are now engaged in what may be the final act of containing and controlling the world's fresh water systems. Large dams and water diversions are being built, planned, or proposed for every major river and tributary on both sides of the Himalaya and throughout Africa, the Americas, Australia, and Southeast Asia—truly, across the world. Lost in this reframing of the environmental and social "good" that large water infrastructure provides is the attention to the very biocultural issues that generated global protest only a few short years ago.

Despite the assurances of the hydropower lobby, these biocultural impacts of large dam development cannot be simply "mitigated." Indeed, our understanding of the devastating effects of the 20th-century dam building boom is still being refined with alarming new information. Consider, for example, reassessments of the total number of people displaced by dam development: In India 14 million were originally acknowledged as officially displaced by dam development through 1999, but a recent reassessment of development records puts the number at 60 million. The majority of the unacknowledged displacees were ethnic minorities living on common land claimed by the state and were not officially eligible for compensation or relocation assistance.[14]

In China 1999 estimates of dam displacement totaled some 10 million people. Yet the 2007 budget announced by Chinese Prime Minister Wen Jiabao included annual stipends for some 23 million rural migrants who are now officially recognized as "dam-displaced without adequate compensation." More have been forcibly displaced in the years since. Resettlement from Three Gorges Dam alone is officially reported to be 1.3 million. Displacement numbers will most assuredly grow. The greatest untapped hydropotential in the world lies in China, where, despite growing concern over the seismic impact of large dams, they continue to be built.[15] For example, the north-south water diversion now under construction, a massive project that will be the world's longest aqueduct, will require the relocation of hundreds of thousands of people.

Reassessments of displacement statistics in India and China suggest, at the very least, a doubling of WCD estimates. This number is further expanded when considering the outcome of a 2010 study on dam-induced alterations of river flow and its human consequences that found that disruption of the natural riverine-based production systems adversely affected the livelihoods of a conservatively estimated 472 million river-dependent people living downstream from large dams.[16] Given the location of existing and proposed dam projects in remote regions and the documented demographics of development refugees, water development will continue to be a driving force in the rise of global poverty and decline in biocultural diversity.

Emerging Trends in Water, Culture, and Power

In the wake of the global economic collapse, financing for some large water infrastructure projects has evaporated. Other projects have been cancelled as a result of increased advocacy, documentation of corruption, and violations of loan agreements. In 2003 the Asian Development Bank cancelled 80% of its projects in Nigeria because of concerns about corruption. Guatemala's request for construction bids for a second dam on the Chixoy (Xalala Dam) closed in 2005 with no offers, reportedly because of the global economy. A second effort to secure bids in 2009 failed because of the government's failure to manage local community opposition (a third request for bids is now pending).

For much of the first decade of the 21st century resurgent nationalism and militarism meant a decline in development aid, especially bilateral aid between the United States and nations in Africa, Latin America, and Southeast Asia, as well as a decline in national contributions to the development banks. In some instances this loss presented an opportunity for new bilateral partnerships. China, whose engineering and construction expertise expanded considerably as a result of the need to build Three Gorges Dam largely on its own, has emerged as a major player in water infrastructure. Bilateral deals in Africa, Latin America, and Southeast Asia typically reward China with extractive resource rights in exchange for financing, technical assistance and construction of dams, diversions, and supporting infrastructure (highways, power grids). As of April 2009 China was financing the building of 219 large dam projects in 49 countries.

Stimulus financing of international and regional development banks announced in 2009 is breathing new life into some stalled projects. In June 2009 the World Bank announced its intent to scale up its financing of hydrodevelopment. A close examination finds that the major goals of these projects are to allow energy and extractive resource development, to export electricity and water to sustain the high-energy and high-water consumer lifestyles of some first-world nations, and to develop water futures, or the capturing of water to sell in a future world water market. In Canada, for example, hydrodevelopment is closely linked with mining and energy development: 63% of all surface water is used for energy production. Proposals include water diversions and containment to support nuclear power plant operations, which in turn produce the electricity and the steam to support oil extraction from the Alberta Tar Sands deposits. In Guatemala hydrodevelopment is promoted as a poverty alleviation tool because it provides electricity to rural households; in fact, it supports the urban and regional grids (with power flowing north through Mexico to the United States), and even local transmission often is used for mineral mining and processing.

Privatization protests and failures of the 1990s and early 2000s led to increased demand for the recognition of water as a human right, respect for the inherent environmental rights of water, and resurgence of a commons approach to water management. In 2003 the United Nations Committee on Economic, Social, and Cultural Rights recognized that the right to drinkable water and adequate sanitation was an essential part of the right to health and the right to an adequate standard of living. In 2006 the UN General Assembly recognized water as a fundamental human right, and in 2010 it adopted a resolution declaring access to clean water and sanitation a basic human right.[17]

Despite decreased support in the notion that effective and sustainable management of water can best be achieved by market forces and for-profit, as opposed to public, utilities, efforts to strengthen the legal framework that prioritizes privatization continue. For example, Italian legislation coming into effect in 2012 redefines the role of local government in developing and managing water utilities from public utilities to public-private partnerships that compete on the market. Public ownership of water utilities can occur only in those situations where there is no corporate or commercial interest.[18]

Another major trend is, as mentioned, the increased effort by governments to imposition of a security framework over water to insure the priority of sovereign rights to manage and use strategic resources.[19] Defining water as a national security resource this approach militarizes the water commons. People who protest the consequences of dams have been charged with crimes against the state under the Patriot Act, legislation that the United States pressured other nations to adopt following 9/11.[20] For example, the previously mentioned Southeast Anatolia project in Turkey (22 dams in the Tigris and Euphrates river basins) lies in the heart of ancient Kurdistan. Turkey's water development projects will create an easily secured border and capture and store a critical resource of potential marketable value for thirsty downstream and distant countries who until now relied on the Tigris and Euphrates for water, energy, and food. The rising waters will also drown ancient cities, create a watery barrier between Kurdish populations in Iraq and Syria, and forcibly displace many of the remaining Kurdish communities within Turkey. The construction of the Ataturk Dam alone displaced some 11,000 Kurds. The Ilisu Dam project promises the dispossession of about 36,000 people. At this writing Ilisu construction is on hold following a loss of international financing in 2009 owing to human rights complaints. Protest at the World Water Forum in Istanbul resulted in the arrests of 39 Kurdish rights activists. Their charge, attempting to influence public option, is punishable by a three-year jail term.[21]

In Chile between 2006 and 2009 at least seven Mapuche activists protesting state development and related loss of traditional lands and resources have been arrested and charged under Pinochet-era antiterrorism laws. Some argue that the culture of governance accompanying the Bush war on terror and the related campaign to establish and utilize Patriot Act laws in other nations has reignited and legitimized this kind of heavy-handed treatment of internal dissidents.[22]

Not all trends in hydrodevelopment have been rights repressive. Increased communication between project-affected communities and distant populations (civil downstream, nationally, and internationally) has transformed dam-affected peoples and, to some degree, created rights-protective space. This increased awareness has prompted the formation of local and regional movements, including Movement of Dam Affected Peoples in Brazil (MAB); African Rivers Network; Latin American Network Against Dams and for Rivers, Communities and Water (REDLAR); Himalayan and Peninsular Hydro-Ecological Network (HYPHEN); and Rivers for Life international meetings of dam-affected peoples. The resurgent push to develop energy and other critical resources and related rise in oppressive actions by the state have, in many cases, strengthened these movements. In some cases civil society protests have transformed governance, as illustrated by the aforementioned social entitlement program for China's dam-displaced peoples. In establishing an annual pension for dam-displaced people in the countryside, the government has formally acknowledged its obligation to provide redress for the abuses accompanying past development projects.

Sometimes civil society protests over proposed hydrodevelopment lead to changes in planning and decision-making processes. For example, a growing number of project-affected communities in Latin America have held *consultas* (consultations that serve as a local referendum) over the question of their support for new dams and mining projects. Originally a participatory element of financing agreements, with the incorporation of consultation and informed consent language in national legislation, *consultas* are increasingly taking on the status of a plebiscite, which is a legally binding vote by communities for or against development proposals. Such efforts are testing the question of whether local peoples truly do have a right to free and prior informed consent as stipulated in international human rights law.[23] When the results are ignored by the state, the InterAmerican Human Rights Commission has increasingly taken a stand.[24]

Finally, in a few instances, efforts to transform the power of dam-affected peoples within development projects from stakeholder (someone who must be consulted and might have some sort of influence or interest in the outcome) to rightsholder (someone with the right to materially benefit from development income) are gaining traction. Host communities in the James Bay region have recently negotiated a share of hydroelectric energy profit as a means mitigating the adverse social and environmental damages of large infrastructure development.[25]

A Final Question on Water and Human Rights

Water is a human need and economic good. We have a societal imperative to provide for that need. Typically we do so through large-scale, technologically intensive projects designed to sustain industry, the economy, and the nation. This approach to water reflects one end of the conceptual continuum in the debate over how best to achieve a viable future.[26]

At the other is a notion of water as a commons resource, a sustaining element in cultural diversity *and* biodiversity. It is a fundamental human right for individuals *and* cultural groups and it has inherent environmental rights that support and sustain the world and that supersede the short-term needs of the state and its economy.[27]

Can we find a middle ground, meeting the societal need for water in ways that support and sustain biocultural diversity? Answering this question requires us to:

- Reconceptualize development priorities, identifying the hidden agendas behind large-scale hydrodevelopment and management schemes and assessing in holistic terms the cumulative and synergistic impact of proposed change.
- Restructure priorities in decision-making frameworks to insure that water is valued, accessed, used, and managed in ways that sustain the ways of life of cultural groups and local communities and their environments.
- Utilize a watershed approach to water management that includes, rather than excludes, and prioritizes the rights and needs of local peoples.

All these actions imply a planning, assessment, monitoring, and management framework in which biocultural health serves as the primary indicator of a sustainable ecosystem.

Notes

1. Portions of this chapter are abstracted from previously published materials. See "Water, Culture, and Power Negotiations at the UN," *Anthropology News* (January 2010, 6, 9) and "Water, Culture, Power: Emerging Trends," American Anthropological Association's blog, http://blog.aaanet.org/2010/01/06/water-culture-power-an-online-feature-from-anthropology-news/, 01/06/10.

   Some of the text on water scarcity was previously published in my chapter "The Commodification of Water and the Human Dimensions of Manufactured Scarcity,"

Globalization, Water, and Health: Resource Management in Times of Scarcity, Linda Whiteford and Scott Whiteford, Eds. (Santa Fe, NM: School for American Research, 2006, 133–52). For similar discussion, see Maude Barlow's 1999 essay "Blue Gold: The Global Water Crisis and the Commodification of the World's Water Supply," *International Forum on Globalization Special Report*, www.ifg.org/bgsummary; John Donahue and Barbara Rose Johnston, Eds., *Water, Culture, & Power: Local Struggles in a Global Context* (Washington, D.C.: Island Press, 1998); Sandra Postel, *Last Oasis: Facing Water Scarcity* (New York: W.W. Norton, 1992, revised 1997); Sandra Postel and Brian Richter, *Rivers for Life* (Washington, D.C.: Island Press, 2003).

2. Catherine Caufield, *In the Rainforest: Report from a Strange, Beautiful, Imperiled World* (Westminster, MD: Alfred A. Knopf, 1984); Marc Reisner, *Cadillac Desert: The American West and Its Disappearing Water* (New York: Viking-Penguin, 1986).

3. The World Bank was part of a steering committee formed in 1986 to supervise the Canadian International Development Agency-financed feasibility study, which included the Canadian International Development Agency and China's Ministry of Water Resources and Electric Power. The World Bank also set up an international panel of experts to evaluate the study. On resettlement, the panel concluded that "feasibility is not yet clearly demonstrated. Unresolved issues pertaining to land availability, job creation and host population, and other issues need further clarification" (Canadian International Development Agency Briefing (transcript), CYJV, *Three Gorges Water Control Project Feasibility Study*, Vol. 1, Appendix A, August 1988).

4. Some of the major financing came from Bank of America, Salomon Smith Barney—now part of Citigroup, Merrill Lynch—with lesser contributions from Chase Securities, JP Morgan, Morgan Stanley; from the Export Credit Agencies of Brazil Canada, France, Germany, Japan, Sweden, and Switzerland; and through the purchase of international bonds by Japan, American banks, European hedge funds, others. See Probe International, "Who's Behind China's Three Gorges Dam: List of International 3G Companies and Financiers," Probe International Report, updated August 2007, http://eprf.ca/pi/3g/Behind3GInternational.pdf, 11/25/09.

5. See, for example, "Changnoi: Not a Picnic for Pak Mool Refugees," reprinted, Probe International, www.probeinternational.org/mekong-utility-watch/changnoi-not-picnic-pak-mool-refugees. See also S. Amornsakchai et al., *Pak Mun Dam, Mekong River Basin, Thailand*, WCD Case Study prepared as an input to the World Commission on Dams, Cape Town, www.dams.org; Patrick McCully, *Silenced Rivers, The Ecology and Politics of Large Dams* (London: Zed Books, 1996, 2001); and Vandana Shiva, *Staying Alive: Women, Ecology, and Survival in India* (New Delhi: Zed Press, 1988); *Ecology and the Politics of Survival: Conflicts over Natural Resources in India* (Thousand Oaks, CA: Sage Publications, 1988); *Water Wars: Privatization, Pollution, and Profit* (Cambridge, MA: South End Press, 2003).

6. Heffa Schücking, "Turning Up the Heat on Export Credit Agencies," *Development Today* (Nordic publication), November 16, 1998, posted on ECA Watch, www.eca-watch.org/eca/heat.html, 11/25/09.

7. World Commission on Dams (WCD), *Dams and Development: A New Framework for Decision Making*, final report of the World Commission on Dams (Cape Town: Earthscan, 2000).

8. WCD, note 27, 226–31; Barbara Rose Johnston, "Reparations and the Right to Remedy," contributing report, *Thematic Review 1.3: Displacement, Resettlement, Reparations, and Development* (Cape Town: World Commission on Dams, 2000).

9. See, for example, Thayer Scudder, *The Future of Large Dams* (London: Earthscan, 2006).

10. Laura Carlsen, "Plan Puebla-Panama Advances: New Name, Same Game" ("El Plan Puebla Panamá Avanza: Nuevo Nombre, el Mismo Juego,") Americas Program, Trans. September 11, 2009, http://americas.irc-online.org/am/6410.

11. Jeoren Warner, "Contested Hydrohegemony: Hydraulic Control and Security in Turkey," *Water Alternatives* 1(2) 2008: 271–88.

12. Thomas Homer-Dixon (2001), and Michael Klare (2003).

13. Water Sector Board of the Sustainable Development Network of the World Bank Group, "Directions in Hydropower: Scaling Up Development," Water Working Notes No. 21, June 2009.

14. Walter Fernandes, "Singur and the Displacement Scenario," *Economic and Political Weekly*, 42(3), January 20–26, 2007: 203–06.

15. China's massive 7.9 Wenchuan earthquake in Sichuan province in 2008 is widely thought to be the catastrophic result of a large reservoir built close to the earthquake's geological fault line. See summation by Richard Stone, "Some Unwelcome Questions About Big Dams," *Science* May 8, 2009 324: 714.

16. Brian Richter, Sandra Postel, Carmen Revenga, Thayer Scudder, Bernhard Lehner, Allegra Churchill, and Morgan Chow, "Lost in Development's Shadow: The Downstream Human Consequences of Dams," *Water Alternatives* 3(2) 2010:14–21.

17. Water, with its key role in sustaining the dignity and the equal rights of human beings and life itself, was recognized as an essential human need under the 1981 *Convention on the Elimination of All Forms of Discrimination against Women* and the 1989 *Convention on the Rights of the Child* (CEDAW Article 14(2)(h) and CROC Article 24(2)(c)). In 2003 the right to drinkable water and adequate sanitation were recognized as essential parts of the right to health and the right to an adequate standard of living in the *International Covenant on Economic, Social and Cultural Rights* (United Nations Committee on Economic, Social, and Cultural Rights, General Comment 15, "The Right to Water," 20/1/2003, UN Doc E/C.12/2002/11, and General Comment 14, as footnote 3). In this covenant the United Nations expressly stated that the human right to water entitles everyone to sufficient, safe, acceptable, accessible, and affordable water for personal and domestic uses (General Comment 15, as footnote 5). In 2010 the UN General Assembly, noting with concern that some 884 million people were without access to safe drinking water and more than 2.6 billion lacked access to basic sanitation, adopted the human right to water and sanitation as a basic right (A/RES/64/292).

18. Tomaso Fernando and Miguel Espichan, "Right over Water or Right to Water: A Global and Local Comparison of Legal Approaches," unpublished paper, International University College, Master of Science in Comparative Law, Economics, and Finance.

19. See Major Randall Reed, *Dehydrated National Security: Water Scarcity, The Emerging Threat of the 21st Century*, MA thesis, School of Advanced Air and Space Studies, Air University, Maxwell Air Force Base, Alabama, June 2004, www.afresearch.org.

20. In preparing this paper I did a Google news search for reports of people being arrested for protesting water development for the calendar year of 2009, finding news accounts of such arrests in Turkey, El Salvador, China, India, Bangladesh, Burma, Thailand, Borneo, Sudan, the United States, Canada, Australia, Greece, and Brazil.

21. The Corner House and Kurdish Human Rights Project 2007; Kurdish Human Rights Project, Ilisu Dam Campaign, The Corner House 2002; Barbara Rose Johnston, "Pulse of the Planet—Water, Culture Wars," *CounterPunch* May 27, 2009, www.counterpunch.org/johnston03272009.html.

22. Elizabeth Benjamin, "Chile Invokes Pinochet-Era Anti-Terrorism Law against Mapuche Demonstrators," Council on Hemispheric Affairs, 2009, www.coha.org/chile-invokes-pinochet-era-anti-terrorism-law-against-mapuche-demonstrators.

23. For an account of recent *consultiva* see Monti Aguirre, "One Person One Vote: The Voice of Community in Development Decisions," *International Rivers Review*, June 2009: 4–5. For a discussion of consultations as an emerging referendum, with growing legal

authority in determining development decisions, see Brant McGee, "The Community Referendum: Participatory Democracy and the Right to Free, Prior, and Informed Consent to Development," *Berkeley Journal of International Law* 27(2) 2009: 570–635.

24. See, for example, the November 2, 2009, Inter-American Commission on Human Rights hearing on dam construction trends in Latin America, where dam-affected peoples and nongovernmental organizations presented information showing that governments continue to build dams with great social, environmental, and economic costs, with disregard for national and international environmental and human rights law. More than 300 large dams are planned for the region: International Rivers, "Inter-American Commission on Human Rights Examines Impacts of Large Dams in Latin America," October 29, 2009, press release, www.internationalrivers.org/en/node/4793.

25. The notion of resident peoples as rights holders with an equity stake in the development project has been explored by the World Commission in Dams (WCD 2000, note 7), the World Bank (*Infrastructure at the Crossroads: Lessons from 20 Years of World Bank Experience*, Washington D.C.: World Bank, 2006), and in Anthony Oliver-Smith, Ed., *Development-Forced Displacement and Resettlement: A Global Human Rights Crisis* (Santa Fe, NM: SAR Press, 2009).

26. See, The Dublin Statement of the International Conference on Water and the Environment, 1992.

27. As argued, for example, by Maude Barlow, *Blue Covenant: The Global Water Crisis and the Coming Battle for the Right to Water* (McClelland & Stewart Ltd., 2007).

SNAPSHOT: From Ecological Disaster to Constitutional Crisis: Dams on Brazil's Xingu River[1]

Terence Turner

Once again the indigenous peoples of the Xingú valley in the Brazilian Amazon are planning to make the long journey to the town of Altamira, where the Trans-Amazonica highway crosses the Xingú. Their ultimate destination is the island of Pimental, a short distance downriver from the town, where the Brazilian government plans to build a huge hydroelectric dam they call Belo Monte (after the nearest Brazilian village). The Indians' bold plan is to prevent the construction of the dam by building a new village directly on top of the proposed dam site and maintaining their occupation until the government abandons its plans.

The planning is being led by the Kayapo, the largest and most politically organized of the indigenous nations of the region, with the participation of other indigenous groups of the Xingú Valley. The Kayapo are not waiting for the 23 groups to reach consensus. They have already seized the ferry that carries Brazil Route 80, an important link in the Trans-Amazonica highway system, across the Xingú River at the Kayapo village of Piaraçú. The ferry and river crossing are now guarded by armed Kayapo warriors, who have announced that they will continue their blockade until the government negotiates with them.

This will not be the first indigenous encampment organized by the Kayapo in their effort to stop the building of dams on the Xingú. In 1989, when the government first set out to implement its plan for a giant hydroelectric complex on the Xingú, with financial support from the World Bank, the Kayapo led a five-day rally of 40 indigenous nations at Altamira. The rally was extensively covered by national and international media and succeeded in persuading the World Bank to withdraw its construction loan. Subsequently the Xingú dam scheme remained dormant, but not dead, for two decades. Two years ago it was revived as the centerpiece of the Lula government's Project for Accelerated Development. As a Brazilian activist remarked at the time: "These big dams are like vampires: you pound a stake through their hearts but they rise again from the grave and you have to do it all over again."

The Xingú River is one of the major tributaries of the Amazon. With its numerous affluents it has created a valley larger than Texas that remains perhaps the least disturbed and most diverse ecosystem in Brazilian Amazonia. It is unquestionably the most culturally diverse. Twenty-three indigenous peoples of distinct cultures and languages make their homes there, most of them among the headwaters of the Upper Xingú, which has been made a national park by the Brazilian state. In the Middle Xingú region just to the north (downriver) of the National Park the large and politically dynamic Kayapo people inhabit seven mostly contiguous reserves totaling 150,000 km² (roughly the size of Austria). Further downriver several other indigenous peoples live in varying degrees of proximity with Brazilian settlers. Some subsist on a technology little different from that of the Indians, and others dwelling in towns they have established along the river and the Trans-Amazonica highway. This variegated system of social and cultural groups and ecosystems, which has evolved a relatively sustainable pattern of coexistence, have now been imperiled by the Federal government's plan to build six giant hydroelectric dams along the Xingu and its largest tributary, the Irirí. Construction on the first and largest of these, Belo Monte, is scheduled to start in January 2011. The master plan for damming the Amazon river system was originally created in the 1970s by the military dictatorship then in power. It essentially treats the Amazon as a reservoir of natural resources to be extracted without regard for environmental destruction or the displacement and pauperization of indigenous and local inhabitants. It has come as a shock to many supporters of the democratically elected government of President Lula Ignacio da Silva that Lula seems not only to have revived this authoritarian relic, with its reliance on technologically problematic and inefficient mega-dams, but also has made it the centerpiece and master symbol of his Accelerated Development Project, his program to make the Brazilian economy one of the world's greatest, and seems intent on carrying it out in defiance of democratic processes and legality.

Belo Monte would be the third largest hydroelectric dam complex in the world, comprising one huge dam and two smaller dams and requiring the diversion of the water from a 60-mile stretch of the river through canals and underground tunnels to two massive arrays of turbines. The whole system would have a peak generating capacity of 11,200 kilowatt hours. Many critics of the project, however, have pointed out that this level of output would be attainable only for four months out of the year, at the height of the rainy season. For the remaining eight months, when the level of the river falls by 30 feet or more, the average output would fall to an annual rate of only 4,000 kilowatt hours. Thus the electricity that the dam would generate, measured against the enormous cost of the dam, would be considerably more expensive than that potentially produced by alternative means. Considering the relatively short life expectancy of dams in the Amazon because of silting and acidic erosion of turbine blades, the Belo Monte Dam does not appear to be economically viable as a stand-alone dam, without another big dam upriver with a large enough reservoir to release a sufficient volume of water during the dry season to keep Belo Monte producing at close to its peak capacity all year. There are plans for such a dam, called Altamira, which would have an enormous reservoir that would flood a vast area of forest, as well as for four more dams upriver.

The government's assurances that Belo Monte is viable by itself are widely disbelieved by engineers, ecological critics, and indigenous inhabitants alike, who suspect that each dam in the series will become a source of pressure for building another dam above it in the series—a hydrological "domino effect." The government's credibility is not helped by its 20-year record of secrecy and misrepresentation of its plans for the Xingú project.

These economic and technical objections, however, are not the only serious problems of the Belo Monte project. The 60-mile section of river that would be diverted now passes through two indigenous reservations (Arara and Paquiçamba-Juruna), whose people depend on the river for fish and transportation. Their villages would become unviable. The Brazilian constitution mandates that indigenous communities be consulted in advance of development projects that are within their reserved territories or affect their livelihoods. Yet government agencies have defiantly refused to comply with this legal requirement, as they have elsewhere in the Xingú. Agencies also have failed to produce a satisfactory environmental impact evaluation, another legal requirement. The construction license was issued in any case under intense political pressure.

This instance, and others, of cutting legal corners to push through the dam project have unleashed bitter and portentous confrontations within the government itself. The Brazilian state is far from monolithically behind the Xingú Dam Project. The Public Ministry, an autonomous governmental agency empowered to decide on the constitutionality and legality of government projects and actions, has openly denounced the Belo Monte Dam project as illegal, in violation of the constitution, and likely to produce an environmental catastrophe. On April 7, 2010, the Public Ministry handed down two devastating decisions, one finding the government's plan to hold the auction at Altamira unconstitutional and in violation of several existing laws, and the other charging that the Belo Monte Project would violate the constitutional and legal rights of indigenous peoples whose territories and communities it would either flood or cut off from access to the river. The ministry called for the annulment of the auction for construction bids.

The attorney general of Brazil, channeling an infuriated Lula, threatened to have the attorneys of the Public Ministry arrested and imprisoned for interfering with the project, but the lawyers of the Public Ministry stood firm. They have not been arrested, but the threat of this illegal attempt at repression of political opposition to state policies remains open and has been repeated by the attorney general. Meanwhile, in another echo of the military regime that preceded his, President Lula defiantly vowed to build Belo Monte. He also brushed aside the criticisms of engineers, biologists and environmentalists, Brazilian and international NGOs, indigenous peoples, and local Brazilian settler organizations.

In the week before the auction a courageous federal judge in Altamira annulled the government's decision to hold the auction. This ruling was immediately reversed by the Regional Appeals Court in Brasília. The Altamira court judge then handed down a second order to cancel the auction, a 50-page document with extensive legal arguments, precedents, and references based on Public Ministry documents. The Appeals Court again reversed the decision, and the auction was held. This blatant corruption of the legal system by political pressure from the government, with the acquiescence of one of the highest courts of the land, outraged of Brazil's legal professionals and further aroused the opposition of the growing array of elements of Brazilian civil society who have been organizing against Belo Monte and the other planned Xingú dams. Many of these groups joined in a march in Brasilia on April 12 that targeted the government ministries implicated in approving the plan for Belo Monte and called for the cancellation of the project. They were joined by James Cameron, writer and director of *Avatar*, and members of the cast of the film, who were struck by the parallels between the Brazilian situation and the battle of Avatar's fictional indigenous people against a giant corporation attempting to extract precious minerals from their planet.

At the time of this writing, a Kayapo delegation led by Chief "Raoni" (or as he pronounces it, Rop-ni) of the Xingu Kayapo is traveling through France, Belgium, and Luxembourg, visiting government ministers and heads of state and appealing for support of the indigenous campaign against the Xingú dams. Other campaigns, some involving other tours by indigenous leaders, are getting under way in Europe and North America. The Brazilian government's attempt to push ahead the Xingú Dam scheme in the face of the mounting storm of opposition is becoming a problem for Brazil's foreign relations. Within Brazil, this issue has already moved from its original status as a localized problem involving indigenous rights and ecological impacts of a dam in a remote part of the Amazon to a major legal, political, and constitutional crisis involving Brazil's political conduct as a democratic state.

At stake in this crisis is Brazil's political ability to reconcile and accommodate the demands of its capital-intensive policy of economic growth, epitomized by its "accelerated development" project, with the principles of constitutional legality and democracy supported by its rapidly growing middle class in alliance with the indigenous and settler groups of its vast Amazonian interior. An irony of the Xingú Dam project is that it has done much to bring this historically unique alliance into political being. In so doing it inadvertently has made a profoundly hopeful contribution to the development of Brazilian democratic civil society. This contribution has been realized only because of to the courage, leadership, and political resourcefulness of the Kayapo, other indigenous groups who have supported them, and the Brazilian social movements of the Xingú Valley.

Whatever the immediate outcome of the struggle over the Belo Monte project, the broad alliance of indigenous peoples, Brazilian settlers and social movements, environmentalists, human rights organizations, and elements of the Brazilian state committed to democratic legality and constitutionality in common opposition to the dam scheme represents a profound social movement. This alliance will continue the fight against the other dams the government hopes to build in the Xingú, dams that would have catastrophic effects on the flora, fauna, and human inhabitants of the Xingú valley.

Statements by Indigenous Leaders on Belo Monte

What follows are two press releases by indigenous leaders on the implications of the Belo Monte Dam. The first is by the Mentuktire Kayapo leader Megaron Txukarramãe; the other is by the Kayapo leader and elder statesman Ropni Mentuktire, in concert with other indigenous leaders of the Xingú.

Letter to the Press from Megaron Txukarramãe

We, the leaders and warriors of our movement, are here in Piaraçu and we will remain here, continuing our blockade of the ferry across the Xingú River so long as President Luis Inácio Lula da Silva continues to insist on building the dam at Belo Monte.

We are outraged to hear Lula say that he will build the dam whatever it takes, even if it means resort to force!

Now we Indians and all of us who voted for Lula are discovering who this man really is. We are not bandits, we are not drug-traffickers that he should treat us this way. All that we want is that the Belo Monte Dam should not be constructed. We here have no weapons to confront an attempt to remove us by force. If Lula wants to finish us off as he seems to be suggesting, the whole world will know that we will have died fighting for our rights.

Lula has shown that he is the Number one enemy of the Indians, and the President of the National Indian Foundation, Marcio Meira, has shown that he is in second place as the enemy of indigenous people. He has failed to demarcate Indigenous lands, or to protect or provide services to existing indigenous territories. We indigenous leaders have been prevented from entering the national offices of the Indian Agency by armed troops.

The Indians of this country have simply been abandoned, we who were the original inhabitants of this country have been forgotten by the government of Lula, who wants only our destruction. This is the conclusion we have drawn from his actions.

(Signed) Indigenous leader Megaron Txukarramãe, Village of Piaraçu, 26 April, 2010

We, the Indigenous People of The Xingú, Do Not Want the Belo Monte Dam, by Chief Ropni Kayapó, Chief Bepkamati Kayapó, and Yakareti Juruna

We, the indigenous people of the Xingú, are here fighting for our people and for our land, but we are also fighting for the future of the world.

President Lula said last week that he is worried about the Indians and about Amazonia, and that he does not want international NGOs speaking out against Belo Monte. Well, we are not international NGOs.

We, 62 indigenous leaders of the communities of Bacajá, Mrotidjam, Kararaô, Terra-Wanga, Boa Vista Km. 17, Tukamã, Kapoto, Moikarakô, Aukre, Kikretum, Potikrô, Tukala, Mentuktire, Omekrankum, Cakamkuben e Pokalmone, have already suffered many invasions and threats. When the Portuguese arrived in Brazil, we Indians were already here and many of us died. We lost enormous territories, the rights we had possessed, and many also lost part of their cultures. Other peoples completely disappeared.

The forest is our butcher shop, the River is our food market. We do not want others meddling with our Xingú and its tributaries, or threatening our villages and our children, whom we want to grow up in our culture.

We do not accept the hydroelectric dam of Belo Monte because we understand that will only bring more destruction to our region. We are not thinking only of the place where they want to build the dam, but of all the destruction that the dam will cause in the future: more industrial enterprises, more ranches, more land invasions, more conflicts and the construction of even more dams. The way the white men are going, they will rapidly destroy everything. We ask: What more does the government want? For what do they need more energy at the cost of so much destruction?

We have already held many conferences and big meetings against Belo Monte, as we did in 1989 and 2008 in Altamira, and in 2009 in the village of Piaraçu, at which many of the leaders assembled here were also present. We have already spoken personally with President Lula and explained to him that we do not want this dam, and he promised us that this dam would not be rammed down our throats. We have also spoken with Eletronorte and Eletrobras, with the National Indian Foundation (FUNAI) and with the Brazilian Institute for the Environment (IBAMA). We have warned the government that if it goes ahead with this dam project, it will mean war. The government did not understand our message and has again defied the indigenous peoples, declaring that it will build the dam whatever it takes. When President Lula says this, he reveals how little importance he attaches to what the indigenous people are saying and that he has no idea of our rights. An example of this lack of respect was the holding of the auction for the construction contracts of Belo Monte in the Week of the Indian.

For these reasons we, the indigenous peoples of the Xingú region, are inviting James Cameron and his crew, and representatives of Xingu Vivo para Sempre (Xingú Alive Forever), the Movement of Women the Xingú, the Socioenvironmental Institute (ISA), the Missionary Council of the Church (CIMI), Amazon Watch and other organizations, to help us spread our message throughout the world, and to the many Brazilians who do not know what is happening in the Xingú. We are issuing this invitation because there are people in many parts of Brazil and in foreign countries who want to support and protect indigenous peoples and their lands. These people are very welcome among us.

We are here fighting for our people, for our lands, for our forests, for our rivers, for our children and for the honor of our ancestors. We fight also for the future of the world, because we know that these forests bring benefits not only for the Indians but for the people of Brazil and the entire world. We also know that if these forests are destroyed many people will suffer much more, because they are already suffering from the destruction that has already been done; because everything is interconnected, like the blood that unites a single family.

The world must know what is happening here, it must see that by destroying the forests and the indigenous peoples they are destroying the world. This is why we do not want Belo Monte. Belo Monte means the destruction of our people.

To conclude, we are prepared, strong and hardened for this struggle, and we remember what a North American indigenous kinsman wrote to the American President many years ago: " Only when the white man has chopped down the forest, killed all the fish, slaughtered all the animals and destroyed all the rivers will he perceive that nobody can eat money."

Note

1. An earlier version of this commentary was published on the *Anthropologyworks* blog and is reprinted with the author's permission. Posted online May 12, 2010, http://anthropologyworks. com/?p=1931#more-1931.

SNAPSHOT: Dam Legacies: Guatemala's Chixoy Dam-Affected Communities

Barbara Rose Johnston

I first met members of the Chixoy dam-affected communities in July 2003 in Pacux, a resettlement village many hours drive northeast of Guatemala City. I was invited by village residents to attend a meeting they had organized with the larger dam-displaced community and their advocates—International Rivers, Rights Action Guatemala, and Reform the World Bank, Italy. Our goal was to craft a participatory strategy for dam-affected people to collaborate in a scientific study of development projects and to address consequential damages, meaningful remedy, and how reparations can bring a more peaceful future. I had already poured over survivor testimonies, project documents, and truth commission findings about Chixoy and other dams for a reparations briefing I wrote for the World Commission on Dams.[1] But I was completely unprepared for the reality of these people, in this place, with its' immense poverty, deep sadness, and almost palpable tension. Death threats and violence were not simply a matter of history, but a fact of daily life.

To enter Pacux we drove through a military compound, past an armed sentry gate, down the singular road to meet in a community hall of a village surrounded by chain link and razor-wire fencing. Similar model villages, as these guarded compounds are called, were built throughout rural Guatemala in the 1980s using the same militarized blueprint first deployed for Pacux. As in Pacux, Mayan massacre survivors were rounded up, kept under armed guard, "re-educated," and used as slave labor. Most of these model villages were demilitarized after the 1996 Peace Accords. In 2003 the only militarized internment camp in the country was the village of Pacux. In later years, as I delved further into the Chixoy Dam history and its consequences, I came to understand that this village of Pacux and the experiences of its residents embodies all that is the worst one can say about the structural violence that accompanies large-dam displacement and the opportunism that international development financing offers to a nation at war against its' own civilian population.

Consider these facts.[2] The Chixoy Dam was built during the most intense period of state-sponsored violence against Guatemala's Mayan civilian population. Financing for this dam, largely provided by the World Bank and InterAmerican Development Bank, was the primary source of income for the military dictatorship. Millions of dollars were included in these loans to acquire land for the development, craft resettlement and compensation plans, acquire replacement land and build resettlement villages, and issue compensatory payments and services; yet these funds were used for other purposes. Development occurred without securing legal title to much of the land supporting the dam, hydroelectric facility, and the reservoir. Residents were flooded out or forced to leave at gunpoint. When the reservoir waters rose in January 1983, 10 communities in the Chixoy River Basin had been destroyed and residents massacred, including the village of Río Negro. Survivors were hunted in the surrounding hills; some were killed, others forcibly resettled. In the few instances where compensatory agreements were made, community leaders were assassinated and the signed *Actas* disappeared when leaders of those communities were assassinated. Resettlement villages were eventually built, though in the case of Pacux, plans developed with resident input and submitted to project financiers were discarded and a militarized guarded compound was built in its place. Compensatory efforts at the time and in later years were grossly inadequate to meet the basic needs of displaced communities, let alone provide redress for the full extent of lost land, property, communal resources, livelihoods, and lives.

The dam was constructed in the midst of a 36-year civil war, during which 200,000 people reportedly died or disappeared. A subsequent United Nations-sponsored investigation determined that by the time the war ended in 1996 acts of genocide had been committed against more than 250,000 Mayan Indians, and the Guatemalan Army was responsible for 93% of these human rights abuses. The U.S. government and U.S. corporations played a key role in maintaining the right-wing military governments in power during most of the war. Despite these findings no high-level military officer has tried and sentenced in Guatemalan Courts.[3]

The second day of my July 2003 trip to Guatemala is now known as Black Thursday. During our meeting about the right to remedy, Guatemala's principle architect of state-sponsored terror, General Efrain Rios Montt, was nominated by his party to run for President. When the Supreme Court ruled that the candidacy violated Guatemala's constitution, Montt called on his supporters to take to the streets. Masked and armed with clubs, guns and machetes, these supporters set up blockades and set fire to cars and buildings, shutting down the streets of Guatemala City's wealthiest district, and breaking into the offices of major human rights organizations, including the Rigoberta Menchú Foundation. Announcements over the radio and mobile speakers urged residents to stay in their homes. The U.S. Embassy and UN Mission closed their doors and evacuated staff before the international airport was shut down. After two days of rioting Guatemala's Constitutional Court reversed the rulings of its' Supreme Court and approved the candidacy of former dictator Efrain Rios Montt for president. (In November 2003 he came in third, and at this writing is still serving as a sitting member of Congress.) A subsequent investigation of these events by the *Procuraduria de los Derechos Humanos*, Guatemala's human rights ombudsman concluded the violence was "supported, planned and executed by public employees and functionaries" of the Rios Montt's party (FRG) and directly blamed the Guatemalan president, vice president, the Minister of Governance, and an ex-chief of the national police.[4]

How could we translate Chixoy Dam injustices into a compelling case for reparation when the rule of law in Guatemala is so fragile? How could such a case be tried when other potentially culpable parties—the development banks whose loans were repaid in full—are international entities that lack standing in national courts? Our strategy was to conduct an independent scientific investigation and produce a report that draws upon multiple sources of evidence to reconstruct the hydroproject history in relation to the legal norms and development requirements of the time, events and related human rights abuses, and the consequential damages for people, families, communities, and the environment. Hundreds of people collaborated in this endeavor, working on community outreach, capacity building, community histories, needs assessments, household surveys, land title searches, archival research, ethnographic interviews, English/Spanish/Mayan translations, data analysis, and peer review. As the principle investigator I conducted an audit of the project records and a consequential damage assessment of the social program failures. The result—was a five-volume, peer reviewed study completed in July 2005—was formally presented to the Government of Guatemala, the World Bank and InterAmerican Development Bank, the InterAmerican Human Rights Commission, and the UN Special Rapporteur on Indigenous Peoples.

What were our major findings? The study demonstrated the failure of developers (INDE), the government of Guatemala, and the major financiers (Inter-American Development Bank [IADB] and World Bank) to achieve their contractual obligations. Project-affected people were not systematically consulted despite repeated protests and petitions. Displacement occurred at gunpoint; there were massacres; financiers continued to disburse funds amid escalating violence. The IADB and World Bank knew of failures in the resettlement process and the risks of impoverishment but, given the opportunity of new loan negotiations, did not revamp the programs. These financiers also were aware that legal title to the land for the hydroelectric facility, the dam and its reservoir had not been secured—a direct violation of loan agreements and bank lending policies.

The lack of viable resettlement and remediation programs contributed to the violence. Communities that attempted to negotiate fair compensation were declared guerrilla-supporting communities and the military and civil patrols were used to forcibly remove people from the reservoir site. (Guerrilla activity did occur in this area, but it did not begin until well after dam construction had begun.)[5] A string of horrors included the March 1980 massacre in Río Negro; February 1982 massacre of Rio Negro community in Xococ; February 1982 massacre of Rio Negro residents in Rio Negro; May 1982 massacre of Rio Negro survivors and their hosts at Los Encuentros; and, the September 1982 massacre of Rio Negro survivors and their hosts at Agua Fria. Other communities in the Chixoy River Basin destroyed by massacre in this period include: La Laguna, Comalmapa, Jocotales, Chitucan, Los Mangales, Pacaal, and Hacienda Chitucan.[6] Demands for compensation from other dam-affected communities were silenced by INDE workers who threatened them with the specter of the Rio Negro massacres.

For survivors, the promises articulated in initial relocation negotiations—fertile lands, adequate housing, just compensation for property losses, electricity and potable water, support for community health and education workers, and effective economic development—failed to materialize. No realistic effort was made to restore the livelihoods of affected people. These failures, their social consequences, and especially the violence are all documented in World Bank and IADB project files and reports. Staff from the World Bank and IADB visited the area to conduct performance evaluations and new feasibility studies in support of additional financing.

An archaeological research team worked in the Chixoy River Basin periodically from 1978 through 1982 and their reports, communications, and concerns are part of the project record. INDE resettlement officers recorded conflicts and other details regarding all families in the affected communities, which they submitted to the IADB throughout the life of the project.

Although survivors have filed complaints and testified in various forums over the years, remedial assistance from the responsible parties has been difficult to secure. As a Guatemala-based World Bank staffer explained to me in 2003, because the loans had been repaid in full the Banks have no legal obligation to survivors. Further, he argued, given international attention and aid to the Rio Negro massacres and the plight of surviving communities, these people are actually better off than other rural Mayan communities. To determine whether this latter assertion was valid, in 2004 we conducted household surveys dam-affected communities using many of the same indicators used by the World Bank in their 2003 assessment of national and rural Mayan poverty rates (including data from villages which have suffered massacres). We found that household production in the pre-dam era (circa 1976) provided for all food needs in 79% of the total survey population. In 2004 household production sustained all food needs for 28% of the survey population. In resettlement communities deterioration of household production was even greater: the numbers were 93% in 1976 and 26% in 2004. The declining ability to produce food is directly related to the loss of productive agricultural land, pastureland, and loss of access to viable river and forest resources. A decreased ability to generate monetary income was also measurable. For displaced residents living in urbanized resettlement villages, productive lands were scarce or, when provided, located at great distances. The consequential damages of these losses are clearly illustrated in household survey data. Significant declines in dietary protein help explain the region's extraordinarily high rates of malnutrition and infant mortality.

Household surveys and archival research also demonstrated a significant undercount of the size of the dam-affected population. Downstream and upstream communities were not considered affected, never compensated, and subjected to intimidation and violence. Some families displaced by the dam were excluded from the initial 1977 census; others were disenfranchised in the 1991 post-project evaluation, because male heads of household were not present at the time of the census (they were in search of work or had been killed). In 2005 people in the resettlement villages were living in extreme poverty, with crumbling homes and few economic opportunities. For those who remained in the Chixoy River Basin, periodic flooding reduced the agricultural season and harvests. Many local fisheries were destroyed. Downstream wells and springs dried up, water was often contaminated, crop failures were common, and flash floods from unannounced dam releases severely eroded riverbanks and agricultural fields and killed people.

What were the driving forces that led people to commit violence and massacre to achieve displacement? Who knew, at the time, of the connections between dam construction and human rights abuse? Where did the money earmarked for resettlement, compensation, and restoration, actually go? What, in concrete human environmental terms, are the damages from inept and abusive development? How might meaningful remedies be achieved?

We conducted our study in an open and transparent fashion, notifying and inviting the government of Guatemala, financiers, and international human rights agencies. Clearly, we needed rights-protective space to pursue dangerous questions, so we made periodic reports to the United Nations Special Rapporter for Indigenous Peoples. Whenever the Special Rapporteur visited Guatemala, the case was on his agenda. The Inter-American Human Rights Commission also placed this case high on their agenda and regularly requested updates from the government of Guatemala on the status of this case. Also important was international media, especially coverage of the September 2004 protest at the Chixoy Dam site, as a result of which the INDE agreed to negotiate reparations. When the INDE orchestrated the arrest of the nine community leaders who signed the reparations negotiation agreement two weeks later, international attention returned to the Chixoy case and the culture of impunity in Guatemala.[7]

The formal presentation of our completed study to responsible parties was an opportunity to transform this negative international attention by demonstrating Guatemala's progress in addressing human rights abuses. In 2006 the Guatemalan government reconfirmed its commitment to Chixoy reparations and in 2008 established a formal negotiations process facilitated by the Inter-American Human Rights Commission. The Chixoy study served as a key evidentiary document in these negotiations. At this writing, an agreement providing reparation for social, economic, cultural, and other consequential damages has been finalized and awaits the signature of Guatemala President Colom. Whether it is fully implemented remains to be seen. Nevertheless, surviving families and the nation have demonstrated that some measure of justice is achievable.

What lessons does this story offer for a troubled world? When most of us hear the term *reparation*, we assume that it simply means monetary compensation. Yet, as a legal and social construct, the term means so much more: reparation as outlined in the United Nations guidelines for Reparation and the Right to Remedy refers to those social, political, and economic actions, mechanisms, and processes that allow for meaningful remedy in all its forms, and thus the restoration of human dignity. Ideally, reparation is both a plan for peace and the process that allows wounds to heal. In Guatemala the process of documenting the Chixoy Dam history, assessing damages, and negotiating a plan for remedy allows the people and their government to move forward, working together to repair, restore, commemorate, and secure the means to rebuild a health way of life.

The lessons we learn from examining the human environmental rights abuses in past dam development and devising meaningful remedy are lessons in the meaning of the term security. Dealing with dam legacy issues and rebuilding a sustainable way of life requires governance and action that prioritizes human *and* environmental security over profit and power. This is a legacy we cannot afford to ignore.

Notes

1. Barbara Rose Johnston, "Reparations and the Right to Remedy," contributing report, Thematic Review 1.3: Displacement, Resettlement, Reparations, and Development (Cape Town: World Commission on Dams, 2000).

2. Barbara Rose Johnston, *Chixoy Dam Legacy Issues Study*; Vol. 1: Executive Summary: Consequential Damages and Reparation—Recommendations for Remedy; Vol. 2: Document Review and Chronology of Relevant Actions and Events; Vol. 3: Consequential Damage Assessment of Chixoy River Basin Communities; Vol. 4: Social Investigation of the Communities Affected by the Chixoy Dam, Iñaqui Aguirre, Ed.; Vol. 5: Estudio Histórico, Catastral, Registral y Geográfico de las Comunidades Afectadas por la Inundación Provocada por la Construcción de la Presa Pueblo Viejo-Quixal, sobre el Río Negro o Chixoy, by Diego Martínez Estrada (Santa Cruz, CA: Center for Political Ecology, 2005), www.centerforpoliticalecology.org, 07/15/10.

3. CEH (Comisión para el Esclarecimiento Histórico), *Informe de la Comisión para el Esclarecimiento Histórico, Guatemala: Memoria del Silencio*. Guatemala: Oficina de Servicios para Proyectos de las Naciones Unidas, 1999, 12 vols.). Also published in English as *Guatemala: Memory of Silence*. Report of the Historical Clarification Commission. American Association for the Advancement of Science, http://shr.aaas.org/guatemala/ceh/report/english/toc.html, 07/15/10.

   Río Negro case is detailed in *Caso ilustrativo número 10: Masacre y eliminación de la comunidad de Río Negro*, Capítulo VI, Casos ilustrativos—Anexo 1, Vol. 1, 48.

4. Despite efforts to disrupt the investigation, including an August 27, 2003 burglary of the Ombudsman's office and seizure of computers and other records, it was widely reported in the Guatemalan press that the *Procuraduria de los Derechos Humanos* investigation confirmed that the FRG drew on social program funds to bankroll the staged protest.

5. See D. Douzant-Rosenfeld, "La vallée du Río Chixoy et le barrage de Pueblo Viejo: Géographie et problèmes de la population déplacée par le lac de retenue (Baja Verapaz)," A. Ichon, Ed., *La vallée moyenne du Río Chixoy (Guatemala), 6: Occupation préhispanique et problèmes actuels* (Paris: Institut d'Ethnologie, CNRS; Santa, Guatemala: Editorial Piedra, 1988, 17–51).

6. CEH, note 3.

7. Amnesty International, "Persecution and Resistance: The Experience of Human Rights Defenders in Guatemala and Honduras," August 2007, www.amnestyusa.org/document.php?lang=e&id=ENGAMR020012007, 08/16/10.

INDEX

9/11: pre-9/11, 20, 446; events of, 37, 46, 173, 372; post-9/11, 21, 142, 171, 173, 373, 446, 449

A

Abramova, V. N., 395
Ackley, Arlyn, 153, 155
Ackley, Charles, 151
Ackley, Chief Willard, 151
Ackley, Fred, 151, 156
adaptation, 10, 427; in agriculture, 105, 196; to climate change, 413, 420–422, n423, 428, 429; and culture 10–11, 12, 414, n423; economic response to globalization, 228; and radiation exposure, 384, 397, 404; society, 131; in subsistence strategies, 105, 243–444
AEC. *See* United States Atomic Energy Commission
Afghanistan, war in, 37, 47, 337, 351, 352, 354
Africa, 9, 18, 19, n24, n25, 43, 44, 81–92, 101–119, 139, 167, 169, 225, 285–304, 311–328, 337, 447, 448, 449; conservation efforts in (*table*), 82; human evolution in, 9–10; human rights in, 90–92. *See also* coercive conservation; mining; refugees; repatriation; resettlement; *specific countries*; violent conflict; wildlife
African American men, U.S. Presidential apology for Tuskegee experiments, 17
African Wildlife Foundation (AWF), 85
agriculture: chemicals, use of, 10, 42, 112, 181, 182, 184, 185, 188, 189, 192, 195, 201, 443; community supported associations (CSAs), 193, 199, 235; and conservation movement, 66, 105, 183, 184, 185, 190, 200, 277, 292; export agriculture, 210, 233, 446;

family farms, 186, 234; gardens, 41, 89, 106, 107, 108, 244, 388, 415, 416, 417; industrial, 182, 183, 195, 196, 197, 199, 234; loans to farmers, 184–185, 233, 446; *milpa*, 243, 244; organic, 92, 181–202, 235, 270; riverine cultivation, 103, 105, 106, 107, 108, 110, 116, 444; sustainable, 117, 187–189, 191, 195, 233, 267, 268; swidden, 29, 34, 35, 59, 132, n229, 255, 278. *See also* Food and Agriculture Organization, biofuels, GMOs
agropastoralists. *See* Viliui Sakha
AIDS. *See* HIV/AIDS
Alaskan natives, and U.S. Presidential apology, 17
Albrecht, W. A., 183
Albrecht Discounts, 189
Alcalay, Glenn, 365
Alfred, Tempo, 357
Amarakaeri, 133
Amazon: 125–142; dams, 127, 128, 444, 454–456, 458; deforestation, 128, 140; environmental health issues in, 129–131; extractive resource industry in, 184; gold mining, 125–142; indigenous groups in, 126, 127, 131–133, 135–137, 139, 169, 174, 454, 455, 457–459; indigenous statements on development, 457–459; mercury contamination in, 128–130, 131, 134, 137, 138, 141; miners in, 125–134, 137, 140, 141, 153. *See also* Amarakaeri; Brazil; Kayapo; Mundurucú; Venezuela; Xingu; Yanomami; Ye'kuana
American Anthropological Association (AAA), 18, 136
Amnesty International, 31, 87, 221, 252, 278, 301, 302, 303

ABOUT THE AUTHORS

Lorraine V. Aragon is an adjunct associate professor in anthropology and Asian studies at the University of North Carolina, and a 2010–11 Fellow at the National Humanities Center. Her research concerns religion, minority politics, development, arts, and intellectual property law in Indonesia. (aragon2@email.unc.edu)

Holly M. Barker, a linguist and ethnographer, is a full-time lecturer in the Anthropology Department at the University of Washington and the former senior policy advisor for the Embassy of the Republic of the Marshall Islands in Washington, D.C. Her current research focuses on the Marshallese Diaspora and nuclear militarism in French Polynesia. (hmbarker@u.washington.edu)

Camilo Perez Bustillo is trained in law and formerly was a research professor at the State of Mexico campus of the Instituto Technológico y de Estudios Superiores de Monterrey.

Melissa Checker is an assistant professor in the Department of Urban Studies, Queens College/City University of New York. Her research concentrates on urban environmental justice movements, climate justice, and urban sustainability. She is currently conducting research that examines sustainability as myth and practice in New York City. (mchecker@qc.cuny.ed)

Susan Crate is an associate professor of anthropology in the Department of Environmental Science and Policy at George Mason University. She is an interdisciplinary scholar specializing in environmental and cognitive anthropology who has worked with indigenous communities in Siberia since 1988 and with Viliui Sakha since 1991. Crate is author of *Cows, Kin, and Globalization: An Ethnography of Sustainability* (2006, AltaMira Press) and senior editor of *Anthropology and Climate Change: From Encounters to Actions* (2009, Left Coast Press). (scrate1@gmu.edu)

Betse Davies participated in a Marin Interfaith Task Force delegation to Bolivia in 2006. She is a researcher at the Center for Global Justice and lives in San Miguel de Allende, Mexico.

Bill Derman is a professor emeritus of anthropology at Michigan State University and a professor in the Department for International Environment and Development Studies at the Norwegian University of the Life Sciences, Aas, Norway. His current work focuses on human rights and land and water reform. (bill.derman@umb.no)

Silvia Elguea is a researcher at the Center for Global Justice, Mexico, and an independent scholar and specialist in environmental ethics and ecofeminism in Latin

America. Until recently she was a profesora titular at Universidad Autonoma Metropolitana-Azcapotzalco, Mexico.

Peter Esainko is an anthropologist and independent scholar interested especially in culture change and human nutrition. His collaborative research with Valerie Wheeler has included following the development of the organic farming movement in northern California and Ohio since the mid-1980s and in France since 2002.

Paula Garb is an anthropologist, adjunct professor of social ecology, and associate director of the Global Peace and Conflict Studies Program at the University of California, Irvine. (pgarb@uci.edu)

Al Gedicks is a professor of sociology at the University of Wisconsin–La Crosse and an environmental and indigenous rights activist and scholar. He has written extensively on conflicts between indigenous communities and multinational mining and oil corporations. (gedicks.al@uwlax.edu)

Ellen Gruenbaum is professor and head of the Department of Anthropology at Purdue University. Her work in Sudan and Sierra Leone has focused on the practice of female genital cutting and the social movements against harmful traditional practices. (gruenbaum@purdue.edu)

Robert K. Hitchcock is professor of geography and adjunct professor of anthropology at Michigan State University. He is an environmentally oriented anthropologist who has worked on southern African development, resettlement, and human rights issues for three decades. (hitchc16@msu.edu)

Marcia C. Inhorn is the William K. Lanman, Jr., Professor of Anthropology and International Affairs at Yale University, where she chairs the Council on Middle East Studies at the MacMillan Center for International and Area Studies. As a medical anthropologist, she focuses her work on gender, reproduction, biotechnology, religion, and public health in the Middle East. (marcia.inhorn@yale.edu)

Jack D. Ives, a Canadian geographer and mountain scholar, has done work in the Nepal Himalayas, Tibet, Tajikistan, the Ecuadorian Andes, Iceland, and the Arctic regions of Canada. He is a professor emeritus of environmental science at University of California, Davis, and an honorary research professor at Carleton University.

Barbara Rose Johnston is an environmental anthropologist and senior research fellow at the Center for Political Ecology in Santa Cruz, California; research associate and lecturer in Sociology at the University of California, Santa Cruz; and adjunct professor of anthropology at Michigan State University. Her research and public praxis includes documenting the linkages between the human rights abuse and environmental crisis. She currently serves as an advisor to the Marshall Islands Nuclear Claims Tribunal on human radiation experimentation and UNESCO International Hydrological Programme on water and cultural diversity. (bjohnston@igc.org)

Thomas L. Leatherman is a professor of biological anthropology at the University of South Carolina and the University of Massachusetts, Amherst. He has conducted several decades of field research in the Peruvian Andes on the political ecology of health in agrarian communities facing extreme poverty, and more recently the impact of armed conflict. He has also conducted research on the dietary, nutrition, and health consequences of tourism-led development in the Yucatán Peninsula of Mexico. (tleatherman@anthro.umass.edu)

Shannon May is a Ph.D. candidate in the Department of Anthropology at the University of California, Berkeley. She has conducted fieldwork throughout China and in sub-Saharan Africa; her recent research and publications focus on political ecology, governance, design, and development. She is cofounder and president of Bridge International Academies, a franchise-like, for-profit, low-cost, network of private primary schools serving impoverished families in informal settlements. (shannon.k.may@gmail.com)

Lucia Ann McSpadden is a medical anthropologist, a cross-cultural researcher and trainer, and founder/director of I-Relate: The Intercultural Leadership Institute, Oakland, California. She is adjunct faculty and coordinator of International Student Support at Pacific School of Religion, Berkeley, California. As director of research at the Life and Peace Institute, Uppsala, Sweden, her work focused on development, gender, environment, refugee repatriation, religion and conflict, and human rights. (lmcspadden@psr.edu)

Joan P. Mencher is a professor emerita of anthropology at the City University of New York's Graduate Center and Lehman College. She is chair of The Second Chance Foundation, which supports rural grassroots organizations in India and the United States. She has conducted research for some 50 years on India ecology, caste, land reform, agriculture, and women and has published widely both in the United States and in India. In 2009 she worked with the Bangalore Film Society to produce a "food movement" film festival. She is currently writing a book *Whose Great-Grandchildren Will Be Able to Eat in 2050?* (JMencher@TheSecond Chance.org)

James Phillips is a cultural anthropologist at Southern Oregon University whose work focuses on issues of social change and social revolution, conflict and peace, refugees, and human rights. He has been a staff member of several international NGOs and has done research in Central America and the Caribbean for several decades. (phillipj@sou.edu)

Oriol Pi-Sunyer is a professor emeritus of anthropology at the University of Massachusetts, Amherst. His research and publications span the field of political and economic anthropology, the modern state, minority nationalism, tourism, and maritime anthropology, with fieldwork focus in Europe and Mesoamerica. (oriol@anthro.umass.edu)

Leslie E. Sponsel is a professor emeritus of ecological anthropology at the University of Hawai'i. He was a founding member and first chair of the American Anthropological Association's Commission for Human Rights and subsequent Committee for Human Rights of the American Anthropological Association, and he has published extensively on anthropological aspects of peace and nonviolence among other subjects.

His latest book is *Spiritual Ecology: A Quiet Revolution* (forthcoming, Praeger). (www.anthropology.hawaii.edu/People/Faculty/Emeritus/Sponsel/index.html)

David Stea is a professor emeritus of geography and international studies and research associate of the Center for Global Justice (CGJ), San Miguel de Allende, Mexico. He is known for his pioneering work in environmental social science, especially participatory planning. (david.stea@gmail.com)

Margaret Byrne Swain is director of the Women's Resources and Research Center at the University of California, Davis. For the past three decades, her research in Yunnan, China has focused on the conditions and challenges of ethnic minorities, women, and the promise and pitfalls of tourism. (http://wrrc.ucdavis.edu/)

Lindsey Swope conducted Masters research in Yunnan, China. Her coauthored article is drawn in part from "Factors Influencing Rates of Deforestation in Lijiang County, Yunnan Province, China," her unpublished Masters thesis, University of California, Davis, 1995.

R. Brooke Thomas is a professor emeritus of anthropology at the University of Massachusetts, Amherst. His research and publications have helped shape the fields of biocultural anthropology, human adaptability, environmental anthropology, and political ecology. His research has included adaptation and exploitation in high Peruvian Andes, tourism on the Yucatán Peninsula of Mexico, and community reforestation in India. His current energies are in support of The Nuñoa Project, which provides humanitarian aid, self-sustaining development, and veterinary support for alpacas and other animals in Nuñoa, Peru (www.nunoaproject.org). (rbthomas@anthro.umass.edu)

Bryan Tilt is an assistant professor in the Anthropology Department at Oregon State University. He is an environmental anthropologist whose research focuses on economic development and environmental protection in China. He has conducted ethnographic fieldwork in Sichuan and Yunnan provinces and has published widely on pollution control, sustainable development, and agricultural systems in China. (Bryan.Tilt@oregonstate.edu)

Terry Turner is a sociocultural anthropologist who has worked with indigenous people in the Amazon for 50 years. He is the president of Survival International USA, a member of the Brazilian Panel of Specialists on the Belo Monte Dam project, a professor emeritus at the University of Chicago, and an adjunct professor at Cornell University. (tst3@cornell.edu)

Valerie Wheeler is a professor emerita of anthropology at California State University, Sacramento. She is a cultural anthropologist whose current work is the ethnography of food production, especially the evolution of organic agriculture in the United States and in France. (wheelerv@csus.edu)

Ben Wisner is a retired geographer based in Oberlin, Ohio, and London, England, who continues to consult, conduct research, and engage in training with a wide range of international and civil society organizations. His research affiliations are

Oberlin College, the Development Studies Institute, London School of Economics, and Aon Benfield UCL Hazard Research Centre. He is lead author of *At Risk: Natural Hazards, People's Vulnerability, and Disaster*, 2nd edition (Routledge, 2004) and *Toward a New Map of Africa* (Earthscan, 2006). (bwisner@igc.org)

Fuquan Yang is an expert in Chinese ethnic history and a Naxi native scholar. He is professor and vice-president of the Institute of Ethnology, Yunnan Academy of Social Sciences in Kunming, China.

Ship To:

Marie Dennan
343 GOODWYN ST
Memphis, TN 381113311 USA

Ship From:

TEXTBOOKSNOW-AMAZON
8950 W PALMER ST
RIVER GROVE, IL 60171

Date: 01/12/2013

SKU	Qty	Condition	Title
541855U 1		Used	Life & Death Matters
			2 9781598743395 Refund Eligible Through= 2/11/2013

Reason for Refund/Return:
Condition Incorrect Item Received Incorrect Item Ordered Dropped Class Purchased Elsewhere Other

Contact Us: For customer service, email us at customerservice@textbooksNow.com.

Page 1 of 1

Refund Policy: All items must be returned within 30 days of receipt. Pack your book securely, so it will arrive back to us in its original condition. Please use the return section and label provided with your original packing slip to identify your return. Be sure to include a return reason. For your protection, we suggest using a traceable, insured shipping service (UPS or Insured Parcel Post). We are not responsible for lost or damaged returns. Item(s) returned must be received in the original condition as sold and including all additional materials such as CDs, workbooks, etc. We will initiate a refund of your purchase price including applicable taxes within 5 business days of receipt. Shipping charges will not be refunded unless we have committed an error with your order. If there is an error with your order or the item is not received in the condition as purchased, please contact us immediately for return assistance.

We are in the process of relocating to our new Aurora Illinois Distribution Facility. You may receive orders shipped from one or both River Grove and Aurora locations until our move is complete. Some orders may be split with a portion fulfilled from our two locations - generating two shipments, each having its own packing slip, but consolidated into a single invoice or charge to your account, whichever is applicable.

Return Information (cut and attach to the outside of return shipment)

Order #: 107-8901851-2065048

TEXTBOOKSNOW-AMAZON
8950 W PALMER ST
RIVER GROVE, IL 60171

(Attn: Returns)

DA51786

Order #: 107-8901851-2065048

	Price	Total
	$ 9.31	$ 9.31

Sub Total	$ 9.31
Shipping & Handling	$ 3.99
Sales Tax	$ 0.00
Order Total	**$ 13.30**

Order #: 107-8901851-2065048